Annotated Index to the Cantos of Ezra Pound

Portrait Drawing of Ezra Pound (1929) by Desmond Chute
Courtesy, the artist and The Leicester Galleries, London

Annotated Index to the
CANTOS
of Ezra Pound

CANTOS I-LXXXIV

By

JOHN HAMILTON EDWARDS
AND WILLIAM W. VASSE

With the assistance of
John J. Espey and Frederic Peachy

UNIVERSITY OF CALIFORNIA PRESS
Berkeley, Los Angeles, London

University of California Press
Berkeley and Los Angeles, California

University of California Press, Ltd.
London, England

© 1957 by The Regents of the University of California
California Library Reprint Series Edition 1971
Second Printing, 1974
ISBN: 0-520-01923-7
Library of Congress Catalogue Card Number: 57-10500

Printed in the United States of America

To James D. Hart,

dreitz hom, πολύμητις

It is said on 67/136 that "a little knowledge of the subject will do us no harm." Surely there have been few readers of the Cantos who have not paused at that line in candid recognition of a fact. That was one reason for this book. Another was that the poem, like the mountain, was there.

J. H. E.
W. W. V.

Berkeley, California
June, 1957

INTRODUCTION

The Annotated Index is both an index to the Cantos of Ezra Pound and an annotation of the indexed materials. Annotations have been kept brief. We have wanted to give the basic information, not Pound's use of that information, in order to let the poetry demonstrate its own purposes. This is a guide to the poem, not a substitute for it. We have sought to establish the denotative center.

The Annotated Index is keyed to the New Directions edition of the Cantos, second printing, second state, dated 1948 but released December 1952. It includes cantos I through LXXXIV, with the exceptions of cantos LXXII and LXXIII, which have never been made public. It does not index Section: Rock-Drill 85-95 de los Cantares (Milan 1955, New York 1956), which was published after the Annotated Index was in final manuscript; however, the annotations in this book will be of service to the readers of Rock-Drill, which continues the major themes of the earlier cantos and builds upon many of the earlier materials.

Containing some 7500 annotated entries, under which are indexed approximately 17,000 references, the book is divided into two main sections:

I. The General Index: containing in alphabetical order names of persons, places and things, quotations in English, and all foreign language expressions except those put in the Appendixes. (For convenience, Greek expressions in roman script are included in both the General Index and Appendix A).

II. The Appendixes

    A. Greek: all Greek expression in Greek or roman script.

    B. Chinese: all Chinese expressions in Chinese characters.

    C. Chronology: all dates, set in a larger chronological framework and selectively annotated.

    D. Genealogy: Italian Renaissance families; Chinese emperors; rulers of England, France and Tuscany; the Renaissance Papal Succession; the American Presidents.

    E. Quotation Index: an index of literary quotations in the poem.

    F. Source Checklist: the major literary and historical sources of the poem.

    G. Text Collation: a comparison of the New Directions and Faber texts.

H. Correlation Table: a comparison of the paginations of the New Directions and Faber editions.

Annotations

All annotations are meant to respect the basic intention of the Annotated Index: to lead toward but not usurp the reading of the poem. The more information given in the text, the less need for annotation. We have, no doubt, annotated the obvious at times. We have tried to make these notes available to various needs, assuming that only those who need to know, will seek to find.

All entries contain three main units:

1. the indexed item: presented as given in the text: Adrian.
2. the location: canto(s) and page(s) in which the indexed item appears in the text: Adrian: 67/135
3. the annotation: Adrian: 67/135: Adrian IV, d. 1159, the first and only English Pope (1154-59).

All entries are annotated except the following:

1. those not needing annotation: Asia, in which case the entry ends with a full stop.
2. those which could not be annotated: Spinder, in which case the entry ends with a colon and space is left for later notes. Less than one percent of the entries remain unannotated.

Some entries are followed by annotations that are meant to designate, not inform. Thus Paris: 24/111 is annotated as the son of Priam, King of Troy as information, but Paris: 18/82 is annotated as the French city as a designation of a particular reference.

Some annotations are qualified by the abbreviations prob or poss:

prob (= probably) is used in two senses:

1. as evidently where the context supports the decision: American Curia: 22/101: prob. the U.S. Congress.
2. as an informed guess: Anne, Lady: 80/93: prob. Lady Anne Blunt, wife of W.S. BLUNT.

poss (= possibly) is used when there is some reason to feel that the annotation is reasonable, but the reason is less than would justify a probable classification:

Allegre: 80/79: <u>poss. Montallegro, a hill above
RAPALLO, Italy.</u>

General Notes

1. The text contains a large number of names and foreign
   language expressions which are not in standard forms.
   Sometimes the variant form seems a matter of poetry,
   sometimes of whimsey, sometimes of error. Changes
   have been made in all recognized cases; the standard form
   of the indexed name or foreign language expression follows the location data and is underscored: Abingdon:
   64/101: <u>Abington</u>. . . .

2. ALL CAPS are used to indicate cross reference.

3. <u>Brackets</u> are used in the following ways:

   a. when an indexed word is bracketed (e.g., [Anor]), it
      is an indication that the indexed word does not appear
      in the text, but that it has been referred to indirectly.
      Thus, the <u>Duchess of Normandia</u> mentioned on 6/21 is
      crossed to [Anor], after which entry the annotation is
      given. Brackets are also used around words which re-
      ceive cross reference from variant spellings.
   b. when a location is bracketed, it is an indication that
      some variation of the indexed item appears in the
      bracketed location. Thus <u>Cythera</u> appearing on 74/8
      is crossed to Aphrodite, in the location list of which
      the [74/8] reference is bracketed. Locations of words
      in variant spellings are also bracketed.

4. <u>Translations</u> follow location data of foreign language expressions. Foreign language expressions are indexed as
   follows:

   a. if single word only, the article is neglected in indexing.
   b. if two or more words, the expression is indexed under
      the first letters of the expression, including the article.
      Expressions broken by interpolations in the text are
      restored in the index.

5. <u>Sources</u> of literary and historical materials are given
   throughout. (See Appendix F for source bibliography).
   Literary sources of quotations from both English and other
   literatures are given wherever known. (See Appendix E
   for index of literary quotations). Historical sources are
   given selectively: one source note will serve a number of
   related entries. When used as source references, Pound's
   writings are noted without author's name: e.g., the references to <u>Confucius</u> in Appendix B refer to his book of
   that title (New Directions, 1951).

6. Chinese names, especially those in cantos 52-61, are drawn largely from Mailla, Histoire Générale de la Chine and have required special attention. Where Pound has incorrectly transcribed from Mailla, the correct Mailla form follows in underscore unless the error is slight, in which case the Mailla form is used in the annotation. In all cases where Mailla differs with Wade, the Wade transliteration follows in parentheses. Other Chinese names, not drawn from Mailla, are followed by the standard English transcription form where necessary.

7. Additional information to annotated entries often appears in the Appendixes. Such entries are crossed to the appropriate appendix.

8. All partial names (last names, titles, abbreviations, first names, descriptive names, familiarizations) are crossed to full name unless the entry is of minor importance, in which case the full name follows in the annotation.

9. Multilingual foreign expressions are kept intact, but the various languages are distinguished in the translations.

10. Treatment of such problems as pseudonyms, puns, poetic inventions and other matters will be evident from an examination of the Annotated Index.

Abbreviations

The following abbreviations have been used:

a. = ante
abb. = abbreviation
Arab = Arabian
b. = born
c. = circa
Ch = Chinese
d. = died
DTC = Disciplinary Training Center
Dut = Dutch
fl. = flourished
fr. = derived from
Fr = French
Ger = German
Gr = Greek
Heb = Hebrew

inv. = invention
It = Italian
Jap = Japanese
L = Latin
lit. = literally
m. = married
ME = Middle English
OE = Old English
O Fr = Old French
Pol = Polish
poss. = possibly
Pr = Provençal
prob. = probably
pub. = published
Russ = Russian
Sp = Spanish

xiii

A Note on Method and Bibliography

It may be of interest to some to know how the Annotated Index was prepared. A copy of the New Directions edition of the Cantos, second printing, second state, was marked for all items to be included in this book. From this marked copy, a typist prepared cards arranged for keysort-type handling, typing one line to the card except when the entry continued beyond the basic line. After the cards were checked against the text, they were punched for canto number, alphabet, person-place-thing designation and, as necessary, the foreign language(s) involved. Once punched, the cards could quickly be distributed by canto number or language or any other key desired.

After the punched cards, numbering about 7500, had been checked for accuracy, the annotations began. The Columbia Encyclopedia was the base work for the spelling of names, supplemented by Webster's Biographical Dictionary, Webster's Geographical Dictionary, and the New Century Cyclopedia of Names. The annotation began with a careful reading of Pound's own sources, especially Mailla's Histoire Générale de la Chine and the Works of John Adams. At the same time, Pound's books were reread; the following proved of most value to this work: the Letters, Guide to Kulchur, Spirit of Romance, Confucius, Make It New, the Literary Essays and the Translations. Special works on Pound were kept at hand: the Analyst series, edited at Northwestern University by Robert Mayo; Hugh Kenner's The Poetry of Ezra Pound and Peter Russell (ed.) An Examination of Ezra Pound. The Yale notes, prepared by a group of students under the direction of Norman Holmes Pearson, were also used.

While these sources were being consulted, inquiries were made in the Pound Newsletter concerning difficult problems; the response was gratifying and informative. Unpublished works, especially Clark Emery's Ideas Into Action, a study of the first thirty cantos, and J.C. Rowan's personal notes on the Cantos were kindly made available; they proved of unique value as intelligent and pointed sources of the kind of information needed.

For particular entries concerning special places or events, more specific works were consulted. Such studies as Jonini's life of Napoleon, Sismondi's work on the Italian Republics, Ricci's magnificent treatment of the Tempio Malatestiana and Paolo D'Ancona's study of the Schifanoia frescoes were used. And, of course, a library of guide books, special dictionaries and histories, the national encyclopedias, and various biographical and autobiographical works was accumulated.

Through the period of annotation, the Cantos remained open on the desk as the constant control. The poem is meant, of course, to be sufficient to itself; it sets both the challenge and the limit of interpretation. All annotations, therefore, were checked against the text in a running test of relevance and value.

The authors of the Annotated Index assume joint responsibility for this book, but to expedite the work some division of the subjects was made. Most of the annotations concerning medieval and renaissance materials, persons associated with Pound's life, and classical references were written by Mr. Edwards; most of the annotations concerning Chinese and American history were written by Mr. Vasse.

When the annotations were nearly completed, but while letters were still bringing clarifications and suggestions, the preliminary manuscript was prepared from the annotated cards. This manuscript was examined by John J. Espey and Frederic Peachy and then given a final editing in which the Annotated Index was checked against the text of the poem for accuracy of index and relevance of annotation, the text was checked selectively against the manuscript, and the final decisions made.

The Annotated Index, a response to challenge and interest, is intended to be of catalytic value to the meeting of that challenge and the nurture of that interest. The Cantos are meant to be a poem. We have hoped that the Annotated Index, both as explication and measurement, will serve as a form of criticism of that poetry, leading toward a more informed and more meaningful reading of one of the most demanding works of our time.

The second printing of the Annotated Index has allowed us to add to some of the previous notes, remove doubts from others, and make a few corrections. The additions and corrections are printed on pp. 327-332.

ACKNOWLEDGMENTS

To name all those who have, in one way or another, contributed to these notes would be to name a multitude. We are grateful, however, for the chance to emphasize our thanks to the following: the Committee on Research of the University of California, which supported this work from its beginning; John J. Espey and Frederic Peachy, each of whom contributed to the annotations through months of notes and comment that ended with careful and cunning readings of the manuscript; a book like this is conceived in doubt and born in error; they have worked for its redemption; Thomas Parkinson, who recognized a need and suggested a way; colleagues at the University of California, especially Elroy Bundy, Francis Carmody, Giovanni Cecchetti, Chen Shih-Hsiang, Arthur E. Gordon, Richard Irwin, Edwin S. Morby, Warren Ramsey, Arturo Torres-Rioseco, Ronald Walpole, and the faculty of the Department of English; readers of the Pound Newsletter who kindly answered queries published there while this work was in progress: all such assistance has been acknowledged in the pages of the newsletter, but we wish to reaffirm our gratitude to the following: Mary Barnard, Richard Bridgman, Desmond Chute, Albert Cook, Hubert Creekmore, Guy Davenport, John Drummond, Clark Emery, Kenneth Hanson, Eva Hesse, Hugh Kenner, James Laughlin, Franz Link, Robert Mayo, D.D. Paige, Mary de Rachewiltz, J.C. Rowan, Olga Rudge, Homer Somers and Hugh Staples.

We also stand in debt to those who contributed to this book by preparing the translations of the foreign language expressions; all translations were subject to later editing and the responsibility for final decisions is ours alone: Fernando Alegría (Spanish), Thomas Bishop (French), Catherine Pirro Feucht (Italian), Frederic Peachy (Greek), Eugene E. Reed (German), Joseph Sheerin (Latin), Ronald Walpole (Provençal and Old French) and Lee Winters (Chinese).

Barbara Flick endured the typing of the annotation cards, Jean Berger, Jeanne Lawson, Kay Sterling and Anne Wigger helped to remove some of the errors from the manuscript and Laurel Fujishige prepared the final typescript with patience and grace. It is a pleasure to acknowledge their assistance.

And, as always, there are our friends, D.S., G.W., J.S., and M.H.

J.H.E.
W.W.V.

CONTENTS

A

A, Mr:62/92, 95: see John ADAMS.

Aaron:74/23: see Aaron BURR.

AA VV:42/5: Altesses Vôtres (Fr) your highnesses. (See: FER-
NANDO II of Tuscany).

Aba tchan, Maen tchan, Tihali tchan:58/66: Manchu general officer
ranks.

abbazia:9/36; 76/39: (It) abbey.

Abbeville:66/126: commune of the Somme department, N France.

Abdul Baha:46/26: see Sir Abdul Baha BAHAI.

Abdul Mejid:48/34: 1824-61, Ottoman sultan (1839-61).

Abelard:80/90: Peter, 1079-1142, the French philosopher and teacher.

Abercrombie:71/160: Sir Robert, 1740-1827, British general in the
French and Indian and the American Revolutionary Wars.

"a better fencer than I was":74/20: from Kumasaka. (See: Translations, 252).

Abigail:62/90, 95: see Abigail ADAMS.

Abingdon:64/101: Abington, town in Plymouth county, Massachusetts.

Abner:77/42: DTC, Pisa.

Abrâm:44/19: Napoleonic representative in Siena, c. 1799.

abuleia:5/19; 54/31: abulia, loss of will power.

Académie Goncourt:77/50: (Fr) the Goncourt Academy (Paris).

a cavallo:79/63: (It) on horseback.

Accademia Romana:11/50: the Roman Academy of Pomponio Leto for
the study of Latin antiquity. In 1469 Pope Paul II (Pietro BARBO)
closed the Accademia Romano, accusing Leto of conspiracy
against the papacy and having Leto and Bartolomeo SACCHI thrown
into prison.

ac ego in harum:39/44; 74/14, [17]: (L) ... haram: and I too in the
pig-sty.

à ce que l'argent circule:53/16: (Fr) that money circulate. (See:
Mailla, Histoire Générale, II, 23).

ac ferae familiares:20/94; 76/35: (L) and domesticated wild animals.

Achaia:74/22, 25: Achaea, region of ancient Greece, N Peloponnesus,
on Gulf of Corinth; later the Roman province, called Achaia,
founded by Augustus.

Achilles:80/80: see PIUS XI.

Acoetes:2/7, 8: the pilot of the ship taking DIONYSUS to NAXOS to
marry Ariadne. The crew, not realizing his identity, attempts
to abduct Dionysus; Dionysus causes tigers and leopards to appear on ship, entwines the mast with vines, and turns the sailors
into dolphins. Only Acoetes is spared. (See: Ovid, Metamorphoses, III; Homeric Hymn VII, To Dionysus).

Acre:6/21: the port in Palestine. ELEANOR of Aquitaine landed
there on the Second Crusade (1146-49).

Actaeon:4/14; 80/79: while hunting he came upon ARTEMIS bathing
in the pool of GARGAPHIA; she changed Actaeon into a stag, and
he was torn to pieces by his own dogs. (See: Ovid, Metamorphoses, III, 138-252).

Acta Sanctorum:71/163, 164: (L) deeds of the saints. The name given

[1]

to collections of biographies of saints and martyrs, especially to
that of the Bollandists.

Actium:21/99: promontory and town, NW Arcanania, Greece; site of the
battle (31 BC) between Octavian and the forces of Antony and Cleopatra.

Actum in Castro Sigismundo, presente Roberto de Valturibus/ . . .
sponte et ex certa scienta: 11/52: (L) Done in the Castle Sigismund,
before Roberto de VALTURIO/ . . . freely and of clear knowledge.

Actum Senis:42/7; 43/13: (L) done at Siena.

actus/ legis nulli facit injuriam:64/102: (L) an act of law does harm
to none. (See: John Adams, Works, II, 159).

Adair:31/5: James, 18th-century trader in Georgia and the Carolinas;
author of The History of the American Indians (1775) in which he
advanced the theory that the Indians were descendants of the Jews.

Adam:22/102; 64/107: the first man.

[Adam]:45/24: architect and sculptor of the Zeno Maggiore, the
Veronese basilica.

Adam, the Brothers:84/118: poss. Brooks Adams [1848-1927, son of
Charles Francis ADAMS, brother of Henry Brooks Adams; American historian] and Henry Brooks ADAMS; or poss. Robert
(1738-92) and James (1730-94) Adam, English architects and de-
signers of furniture in the classical style.

Adamo me fecit:45/24: (It) Adam (L) made me.

Adams:74/11: see Henry Brooks ADAMS.

Adams:74/14; 76/33: DTC, Pisa.

Adams:13/3, 4, 6; 32/7, 9; 50/40; 62/90, 95, 96; 65/110, 117, 118, 122; 69/
150; 71/161, 162, 164, 165, 167: see John ADAMS.

Adams:34/15, 18; 37/31: see John Quincy ADAMS.

[Adams, Abigail]:62/90, 95: 1744-1810, wife of John ADAMS.

Adams, Charles Francis:[42/3]; 48/34; [62/88, 90; 67/138]: 1807-
86, son of John Quincy ADAMS, U. S. statesman, minister to
Great Britain (1861-68); edited letters of Abigail ADAMS, Works
of John ADAMS (10 vol., 1850-56) and Memoirs of John Quincy
ADAMS (12 vol., 1874-77).

Adams, Charles H.:42/3: see Charles Francis ADAMS.

[Adams, Elihu]:64/101: brother of John ADAMS, made deputy sher-
iff of Braintree, Massachusetts, 1761.

[Adams, George Washington]:34/18: ?1801-28, eldest son of John
Quincy ADAMS.

[Adams, Henry]:62/87: d. 1646, founder of the Adams family in America; in 1640 he was granted 40 acres at Mt. WOLLASTON, later
BRAINTREE, Massachusetts.

[Adams, Henry Brooks]:74/11; 84/118(?): 1838-1918, son of Charles
Francis ADAMS; American historian, taught medieval history at
Harvard (1870-77).

Adams, John (J., Johnnie):31/3, 4, 5, 6; 32/7, 9; 33/11; 37/36; 48/34;
50/40; 52/3; 62/87, [89], 90, 91, 92, [93, 95], 96; 63/97; 64/[101],
102; 65/110, 112, 114, [116], 117, 118, [120, 121], 122, [123]; 66/131; 67/
138; 68/[141], 142, 143, [147, 148]; 69/150, [151]; 70/155, 156, [158];
71/161, 162, 164, 165, [166]; 74/17; 76/35; 81/96; 84/116, 118: 1735-
1826, second President of the U. S. (1796-1800). Delegate to
First CONTINENTAL CONGRESS (1774); appointed commissioner

to France (1777-78) and minister to the United Provinces (1780-
82); envoy to Great Britain (1785-88); elected Vice-President
(1788, 1792), serving under George Washington.

Adams, John Quincy (J. Q., J. Quincy):31/5; 34/15,[17],18,19; 37/
31,32; [62/94]; 63/97; [64/104]; 65/115; [68/144]: 1767-1848, sixth
President of the U. S. (1825-29). Son of John ADAMS, member
of the U. S. Senate (1803-08); minister to Russia (1809-11); member of commission to negotiate the peace after War of 1812; minister to Great Britain (1815); Secretary of State under MONROE
(1817-25); after term as President, he served in the House of
Representatives (1831-48).

Adams, Joseph:62/87: 1626?-94, youngest son of Henry ADAMS,
great-grandfather of John ADAMS and Samuel ADAMS.

Adams, Samuel (Sam, Saml):34/17; 62/90; 64/102; 65/110, 119; 66/130;
67/138; 71/165,166: 1722-1803, American patriot. Leader of the
Massachusetts legislature (1765-74); active at the Boston Tea
Party (1773); signer of Declaration of Independence; member of
CONTINENTAL CONGRESS (1774-81); governor of Massachusetts
(1794-97). A radical, he was among the more extreme spokes-
men for independence from England; after the Revolution, his influence declined.

Adams, Thomas:62/87: one of the grantees of the first charter of the
Colony of Massachusetts Bay (1629); he may have been a relative
of Henry ADAMS.

Adamses: [37/36]; 61/85; 64/106: the ADAMS family in the U. S.

Adam Street:62/93: street in central London.

Ade du Lesterplatz:80/79: pun: (Ger) ade du, (Fr) adieu: farewell
Leicester Square; from British war song, Tipperary.

Ade du Piccadilly:80/79: pun: farewell Piccadilly; see entry above.

Adelphi:62/93: the Adelphi Hotel, the Strand, London.

Adelphi:74/12:

a destra:76/35: (It) to the right.

Adet:62/94: Pierre-August, 1763-1834, French envoy to U. S. (1795)
with rank of minister plenipotentiary.

Adige:4/16; 42/7: river in Italy.

Adolf:38/41: see Adolphe SCHNEIDER.

Adonis:23/109; 47/30, 32, 33: a youth loved by APHRODITE; when he
was killed by a boar, she caused the anemone to spring from his
blood. Adonis is the central figure in a number of fertility rites
and myths which celebrate his death and survival; TAMMUZ is
the Babylonian equivalent of Adonis. (See: Bion, Lament for
Adonis; Ovid, Metamorphoses, X).

Ad Orcum autem quisquam?/ nondum nave nigra pervenit...:39/45:
(L) But (has) anyone (yet been) to Hell?/ has not yet come in a
black ship. (See: Odyssey, X, 502).

ad posteros:74/16: (L) to posterity.

Adrian:67/135: Adrian IV, d.1159, the first and only English Pope
(1154-59).

Adriatic:83/110: the Adriatic Sea.

[Aeetes]:17/79: king of Colchis, brother of CIRCE and father of
Medea.

Aegean:16/72: the Aegean Sea.

Aegesta:67/139: town of NW coast of Sicily, said to have been founded by the Trojans; called Egesta or Aegesta by the Greeks, now
called Alcamo.

Aegeus:6/21: legendary king of Athens, father of THESEUS.

Aemelia:30/148: Emilia, district in N Italy.

Aeneas:74/13: the Trojan, hero of the Aeneid; his descendants were
the legendary founders of Rome; son of ANCHISES and APHRO-
DITE.

Aeneas, this:10/46: see Aeneas Silvius PICCOLOMINI.

Aeolus:20/92: the keeper of the winds.

aere perennius:83/112 (L) more enduring than bronze. (See: Horace; Odes, III, 30).

Aeschylus:82/101: 525-456: the Athenian tragic poet.

Aesop's Fables:32/8.

Aethelbert:67/133: d. 616 AD, King of Kent; organized a code of laws
based on Roman law and on the code of INA.

affatigandose per suo piacere o no/ non gli manchera la provixione
mai:8/29; [21/97]: (It) tiring himself, for his pleasure or not/
he will never need provision. (From a letter of Sigismondo
MALATESTA; see: Yriarte, Un Condottiere au XVᵉ Siecle, 381).

Afghans:38/38: see AMANULLAH.

Africa:7/25.

africanus:80/91: (L) from Africa.

Agada:77/43: locality in African Sudan, now Agadez; first stop of
the FASA in the reincarnation of WAGADU. (See: Frobenius and
Fox, African Genesis, 97-110).

Agatha:80/91: Saint Agatha, 3rd century Sicilian virgin, martyred
by Decius.

Agathos:33/11: (Gr) good, well-born. (See: Appendix A).

Agen, la Duchesse d': 65/118: see la Duchesse d'AYEN.

agit considerate: 53/17: (L) he leads with deliberation. (See: A.
Lacharme, Confucii Chi-King, III, 3, ode 9, stanza 3).

Agnesina:24/113: d. c.1430, a matron of Modena who, apparently, had
committed adultery and poisoned her husband; under the edict
(1425) of Niccoló d'ESTE, she was beheaded.

"A good governor is as wind over grass":53/12: from Analects, XII,
xix.

Agostino:9/40; 20/90: see Agostino di DUCCIO.

Agresti:76/30: Signora Olivia Rossetti Agresti, daughter of William
Michael Rossetti; living in Rome, Signora Agresti has for years
been writing on 20th century economic problems.

Agsterburg wal:69/149: Agsterburg Wall, located in Amsterdam.

a guisa de leon. . .quando si posa:32/9: (It) as a lion does. . .when he
rests. (See: Purgatorio, 6, 66).

Ahama:56/50: (Ahma), d.1282 AD, minister of KUBLAI KHAN, used
his power to enrich himself; alarmed at his excesses, several
members of the court, led by OUANG-TCHU, formed a conspiracy and assassinated him.

Ah Monsieur. . .vous allez raser une toile?:80/84: (Fr) Ah, Sir, . . .
are you going to shave (destroy?) a canvas?

Ah, voui, Vive le Roi:34/16: (Fr) Ah, yeah, long live the King.

Ailas e que'm fau miey huelh/ Quar no vezon so qu'ieu vuelh:29/144: (Pr) Alas, that my eyes avail me not/ For they see not what I wish. (See: Sordello, Ailas, e quem fau miey huelh; Cesare de Lollis, Vita e Poesie di Sordello di Goito, 196).

ainé:29/141; 57/60: (Fr) eldest.

Ainley:77/47: poss. a cat, whose name may have been derived from Henry Ainley (1879-1945), British actor. (See: Letters, 336).

Aïulipata:56/52: (Ayuli Palpata), personal name of Emperor GIN-TSONG.

Akers:38/37: poss. Vickers, Sons and Co. , or Vickers-Maxim Co. , British munitions firms.

akouta:56/47: (Mongolian) term for chief of the NUTCHÉ Tartars.

Akouta:55/45: (Akuta) 1069-1123, chieftain of the KIN Tartars. In 1114 he rebelled from the Léao (Liao) dynasty of the KHITAN Tartars and entered into an agreement with Emperor HOEÏ-TSONG; he attacked the Léao, and then invaded the Empire, forcing Hoeï-tsong off the throne. The Kin withdrew to Peiping, which they made their capital.

Akra:40/49: town on Atlantic coast of North Africa, founded by HANNO, just south of GUTTA.

A Lady asks me. . .:36/27-29: from Cavalcanti, Donna mi prega. (See: Translations, 132-141).

a la marina:74/21: (Sp) in the naval manner.

à l'Amitié:80/83: (Fr) to Friendship.

à la Valturio:54/29: (Fr) in the manner of VALTURIO.

à la Wörgl:78/60: (Fr) in the manner of WÖRGL.

Alberic:29/141,142: see Alberic da ROMANO.

Albert:19/86, 87: Prince Albert, 1819-61, Prince Consort of England, husband of VICTORIA.

Albert:24/114: see Alberto d'ESTE.

Albert:9/38: see Leon Battista ALBERTI.

Alberti:9/38: Leon Battista, 1404-72, Italian architect, designer of the TEMPIO.

Albigenses:74/7: a religious sect of S France in the Middle Ages; although officially designated as Christian heretics, they were adherents of a form of Manichaeism. The Albigenses appeared in the 11th century, in 1208 Innocent III proclaimed the Albigensi-an Crusade to stamp them out, and, by 1233, the Albigenses were finished.

Albigeois:74/4: (Fr) the ALBIGENSES.

Albizzi:26/125: a Florentine family of the late 14th century, members of the Parte Guelfa.

alcalde:67/140: (Sp) chief administrator.

Alcazar:81/95: prob. Alcázar de San Juan, town in Ciudad-Real province, central Spain.

Alcides:82/101: error for ATREIDAES. (See: Aeschylus, Agamem-non, I, 3).

Alcmene:74/9, 21; 76/30: the wife of Amphitryon; Zeus loved her and visited her in the shape of her husband; by Zeus she bore HERACLES; by Amphitryon, Iphicles. ODYSSEUS sees her in the underworld. (See: Odyssey, XI, 266).

[Aldobrandino, Ugo]:24/110,112: 1405-25, bastard son of Niccoló
d'ESTE and stepson of Parisina MALATESTA; he and Parisina
were beheaded when Niccoló discovered their adultery.

Aldous:30/148: see Aldus MANUTIUS.

Aldovrandino: 24/112: see Ugo ALDOBRANDINO.

Alessandria:80/88: see ALEXANDRIA.

Alessandro:5/19; 7/27; 8/28; 84/117(?): see Alessandro de'MEDICI.

Alessandro:9/37: see Alessandro SFORZA.

Aletha:17/78: prob. an invention; a sea deity.

Alex:9/35: see Alessandro SFORZA.

Alexander:32/7: see ALEXANDER I.

Alexander:44/17: see ALEXANDER III.

Alexander:80/90: Cicely Henrietta, who sat for WHISTLER's
Arrangement in Gray and Green.

[Alexander I]:32/7; 34/15: 1777-1825, emperor of Russia (1801-25)
during the Napoleonic wars.

[Alexander III]:44/17: Orlando Bandinelli, d. 1181, Pope (1159-81).

[Alexander VI]:30/149: Rodrigo BORGIA, 1431-1503, Pope (1492-
1503).

Alexandria:14/62; [80/88]: the Egyptian city.

Alexi:35/23:

Alf:20/91: see ALFONSO.

Alfonso:8/28; 9/35; 10/46: Alfonso V (Alfonso the Magnanimous)
1396-1458, King of Aragon and Sicily (1416-58) and of Naples
(1443-58). Sigismondo MALATESTA fought for Alfonso against
Venice and Florence, but later changed sides.

[Alfonso]:20/91: character in Lope de Vega's play, Las Almenas
de Toro; brother of King SANCHO. (See: Spirit of Romance, 191-
193).

Alfonso:30/148: see Alfonso d'ESTE.

Alfred:38/41: see Alfred Peirrot DESEILLIGNY.

Algernon:82/101: see Algernon Charles SWINBURNE.

Algiaptou:56/52: prob. AÏULIPATA, Emperor GIN-TSONG, who
ruled 1311-20 and who did honor to CONFUCIUS by restoring the
ceremonies (1313) instituted to honor him.

Alhambra:74/25: the famous group of buildings above Granada,
Spain.

Alice:77/48: poss. Alice of Montpellier, see VENTADOUR, LADY
OF.

aliofants:9/40: reference is to the elephant motifs in the TEMPIO.

Aliscans:80/90: the Alyscamps or Aleschans, necropolis of Arles,
France. (See: Inferno, 9, 112).

Alix:6/22: Alais Capet, second daughter of LOUIS VII; betrothed to
RICHARD I of England, 6 January 1169; in 1191 Richard was released from this agreement and her dowry was returned.

alixantos, aliotrephes, eiskatebaine:23/107: (Gr) worn by the sea,
feeding in the sea (sea-reared), he went down into. (See: Appendix A).

alla fuente florida:76/34: (It) to the (Sp) flowery fountain.

"alla" non "della":78/56: (It) "to the, " not "of the". (Reference is
   to the statement in the PROGRAMMA DI VERONA: è un diritto
   alla proprietà, it is a right to property).
alla terra abbandonata:78/56: (It) to the abandoned earth.
Allegre:80/79: poss. Montallegro, a hill above RAPALLO, Italy.
Allingham:79/63: DTC, Pisa.
Alma-Tadema:80/86: Sir Lawrence, 1836-1912, English painter.
[Almeida, Don Joas Theolomica de]:65/122: envoy extraordinary
   of Portugal at the Paris Treaty Conference, 1782.
Alphonse le roy d'Aragon:9/35: (Fr) ALFONSO, king of Aragon.
Al poco giorno ed al gran cerchio d'ombra:5/20: (It) at the dim day-
   light and at the large circle of shadow. (See: Dante, Canzoniere,
   Sestina I, 1).
Altaforte:80/87: castle in Lemousin, 20 miles NE of Periguex,
   France. The castle of Bertran de Born. Also poss. reference
   to Pound's poem, "Sestina: Altaforte, " hence, as adverb, loud-
   ly, riotously, belligerently.
Althea:81/97: reference to the Althea in Lovelace's poem, "To Al-
   thea from Prison": And my divine Althea brings / To whisper at
   the grates; also poss. reference to Althea, mother of MELEAG-
   ER, who destroyed him by burning a fated log on her grates.
al triedro:78/61: (It) in the corner.
A Lume Spento:76/38: title of Pound's first book of verse, published
   in Venice, 1908. (It) with tapers quenched; at extinguished light.
   (See: Purgatorio   3, 132).
Alviano:5/20: Ser Bartolomeo d', 1455-1515, a general of the Orsi-
   nis, suspected for a time of the murder of Giovanni BORGIA.
[Alvise, Giovanni]:9/38: son of Luigi ALVISE.
[Alvise, Luigi]:9/37: carpenter on the TEMPIO.
Alwidge:9/37: see Luigi ALVISE.
Alwise:9/38: see Giovanni ALVISE.
à Madame la veuve de M. Henry Schorn/ op de Agsterburg wal by
   de Hoogstraat:69/149: (Fr) to Madame, the widow of M. Henry
   SCHORN/ (Dut) up near the AGSTERBURG wall in the HOOG-
   STRAAT.
[Amanullah]:38/38: 1892-   , emir (1919-26) and king (1926-29) of
   Afghanistan; called Amanullah Khan; made treaties with Russia
   and Great Britain at Geneva (1921).
Amari-li:79/62: (It) Amaryllis; prob. associated in Pound's mind
   with a song heard at Salzburg.
a marito subtraxit ipsam. . . /dictum Sordellum concubuisse:6/23:
   (L) she withdrew herself from her husband. . . / SORDELLO said
   to have lain with (her). (See: Rolandini, V, 3 in Chabaneau,
   Les Biographies des Troubadours, 315).
Ambassador:66/126: the ambassador mentioned in John Adams,
   Works, III, 392.
Ambassador (french):34/15: see Armand Augustin-Louis de CAUL-
   AINCOURT.
Ambassador Manchester:65/125: see George MONTAGU.
Ambrosiana:20/89: the Ambrosian Library in Milan.
amendment Number XVIII:78/59: see EIGHTEENTH AMENDMENT.

America:21/98; 31/5; 34/16; 50/41; 62/93; 64/101,102,105; 65/110,112,
    113,114,116,119,122,125; 66/126,129; 67/139,140; 68/141,143,145,147;
    69/151; 70/156; 71/165,166; 80/78.
America del Sud:38/37: (Sp) South America.
American, the:84/118: see Harry S. TRUMAN.
American Army:77/49: the American Army of Occupation in Italy,
    1945.
American civil war:48/35.
American Curia:22/101: prob. the U.S. Congress.
[American Indians]:31/5.
American Legislature:65/110: the CONTINENTAL CONGRESS.
Américas, Las:80/72: bazaar in Madrid, Spain.
Ames, Fisher:69/153: 1758-1808, member of the House of Represent-
    atives (1789-97), where he was a supporter of the financial poli-
    cies of Alexander HAMILTON.
Amherst:71/160: Lord Jeffrey, 1717-97, English general; commanded
    at the capture of Cape Breton from the French (1758); took Ticon-
    deroga (1759); made commander-in-chief of British forces in
    America (1759).
Amiens:66/126: manufacturing city of Somme department, N France.
ammassi:53/8; 56/49; 61/81: (It) piles (of things); grain pools. (See:
    What is Money For?, 13).
amo ergo sum:80/71: (L) I love, therefore I am.
Amphion:62/95: a musician, so excellent that he drew stones after
    him with the music of his lyre.
Amphitrite:32/7: French ship belonging to BEAUMARCHAIS; car-
    ried supplies to the colonists during the Revolutionary War.
Amsterdam:62/92,93; 65/121; 68/146,147,148; 69/149,150,151, [152];
    70/158: the Dutch city; John ADAMS served there as American
    minister to the Netherlands (1780).
Amur:59/73: river in NE Asia, forming the boundary between Man-
    churia and the Chita region and Khabarovsk Territory of the USSR.
Anacreon:83/113: fl. 521 BC, the Greek lyric poet.
Anafeste:67/140: Paul Luc, d. 717 AD, early tribune of Venice and
    first Doge; reputed to have been a just magistrate.
Anastasia:80/91: Saint Anastasia, 4th century Roman noblewoman
    martyred under DIOCLETIAN.
Anatoth:74/18: a city of BENJAMIN, home of JEREMIAH.
Anaxiforminges:4/13: (Gr) Lords of the lyre. (See: Appendix A).
Anchises:23/109; 74/13; 76/34: father of AENEAS.
Ancona:8/31; 26/127: the Italian city.
Ancures:20/91: companion of SANCHO in Lope de Vega's play, Las
    Almenas de Toro.
"and all their generation":74/11: from Ford Madox Ford, The Three-
    Ten.
and belt the citye quahr of nobil fame:78/56: from Gavin Douglas,
    Aeneid. (See: Literary Essays, 245).
And by the beach-run, Tyro,...:2/6: from Odyssey, XI, 235-59.
Andiamo:15/66: (It) let's go.
André:77/50: see André SPIRE.
Andromeda:52/5; [55/41]: a constellation, between Pegasus and

Perseus, in the northern skies; represented as a chained woman.
and the greatest is charity:74/12: see I Corinthians 13, 13.
And then went down to the ship...:1/3-5: from Odyssey, XI, 1-104.
(See: Literary Essays, 259-264).
and the pleasure of having it hot:83/112: poss. variation of T. S.
Eliot, The Waste Land, II, 167: to get the beauty of it hot.
Angelico:45/24; 51/44; 76/40: Giovanni da Fiesole, Fra Angelico,
1387-1455, Florentine painter.
angelos:12/54: (Gr) messenger.
Angevins:10/46: members of two medieval dynasties which originat-
ed in France. The older house issued from Fulk, who became
Count of ANJOU in the 10th century; the second house was a
branch of the Capetians and began with Charles, younger brother
of Louis IX of France. Text reference is to René of Anjou, who
became Duke of Anjou in 1434 and sought control of Naples and
Sicily.
Angleterre:18/82: (Fr) ENGLAND.
Angliae:67/135: (L) ENGLAND.
Angold:84/115: J. P., 1909-1943, British poet; killed in World War
II.
animae:74/16: (L) of the soul.
Anjou:36/30: region and former duchy of W France.
Annam:56/50: section of Vietnam.
Annapolis:31/3: port in Maryland; seat of the CONTINENTAL CON-
GRESS (1783-84).
Anne:66/129: 1665-1714, Queen of England (1702-1714).
Anne, Lady:80/93: prob. Lady Anne Blunt, wife of W. S. BLUNT.
anno seidici:52/3: (It) sixteenth year (of Era Fascista: 1938).
anno undecesimo:59/70: (It) eleventh year.
a noi:58/69: (It) ours.
anonimo:74/4: (It) anonymous.
[Anor]:6/21: daughter of the Countess of Chatellerault; mother
of ELEANOR of Aquitaine.
Anschluss:38/39; 50/41: political merger of two countries; particu-
larly, the merger (1938) of Austria and Germany.
Anselm, Meyer:74/17: see Mayer Amschel ROTHSCHILD.
Antares:52/5: the principal star of Scorpio, called Scorpio's Heart.
ante mortem no scortum:76/33: (L) before death no prostitute.
Antheil:74/5: George, 1900-   , American composer and pianist.
(See: Antheil and the Treatise on Harmony).
Anticlea:1/4, 5: wife of Laertes and mother of ODYSSEUS. (See:
Odyssey, XI, 84-85; 152-153).
Anti-Hellene:9/34: see Parcellio PANDONE.
Antille, Nicolo de:42/6; 43/15: Niccolò dell' Antella, Auditore of
the BALIA of Siena, 1622.
Antioch:60/76: ancient city on the Orontes, Turkey.
Antis:70/156: anti-Federalists, opposed to the adoption of the U. S.
Constitution; followers of Thomas JEFFERSON.
Antoninus:42/3; 46/28; 78/57: Antoninus Pius, 86-161, Roman Emper-
or (138-161); administered the empire with ability, kept the peace,
and carried out an extensive building program.

Antwerp:71/163: the Belgian city.

Antzar:55/46: Antsar, fl. 1231, Mongolian general serving under Emperor OGOTAI KHAN during the great Mongol campaigns against the KIN Tartars in Honan province.

Aoi:79/68; 81/97: an expression of uncertain meaning; it occurs 172 times in the Oxford manuscript of the Chanson de Roland, generally following the last line of a laisse. (See T. Atkinson Jenkins' edition of the poem, Boston, 1924, p. 4, for comment).

Apaoki:55/39: see YÉ-LIU-APAOKI.

Apaoki:55/39: see YÉ-LIU-TÉ-KOUANG.

apaoki:56/47: (Mongolian) term for the chief of the KHITAN Tartars.

Apeliota:47/32; 74/16, 21, 22, 27: the East Wind.

Aphrodite:1/5; 24/111; [27/131; 74/8, 22]; 76/[34, 36], 37, 40; [77/ 46]; 79/[67, 68], 69, 70; [80/79, 88, 89; 81/95; 82/103; 84/116]: the goddess of love, beauty and fertility. Born of blood and the sea foam (from which comes her name), she was the mother of AENEAS, lover of ADONIS and ANCHISES in the various Greek legends in which she appears. In Cyprus especially she was worshipped, with Adonis, as goddess of fertility. (See: Homeric HYMN V; see also VENUS).

Apollo: [4/13]; 20/94; [21/99]; 24/114; [29/145]; 77/49; 84/116: Phoebus Apollo, Olympian god of light, music, prophecy and pastoral matters.

Apovitch:12/55:

Aquabello, Enricho de:11/52: Enrico Acquadelli, steward to Sigismondo MALATESTA.

aqua morta:16/69: (It) dead water.

aquarelle:26/127: water color.

Aquinas:36/29: Saint Thomas, 1225-74, scholastic philosopher and Doctor of the Church, author of the Summa Theologiae.

Aquitain:6/21; 67/135: Aquitaine, once a duchy and kingdom in SW France; established as kingdom by Charlemagne, it became a duchy under the Counts of Poitiers; in the late 9th century, it came under the control of William, count of Auvergne. The marriage of ELEANOR of Aquitaine to HENRY II of England gave England claim to Aquitaine and led to the Hundred Years War.

Arabia Petra:74/22: Arabia Petraea (Rocky Arabia), the NW part of Arabia, including the Sinai Peninsula; not part of modern Arabia.

arachidi:74/26: (It) peanuts.

Arachne:74/24; 76/39: the girl who challenged ATHENA to a weaving contest; because the girl dared to contest the gods, Athena changed her into a spider so she should weave forever; hence, a spider.

[Aragon]:8/28; 9/35: the medieval kingdom in N Iberian peninsula.

Arambo:40/49: Arambys, a town on the Atlantic coast of N Africa, founded by HANNO, just south of MELI.

aram nemus vult (aram vult nemus):74/24; 78/59; 79/70: (L) the grove needs an altar.

Arbia:77/51: river in the vicinity of Siena.

Archbishop:44/19: see Anton-Felice ZONDADARI.

Archbish of Antioch: 60/76:   see Charles-Thomas Maillard de
   TOURNON.
Archbishop of Morea Lower: 26/123: Orthodox delegate to the Coun-
   cil of Ferrara-Florence (1438-45). (See: MOREA).
Archbishop of Salzburg: 26/128: see Graf Hieronhymus Joseph
   COLLOREDO.
Archbishop of Sardis: 26/123: Orthodox delegate to the Council of
   Ferrara-Florence (1438-45). (See: SARDIS).
Archbishops of Athens, Corinth and of Trebizond: 26/123: Orthodox
   delegates to the Council of Ferrara-Florence (1438-45). (See:
   ATHENS, CORINTH, TREBIZOND).
Archivio Storico. . . La Guerra dei Senesi col conte di Pitigliano: 10/
   42: (It) Historical Archives. . . The War of the Sienese against the
   Count of PITIGLIANO.
Archon: 68/141: the chief magistrate of Athens.
Arcturus: 77/43: chief star of the constellation Boötes.
Arena: 4/16; 29/145; 78/59: see DIOCLETIAN'S ARENA.
Arena romana: 12/53: see DIOCLETIAN'S ARENA.
Arezzo: 44/19; 50/43; 76/40: city in central Italy.
Arezzo, Gui d': 79/65: Guido d'Arezzo, ?995-1050?, Benedictine
   monk and musician; supposed to be inventor of the medieval
   "great scale" or gamut, the hexacord, and hexacord solmization.
Argicida: 1/5: see HERMES.
arguendo: 67/133: (It) accusing.
Arimino: 9/37; 24/111: (It) RIMINI.
Ariminium: 9/36: (L) RIMINI.
Aristotle: 36/29; 73/19; 74/22: 384-322, the Greek philosopher.
Arlechino: 77/48: (It) harlequin.
[Arles]: 80/86: town in Provence, France.
Arli: 80/86: (It) ARLES.
Armenonville: 74/14; 76/31; 78/58: Pavillon d'Armenonville, fashion-
   able restaurant in the Bois de Boulogne, Paris.
[Armour]: 33/14: Chicago meatpacking firm, among those investi-
   gated by Upton Sinclair for his novel, The Jungle (1906).
Armstrong: 80/91: DTC, Pisa.
Army: 65/111: see CONTINENTAL ARMY.
Arnaut: 6/21; 20/89; 29/145: see Arnaut DANIEL.
Arno: 77/48, 51: river in Tuscany, central Italy.
Arnold: 69/153: Benedict, 1741-1801, American army officer and
   traitor; in the Revolutionary War, he received the rank of brigadier general in the Continental Army. In 1779 he began corre-
   spondence with the British forces and in 1780, while he commanded West Point, he arranged for the surrender of the fort to the
   British. The plot was discovered and Arnold fled to British protection.
arpens: 61/83: (Fr) acres.
Ararat: 34/21: Mount Ararat in Turkey, identified as the landing
   place of Noah's Ark.
arriba: 62/96: (Sp) hail!
Arry: 74/22: see ARISTOTLE.
Ars Amandi: 63/98: (L) The Art of Love. (See: OVID).

Artemis:[4/14]; 30/147, [148(?)]; 35/25]; 76/35, 36(?); 79/70: the
    goddess of wildlife and the hunt. See ACTAEON.
Arthur:80/89: see Arthur SYMONS.
arti:80/75: (It) guilds.
"a S. Bartolomeo mi vidi col pargoletto, / Chiodato a terra colle
    braccie aperte/ in forma di croce gemisti. / diss'io: Io son' la
    luna. "/ Coi piedi sulla falce d'argento/ mi parve di pietosa
    sembianza:80/78: (It)" at St. Bartholomeo I found myself with
    the little boy/ nailed to the ground with his arms spread/ as on
    the cross, (you) groaned/ I said: I am the moon. "/ With my
    feet on the silvery scythe/ he looked pitiful to me.
Ascension:25/116: Ascension Day, fortieth day after Easter.
a schavezo:35/25: (It) a scavezzo: quickly, hurriedly; at wholesale
    price.
Asia:61/85.
Aso iqua me:28/133: prob. (It: Romagna dialect) It's me.
Asquith:77/47: Herbert Henry Asquith, 1st Earl of Oxford and As-
    quith, 1852-1928, British statesman; Prime Minister (1908-16).
[Asquith, Margot]:38/38(?); 80/71: 1864-1945, second wife of
    Herbert Henry ASQUITH.
assez mal propre:59/72: (Fr) rather slovenly. (See: Mailla, His-
    toire Générale, XI, 113, note).
Assisi:74/26; 79/64: town in Umbria, central Italy; birth place of
    St. Francis of Assisi; above the Saint's tomb, two Gothic church-
    es were built, both decorated with frescoes by Cimabue, Giotto,
    and others.
Astafieva:79/62, 67: Serafima, 1876-1934, Russian dancer and teach-
    er; member of the corps de ballet of the Maryinsky Theatre
    (1895-1905) and of the Diaghilev Company (1909-1911); opened a
    ballet school in London.
Astor:34/17: John Jacob, 1763-1848, American merchant and fur
    trader.
Astorga:65/120: town in León province, NW Spain.
Asturias:65/121: mountain region, NW Spain.
as under the rain altars:78/59: from Analects, XII, xxi, 1.
atasal:76/36, 37: the word is said to mean "union with God" and to
    come from the writings of Avicenna, the Mohammedan physician
    and philosopher.
Atchen (Atkins) Chelisa:54/32: see CHÉ-POU-KIU-ATCHEN.
Atesten:20/91: commune in NE Italy. (See: ESTE).
Athame:21/100: prob. inv.: a daughter of the Sun. (See: PHAE-
    THUSA).
Athelstan:48/36: Æthelstan, d. 940, king of the English (924-40).
Athena:17/77, 78; [21/99; 74/16]; 76/39; 78/57; 79/64: the goddess
    of wisdom; Pallas Athena; patron of the arts of peace and of war;
    guardian of cities, especially of ATHENS.
Athenae:74/16: see ATHENS.
Athens:26/123; 43/12; 46/28; 74/18: the Greek city.
A tiels leis ... en ancien scripture: 31/6: (Pr) according to such
    laws ... (Fr) in old handwriting.
A traverso le foglie:39/46: (It) through the leaves.

Atreides:8/32; [82/101]: Atreidaes, sons of ATREUS.

Atreus:77/49: king of Mycenae; son of Pelops, who brought a curse
   on his house. Thyestes, Atreus' brother, seduced Atreus' wife;
   Atreus murdered three of the four sons of Thyestes and served
   them to their father. Thyestes laid a curse on the house of
   Atreus, which descended upon his sons, Agamemnon, Menelaus.

atrox Ming, atrox finis:58/68: (L) frightful MING, frightful end.

Atthis:5/18: poss. one of the young girls of whom SAPPHO sang;
   prob. Attis, a priest of Cybele, who castrated himself in a fit of
   religious fanaticism. (See: Catullus, LXIII).

Atti, Antonio degli:9/40 fl. 1448, brother of Isotta degli ATTI.

Atti, Isotta degli:9/38, 39, 41; 20/94; 74/8, 26; [76/30, 37, 40]: ?1430-
   1470, first the mistress, then the third wife (1456) of Sigismondo
   MALATESTA. She bore him at least two sons, both illegitimate:
   SALLUSTIO (b. 1448) and Valerien (b. 1454). It was in her honor
   that Malatesta built the TEMPIO.

Attlee:79/64: Clement Richard, 1883-   , British statesman; leader of the Labor Party; Prime Minister (1945-51).

Aubeterre:76/33; 80/87: a church just outside Poitiers, France.

Auchmuty:64/105: Robert, d. 1788, colonial jurist and loyalist; appointed judge of the vice-admiralty for Massachusetts and New
   Hampshire. With John ADAMS, he was counsel for Captain
   PRESTON in the case of the Boston Massacre (1770). He returned to England in 1776.

auctor:79/65: (L) author.

Au douce temps de pascor:54/22: (Fr) in the fair Eastertime. (See:
   Joios of Tolosa: Lautrier el dous temps de pascor).

auf dem Wasser:34/15: (Ger) on the water.

augean stables:74/17: the stables of Augeas, king of Elis; cleansed
   by HERACLES.

Augusta:41/55: one of the three principal characters in René
   CREVEL's Les Pieds dans le plat (1933), where she is an Austrian archduchess.

Augusta Victoria:41/53: see VICTORIA.

Augustine:16/68: Saint Augustine, 354-430.

Augustus:80/80: BC 63-14 AD, first Roman emperor (BC 27-14 AD).

Aula regum:67/133: Aula Regis, the chief court of England during
   early Norman times. The single court split into four parts: the
   High Court of Chancery, the Queen's Bench, the Exchequer, and
   the Court of Common Pleas.

aulentissima rosa fresca:79/64: (It) thou sweetly-smelling fresh
   red rose. (See: Ciullo d'Alcamo, Dialogue, the first line of
   which runs: Rosa fresca aulentissima).

Aunt F.:80/86; 84/117: Aunt Frank, great aunt (by marriage) of
   Ezra Pound; she took him to Europe when he was a child.

Aurelia:76/30: the Aurelian Way (Via Aurelia), the Roman highway
   which runs along the coast to Pisa and then north to Genoa.

Aurunculeia:4/13,15; 5/17: Vinia Aurunculeia, a bride praised by
   Catullus. (See: Catullus, LXI).

Austini, Marcellus:42/8: prob. member of the Sienese BALÍA, 1622.

Austors:23/108: see Austors de MAENSAC.

Auss'ralia: 74/5: Australia.

Austria: 16/71; 32/9; 38/38, 41; 50/42; 80/71.

Authority comes from right reason: 36/29: from Johannes Scotus
ERIGENA, De Divisione Naturae, I, chapter 69.

Auvergnat: 5/18; 23/109: see AUVERGNE.

Auvergne: 23/109: a section of Provence, SE central France.

Auxerre: 34/16; 77/45: capital of Yonne department, NE central
France.

avenément révolution allemande posait des problèmes nouveaux, /
routine commercial être remplacée par création de deux/ fonds or
et blé destinés au proletariat victorieux (allemand): 33/13: (Fr)
beginning German revolution posed some new problems, / commercial routine to be replaced by the creation of two/ funds (of)
gold and wheat destined to the victorious (German) proletariat.

Avernus:1/4: lake near Cumae and Naples; close to it was the cave
by which AENEAS descended to the lower world; sometimes, as
here, used as the name of the lower world itself.

Avignon:21/96; 78/55; 80/87: capital of Vaucluse department, SE
France, on the left bank of the Rhone; was the Papal See during
the "Babylonian Captivity" (1309-78) and residence of several
antipopes during the Great Schism (1378-1408); under Papal rule,
it became a great trading city.

avoyer:67/140: (Fr) chief magistrate of a free city or a canton in
French Switzerland.

Awoi:77/43: the Lady Awoi, first wife of GENJI in Lady Murasaki's
Tale of Genji. Also: character in the Noh play, Awoi no Uye.
(See: Translations, 323-331).

Axon:35/23:

[Ayen, la Duchesse d']:65/118: prob. Henriette-Anne-Louise d'Ag-
uesseau de Fresne, Duchesse d'Ayen, wife of Jean-Paul-François
de NOAILLES.

Ayers, Severn:64/106: member of the Virginia House of Burgesses
in 1770.

Ayliffe:70/157: John, 1676-1732, English jurist and writer on law.

Azeglio:50/43: Massimo Taparelli, the Marchesse d'Azeglio, 1798-
1866, Italian statesman and author, leader in the Risorgimento
(1848); assisted early liberal reforms of PIUS IX, with whom he
joined in support of the House of Savoy.

Azores:28/140: the islands in the Atlantic.

B

Baastun:65/121: see BOSTON.

Baastun Gazette:66/128; 67/133: see BOSTON GAZETTE.

babao:74/17: (It) bugbear.

Babylon:15/66; 74/15; 76/31, 40: the ancient city.

Bacchus:78/59: see DIONYSUS.

Bach, Johnnie:59/72; 80/82, 88: Johann Sebastian, 1685-1750, the German organist and composer.

Bacher:74/26: prob. pseudonym for an inhabitant of Gais, near Brunico, in the Italian Tyrol.

Bacon, Baldy:12/53: Francis S. Bacon, fl. 1910, American business man.

Bacon, Lord:64/102; 77/47: Sir Francis, 1st Baron Verulam, 1561-1626, English philosopher and statesman.

Baghdad:56/49; 74/22: city in Iraq, on the Tigris river. The Germans once projected a railroad from Berlin to Baghdad.

Bagni Romagna:78/60: Bagno di Romagna, commune in Forlí province, N Italy.

Bagot:34/17: Sir Charles, 1781-1843, British diplomat; minister to the U. S. (1815-20) when he negotiated the Rush-Bagot Convention (1817) limiting armaments on the Great Lakes.

[Bahai, Sir Abdul Baha]:46/26: 1844-1921, leader of the religion known as Bahaism, founded by his father Baha Ullah. Bahaists believe in the unity of all religions, universal education, world peace and the equality of sexes.

Bailey:42/3, 4, 5, 6; 43/9, 12, 13, 14, 16: see BALÍA.

baily:40/51: bail, the outer wall of a feudal castle, or the court thereby enclosed.

Baker:40/48: George Fisher, 1840-1931, American financier and philanthropist; one of the founders (1863) of the First National Bank of New York, president of the bank in 1877, chairman of its board of directors in 1909; he was closely associated with the house of MORGAN.

balascio:36/29: (It) a variety of ruby.

baldacchino:[8/31]; 52/4: (It) canopy.

baldachino:8/31: see BALDACCHINO.

Baldy:12/53: see Baldy BACON.

Balfour:46/26: Arthur James, 1848-1930, British statesman; foreign minister (1916-1919); author of the Balfour Declaration which pledged British support to the founding of a Jewish state in Palestine.

Balía: [42/3, 4, 5, 6; 43/9], 10, [12, 13, 14, 16]: (It) authority, power, bench of magistrates; here the reference is to the Balía, ruling authority of SIENA in the early 17th century.

Balista:26/124: (It) catapult.

Baluba:38/39; 53/10; 74/12, 14; 77/43: name of a tribe (and of the place of residence) in the upper valley of the Kassai river, a tributary of the Congo, in the SW Belgian Congo.

banco di giro:42/3: (It) a bank specializing in the endorsement and transfer of credit.

[15]

Bancroft:65/118; 69/153: Edward, 1744-1821, American scientist and
    secret agent; during the American Revolution he served as a se-
    cret agent for the American commissioners in Paris; it was al-
    leged that he sold information to the British government.
Bandini:44/21: poss. Carlo Bandini, author of Roma e la nobilita ro-
    mana nel tramonto del secolo XVIII (1914).
Banditore, il:43/12: (It) the public cryer.
Bank:37/32, 33, 34, 35, 36: see SECOND NATIONAL BANK OF THE
    UNITED STATES.
Bank:43/13: see MONTE DEI PASCHI.
Bank:80/92: see BANK OF ENGLAND.
Bankers:80/91: corporal in the Provost section, DTC, Pisa.
Bankhead:84/115: John Hollis, 1872-1946, U. S. Senator from Ala-
    bama (1930-46).
Bank of Egypt:80/88.
Bank of England:37/32; [80/92]: founded 1694 by William PATERSON;
    the central bank of England.
Bank of the Paris Union:38/42: La Banque de l'Union Parisienne, an
    investment bank founded in 1874 and reorganized in 1904; controlled
    by ZAHAROFF and SCHNEIDER-CREUSOT.
Bank president:37/34: see Nicholas BIDDLE.
Baptist learnery:28/136: poss. Baylor University, Waco, Texas, a
    Baptist school.
Barabbas:74/5, 14: the bandit held in jail at the time of the arrest of
    Christ.
Barabello:5/19: a poetaster of the time of Pope Leo X; he asked to be
    crowned with laurel in the Capitol; during the mock ceremony the
    Pope's elephant, on which Barabello was riding, became fright-
    ened by the fireworks and refused to move.
barbarisci:24/110: (It) wild horses (?).
Barbary:69/152: the Barbary States, North Africa. In the Algerine
    War (1815) the U. S. forced concessions from the dey of Algiers.
barbiche:74/25: (Fr) goatee.
Barbier de Séville:65/119: the play by BEAUMARCHAIS, first per-
    formed in 1775.
Barbo:11/51: Pietro, 1417-71, Pope Paul II (1464-71).
Bard:80/79: William Shakespeare.
Bard, Jo:81/96: prob. Joseph Bard, 1892-   , English essayist.
Bariatinsky, Princess:79/66: prob. Lydia YAVORSKA, 1874-1921,
    wife of Prince Vladamir Bariatinsky; poss. Princess Anatole
    Marie Bariatinsky, author of My Russian Life (1923).
Barilli:80/74: Bruno, 1880-1952, Italian music critic and composer.
Barlow:31/5: Joel, 1754-1812, American writer and diplomat; ap-
    pointed U. S. consul to Algiers (1795); he succeeded in releasing
    American prisoners and negotiating treaties with Algiers. In 1811
    he was sent to Europe to negotiate a commercial treaty with
    Napoleon.
[Barney, Natalie]:80/83; 84/117: 20th century American writer living
    in Paris.
Barre, Mass.:74/25: town in central Massachusetts, NW of Worces-
    ter.

Bartók:84/116: Bela, 1881-1945, Hungarian composer, pianist and collector of folk music.

Barzun:77/50: Jacques, 1907-   , American historian and teacher.

Basil:77/52; 81/96: see Basil BUNTING.

Basinio:9/34; 82/102: Basinio de Basanii, 1425-1457, Italian poet patronized by Sigismondo MALATESTA, wrote L'Isottaeus, a poem modeled after Ovid's Heroides, which represents Sigismondo's love for Isotta degli ATTI (Paris: 1539). In 1456, Basinio defeated Parcelio PANDONE in a literary debate; Pandone argued for the thesis: "One may be an elegant Latin poet without having studied assiduously the Greek authors. "

bassarids:79/66, 68: Thracian maenads.

Basse Cour:65/118: the house in Passy, formerly the Hotel de Valentinois, donated to the American ministers (1778) by Donatien le Ray de CHAUMONT.

Bassier:84/115: DTC, Pisa.

Bastun:62/88, 89: see BOSTON.

Batavia:60/76: city on NW coast of Java.

[Bathsheba]:8/30: wife of Uriah, the Hittite. David seduced her, had her husband killed, and then married her out of remorse. She was the mother of Solomon.

Batsabe:8/30: see BATHSHEBA.

Battista:9/38: see Leon Battista ALBERTI.

battistero:79/62: (It) baptistery; text reference is evidently to that of Pisa.

Battle Hymn of the Republic:80/76: the famous marching song of the American Civil War, written in 1861 by Julia Ward Howe.

Battle of Lexington:64/105; 66/127: see LEXINGTON AND CONCORD, Battles of.

Battle of Waffenschlag:41/54: inv. ; note: waffe = (Ger) weapon + schlag = (Ger) strike.

Baur, Wilhelm:41/53: 1826-97, author of Geschichte und Lebensbilder aus der Erneuerung des Religiösen Lebens in Deutschen Befreiungskriegen, Hamburg, 1864. (See: IN DEN DEUTSCHEN BEFREUDENSKRIEGEN).

Bayard:34/16: James Asheton, 1767-1815, American statesman; member of the House of Representatives (1797-1803), U. S. Senate (1804-13), and of the commission which negotiated the Treaty of Ghent (1814), ending the War of 1812.

Bayard:65/113: John Bukenheim, 1738-1807, Philadelphia merchant; colonel in the Philadelphia Volunteers during the Revolution; member of the CONTINENTAL CONGRESS (1785-87).

Bayle:28/139: Pierre, 1647-1706, French philosopher and critic.

Baymont, Tommy:19/86, 87: see Thomas LAMONT.

Bay of Naples:54/26.

B. B. C. :76/36: the British Broadcasting Corporation.

bé:54/35: (Fr) well!

Beard, Charles:84/116: Charles Austin, 1874-1948, American historian.

Beardsley, Aubrey:74/22; 80/89: Aubrey Vincent, 1872-98, English illustrator and writer.

Beardsley, Mabel: [80/85]; 82/102: 1872-1913, sister of Aubrey
    BEARDSLEY.
Bearing the golden bough of Argicida:1/5: from Homeric Hymn V, To
    Aphrodite, 117-118. (Prob. a translation from the Latin version of
    Georgius Dartona Cretensis).
Beauchamps:66/132: Richard de Beauchamp, ? 1430-81, Bishop of
    Hereford and Salisbury, Chancellor of the Order of the Garter.
Beaucher, Sergeant:76/33: DTC, Pisa.
Beaugency:56/49: town in Loiret department, on the Loire river,
    France. There is an old French song which runs:
    Orléans, Beaugency!
    Notre Dame de Cléry!
    Vendôme! Vendôme!
    Quel chagrin, quel ennui
    De compter toute la nuit
    Les heures -- les heures!
Beaumarchais:31/4; 32/7; 65/118; 68/143; 71/161: Pierre Augustin
    Caron de, 1732-99, French playwright and man of affairs.
beauté, la:80/98: (Fr) beauty.
Beauties of Mougden:61/86: the Eulogy on MUKDEN, a poem written
    by Emperor KIEN-LONG in 1743 after a visit to Mukden to honor
    the tomb of his ancestors.
Beauvais:34/16: capital of Oise department, N France.
Beccaria:64/106: Cesare Bolnesana di, ?1735-1794?, Italian econo-
    mist and jurist; author of Tratto dei Delitti e della Pene (1764).
Bechstein:79/63: a make of piano.
Becket:67/135: Thomas à Becket, 1117-70, Archbishop of Canterbury
    (1162-70); murdered by the agents of Henry II.
Beddoes:80/75, 76: Thomas Lovell, 1803-49, the English poet.
Bedell:80/91; 84/115: lieutenant in the Provost section, DTC, Pisa.
Bedlam:68/141: Bethlehem Royal Hospital in London.
Beebe:38/39: William, 1877-   , American scientist, explorer and
    author, famous for his underwater explorations in the bathysphere.
Beecher:40/48: Henry Ward, 1813-87, American Congregational
    preacher, orator and lecturer; held the pulpit of the Plymouth
    Church, Brooklyn, New York, from 1847; leader in the Abolition-
    ist movement.
Beethoven:79/63: Ludwig van, 1770-1827, the German composer.
Begin thy plowing... think of plowing:47/31: from Hesiod, Works and
    Days, 383-391; 448.
Be glad, poor beaste:82/103: poss. variation on Chaucer, Balade de
    Bon Conseyl, translated by Henry Van Dyke in SPEARE, Pocket
    Book of Verse: Therefore, poor beaste....
Bekford:71/167: William Beckford, 1709-1770, West Indian planter;
    member of Parliament; alderman and Lord Mayor of London.
Belcher, Governor:64/107: Jonathan, 1682-1757, colonial governor
    of Massachusetts and New Hampshire (1730-41); governor of New
    Jersey (1747-57).
Bel Fiore:10/43: Belriguardo, a villa of Borso d'ESTE.
Bell, Miss:52/3: Gertrude Margaret Lowthian Bell, 1868-1926, Brit-
    ish authority on, and government servant in, the Near East.

Bella, Piero della:11/48, [49]: officer in the forces of Sigismondo
  MALATESTA. (Note: Pound's description: that gay bird... is a
  misreading of his source, which describes Piero della Bella as a
  gagliardo, or brave, valiant. See: Tonini, Rimini nella Signoria
  de' Malatesti, II, 281, who quotes Pound's source, the Cronaca of
  Gaspare Broglio, an unpublished manuscript in the Gambalunga
  Library, Rimini).
Belle Poule:65/120: a French frigate anchored at Corunna; John
  ADAMS dined aboard 24 December 1779.
Bellin, Zuan:25/120; 45/24; 74/3: see Giovanni BELLINI.
[Bellini, Giovanni]:25/120; 45/24; 74/3: 1426-1516, leading painter of
  the Venetian school, noted for his altarpieces and Madonnas.
Belotti:80/79: owner of Belotti's Ristorante Italiano, 12 Old Compton
  Street, London, where Pound and his friends dined, 1910-1920.
Belmont:40/48: August, 1816-1890, American banker and politician;
  head of August Belmont and Company.
bel seno (in rimas escarsas, vide sopra):77/47: (It) beautiful bosom
  (Pr) (in rare rimes, (It) see above).
bel seno...copulatrix:77/48: (It) beautiful bosom...(L) who copulates.
benché:42/4: (It) although.
Benche niuno cantasse:24/112: (It) although no one was singing.
benecomata dea: [74/15]; 76/38: (L) the fair-tressed goddess. (See:
  CIRCE).
Benedetto:5/19: see Benedetto VARCHI.
[Benedict XIII]:61/81: Pope (1724-1730).
benedicti:84/115: (L) the blessed ones.
Benette joue la Valse des Elfes:27/130: (Fr) Benette plays the Waltz
  of the Elves. (See: Francis Jammes, Le Poète).
Bengal:57/57.
Ben:52/3: prob. Benjamin FRANKLIN; poss. Benito MUSSOLINI.
Ben:67/134: see Benjamin FRANKLIN.
Ben:74/3: see Benito MUSSOLINI.
[Benckendorff, Aleksandr Konstantinovich]:19/87: 1849-1917, Russian
  ambassador to London (1903-16).
Benin:81/96: DTC, Pisa.
Benito:80/73: see Benito MUSSOLINI.
Benjamin:74/18: the plateau of E central Palestine, near the Jordan
  river, between Jerusalem and Bethel.
Bennett, Arnold:80/84: Enoch Arnold, 1867-1931, English novelist.
Bentinck, Colonel:65/122: Berend Henrik, 1753-1830, one of the
  Dutch negotiators of the Treaty of Paris (1783).
Bentinck:50/43: Lord William Cavendish, 1774-1839, British states-
  man and soldier; governor-general of Madras, India (1803-07);
  commander in Sicily (1811); governor-general of India (1833).
Benzi, Andreas:10/44: Andrea, fl. 1460, a fiscal agent of Pope PIUS
  II; delivered the papal accusation against Sigismondo MALATESTA.
Benzo, Nic:11/48: officer in the household squadron of the forces of
  Sigismondo MALATESTA.
Berchthold:76/37:
Berdsma:69/150: Bergsma, fl. 1780, an official of the Province of
  Friesland.

Berettino:26/127: (It) small cap.

Berlin:33/13; 38/38; 74/16, 22; 84/118.

Berlitz:58/66: the school of language studies, founded by Maximilian
   Delphinus Berlitz, 1852-1921.

Bernard:[64/102]; 67/134: Sir Francis, 1712-79, colonial governor of
   New Jersey (1758-60), and Massachusetts (1760-69). His policies
   aroused bitter opposition and he was removed from office in 1769
   and returned to England.

Bernart:23/109: see Bernart de TIERCI.

Bersolle:68/143: fl. 1778, a Frenchman engaged in the repair of ships.

Bessedovsky:33/13: Grigorii Zinovevich, a former Soviet diplomat;
   author of Revelations of a Soviet Diplomat (1931).

bestialmente:8/32; 9/35: (It) in a beastly manner.

Bethlehem:65/111: a town in Pennsylvania.

Betuene April and Merche:39/45: from the 14th-century lyric Alysoun: "Bytuene Mersh and Averil/ When spray beginneth to spring."

Beveridge, Senator:81/97: Albert Jeremiah, 1862-1927, U. S. Senator (1899-1911) and historian; supported the policies of Theodore
   Roosevelt; an organizer of the Progressive Party (1912).

bezant:18/80: gold coin issued by the Byzantine emperors, circulat-
   ing in Europe between 6th and 15th centuries.

B. F.:68/143: see Benjamin FRANKLIN.

B. Fr.:68/143 see Benjamin FRANKLIN.

bhud:54/28; 55/44; 58/64: see BUDDHA.

Bhudd-ha:38/39: see BUDDHA.

bhuddists:54/26, 27, 29, 30, 31: followers of BUDDHA.

Bible:74/8; 76/32; 77/51.

Bicker:68/146,147: H., fl. 1780, a Dutch statesman, friendly to the
   American Revolutionary cause.

Biddle, Nicholas:34/19; 37/33, 34: 1786-1844, American financier; ap-
   pointed director of the SECOND NATIONAL BANK OF THE
   UNITED STATES (1819) and became its president (1822). He was
   President JACKSON's chief antagonist in the Bank War.

bidet:80/72: (Fr) sitz bath.

Biers:18/81: poss. Hiram MAXIM.

bifronte:78/55: (It) double-faced.

Big Beaver:31/3: a river in W Pennsylvania.

biglietti:56/47: (It) paper bills.

Billi:8/30: see PENNABILLI.

Bill of Rights:65/110; [80/92]: the British Bill of Rights, drawn up in
   1689.

Billyum:80/74: see William Butler YEATS.

Bimmy:16/72: an invented name with no particular reference.

Bingen:80/77: city in W Germany, located on the Rhine above the
   whirlpool known as the Binger Lock.

Bingen on the Rhine:80/77: a poem by Caroline Elizabeth Sarah Norton.

Bingham:69/153: William, 1752-1804, American politician; founder of
   the Bank of North America (1781); U. S. Senator (1795-1801).

Binis, Johnny something or other de:42/7:

Binyon:80/84, 85: Laurence, 1869-1943, English poet, Keeper of the

Prints and Drawings, British Museum; authority on Oriental art; translator of DANTE.

Birch:71/165: an English agent in Boston, 1776.

Birrell:82/102: Augustine, 1850-1933, English essayist and public official.

Bishop:80/87: poss. Samuel Wilberforce, 1804-1873, Bishop of Oxford and of Winchester; in 1860 Wilberforce attacked the Darwinian theory and was challenged and defeated in argument by T. H. Huxley.

Bishops of Lacedaemon and of Mitylene, / of Rhodos, of Modon Brandos: 26/123: all Orthodox delegates to the Council of Ferrara-Florence, (1438-45). (See: LACEDAEMON, MYTILENE, RHODES, MODON BRANDOS).

Bishops of Lampascus and Cyprus:26/124: Orthodox delegates to the Council of Ferrara-Florence (1438-45). (See: LAMPASCUS, CYPRUS).

Bismarck:48/34; [80/81]: Otto von, 1815-98, the German soldier and statesman.

Bismark:80/81: see Otto von BISMARCK.

Bithynia:48/35: Bythnia, ancient country of NW Asia Minor; became a Roman province in BC 74 when Nicodemus willed his kingdom to Rome.

Bivar:3/11: village in Old Castile, near BURGOS, N Spain.

B-J:80/89: see Sir Edward BURNE-JONES.

Blake:16/68: William, 1757-1827, English mystic poet and illustrator.

Blaydon:62/88: Colonel Bladen, fl. 1740, member of the British Board of Trade and Plantations.

Blaye:65/117: a French village near BORDEAUX.

[Blitterswyk, Baron de Lynden de]:65/122: fl. 1782, deputy from ZEELAND at the Conference of Paris.

Blodgett:38/40: poss. Lorin Blodget, author of The Textile Industries of Philadelphia (1880).

Blomberg:68/147: fl. 1780, a banker in Amsterdam.

Blood:78/57: DTC, Pisa.

Blount:70/155: William, 1749-1800, American political leader; U. S. Senator from Tennessee (1796-97); expelled from the Senate on the charge of plotting to aid the British to get control of Spanish Florida and Louisiana.

Blum:80/72: Léon, 1872-1950, the French Socialist statesman and writer.

Blunt:81/100; 82/101: Wilfrid Scawen, 1840-1922, English poet and political writer; admired for his independence of mind.

B. M.:80/84: see BRITISH MUSEUM.

Boardman, Andrew:66/130: town clerk of Cambridge, Massachusetts, 1772.

Board of War:65/114: a special council established during the American Revolution, acting as intermediary between the CONTINENTAL CONGRESS and the armed forces.

Boccata:20/90: Giovanni Boccatti, ?1435-1480?, Umbrian painter.

Boche:16/73; 19/85: Franco-British term for the German.

Boeotians:67/139: people of the ancient republic of Boeotia, E central Greece.

Boer War:80/81: (1899-1902).

Bohea:64/108; 70/156: a kind of tea.

Bohlem und Halbach:38/41: see Gustave KRUPP VON BOHLEN UND HALBACH.

Bohon:80/92: DTC, Pisa.

Bois de Boulogne:66/126: a large park containing the racetracks of Longchamp and Auteuil, just W of Paris.

Boja d'un Dio!:28/133: (It) damn it!

bojar:33/11; 35/24; 56/47: (Russ) member of a Russian aristocratic order, favored with certain exclusive privileges.

Bokara:60/75: see BUKHARA.

Boleyn:80/94: Anne, ?1507-1536, second wife of Henry VIII and mother of Queen Elizabeth I; she was beheaded; also: the Boleyn family.

Bolgarini, Paris:43/13: prob. Sienese representative at the negotiations leading to the establishment of the MONTE DEI PASCHI.

bolge:15/65; 25/118: (It) infernal circle.

Bolingbroke:68/144: Henry St. John, Viscount Bolingbroke, 1678-1754, English statesman and orator; author of Idea of a Patriot King (1749).

Bolivia:27/130.

Bologna:9/36; 24/110; 26/126; 78/56: the city in N central Italy.

Bologna, Francesco da:30/148: a printer of whom little is known; poss. he is the same as Francesco Griffi, who was a printer in BOLOGNA in 1516-17.

Bolsano:74/11; 83/113: Bolzano, capital of Bolzano province, N Italy.

bolsheviki:16/74: members of the majority group of the Russian political group led by Lenin, the Workers Social Democratic Party (1903).

Bonaparte:31/6; 33/11; 34/15,16; 71/163,164: see NAPOLEON.

[Bonaparte, Maria Anna Elisa]:44/20, 21: 1777-1820, sister of NAPOLEON; made Grand Duchess of Tuscany (1809); exiled 1810.

Bondeno:24/113: commune, Ferrara province, N Italy.

Bond St.:80/80: a street in LONDON noted for its fashionable shops.

Bonius:29/142: a soldier from Treviso with whom Cunizza da ROMANO took up after SORDELLO had left her.

bonzes:55/40: Buddhist monks.

bonzesses:55/40: Buddhist nuns.

Book of the Council Major:25/115: the records of the Great Council of Venice.

Book of the Mandates:24/110: the mandates of the ESTE family.

Boracchios, Los:80/71: Los Borrachos, a painting by VELÁSQUEZ in the Prado, Madrid.

Borah:84/115: William Edgar, 1865-1940, U. S. Senator (1907-40) a leading spokesman on international affairs.

Bordeaux:37/33; 62/92; 65/117: port city of Gironde department, SW France.

Boreas:74/16; 77/43: the north wind.

Borgia, Pope Alessandro:30/149: see ALEXANDER VI.

Borgia, Caesare:30/148: 1476-1507, Italian nobleman; son of Pope ALEXANDER VI.

Borgia, Giovanni (John):5/18,19: d.1497; son of Pope ALEXANDER
   VI; brother of Caesare BORGIA. His body was found in the Tiber;
   it was generally held that Caesare instigated his murder.
[Borgia, Lucretia]:38/37(?); 74/24(?): 1480-1519, sister of Caesare
   BORGIA, daughter of Pope ALEXANDER VI.
Borr:80/87: prob. a surname, reminding Pound of Bertran de Born
   of ALTAFORTE.
Borso:10/43, 45, 46; 17/78, 79; 20/91, 95; 21/96; 24/114; 26/121: see
   Borso d'ESTE.
Boss, the:41/52, 53: see Benito MUSSOLINI.
Boston:62/88, 89; 64/103, 104, 105; 65/109, 121; 68/145; 70/157, 158;
   71/164, 165; 81/97.
Boston, the:65/114: the frigate that carried John ADAMS to his post
   as commissioner to France in 1778.
Boston Gazette:62/90; 64/104; 66/128; 67/133, 136: a Boston news-
   paper, published 1719-98; the paper was strongly in favor of the
   American Revolution.
Bott:62/96: prob. Timothy PICKERING.
[Botticelli, Sandro]:20/90; 80/89: 1444-1510, the Florentine painter.
Bottom:80/80: see BOTTOMLY.
Bottomly:80/80: DTC, Pisa.
Boucaria:61/85: see BUKHARA.
Boudha:54/29: see BUDDHA.
Boud-hah:28/137: see BUDDHA.
Bouiller:74/11: the Bal BULLIER.
Bourbon:32/9; 34/16; 65/125: royal family of France, branches of
   which ruled Spain, Sicily and Parma at various times.
Bourbon, Mlle: 65/123, 124: a member of the BOURBON family, liv-
   ing at VERSAILLES in 1783.
Bournat:60/74: see Joachim BOUVET.
Bourrienne:18/80: Louis Antoine Fauvelet de, 1769-1834, French dip-
   lomat and writer; he was private secretary to NAPOLEON (1797-
   1802); his memoirs (10 vol., 1829) give a somewhat inaccurate
   account of Napoleon.
Boutwell:40/48: George Sewall, 1818-1905, American politician; member of House of Representatives (1863-69); one of the leaders in the
   move to impeach President JACKSON; Secretary of the Treasury
   (1869-73), during which term he averted the attempt to corner the
   gold market on Black Friday (24 September 1869) by releasing
   government gold.
Bouvet:60/[74], 78: Joachim, fl. 1732, Jesuit missionary in China.
   With GERBILLON and four other Jesuits, he arrived in Peiping in
   1688. Bouvet and Gerbillon were made professors of mathematics
   by KANG-HI and translated several TARTAR works on mathematics
   into Chinese. He also served as a surveyor and cartographer in
   the Chinese provinces.
Bowdoin:62/90: James, 1726-90, American statesman; nominated to
   the CONTINENTAL CONGRESS (1774), he was too ill to serve;
   he became a leading figure in the Massachusetts councils during the American Revolution and became governor of the state
   in 1785.

Bowers:81/95: Claude Gernade, 1878 -   , American journalist,
    historian and diplomat; ambassador to Spain (1933-39).
Bowery, the:28/135: section of lower MANHATTAN, New York,
    famous for its bars and its derelicts.
Bowring:50/43: Sir John, 1792-1872, English statesman and linguist;
    in 1836 he went to Italy to study England's commercial relations
    with Tuscany, Lucca, the Lombardian and Papal states; he re-
    turned to Italy in 1860 to discuss trade relations with Cavour.
Bozen:83/113: (Ger) BOLSANO.
bozze, le:76/38: (It) the rough draft, copy.
Bracelonde:83/110: poss. Brocéliande, the forest mentioned in the
    Arthurian legends.
Bracken:76/36: Brendan, 1901 -   , British publisher and politician,
    Minister of Information (1941-45).
Brackett:64/105: Brackett's Tavern, The Cromwell Head Inn, Boston.
Bracton:63/99; 67/133; 70/157: Henry de Bracton (or Bretton) d. 1267,
    English jurist; author of the first systematic treatise of law in
    England, De Legibus et Consuetudinibus Angliae.
Bracton:67/138: see Carter BRAXTON.
Braddock:71/160: Edward, 1695-1775, commander-in-chief of British
    forces in America (1754).
Braddon:80/86: see Mary Elizabeth Braddon MAXWELL.
[Brady, James Buchanan]:19/87: 1856-1917, American financier,
    commonly known as Diamond JIM.
Braganza:29/142; 32/9: capital of Bragança district, NE Portugal;
    seat of the house of Bragança, former rulers of Portugal.
Braintree:62/87; 63/99; 64/107; 66/129; 70/157: town in Massachusetts
    (now QUINCY), home of the ADAMS family; incorporated (1640).
Braintree House:37/36: a reference to the ADAMS family, whose
    home was in BRAINTREE, Mass.
branda:78/56: (It) hammock.
Brandolino, Cetho:11/48: Cecco Brandolino, a captain serving in the
    forces of Sigismondo MALATESTA.
Brassitalo:76/39: poss. Italico Brass, 1870-1943, Italian painter.
Brattle:66/131; 67/133: William, 1702-76, brigadier-general in the
    Massachusetts militia. In 1773 John ADAMS and William Brattle
    engaged in a debate, published in the Boston newspapers; their re-
    marks, collected under the title The Independence of the Judiciary,
    appear in the Works of John Adams, III. A loyalist, Brattle went
    to England during the Revolution.
Brattle Street:62/88; 64/104: a street in BOSTON, Mass., on which
    John and Abigail ADAMS lived (1768).
[Braxton, Carter]:67/138: 1736-97, American statesman, Virginia
    delegate to the CONTINENTAL CONGRESS.
[Brazil]:12/55; 46/28.
Breda:80/71: see SURRENDER OF BREDA.
Breisgau:20/89: the region in SW Germany.
Brescia:11/48; 35/25: the capital of Brescia province, N Italy.
Brest-Litovsk:16/74: a town in Russia where the treaty between Ger-
    many and the BOLSHEVIKI was signed (March 1918).
bride, the:5/17: see DANAË.

Bridges, Robert:80/85: 1844-1930, the English poet.
"brings the girl to her man":5/17: from Catullus, LXI, 56-60.
Brisset:27/129; 80/84: Jean-Pierre, French philologist and writer,
  among whose works is Les Origines humaines, deuxième edition
  de la science de Dieu (1913) in which he "demonstrated" that man
  is descended from the frog.
Bristol:65/113: port city, Gloucestershire, England; important center
  of trade with colonial America.
Britain:38/40; 44/20; 62/87, 89, 91, 93, 96; 64/108; 65/113, 125; 66/128;
  67/134; 68/142; 69/149; 70/156; 71/165: see GREAT BRITAIN.
British constitution:65/110; [71/160, 161]: a flexible constitution con-
  tained implicitly in the body of common and statutory law of the realm.
[British Empire]:65/110; 66/129.
British Islands:69/153.
British Museum:80/84.
British Statutes:64/105; [71/165]: prob. State Trials and Statutes at
  Large, edited by John Selden.
brits:78/59: slang term for the British people.
Britten:63/99: John le Britton (or Breton) d. 1275, Bishop of Here-
  ford; author of the treatise on English law, Britton.
Broadway:65/109: the street in New York.
broccatelli:40/49: (It) types of brocade.
Broglie:68/142: Victor-François, le Comte de, 1718-1804, Marshal
  of France (1759), Minister of War (1789).
Broglio:8/32; 9/37; 10/43: Gaspare, soldier in the forces of Sigismondo MALATESTA; author of Cronaca, an account of Malatesta's
  campaigns and life in RIMINI, the manuscript of which is at the
  Gambalunga Library, Rimini.
Bromley, Joe:28/136: prob. an acquaintance of Pound in Philadelphia,
  c. 1908.
Bronzino:79/63: Il Bronzino (Agnolo di Cosimo), 1502-72, Florentine
  painter in the court of Cosimo I.
Brookhart:33/14: Smith Wildman, 1869-1950, U.S. Senator from Iowa,
  (1928-32), spokesman for farm interests.
brother of Circe:17/79: see AEETES.
Brother Percy:16/70: prob. Percy Bysshe SHELLEY; poss. Lord
  Algernon PERCY.
Browning, Robert:2/6; 48/34: 1812-89, English poet, author of Sor-
  dello (1840), etc.
Bruge:65/122: Bruges, capital of W Flanders, NW Belgium, once a
  great trading city.
Bruhl:38/39: see Lucien LÉVY-BRUHL.
Brumaire:27/131; 44/20; [50/41]: one of the French Revolutionary
  months, running between 22 October and 20 November.
Brumale:50/41: see BRUMAIRE.
Brunik:77/48: town in the Tyrol, N Italy.
Brussels:33/12; 65/122: city in central Belgium.
Brutus:5/19: Marcus Junius, ?78-42 BC, one of the principals in the
  murder plot against Julius Caesar.
Buardino of Brescia:11/48: Sovardino da Brescia, soldier in the forces
  of Sigismondo MALATESTA.

Buc(c)entoro:3/11; 27/129: see BUCINTORO.

Buchanan:34/21: James, 1791-1868, President of the U. S. (1857-61).

Buchio:11/49: locality in central Italy taken from Sigismondo MALA-
     TESTA by the peace terms imposed by PIUS II (c. 1460).

[Bucintoro]: 3/11; 27/129: orig. the special ship used by the Doge of
     Venice during the ceremony of the marriage of Venice to the
     Adriatic; now the name of a Venetian rowing club.

Buddha:28/137; 38/39; 54/29, 30, 31, 33; 56/52; 77/49: direct or indi-
     rect references to the Buddha, fl. BC 563-483, who, born of a
     noble family, renounced luxury and became a hermit at the age of
     29. While sitting under a bo (i. e. pipal) tree, he received the
     "great enlightenment" and became a teacher. Buddhism teaches
     that suffering is inherent in life and that the greatest good is re-
     lease from life and suffering through the attainment of nirvana, a
     state of nonexistence in which the individual loses all sense of self
     and becomes identified with the Oneness of being.

Buddhists:54/26, 27 [29], 30, 31; [55/37, 40]44; 58/64: followers of
     BUDDHA.

Buffon:66/127: Comte Georges Louis Leclerç de, 1707-88, the French
     naturalist.

Bufford:80/92: DTC, Pisa.

[Bukhara]:60/75; 61/85: city in W Uzbek S. S. R., once a center of
     Moslem worship.

Bukos:22/101, 102: prob. John Maynard KEYNES.

Bulagaio:83/110: prob. an acquaintance of Pound in Venice.

Bull, Johnny:46/26; 71/163: nickname for GREAT BRITAIN.

Bull:64/106: William, 1710-91, colonial Lt. Governor of South Carol-
     ina (1760-75).

Bullier: [74/11]; 76/31: the Bal Bullier, a dance hall on the Boulevard
     Saint-Michel, Paris.

Bullington:74/17: DTC, Pisa.

[Bulwer-Lytton]:82/101: Edward Robert, 1st Earl of Lytton, 1831-91,
     English diplomat and poet.

Bunting:74/9, 10; [77/52; 81/96]: Basil, 20th century British poet who
     lived in the Near East; author of Redimiculum Matellarum (1930),
     Poems (1951).

bunya:77/52: (Hind) moneylender. Also: banya.

buonuomini:43/15: (It) good men.

Buovilla:7/26: poss. residence of William of Buovilla, a noble of
     Gascony whose wife was loved by Arnaut DANIEL.

bureaucrat paisable, Van Tzin Vei se montra, tout à fait incapable
     d'assumer le role de chef d'une revolution sanguinaire:33/13: (Fr)
     a peaceful bureaucrat, VAN TZIN VEI showed himself, completely
     incapable of assuming the role of chief of a bloody revolution.

Burgh, de:67/113: Hubert, d. 1243, earl of Kent, chief justice of
     England under Henry III (1216).

Burgos:3/11; 52/4; 65/121: capital of Burgos province, N Spain, in
     Old Castile; home and burial place of the CID.

Burgundy:21/97: province in E France, divided into the departments
     of Yonne, Côte d'Ore, Saône-et-Loire, and Ain.

Burke:62/87, 89; 68/144: Edmund, 1729-97, the British statesman

and writer; one of the prominent Whigs under GEORGE III; favored liberal treatment of American colonies.

Burne-Jones:80/89: Sir Edward, 1833-98, English painter and deco-
rator; strongly influenced by the ROSSETTIs; exponent of Pre-
Raphaelite doctrines.

Burnes:76/33: DTC, Pisa.

Burnet:67/137: Sir Thomas, ?1694-1753, English judge and political
writer.

Burr:74/23: DTC, Pisa.

Burr:32/7; 66/127; 70/156,159; 71/164: Aaron, 1756-1836, American
Revolutionary officer and political leader; U. S. Senator (1791-97);
ran for President (1800) and received same number of electoral
votes as JEFFERSON; the election was thrown into the Congress,
and Burr withdrew from the race to become Vice-President under
Jefferson. He was tried for treason after conspiring to seize territory from Spanish America to form a new republic in the South-
west, but was acquitted (1807).

Bushnell:31/3: David, ?1742-1824, American inventor, noted for his
invention of a submarine.

buttato via:8/28: (It) thrown away.

Buxtehude:75/28: Dietrich, 1637-1707, the North German composer
and organist.

Byers:28/136: prob. an acquaintance of Pound in Philadelphia, c.1908.

Byles:64/104: Mather, 1707-88, American Congregationalist clergyman and writer of light verse.

Byron, Lord:16/71; 63/97; 77/46: George Gordon, 1788-1824, the
English poet.

Byzance:79/67: see BYZANTIUM.

Byzantium:74/17; [79/67]: ancient city on the Bosphorus; site of modern Istanbul.

C

C, Monsieur:80/83: poss. Paul Claudel, 1868-1955, French poet and diplomat.

Ca':83/110: (It) house (casa).

Cabestan:4/13,16: Guillem da Cabestanh, a late 12th century Provençal troubadour; because he loved Marguerite (or Triclime or Soremonda), wife of Raymond of Chateau Roussillon, Raymond killed Guillem and had his heart cooked and served to Marguerite; upon learning what she had eaten, Marguerite declared that since she had eaten such noble food, her lips should touch no other and threw herself out the window. Some versions of the story claim she stabbed herself; others that she starved herself to death.

Cabot:69/153: George, 1752-1823, American businessman and politician; U. S. Senator from Massachusetts (1791-96).

Cabot, J.:65/109: John Cabot, ?1451-1498?, Venetian explorer; sailing under the English flag, he discovered areas of North America.

Cabranez:81/96:

Cade, Jack:33/11: d.1450, English rebel leader of the Kentish rebellion (May-June, 1450) in protest against corruption in the court.

Cadmus:2/9; 4/13; 27/132; 62/88: the founder of THEBES; a dragon guarding a spring killed the companions of Cadmus and he in turn killed the dragon; by ATHENA's instruction, he sowed the dragon's teeth, and from them armed warriors sprang up; these were set fighting each other until only five remained, the Sparti, ancestors of the noble families of Thebes. Cadmus is said to have civilized the BOEOTIANS and to have taught them the use of letters. He was the grandfather of PENTHEUS.

Cadore:25/119,120: Preve di Cadere, village in Venezia, NE Italy, birthplace of TITIAN.

caesia ocula:79/64: (L) caesii oculi: grey eyes.

Cafe Dante:78/59: a cafe in Verona.

Cagnascis, Nicolaus Ulivis de:42/7: a notary public of Florence, early 17th century.

Cahors:76/33: city in S central France, on the Lot river; important financial city in the Middle Ages, noted for its usurious practices.

Caïfon fou:55/40: see CAÏ-FONG-FU.

Caïfong:55/44: see CAÏ-FONG-FU.

Caï Fong:56/49: see CAÏ-FONG-FU.

[Caï-fong-fu]:55/40, 44; 56/49: (Kaifeng) city in HONAN province, E central China; served as the capital of the empire during the period of the Five Dynasties (907-960).

Caina attende:5/19: (It) Caina is waiting (Inferno, 5, 107). (Caina is a division of the lowest circle in the Inferno, containing those who have betrayed their country, family, master, or benefactor.)

Caine, Hall:35/23: Sir Thomas Henry Hall Caine, 1853-1931, English novelist, friend of Dante Gabriel ROSSETTI.

Caio e Tizio:76/32: (It) this (man) and that man; John Doe and Richard Roe.

Cairels:6/23: Elias, a Provençal troubadour of the 13th century.

Cairo:80/75: the city in Egypt.

Cai Tsong Hien Hoang Ti:61/85: see CHI-TSONG-HIEN-HOANG-TI.

Calabria:5/20: a region in ancient Italy.

Calhoun:79/67: DTC, Pisa.

Calhoun, J.:34/18,19, 20; [37/31]; 79/67: John Caldwell Calhoun,
    1782-1850, member of House of Representatives (1811-17), Secre-
    tary of War (1817-25), Vice-President (1825-32), Senator (1832-43),
    Secretary of State (1844-45), Senator (1845-50). From South Caro-
    lina, Calhoun was a champion of slavery and the Southern cause.

Calhoun, Mrs.:34/19; [37/31]: Floride Calhoun, wife of John CAL-
    HOUN, to whom she was married 8 January 1811.

Calhouns:37/31: see John and Floride CALHOUN.

Calixte:10/46: see CALIXTUS III.

[Calixtus III]:10/46: 1378-1458, Pope (1455-58), preceding PIUS II;
    quarreled with ALFONSO V of Aragon and Naples, who wanted
    Ancona in return for his friendship; Calixtus refused.

Calkoen:62/92; 68/146: Hendrik, 1742-1818, Amsterdam lawyer; in-
    strumental in swaying Dutch opinion in favor of the American
    colonies during the American Revolution.

calle:22/103: (Sp) street.

Calliope:8/28; 80/76: the muse of epic poetry. Also: a steam pipe
    organ usually used in circus parades.

Calpe (Lyceo):22/103: Mount Calpe is the Rock of Gibraltar; the Calpe
    Club, Church Street, Gibraltar.

Calunnia, La: 45/24; 51/44: painting by BOTTICELLI in the Uffizi
    Gallery, Florence.

calvario:80/75: (It) Calvary.

Calvin:14/62; 62/87: John, 1509-64, the French Protestant theologian.

[Calypso]:20/94: in the Odyssey, a nymph who entertained ODYSSEUS
    seven years and offered to make him immortal. He refused.

Cambaluc:18/80: (Khanbalik), capital city of KUBLAI KHAN; the
    "City of the Great Khan" was built (1264-67) on the site of the
    earlier city of Yen by Kublai Khan; site of modern Peiping.

Cambrai:51/46: city in Nord department, N France. (See: LEAGUE
    OF CAMBRAI).

Cambreling:37/35: Churchill Caldom Cambreleng, 1786-1826, mem-
    ber of House of Representatives (1821-39); influential leader of the
    House under JACKSON and VAN BUREN; appointed minister to
    Russia (1840-41).

Cambridge:66/130: the city in Massachusetts.

Cambuskin:56/51: Cambyuskan or Cambiuskan, the Tartar king in
    Chaucer's Squire's Tale (line 12); usually identified as either
    GENGHIS KHAN or KUBLAI KHAN.

Camden:80/86; 82/104: city in New Jersey; Walt WHITMAN lived his
    last years there.

camion:77/43: (Fr) dray, truck.

Campari:77/47: the famous cafe in Milan.

[Campbell, John, 4th Earl of Loudoun]:71/160: 1705-82, a command-
    er of British forces in the French and Indian War; forced the
    people of Boston to quarter his troops.

Campestribus locis:53/17: (L) in country places. (See: A. Lacharme,
    Confucii Chi-King, II, 3, ode 10, stanza 1).

Campiglia:10/42: town in Livorno province, Italy.

Campo, Luchino del:24/112: Luchino dal Campo, companion of Nic-
    colò d'ESTE on a journey to Jerusalem, and author of an account
    of the trip: Viaggo a Gerusalemme di Niccolo da Este, descritto
    da Luchino dal Campo, ed. by G. Ghinassi, 1861.

canaglia:61/84: (It) rascals.

Canal Company:34/19: see CHESAPEAKE AND OHIO CANAL COMPA-
    NY.

Canal Grande: [10/46]; 25/120; 76/34, 38: the major canal of VENICE.

Canaries:60/76; 81/96: the Canary Islands.

cancellarius:43/13: (L) secretary.

Candide:74/16: reference to Voltaire's Candide (1759).

Cane e Gatto:83/107: (It) dog and cat.

Can Grande:78/59: prob. Can Grande della SCALA.

Cannabich:26/128: Rosa, 1764- ?, elder daughter of Christian Can-
    nabich (1731-98), composer and leader of the Mannheim orchestra;
    for Rosa, MOZART wrote the piano sonata in C (K. 309) in 1777.
    Of this sonata, Mozart wrote: "Als wie Andante, so is sie. "

Cannes:50/43: resort town on the French Riviera.

Cannon:71/161: James, member of the group which framed the con-
    stitution of the state of Pennsylvania (1776).

Canossa, Rioberto da:11/48: Nicolecto de Canosa, officer in the forces
    of Sigismondo MALATESTA.

Canton:60/76, 77; 61/84: city and port of Kwangtung province, SE
    China.

Cao:53/19: poss. KAO-YAO.

Capaneus:79/65: one of the Seven Against THEBES; he defied Zeus
    to prevent him from scaling the wall, so Zeus killed him with a
    thunderbolt.

Cape Breton:71/160: Cape Breton Island, NE Nova Scotia, retained by
    the French after the Peace of Utrecht (1713); attached to Nova
    Scotia after France ceded Canada to the English (1763).

Cape Cod:64/106: the peninsula in SE Massachusetts.

Capellen:69/150: see CAPELLEN TOT DEN POL.

Capellen de Pol:68/148: see CAPELLEN TOT DEN POL.

Capellen, van der:68/147: see CAPELLEN TOT DEN POL.

[Capellen tot den Pol, Joan Derk van der]:62/92; 65/122; 68/147, 148;
    69/150: Dutch statesman; friend of American interests during late
    18th century.

Capello, Bianca:74/5: ?1542-87, mistress of Francesco de' MEDICI,
    Duke of Tuscany; married to him (1579), proclaimed Grand Duch-
    ess of Tuscany four months later; said to have been poisoned by
    Francesco's brother, Ferdinand.

Capello, Philippus:25/119: Filippo Capello, fl. 1522, Venetian noble-
    man.

Capello, Vittor:26/126: member of the Privy Council of Christoforo
    Moro, who became Doge in 1462.

Cape Sable:65/123: Cape Sable Island, off SW tip of Nova Scotia.

Capet:67/133: Hugh, ?940-996, son of Hugh the Great; Duke of
    France (959-996); King of France (987-996); founder of the Cape-
    tian line of French kings.

capitaneo:67/140: (It) an administrative official in Italy.

Capitolare:74/26: (It) city hall.

Capo, il:84/117: (It) the head, the leader. (See: MUSSOLINI).

Capoquadri:74/24: name of house in Siena where Pound used to stay during visits to the town.

capriped:23/108: capripede, goat-foot, a satyr.

Cardinal of Bologna:9/36: Filippo Calandrini, fl. 1450, Cardinal Bishop of Bologna.

Cardinal, Peire:16/68: 13th century Provençal poet and satirist.

Careggi:10/42: see Ghiberto da CORREGIO.

Caressor:80/79: EDWARD VII of England.

Carissimi nostri:24/110: (It) our dearest ones.

caritas:80/79: (L) love, esteem.

Carleton:80/91: poss. DTC, Pisa.

Carlos, Don:76/38: the Bourbon Don Carlos, Duke of Madrid, 1848-1909, who in 1908 was living at the Palazzo Loredan, Campo San Vio, Venice.

Carmagnola:10/42; 17/78,79: Francesco Bussone da, fl. 1380-1432, Italian militarist, serving under Filippo VISCONTI, Duke of Milan; later he led the forces of FLORENCE and VENICE against Visconti; his strange conduct led the Venetians to try him for treason before the Council of Ten, after which he was executed.

Carman:80/73: Bliss, 1861-1929, the Canadian poet and journalist.

Carmathen, Lord:66/126: Francis Osborne, 5th Duke of Leeds, 1751-99, known until 1789 as Marquis of Carmathen; foreign secretary under Pitt (1783-91).

Carolina:64/106: American colony; first charter granted by Charles I in 1629.

Caroline:67/138: Caroline County, Virginia.

Carolus:80/84: see Charles Auguste Émile CAROLUS-DURAN.

Carolus, King:74/7; 83/106: see CHARLES II, Holy Roman Emperor.

[Carolus-Duran, Charles Auguste Émile]:80/84: ?1838-1917, French portrait and genre painter.

caro mio:9/36; 10/43: (It) my dear one.

Carpaccio, the:76/39: reference to a painting by Vittore CARPACCIO in the Church of San Giorgio degli SCHIAVONI, Venice.

[Carpaccio, Vittore]:26/127: c. 1450-1522, Venetian painter; pupil of Lazaro Bastiani and follower of BELLINI.

Carpathio, Victor:26/127: see Vittore CARPACCIO.

Carpatio:26/127: see Vittore CARPACCIO.

Carpegna:8/30: a mountain near Rimini.

Carr, D.:31/6: Dabney, 1773-1837, American jurist; nephew of Thomas JEFFERSON; justice of the Virginia supreme court of appeals (1824-37).

Carrara:74/6; 76/36; 84/116: the city in Tuscany, Italy; famous for its marble.

Carrière:80/84: Eugène, 1849-1906, French painter and lithographer; known for his Portrait of Verlaine and for decorations in the Sorbonne.

carroccio:[40/50]; 43/10, [11; 57/58; 80/75]: (It) flag car of an army; triumphal car.

carroch:40/50; 43/10,11; 57/58: see CARROCCIO.

carrochio:80/75: see CARROCCIO.

Carrol of Carrolton:69/153; [74/15]:   Charles Carroll of Carrollton,
    1737-1832, Revolutionary leader from Maryland; member of the
    CONTINENTAL CONGRESS (1776-78), signer of the DECLARA-
    TION of Independence; member of the U. S. Senate (1789-92).

Carrolton:69/153; 74/15: Carrollton, Maryland, residence of Charles
    CARROL(L) OF CARROL(L)TON.

carrozze:48/36: (It) carriages.

Carson:84/116: prob. a pseudonym.

Carthage:40/49,51; 65/113: ancient city of N Africa, near modern
    Tunis. (See: HANNO).

cartouche:60/76: a scroll or tablet in ornamental form; also an oval
    monument form.

Carver:74/26: George Washington, ?1864-1943, American agricult-
    ural chemist who discovered many new uses for products of the
    South.

Ça s'appelle une mansarde:80/83: (Fr) that is called an attic.

Casey, Corporal:74/16, 23; 79/66(?): DTC, Pisa.

Caspian:54/25, 26, 32: the Caspian Sea.

Cassandra:77/53; 78/55, 60: the Trojan prophetess.

Cassini:24/114: poss. Gherado Casini, the Roman publisher.

Cassio:69/153: see Caius CASSIUS LONGINUS.

[Cassius Longinus, Caius]:69/153: d. BC 42, partisan of Pompey;
    one of the murderers of Caesar. Dante places Cassius (whom he
    describes as membruto, apparently in confusion with Lucius
    Cassius) with Brutus and Judas Iscariot in the jaws of Lucifer in
    Giudecca. (See: Inferno, 34).

cassoni:76/40: (It) treasure chests, coffers.

Castaldio:25/115: (It) (?) castaldo: head steward.

Castano, Nicholas:12/53: prob. a Cuban banker.

castelan:11/51: (It) (?) castellano: governor.

castellaro:74/16; 76/30: (It) (?) castellare: ruined castle.

Castelli:74/21: the hills around Rome.

castello:11/49: (It) castle.

Castro, Ignez da:3/12; 30/148: Inés (Inéz) de Castro, ?1320-1355, a
    Castillian noblewoman whom Pedro, heir to the throne of Portugal,
    secretly married after the death of his wife, Constance, in 1345;
    she was distrusted by King Alfonso IV and murdered; after Alfon-
    so's death, Pedro had her body exhumed and placed on a throne at
    his side while the court paid homage to the dead queen. (See:
    Spirit of Romance, 231).

castrum romanum:79/63: (L) a Roman fortified camp.

casus bellorum:78/60: (L) cause of wars.

casus est talis:9/36: (L) this is the case.

casus omissus:67/134: (L) omitted case.

[Catilina, Lucius Sergius]:63/99: BC ?108-62, Roman politician; in
    BC 63 he entered into a conspiracy to assassinate the consuls and
    plunder Rome, but his plot was stopped by Cicero.

Cataline:63/99: see Lucius Sergius CATILINA.

Cathcart, Lord:34/16: William Schaw, 1st Earl of Cathcart, 1755-

1843, English soldier and diplomat; served in American Revolutionary War; ambassador to Russia (1813-21) when he organized the last coalition against NAPOLEON (1813).

Catherine:32/9; 69/150: Catherine II, 1729-96, Empress of Russia (1762-96).

Cats, V.:69/152: fl. 1783, official of the State of FRIESLAND; member of the SOCIÉTÉ BOURGEOISE at LEEUWARD.

Catullus:76/34: Gaius Valerius, BC ?84-54, the Roman lyric poet.

[Caulaincourt, Marquis Armand Augustin Louis de]:34/15: 1772-1827, French diplomat; ambassador to Russia (1807-11).

cautele:43/16: (It) caution.

cauteles:42/8: (It) precautions.

Cavalcanti:29/142: Cavalcanti di Cavalcanti, d. c. 1280, father of Guido CAVALCANTI.

Cavalcanti:4/16; [36/27, 28, 29]: Guido, fl. 1250-1300, Tuscan poet, friend of DANTE. His best known poems are in the Canzone d'amore. (See: Sonnets and Ballate of Guido Cavalcanti, 1912).

caveat ire ad Turchum:26/121: (L) let him beware of going to the Turk. (See: MOHAMMED II).

Cavour, Count:61/82: Camillo Benso di, 1810-61, Italian statesman; premier (1852-59).

Cawdor:48/35: prob. Cawdor Castle, Nairnshire, N Scotland.

Cayohoga:31/3: Cayuga Lake, W central New York, connected with Lake Seneca by a canal.

c'è il babao:74/16: (It) there's the bugbear.

Cellesi, Sebastiano:42/6; 43/15: prob. member of the BALÍA of Siena, c. 1622.

Celso:43/13: Celso Cittadini, poss. member of the BALÍA of Siena.

Celtic:80/85: reference to the Celts or their language; modern Irish.

cendato:26/123,124: (It) silk cloth.

Centaur:4/16; 79/69: a mythical creature with the body of a horse and the head of a man.

[Cephalonia]:24/111: largest of the Ionian Islands off Greece.

Ceres:47/30; [74/9; 77/48; 79/68; 80/91]; 81/95: see DEMETER.

Ceres' daughter:47/30: see PERSEPHONE.

Cerinthe:25/117: Cerinthus, the lover of SULPICIA and the subject of her verses. (See: Tibullus III, x, 15).

ce rusé personnage:78/60: (Fr) that shrewd character.

Cesena:8/33; 9/40; 11/49, 50; 26/122; 74/24: town in Forli province, Emilia, Italy; controlled by the MALATESTAs from 1385-1465.

ce sont les moeurs de Lutèce:80/83: (Fr) these are the morals of Lutetia. (See: PARIS).

Ce sont les vieux Marsouins!:28/137: (Fr) It's the old Marines!

c'est nôtre comune:80/87: (Fr)... commune: it's our bailiwick.

cette mauvaiseh venggg:76/30: (Fr) ce mauvais vent: that rotten wind (in Provençal accent?).

Ceylon:28/136.

C. H.:22/101,102; 41/55: see C. H. DOUGLAS.

[Cha-hou-kéou]:59/72: (Shaho), town just south of MUKDEN, Manchuria.

Cha houkoen:59/72: see CHA-HOU-KÉOU.

Chaise Dieu:23/109: the abbey of Chaise Dieu, founded in 1046, in
  Brionde, near the Languedoc-Auvergne border.
Chalus:76/33: a château in the town of Chalus, S France, where
  RICHARD Coeur de Lion was killed.
[Chamber of Deputies]:27/129; 38/41: lower house of the French
  national assembly.
Champs Elysées:18/81; 19/84: the street in Paris.
Chan:53/10: (Shan), prob. reference to CHAO-HAO.
chançons de gestes:55/38: (Fr) chansons de geste: songs of (heroic)
  deeds.
Chandler, Colonel:63/99: a leader of the Boston pre-Revolutionary
  troops with which John ADAMS sometimes served.
Chang:56/51, 54: (Shang), ancient Chinese dynasty (c. BC 1766-1121)
  which preceded the great TCHEOU dynasty; while usually called
  the "second" dynasty, the Chang has not yet been definitely designated this by historians.
Chang Ti: [52/4(?), 7(?)]; 53/9, 10, 11; 54/23; [58/65]; 60/76: (Shang
  Ti), the Supreme Ancestor or the Ruler of Heaven; may be distinguished as the "God Active" from the Ti'en, or "God Passive."
  Chang Ti, a personalized deity, is associated with a heaven for
  departed spirits.
Chang-tou:56/53: (Shang-tu, modern Chengteh), city in Mongolia not
  far north of the China border; this is the city which Coleridge
  called Xanadu, the famous summer residence of KUBLAI KHAN
  and other Mongol emperors, from 1260.
Channel:66/126: the English Channel.
Chan-si:61/81: see SHANSI.
Chantiers de la Gironde:38/42: the Gironde Shipyards, prob. near
  Bordeaux.
Chantong:56/54; 58/68: see SHANTUNG.
[Chao-hao]:53/10: (Shao Hao) (reign: 2598-2514), fourth of the five
  legendary emperors of China.
Chao Kang:53/10: (Shao Kang) (reign: 2079-2055); this emperor came
  to the throne after the Interregnum of forty years when Tsuh had
  been deposed by the people; he quelled disorder in the Empire and
  gave the state of Shang its first prominence; son of Empress MIN.
Chao Kong:53/13, 14, 15, 16: (Shao Kung) d. BC 1053; the Duke of Shao,
  a kinsman of WU WANG; a counsellor famous for his justice dis-
  pensed from his seat under a wild pear tree.
Chaomoukong:53/16: (Shao Mu-kung) fl. BC 826; the name, which
  means Mou, Prince of Chao, was given to Chao-hou (Shao Hu) after
  his death; Chao-hou was a general in the service of SIUEN-OUANG.
  (See: Mailla, Histoire Générale, II, 30; A. Lacharme, Confucii
  Chi-King, 308).
[Chao-tching-mao]:53/19: (Shao Ching-mao) d. BC 497; a government
  official in the state of LOU; when CONFUCIUS was appointed minister of the state of Lou, he found Chao-tching-mao was causing
  great disorder; Confucius had him arrested and beheaded. When
  the followers of Chao protested, Confucius said that Chao had been
  a man of five vices: a man deceitful in heart, artificial in manner,
  vain and false in language, of vicious gossip and with a natural turn
  for evil.

[Chao-t'o]:54/22: (Shao T'o) fl. BC 196, the overlord of NAN-YUEI; in 196 he proclaimed himself Prince of Yuei, but when LOU-KIA, the envoy of Emperor KAO-HOANG-TI, presented Chao-t'o with the imperial seal of office, he gave his allegiance to the emperor again.

Charent:65/121: the Charente river, W France, flowing into the Bay of Biscay.

Charles:24/113: see CHARLES VII of France.

Charles the Mangy:36/30: see CHARLES I OF NAPLES AND SICILY.

[Charles I of England]:67/136: 1600-1649, King of England (1625-49); granted the first charter of the Colony of Massachusetts (4 March 1629).

[Charles I of Naples and Sicily]:36/30: 1226-85, King of Naples and Sicily, and count of Anjou; with consent of Pope CLEMENT IV, he attacked and defeated Manfred, King of Naples (1266) and ascended the throne of Naples. SORDELLO served in his army.

Charles II:64/106; 67/136: 1630-85, King of England (1660-85).

[Charles II, Holy Roman Emperor]:74/7; 83/106: Charles le Chauve (the Bald), 823-877, (reign: 875-77).

[Charles III of Spain]:68/147: 1716-88, King of Spain (1759-88).

[Charles IV of Spain]:32/9: 1748-1819, King of Spain (1788-1808); subservient to NAPOLEON; forced to abdicate (1808).

[Charles VII of France]:24/113: 1403-61 (reign: 1422-61).

Charles le Chauve:83/106: see CHARLES II, Holy Roman Emperor.

Charleston:68/146,148: city in South Carolina, captured 12 May 1780 by Sir Henry Clinton and held by British forces until 14 December 1782.

Charlie:74/4: see Charles Jones SOONG.

[Charlotte, Sophia]:66/126: 1744-1818, wife of GEORGE III of England.

Charondas:71/163: Sicilian jurist of 6th century BC.

Charter:66/131: see MASSACHUSETTS STATE CONSTITUTION.

Charter Oak:74/25: a white oak which stood in Hartford, Conn., until 1856. There is a story that when Sir Edmund Andros, governor general of New England, demanded (1687) that the charter of Connecticut be surrendered, the Hartford citizens hid the document in this oak.

Charter, old:80/92: see BILL OF RIGHTS.

Charybdis:74/9: reference to the whirlpool, opposite SCYLLA, off coast of Sicily, by which ODYSSEUS had to pass. (See: Odyssey, XII).

Chase:62/91; 65/112: Samuel, 1741-1811, American patriot; signer of the DECLARATION of Independence; delegate to the First and Second CONTINENTAL CONGRESSes; appointed Associate Justice of Supreme Court (1796).

Chas Francis:62/90: see Charles Francis ADAMS.

Chas Second:64/106: see CHARLES II of England.

Château Margaux:65/117: one of the great wines of Bordeaux.

Chatham:65/124: William Pitt, 1st Earl of Chatham, 1708-78, English statesman known as "the Elder Pitt" and, later, as the "Great Commoner".

Chatham, the:68/143: an English ship captured during the American
  Revolution.
Chato:55/40: (Shato) a Tartar tribe.
Chaumont, Ray de:65/114; 68/143: Donatien le Ray de Chaumont, who
  in 1778 donated his house at PASSY to the American legation in
  Paris; Chaumont was influential and friendly toward the American
  Revolution and contributed supplies to the American forces.
Chawles Fwancis:62/88; 67/138: see Charles Francis ADAMS.
chazims:52/3: prob. variation of (Heb) hazirim: pigs; a term of
  abuse.
cheek bone, by verbal manifestation:74/24: from Hugh Selwyn
  Mauberley.
Cheever:76/31: see Ralph Cheever DUNNING.
Chef d'Escadre:71/162: see Hippolyte de SADE.
Ché-heng:57/58: (Shih Hêng) d. AD 1460, one of the generals of Em-
  peror KING-TI who defended Peiping against the Mongols in 1450.
  He later plotted against the Empire and died of poison.
Chéking-Tang:55/39: (Shih Ching-t'ang) 892-944, general and governor of Shantung province. He bribed the KHITAN Tartars with a
  promise of half of Chihli and Shansi to help him to the throne. In
  936 he proclaimed himself emperor, ruling under the name of Kao
  Tsu (reign: 936-44); he was the founder of the Later TSIN (Chin)
  dynasty.
che le donne:11/50: (It) that the women.
che mai da me non si parte il diletto/ Fulvida di folgore:39/44: (It)
  who is never departed from the pleasure/ of bright lightning. (See:
  Paradiso, 23,129; 30,62).
che mi porta fortuna:[74/24]; 76/39: (It) who brings me good luck.
ch'êng:77/53: (Ch) to complete. (See: Appendix B).
Chennevière:80/84: Georges, 1884-1927, French poet.
Chensi:56/47; 58/66: see SHENSI.
Cheou-lang:53/18, 20: (K'ung Shu-liang Ho) d. BC 548, father of
  CONFUCIUS; chief magistrate of Tsu in Shantung province. He
  was remarkable for his gigantic stature and great strength; after
  fathering nine daughters by his first wife, he remarried at seventy
  and his second wife, Chêng Tsai, bore him Confucius.
Cheou-sin:53/12: (Chou Hsin) (reign: 1154-22), last emperor of the
  SHANG (or YIN) dynasty; his career was one of extravagance, lust,
  and cruelty; overthrown by WU WANG, he perished in the flames
  of his palace.
che pende:74/21: (It) leaning.
[Ché-pou-kiu-atchen]:54/32: (Shih Pu-chü Atchen) fl. 647, first
  officer of Che-li-sa (Shih-li-sa) of the KIEÏ-KOU; ambassador to
  the court of Emperor TAÏ-TSONG; demanded that the emperor give
  him the title of grand mandarin: since titles cost nothing, the emperor made him grand general of the army as well.
Chépoutching:54/34: (Shih-pu-chêng), city in N China.
Cherokee Nation:[32/8]; 34/21: formed under the constitution (1820)
  by the Cherokee Indians, the largest and most important tribe in
  SE United States; the tribe was deported to the Indian Territory
  (Oklahoma) in 1838.

Cherokees:32/8: see CHEROKEE NATION.

[Chesapeake and Ohio Canal Company]:32/7; 34/19: chartered 31 Jan-
    uary 1825, the Company began work on the canal 4 July 1828; John
    Quincy ADAMS broke ground.

Chester:67/136: city in Cheshire county, NW England; last place in
    England to surrender to William the Conqueror (1070).

Chesterton: [46/26]; 80/93: Gilbert Keith, 1874-1936, English jour-
    nalist, writer, and defender of Catholicism; a brilliant represen-
    tative of Edwardian England.

che sublia es laissa cader:74/9: (Pr) que s'oblid' es laissa chazer:
    and faint away and fall. (From a canzone of Bernart de Ventadour).

Chi:55/40: see CHI-TSONG.

chi:56/49: (Ch) a winnowing basket.

Chi:74/17: (Ch'i), principality in SHENSI province; ruled by WEN
    WANG.

Chi:84/117: see CHI TZŬ.

chiaccierona:79/65: (It) a great babbler.

Chiasso:28/134,135: commune in Switzerland, W end of Lake Como;
    a custom station on the St. Gotthard railroad.

Chicago:12/55.

Chief Justice:65/109: see Peter OLIVER.

Chief Justice:65/119: president of the Sovereign court of GALICIA
    (c. 1780).

chiexa:10/44, 45; 11/49: (It) chiesa: church.

Chigi:42/8: member of the famous Chigi family of Siena; member of
    the BALÍA (c. 1622).

chih:52/7: (Ch) to stop, desist. (See: Appendix B).

Chi Hoang Ti:54/21: see TSIN-CHI-HOANG-TI.

Chi king:54/22, 24; 59/70: see SHIH CHING.

Chilanti:77/48: Felice Chilanti, an Italian journalist.

Child:66/127: a descendant of Samuel Child, son of Sir Francis Child
    (1642-1713), a banker and Lord Mayor of London.

Chile:27/130; 46/28.

Chin:55/44: see CHIN-TSONG.

China:53/16; 54/21, 31; 55/45; 56/51, 52; 58/63, 64, 65, 66, 69; 62/90.
    (See: CHINESE EMPIRE).

[Chinese Empire]:53/12,14,17; 54/21,25,26,30,33,34; 55/37,39; 56/51,
    54; 57/57,59; 58/69; 60/74,77; 61/83,86; [77/45]: (references to
    various areas of China that bore the name of "empire").

Chinese rites:60/76: the Chinese rites of worship and government.

Ching: [63/89]; 67/133: (Ch) (Chêng): upright, true. (See: Appendix B).

Ching Ming: [51/46]; 60/79; 66/128; 68/146: (Ch) (Chêng-ming): to
    regulate the name; to define the correct term; precise definition.
    (See: Appendix B).

Ching-nong:53/10: see CHIN-NONG.

Chin lo-koan:57/57: (Shên-lo-koan), a Buddhist temple outside the
    city of Nanking.

Chin Nong:53/8, [10]: (Shên Nung) (reign: 2838-2698), second of the
    Five Emperors of legendary China; taught the art of agriculture;
    known as the "Prince of Cereals"; introduced system of barter;
    aided by his glass-covered stomach, through which he could watch

his own digestion, he studied the properties and effects of herbs.

Chinon:24/113: commune, Indre-et-Loire department, NW central France.

Chin Song:58/63: see CHIN-TSONG.

ch'intenerisce/ a sinistra la Torre:74/9: (It) that softens/ the Tower at the left. (See: Paradiso, 8, 2).

Chin-Tsong:55/42,[43], 44: (Shên Tsung) (reign: 1068-1086), an able administrator, ambitious for his empire, his people, and himself. His chief ally was the minister, OUANG-NGAN-CHE; they tried, however, to move too quickly and their program of sweeping reforms met stiff resistance and ended in failure.

Chin Tsong:58/63, 64: (Shên Tsung) (reign: 1573-1620), his long reign ushered in the ruin of the MING dynasty. After the death of TCHANG-KU-TCHING, the regent, Chin-tsong abandoned himself to sensuality and extravagance; from 1585-1610 no one except the court eunuchs saw the emperor. High taxes ruined the middle class, Manchu hordes raided from the north, Japanese from the southeast; there were floods, droughts, famines and corrupt officials.

chiostri:20/95: (It) cloisters.

Chisio, Augustino:43/11: prob. Agostino CHIGI, ?1465-1520, Sienese banker; built the Villa Farnesina in Rome; founder of the princely family of Chigi. The Latin form of the name is Chisius; the Italianized form of the Latin is here rendered Chisio.

Chi-tsong:55/40: (Shih Tsung) (reign: 954-959), a benevolent and generous emperor. He waged successful wars against the KHITANS and Northern HANS and enlarged the empire. When there was a scarcity of money, he ordered all copper utensils be given up for imperial uses; he also seized all the bronze images of BUDDHA and converted them into coin, remarking that Buddha, who had given up so much to mankind, was not likely to object.

[Chi-tsong]:55/45: (Shih Tsun, also known as Oulo and as Wan-yen P'ou) fifth emperor of the KIN dynasty of the NUTCHÉ Tartar. During his reign (1162-90) the Kin gained much territory in China, mainly in the control of HONAN province. An exceptional man, wise and benevolent, he was sometimes called the "Little YAO and SHUN".

Chi Tsong:57/60: (Shih Tsung) (reign: 1522-66). Like many other MING Emperors, Chi-tsong consistently picked poor advisers and refused to listen to the most able men of his kingdom.

[Chi-tsong-hien-hoang-ti]:61/85: (Shih Tsung Hsien Huang Ti), dynastic title of Emperor YONG-TCHING.

Chi-Tsou:55/45: (Shih Tsu), the name which KUBLAI KHAN took when he began his reign over China (1280).

Chittenden:74/25: poss. Kate Sara Chittenden, 1856-1949, American organist, composer and lecturer.

[Chi Tzŭ]:84/117: Viscount of the principality of CHI, 12th century BC. Uncle of CHEOU-SIN, last sovereign of the YIN dynasty; because he protested against the practices of the emperor, Chi was put into prison. (See: Analects, xviii, 1).

Chiyeou:61/84: (Shih Yeu) fl. AD 1727, a poor laborer of SHENSI province who found a purse and gave it back to its owner without accepting a reward. Emperor YONG-TCHING was so impressed when he heard of this that he rewarded the man with a hundred ounces of silver and used the honesty of Chiyeou as the text of a long letter to his people, urging them to reform their morals. (See: Mailla, Histoire Générale, XI, 487-89).

Chocorua:74/18: Mount Chocorua, E New Hampshire, in the Sandwich Range of the White Mountains.

Cholkis:74/8: prob. Colchis, the kingdom of AEETES; land of the Golden Fleece.

choros nympharum:4/13; 17/77: (L) chorus of nymphs.

"Chose Kao-yao...the crooks toddled off":78/59: from Analects, XII, xxii, 6.

Chou:55/39: (Chou), a principality in the province of SZECHWAN, S central China.

Chou:55/40: (Chou), the After Chou dynasty (951-59).

Chou:55/41: see HEOU-CHOU.

Chou:56/54: see TCHEOU.

[Chouliu]:55/38, 39: (Shulü), d. c. AD 945, queen of the KHITAN chieftain, YÉ-LIU-APAOKI. She was a woman of great beauty and wisdom, and her husband often depended on her advice in matters of state and military operations.

Christian, Herbiet:80/88: French translator of Pound, c. 1922-24.

Christ: [10/46; 22/102]; 24/112; 28/137; 34/20; 80/91; [83/111].

Christers:61/82: see CHRISTIANS.

[Christians]:58/62; 59/71, 73; 60/76; 61/80, 82, 83; 76/32. (Note that text generally uses X for the Greek letter chi: Xtians.)

Christmas:80/93.

Christophoro, Joanne:42/7: Giovanni Christophoro, prob. Florentine representative at the negotiations leading to the establishment (1622) of the MONTE DEI PASCHI.

Christu:22/102: see CHRIST.

chrysalids:74/10: chrysalis: the pupa stage of insects, especially of butterflies.

Chrysophrase:17/76: an apple-green chalcedony, used in jewelry.

Chu Hsi:80/89: 1130-1200, Chinese philosopher during the Southern SUNG dynasty; author of many works on the classics of CONFUCIUS.

Chu King:53/15; 54/22, 24: see SHU CHING.

Chuliu:55/38, 39: see CHOULIU.

Chun:53/9, 10, 13, 14, 15; 54/24; 55/44; 56/48, [49, 55; 57/59; 58/66; 74/7, 17, 18, 20; 77/45]: (Shun) (reign: BC 2255-2205); after serving a three-year apprenticeship, Shun was selected as emperor to follow YAO; noted as a governor, astronomer, and as one who regulated the order and ceremony of religious service.

Chung:76/32; 77/42: (Ch) center, middle, point of balance. (See: Appendix B).

Chun King:56/49: (Shun-ching-fu), the modern city of Chunking in SZECHWAN province.

Chung Ni: [53/18]; 56/54; 76/32; 77/48: (Ch) CONFUCIUS. (See: Appendix B).

Chun Tchi:59/70, 71: (Shun Chih), first emperor of the MANCHU dynasty (reign: 1644-61) to rule over China. His reign was occupied
in consolidating the Manchu power by crushing the remains of the
MING dynasty; in 1645 Manchu troops took Nanking, a stronghold
of Ming power, and in 1662 the "last" emperor of the Ming dynasty, KUEI-WANG, was defeated. Good and generous, Chun-tchi
eliminated eunuchs from the court, set up a civil administration,
and treated Catholic missionaries with favor. In the last year of
his reign the Dutch were expelled from Formosa.
Chunti:56/52, 53: (Shun Ti) (reign: 1333-68), also known as Tohan
Timur, last Mongol emperor of the YUAN dynasty. Weak and
pleasure loving, he was incapable of action and his reign was
marked by continual rebellion from the Chinese. In 1368 the rebels took Peiping, capital of the Yuan dynasty, and Chunti fled
north, bringing the dynasty to an end. He died in 1370.
Churchill: [41/54]; 74/4, 18; 78/59; [80/92; 84/118]: Winston Leonard
Spencer, 1874-   , the British statesman and author.
Church of England:63/98.
Church St.:80/81: a street in the Royal Borough of Kensington, London, in a court off which Pound lived (1909-1914).
Ciano:77/48: Conte Galeazzo Ciano di Cortelazzo, 1903-44, Italian
statesman, secretary of state for press and propaganda (1935),
minister of foreign affairs (1936-43), ambassador to the Holy See
(1943). He was the son-in-law of MUSSOLINI.
Cicero:63/99; 67/139: Marcus Tullius Cicero, also known as TULLY,
106-43 BC, Roman orator and philosopher.
Cici:41/52: a child. (See: Jefferson and/or Mussolini, 53).
Cid:3/11: see Ruy DIAZ.
cielo di Pisa:84/117: (It) sky of Pisa.
Cigale, La:74/13: the dance hall and restaurant near the Place
Pigalle, Montmarte, Paris.
Cigna:11/49: locality in central Italy taken from Sigismondo MALA-
TESTA by the peace terms imposed by PIUS II (c. 1460).
Cimbica:79/70: prob. an invention; the lynx(?).
cimier:6/21: an ornament forming the apex or crest on a helmet.
ciocco:5/17; 7/24: (It) log.
Ciola:11/49: locality in central Italy taken from Sigismondo MALA-
TESTA by the peace terms imposed by PIUS II (c. 1460).
Circe:1/3, 4, 5; 17/79; 20/94; 39/43, 44; 74/14, [15;   76/38]; 80/72:
the enchantress who turned men into swine. ODYSSEUS avoids
her spell with the aid of the herb, MOLY, and becomes her lover.
She informs him that to return to ITHACA he must first seek out
TIRESIAS in Hades. (See: Odyssey, X-XII).
Circeo:39/45; 41/52: Monte Circeo, N side of the Gulf of Gaeta, W
Italy; once the island called Aeaea, home of CIRCE.
Circe Titania:20/94: Titanian CIRCE (as Circe is daughter of the Sun).
(See: Ovid, Metamorphoses XIV, 382, 438).
cisclatons:80/88: (Pr) a kind of gown.
Cithera:24/111: see CYTHERA.
cittadini:21/96: (It) citizens.
City, the:74/8; 77/43: see WAGADU.

Civis Romanus:25/118: (L) Roman citizen.

Clara, la:74/3: see Clara PETACCI.

Clara Leonora:28/135: prob. a graduate student at University of Pennsylvania, 1906.

Clarendon, Earl:66/128: a pseudonym used by John ADAMS in a series of letters sent to the BOSTON GAZETTE in 1765.

Claridge's:80/93: the fashionable hotel on Brook Street, London.

Clarke, Gen.:44/20: Henri Jacques Guillaume, 1765-1818, Duke of Feltre, Napoleonic general.

Classe:9/36: a town in Ravenna, Italy. Sigismondo took marble for the TEMPIO from the church of SANT APOLLINAIRE in Classe, though against the wishes of the people of Ravenna.

Clay:34/18,19, 20; 37/32, 36; 71/163: Henry, 1777-1852, American lawyer and statesman; member of the House of Representatives (1811-14; 1815-21; 1823-25); supported John Quincy ADAMS in the Presidential election of 1824; served as Secretary of State (1825-29); U. S. Senator (1849-52).

Clemens:60/76: see CLEMENT XI.

Clement:74/6: Saint Clement I, Pope ?88-97?; also known as Clement of Rome.

[Clement IV]: 36/30: Pope (1265-68).

[Clement XI]:60/76: 1649-1721, Pope (1700-21); he condemned the custom of Chinese ancestor worship and denied the Jesuit petition that the Mass might be said in the Chinese language.

Cletus:74/6: Saint Cletus (or Anacletus), Pope (?76-88).

Clinton, DeWitt:34/17; 37/36: 1769-1828, New York lawyer and statesman; U. S. Senator (1802-03); mayor of New York, unsuccessful candidate for the Presidency (1812); governor of New York (1817-21; 1825-28).

Clinton, George:34/18: 1739-1812, New York lawyer and statesman; member of the CONTINENTAL CONGRESS (1775-76); brigadier general (1777); governor of New York (1777-95; 1801-04); Vice-President (1805-12).

Clinton:70/157: Sir Henry, ?1738-95, English soldier; succeeded Howe as commander-in-chief of British forces in North America (1778).

Clinton:77/42: small town in N central New York, near Utica; site of Hamilton College, at which Pound was in residence 1903-1905.

Clio:74/23: the muse of history.

Clower:83/109: see CLOWES.

Clowes:82/102; [83/109]: a member of the English printing firm of William Clowes and Sons, Ltd., London.

Cnidos:82/103: Cnidus, the ancient town at Cape Krio, SW Asia Minor; once a Dorian city noted for its wealth, sculpture and architecture. Praxiteles' statue of APHRODITE was at Cnidus.

Cochran, Tommy:78/59:

Cocito:69/153: (It) COCYTUS.

Cockle:63/100: James, fl. 1761, an officer of the customs in Salem, Massachusetts, who petitioned the court to grant him WRITS OF ASSISTANCE to let him search for prohibited merchandise. James OTIS and Oxenbridge THACHER represented the protesting Boston merchants; Jeremiah GRIDLEY appeared for Cockle in support of

COCTEAU [42]

the writs. Cockle won his case, known as the Paxton case.
Cocteau:[74/14]; 76/31; 77/47, 50; 80/90: Jean, 1891 -   , French
poet, playwright and man of letters.
[Cocytus]:69/153: the river of Hell; in the Inferno, it is a marsh
formed by the tears of this world.
Coke, Lord:62/89; 63/98; 64/102; 66/130,131; 67/133: Sir Edward,
1552-1634, English jurist, best known for his four Institutes (1628-
44), the first of which is called Coke upon Littleton.
Col credito suo ... / Napoli a Venezia di danari ... / Costretti ...
Napoli e Venezia ... a quella pace:21/96: (It) with that debt ... /
Naples and Venice of money ... / forced ... Naples and Venice ...
to that peace.
Cole, G. D. H.:81/96: George Douglas Howard, 1880-   , English
economist and novelist.
Cole, Horace:80/80; 81/96: poss. the Horace Cole, 1874-   , who
was secretary of Geo. Newnes Ltd. and other companies, and a
contributor to 20th Century Business Practice, The Hub, etc.
College, Illustrious:42/3: see BALÍA.
[Colloredo, Graf Hieronhymus Joseph]:26/128: 1732-1812, Arch-
bishop of Salzburg in 1772; was patron of MOZART for a time.
Cologne:74/25: German manufacturing city. The Cologne Cathedral,
a Gothic structure, was begun c. 1248, completed 1880.
color di luce:74/10: (It) color of light.
Colum, Padraic:80/74: 1881-   , Irish poet and playwright.
Comédie (Nantes):65/119: the Theater in NANTES.
Come pan, niño:80/71; 81/95: (Sp) eat bread, boy.
comes miseriae:74/14: (L) companion of misery.
Comfort:80/91: DTC, Pisa.
Comité des Forges:38/42: the French Steel Trust.
comites:74/14: (L) companions.
Comley:28/136: poss. associated with Cheltenham Military Academy,
Ogontz, Pa., at which Pound was a student, c. 1900.
commandante della piazza:41/52: (It) commander of the square.
Commendatore:24/114: (It) a knight of a chivalric order.
Comment! Vous êtes tombés si bas?:35/24: (Fr) What! You have
fallen so low?
commerciabili:65/112: (It) for trade.
commerciabili beni:52/3: (It) goods for trade.
commercianti:27/130: (It) merchants.
Commission to France:68/142: the commission sent by the Colonies
to France in 1776; members: Benjamin FRANKLIN, Arthur LEE,
and Silas DEANE. Later in the year, John ADAMS replaced Deane.
commons:62/91; 66/129: see HOUSE OF COMMONS.
commune sepulchrum/ Aurum est commune sepulchrum. Usura,
commune sepulchrum:46/28: (L) the common sepulchre/ Gold is
the common sepulchre. Usury, the common sepulchre.
Como:28/134: Lake Como in Lombardy, N Italy.
Compleynt, compleynt I hearde upon a day.... Nothing is now clean
slayne/ But rotteth away:30/147: poss. variation of Chaucer, The
Complaint Unto Pity.
concha, la:76/40: (Sp) the shell.

Concord: 28/134: the town in NE Massachusetts, famous for its liter-
ary associations.
Concorde, La: 80/82: see PLACE DE LA CONCORDE.
concret Allgemeine: 8/31: (Ger) concrete universal. (Hegelian term).
Condillac: 65/119: Etienne Bonnot de, 1715-80, French philosopher.
condit Atesten: 20/91: (L) founded Ateste. (See: ESTE).
Condor, Charles: 80/82: Charles Conder, 1868-1909, English decora-
tive painter.
Condorcet: 31/5; 33/11; 65/118; 71/161: Marie Jean Antoine Nicholas de
Caritat, Marquis de, 1743-94, French philosopher, mathematician
and politician.
Coney Island: 80/85: the amusement park in Brooklyn, N. Y.
confine: 41/52: (It) exile.
confino: 55/43; 61/82: (It) in exile.
Confucius: [13/58, 59, 60; 52/4]; 53/14, [18, 19, 20; 54/22, 30, 31], 32, [34;
55/39, 40, 44; 56/48, 51, 52], 54; [57/58, 59; 58/66]; 59/70; 60/76;
[61/80; 67/137; 76/32; 77/42, 46]; 80/73, 76, 77: (K'ung Ch'iu or
K'ung Fu Tzŭ or K'ung) 551-479, Chinese philosopher and statesman. Confucianism is an organized series of precepts dealing
with morals, the family system, social reforms, statecraft, and
ceremonials; considers action, directed by right thinking, to be the
highest good; postulates the innate virtue of man. It opposes the
passivity of Buddhism and the mysticism of Taoism. A philosophy
of reason, it influenced the thought of the French Enlightenment.
Cong-ho: 53/16: (kung-ho), the historical name for the interregnum
(BC 841-27) between the reign of LI-WANG and SIUEN-OUANG, his
son.
con gli occhi onesti e tardi: 7/24: (It) with eyes honest and slow. (See:
Purgatorio, 6, 63, where text reads: E nel muover degli occhi
onesta e tarda).
Congo: 70/156: a kind of tea.
Congress: 31/3; 62/91, 96; 65/109, 110, 112, 117, 121; 66/126; 68/143, 147;
69/49; 70/156; 71/160, 163: see CONTINENTAL CONGRESS.
Congress: 34/18; 37/32, 36; 65/125; 71/161: see CONGRESS OF THE
UNITED STATES.
[Congressional Globe]: 37/35: Containing the Debates and Proceedings, 1833-73, a newspaper published in Washington, D. C., 109
vol.
[Congress of the United States]: 22/101(?); 34/18; 37/32, 36; 65/125;
71/161: the legislative branch of the Federal government; instituted
(1789) by the CONSTITUTION OF THE UNITED STATES.
Connecticut: 31/3; 64/106; 65/124.
Connecticut constitution: 65/124: the Connecticut Charter, granted
(1662) to John Winthrop.
connubium terrae... mysterium: 82/104: (L) the marriage of the
earth... mystery.
consiros: 83/107: (Pr) with grief. (See: Purgatorio, 26, 144).
Constans proposito... / Justum et Tenocem: 34/21: (L) ... tenacem:
constant in purpose... / just and enduring. (See: Horace, Odes,
III, 3; J. Q. Adams, Diary, 568; see also ET AMAVA PERDUTA-
MENTE....

Constantinople:18/80; 26/121,125: formerly BYZANTIUM, now Istanbul.

Constitution:62/95; 66/130; 70/155; 74/4,12; 79/64: see CONSTITUTION OF THE UNITED STATES.

Constitution:64/108: see MASSACHUSETTS COLONIAL CHARTER.

constitution: 71/160: see BRITISH CONSTITUTION.

Constitution of Massachusetts:67/138: see MASSACHUSETTS STATE CONSTITUTION.

[Constitution of the United States]:37/35; 62/95; 66/130; 67/139; 70/155; 74/4,12; 79/64: the document which established the system of Federal government in the United States; drawn up at the FEDERAL CONSTITUTIONAL CONVENTION at Philadelphia (1787) and ratified by the required number of states (nine) by 21 June 1788.

Consules, Iudices ... pro serenissimo:42/4: (L) consuls, judges ... for his most serene.

consuls:68/141: the joint magistrates of the Roman Republic.

[Contarini]:76/38: ancient Venetian family which produced eight doges, a cardinal and several artists; most celebrated member of the family was Andrea Contarini (?1300-82), Doge at the time of the War of Chioggia between Venice and Genoa. Text reference is to the Palazzo Contarini, Calle della Vida, Venice.

[Continental Army]:65/111; 70/157: American army during the Revolution; created in 1775 by the CONTINENTAL CONGRESS, it was commanded by George WASHINGTON.

[Continental Congress]:31/3; 62/91,96; 65/109,110,112,117; 66/126; 68/143,147; 69/149; 70/156; 71/160,163: 1774-89; the Federal legislature of the Thirteen Colonies and, later, of the United States. The First Continental Congress (5 September-26 October 1774) met in Philadelphia. The Second Continental Congress met at Philadelphia on 10 May 1775. The Congress issued the DECLARATION of Independence (4 July 1776) and carried on the Revolutionary War.

contra barbaros/ legat belli ducem:53/16: (L) against the barbarians/ he appoints a leader in war. (See: A. Lacharme, Confucii Chi-King, 308).

contrade:43/10; 44/18; 80/75: (It) neighboring towns, regions; districts.

Contra naturam:45/24: (L) against nature.

contrappunto:74/9: (It) counterpoint.

Contrarini:76/38: see CONTARINI.

Contrarini, Ugaccion dei:26/123: a member of the CONTARINI family of Venice.

contre-jour, le:74/22: (Fr) false light.

Contre le lambris, fauteuil de paille, / Un vieux piano, et sous le baraomètre:7/24: (Fr) Against the panelling, straw arm-chair, / An old piano, and under the barometer. (See: Flaubert, Un Coeur Simple).

contrordine e disordine:41/54: (It) counter order and disorder.

Convention of '87:34/17: see FEDERAL CONSTITUTIONAL CONVENTION.

Conversations upon Political Economy:34/20: Illustrations of Political Economy (1832-34), by Harriet MARTINEAU.

coram non judice:32/7: (L) not in the presence of a judge.

Corcoran, Captain:16/72: a pseudonym having no particular reference.

Córdoba:80/71: capital of Córdoba province in S Spain.

Corea:54/32; 55/45; 56/53; 58/62,67: see KOREA.

Corey:40/48: William Ellis, 1866-1934, American industrialist, president of Carnegie Steel Co. (1901-03) and U. S. Steel Corp. (1903-11).

Corfu:24/111,112; 26/122: island in the Ionian Sea.

Corinth:26/123: city in S Greece; one of the cities represented at the Council of Ferrara-Florence (1438).

Corles, Mr.:35/22: Alfred Perlès, 20th century writer and biographer.

Cornelison:80/91: sergeant in the Provost section, DTC, Pisa.

Cornwallis:62/92; 69/150: Charles, 1738-1805, British general defeated by the Americans and French at Yorktown, 1781.

corps diplomatique:34/15; 62/92: (Fr) diplomatic corps.

Corpus:77/45: Corpus Christi: a feast of the Catholic Church, honoring the institution of the Eucharist; the Thursday after Trinity Sunday.

Corre, volpe corre, Christu corre, volpecorre, / Christucorre, e dav' un saltu, ed ha preso la coda/ Della volpe:22/102: (It) Runs, the fox runs, Christ runs, fox runs, / Christ runs, and made a jump, and took the tail/ Of the fox.

[Correggio, Ghiberto da]:10/42: one of the officers of Sigismondo MALATESTA when he was employed by the Sienese.

Correze:6/22: department and river in S central France.

Corriere di Domenica:41/54: (It) the Sunday Courier (a newspaper).

corruptio:14/63: (It) corruption.

cortile:78/58: (It) court, patio.

Cortona:52/4; 76/40: town in Tuscany, central Italy; its churches have paintings by Fra ANGELICO and Luca Signorelli.

Corunna:65/119,120,121: seaport commune of Coruna province in NW Spain.

corvées:53/20; 54/32,35; 56/51: (Fr) forced labors.

Cosa deve continuare? Se casco... / non casco in ginnocchion:74/5: (It) Why must it go on? If I fall... / I will not fall on my knees.

cosi discesi per l'aer maligno/ on doit le temps ainsi prendre qu'il vient:80/77: (It) so it is said through the spiteful air/ (Fr) one must take the weather as it comes. (See: Inferno, 5, 1 and 86).

cosi Elena vedi:20/92: (It) thus HELEN sees. (See: Inferno, 5, 64).

Cosimo:10/43; 21/96,97; 26/124: see Cosimo de' MEDICI.

Cosimo:41/55: see Cosimo I de' MEDICI.

Cosimo, Johanni di:8/30: see Giovanni de' MEDICI.

Cossa:77/51,53; 78/55; 79/62,63: Francesco del, fl. 1435-1477?, Italian painter; his Glorification of March, April and May frescoes are in the SCHIFANOJA Palace, Ferrara.

cossacks:16/75: Russian peasant cavalrymen serving the czars.

Cotsworth:62/94: see Charles Cotesworth PINCKNEY.

Cott:62/96: prob. Oliver WOLCOTT.

Cotta:5/20: Johannes, 1480-1510, Italian poet and humanist; a friend of Girolamo FRACASTORO; helped Bartolomeo d'ALVIANO found an academy of arts.

Council: 64/108: see MASSACHUSETTS COLONIAL LEGISLATURE.

Council: 25/115, 117, 119, 120: see DIECI, Consiglio de.

counties palatine: 66/132; 67/136: counties in England in which the
    earl ruled under exclusive royal powers in law; such powers are
    now mostly abolished.

[Coupataï]: 61/84: (Cupat'ai) d. 1735 AD, a general and president of
    the Tribunal of Rites; he had been picked by KANG-HI to be tutor
    to YONG-TCHING.

Coupetai: 61/84: see COUPATAÏ.

[Couplet, Philippe]: 60/74: fl. 1680, Jesuit missionary in China; he
    arrived in Peiping with VERBIEST (1660) and served as procurator
    of the China missions. In 1680 he returned to Rome, carrying
    Verbiest's plea for ordination of Chinese priests and a vernacular
    Mass.

Cour de Londres, la: 69/150: see ST. JAMES's Palace, London.

Court House: 63/98; 66/129: the Court House in Boston, Mass.

Coxie: 84/115: Jacob Sechler Coxey, 1854-1951, American reformer
    and politician.

cramoisi: 45/24; 61/83: (Fr) crimson cloth.

Crawford, Carrol: 74/15; 76/33; 77/51: DTC, Pisa.

Crédit Agricole: 81/96: (Fr) Agricultural Bank.

Creeks: 32/8: American Indian confederacy, located in the south-east
    U. S.

[Cremona]: 8/29: fortified commune in Lombardy, N Italy, on the Po
    river.

Cremonam: 8/29: see CREMONA.

Cremonesi: 35/25: people of CREMONA.

Cretan, the: 1/5: see Georgius Dartona CRETENSIS.

[Cretensis, Georgius Dartona]: 1/5: made a Latin translation of the
    Homeric Hymns. (See: Make It New, 145-146).

Creusot: 38/41; 41/56: Le Creusot, city in Saône-et-Loire department,
    E central France; location of the SCHNEIDER iron and steel mills
    and munitions plants.

Crevel: 41/55; 80/88: René, 1900-   , French author; Les Pieds dans
    le plat (1933).

Crimea: 38/41: peninsula in S Soviet Russia, extending into the Black
    Sea; scene of the Crimean War (1854-56).

crimen est actio: 16/68: (L) crime is action.

Cristo Re, Dio Sole: 83/111: (It) Lord Christ, Sun God.

Croat: 27/130: Croats, a south Slavic people.

croce di Malta, figura del sol: 80/76: (It) cross of MALTA, image of
    the sun.

croceo: 20/93: (It) saffron-colored.

Crommelins: 69/150: a Dutch banking house, c. 1780.

Cromwell: 33/11; 64/101: Oliver, 1599-1658, Lord Protector of Eng-
    land (1653-58).

crotale: 79/68: (It) rattlesnake.

crotales: 79/69: (It) rattlesnakes.

Crowder, H.: 84/115: DTC, Pisa.

Cuba: 12/53, 54; 70/155.

Cul de Sac: 31/5: the cul-de-sac Tete-bout, Paris, in the hotel at
    which Jefferson stayed (October, 1784).
[Cumae]: 64/106: site of the grotto of the Cumaen Sibyl, on a promon-
    tory in Campania; the earliest Greek colony in Italy, founded in the
    8th century BC.
cum delegans revocarit: 67/133: (L) when one who sends a delegate
    calls him back. (See: Bracton, De Legibus, III, 10, where text
    reads: Item cum delegans revocaverit jurisdictionem; John Adams,
    Works, III, 546).
Cumis: 64/106: see CUMAE.
Cummings: 74/10; 80/85, 86: Edward Estlin, 1894-   , the American
    poet.
Cummings: 46/29: Homer Stille, 1870-1956, the American lawyer and
    politician; U. S. Attorney General (1933-39).
[Cunard, Nancy]: 80/73: 1896-   , contemporary American poet.
Cunizza: 29/141, 142; 74/16, 21; 76/30; 78/61: see Cunizza da ROMANO.
cunnus: 47/32: (L) pudendum muliebre.
Curia: 25/115: (It) court.
Curie: 23/107; 27/129: Pierre, 1859-1906, French chemist and physi-
    cist.
Cushing: 62/90; 65/111; 66/130: Thomas, 1725-88, American political
    leader; member of the Boston Committee of Correspondence (1773)
    and of the CONTINENTAL CONGRESS (1774-76).
custode: 76/38: (It) guard.
custos rotolorum: 66/131: (L) custos rotulorum: keeper of the rolls
    (of peace). (See: John Adams, Works, III, 527).
Cypri munimenta sortita est: 1/5: (L) The citadels of CYPRUS are
    her appointed realm. (See: Georgius Dartona Cretensis, Homeric
    Hymn VI, To Aphrodite, 2).
Cyprus: [1/5]; 25/112; 26/124: island in the E Mediterranean; a center
    of the worship of APHRODITE.
Cyrne: 40/49, 50: island of Cerne, or Herne, in the mouth of the Rio
    de Oro on the west coast of Africa; HANNO stopped there on his
    periplus.
Cyrenians: 67/139: people of the ancient city of Cyrene in the part of
    Africa known as Cyrenaica, the modern Barca.
Cythera: 24/111; 74/8, 22; 76/34, 36; 77/46; 79/68, 69, 70; 80/79, 88, 89;
    81/95; 82/103; 84/116: epithet of APHRODITE, from the associa-
    tion of the goddess with the island of Cythera, off the SE coast of
    Laconia.
Cythera egoista: 80/79: (L) proud CYTHERA. (See: APHRODITE).
Cythera potens: 76/34: (L) powerful CYTHERA. (See: APHRODITE).

D

Dafne: 2/9: see DAPHNE.

Dafne: 76/39:

Dahler, Warren: 80/86: 1897- , New York painter and muralist.

Dai: 58/62: (Jap) great. The term is used to refer to the Dairi dynasty of Japan and by extension to the Japanese emperors.

Daimio: 77/44: (Jap) a Japanese feudal baron.

Dai Nippon Banzai: 74/20: (Jap) Long live the Japanese Empire; Hail to the greatness of Japan.

Dakruon: 83/110: (Gr) weeping. (See: Appendix A).

D. Alighieri: 50/43: see DANTE.

Dalmatia: 17/79; [67/140]; 77/48: territory on the E shore of the Adriatic Sea.

Danaë: 4/16: daughter of Acrisius, king of Argos; having been told by an oracle that he would be killed by his daughter's son, Acrisius had Danaë imprisoned in a bronze tower. But Zeus took pity on her and visited her in a shower of gold; as a result of this visit, Danaë bore a son, Perseus. Acrisius set Danaë and Perseus adrift in a sea chest. After many adventures, Perseus returned and accidentally killed Acrisius with a discus, thus fulfilling the oracle.

danar: 9/38; 25/115: an early Italian coin (fr. (It) danaro: money).

Danegeld: 66/128: (OE) an annual tax paid by the Britons to the Danes; continued in later history as a land tax.

[Daniel, Arnaut]: 6/21; 20/89; 29/145: 12th century Provençal troubador. (See: Spirit of Romance, 22-38).

D'Annunzio: 76/34, 39: Gabriele, 1863-1938, Italian author and soldier.

Dante: 7/24; [16/68] ; 74/21: Dante Alighieri, 1265-1321: the Florentine poet.

Da nuces! / Nuces!: 5/17: (L) give nuts! / nuts! (See: Catullus, LXI, 131).

Danzig: 76/33: city in N Poland.

da parte/ de non... / ...non sincere: 25/117: prob. (It) on the side (i.e., affirmative)/ of no (i.e., negatively)/ ...unverified (or not genuine).

[Daphne]: 2/9: Daphne, pursued by APOLLO, was at her entreaty changed into a bay tree (the Greek laurel), which thus became sacred to Apollo.

D'Arcy: 38/38; 40/47: William Knos, Australian oilman, founded the Anglo-Persian Oil Company after first obtaining (1901) the oil concession from the Shah of Persia.

Darwin: 29/114: Charles Robert, 1809-1882, the English naturalist.

Das Bankgeschaft: 77/52: (Ger) the banking business. (See: Georg Obst, Das Bankgeschäft, 1914).

Das heis Walterplatz: 83/113: (Ger) that is called Walter Square.

Das Kapital: 19/84; 33/12: the economic study by Karl MARX.

Das thust du nicht?: 19/86: (Ger) Don't you do that?

Daudet: 77/50: Alphonse, 1840-1897, the French novelist.

daughter of Ocean: 2/6: any sea nymph sired by OCEAN.

Dauphin: 5/18; 23/109: see ROBERT, Dauphin of Auvergne.

Dave:18/83: prob. Dave HAMISH.

David rex:74/7: (L) King David, d. c. BC 972, king of the Hebrews.

Davila:68/141: Enrico Caterino, 1576-1631, Italian soldier and historian; author of History of French Civil Wars (1630); on Davila's work John ADAMS based his Discourses on Davila (1790), a series of papers written to demonstrate that a government must be strong if it is to survive faction.

Davis, Jeff:77/49: Jefferson Davis, 1808-89, President of the Confederate States of America (1861-65).

Dawley:79/67: DTC, Pisa.

Dawn in Britain, The:83/112: an epic poem by Charles Montague DOUGHTY (1906).

Dawson:31/3: John, 1762-1814, member of the House of Representatives (1797-1814), the bearer to Paris of the ratified Convention with France (1800).

D. de M.:9/38: abb. for (L) D(ominus) de M(ALATESTA).

Deane:65/112,114,118,119: Silas, 1737-89, American diplomat; commercial representative in France (1776). Charged with profiteering (1778), he was not able to clear himself and spent the rest of his life in exile. In 1842 Congress granted restitution to his heirs.

De Banchi(i)s cambi tenendi:40/47; 48/34: (L) from the exchange mart.

d'''e b'''e colonne:11/50: prob. double (It) columns.

Debussy:80/71: Claude, 1862-1918, French composer.

decaduto, il:29/145; 78/59: (It) the decadent one.

Decennio:46/25: the tenth anniversary celebration of Italian Fascism (1932).

Declaration:57/137: the American Declaration of Independence (1776).

Degas:74/13; 80/82: Edgar, 1834-1917, the French painter.

Deh! nuvoletta:29/144: (It) Oh! little cloud.

Dei Greci:76/39: see SAN GIORGIO DEI GRECI.

dei ministri:42/3: (It) of the ministers (political).

dei Miracoli:83/107: the Santa Maria dei Miracoli, a church in Rome.

[De la Lande and Fynje]:62/92; 69/151: a Dutch banking house (c. 1780).

De Lara:80/79:

Delaware:71/161: the Delaware River.

Del Carmine:5/19: Giuliano del Carmine, an astrologer who predicted the murder of Alessandro de' MEDICI.

[Delia]:76/35, [36(?)]; 79/70: a reference to ARTEMIS, the goddess of Delos.

De libro Chi-King sic censo... Ut animum nostrum purget, Confucius ait, dirigatque/ ad lumen rationis/ perpetuale effecto... Chi King ostendit incitatque. Vir autem rectus/ et libidinis expers ita domine servat... obsequatur parentis/ nunquam deflectat... igitur meis encomiis,... Chun Tchi anno undecesimo:59/70: (L) ... ita domino...: Concerning the book SHIH CHING I think thus... To purge our minds, CONFUCIUS says, / and guide (them) to the light of reason with perpetual effect... The Shih Ching shows and exhorts. But the just man/ and the one free of lust so serves his master... obeys his parents/ never turns aside... therefore in my eulogies,..

CHUN TCHI (It) eleventh year. (See: A. Lacharme, Confucii Chi-
King, xi-xii; Guide to Kulchur, 249).

Delille, Abbé:34/15: Jacques, 1738-1813, French poet and translator.

de litteris et de armis, praestantibusque ingeniis:11/51: (L) about
letters and arms, and men of outstanding genius. (From Platina:
Petunt quid mihi colloquii fuerit cum Sigismundo Malatesta, qui
tum in Urbe erat. De litteris, inquam, de armis, de praestanti-
bus ingeniis tum veterum, tum nostrorum hominum loquebamur,
deque his rebus, quae in hominum colloquia cadere possunt. (See:
Muratori, Rerum Italicarum Scriptores, III, part I (1923), 384;
also quoted in Yriarte, Un Condottiere au XVe Siècle, 319).

della gloria:21/96: (It) of (the) glory.

dell' Italia tradita:74/8: (It) of the betrayed Italy.

de lonh:65/117: (Pr) far-off. (From a song of Jaufre Rudel; see:
Spirit of Romance, 42).

Delort:44/20: Jean-Francois Delort de Gléon, 1769-1812, officer in the
Napoleonic Army of Italy, serving under General Pierre Antoine
Dupont de l'ETANG.

Delphos:8/31: ancient shrine of APOLLO, on Mt. Parnassus.

Demattia:83/115: DTC, Pisa.

Demeter:[47/30]; 74/9; [77/48]; 79/68; 80/91; [81/95]: the goddess
of corn, of the harvest, of fruitfulness; the mother of PERSEPHONE.

de mis soledades vengan:80/88: (Sp) out of my solitude let them come.
(From a poem of Lope de Vega: de mis soledades vengo...; see
Spirit of Romance, 208).

[Democritus]:77/47: the Greek philosopher.

Demokritoos:77/47: see DEMOCRITUS.

de mortuis:37/34: (L) about the dead; (de mortuis nil nisi bonum).

Dempsey, Jack:77/47: William Harrison Dempsey, 1895-   , the
American heavyweight boxing champion (1919-1926).

denar:54/32; 55/43; 56/49: a coin.

Denmark:68/144; 82/104.

Dennis:28/140: see Dennis WYNDHAM.

Deo similis quodam modo/ hic intellectus adeptus:51/45: (L) Godlike
in a way/ this intellect that has grasped. (From Albertus Magnus;
see: Literary Essays, 186).

dépopulariser:70/158: (Fr) to make unpopular.

de province:27/130: (Fr) provincial.

depuis qu'il...est enfermé à la Tour:68/147: (Fr) since he...has been
locked up in the TOWER. (See: John Adams, Works, VII, 323).

Deputies:27/129; 38/41: see CHAMBER OF DEPUTIES.

Deputies of Holland and Zeeland:65/122: Baron de Lynden de BLIT-
TERSWYK and Baron Van den Santheuvel.

[De Re Militari]:26/121: treatise by Roberto VALTURIO (1472).

Der im Baluba das Gewitter gemacht hat:38/39; 53/10; 74/14; [77/43]:
(Ger) (He) who made the tempest in BALUBA.

Desdemona:83/110: wife of Othello in Othello. The so-called Ca'
Desdemona is the Contarini-Fasan palace, Grand Canal, Venice.

[Deseilligny, Alfred Pierrot]:38/41: 1828-75, son-in-law of Joseph-
Eugène SCHNEIDER, and co-manager of the iron works with Henri
Schneider, son of Joseph-Eugène.

[Despenser, Hugh le]: 62/89: Earl of Winchester, 1262-1326, supported Edward III and was beheaded as a traitor.
[Despenser, Hugh le]: 62/89: d. 1326, son of Hugh le Despenser
the elder; was beheaded as a traitor.
des Petits Augustins: 65/123: the rue des Petits Augustins, Paris;
the Hôtel d'Orleans was on this street. John JAY stopped there.
[Destournelles]: 65/121: French consul at Corunna in 1780.
[Destutt de Tracy, Comte Antoine Louis Claude]: 71/166: 1754-1836,
French philosopher and member of the States-General (1789).
desuete: 74/16: obsolete, out of date.
de suite: 60/74: (Fr) consecutively.
Des valeurs,/ Nom de Dieu, et/ encore des valeurs: 29/144-145: (Fr)
stocks and bonds,/ for God's sake, and/ more stocks and bonds.
Detroit Michilimakinac: 66/126: a military fort controlled by the
British on the Strait of Mackinac, near Detroit, Michigan; final-
ly relinquished to the Americans.
deus nec laedit amantes: 25/118: (L) nor does God harm lovers.
(See: Tibullus, III, x, 15).
Deux Avares, Le: 65/117: a play by Fenouillot de Falbaire de Quing-
ey (1770).
Dhu Achil: 48/35: prob. a dog.
diafan: 36/27: diaphane, a diaphanous substance.
Dial: 80/82: the American magazine (1880-1929).
Diana: 4/14: see ARTEMIS.
diaspre: 20/95: (It) jasper.
Diaz, Ruy: 3/11: Rodrigo Diaz de Bivar (or Vivar), ?1040-1099, the
Cid, Spanish soldier of fortune who served under Sancho IV of
Navarre and Alfonso VI; banished by Alfonso, he served the Arab
kings of Sargossa, capturing and ruling Valencia and Murcia until he was overthrown and killed; hero of the Spanish epic Poema
del Cid.
Dickens: 82/103: Charles, 1812-70, the English novelist.
Dickenson: 65/110: John Dickinson, 1732-1808, American statesman;
member of the CONTINENTAL CONGRESS (1774, 1775, 1779) and
delegate from Delaware to the Federal Constitutional Convention.
In the Continental Congress Dickinson was a leader of those who
desired conciliation with England at almost any cost. (See: John
Adams, Works, II, 414-29).
dicto millessimo: 25/115: (L) in the forementioned date (year).
Di cui...godeva molto: 8/31: (It) in the which...very much enjoyed
himself.
Dido: 7/26: the legendary queen of Carthage who loved Aeneas.
[Dieci, Consiglio de]: 25/115, 117, 119, 120: the Council of Ten of
Venice; supreme Venetian authority, founded in 1310.
[Dieci della Balía]: 8/29, 30; 24/112: the Council of Ten of the Balía;
the ruling authority of Florence.
die decima ottava: 42/8: (L) on the eighteenth day.
Dieudonné: 74/11; 76/31; 77/47: a restaurant in London.
Digenes: 48/35; 74/3: (Gr) digonos: twice born. (See: Appendix A).
Dilectis miles familiaris... castra Montis Odorisii/ Montis Sancti
Silvestri pallete et pile .../ In partibus Thetis: 36/30: (L) (My)

beloved and familiar soldier ... the castles of MONTE ODORISO (and) MONTE SAN SILVESTRO to have and to hold (?).../ in the district of Thetis. (See: Cesare de Lollis, Vita e Poesie di Sordello di Goito, 61).

dilettissimo: 43/9: (It) most beloved.

dilly cavalli tre milia: 11/48: (It) degli...: of the three thousand horses.

Dioce: 74/3, 12; 80/88: Deioces. (See: ECBATAN).

Diocletian: [4/16]; 12/53; [29/145; 78/59]: Gaius Aurelius Valerius Diocletianus, 245-313, Roman Emperor (284-306).

[Diocletian's arena]: 4/16; 12/53; 29/145; 78/59: the Theatrum in the Baths of Diocletian, which are situated at the junction of the Quirinal and Viminal Hills in Rome; begun by Diocletian about 302.

[Diodorus Siculus]: 67/139: Sicilian historian of the first century BC; author of Biblioteca Historica (40 vol.)

Diona: 47/30, 33: see DIONE.

Dione: [47/30, 33]; 76/36: an obscure Greek deity, thought to be either a local form of Earth Mother or a sky goddess; consort of Zeus, mother of APHRODITE.

Dionysius of Syracuse: 8/31: Dionysius the Elder, 430-367, tyrant of Syracuse (405-367); PLATO lived at his court for a time during 388 as tutor to Dionysius the Younger.

[Dionysus]: 2/8; 17/76, 77; 77/53; 78/59; 79/67, 68: the god of wine, fertility and ecstasy.

Diotisalvi: 21/96: see Dietisalvi NERONI.

Dirce: 50/43; 76/30; 82/101, 103: in Greek mythology the wife of Lycus, king of the city later called Thebes; she was put to death by Amphion and Zethus, who tied her on the horns of a bull.

directio voluntatis: 77/45: (L) direction of the will. (See: Dante, De Vulgari Eloquentia, II, 2).

Directory, the: 71/164: a five-man executive committee during the French Revolution; abolished by Napoleon after the coup of 18 BRUMAIRE.

Dis: 21/100: the god of the underworld, the Greek Pluto; consort of PERSEPHONE.

Discobolus: 28/139: statue of the discus thrower by the Greek sculptor, Myron; only copies exist, the best known of which is the Lancelotti Discobolus.

Disraeli: 48/31: Benjamin, 1st Earl of Beaconsfield, 1804-1881, the British statesman and author; prime minister (1874-80).

di sugello: 21/96: (It) as final payment.

Divae Ixottae: 76/37: (It) Divine Isotta. (See: Isotta degli ATTI).

Divina Commedia: 74/19: the Divine Comedy by DANTE (c. 1302-1320).

Divus, Andreas: 1/5: author of a Latin translation of the Odyssey, printed in Paris, 1538. (See: Make It New, 137-146).

dixit: 37/31; 74/7: (L) said.

dixit sic felix Elias?: 35/24: (L) thus said the happy ELIAS?

djassban: 29/143: prob. jazz band.

Doctor, the: 65/124: see Benjamin FRANKLIN.

documento: 41/53: (It) document.

dogana: 43/13: (It) customs house.

Dogana's steps: 3/11: the Dogana di Mare, custom-house in Venice.

Doge: 25/115, 116: see John SORANZO.

Doge: 25/117: see Michele STENO.

doivent tousjours crier la Liberté, -- amis de la France: 62/92: (Fr) (they) ought always to cry Liberty -- friends of France. (See: John Adams, Works, I, 345 note).

Dolmetsch: 80/82; 81/97, 98: Arnold, 1858-1940, French musician and instrument maker, especially of early stringed and keyed instruments; the Dolmetsch Foundation (1928) was founded to encourage interest in old music.

Dolores: 37/35; 81/95:

Domat: 70/157: Jean, 1625-95, French jurist; author of The Civil Laws in their Natural Order (1689-94).

Dome Book: 67/133: The Domesday Book, started about 1066 by William the Conqueror; a record of lands owned in England, their values, and their owners.

Domenica: 65/110: island and British colony in the British West Indies.

Dominant, The: 35/25, 26: traditional term applied to Venice: Venezia Dominante.

Domino: 43/9: (It) Lord, master.

domna jauzionda: 6/22: (Pr) the gay mother; the pleasure-seeking, pleasure-giving mother. (See: Bernart de Ventadour, Tant ai mo cor ple de joya, 53).

Donatello: 79/65: Donato di Niccolò di Betto Bardi, ?1386-1466, Italian sculptor of the early Renaissance; or poss. the character in Hawthorne's Marble Faun.

Don Ferdinandus Secundus Dux Magnus: 42/8: (L) Lord Ferdinand the Second, Mighty Leader. (See: FERDINAND II of Tuscany).

Don Juan: 80/71: see JOHN OF AUSTRIA.

donna, la: 41/52; 74/5; 76/36: (It) the woman.

donne, le: 11/50: (It) the women.

Don Quixote: 71/162: the novel by Cervantes (1605-15).

dont la fâcheuse catastrophe me désole.../ un parent me témoigne de l'inclination d'y placer/ vingt mille florins d'Hollande/ Ven der Kemp peut être de grand utilité pour le Congrès: 68/147: (Fr) whose regrettable catastrophe makes me most unhappy.../ a relative indicates to me that he is inclined to invest twenty thousand Dutch florins in it/ VEN DER KEMP can be very useful to the Congress. (See: John Adams, Works, VII, 317-318).

don't work so hard: 76/39; 83/109: variation of Mencius, II, I, ii, 16: "Let not the mind forget its work, but let there be no assisting the growth of that nature."

Dorata, la: 52/4: see GOLDEN ROOF.

Dortmund: 35/23: a German beer, Dortmunder Aktien Brauerei.

Dottore: 76/39: (It) doctor.

douanes: 53/20; 55/41: (Fr) custom houses, custom duties.

Doughty: 83/112: Charles Montagu, 1843-1926, English traveler and writer, author of Arabia Deserta (1888) and an epic poem, The Dawn in Britain (1906).

Douglas: [22/101, 102]; 38/40; [41/55; 46/25]: Clifford Hugh, 1879-
1952, British engineer and social economist; founder of Social
Credit.
dove è Barilli?: 80/74: (It) where is BARILLI?
dove fu Elena rapta da Paris: 24/111: (It) where HELEN was kidnapped by PARIS.
Dover: 66/126: borough of Kent in SE England, on the Strait of Dover.
dove sta memora: 63/99; 76/30: see DOVE STA MEMORIA.
dove sta memoria: [63/99; 76/30]; 76/35: (It) where one remembers.
(See: ₄Cavalcanti, Donna mi prega in Translations, 134).
Dovizia annonaria: 44/19: (L) the hand-out of food.
Dowland: 81/98: John, 1563-1626, the English composer and lutanist.
Drake, the: 68/143: an English ship captured by John Paul JONES in
1779.
Drecol: 74/13: a Parisian dress designer.
dreitz hom: 5/18: (Pr) a right good man, a man of upright character.
dreory: 1/4: (OE) dreorig: bloody, dripping blood.
Drusiana: 10/43: see Drusiana SFORZA.
Dryad: [3/11; 76/30]; 83/108: a tree nymph which lived only as long
as the particular tree it was associated with.
Dryas: 3/11; 76/30: see DRYAD.
D.T.C.: 76/33: Disciplinary Training Center, near Pisa, Italy; U.S.
Army prison camp, 1945.
Duane: 34/17: William, 1760-1835, American journalist interested in
South America.
du Barry: 65/119: Jeanne Bécu, comtesse du Barry, 1743-93, mis-
tress of Louis XV of France.
Dublin: 77/47: the capital of Ireland.
Dublin pilot: 77/47:
ducatorum? no. ducentorum: 43/11: (L) of ducats?   No.   of two
hundred.
[Duccio, Agostino di]: 9/40; 20/90: ?1418-81, Italian sculptor noted
for his bas-reliefs in the TEMPIO.
Duccio: 45/23; 51/44; 74/3: Duccio di Buoninsegna, 1278-1319, Ital-
ian painter and leading representative of the Sienese school.
[Duccio, Ottaviano d'Antonio di]: 9/40: 1418- ?, Florentine sculptor;
went to Rimini in 1446 to work on the TEMPIO; major designer of
the Tempio decorations.
Duchess of Normandia: 6/21: see ANOR.
Dudley: 66/130: Edmund, a justice during the reign of Henry VII of
England.
Duett: 80/91: DTC, Pisa.
Duke: 43/14: see FERDINAND II of Tuscany.
Duke: 50/42; 79/64; 80/75: see Duke of WELLINGTON.
Duke: 62/93: see John Frederick SACKVILLE.
Duke of Milan: 8/29: see Francesco SFORZA.
Dukes: 74/14: tobacco, "Duke's Mixture."
Dulac: 80/81, 82: Edmund, 1882- , the French artist and illustrator.
Dumas: 62/92; 69/151: Charles William Fredrick, d.c. 1794, Swiss
man of letters whom Franklin employed as an agent to promote
American affairs in Holland (1775); he acted as secretary for John

Adams in Holland (1780-82) and remained there as American
chargé d'affaires.

Dumas: 80/78: Alexandre--Dumas fils--, 1824-95, the French playwright and novelist.

dum capitolium scandet: 77/45: (L) as long as he goes up the Capitol
Hill. (See: Horace, Odes 3, 30).

Dum spiro/... Dum spiro amo: 70/159: (L) While I breathe/... while
I breathe I love. (See: John Adams, Works, IX, 569).

Dunlap, John: 67/137: 1747-1812, a printer in Philadelphia; printed
the first edition of John ADAMS' Thoughts on Government (1776).

[Dunning, Ralph Cheever]: 76/31: d. 1930, English poet.

duomo: 27/130: (It) cathedral.

Duomo, the: 43/11; 44/18: the Cathedral of Siena.

Dupont: 44/20: See Pierre Antoine Dupont de l'ETANG.

Durand: 80/84: see CAROLUS-DURAN.

Durham: 67/136: a county in N England.

Dutch: 60/76, 77, 78; 65/122; 68/148; [69/150]; 78/59.

Dutch constitution: 68/147: the agreements which bound the states of
the Netherlands together under the STADTHOLDER; the Netherlands' Constitution was promulgated in 1814 and established a
constitutional monarchy.

dwarfs, the: 80/71: reference to El Primo, a portrait by VELÁS-
QUEZ in the PRADO.

E

"each one in the name of its god" (each one in his god's name): 74/13,
  21; 76/32; 78/57; 79/65; 84/118: from Micah, 4, 5: "For all
  people will walk everyone in the name of his god."
E al Triedro, Cunizza/ e l'altra: "Io son' la Luna": 74/16: (It) And
  in the corner, CUNIZZA/ and the other (woman): "I am the Moon."
East End of London: 35/23: that part of London lying east of the Bank
  of England.
Eaton: 37/32: John Henry, 1790-1856, American lawyer and politician; member of the U. S. Senate (1818-29), Secretary of War
  (1829-31), minister to Spain (1836-40). His second wife was
  Peggy EATON, whom he married in 1829.
Eaton: 64/103: Joseph. fl. 1766, a Massachusetts lawyer of doubtful
  character.
Eaton, Peggy: 34/19; 37/31: Margaret Eaton, known as Peggy, 1796-
  1879, the daughter of a Washington, D.C. innkeeper; she married
  John B. Timberlake (d. 1828) and then John Henry EATON in
  1829. When Eaton became U. S. Secretary of War (1829) the
  wives of the other cabinet members refused to accept Mrs. Eaton
  socially. Although President JACKSON tried to quiet the matter,
  Eaton was forced to resign in 1831.
E biondo: 7/27: (It) (He) is blond. (See: Inferno, 12, 110).
Eblis: 6/22; 27/132: Eblis II, Viconte of VENTADOUR, a 12th century Provençal nobleman.
Ecbatan: 4/16; 5/17; [74/3, 12; 80/88]: Ecbatana, ancient capital of
  Media Magna, founded in 6th century BC by the legendary first
  king of the Medes, Deïoces. According to Herodotus, the city
  was surrounded by seven concentric walls, each a different color,
  and the citadel was a treasure house.
Ecco il tè: 74/26: (It) Here is the tea.
e che fu chiamata Primavera: 76/30: (It) and who was called Spring.
  (See: Dante, La Vita Nuova, XXIV, 20-23).
Echelles: 32/7: Echelles du Levant, the commercial ports of the
  Near East on the Mediterranean; they were long under Turkish
  control.
Echo de Paris: 38/42: a contemporary Paris newspaper.
École Militaire: 80/83: building at the southern end of the Champ-de-
  Mars, Paris; built by Louis XV and used since as the French
  General Staff College.
Ed ascoltando al leggier mormorio: 81/98: (It) And listening to the
  light murmur.
[Edgar]: 67/135: Edgar the Peaceful, 944-75, King of the English
  (959-75).
Edgardus: 67/135: see EDGAR.
Edgardus Anglorum Basileus/ insularum oceani imperator et dominus
  gratiam ago/ Deo omnip. qui meum imperium/ sic amplicavit et
  explicavit super regnum patrum meorum/ concessit propitia di-
  vinitatis.../ Hibernia habet parliamentum: 67/135: (L) EDGAR,
  King of the English,/ emperor and ruler of the isles of the ocean,
  I thank/ almighty God who so enlarged and extended my kingdom

beyond the kingdom of my fathers, / granted the good offices of
divinity... / Ireland has a parliament. (See: Coke, Reports, 7,
22b; John Adams, Works, IV, 161).

E difficile, / A Firenze difficile viver ricco/ Senza aver lo stato. / "E
non avendo stato Piccinino/ "Doveva temerlo qualunque era in
stato": 21/97: (It) It is difficult/ in Florence to live in wealth/
without having possessions. / "And PICCININO, having none, /
"had to be feared by anyone who had them. "

e di questu/ Fu fatta, / e per questu/ E la donna una furia, / Una
fuRRia-e-una rabbia: 22/102: (It) and of this/ Was made, / and
for this/ And the woman is a fury, / A fury and a rage.

editio terza: 63/98: (It) third edition.

e di tutte le qualità: 44/18: (It) and of all qualities.

Edmée: 77/48:

Edvardus: 74/22: see EDWARD VIII of England.

[Edward the Confessor]: 67/135: ?1002-66, last of the Anglo-Saxon
monarchs of England; ruled 1043-66.

Edward I: 66/131: 1239-1307, King of England (1272-1307).

Edward IV: 66/132: 1442-83, King of England (1461-83).

Edward VII: 22/104: 1841-1910, King of England (1901-10).

[Edward VIII]: 74/22: 1894-   , King of England (20 January-11 December 1936).

Edward, Sir: 66/131: see Sir Edward HALES.

Edwards: 83/114: Ninian, 1775-1833, U. S. Senator from Illinois
(1818-24).

Edwards, Mr.: 74/12, 14: DTC, Pisa.

Edwardus: 67/135: see EDWARD the Confessor.

Edwardus Deo Gratia Angliae/ Dom. Hib. et Dux Aquitaniae terram
Walliae cum incolis suis/ in nostrae proprietatis dominium:
67/135: (L) Edward by the Grace of God (King) of England, /Lord
of Ireland, and Duke of Aquitaine (holding) the land of Wales together with its inhabitants /in possession of our private ownership.
(See: John Adams, Works, IV, 134).

Eetaly: 22/104: see ITALY.

E.F.: 48/36: Era Fascista (the Fascist Era) (1922-1943).

e faceva bisbiglio: 22/105: (It) and whispered.

e "fa di clarita l'aere tremare": 74/[22], 26; 78/59: (It) and makes
the air tremble with light. (See: Cavalcanti, Sonnet VII).

E fu sepulto nudo: 24/113: (It) and was buried naked.

Egeria: 35/23: the nymph who in Roman legend gave advice to King
Numa in the Arician wood. (See: Livy, I, xix, 5). Also a
classical idealization of a mistress.

Ego: 42/7: (L) I.

ego scriptor: 76/36: (L) I, writer.

ego, scriptor cantilenae: 24/112; 62/96; 64/106: (L) I, the writer of
the canto.

E gradment li antichi cavaler romanj/ davano fed a quisti annutii:
10/47; 11/48: (It) and greatly the ancient Roman Knights believed
these signs. (See: Tonini, Rimini nella Signoria de' Malatesta,
283, for this transcription from Broglio).

Egypt: 5/17; 21/98; 38/41; 80/75, 88.

[Eighteenth Amendment]: 78/59: the Eighteenth Amendment to the
    CONSTITUTION OF THE UNITED STATES, prohibiting the manu-
    facture and sale of intoxicating liquors; ratified 16 January 1919
    by Nebraska, the 36th state to do so; repealed 1933.
eijen: 58/69: (Ch) barbarian (?); poss. misspelling of ELJEN (Mag-
    yar) Hail!
e il Capo: 84/117: (It) and the leader. (See: MUSSOLINI).
Eileen: 76/31:
Eire: 67/135: see IRELAND.
eiusdem civitatis Senen: 43/9: (L) of the same city of Siena.
E la Miranda: 77/49: (It) and the MIRANDA.
Elba: 50/42: Italian island in the Mediterranean on which Napoleon
    was confined in 1814.
elder brother: 8/33: see Galeazzo Roberto MALATESTA.
Eleanor: 2/6(?); 6/21, 22; 7/24, 25: Eleanor of AQUITAINE, 1122-
    1204, daughter of William X of Aquitaine; married LOUIS VII of
    France (1137) and Henry of ANJOU (afterward HENRY II of Eng-
    land) in 1152; mother of Henry, Richard I and John of England.
Eleanor: 2/6: see HELEN of Troy.
elegantissimam: 62/91: (L) very elegant.
Elena: 20/92; 24/111: see HELEN of Troy.
Eleusis: 45/24; 51/44; 52/4; 53/18: town in Attica where the Eleusin-
    ian Mysteries of Demeter were held. Originally an agrarian
    festival, the Eleusinian Mysteries came to be concerned with the
    underworld deities, descent into Hades and mystic visions of fut-
    ure life.
Eleutes: 59/72; 60/74, 75: or Eleuths, a nomadic tribe to the north
    and northwest of China; the period of their greatest power was
    1680-96, when they were led by KALDAN.
Elias: 74/4: (Ger) Elijah; the Hebrew prophet.
Elias, Mr.: 35/23, 24:
e li mestiers ecoutes: 7/24: (O Fr) and the mysteries heard.
Elinus, Don: 6/22: a son of FARINATO DE FARINATI.
Eliot: 46/25; 65/124(?); [74/3, 14]; 77/44; 80/75, 76; [81/96]:
    Thomas Stearns, 1888-   , the poet and critic; also referred to
    as POSSUM.
Elizabeth: 66/129; [67/136]: Elizabeth I, 1533-1603, Queen of Eng-
    land (1558-1603).
Elizondo, Padre José: [77/44]; 81/95: José Maria de, Spanish priest
    who helped Pound get a photostat of the Cavalcanti manuscript in
    the Escorial, Madrid. (See: Guide to Kulchur, 158).
Eljen! Eljen Hatvany!: 35/24; [58/69(?)]: (Magyar) Hail, Hail HAT-
    VANY.
Elkin: 82/101: see Elkin MATHEWS.
Ellébeuse, Clara d': 27/130: character in the novel Clara d'Ellébeuse
    ou l'histoire d'une ancienne jeune fille (1899) by Francis Jammes;
    also the name is to be found in Jammes' De l'angélus de l'aube à
    l'angélus du soir (1898).
Elleswood: 62/95: see Oliver ELLSWORTH.
[Elliot, Sir Henry George]: 50/43: 1817-1907, English diplomat who
    was sent on special missions to Naples (1859) and to Greece (1862);

ambassador at Vienna (1877-84); son of the second earl of Minto.

Ellsworth: [62/95]; 63/97: Oliver, 1745-1807, American statesman and jurist; delegate to the CONTINENTAL CONGRESS (1777-84), Chief Justice of the U. S. (1796-99); sent to France to negotiate with NAPOLEON (1800).

E'l Marchese/ Stava per divenir pazzo: 20/90: (It) And the Marquis/ was about to turn crazy. (See: Niccolò d'ESTE).

el mirador de la reina Lindaraja: 74/25: (Sp) the gallery of Queen LINDARAJA.

e l'olors/...d'enoi ganres: 20/90: (Pr) and the smell/...of weariness (wretchedness) you will win (gain) (See: Arnaut Daniel, Er vei vermeils..., in Literary Essays, 139).

e lo soleils plovil: 4/15: (Pr) the sun with the rain in it. (See: Arnaut Daniel, IV: Lancan son passat li giure).

E lo Sordels si fo di Mantovana: 61/22: (Pr) and the SORDELLOs are from Mantua. (From a manuscript in the Ambrosian Library, Milan; see: Literary Essays, 97).

Elpenor: 1/4; 20/94; 80/92: a companion of ODYSSEUS who fell off the roof of CIRCE's dwelling, was killed and left unburied. His is the first shade met by Odysseus in Hades; he asks that he be buried and that his oar be planted on his grave. (See: Odyssey, X-XII).

Elsie: 28/140: see Elsie MACKAY.

Elskamp: 76/33: Max, 1862-1931, Belgian symbolist poet associated with the Catholic renaissance in Belgium.

Elson: 74/10: a missionary known by Pound in Gibraltar, 1906? 1908?

el triste pensier si volge/ ad Ussel. A Ventadour/ va il consire, el tempo revolge: 74/6: (It) the sad thought goes/to USSEL. To VENTADOUR/ goes his counsel, time returns.

Elvira: 20/91: sister of King SANCHO in de Vega's Las Almenas de Toro.

Elysée: 7/25: the Palais de l'Elysée on the Rue du Faubourg-Saint-Honoré, residence of the President of the French Republic; or the CHAMPS ELYSÉE; also the classical ELYSIUM.

Elysium: 80/90; 81/99: in Greek mythology the Islands of the Blest, where heroes and patriots enjoy eternal ease; Virgil places it in the lower world.

e maire del rei jove: 6/21: (Pr) and mother of the young king. (From a Provençal biography of Guillaume POITIERS).

[Emerson, Ralph Waldo]: 28/134: 1803-82, the American essayist and poet; called the Sage of Concord.

eminent Irish writer: 76/34: see James JOYCE.

Emo, Leonardus: 25/119: fl. 1522: a Venetian noble.

Emperor: 9/34: see SIGISMUND V, Holy Roman Emperor.

Emperor: 18/80: see KUBLAI KHAN.

Emperor: 34/15: see ALEXANDER I, of Russia.

Emperor: 38/41: see NAPOLEON III.

Emperor: 54/22: see KAO-HOANG-TI.

Emperor: 54/25: see HAN-SIUEN-TI.

Emperor: 54/28: see TCIN OU TI

Emperor: 54/32: see TAÏ-TSONG.

Emperor: 55/39: see CHEKING-TANG.
Emperor: 55/41: see TAI-TSOU.
Emperor: 55/43, 44: see CHIN-TSONG.
Emperor: 56/52: see GIN-TSONG.
Emperor: 56/56: see NGAÏYCOU-CHILITALA.
Emperor: 57/60: see OU-TSONG.
Emperor: 58/63: see CHIN-TSONG.
Emperor: 58/65: see TAÏ-TSONG.
Emperor: 60/74, 78: see KANG-HI.
Emperor: 61/80, 81, 82: see YONG-TCHING.
Emperor: 61/85: see KIEN-LONG.
Emperor: 65/125; 69/150, 151: see FREDERICK II, of Prussia.
Emperor of the Occident: 53/20: see TCHAO-SIANG.
Empire: 52/3; 65/110; 66/129: see BRITISH EMPIRE.
Empire: 53/14, 17; 54/21, 22, 25, 26, 30, 33, 34; 55/37, 39; 56/51,
    54; 57/57, 59; 58/69; 60/74, 77; 61/83, 86: see CHINESE EM-
    PIRE.
Empress: 53/10: see MIN.
Empress: 54/26: fl. AD 90, wife of HAN HO TI. (See: Mailla,
    Histoire Générale, III, 378).
Empress: 54/29: the empress of OU-TI.
Empress: 54/33: see OU-HEOU.
Empress: 57/60: see TCHANG-CHI.
Empress: 61/86: see HIAO-CHING, HIEN-HOANG-HÉOU.
Empress from Elba: 50/42: see MARIE LOUISE and ELBA.
Empson: 66/130: Sir Richard, a judge during the reign of Henry VII
    of England.
en casque de crystal rose les baladines: 78/58; 80/82: (Fr) in pink
    crystal helmets the mountebanks. (See: Ballet by Stuart Merrill
    in Make It New, 232).
Endicott: 64/107: John, ?1589-1665, one of six persons who bought
    the patent from Plymouth Council in England for territory on
    Massachusetts Bay; acted as first governor of the colony (1628)
    until Winthrop took charge (1630); served as assistant governor,
    deputy governor, and governor at various times (1630-64).
En fait de commerce ce (Bonaparte) est un étourdi: 34/15: (Fr) as
    regards commerce this (Bonaparte) is a scatterbrain. (See:
    J. Q. Adams, Diary, 67-68).
England: 5/18; [18/82]; 19/84; 22/101; [26/122]; 27/129; 31/6; 34/16,
    17, 18; 37/32; 38/37, 38; 40/47; 41/56; 46/26, 29; 50/40, 42; 62/88,
    91, 93; 63/98; 64/103; 65/109, 111, 112, 121, 123, 125; 66/130; 67/135,
    136, 140; 68/144, 146, 147, 148, 149, 150; 71/160, 161, 162, 164;
    74/4; 80/78, 92, 93, 94.
[English Channel]: 66/126.
English Constitution: 71/161: see BRITISH CONSTITUTION.
Englishman Duke: 65/125: see George MONTAGU.
Ennemosor: 83/112: Joseph, 1787-1854, author of Geschichte der
    Magie, Leipzig, 1844.
En son Palais divers ateliers: 60/79: (Fr) In his Palace various
    workrooms. (See: Mailla, Histoire Générale, I, 93).
Entha hieron Poseidōnos: 40/49: (Gr) There (is) a temple of

POSEIDON. (See: <u>The Periplus of Hanno</u>, 4).

entrate: 43/13: (It) enter.

entrefaites: 52/3: (Fr) interval; events.

Entrez donc, mais entrez,/ c'est la maison de tout le monde: 80/83:
     (Fr) Enter then, go on in,/ it is everyone's house.

Eos: [74/22]; 79/66; 80/77, [89]: the goddess of dawn.

E. P.: 42/3: see Ezra POUND.

e pensava: 22/102: (It) and was thinking.

ephèbe: 29/143: (Fr) youth.

Ephesus: 67/139; 80/78: one of the principal Ionian cities on the
     coast of Asia Minor.

Epictetus: 77/43: fl. 60-140, the Stoic philosopher; author of the
     <u>Lectures or Diatribai</u> on the values of endurance and abstention.

Epicurus: 31/6: ?342-270, the Greek philosopher.

(Epi purgo) peur de la hasle: 20/91: (Gr) (upon the wall) (Fr) Fear
     of the (O Fr) sunburn. (See: Appendix A; <u>Literary Essays</u>, 254).

Episcopus: 14/63; 15/64: (L) bishop.

e poi basta: 79/64: (It) and then nothing else.

E poi ha vishtu una volpe: 22/102: (It) And then he saw a fox.

e poi io dissi alla sorella/ della pastorella dei suini:/ e questi ameri-
     cani?/ si conducono bene?/ ed ella: poco./ Poco, poco./ ed io:
     peggio dei tedeschi?/ ed ella: uguale: 84/118: (It) and then I
     asked the sister/ of the little shepherdess of the hogs/ and these
     Americans?/ do they behave well?/ and she: not very well/ not
     very well at all/ and I: worse than the Germans?/ and she: the
     same.

Eppes: 31/5: John Wayles, 1773-1823, nephew and son-in-law of
     Thomas JEFFERSON.

e quel remir: 7/26: (Pr) into which I gaze. (See: Arnaut Daniel:
     XII: <u>Doutz brais et critz.</u>

equites: 43/11: (L) knights.

Era, the: [48/36] 76/38: the Era Fascista: proclaimed by MUSSO-
     LINI in 1922, lasted until 1943.

Erard: 7/25: <u>Érard,</u> a make of piano; Sebastien Érard, 1752-1831,
     French maker of musical instruments.

Erebus: 1/3: in Greek mythology a place of darkness in the under-
     world through which souls pass on the way to Hades.

"Ere he his goddis brocht in Latio": 78/57: from Gavin Douglas,
     <u>Aeneid.</u> (See: <u>Literary Essays</u>, 245).

Erie, Lake: 31/3, 4.

[Erigena, Johannes Scotus]: 36/29; [74/7]; 83/106: ?815-877?, the
     Medieval philosopher and theologian.

Eri men ai de kudoniai: 39/45: (Gr) In the spring the quinces. (See:
     Appendix A).

Eripuit caelo fulmen: 63/98: (L) He snatched the lightning from the
     sky. (<u>Note</u>: the original, Turgot's epigram on Benjamin Franklin,
     reads, <u>Eripuit coelo fulmen; mox sceptra tyrannis;</u> see: John
     Adams, <u>Works,</u> I, 662).

Eriugina, Scotus: 36/29: see Johannes Scotus ERIGENA.

Erizio, Marc: 25/117: prob. a member of the Consiglio dei DIECI,
     Venice.

[Ermentrude]: 83/106: d. 869, first wife of CHARLES II of France
   (Charles le Chauve). She was noted for her ornamental needle
   work, and Johannes Scotus ERIGENA compared her with ATHENA.
Erneung des Religiosen Lebens: 41/53: Erneuerung des religiösen
   lebens (Ger) Revival of Religious Life. (See: Wilhelm BAUR).
Eros: 7/27: the god of love; son of APHRODITE.
err' un'imbecille; ed ha imbecillito/...il mondo: 48/35: (It) he was
   an imbecile; and he has made imbecile/ ...the world.
Escort, Sier: 6/22: father of SORDELLO.
escrime: 58/62: (Fr) fencing.
Eso es luto,...!/ mi marido es muerto: 81/95: (Sp) That is mourning,
   ...!/ my husband is dead.
Esperanza: 41/55: Espéranza, Duchess of Monte Putina, one of the
   main characters in René CREVEL's Les Pieds dans le plat (1933).
est agens: 74/27: (L) it is an agent.
Estaing: 70/157: Comte Jean Baptiste Charles Henri Hector d', 1729-
   94, French naval commander who led a squadron aiding the Amer-
   icans during the Revolutionary War.
Est consummatum, Ite: 74/10: (L) It is finished, go.
Este: 8/32: see Niccolò d'ESTE.
[Este]: 20/91: variant spelling for Ateste, commune in N Italy.
Este, the: 18/81: a reference to the Este family.
[Este, Alberto d']: 24/114: 1347-1393, father of Niccolò d'ESTE;
   Marchese and Vicar of Ferrara.
[Este, Alfonso d']: 30/148: 1476-1534, Alfonso I, third husband of
   Lucrezia BORGIA; became third Duke of Ferrara in 1505 and
   made it a center of the arts.
[Este, Borso d']: 10/43, 45, 46; 17/78, 79; 20/91, 95, 96; 24/114;
   26/121: 1413-71, son of Niccolò d'ESTE; Lord of Ferrara and a
   patron of learning; he was unable to keep peace between Sigis-
   mondo MALATESTA and Federigo d'URBINO.
[Este, Ercole d']: 24/113: 1431-1505, Ercole I, second duke of
   Ferrara, son of Niccolò d'ESTE; patron of Ariosto.
[Este, Ginevra d']: 9/34: d. 1440, daughter of Niccolò d'ESTE;
   married to Sigismondo MALATESTA on 15 March 1433; when she
   died, PIUS II accused Sigismondo of poisoning her, but there was
   no conclusive evidence of such a crime.
Este, Leonello: 25/110; [76/40(?)]: Lionello d'Este, 1407-50, son of
   Niccolò d'ESTE, brother of Borso d'ESTE; patron of PISANELLO.
[Este, Margarita d']: 24/111: d. 1452, sister of Lionello d'ESTE.
[Este, Niccolò d']: [8/32]; 20/[90], 91; 24/111, [112, 114]; 26/123;
   [82/104]: Nicholas III of Ferrara, 1384-1441, ruler of Ferrara,
   Modena, Parma, Reggio, and Milan; father of Borso, Lionello,
   and Ercole d'ESTE; husband of Parisina MALATESTA.
Este, Niclaus: 24/111: see Niccolò d'ESTE.
Esten, Nicolai: 24/111: see Niccolò d'ESTE.
es thalamon: 39/44: (Gr) into the bedroom. (See: Appendix A).
estoppel: 46/28: (law) a bar to one's alleging or denying a fact because of his own previous action by which the contrary has been
   admitted, implied or determined.
"et amava perdutamente Ixotta degli Atti"/ e "ne fu degna"/ "constans

in proposito/ "Placuit oculis principis/ "pulchra aspectu"/ "populo grata (Italiaeque decus): 9/41: (It) and he loved Isotta degli
ATTI to distraction/ and "she was worthy of him"/ "constant in
purpose/ "she was pleasing to the eyes of the prince/ "beautiful
to look at"/ "she was liked by the people (and the honor of Italy).
(See: Yriarte, Un Condottiere au XVe Siècle, p. 155: "Il a aimé
éperdument Isotta et elle en était digne." La chronique de Rimini
l'a caracterisé ainsi: "Erat haec pulchra aspectu, plurimus doti-
bus locupletata, foemina belligera et fortis, et constans in proposito, grata populo et placita oculis principis." Italiaeque decus:
epithet of Isotta; inscription on Matteo da Pasti medal (1446) reads:
Isote Ariminensi Forma Et Virtute Italie Decori.

[Etang, Pierre Antoine Dupont de l']: 44/20: 1765-1840: French
   general under NAPOLEON.

Et/ "anno messo a saccho el signor Sigismundo": 10/42: (It) and/
   "they fooled master Sigismondo. (See: Sigismondo MALATESTA).

Etats de Frise, des: 69/152: (Fr) FRIESLAND.

Etats Unis, des: 69/150: (Fr) UNITED STATES of America.

et des dettes des dites Echelles.../... peu délicat sur les moyens:
   32/7: (Fr) and of the debts of the said ECHELLES.../... in the
   principal decrees of the Council, December [17]66/ weapons and
   other implements which can only be for/ the government's account
   ... M. Saint-Libin/ well versed in the languages of the country,
   known by the Nabobs/..to excite him, and to follow hot upon the
   enemy (to the) English/ not very delicate about the means.

et effectu: 55/44: (L) and in effect.

Et/ En l'an trentunième de son Empire/...Faictes moi mes funér-
   ailles: 56/56: (Fr) And/ in the thirty-first year of his Rule/
   the year sixty of his age/ HONG VOU, seeing his strength weaken/
   said: May virtue inspire you, TCHU-OUEN,/ you faithful mandarins, cultivated people, soldiers/ Help my grandson sustain/ the
   dignity of this power, the weight of his office/ And as to Prince
   OUEN TI of the HAN in former times,/ make me my funeral.
   (See: Mailla, Histoire Générale, X, 104).

et fils: 76/34: (Fr) and son.

et j'entendis des voix: 16/70: (Fr) and I heard voices.

Et les angloys ne povans desraciner...venin di hayne: 10/46: (O Fr)
   And not being able to root out the English...poison of hatred.

Et les Indiens disent que Boudha: 54/29: (Fr) and the Indians say that
   BUDDHA.

et libidinis expers: 76/35: (L) to whom passion is unknown.

Et ma foi, vous savez,/ tous les nerveux.../ Faut que ça soit bien
   carré, exact: 16/72-74: (Fr) And really, you know,/ all the
   nervous (or nervy) ones. No,/ there is a limit; animals, animals
   are not/ made for that, a horse doesn't amount to much./ The
   men of 34, on all fours,/ who cried "Mommy". But the tough
   guys,/ at the end, there at Verdun, there were only those big boys/
   and they knew exactly what the score was./ What are they worth,
   the generals, the lieutenant,/ they weigh out at a centigramme,/
   they are nothing but wood./ Our captain, all shut up in himself
   like/ the old military engineer he was, but strong,/ a strong head.

There, you know,/ everything, everything runs in order, and the
thieves, all the vices, but the birds of prey,/ there were three
in our company, all killed./ They went out to plunder a corpse,
for nothing,/ they would have gone out for nothing but that./ And
the Jerries, you can say anything you want,/ militarism etc...
etc.../ All that, but, BUT/ the Frenchman, he fights when he has
eaten./ But those poor guys/ at the end they attacked each other
so they could eat,/ Without orders, wild animals, they took/
prisoners; those who could speak French said:/ "Poo quah? Well,
we attacked so we could eat."/ It's the grease, the grease/ their
supplies come forward at three kilometers an hour,/ and they
creaked, they grated, could be heard five kilometers away./
(That's what finished the war.)/ The official list of dead:
5,000,000/ He tells you, Well yeah, it all smelled of oil./ But,
No! I bawled him out/ I said to him: You're a jerk! You missed
the war./ O Yeah! all the people with taste, I admit,/ all of them
in the rear/ But a guy like you! / That fellow, a guy like that!/
What he couldn't have taken! He was in a factory./ What, bury-
ing squad, ditch diggers, with their heads/ thrust back, looking
like this,/ they risked their life for a shovelful of dirt./ Must be
nice and square, accurate.

et nulla fidentia inter eos: 15/65: (L) and no confidence among them.

et omnia alia juva: 43/9: (L) and everything else, support.

Et omniformis,...omnis/ Intellectus est: [5/17]; 23/107: (L) And
   every intellect is capable of assuming every shape. (See:
   Porphyry, De Occasionibus, the 13th chapter of which is titled:
   "Omnis Intellectus Est Omniformis").

Et quand lo reis Lois lo entendit/ mout er fasché: 6/21: (O Fr) And
   when King Louis (LOUIS VII) heard it,/ he was very angry.

Et quant au troisième/ Il est tombé dans le/ De sa femme, on ne le
   reverra/ Pas: 27/129: (Fr) And as to the third/ he fell into the/
   of his wife, (and) won't be seen again.

et/ quod publice innotescat: 25/115: (L) and which may be publicly
   made known.

Et sequelae: 76/38: (L) and the consequences.

e theos e guné...ptheggometha thasson: 39/43: (Gr) either a goddess
   or a woman...let us raise our voices without delay. (See: Appendix A).

e tot lo sieu aver: 12/54: (Pr) and all his possessions.

Et sa'ave, sa'ave, sa'ave Regina!: 4/16: (L) And hail, hail, hail
   Queen!

Etruria: 44/20: ancient country in central Italy; the kingdom of
   Etruria was erected by NAPOLEON in 1801 and incorporated into
   the French Empire in 1808.

Et ter flebiliter: 4/13; [78/55]: (L) and thrice with tears. (See:
   Horace, Odes, IV, xii, 5).

Euclid: 62/93: fl. c. 300BC, Greek mathematician.

Eulh: 54/21: Eulh-chi-hoang-ti (Êrh Shih Huang Ti) (reign: 209-206),
   an extremely inept emperor; he was controlled by the eunuch
   Chao Kao, who finally murdered him.

Euné kai philoteti ephata Kirkh: 39/44: (Gr) Making love in bed, said
   CIRCE. (See: Appendix A).

eunuchs: 54/21; 55/37, 38, 40; 56/48, 53, 55; 57/58, 59; 58/64, 68;
    59/71: the eunuchs of the imperial palace of China; whenever
    they gained control over an emperor, the government would de-
    cline in quality.
Eurilochus: 39/44: see EURYLOCHUS.
Europa: 74/21, 25: in Greek mythology the daughter of Agenor, king
    of Tyre; she was courted and captured by Zeus, who assumed the
    form of a bull.
Europa nec casta Pasiphaë: 74/21: (L) EUROPA nor chaste PASI-
    PHAË. (See: Propertius, II, xxviii, 52).
Europe: 31/5; 32/9; 34/15, 18; 37/33; 50/41; 58/64; 59/73; 60/74, 78;
    61/83; 62/87, 96; 64/107; 65/116, 123, 125; 66/126; 67/137, 139;
    68/143, 145, 146; 69/152; 70/156, 157, 158; 71/161, 164, 166; 74/19,
    26; 76/36; 84/117.
Eurus: 74/21; 76/38: the east, or south-east, wind.
Eurylochus: 1/3; [39/44]: a member of the crew of Odysseus who,
    with PERIMEDES, performs the rites of sacrifice on the banks
    of OCEAN. (See: Odyssey, XI, 23-24).
Evelyn: 34/19: John, 1620-1706, the English writer.
Evviva: 44/17, 18; 50/43; 55/39: (It) hurrah!
Evviva Ferdinado il Terzo: 44/18: (It) Hurrah for FERDINAND III.
Evviv' Indipendenza: 50/43: (It) Hurrah for Independence.
exarchate: 21/98: the office of an exarch, a viceroy of a Byzantine
    emperor.
Ex Arimino die xx Decembris/ "Magnifice ac potens domine, mi sin-
    gularissime: 9/37: (L) from RIMINI the 20th of December/ "My
    very excellent lord, magnificent and potent.
ex certe scientia et: 42/8: (L) with certain knowledge and.
Excideuil: 80/88: village of Dordogne department, SW France, near
    Perigreux.
ex nihil: 46/27, 28; 76/40: (L) from nothing. (Reference is to the
    statement attributed to William PATERSON: "the bank [of
    England] hath benefit of the interest on all moneys which it cre-
    ates out of nothing." (See: A Visiting Card, 9).
Exso et Dno sin Dno Sigismundum Pandolfi Filium/ Malatestis Capi-
    tan General: 9/39: (L) Most excellent, and Lord without Lord,
    SIGISMONDO son of PANDOLFO/Captain General MALATESTA.
eyetalian peninsula: 80/88: see ITALY.
Ez, Old: 79/66: see Ezra POUND.
Ez. P: 64/106: see Ezra POUND.

F

Fabbizio bollo/ vedo/ Governatore: 42/6: (It) needs a stamp/ see/ Governor.

fabians: 15/64: the Fabian Society, a group of socialists, organized in England in 1884.

Fac deum! Est factus!: 39/45: (L) Make God! He is made!

facilius laudari quam invenire/ vel haud diuturna/ optime modice confusa.../ concors tamen efficitur...civitas consensu/ ubi justitia non est, nec jus potest esse: 67/139-140: (L) it is more easily praised than discovered/ or not lasting/ excellently blended in moderation.../ is nevertheless brought about in unison... a state by agreement/ where there is no justice, there can be no law. (For sources of these fragments see: Tacitus, Annales, IV, xxxiii, 20, where text reads: ...laudari facilius quam evenire, vel si evenit, haud diuturna esse potest; Cicero, De Re Publica, II, xxiii, 41, where text reads: statu esse optimo...confusa modice...; Cicero, De Re Publica, II, xlii, 69; and Cicero, De Re Publica, III, Fragmenta, where text reads: Ubi justitia vera non est, nec jus potest esse, a quotation from St. Augustine, De Civitate Dei, XIX, 21; see also: John Adams, Works, IV, 294-296).

Factory Act: 33/13: the British act passed in 1825, shortening the hours of child labor; amended (1829, 1831) specifically to regulate child employment in cotton mills. (See: John HOBHOUSE).

"Fades light from sea-crest,...and brought to mind of thee": 5/17-18: from Sappho. (See: C. R. Haines, Sappho: the poems and fragments, 84-86).

Faece Romuli non Platonis republica: 65/113: (L) in the dregs of ROMULUS, not in PLATO's republic. (See: Cicero: Epp. ad Atticum: II, i, 8).

Faenza: 9/34: town in Romagna, N central Italy; ruled by the MANFREDIs (14th and 15th centuries).

Fa Han: 23/108: prob. invention; poss. Fa Hiän, an early Chinese pilgrim to India who is remembered for his travelogues.

faire passer ces affaires/ avant ceux de la nation: 38/42: (Fr) to make these matters come/ before those of the nation.

Falange, La: 80/83: (Sp) the Falange, Spanish fascist organization.

Fa me hora tagliar la testa/ dapoi cosi presto hai decapitato il mio Ugo: 24/112: (It) now let my head be cut off/ being that so quickly you decapitated my UGO.

Fan-chungin: 55/43: (Fan Shun-jen) fl. AD 1069, Chinese minister sent by Emperor CHIN-TSONG to inspect the progress of OUANG-NGAN-CHÉ's reforms in the province of SHENSI; Fan-chungin complained of the new regime because it did away with the form of government that had always been in China.

fane: 30/148: temple, sacred building.

Fanesi: 10/42: citizens of FANO.

[Fang-koué-tchin]: 56/53: (Fang Kuei-chên) fl. AD 1358, a Chinese pirate during the reign of CHUNTI. He operated a fleet of junks off the South China coast and added his bit to the general rebellion which ended the Mongol dynasty.

Fan-kouai: 54/22: (Fan Kuai) d. BC 189, a dog-butcher of P'ei (in modern Kiangsu) who early attached himself to the fortunes of LIEOU-PANG and became one of his advisers when he attained the rank of emperor. When Emperor Kao was old, he shut himself in the palace; Fan-kouai found him sleeping pillowed on a eunuch. Fan-kouai burst into tears and said: "Sire, think of Chao Kao!" (See: EULH). The emperor then got up and went back to work.

Fan-kuang: 57/58: (Fan Kuang) fl. AD 1450, Chinese commander in the imperial troops defending Peiping from the Mongol warriors.

[Fan-li]: 53/20: (Fan Li) fl. BC 474, Chinese minister of Kou Chien, Prince of YUEI State. Kou Chien had been attacked by the troops of Wu some years before and Fan-li urged him to take revenge; he did so and was victorious.

Fano: 9/34; 11/48, 50; 30/148; 76/40; 80/79: town of the Marches, E central Italy; once in the possession of the MALATESTAs.

Fano Caesaris: 30/148; 80/79: poss. reference to the triumphal arch of AUGUSTUS in FANO; poss. merely reference to fact that Fano was once a Roman settlement.

[Fan-tchin]: 54/29: (Fan Chên) fl. AD 484, Chinese intellectual, one of a group that gathered about Hsiao Tzǔ-liang, son of Emperor OU-TI. The prince was a BUDDHIST, but Fan-tchin took it upon himself to discourse on the methods which the Buddhist monks (BONZES) used to deceive the people.

fanti: 11/48: (It) foot soldiers; infantrymen.

Fan Tsuyu: 55/44: (Fan Tsu-yu) fl. AD 1084, Chinese historian in the court of Emperor CHIN-TSONG; one of those who helped SSE-MA-KOUANG compile The TSÉ-TCHI-TONG-KIEN.

Fara Sabina: 78/56: a locality near Rome.

Farben works: 74/12: the I. G. Farben (Interessen Gemeinschaft Farbenindustrie Aktiengesellschaft) works, German chemical and dye cartel, officially organized as a monopoly in 1925 at Frankfurt-on-Main.

Farinata: 78/58: see Farinata degli UBERTI.

Farinato de' Farinati: 6/22: see Farinata degli UBERTI.

Farinatis, Picus de: 6/22: a son of Farinata degli UBERTI.

Farley: 46/29: James Aloysius, 1888-   , American politician.

Fasa: 74/5, 8, 9; 77/43: a tribe of heroes in N Africa. (See: Frobenius, Erlebte Erdteile).

[Fates]: 47/33: the three goddesses supposed to determine the course of human life; their names were Clotho (the Spinner), Lachesis (the Disposer of Lots) and Atropos (the Inflexible).

Fatty: 11/51: see Pietro BARBO.

Faunus: 79/69: Roman god of herdsmen.

faute de: 74/21: (Fr) in lieu of.

Favonus, vento benigno: 80/90: (L) west wind, with kindly breeze.

Faziamo tutte le due: 29/144: (It) let's do both of them.

Fazzio: 84/115: DTC, Pisa.

feconda: 79/65: (It) fruitful.

Feddy: 9/35, 36, 37: see Federigo d'URBINO.

fede, la: 78/56: (It) faith.

[Federal Constitutional Convention]: 34/17: the convention which met
  at Philadelphia in 1787; the Convention was to examine and improve the Articles of Confederation, but the Articles were quickly recognized to be inadequate, and the Convention abandoned
  them and wrote the CONSTITUTION OF THE UNITED STATES.

federalists: 70/156: supporters of U. S. CONSTITUTION; anti-
  Jeffersonians.

Federal Reserve banks: 33/14: the United States Federal Reserve
  Bank, organized to serve as a bank of reserve and rediscount for
  member banks (all national banks and many state banks and trust
  companies). Federal reserve banks have the power to issue currency.

Feigenbaum: 28/136: prob. an acquaintance of Pound in Philadelphia,
  c. 1908.

Fei-tsei: 53/16: Fei-tsé (Fei Tzŭ) fl. BC 900, an ancestor of Yih,
  an official of the great CHUN. Fei-tsei was given charge of Emperor Hiao-wang's studs. When he was appointed head of his
  clan, there was a great fall of hail in SHENSI, so that oxen and
  horses died in great numbers and the Han river was frozen; these
  seemed to be unlucky omens for the CHOU dynasty. Fei-tsei was
  given a small portion of land in Kansu province, the chief town of
  which was Ts'in; thus he became the Prince of Ts'in (Ch'in).

feitz Marcebrus: 28/137: (Pr) MARCABRU made it.

femina: 74/9: (L) woman.

Fen-li: 53/20: see FAN-LI.

Fen-yang: 53/19: (Fén Yang) fl. BC 520, Chinese general and counsellor of KING WANG (BC 544-519), and of his grandson, KING-OUANG.

Ferd. I: 43/10: see FERDINAND I of Tuscany.

Ferd. III: 44/19: see FERDINAND III of Tuscany.

[Ferdinand I of Austria]: 50/42: 1793-1875, emperor of Austria
  (1835-48); son and successor of Emperor Francis II. Subject to
  fits of insanity, he was dominated by a council led by Metternich,
  which ruled in his name; he was forced to abdicate (1848) in favor
  of his nephew, FRANZ JOSEPH.

[Ferdinand I of Naples]: 10/43, 46: 1458-94, natural son and successor to ALFONSO V of Aragon and Naples.

[Ferdinand I of Naples and Sicily]: 32/9: 1751-1825, King of Naples
  (1759-1806; 1815-25) as Ferdinand IV; because he remained hostile
  to NAPOLEON, he fled to Palermo while the French established
  the short-lived Parthenopean Republic at Naples (1799); in 1806 he
  fled to Sicily where he ruled as Ferdinand III while Naples was
  ruled by Joseph Bonaparte and Murat; he was restored to the
  throne of Naples in 1815 and was made king of the Two Sicilies in
  1816 as Ferdinand I.

[Ferdinand I of Tuscany]: [42/5]; 43/10: Ferdinand de'MEDICI, 1549-
  1609, Grand Duke of Tuscany (1587-1609); responsible for the
  founding of the real strength and prosperity of the grand duchy.

[Ferdinand II of Tuscany]: 42/[3, 5, 6, 7,] 8; 43/[9], 10, [12, 14],
  15; 50/42: Ferdinand de'Medici, 1610-1670, Grand Duke of Tuscany
  (1620-70); patron of arts and letters.

[Ferdinand III of Tuscany]: 44/17, 18, 19, 22; 50/41: 1769-1824,
    Grand Duke of Tuscany (1790-99; 1814-24) and Archduke of
    Austria.
Ferdinandi: 44/19: see FERDINAND III of Tuscany.
Ferdinando: 10/43, 46: see FERDINAND I of Naples.
Ferdinando: 44/17, 18, 22; 50/41: see FERDINAND III of Tuscany.
Ferdinando of Naples: 10/43: see FERDINAND I of Naples.
Ferdinandus Secundus: 42/8: see FERDINAND II of Tuscany.
Fernando: 84/117: see FERDINAND III of Tuscany.
Ferrara: 8/31; 9/40; 10/43; 24/110, 112, 114; 25/118; 26/121, 123; 30/148;
    [77/53]; 82/104: the town in N Italy.
Ferrara, paradiso dei sarti, "feste stomagose": 24/114: (It) Ferrara,
    heaven of the tailors, "disgusting festivals".
Feyenkopf: 60/74, 75: see FÉYANKOU.
[Feyankou]: 60/74, 75: (Fei Yang-ku) d. AD 1701, Chinese grand-
    general in the service of Emperor KANG-HI. His greatest mili-
    tary feat was his part in the campaigns against KALDAN, the
    chief of the ELEUTES. In 1696 he pursued Kaldan's forces
    through the Gobi desert and defeated them at Chaomoto, to the
    north of the desert. In 1697 Kaldan committed suicide and his
    followers submitted to the emperor all the country east of the
    Ordos.
Ficino: 21/96: Marsilio, 1433-99, the Italian Platonist philosopher.
Fidascz: 35/22:
Figlia di Jorio, La: 76/34: (It) Jorio's Daughter; a play (1904) by
    D'ANNUNZIO.
Filippo: 9/36: see Filippo Maria VISCONTI.
filius: 42/7: (L) son.
finito: 76/31: (It) finished.
Finlandia: 80/71: a tone poem (1900) by the Finnish composer,
    Sibelius.
fin oreille: 77/50: prob. (Fr) fine oreille: a good ear.
fiolo del Signore: 24/110: (It) son (bastard) of the Lord.
Fiorentino, Il: 16/68: see DANTE.
fiorini di Camera: 8/30: (It) public money.
[Firdausi]: 77/52: fl. 940-1020, Persian poet, author of the SHAH
    NAMAH, the great Persian epic; his real name was Abul Kasim
    Mansur.
Firdush': 77/52: see FIRDAUSI.
Firenze: 21/97; 42/5; 43/13, 15, 16; 44/17: (It) FLORENCE.
First Consul: 50/41: see NAPOLEON.
First honey and cheese...honey and wine and then acorns: 39/44:
    from Odyssey, X, 234, 242.
First must thou go the road/   to hell...Knowing less than drugged
    beasts: 47/30: from Odyssey, X, 490-95.
Fiseaux: 69/150: a Dutch banking house (c. 1780).
Flanders: 50/40, 43: formerly a country in the Low Countries; now
    divided between Belgium and France.
Flassans: 62/92: Jean Baptiste Gaëton de Roxis de Flassan, 1760-
    1845, French diplomat and historian; author of Histoire Générale
    et Raisonée de la Diplomatie Française (1808).

Flaubert: 80/72; 82/102: Gustave, 1821-1880, the French novelist.

Fleet Prison: 71/163: a debtor's prison on Fleet Street, London.

Fleta: 63/99: name of a Latin textbook on English law, Fleta, seu
     Commentarius Iuris Anglicani (c. 1290); believed to have been
     written in FLEET PRISON by one of the corrupt judges im-
     prisoned by Edward I.

Flora: 39/45: an old Italian deity of fertility and flowers.

Floradora: 27/130: a musical comedy written by Leslie Stuart (1900),
     famous for the Floradora Sextette which sang and danced the hit
     number of the show, "Tell Me Pretty Maiden."

Florence: 5/19; 8/28, 29, 31; 9/35, 37; 10/42, 46; [21/97]; 26/126;
     [42/5]; 43/13[15, 16]; [44/17]; 77/5: capital of FIRENZE prov-
     ince, Tuscany, central Italy.

Florentine Baily: 24/112: see DIECI DELLA BALÍA.

Florian's: 76/34; 80/88: a restaurant in the Piazza di San Marco.
     Venice.

Florida: 34/16: the state on extreme SE tip of the United States;
     formerly a Spanish possession.

Foé: 54/30, 31; 56/52; 57/59: the name of BUDDHA and more com-
     monly the name given to Buddhist priests, foés, foéist, in French
     transliteration.

Foglia: 8/33: the river in Italy.

folcright: 67/133: (OE) folcriht: common law, public rights.

Folies, Les: 74/13: see FOLLIES. Text reference is to the painting
     of Manet: Un Bar aux Folies-Bergère (1882).

Follies: [74/13]; 80/82: the Folies-Bergère in the rue Richer, Paris.

Fonda: 76/38: prob. reference to the various (It) fondamenti (streets,
     passageways) in Venice; poss. a contraction of (It) fondaco
     (warehouse), especially the Fondaco dei Turchi, 13th century
     Venetian-Byzantine building on the Grand Canal, opposite the
     VENDRAMIN Callergi Palace.

Fondamento dei (delli) Thodeschi: 25/119, 120: a street in Venice.

Fondecho: 76/38: prob. (It) fondaco. (See: FONDA).

fondego: 61/81: (It) chamber.

fondo: 43/13: (It) bottom.

Fong: 54/26: see FONG-CHI.

Fong-chi: 54/26: (Fêng Shih) fl. BC 6, concubine of HAN-YUEN-TI;
     prominent in the reign of Emperor Han Ngai Ti (BC 6-1 AD).

[Fontaney, de]: 60/74: fl. 1693, a Jesuit missionary in China.

Fonte Giusta: 44/17: the Madonna of Fontegiusta, a church (1479) in
     Siena.

Fontego: 35/24; 48/36; 61/81: (It) chamber.

[Ford, Ford Madox (Hueffer)]: 74/10; 80/86, 88; 82/103: 1873-1939,
     the English novelist, critic, poet and editor.

Ford, Henry: 74/19: 1863-1947, the American industrialist.

Ford, Henry, Life of: 74/19: prob. My Life and Work by Henry FORD
     (1923).

Fordie: 74/10; 80/86, 88; 82/103: see Ford Madox FORD.

Forest: 64/105: James, fl. 1770, a Boston merchant and Loyalist,
     born in Ireland.

Foresteria: 78/56: (It) the part of a monastery (or club) where visi-
     tors are housed.

"forloyn": 80/85: a term in hunting (also forloin), meaning to leave the pack behind; used in reference to a stag or to individual hounds. (See: Sonnets and Ballate of Guido Cavalcanti, 61).

Formando di disio nuova persona: 27/129: (It) forming with desire a new person. (See: Sonnets and Ballate of Guido Cavalcanti, 126).

formato loc(h)o: 70/156; 74/24: (It) in a prepared place. (See: Cavalcanti: Donna mi prega in Make It New, 366).

Formosus: 11/51: see Pietro BARBO.

fornicarium ac sicarium/ proditor, raptor, incestuosus, incendiarus ac/ concubinarius: 10/44: (L) fornicator and murderer,/ betrayer, rapist, incestuous, arsonist and/ liver in concubinage.

Fortean Society: 74/24: a society, organized in 1931, directed by Tiffany Thayer, devoted to the study of the works of Charles Fort (1874-1932).

Fortescue: 66/131; 67/133: Sir John, ?1394-1476?, English jurist and one of England's first constitutional lawyers.

"For this hour, brother of Circe": 17/79: poss. variation of Odyssey, X, 137.

Forti dei Marmi: 76/37: a small Italian town, Lucca province, Italy.

Fortinbras: 26/122: Carlo Fortebracci, Count of Montone, Venetian condottiere during the wars between the forces of Sigismondo MALATESTA and PIUS II; he was granted 2000 ducats for enlistment of soldiers into the Venetian forces.

42nd Street: 74/25: a major street in midtown MANHATTAN; the only tunnel on 42nd Street is a subway tube.

Foscari: 9/36: Francesco, ?1372-1457, doge of Venice (1423-57); extended the power of Venice into northern Italy by a series of successful wars (1426-54).

Foscari, Ca': 83/110: the famous palace in Venice, on the Grand Canal.

Fossembrone: 9/35: town in the Marches, central Italy, near the Metauro river.

Foster: 67/133: Sir Michael, 1689-1763, English jurist.

Fou: 54/31: see FOU-Y.

Fou: 56/49: see TCHONG-KING-FOU.

Fou-chi: 54/26: (Fü Shi) fl. BC 6, concubine of HAN-YUEN.

Fou Hi: 53/8, 10: (Fü Hsi) (reign: BC 2953-2838), the first of the Five Emperors of the legendary period of China; he taught his people to hunt, fish, and keep flocks; he invented a calendar, formed musical instruments, and developed the marriage contract.

Fou-kien: 57/61: (Fukien), a province in SE China.

Foundation of Regius Professors: 46/27: Royal endowment of professorships at Oxford and Cambridge Universities.

Fou-Píe: 55/42: (Fü Pi) d. AD 1085, Chinese scholar and diplomat serving Emperor GIN-TSONG. In 1042 the KHITAN Tartars demanded ten counties of the empire and threatened war if the emperor refused. Fou-píe was sent to negotiate with the Khitan. Fou-píe's treaty enjoined the Khitan to keep peace and promised them a tribute each year of 100,000 ounces of silver and 100,000 pieces of silk in addition to the previous tribute promised by Emperor TCHIN-TSONG (1006). Fou-píe's treaty was humiliating to the empire, but a masterpiece of diplomacy.

Fouquet: 74/25: prob. a resident in a New York boarding house, c. 1890. (See: Indiscretions, in Quarterly Review of Literature, V, 2 (1949) 124).

Foutères: 60/74: see FONTANEY.

Fou-Y: 54/31: (Fü I) fl. AD 626, Chinese minister of Emperor KAO-TSEU who petitioned that all Buddhist establishments be abolished and that all Buddhist monks and nuns be sent to their homes; he argued that Buddhism demoralized the empire by de-emphasizing the proper relationships between ruler and people, between parents and children.

Fox: 68/144: Charles James, 1749-1806, the English statesman; sided with BURKE against NORTH's policies toward the American Colonies.

Fracastor: 5/20: Girolamo Fracastoro, 1483-1553, Italian physician, astronomer and poet; wrote Syphilis sive Morbus Gallicus in which the hero's mother is struck by lightning while he is a child in arms.

France: 31/4; 41/55; 46/29; 62/92,94; 65/111, 112, 113, 115, 118, 119, 123, 124; 67/136; 68/142, 144, 145; 69/151, 153; 70/155, 158; 71/160, 161, 162, 163, 166; 74/13, 26; 76/33; 80/94.

Francesca, Pier della: 45/20: see Piero dei FRANCHESCHI.

Francesco: 8/31, 32; 9/35, 36; 10/46: see Francesco SFORZA.

[Francheschi, Piero dei]: 8/28; 45/20: ?1420-92, the Italian painter.

[Franchet d'Esperey], Louis Félix Marie: 35/24: 1856-1942, Marshal of France; commanded the French 5th Army in the battle of the Marne (1914); in 1918 he led the Allies to victory in the Balkans.

Franchet de Whatshisname: 35/24: see FRANCHET D'ESPEREY.

Franco: 81/95: Francisco, 1892-   , the Spanish general and dictator.

François Guiseppe: 35/22; 38/38: see FRANZ JOSEPH.

franco-japanese bank: 38/42: the Franco-Japanese Bank, closely connected with the SCHNEIDER interests.

[Francy, John Baptiste Lazarus de Theveneau de]: 68/143: commercial agent of BEAUMARCHAIS.

Frankfurt: 81/97: Frankfurt-am-Main, a manufacturing and commercial city in Wiesbaden district of Germany; location of the Institute for Cultural Morphology, founded by Leo FROBENIUS.

Franklin, Benjamin: 31/3, 5; 33/11, 12; 34/16; [52/3(?)]; 62/92; 63/97, 99; 64/108; 65/113, 117, 118, 123, 124, 125; 67/133,[134]; 68/143, 144, 147; 69/150; 71/161: 1706-90, American statesman, printer, scientist, and writer; member of the committee which drafted the DECLARATION of Independence (1776); negotiated the Treaty of Paris (1781-83) with John ADAMS and John JAY; member of the FEDERAL CONSTITUTIONAL CONVENTION (1787).

Franklin, Billy: 65/124: William Temple Franklin, d. 1823, grandson of Benjamin FRANKLIN; served as secretary to his grandfather in Paris; published editions of Franklin's works (1816-19).

Franklin Inn Club: 80/85: the Philadelphia literary club, founded by Dr. S. Weir MITCHELL (1902).

Franks: 68/141: a group of Germanic tribes; the Western Franks
    consolidated into France; Eastern Franks into Germany.
Franz, Joseph: 16/71; [35/22; 38/38]; 50/41: Emperor of Austria,
    1830-1916, whose policies were contributory to the outbreak of
    World War I; he rejected the Serbian note after Sarajevo and de-
    clared war 28 July 1914.
Frascati: 77/52: town in Roma province, Latium, central Italy.
Frater tamquam/ Et compater carissime; tergo/ ...hanni de/ ...
    dicis/ ...entia: 8/28: (L) like a brother/ and co-father most
    dear: on the back (?)/ (Jo)hanni de/ (Me)dicis/ (Flor)entia. (See:
    Giovanni de' MEDICI).
Frau Burgomeister: 74/19: the wife of the mayor of WÖRGL.
Fraulein Doktor: 35/22:
Frederic: 62/93; 64/101: see FREDERICK II of Prussia.
[Frederick II of Prussia]: 32/9; 62/93; 64/101; [65/125; 69/150, 151]:
    Frederick the Great, 1712-86, King of Prussia (1740-86).
[Frederick II of Sicily]: 25/115: 1272-1337, King of Sicily (1296-1337);
    waged war against CHARLES II of Naples (1296-1302) and against
    the ANGEVINS (1325).
Frederic of Prussia: 32/9: see FREDERICK II of Prussia.
Frederic of Sicily: 25/115: see FREDERICK II of Sicily.
Freer: 22/103:
Freiburg im Breisgau: 20/89: town, SW Germany.
French army: 34/15: the Napoleonic forces.
French consul: 65/121: see DÉSTOURNELLES.
French fleet: 68/145: the fleet at the time of the American Revolution.
French Revolution: 71/165; 79/64.
French States: 44/20: the kingdoms established by NAPOLEON in the
    wake of his victories.
Freud: 77/47: Sigmund, 1856-1939, the Austrian psychiatrist.
Fries: 62/96; 63/97: John, ?1750-1818, American insurgent who op-
    posed a federal property tax by leading a force of Pennsylvania
    Germans against the assessors in 1799; Fries was arrested by
    government troops, tried, and found guilty of treason; John
    ADAMS pardoned him in 1800.
Friesland: 69/150, [152]: a province in N Netherlands.
Fritz: 7/25; 80/88: see Fritz-René VANDERPYL.
Fritz: 41/54: see Fritz von UNRUH.
Frobenius: 38/39; 74/5, 14: Leo, 1873-1938, German archeologist
    and anthropologist largely interested in Africa; author of the
    seven-volume study, Erlebte Erdteile. (See: WAGADU, FASA,
    GASSIR).
frog (frogs, froggies): 59/72, 73; 60/76; 65/125; 74/22; 78/59: slang
    reference to the French people.
From Fancy's dreams to active Virtue turn: 63/97: from the verse
    on the tombstone of Abigail Adams. (See: John Adams, Works,
    I, 644).
from the tower of Hananel unto Goah/ unto the horse gate...in Anatoth/
    which is in Benjamin: 74/18: from Jeremiah, 31, 38-40; 32, 8.
Frontenac: 65/120: prob. Frontignac, a French muscatel of the
    Pyrenees region.

Fructidor: 27/131: one of the French Revolutionary calendar months, running from 18 August to 16 September.

Frumentorum licentia/ coercita de annonaria laxata Pauperum aeque/ divitium bono conservit: 44/19: (L) free grain/ dole restrictions relaxed for the good of the poor/ and the rich.

Fu: 61/84: (Ch) Happiness, prosperity. (See: Appendix B).

Führer: 62/91(?); 76/35: see Adolf HITLER.

Fujiyama: 41/52; 74/5; 76/36: sacred mountain in Honshu, Japan.

Fulano, Don: 76/32: (Sp) John Doe; a general nonexistent name.

fumée maligne: 55/46: (Fr) evil smoke. (See: Mailla, Histoire Générale, IX, 85).

funge la purezza: 74/24: (It) purity acts.

fu Nicolo/ e di qua di la del Po: 82/104: (It) late Niccolò (d'ESTE)/ and on this side and the other side of the Po.

Furnivall: 80/85: Frederick James, 1825-1910, the English philologist.

Fynje: 62/92; 69/151: see DE LA LANDE AND FYNJE.

G

gabelle: 43/13; 44/21: (Fr) salt tax.

Gabriel, Claude: 34/16: fl. 1812, a negro in the service of ALEXANDER I; on a trip to America he was insulted and even beaten by people who were offended by his official uniform. (See: J. Q. Adams, Diary, 96-97).

Gaddy: 80/80: DTC, Pisa.

Gadsden: 65/113: Christopher, 1724-1805, American Revolutionary leader; delegate from South Carolina to the CONTINENTAL CONGRESS (1774-76) where he supported John ADAMS' proposal to negotiate a treaty with France. He served as a brigadier general in the Continental Army (1776-78).

Gais: 77/48: village in the Tyrol, N Italy.

Galeaz: 8/32; 9/45: see Galeazzo MALATESTA.

Galeaz, Duke: 21/98: prob. Galeazzo Maria SFORZA.

Galeazzo, Sr.: 9/38: prob. a man whose daughter was seduced by Sigismondo MALATESTA, c. 1454.

Galicia: 65/119, 120: region and ancient kingdom, NW Spain.

Galileo: 48/35; 59/71; 60/74: Galileo Galilei, 1564-1642, the Italian mathematician and astronomer.

Galla: [21/98]; 76/33: Galla Placidia, 388-450, Roman empress; the Mausoleum of Galla Placidia is the church of St. Nazario Celso, Ravenna.

Gallatin: 31/5; 34/16; 41/56; 71/163: Abraham Alfonse Albert, 1761-1849, Swiss-born financier and statesman who came to the U. S. in 1780; served as member of the House of Representatives (1795-1801); member of committee negotiating with England after War of 1812; U. S. Minister to France (1816-23); U. S. Minister to Great Britain (1826-27).

gallice: 58/68: (L) in French.

Gallifet: 16/70: Gaston Alexandre Auguste de Galliffet, 1830-1909, French army commander who led the charge of the Chasseurs d'Afrique at Sedan in the War of 1870.

Gallipoli: 28/138: the Gallipoli campaign (1915) in which the Allied forces made a futile attempt to capture the Dardanelles.

Galloway: 65/109: Joseph, ?1729-1803, American lawyer and loyalist; member of the Pennsylvania colonial legislature (1756-64; 1765-75); member of the CONTINENTAL CONGRESS (1774-75), where he opposed the independence of the colonies.

Gama, De: 7/25; 35/25: Vasco da Gama, 1460-1524, the Portuguese navigator.

Gamaliel: 67/133: reference to the great teacher of Jewish law, d. AD 88; thus, any great teacher, especially of law.

Gandhi: 38/38: Mohandas Karachand, 1869-1948, the Indian political and religious leader.

Ganelon: 20/91: one of the Twelve Peers in the Song of Roland; prompted by jealousy, he betrayed the presence of Roland's rearguard forces to the Moslems.

Ganna: 77/43: locality in the African Sudan, west of Timbuctoo; second stop of the FASA in the reincarnation of WAGADU.

Garda, Lake: [76/34]; 78/58: lake in E Lombardy, N Italy.

Gardasee: 76/34: Lake GARDA.

[Gardiner, Sylvester]: 63/98: 1708-86, American colonial physician;
    he was a loyalist and fled America during the Revolution.

Gardone: 74/5; 76/36; 78/56: prob. Gardone Val Trompia, a town in
    Brescia province, N Italy.

Gargaphia: 4/15: Gargraphie, a vale and spring in Boeotia, sacred
    to ARTEMIS who was bathing there when surprised by ACTAEON.
    (See: Ovid, Metamorphoses, III, 156).

Garonne: 4/16; 84/116: the river in France.

Garry Yeo: 48/35: see GALILEO.

Gassir: 74/5, 8, 20: Gassire, son of Nganamba FASA, king of the
    Fasa tribe; the story of Gassire's envy and its consequences is
    told in the legend collection, the Dausi, which deals with the his-
    tory of WAGADU. (See: Frobenius and Fox, African Genesis,
    97-110).

Gassir, Lute of: 74/5: the introductory song to the legend collection,
    the Dausi. (See: GASSIR).

Gaubertz: 48/37: see Gaubertz de POICEBOT.

Gaudier: 16/71; 77/47; 78/57; 80/82: Henri Gaudier-Brzeska, 1891-
    1915, Franco-Polish sculptor; killed in World War I.

Gauthier-Villars: 78/58; 80/[81], 82: Henri, 1859-1931, French
    novelist, essayist and biographer; generally known as "Willy".

[Gautier, Judith]: 80/82: 1850-1917, French poet and novelist,
    daughter of Théophile GAUTIER.

[Gautier, Théophile]: 76/31; 80/82: 1811-72, French poet, novelist,
    and man of letters; leader of the Parnassian poets; author of
    Emaux et Camées, etc.

Gay de Lussac, rue: 80/88: the rue Gay-Lussac, street on Left Bank,
    Paris.

Gazette de Madrid: 65/121: a newspaper in Madrid, Spain, in late 18th
    century.

G.B.S.: 46/26: see George Bernard SHAW.

Gea: 77/46; 79/65; 82/104: (Gr) earth. (See: Appendix A).

Gedichte: 74/19: (Ger) poems.

Geheimrat, der: 74/14: (Ger) privy councillor.

[Gelderland]: 62/92: province in E Netherlands.

Gemini: 52/4: the third zodiacal constellation, represented as the
    twins, Castor and Pollux. The sun enters Gemini about May 21.

Gemisthus Plethon: 8/31: see Georgius GEMISTUS.

Gemisto: 23/107; 26/123; 83/106: see Georgius GEMISTUS.

[Gemistus, Georgius]: 8/31; 23/107; 26/123; 83/106: fl. early 15th
    century, Greek Platonic philosopher, sometimes called Plethon,
    who led Cosimo de' MEDICI to found the Florentine Academy for
    classical studies; Sigismondo MALATESTA brought his remains
    back from the MOREA and placed them in the TEMPIO.

Genare: 9/38: see Pietro di GENARI.

[Genari, Pietro di]: 9/38, 40: secretary of Sigismondo MALATESTA.

Genariis, Petrus: 9/40: see Pietro di GENARI.

Genêt: 65/119; 68/144: Edmé-Jacques, d. 1781, head of the Bureau of
    Correspondence of the French Department of Foreign Affairs
    (1762); he was a close friend of John ADAMS when Adams was in

France, and he supported American independence.
Geneva: 38/38; 67/140; 78/59: the city in Switzerland.
Genevra: 9/34: see Ginevra d'ESTE.
Genghis: 56/47: see GENGHIS KHAN.
[Genghis Khan]: 55/41, 45, 46; 56/47, 49, 50, 51, 53, 54; 58/68:
     (also: Jenghiz or Chingiz) 1162-1227, Mongol emperor. His
     personal name was Temougin (Temuchin) and his imperial title
     Tai-Tsou (T'ai Tsŭ). He proclaimed himself emperor of the
     Mongols in 1206. Through a series of wars with the various
     Tartar tribes (mainly the KHITAN and NUTCHÉ) he became by
     1214 master of all the territory north of Hwang-ho, except for
     Peiping, the capital of the KIN dynasty of the Nutché; he con-
     quered Korea and by 1221 controlled much of central Asia. During
     his career of conquest he established the power of the Mongol in
     Asia.
Genji: 74/21: central character in Lady Murasaki's Tale of Genji;
     also mentioned in some of the Noh plays. Historically, the Genji,
     or Minamoto, were a Japanese feudal clan. (See: Translations,
     231).
Genoa: 18/80; [43/9]; 50/40, [42, 43; 76/30]: the seaport, NW Italy.
Genova: 43/9; 50/42, 43; 76/30: (It) GENOA.
gente di cavallo e da pie: 8/30: (It) horsemen and people on foot.
gentildonna: 78/60: (It) a lady.
George: 34/18: see George Washington ADAMS.
George: 64/101: see GEORGE III of England.
George: 81/97: see George Horace LORIMER.
George III of England: 32/9; 64/[101], 108; [65/109; 68/148; 69/150,
     152]: 1738-1820, King of England (1760-1820).
George Horace: 81/97: see George Horace LORIMER.
George, Uncle: 74/11; 76/39; 80/87: see George Holden TINKHAM.
Georgia: 34/21; 64/102: the southern state of the U.S.
Gerbillon: 59/72, 73; 60/74, 75, 78; 61/80: Jean-François, 1654-
     1707, Jesuit missionary in China. He arrived in Peiping in 1688,
     and his talents at once impressed Emperor KANG-HI. He served
     with PÉREIRA on the commission to negotiate a border treaty
     between China and Russia in 1689, the Treaty of NIPCHOU. He
     was a skilled linguist and mathematician and wrote an account of
     his journeys in Tartary.
Gerhart: 75/28: see Gerhart MÜNCH.
German Ambassador: 71/160: (see John Adams, Works, IX, 588).
German-Burgundian female: 9/36: a noblewoman assaulted and killed
     while on the way to Rome for the Jubilee (1450). Sigismondo
     MALATESTA was thought to have done it, but the evidence was
     not conclusive.
German princes: 68/144: the petty princes of the various German
     states, c. 1780.
[Germans]: 18/83; 41/56; 80/[81], 82: the German peoples.
Germany: 64/101; 68/141.
Gerry, Elbridge: 34/18; 70/155: 1744-1814, American statesman;
     member of the CONTINENTAL CONGRESS (1776-81; 1782-85);
     signer of the DECLARATION of Independence; delegate to the

FEDERAL CONSTITUTIONAL CONVENTION (1787); member of
the XYZ mission to France; Governor of Massachusetts (1810,
1811).

Gervais: 80/71: brand name of a French dairy company.

Geryon(e): 46/29; 49/39; 51/45: Geryon, (1) the three-headed or
three-bodied monster, living on the island of Erythia, killed by
HERACLES; (2) the symbol of fraud and guardian of the eighth
circle of hell in the Inferno; sometimes a symbol of usury, violence against nature and art, etc. (See: Inferno, 17).

Geschichte und Lebensbilder: 41/53: (Ger) history and pictures
(images) from (of) life. (See: Wilhelm BAUR).

Gesell: 74/20; 80/85: Silvio, 1862-1930, German merchant and
economist known especially for his emphasis on the theory of
velocity of money circulation and his advocacy of stamped paper
currency as a medium of exchange; author of Die Verstaatlichung
des Geldes (1891).

Gethsemane Trebizond Petrol: 18/82: poss. pseudonym for the
Anglo-Persian Oil Company, in which ZAHAROFF had an interest.

Gettysburg: 40/48: the battle of Gettysburg, June-July 1863, a major
battle in the Civil War at Gettysburg, Pennsylvania.

ghazel: 58/64: (Arab) ghazila: a form of Persian love poetry in
couplets riming on the same sound: aa, ba, ca, etc.

Ghengis: 55/41; 58/68: see GENGHIS KHAN.

Ghengiz Khan: 55/45; 56/49, 50, 51, 53, 54: see GENGHIS KHAN.

Ghenso: 56/49: see GENGHIS KHAN.

Ghingiz: 55/46: see GENGHIS KHAN.

Giacomo: 10/43, 47: see Giacomo PICCININO.

Gianfiglioli, Horatio: 43/15: see Horatio GIONFIGLIOLI.

Gianozio: 8/28: prob. chancellor to Sigismondo MALATESTA.

Gibbon: 62/87: Edward, 1737-94, the British historian.

Gibel Tara: 22/103; 40/49: see GIBRALTAR.

Gibraltar: [22/103; 40/49]; 74/25; 76/32.

Giddings: 18/81:

Gignetei kalon: 21/99: (Gr) a beautiful thing is born. (See: Appendix
A).

Giles: 62/95: William Branch, 1762-1830, American statesman;
member of House of Representatives (1790-98); opposed the founding of the First Bank of the United States and brought charges of
corruption against HAMILTON (1793); the charges were dismissed;
U. S. Senator (1804-1815).

Gill, Moses: 65/109: d. 1800, Lieutenant Governor of Massachusetts
(1794-1800).

Gin Cheou: 54/30: poss. reference to the Ch'ên dynasty (557-89).

Ginger: 22/103, 104:

Gin Tsong: 55/42: (Jen Tsung) (reign: 1023-64). He had to contend
with internal rebellions and invasions which weakened the empire;
in 1042 he was forced to make a humiliating peace with the KHI-
TAN Tartars to keep them quiet. A patron of literature, he encouraged a golden age of Chinese literature in which many of the
most noted poets, historians and scholars wrote.

Gin-tsong: 56/51, 52: (Jen Tsung or Ayuli Palpata) (reign 1312-21).

The eighth emperor of the Yüan dynasty. An able administrator,
well read in Confucius and Buddha and averse to war, he tried to
improve the government and abolished those abuses brought to his
notice, but the practice of giving the highest government posts to
Mongols was not effective and the people were oppressed. He
enacted sumptuary laws and established regular examinations for
officials.

Gin-tsong: 57/57: (Jen Tsung) (reign: 1425-1426), came to the throne
at the age of forty-seven and ruled only a little over nine months.

Giohanni: 8/28: see Giovanni de' MEDICI.

Gionfiglioli, Horatio: 42/6; [43/15]: prob. member of the BALÍA of
Siena, 1622.

Giovane: 9/38: see Giovanni ALVISE.

Giovanna: 76/39; 83/109: servant in a Venetian house where Pound
used to stay.

giribizzi: 80/74: (It) fancies.

Gisors: 6/21; 10/46: town, 20 miles NW of Paris; medieval capital of
the Vexin district, France.

Giudecca: 83/110: a major canal in Venice.

Giuliano: 21/97: see Giuliano de' MEDICI.

[Giustinian, Bernardo]: 26/122: Venetian ambassador to PIUS II;
charged to press for peace between the Pope and the MALATESTA
family.

Giustinian, Ca': 26/124; 83/110: a palace in Venice.

Glanville: 63/99: Ranulf de, d. 1190, English statesman and jurist;
advisor to Henry II of England.

Glaucus: 39/44: Glaucus of Anthedon; he became immortal by a magic
herb, then for some reason he leaped into the sea and became a
sea-god and was famous for his gift of prophecy. The name is
also an epithet of the sea.

Glielmo ciptadin: 27/130: (It) Guglielmo citizen. (Reference is to
the inscription over the altar of the Cathedral of Ferrara.)

Gluck: 80/82: Christoph Willibald, 1714-87, German composer; best
known for his operas, IPHIGÉNIE en Tauride, etc.

gli onesti: 76/38: (It) the honest ones.

Globe Extra: 37/35: see CONGRESSIONAL GLOBE.

Goah: 74/18: Goath, a locality near or in Jerusalem.

God: 10/45, 46; 23/107; 28/133; 34/20; 38/38, 42; 40/47; 43/9, 11, 12;
44/21; 51/44; 58/64; 59/73; 65/117; 70/157; 71/164; 74/14, [18];
79/64.

Goddess: 79/70: see APHRODITE.

Godio: 36/30: see GOITO.

Goedel: 78/56; 79/62: prob. a German soldier whom Pound met when
he hitchhiked north from Rome after the 8 September 1943 armi-
stice.

Goffe: 64/103: see Edmund TROWBRIDGE.

Goito: 36/30: name of castle and town, ten miles from Mantua;
birthplace of SORDELLO.

Golden Bough: 1/5: the golden wand of HERMES.

Golden Roof: 52/4: reference to the church of La Daurade, Toulouse,
France. The Italian name, La Dorata (= the Golden One).

golden wand: 1/4: the golden wand of TIRESIAS. (See: Odyssey, XI,
    91.
Gold Mirror: 55/38: the Kin-king (Chin-ching) or The Mirror of Gold,
    a work by the emperor, TAÏ-TSONG. This work may be the same
    as Tai-tsong's NOTES ON CONDUCT.
Goncourt: 79/64: Edmond Louis Antoine de, 1822-96, and Jules
    Alfred Huot de, 1830-70, French novelists and historians. (See:
    ACADÉMIE GONCOURT).
gonfaron/ et leurs fioles chargies de vin: 26/122: (Fr) poss. gan-
    falon: banner/ and their flasks full of wine.
Gonzaga: 45/23: prob. Ercole GONZAGA; poss. Francesco GON-
    ZAGA.
Gonzaga, Carlo: 10/42: 15th century soldier of Mantua, member of
    the Gonzaga family, rulers of Mantua; he betrayed Milan by ad-
    mitting to the city the troops of Francesco SFORZA.
Gonzaga: 26/126; [45/23]: Ercole, 1505-63, cardinal of the Roman
    Church and regent of the Duchy of Mantua; a patron of the arts
    and learning; presided over the Council of Trent.
Gonzaga, Francesco: 26/123; 45/23(?): d. 1444, Lord of Mantua.
Gonzaga, Franᵒ: 26/127: Gian Francesco, d. 1519, Lord of Mantua
    (1484-1519).
Gonzaga, Luigi: 26/124: 1267-1360, founder of the house of Gonzaga,
    which ruled Mantua from 1328 to 1708; Luigi became captain-gen-
    eral of Mantua in 1328.
Good Hope: 48/35: the cape at tip of South Africa.
Goodwin: 66/129: Sir Francis, principal of the Goodwin Case (1604)
    in which Parliament asserted its right to be the sole judge of the
    election returns of its own members.
Gordan, Dr.: 63/98: see Sylvester GARDINER.
Gosindi: 31/6: Pierre Gassendi, 1592-1655, French philosopher,
    theologian and physicist; author of the Syntagma Philosophicum.
Gospel Society of London: 71/163: the Society for the Propagation of
    the Gospel in Foreign Parts, a missionary arm of the Church of
    England; it was powerful but disliked in colonial America.
Gould, Joe: 74/10: Greenwich Village, N.Y., bohemian and writer.
Gourdon: 4/15: city in Provence, N of Toulouse; associated with
    troubadour poetry.
Governor: 34/17: see DeWitt CLINTON.
Governor: 61/84: a viceroy of Honan province in AD 1728.
Governor: 62/89: see Thomas HUTCHINSON.
Governor: 64/102: see Sir Francis BERNARD.
goyim: 52/3; 74/17, 21; 79/65: (Heb) gentiles.
G.P.: 79/62: poss. Gaby Picabia, wife of Francis Picabia, French
    painter; Madame Picabia was a member of the French Resistance
    in World War II.
[Graces]: [27/131; 74/21]; 79/69; [80/79]: the Charites, three
    Greek goddesses, Aglaia, Thalia and Euphrosyne, personifica-
    tions of beauty and charm; often associated with the MUSES,
    DIONYSUS, EROS and APHRODITE.
Gradara, Gentilino da: 9/39: an agent for Sigismondo MALATESTA.
gradins, les: 12/53; 21/98; 29/145: (Fr) the steps.

Gradonico, Tomasso: 25/117: prob. Gradenigo, a member of the
    Consiglio dei DIECI in Venice.
Graham: 74/12: prob. R. B. Cunninghame Graham, 1852-1936,
    Scottish essayist, biographer, and world traveler, noted for his
    journey by horse through South America.
Granada: 22/104: city in S Spain.
Grand Canal: 10/46: see CANAL GRANDE.
Gd Ducal Palace: 42/7: the Grand Ducal Palace in Siena.
Grand Duchy: 44/17: the Grand Duchy of Tuscany.
Grand Duke: 33/11: see LEOPOLD II, Holy Roman Emperor.
Grand Duke: 42/5: see FERDINAND I of Tuscany.
Grand Duke: 42/5, 6, 9; 43/15: see FERDINAND II of Tuscany.
Granham: 51/45: a trade name for a type of fly used in fishing.
Granville: 74/23: prob. Harley Granville-Barker, 1877-1946, Eng-
    lish actor, manager and playwright.
Grasse: 15/64: city in France where soap and other products are
    manufactured from fats; it is also the center of the perfume in-
    dustry of Provence.
gratia: 80/91: (L) thanks to, on account of.
Grave incessu: 7/24: (L) gravi incessu: with heavy gait.
Grcolini, Cenzio: 42/6: prob. a notary of Florence in 1622.
Grcolini, Orazio: 43/16: fl. 1622, prob. secretary of MARIA MAG-
    DELENA and Orazio della RENA.
Great Britain: [38/40; 44/20; 62/87, 89, 91, 93, 96; 64/108; 65/113],
    125; [66/128; 67/134; 68/142; 69/149; 70/156; 71/165].
great domed head: 7/24: see Henry JAMES.
Great Duchy: 43/12: see GRAND DUCHY.
Greater Council: 25/120: see DIECI, Consiglio de.
Great Khan: 18/80: see KUBLAI KHAN.
Gt Tichfield St: 80/80: street in central London, crosses Langham
    Street, where Pound once lived (1908).
Gt Tower Hill: 66/126: hill near the Tower of London where the
    gallows formerly stood; in the 18th century it was an area of fine
    residences.
Great wall: 59/72: see GREAT WALL OF CHINA.
[Great Wall of China]: 54/21, 31; 59/72: (Ch.: Chang-chêng), the de-
    fensive wall of China, extending 1250 miles from Mongolia to
    China Proper; started in the 3rd century BC and finished in BC
    204 by Emperor TSIN-CHI.
Greece: 67/139; 68/141.
Greek: 21/96; 30/148; 63/98; 71/166; 80/106: the Greek language.
Greek armies: 80/81: the armies of Agamemnon in the Trojan War.
Greek classics: 74/22: the classic works of Greek literature.
Greek Emperor: 8/31; 26/123: John VIII Palaeologus, 1391-1448, son
    of Manuel II; Emperor (1425-48); attended the Council of Ferrara-
    Florence (1438) with GEMISTUS.
Greeks: 23/107; 26/124; 46/26; 68/141; 76/39: the Greek peoples.
Green: 74/14; 77/51: prisoner in a "security cage" near Pound; DTC,
    Pisa.
Gregorio: 76/39: see SAN GREGORIO.
Gregory: 52/4: Theodor Emanuel Gugenheim, 189?-   , English

economist; author of <u>Gold, Unemployment and Capitalism</u> (1933).
Greif, der: 74/11; 76/31: a restaurant in BOLSANO.
Grenville: 64/103; 67/134: George, 1712-1770, Prime Minister under
   GEORGE III (1763-65); his most famous act was the creation of
   the Stamp Act (1765); he also tried to enforce the Sugar Act.
   Neither did him much good.
Grey: 66/127: a casual acquaintance made by John ADAMS in Eng-
   land.
Gridley: 63/98; 64/102, 108: Jeremiah, 1702-1767, American lawyer
   and attorney general of Massachusetts Bay Province; in 1761 he
   defended the legality of the WRITS OF ASSISTANCE.
Gridley: 64/108: Benjamin, fl. 1768, loyalist lawyer practicing in
   Boston; left America in 1776.
Gridley of Abingdon: 64/101: a farmer (?) named <u>Greenleaf</u>, resident
   of Abington, Mass.
Griffiths: 78/59: Arthur <u>Griffith</u>, 1872-1922, Irish political leader;
   founder and editor of the United Irishmen, a journal; founder and
   leader of the Sinn Fein Movement (1906), which worked for the establishment of an Irish parliament united to the British Parlia-
   ment only by the Crown.
Grill--: 28/135: see Franz GRILLPARZER.
grillo: 78/58: (It) cricket.
Grillparzer: 28/135: Franz, 1791-1872, the Austrian playwright and
   poet.
Grimaldi: 60/74, 75: Philippe, fl. 1691, Jesuit missionary in China.
Grishkin: 77/44: allusion to character in T.S. ELIOT's poem,
   <u>Whispers of Immortality.</u>
[Groningen]: 62/92: province in NE Netherlands.
Gronye: 62/92: prob. GRONINGEN.
gros blé: 53/8: (Fr) coarse wheat.
Grosseto: 43/15: town in Tuscany, central Italy.
Grosvenor Sq.: 66/126; 67/139: the fashionable square in London,
   residence of John ADAMS when he was in London.
Grouchy: 50/43: Emmanuel, Marquis de, 1766-1847, French general
   in the French Revolution and the Napoleonic wars. Because he
   failed to prevent the Prussians from joining the British, he was
   largely responsible for Napoleon's disaster at Waterloo.
"Gruss Gott," "Der Herr!" "Tatile is gekommen!": 78/56: (Ger)
   "Good day," "The master!" "Tatile has come!"
Guadaloupe: 65/112: the name applied to two islands of the French
   West Indies: Basse-Terre and Grande Terre; the two are sepa-
   rated by a narrow channel.
Gualdo: 24/111: Gualdo Tadino, town in Perugia province, central
   Italy.
Guardia regia: 12/53: (Sp) royal guard.
Gubberton: 46/26: prob. reference to Surbiton, a town on the Thames,
   Surrey, England.
Guiduccioli: 24/111: prob. the representative of Carlo MALATESTA
   at the arrangements for the marriage of Carlo's daughter, Para-
   sina MALATESTA, to Niccolò d'ESTE in 1418.
Guilderland: 62/92: see GELDERLAND.

Guillaume: 6/21: see Guillaume POITIERS.

Gulf of St. Lawrence: 65/123: the gulf off E coast of Canada.

Gustavus: 32/9; [65/124]: Gustavus III of Sweden, 1746-92, King (1771-92).

"Guten Morgen, Mein Herr": 82/101: (Ger) Good morning, sir.

Gutta: 40/49: Gytta, a town on the Atlantic coast of North Africa, founded by HANNO; just S of KARIKON.

Guys: 74/13; 80/82: Constantin, 1802-92, newspaper illustrator for the Illustrated London News during the Crimean War; settled in Paris (c. 1865) where he sketched the life and manners of the Second Empire.

Gyges: 4/16: a Lydian secreted by Candaules, king of Lydia, so Gyges could see the beauty of the naked queen; discovering his presence, the queen forced Gyges to kill Candaules and marry her.

H

H., Captain: 14/62: prob. an English officer of the Black and Tans at the time (1916) of the Irish Rebellion.

H., Mr.: 66/127: see Thomas Brand-HOLLIS.

H.: 74/14: poss. Ernest HEMINGWAY; poss. Adolf HITLER; poss. Henri GAUDIER-Brezska.

H., old: 74/17: poss. Henry MORGENTHAU; poss. Sisley HUDDLE-STON.

H., young: 74/17: poss. Henry MORGENTHAU, Jr.; poss. Ernest HEMINGWAY.

[Haarlem]: 62/92: city of North Holland province in W Netherlands, near Amsterdam.

Habana: 12/53: La Habana (Sp) Havana, capital of CUBA.

Habitat cum Quade: 12/54: (L) lives with QUADE.

Habsburg-Lorraine: 42/22; [50/42]: see HAPSBURG-LORRAINE.

hac dextera mortus: 82/101: (L) hac dextera mortuus: dead by this right hand. (See: Literary Essays, 270).

hac loca fluvius alluit: 53/17: (L) haec loca...: these places the river washes.

Haec sunt fastae: 74/12: (L) haec sunt fasti (?): these are the festivals (?)

haec sunt infamiae: 34/21: (L) these are infamies.

haec traditio: 9/35: (L) this tradition.

Hagoromo: 74/8; 79/63: the Noh play, Hagoromo. (See: Translations, 308-14).

hagoromo: 80/78: the feather-mantle in the Noh play, Hagoromo.

Hague: 66/126; 70/155: The Hague, Netherlands.

Haig: 16/75: Douglas, 1861-1928, British marshal, commander-in-chief of expeditionary forces in France and Flanders (1915-19); he served under French Marshal Foch during final stages of the Allied advance.

[Haile Selassie]: 80/88: 1891-   , Haile Selassie I, emperor of Ethiopia (1930-   ).

Hai men: 57/60: (Hai-men), a department of what is now Kiangsu province, China.

Haitse: 60/78: (Hai-tzŭ), a game preserve near Peiping.

Hakluyt: 65/109: Richard, ?1552-1616, the English historian and geographer.

Halbach: 38/41: see Gustav KRUPP VON BOHLEN UND HALBACH.

Hales: 66/131: Sir Edward, fl. 1686, principal in a law case by which JAMES II attempted to establish the Crown's dispensing power in regard to the Test Act; having failed to gain support for such power from Parliament, James tried to secure it by verdict of the judiciary (1686).

"half dead at the top": 79/65: from W. B. Yeats, Blood and the Moon, I, IV.

Ham: 62/95, 96: see Alexander HAMILTON.

Hamadryas: 74/9; 76/30: (L) Hamadryad, tree nymph.

Hamadryas ac Heliades: 76/30: (L) HAMADRYAD and HELIADS.

Hamilcar: 80/80: Hamilcar Barca, ?270-228, Carthaginian general

who commanded in Sicily (247-41) and in Spain (237-28); father of
HANNIBAL.

Hamilton: 37/33, 34, 35; [62/95, 96]; 63/97; 66/126, 127; 69/153;
70/155, 156; 71/161, 164: Alexander, ?1753-1804, American
statesman, member of the CONTINENTAL CONGRESS (1782, 83,
87, 88), first U. S. Secretary of the Treasury (1789-95). As a
supporter of a strong federal government, Hamilton was instrumental in securing the ratification of the CONSTITUTION OF THE
UNITED STATES, especially in New York. Under WASHINGTON's
administration he established a national fiscal system and placed
public credit on a sound basis; retaining much of his control of
the Cabinet during John ADAMS' administration, he hampered
Adams' attempts to maintain peace and fostered the emergence
of political parties. Hamilton was wounded in a duel with Aaron
BURR on 11 July 1804 and died 12 July.

Hamish: 18/82, 83: prob. Dave Hamish (or Fowler in Faber text);
evidently associated with MENELIK II of Ethiopia, but exact information unknown.

Hammerton, Cyril: 16/72: a pseudonym having no particular reference.

hamomila de hampo: 80/75: (It) prob. campanile de campo: bell
tower of the Campo (Siena) (in Tuscan dialect); poss. camamilla
de campo: the camomile of the field (in Tuscan dialect).

Han: 53/17: see HAN-HOU.

Han: 54/21; 56/51, 54, 55, 56: the Former Han dynasty (BC 206-AD 25).

Han: 54/27: the After Han dynasty (25-221).

Han: 54/27: the Minor Han dynasty. (221-263).

Han: 54/28: a feudal kingdom of China, roughly the area of SZECH-
WAN province, formerly one of the THREE KINGDOMS.

Han: 55/40, 42: a principality in the provinces of SHENSI and HONAN
on both sides of the Hwang-ho; established in BC 453.

Han: 55/40; 56/48(?): prob. the After Han dynasty (947-51); (Yin Ti,
the last emperor of the After Han, was eighteen when he came to
the throne).

Han: 56/49: see HAN-TCHÉOU.

Han: 74/3: see HAN-KIANG.

Hananel: 74/18: (Heb) God is gracious. (See: TOWER OF HANANEL).

Hancock: 64/104; 65/110, 124; 66/130; 71/160, 165, 166; 77/52: John,
1737-93, American merchant and statesman, member of the
CONTINENTAL CONGRESS (1775-80; 1785, 86), first signer of
the DECLARATION of Independence, governor of Massachusetts
(1780-85; 1787-93).

Han Ho Ti: 54/26: (reign: 89-106); during his reign the military fame
of China was higher than ever before; and at this time the first
eunuch was raised to the rank of mandarin, thus setting a prece-
dent that led to many seditions and intrigues in later years of the
Empire.

[Han-hou]: 53/17: (Han Hu) fl. BC 800, a military officer during the
time of SIUEN-OUANG; for his services in battle Han-hou was
given the districts of YUEI and Me, which he developed into important principalities.

[Han-houon-ti]: 54/27, 28: (Han Huan Ti) (reign: 147-168), in 158
he did away with his corrupt prime minister, LEANG-KI, and
confiscated his estate, which amounted to three hundred million
TAEL. Because he had so much money, Han-houon-ti remitted
the land tax for a year; he also built a temple to honor LAO-TSE.

Hanibal: 26/122: Annibale di Constantino Cerboni da Castello, agent
of Domenico MALATESTA to the Venetians.

Han-kiang: 53/16; [74/3]: the Han river, which flows through SHENSI
and Hupeh provinces and into the YANGTSE river at Hankow;
(kiang = river in Chinese).

Han-king-ti: 55/37: see HIAO-KING.

Hanjong: 56/52: (Han Jung) fl. AD 1347, an imperial inspector serving Emperor CHUNTI. When Hanjong found temples on land
needed for cultivation, he had the temples destroyed; when he
found young people who wanted to learn, he had schools established.

[Han-lin-eul]: 56/53: (Han Lin-êrh) d. AD 1367. In 1355 the WHITE
LILY SOCIETY proclaimed him emperor of a new Sung dynasty
and he set up a capital at Po-chou in Anhwei province, calling
himself by the dynastic title Ming Wang. This new Sung dynasty
was created in opposition to Emperor CHUNTI of the YUAN dynasty and was one of many such ventures during the reign of this
last Mongol emperor. As a symbol of revolt, Han-lin-eul's dynasty was effective, but it was not permanent.

Han Ling: 54/27, [28]: Han-ling-ti (Han Ling Ti) (reign: 168-90).
His reign was distinguished while TÉOU-CHI was regent and her
father Tou Wu (d. AD 167) prime minister; but the chief eunuch
persuaded the emperor that Tou Wu was dangerous, so Han-ling-
ti executed the prime minister and banished the queen dowager.
In 184 an outbreak in the northern provinces started the series of
calamities that brought the downfall of the HAN dynasty.

Han Ming: 54/26: Han-ming-ti (Han Ming Ti) (reign: 58-76). This
emperor has the reputation of having introduced Buddhism, and
consequently idolatry, into China. Hearing that there was a holy
man in the west named FOÉ, he sent ambassadors to discover
his teachings and bring back books of his doctrines.

Han Ngan: 54/26: Han-ngan-ti (Han An Ti) (reign: 107-25). He was
a very just emperor; but unfortunately he elevated women to the
rank of court officials, and from this time there was great corruption in the court, justice was perverted, and honest men driven
from the government.

Hannibal: 9/40; 80/80: 247/182, Carthaginian general who led the
forces of Carthage against Rome in the Second Punic War (218-
201).

Hanno: 40/49: c. BC 470, the Carthaginian navigator who led an expedition through the Straits of Gibraltar and founded seven towns
on the Atlantic shore of Morocco; the account of his voyage is
The Periplus of Hanno.

Han Ou: 54/24: Han-ou-ti (Han Wu Ti) (reign: 140-86). Had not this
emperor been a believer in the Taoist magicians, the philosophy
of Confucianism might have become supreme in the empire; Han-
ou-ti laid the first general property tax in China.

Han-ouen: 55/37: see HIAO-OUEN.

Hanover: 37/36: an electoral house of Germany and a royal family
of England. Hanoverian Kings of England were: George I, George
II, GEORGE III, George IV, William IV, and VICTORIA (1714-1801).

Han Ping: 54/26: Han-ping-ti (Han Ping Ti) (reign: 1-6). Since he
was only nine when he came to the throne, the empire was ruled
by Wang Mang, an evil minister who usurped all power and finally
murdered Han-ping-ti.

Hanseatic, the: 69/150: the German commercial cities which formed
the Hanseatic League.

Han Sieun: 54/25, 26: see HAN-SIUEN-TI.

[Han-Siuen-ti]: 54/25, 26: (Han Hsüan Ti) (reign: 73-48), an able
emperor who, in 65, sent out Kung Su to deal with the many men
who had turned brigand during a famine; Kung-su said that every
man with a hoe on his shoulder would be treated as an honest man;
every poor man was invited to present his case to the emperor,
and farmers without seed were assisted.

Hans of Kalkas: 59/72: the kings (Han is a title) of the KALKAS.

Han Tchao Ti: 54/25: (Han Chao Ti) (reign: 86-74). In the second
year of his reign he remitted the land tax in impoverished areas.
When crops failed in 80 BC the emperors' ministers said, "pay
more attention to the good government of the people." The people said they wanted taxes on salt, iron, spirits, and property
abolished. Han-tchao-ti compromised and abolished taxes on
spirits and property.

[Han-tchéou]: 56/49: (Han-ch'ou), a large town in SZECHWAN province.

Han Yu: 58/64: (Han Yü) fl. AD 819, judge of a tribunal which, in
the time of emperor HIEN-TSONG, investigated Buddhism in the
Empire. In a memorial to the emperor, Han-yu said that the
Buddhists had been the ruin of many dynasties, that they had perverted the old ways of the Chinese, that they were a pernicious
influence in the Empire, and that they and their temples should be
stamped out.

Han Yuen: 54/26: Han-yuen-ti (Han Yuän Ti) (reign: 48-32). This
emperor started his reign by cutting taxes and forcing the court
to be economical; but he later came under the control of the eunuch Shih Hsien, who "seduced the emperor into immoral habits."

Hao tse: 53/20: poss. (Ch) Tai-tsé (T'ai-tzǔ): chief prince or noble;
a reference to Kong-sung-yang (Kung Sung-yang) who died in
338 BC. (See: Mailla, Histoire Générale, II, 269-280. Note:
the figure 280 in text refers not to the date of 280 BC, but to page
280 in Mailla, on which page the death of Kong-sung-yang is re-
corded). However, Hao tse is poss. an abbreviation of (Ch) hao
han tse: a true Chinaman, a good type.

[Hapsburg-Lorraine]: 42/22; 50/42: a ducal and ruling house of
Europe, founded by Joseph II (1741-90) Holy Roman Emperor and
King of Bohemia and Hungary.

Harbell: 82/101: DTC, Pisa.

Hard night, and parting at morning: 5/18: variation of the titles of
Browning's two poems, Meeting at Night and Parting at Morning.

Hardy, Thomas: 80/78; 83/107: 1840-1928, the English novelist.

Harlem: 62/92: see HAARLEM.

Harley: 82/101: DTC, Pisa.

harpes et luthes: 45/23: (L) harps and lutes. (See: Villon, Au
    moustier voy dont suis paroissienne/ Paradis paint, où sont
    harpes et luz...).

Harriet: 78/60: poss. Harriette Wilson, 1789-1846, in whose Mem-
    oirs (1825; ed. J. Laver, 1929) there is an account of a discussion
    between Wellington and Harriette Wilson concerning the propriety
    of boots. It is to be noted, however, that the story the text seems
    to refer to is usually associated with the Duke and Duchess of
    Marlborough.

Harrison: 34/21; [37/33]: William Henry, 1773-1841, ninth president
    of the U. S. (1841), serving only one month of his term in office
    before he died of pneumonia. He first gained fame in wars against
    the Indians (1811-12) and was known as "Tip" for his successful
    battles against the Indians at Tippecanoe (1811).

Harry: 6/21: see HENRY II of England.

Hartford: 64/107: city in N Connecticut on the Connecticut river.

Hartley: 65/125: David, 1732-1813, English diplomat who, with
    Benjamin FRANKLIN, drafted and signed the peace treaty between
    the U. S. and Great Britain in 1783.

Hartmann: 80/73: Sadakichi, 1867-1944, American poet, playwright
    and art critic.

Harvard: 74/11: Harvard University.

Hashan: 61/85: see KASGAR.

[Hashar]: 61/85: a petty court in the Bukhara region, W Asia.

Haskai: 61/85: see HASHAR.

Hast 'ou seen the rose in the steel dust/ (or swansdown ever?): 74/27:
    variation of Ben Jonson, The Triumph of Charis: "Have you seen
    but a bright lily grow... Or swan's down ever?"

Hatfield: 41/56:

Hathor: 39/44: an Egyptian fertility goddess, sometimes represented
    as a cow, sometimes as a combination of a cow and a woman.

Hatvany: 35/24: prob. Bernhard and Joseph Deutsch, Jewish bankers
    of the town of Hatvan, titled 15 January 1879 as Deutsch de Hat-
    vany. Bernhard Deutsch de Hatvany was Director of the Oster-
    reich-Ungarische Bank in 1888. The sons were made Barons in
    June 1908.

Haute Brion: 65/117: Haut Brion, a wine of Bordeaux.

Hawkesby: 74/11: Henry JAMES' housekeeper at Rye.

Hawkins: 63/99: William, 1673-1746, English lawyer, author of
    Treatise of the Pleas of the Crown (1716).

Hawkwood: 38/42: Sir John de, d. 1394, an English soldier who
    fought in France with the Black Prince. With his "white company"
    of mercenaries Hawkwood entered Italy in 1362 and became a con-
    dottiere, serving any and all republics; finally he accepted a pen-
    sion from Florence. (See: Spirit of Romance, 70, note).

Hawley, Joseph: 64/104; 71/166: 1723-88, American political leader
    who was associated with James OTIS, Samuel ADAMS and
    John ADAMS. He was one of the first to urge a declaration

of independence and a unified colonial administration.

Haworth: 64/108: Colonel Howarth, fl. 1775, American army officer.
(See: Adams, Works, II, 232).

Hay aquí mucho catolicismo.../ y muy poco reliHion/ ...Yo creo que
los reyes desparecen: 81/95: (Sp) desaparecen: Here is much
Catholicism/ ...and very little religion/ ...I believe that kings
disappear.

Hayes, Rutherford: 76/39: Rutherford Birchard Hayes, 1822-93,
nineteenth President of the U. S. (1877-81).

H.B., Mr.: 22/102: see John Maynard KEYNES.

H.C.L.: 22/101: the high cost of living.

heaven: 80/72, 73, 78.

Heaven's Son: 52/7: see SON OF HEAVEN.

Hebrew: 30/148; 34/21: the language.

hebrews: 44/19: the Jewish peoples.

Hebrew scriptures: 80/76: either the Pentateuch or the Old Testament.

He heard the wild goose crying sorrow: 53/17: from Shih Ching, ode
181.

Heine: 74/19: Heinrich, 1797-1856, the German lyric poet and literary critic.

hekasta: 74/19: (Gr) particulars. (See: Appendix A).

helandros kai heleptolis kai helarxe: 46/29: (Gr) destroyer of men,
and destroyer of cities, and destroyer of governments. (See:
Appendix A).

Helen: [2/6; 5/18; 7/24, 25]; 8/30; [20/92; 24/111]; 77/51; 79/65:
Helen of Troy.

Helia: 76/36: poss. misprint for DELIA.

Heliads: [76/30]; 79/68, 69; 83/108: the daughters of HELIOS; they
were changed into poplar trees as they mourned for their brother,
Phaethon.

Helios: [15/67; 23/107, 108]; 27/131; 29/145; 39/43; 74/24; 79/70:
(Gr) the sun; the god of the sun who drove a four-horse chariot
through the heavens.

Hellene: 40/48: a Greek.

Helvetius: 65/118, 119: Anne Catherine, Countess of Ligniville
d'Autricourt, 1719-1800; wife of Claude Adrien Helvetius, the
French philosopher.

Hemingway: 74/5, [14(?)]: Ernest, 1898-   , the American novelist.

Hempire, the: 54/33: the CHINESE EMPIRE.

hennia: 77/43: (Jap) hannya: an evil spirit in Noh drama.

Hennique: 80/72: Léon, 1851-1935, French dramatist and novelist.

Henri, Herr: 38/42: prob. Henri de Wendel, grandson of the original François de WENDEL and thus influential in French steel and
banking circles.

Henriot: 84/117: prob. Emile Henriot, (pseudonym for Emile
Maigrot), 1889-   , the French novelist and poet.

Henry: 6/21; 67/135: see HENRY II of England.

Henry: 11/52: see Enricho de AQUABELLO.

Henry: 12/53: poss. Henry JAMES; poss. Henry Wadsworth Long-
fellow; poss. Henry NEWBOLT.

Henry: 26/122: see HENRY VI of England.

Henry: 62/87: see Henry ADAMS.

[Henry II]: 6/21; 67/135; 1133-89, King of England (1154-89); m.
ELEANOR of Aquitaine (1152).

Henry V: 67/135: 1387-1422, King of England (1413-22).

[Henry VI]: 26/122: 1421-71, King of England (1422-61; 1470-71).

Henry VIII: 67/134: 1491-1547, King of England (1509-47).

Henry, Patrick: 31/6; 33/10; 62/94; 65/109, 110; 66/127; 67/137; 71/163:
1736-99, American Revolutionary leader, member of the CON-
TINENTAL CONGRESS (1774-76), governor of Virginia (1776-79;
1784-86), U. S. Secretary of State (1795) and justice of the U. S.
Supreme Court (1795).

Heoi-king: 55/43: see LIU-HOEI-KING.

Heou: 54/30: see HEOU-TCHU.

[Heou-chou]: 55/41: (Hou-chou), a principality combining parts of
the provinces of SHENSI and SZECHWAN; known as the Second
Chou and lasted 925-65.

[Heou-tchu]: 54/30: (Hou Chu) (reign: 583,-89). Not heeding the
signs that his dynasty was at its end, this emperor pursued a
course of extravagance and debauchery; he built three great
buildings for his favorite concubines. When he was told that the
Duke of Soui was about to overthrow the dynasty, Heou-tchu told
his ministers not to worry because the rebellion would probably
be unsuccessful -- it wasn't.

Heou-Tsie: 53/16: (Hou Chi) fl. BC 2357, chief minister of agriculture and animal husbandry under Emperor YAO.

[Heracles]: 40/49; 74/3; 82/101: the Greek hero.

[Heraclitus]: 77/47: Greek philosopher of the 6th-5th century BC,
known as the "Weeping Philosopher".

Heragleitos: 77/47: see HERACLITUS.

Herakles: 40/49; 74/3: see HERACLES.

Herakles: 74/3: see PILLARS OF HERACLES.

herbal: 53/8: a book in which plants are named, described, and their
officinal properties noted.

Herculaneum: 37/33: ancient city of Italy at the NW foot of Mt. Vesuvius, destroyed by the eruption of AD 79.

Hercules: 24/113: see Ercole d'ESTE.

Her Majesty: 66/129: see ANNE, Queen of England.

Hermes: [1/5]; 12/54; 17/77, 79; 74/16; [77/49]; 79/70: the messenger and herald of the gods; the patron of merchants and thieves
and the god of luck and wealth.

Hé Sloveny: 19/85: (Russ) Hail the Slavic Peoples. (There are many
Russian songs of this title).

Hesperus: 2/10; 5/17; 79/66, 70: the evening star. (See: Sappho,
Ode to Hesperus).

hetman: 58/65: (Pol) a headman; chieftain.

Hewlett, Maurie: [74/11]; 80/93: Maurice Henry Hewlett, 1861-1923,
English essayist, novelist and poet.

[Heyman, Katherine]: 76/39: 1877-1944, American pianist; special-
ist in works of Scriabin; friend of Pound, London, 1908.

H.G.: 42/3: see H.G. WELLS.

Hia: 53/11; 54/24; 56/51: (Hsia), usually designated as the first dynasty of China (2205-1766).

Hia: 55/45: (Hsia) a minor kingdom or principality in the region of
Ordos, the island bordered on one side by the Hwang-ho and on
the south by the GREAT WALL; the territory is on the north border of SHENSI and was occupied by Tartars.

Hianglou: 56/50: (Hsiang-lu), a mountain near the KIANG river,
probably in the province of HONAN.

Hiang-yu: 54/22: (Hsiang Yü or Hsiang Chi) 233-202, a general who
at first fought with LIEOU-PANG against the TSIN dynasty and
then turned against him when the dynasty had been overthrown.
Hiang-yu's forces were crushed in 202, and he killed himself.

Hiao Ching Hien Hoang Héou: 61/[85], 86: (Hsiao-shêng, Hsien-
huang-hou) d. AD 1777, empress dowager, mother of Emperor
KIEN-LONG; after her death, she was given great honors by her
son.

Hiao Hoei Ti: 54/23: (Hsiao Hui Ti) (reign: 194-87), the son of KAO-
HOANG-TI; he was a kind-hearted youth, but rather feeble mind-
ed, and was completely controlled by the queen dowager, LIU-
HEOU.

Hiao King: 54/24; [55/37]: Hiao-king-ti (Hsiao Ching Ti) (reign: 156-
140). In his second year as emperor there was a rebellion of
feudal lords; they said they would disband their forces if the emperor would execute his chief counselor, Chao Tsu, who had
urged the emperor to abolish all feudal dependencies. The peace
terms were met, but the feudal lords attacked again and were not
defeated until later.

[Hiao-ouang]: 53/16: (Hsiao Wang) (reign: 909-894), known as "The
Filial", the brother of Y-OUANG. He was an undistinguished
ruler whose reign was marked only by the appearance of FEI-TSEI,
whose descendants were later to overthrow the Chou dynasty.

Hiao Ouen: 54/23, 24; [55/37; 56/56]: Hiao-ouen-ti (Hsiao Wên Ti)
(reign: 179-56), an emperor famous for his generosity, humanity
and economy. He decreed that a man's family should not suffer
for his crimes; he established the unit of money in the Empire
and reserved for the government the sole right to coin money; for
the punishments of mutilation, he substituted flogging and made
beheading the only great punishment. He also ordered that the
classical books be hunted out again and that scholars start study-
ing them.

[Hiao-ou-ti]: 54/29: (Hsiao Wu Ti) (reign: 453-464) Little happened
during his reign, and he had no able minister to spur him to ac-
tivity. The emperor was very frivolous, giving people of the
court nicknames and having his servants chase the mandarins
with a stick. Thus, there was no respect given the emperor, and
Hiao-ou-ti is known as the "Discarded."

Hiao Tsong: 57/59: (Hsiao Tsung) (reign: 1488-1505). He had able
ministers and was able to institute several administrative reforms, stop internal rebellions, deal with Mongol invasions, and
curtail the power of the eunuchs.

Hiao wang: 53/16: see HIAO-OUANG.

Hib.: 67/135: see IRELAND.

Hibernia: 67/135: (L) IRELAND.

Hic est hyper-usura: 46/28: (L) this is over-usury.

hic est medium mundi: 24/112: (L) here is the center of the world.

Hic Explicit Cantus: 31/6: (L) Here the Canto ends.

Hic Geryon est. Hic hyperusura: 46/29: (L) Here is GERYON.
    Here over-usury.

Hic/ Jacet/ Fisci Liberator: 37/36: (L) Here/ Lies/ the Liberator
    of the Treasury.

Hic mihi dies sanctus: 25/118: (L) This day a holy one for me.

Hic nefas...commune sepulchrum: 46/28: (L) Here is wickedness
    ...the common sepulchre.

hidalgo: 28/135: (Sp) nobleman.

[Hideyashi Toyotomi]: 58/62, 63: d. AD 1598, in Japanese his name
    means "the man found under a tree," known to the Chinese as
    Ping Hsiu-ki. Born of poor parents he rose through his military
    exploits to be the greatest power in Japan. In 1586 he was named
    Kwambaku (commander-in-chief) of Japan and held power far
    greater than the emperor. He is noted for his toleration of
    Christianity, but in 1587 he expelled the Portuguese Jesuits from
    Japan, for he thought they might make his country a vassal of
    Portugal. In 1592 he declared war on Korea, hoping to destroy
    Korean control of the sea and to re-open trade with China, but
    was unable to subdue Korea completely.

Hien: 55/37, 38; 57/59: see HIEN-TSONG.

Hien-Tsong: 55/36, 37, [38; 57/59]: (Hsien Tsung) (reign: 806-821).
    He started his reign by regulating the revenue of the Empire,
    stopping presents, forbidding slavery, and remitting taxes. In a
    series of wars (814-19) he re-established imperial control over
    the provincial governors. However, the emperor was controlled
    by the court eunuchs, who often opposed his reforms. Toward
    the end of his reign he became a Buddhist and died suddenly after
    taking some pills that were supposed to insure his immortality.

[Hien-tsong]: 56/49: (Hsien Tsung), imperial title of MANGU KHAN.

Hien Tsong: 57/58, 59, 60: (Hsien Tsung) (reign: 1465-88), a weak
    emperor who was ruled by his concubine and by eunuchs; during
    his reign there were rebellion in the northern provinces. How-
    ever, he did repair the GREAT WALL, improve the Grand Canal,
    and restore the reputation of YUKIEN with posthumous honors.

Hien-yang: 54/22: (Hsien-yang), the capital city during the Former
    HAN dynasty and several other dynasties; today it is the city of
    Sian, capital of SHENSI province in NE central China.

hieri: 80/91: (It) ièri (?): yesterday.

Hier wohnt: 80/86: (Ger) here lives.

Hieun: 54/33: see HIUEN-TSONG.

Hieun Tsong: 54/34: see HIUEN-TSONG.

High Libya: 40/49: corresponds roughly to what is today Algeria.

High Wycombe: 66/126: Chepping Wycombe, municipal borough of
    Buckinghamshire in SE central England.

Hilaritas: 83/106: (L) hilarity.

Hildebrand: 80/91: major in charge of Post utilities, DTC, Pisa.

Hill, the: 42/8: see MONTE DEI PASCHI.
Hillhouse: 68/142: James A., 1754-1832, American lawyer, member
of the House of Representatives (1791-1808).
hillock: 53/18, 20: see CHEOU-LANG.
Hinchcliffe: 28/140: Captain Walter G. Hinchliffe, d. 1928, a one-
eyed English pilot who was hired by Charles A. LEVINE to pilot
the Columbia; bad weather defeated their attempt to fly the Atlan-
tic. Hinchliffe acquired a small plane and made plans to fly the
Atlantic himself. On the morning of 13 March 1928 he smuggled
Elsie MACKAY aboard and the two started over the Atlantic.
Crowds awaited them in New York; they never arrived.
Hindenburg: 41/54: Paul von, 1847-1934, the German general and
president of the German Republic (1925-34); his greatest military
success was his victory over the Russians at Tannenberg (1914).
Hiong-nou: 54/24, 25: (Ch) (Hsiung-nu): Hungarian slaves, TAR-
TARS.
His Holiness: 36/30: see CLEMENT IV.
His Holiness: 38/37: see PIUS XI.
His Majesty: 65/109; 69/152: see GEORGE III of England.
His Majesty: 65/119: see LOUIS XVI of France.
[Hitler, Adolf]: 62/91(?); 76/35: 1889-1945, the German dictator.
Hi-Tsong: 55/38: (Hsi Tsung) (reign: 874-89). He left the govern-
ment to eunuchs while he devoted himself to sport, music and
mathematics. During his reign the greatest rebellions of the
TANG dynasty occurred; they devastated much of China and led to
the ruin of the dynasty.
Hiu: 55/38: see LI-TSUN-HIU.
[Hiuen-tsong]: 54/33, 34: (Hsüan Tsung) (reign: 713-56). The reign
of this emperor is one of the most celebrated in Chinese history;
he paid great attention to governing his people and made sumptuary laws for the court to cut down state expenses. ·In 740 he
ordered that CONFUCIUS be elevated to the rank of prince. But
his reign ended in rebellion and palace politics, and Hiuen-tsong
resigned in favor of his son, SOU-TSONG.
H. J.: 79/66: see Henry JAMES.
Hoa-chan: 53/12, 13: (Hoa-shan), a mountain in SHENSI province.
Hoadly: 67/137: Benjamin, 1676-1761, Bishop of Bangor and Hereford;
author of religious and political treatises, among them An Essay
on the Origin of Civil Government.
Hoai: 53/16: see HOAÏ-HO.
[Hoai]: 53/16; 55/37: (Huai), the territory roughly identical with the
old province of KIANG-NAN; the rich agricultural area watered
by the HOAÏ-HO, S HONAN and NW Anhwei provinces of modern
E China.
Hoai: 57/59: see HOEÏ-TSONG.
Hoaï-ho: [52/6; 53/16]; 55/40: (Huai-ho), river in S HONAN and NW
Anhwei provinces in E China, flows into the HOANG-HO above
Hungtze Hu.
Hoailand: 53/16: see HOAI.
Hoailand, fed by Hoai river/ dark millet, Tchang wine for the sacri-
fice: 53/16: from A. Lacharme, Confucii Chi-King, 308.

Hoaï-nan: 54/24; 55/40: (Huai-nan), a former city on the south bank
    of the Huai River (HOAÏ-HO) in Anhwei province.
Hoai-ngan: 57/58: Hoaï-nghen (Huai Ên) fl. AD 1487, a palace eu-
    nuch who became president of the tribunal of mandarins and then
    minister of state under Emperor HIAO-TSONG.
Hoai Ti: 54/28: see TÇIN-HOAI-TI.
Hoai Tsong: 58/65, [68]: (Huai Tsung) (reign: 1628-1644), last true
    emperor of the MING dynasty. He made an attempt to rule well,
    but heavy taxes and poor harvests drove the north-west into re-
    volt. The emperor managed to keep peace with the Manchus, but
    the revolutionaries, led by Li Tzǔ-ch'êng, captured the province
    of HONAN and by 1642 advanced into SHENSI. In 1644 Peipingfell,
    and the emperor killed himself.
Hoang-ho: 53/20; 54/27, 31; 55/45; 56/47, 50, 52, 53; 60/75: (Hwang
    Ho), the second largest river of China; known as the Yellow River.
Hoang miao: 58/64: see HONG-MAO.
Hoang Tchang: 60/74: Hoang-tching (Huang-chêng), a region within
    the walls of the imperial palace at Peiping; in 1693 the first per-
    manent church and residence of the Jesuits in China was estab-
    lished there at the expense of Emperor KANG-HI.
Hoang Ti: 53/8, 10: (Huang Ti) (reign: 2698-2598), the Yellow Em-
    peror, from whom all later kings and princes of China claimed
    to be descended; he was a practical and beneficent ruler.
Hobhouse: 33/13; 71/167: John Cam, Baron Broughton de Gyfford,
    1786-1869, British administrator and liberal pamphleteer.
Ho Bios: 20/92: (Gr) Life. (See: Appendix A).
Hobo Williams: 77/51: DTC, Pisa.
hoc die decim' octavo: 43/13: (L) on this eighteenth day.
hochang (hochangs): 54/29, 30, 31, 33; 55/37, 40, 44; 56/48, 53;
    57/57, 58; 60/74; 61/80: (Ch) (ho-shang): BUDDHISTS.
Ho-che: 58/66: see HOCHÉ-TÉ-KELEÏ.
[Hoché-té-keleï]: 58/66: (Hoshih Tê-keleï) fl. AD 1643, a Mongol
    prince who allied himself to the Manchu leader TAÏ-TSONG during
    one of the latter's many raids on SHANSI province.
Ho Ci'u: 84/116: poss. Hoku (Ho-ch'ü), a town in NW SHANSI prov-
    ince near the GREAT WALL.
Hock Shop: 42/4: see MOUNT OF PITY.
Hodshon: 69/150: a Dutch banking house (c. 1780).
Hoei: 55/43: see LIU-HOEÏ.
Hoei: 55/45; 56/47: see HOEÏ-TSONG.
Hoei: 58/68: see HOAI-TSONG.
Hoei-tsong: [55/45; 56/47]; 57/59: (Hui Tsung) (reign: 1101-26). He
    was a clever artist and collector of antiques -- but not much of
    an emperor. He was dominated by his minister, TSAÏ-KING, who
    led him into Taoism. Unable to resist the KIN Tartars, the em-
    peror abdicated and surrendered himself to the invaders; they
    gave him the title of "Besotted Duke."
ho fo: 59/72: (Ch) (huo-fo): living BUDDHA. (See: Mailla, Histoire
    Générale, XI, 112 note).
hoi barbaroi: 76/37: (Gr) the barbarians. (See: Appendix A).
Ho-kien: 54/24: (Ho-chien) prob. a district city in the province of
    Hopeh.

Ho-Kien: 84/116: poss. LIEOU-TÉ.

Holans: 60/76: (Ch) the DUTCH.

Holland: 62/93; 64/107; 65/122, 125; 66/127; 68/147, 148; 69/[150], 153; 70/157.

Holland Park: 80/81: on Kensington Road, London; site of Holland House.

Hollis, Thomas: 66/128: 1720-74, English student of political philosophy and an ardent supporter of republican principles. In 1765 he had John ADAMS' Dissertation on the Canon and Feudal Law published in England; Hollis attributed Adams' work to Jeremiah GRIDLEY, however.

[Hollis, Thomas Brand-]: 66/127; 70/158: c. 1790, English friend of John ADAMS and a sympathizer with republican forms of government. He inherited the property of Thomas HOLLIS and took the name of his benefactor.

Hollis Brook: 70/158: the proposed name for a brook on John ADAMS' property at BRAINTREE; it was to be a compliment to Thomas Brand-HOLLIS.

Holt, Charles: 63/79: fl. 1800, editor of the Bee, a Republican newspaper in Connecticut, who was imprisoned under the Sedition Act (1798) for his attacks on the administration of John ADAMS.

Holy Scripture: 31/6: the Bible.

Homer: 1/5; 2/6; 7/24; 68/141; 80/81: the Greek epic poet.

Honan: 57/58: 58/68: a province in E central China.

hong-mao: [58/64]; 59/71; 60/76: (Ch) (hung-mao): Red-heads; the name used by the Chinese to designate the English and Dutch.

Hong-pi: 53/13: (Hung-pi): a precious stone.

Hong Vou: 56/54, 55; 57/57, 58, 60; 58/67: (Hung Wu) (reign: 1368-99), founder of the MING dynasty. He started his career as a rebel against the Emperor CHUNTI; in 1368 he overthrew the YÜAN dynasty and took the throne, changing his name from TCHU-YUEN-TCHANG to Hong-vou. Once emperor, he showed himself an able administrator; he reformed the law code and the system of taxation, re-established government coinage on a sound basis, prohibited eunuchs from holding office, and patronized literature and education.

Hoogstraat: 69/149: a street in Amsterdam.

Hooo: 74/5, 8, 9; 77/43: (African) Hail!

Hooper: 65/113: William, 1742-90, member of the CONTINENTAL CONGRESS (1774-77), signer of the DECLARATION of Independence.

Horace C.: 80/80: see Horace COLE.

Horn, the: 48/35: Cape Horn.

Horner, Leonard: 33/13: 1785-1864, English geologist and educational reformer; appointed in 1833 to a commission on child employment and until 1856 was a chief inspector under the FACTORY ACT.

Hortalez, Roderique: 68/143: see RODERIQUE HORTALEZ.

Ho-tcheou: 56/49: (Ho-ch'ou), city on the Kialing river, 60 miles N of Chunking.

Hotel Angioli: 27/130: a hotel in Milan, Italy.

Hôtel de Valois: 65/118: a hotel in Paris.

Hôtel Valentinois: 65/118: on the Rue Raynouard; Benjamin FRANK-
   LIN and John ADAMS stopped there while in Paris; later known
   as the BASSE COUR; it no longer exists.

hotien: 61/85: Khotan, town in NW China, important as caravan
   junction. (See: Mailla, Histoire Générale, XI, 570).

Houai: 52/6: see HOAI-HO.

Hou-chi: 54/30: (Hu Shih) d. AD 552, empress of the state of OUEI
   who built many Buddhist temples and often waged war against the
   Empire.

[Hou-han-yé]: 54/25: (Hu Han-yeh) fl. BC 55, a tartar chief of
   great importance who became a vassal of Emperor HAN-SIUEN-
   TI in BC 55.

Houille blanch/ Auto-chenille: 23/107: (Fr) water power/ caterpillar
   tread vehicle.

"Hound of Heaven, The": 74/23: poem by Francis Thompson (1859-
   1907); appeared in the volume Poems (1893).

House, the: 62/95; 83/114: see HOUSE OF REPRESENTATIVES.

House, the: 64/108: see MASSACHUSETTS COLONIAL LEGISLATURE.

[House of Commons]: 62/91; 66/129: the lower house of the English
   PARLIAMENT.

[House of Lords]: 62/91: the upper house of the English PARLIA-
   MENT.

House of Lorraine: 50/42: see HAPSBURG-LORRAINE.

[House of Representatives]: 62/95; 69/154; 83/114: the lower house
   of the CONGRESS OF THE UNITED STATES.

House ov reppyzentativs: 69/154: see HOUSE OF REPRESENTATIVES.

Hovey: 80/73: Richard, 1864-1900, American poet.

Howard: 80/94: Catherine, ?1521-1542, Queen of England, fifth wife
   of HENRY VIII; she was accused of immoral conduct before her
   marriage and was beheaded. Or poss. reference to the entire
   Howard family.

Howe: 65/114: Richard, Earl Howe, 1726-99, English naval officer
   engaged in the American Revolution (1776-78).

"How is it far, if you think of it?": 77/43, 51; 79/66: from Analects,
   IX, xxx, 2.

"how stiff the shaft of your neck is"...each his own way: 74/20: from
   Kagekiyo. (See: Translations, 321).

Hoy mismo han llegado/...los Americanos tomaron: 65/120-121: (Sp)
   Today have arrived at this square the knight/ John ADAMS mem-
   ber/ etc/ the Englishmen evacuating RHODE ISLAND/ the Americans took over. (See: John Adams, Works, III, 247).

Huai: 53/16: see HOAI-HO.

[Huddleston, Sisley]: 74/17: 1883-1952, the English journalist.

Huddy: 74/11: see William Henry HUDSON.

Hudibras tavern: 65/109: inn near Nassau Hall College, Princeton,
   New Jersey; John ADAMS stopped there in 1774.

Hudor et Pax: 83/106, [109]: (Gr) water (L) and peace. (See: Appendix A).

Hudson: 19/84; 70/159; [71/161]: river in E New York State.

Hudson Bay Company: 65/125: Hudson's Bay Company.

Hudson, Henry: 74/14: DTC, Pisa.

[Hudson, William Henry]: 74/11: 1841-1922, naturalist and author.

Hulme: [16/71]; 78/57: Thomas Ernest, 1883-1917, the English
  philosopher and poet, killed in World War I.

humanitas: 82/103; 84/117: (L) humanity, the sum of humane qualities; virtù.

Humbers: 18/81: pseudonym for VICKERS.

Hume: 67/133, 139; 68/141: David, 1711-1776, the Scottish philosopher
  and historian.

Humphries: 33/10: David, 1753-1818, colonel in the American Army
  during the Revolution, aide-de-camp to George WASHINGTON;
  minister to Spain (1794); recognized as an expert on raising
  merino sheep.

Hun: 41/54: German.

Hungary: 26/124; 56/49.

[Hunt, Violet]: 38/38: 1866-1942, English writer; companion of Ford
  Madox FORD.

Huntington: 68/144; 69/149: Samuel, 1731-96, president of the CON-
  TINENTAL CONGRESS (1779-81), signer of the DECLARATION
  of Independence, member of the Continental Congress (1776-83).

Huon: 54/27, 28: see HAN-HOUON-TI.

Hutchinson: [62/89]; 64/[101], 103, 106, 107, 108; 66/129; 67/136;
  68/144; 71/165: Thomas, 1711-80, American colonial administrator; member of the Massachusetts governor's council (1749-66);
  accepted the legality of the STAMP ACT (1765); Royal Governor
  of Massachusetts (1771-74). Hutchinson was a firm believer in
  British authority, and his policies in Massachusetts did much to
  hasten the American Revolution.

Hyades: 52/4: a cluster of stars in the constellation Taurus; their
  rising with the sun was supposed to indicate rainy weather.

Hyder Ali: 32/7: or Haider Ali, d. 1782, Indian maharaja of the
  Hindu state of Mysore.

Hydra: 52/5, 6: a southern constellation having the form of a ser-
  pent.

hyght: 18/80: (ME) was called.

Hymen: 4/15; [5/17]: Greek god of marriage.

Hymenaeus: 5/17: (L) HYMEN.

Hymenaeus Io! / Hymen, Io Hymenaee!: 4/15: (L) Hail HYMEN! (See:
  Catullus, LXI).

[Hyperion]: 23/107: a Titan, father of the Sun, Moon, and Dawn;
  also a reference to the sun itself.

Hyson: 70/156: a kind of tea.

I

[Iacchos]: 79/67, 68: a mystic name of DIONYSUS. (See: Appendix A).

Iamblichus: 5/17: c. AD 330, the Greek neo-Platonic philosopher.

"I am noman, my name is noman": 74/4: from Odyssey, IX, 366.

"I am the torch...she saith": 80/89: from Arthur Symonds, Modern Beauty in Images of Good and Evil, 257.

Ibsen: 28/136: Henrik, 1828-1906, the Norwegian poet and dramatist.

Ida: 77/45, [49]; 78/55: a hill in the Troad, scene of the marriage between ANCHISES and APHRODITE; also the scene of the Judgment of Paris.

id est: 37/34; 42/5: (L) that is.

id est Burgundy: 21/97: (L) that is BURGUNDY.

id est, più utilmente: 42/4: (L) that is (It) more usefully.

igitur meis encomiis...: 59/70: see DE LIBRO CHI-KING SIC CENSO ....

Ignez: 30/148: see Inez da CASTRO.

I had not loved you...: 79/62: from Lovelace, To Althea from Prison.

il cardinale di San Pietro in Vincoli: 10/45: (It) the Cardinal of SAN PIETRO IN VINCOLI. (i.e., Nicholas of Cusa, 1400-64, German churchman named cardinal in 1448 by Pope Eugene IV).

il danaro c'è: 74/20: (It) there is the money.

il duol che sopra Senna/ Induce, falseggiando la moneta: 38/37: (It) the grief that over the Seine river/ Induces, forging the money. (See: Paradiso, 19, 118-119).

Ile St. Louis: 80/90: Île de Saint-Louis, one of the islands of Paris.

Il est bon comme le pain: 80/82: (Fr) it is good as bread; proverbial: it is good as gold.

Ileuthyeria: 2/9: prob. inv., a sea nymph.

il Gran Maestro: 28/135: (It) the Great Master. (See: Franz LISZT).

Ilion: 23/109: see TROY.

illa dolore obmutuit, pariter vocem: 39/44: (L) she hushed with grief, and her voice likewise. (See: Ovid, Metamorphoses, XIII, 538-540).

Illmo ac ex^{mo} (eccellentissimo) princeps et d^{no}: 26/125: (L) ... principi...: To the most illustrious and excellent prince and lord.

Ill^{us} Balia eseguisca in tutto: 43/13: (It) Illustrious BALÍA that acts in everything.

Illustrae Dominae Parisinae Marxesana: 24/111: (L) Of the illustrious Lady Parisina, Marchioness. (See: Parisina MALATESTA).

Illustre signor mio, Messire Battista: 9/38: (It) My dear sir, Master Battista. (See: Leon Battista ALBERTI).

Il me paraît...un curé déguisé: 80/83: (Fr) He appears to me ... a disguised priest.

Il Papa mori: 30/149: (It) The Pope died. (See: ALEXANDER VI).

il più galantuomo del paese: 44/19: (It) the best gentleman of the town.

Il Popolo: 46/25: Popolo d'Italia, newspaper started by MUSSOLINI in 1914.

[98]

il Pozzetto/ al Tigullio: 74/17: (It) the Little Well/ at TIGULLIO.

Il Scirocco è geloso: 77/43: (It) and the south-west wind is jealous.

il sesso femminile: 50/43: (It) the female sex.

Ils n'existent pas, leur ambience leur confert/ une existence: 77/49:
    (Fr) ...ambiance...: They don't exist, their surrounding con-
    fers/ an existence upon them.

ima vada noctis obscurae: 23/107: (L) the lowest depths of dim night.

immacolata: 74/7; 80/78: (It) immaculate.

Immaculata, Introibo: 80/91: (L) immaculate, I shall enter. (Intro-
    ibo from the Preparation of the Roman Mass).

Imperial Chemicals: 78/55; 84/117: the British chemical combine.

Imperial Seal: 54/23: the seal of the Emperor of China during the
    Former HAN dynasty.

im Westen nichts neues: 74/4: (Ger) im Westen nichts Neues: noth-
    ing new in the West. (Novel by Erich Maria Remarque; the Eng-
    lish translation is All Quiet on the Western Front, 1929).

In: 53/13: see YIN.

Ina: 67/133: King of the West Saxons (689-728); organized a code of
    laws.

In campo Illus. Domini Venetorum die 7/ aprilis 1449 contra Cremo-
    nam: 8/29: (L) In the field of the Illustrious Lord of the Vene-
    tians, 7 April 1449, opposite CREMONA.

in capite: 65/109: (Law) referring to the holding of land under direct
    grant of the lord or king; lit.: in chief. (See: John Adams,
    Works, II, 372).

In carta di capretto: 21/96: (It) on parchment.

in coitu inluminatio: 74/13: (L) coition maketh the light to shine.

Incostante: 50/42: The Inconstant, the ship on which NAPOLEON left
    Elba in 1815.

In den Deutschen Befreudenskriegen: 41/53: (Ger) Befreiungskriegen:
    In the German Wars of Liberation. (See: Wilhelm BAUR).

India: 74/4.

Indian army: 19/87: the British forces in India.

Indians: 31/5; 32/8; 71/162: the American Indians.

[Indians]: 54/29: East Indians.

in discourse what matters is to get it across: 79/64: from Analects,
    XV, xl, 1.

in excelsis: 12/55: (L) in the highest.

Infante: 38/39: prob. the son of Alfonso XIII, last king of Spain.

inficit umbras: 35/25: (L) tinges with a darker shade. (See: Ovid,
    Metamorphoses, X, 596).

Inghilterra: 26/122: (It) ENGLAND.

in giro per il paese: 48/36: (It) going around the town.

in gran dispitto: 77/51: (It) with great spite.

in harum ac ego ivi: [39/44]; 74/[14], 17: ...haram...: into a pig-
    sty I too have gone.

In libro pactorum: 25/115: (L) In the book of the agreements.

in margine: 69/153: (L) in the margin.

"in meteyard in weight or in measure": 74/12, 18; 76/32: from Levi-
    ticus, 19, 35.

Innes: 80/80: George Inness, 1825-94, American landscape painter, member of the Hudson River School; or his son George, 1854-1926, also a painter.

Innsbruck: 74/19: capital of the Tyrol, W Austria.

In officina Wecheli: 1/5: (L) At the workshop of WECHEL. (See: Homeri Odyssea, adverbum translata, Andrea Divo Iustinopolitano (Andreas DIVUS) interprete, Paris, 1538, title page).

inoltre: 78/56: (It) also.

Inopos: 21/99: Inopus, a river of Delos; it is said to rise and fall at the same time as the Nile, and the two rivers were supposed to be connected in some way.

in principio verbum/...verbum perfectum: sinceritas: 74/5: (L) In the beginning was the Word/...the perfect Word: sincerity. (See: John 1, 1).

in quella parte/ dove sta memora: 63/99; [76/30, 35]: (It) memoria: in that part/ where the memory is. (See: Cavalcanti, Donna mi prega).

Inquisition: 50/40: the systematic punishment of religious heretics during the period between the 13th and 18th centuries; especially the Spanish Inquisition.

Institutes: 63/98: comprehensive summaries of legal principles and decisions; here prob. a particular reference to COKE's Institutes of the Laws of England.

Institutes Digest Roman: 66/128: the institutes, digests, and codes of the Roman law.

in tabernam: 80/85: (L) to the tavern.

intellex: 38/40: intellects.

Interea pro gradibus Basilicae S. Pietri ex arida materia/ ...et pyra simulacrum repente flagravit./ Com. Pio II, Liv. VII: 10/43-44: (L) Meanwhile in front of the steps of the Basilica of ST. PETER, from dry stuff/ a huge pyre was built and on top of it was placed an effigy of Sigis/mondo, imitating so exactly the man's features and style of dress/ that it seemed rather to be the real person/ than his effigy; but so that the effigy could not fool anyone,/ some writing came from his mouth which said:/ Here am I, Sigismondo/ MALATESTA, son of PANDOLFO, king of traitors,/ naked before God and men, by decree of the Sacred Senate/ condemned to the flames;/ would write. Many read (the words). Then as the people stood by, a fire was lit beneath it,/ and the pyre of a sudden set the the likeness on fire. Commentaries of Pius II, Book VII.

Inter lineas: 26/128: (L) between the lines.

in terrorem: 65/112: (L) in terror; for the purpose of terror (?).

Intorcetta: 60/74: fl. 1691, an Italian Jesuit missionary in China.

Invention-d'entités-plus-ou-moins-abstraits-/en-nombre-égal-aux-choses-à-expliquer.../ La Science ne peut pas y consister. "J'ai/ Obtenu une brulure".../ "Qui m'a côuté six mois de guérison": 23/107: (Fr) Invention of more or less abstract entities/ in number equal to the things to be explained.../ Science can not be composed of it. "I/ got a burn".../ "from which it took me six months to recover."

Invidia: 14/63: (It) envy.

Io: 4/15; 79/67: (Gr) (an exclamation). (See: Appendix A).

Ione: 7/25: (See: "Ione, Dead the Long Year," Personae, 112).
Ionides: 40/48: prob. Luke Ionides. (See: Guide to Kulchur, 227).
Io son la luna: 74/16, 21; 76/31: (It) I am the moon.
Io venni in luogo d'ogni luce muto: 14/61: (It) I came to a lightless
    place. (See: Inferno, 5, 28).
Iphigénie: 80/82: Iphigénie en Tauride, an opera by Christoph Willi-
    bald GLUCK (1779).
Ipswich, Agot: 38/38: poss. Margot ASQUITH; (however, the 1954
    Faber edition of the Cantos substitutes the name Minny Humbolt
    for Agot Ipswich).
Ipswich Instructions: 64/103: the instructions given by the people of
    Ipswich, Massachusetts to Dr. John Calef, their representative
    to the STAMP ACT Congress (1765).
Ira: 63/99: (L) anger.
Ireland: 65/124; 67/135, 136; 68/144; [80/74].
Iriquois, Frank Robert: 28/137: prob. an American expelled from
    France c. 24 July 1928.
Irish Nation: 67/135: IRELAND.
[Irish Parliament]: 67/135: the quasi-legislative body of Ireland; the
    Irish Parliament had been curbed by POYNINGS's Law in 1495 and
    made dependent upon the English Parliament for legislative ini-
    tiative; the law was not rescinded until 1782.
Irol: 23/107: Iroline, a French motor fuel.
Irritat mulcet et falsis terroribus implet: 67/134: (L) annoys, soothes,
    and fills with false fears. (See: Horace: Epistles II, i, 212).
Isaiah: 74/7; 77/50; 80/85: fl. BC 710, the Hebrew prophet.
Isé: 4/15; 21/99: the two sacred Shinto shrines to the Sun Goddess;
    located at Ujiyamada, S Honshu, Japan.
Ismarus of the Cicones: 79/63: Ismarus, a city of the Cicones, at-
    tacked by ODYSSEUS shortly after his leaving Troy. After an
    initial defeat, the Ciconians rallied and drove the Greeks back
    to their ships. (See: Odyssey IX, 39ff).
[Isolde]: 8/30: the heroine of the legend of Tristam and Isolde.
Isotta: 9/38, 39: see Isotta degli ATTI.
Issy: 66/126: Issy-les-Moulineaux, SW suburb of Paris, on the Seine.
Istria: 9/37: the Istria Peninsula on the NE coast of the Adriatic Sea.
Italia: 35/22; 74/8: (It) ITALY.
Italy: 2/7; 20/89; 22/104; [35/22]; 44/20; 50/43; 62/95; 74/[8], 20;
    76/34; 80/78, 80, 85, [88].
I-Tching-tcheou: 56/48: Tching-tcheou (Ching-ch'ou), a village in
    the district of CAÏ-FONG-FOU.
Ithaca: 1/3: the island-kingdom of ODYSSEUS in the Ionian Sea.
"I think you must be Odysseus...Always with your mind on the past...:
    39/44-45: from Odyssey, X, 456-64.
[Ito, Miscio]: 77/47: a Japanese dancer known to Pound. (See:
    Guide to Kulchur, 217).
Ito Yen: 56/53: poss. Ho-yan, a town in what is now Anhwei province.
    (See: Mailla, Histoire Générale, IX, 615).
Ityn: 4/13; 78/55: see ITYS.
[Itys]: 4/13, 14; 78/55: son of Procne, who was married to Tereus,
    king of Thrace. Tereus seduced Philomela and cut out her

tongue; to revenge her sister, Procne killed Itys and served his flesh to her husband.

ivi in harum ego ac vidi cadaveres animae: [39/44]; 74/14, [17]: (L) <u>haram</u>: I went into the pig-sty and saw soul-corpses.

i vitrei: 17/78: (It) the makers of glass.

Ixion: 80/81: a Thessalian who courted Hera illicitly; as punishment for his crimes, Ixion was bound to an ever-turning wheel in the underworld.

Ixotta: 9/38; 20/94; 74/8, 26; 76/30, 40: see Isotta degli ATTI.

Ixottae: 76/37: see Isotta degli ATTI.

I Yin: [53/11]; 78/59: 18th century BC, a minister of TCHING TANG, first emperor of the CHANG dynasty. I Yin was instrumental in putting an end to the HIA dynasty.

J

J.: 65/113: see Thomas JEFFERSON.

J. A.: 33/11; 62/91; 63/97; 65/116, 123; 68/141, 142, 143, 147, 148;
   69/151; 70/155, 158; 71/166: see John ADAMS.

Jackson: 34/19, 20; 37/32, [33, 34]; 80/75: Andrew, 1767-1845,
   seventh President of the U.S.; member of the House of Representatives (1796-97) and of the U.S. Senate (1797-98; 1823-25); successfully defended New Orleans against the British (1814); President (1828-36).

Jackson, Colonel: 80/82: prob. acquaintance of Pound. (See: Guide
   to Kulchur, 227).

Jackson, Jim: 69/154: James Jackson, 1757-1806, American statesman, member of the House of Representatives (1789-91), govern-
   or of Georgia (1798-1801); he was an opponent of HAMILTON's
   financial measures.

Jacob, rue: 80/83: street on the Left Bank, Paris.

Jacopo: 20/90; 80/89: see Jacopo SELLAIO.

Jacques, Henri: 4/16: a French Jesuit priest. (See: Letters, 180).

Jaffa: 28/136: a subdistrict of S Palestine; ancient Joppa was a seaport of Palestine.

Jah, (the Bard's pedestal) ist am Lesterplatz: 80/79: (Ger) Yes,
   (the BARD's pedestal) is in LEICESTER SQUARE.

J'ai eu pitié des autres/ probablement pas assez: 76/38: (Fr) I had
   pity for the others/ probably not enough.

J'ai honte d'être Hollandais: 69/150: (Fr) I am ashamed of being
   Dutch.

J'ai obtenu: 27/129: (Fr) I got.

jambe-de-bois: 80/83: (Fr) wooden leg.

James: 80/86: prob. a negro servant of Pound's AUNT FRANK.

[James, Henry]: [7/24; 12/53(?)]; 74/11; 79/66: 1843-1916, the American novelist.

James, King: 66/131: see JAMES II of England.

James I: 66/129, [131]: 1566-1625, King of Great Britain and Scotland (1603-25).

James II: 66/128, 131: 1633-1701, King of Great Britain and Scotland
   (1685-88).

[Jan Ch'iu]: 13/58: a disciple of CONFUCIUS. (See: Analects, XI,
   25).

Janequin: 79/63: Clement Jannequin or Janequin: 16th-century French
   composer of both secular and church music.

Janus: 78/55: the god of beginnings, the guardian of the gate or the
   gate itself; usually represented as bifrons, with two faces, looking both before and behind. The closing of the Janus geminus, in
   the Roman Forum, signified peace.

Japan: 38/38; 56/47, 50; 58/62; [63]; 60/76, 77; 62/90; [74/20].

Jason: 56/52: poss. Jason, Tyrant of Pherae, c. 380-70; a man of
   great ability who started to unite northern Greece into a strong
   Thessalian hegemony but was assassinated before he could carry
   out his plans.

Jassy: 19/87: a commercial town in NE Rumania.

Jay: 62/94; 65/112, 121, 123; 69/152; 71/166: John, 1745-1829, American jurist and statesman; member of the CONTINENTAL CON-
GRESS (1774-77, 78, 79); aided in peace negotiations with Great
Britain (1782-3); Chief Justice of the U.S. Supreme Court (1789-
95); negotiated Jay's Treaty with Great Britain (1794-5).

Jean, M.: 74/14; 80/83: see Jean COCTEAU.

Jeen-jah: 22/103: see GINGER.

Jeff: 62/95: see Thomas JEFFERSON.

Jeffers: 82/101: DTC, Pisa.

Jefferson: 21/97; 31/3, 4, 5, 6; 32/9; 33/[10], 11; 34/17; 37/32, 35;
41/56; 46/28; [60/76]; 62/95; 63/97; 65/113; 66/126, 127; 68/145;
69/151, [152], 153, [154]; 70/156, 157, 159; 71/164, 165; 81/96:
Thomas, 1743-1826, third President of the U.S.; member of the
CONTINENTAL CONGRESS (1775, 76; 1783-85); chairman of the
committee to draft the DECLARATION of Independence (1776);
U.S. minister to France (1785-98); Secretary of State (1790-93);
Vice-President (1797-1801); President (1801-09).

Jehoveh: 74/18.

Jelly Hugo: 55/41: see YÉLIU-HIÉOU-CO.

jen: 82/103; [84/117(?)]: (Ch) jên: virtue, benevolence, humanity.
(See: Appendix B).

Jena: 41/56: city in Thuringia, Germany.

Jenkyns: 81/97, 98: John Jenkins, 1592-1678, English composer and
musician to CHARLES I and CHARLES II; composed many Fancies for viol and organ.

Jenny: 38/38:

Jepson: 74/11; 78/80: Edgar, 1863-1938, English novelist.

Jeremiah: 74/18: ?650-587?, the major Hebrew prophet.

[Jerome, Jennie]: 41/54: mother of Winston CHURCHILL, married
Randolph Henry Spencer Churchill in 1874.

Jerusalem: 24/111, 112; 82/102: the city in Palestine.

Jerusalem: 26/127: a painting of Jerusalem by Vittore CARPACCIO;
poss. his St. Stephen Preaching at Jerusalem, in the Louvre.

Jesu Christo! / Standu nel paradiso terrestre/ Pensando come si fesse
compagna d'Adamo!: 22/102: (It) Jesus Christ/ being in the
terrestrial paradise/ thinking how to make Adam's mate!

Je suis au bout de mes forces: 80/90: (Fr) I am at the end of my tether.

Je suis.../ plus fort que.../ ...le Boud-ha!/ Je suis.../ ...plus
fort que le.../ ...Christ!/ J'aurais.../ aboli...le poids!: 28/137:
(Fr) I am/ stronger than/ BUDDHA/ I am/ stronger than/ CHRIST/
I would have/ abolished weight!

Jesuit church: 60/74: a church and residence in Peiping. (See:
HOANG-TCHANG).

Jesuits: 50/40; 60/74, 78; 61/84: the Society of Jesus, founded by
St. Ignatius Loyola in 1534.

Jesuits: 60/74, 78; 61/84: (see entry above), the Jesuit missionaries
in China who established the modern Roman Catholic missions
there. First to arrive was Matteo RICCI (1582), followed by
Johann Adam Schall von Bell (1619). The period of greatest missionary effort began in 1688 when GERBILLON and VERBIEST
gained the favour of Emperor KANG-HI.

jeu de paume: 58/62: (Fr) court tennis.
Jevons, Mrs.: 74/26:
Jew (Jews): 10/44; [22/105]; 31/5; 34/18; 35/24, 26; [44/19]; 48/35;
    50/41, 42; 52/3; 65/112; 74/21.
Jewish Hungarian baron: 35/24: see HATVANY.
Jim: 19/87: see James Buchanan BRADY.
Jim: 74/11; 76/34: see James JOYCE.
Jim: 74/25; 80/86: see JAMES.
[Jimmu Tenno]: 58/62: 711-585, first of the legendary emperors of
    Japan (660-585). Jimmu is regarded as a direct descendent of
    the Sun Goddess and as the founder of the Japanese imperial dy-
    nasty, which has remained unbroken since his accession to the
    throne. The Japanese Era is dated from the beginning of his
    reign: 11 February 660 BC.
Jim X: 12/55, 56: see John QUINN.
Jin: 84/117: prob. JEN.
Joannis: 43/12: see SAN GIOVANNI di Siena.
Jockey Club: 38/38: the leading social club of Paris.
Joe: 22/101:
Joe: 28/136: see Joe BROMLEY.
Johanni di Cosimo: 8/30: see Giovanni de' MEDICI.
John: 62/91, 92, 93, 95; 64/101; 65/114, 121: see John ADAMS.
John: 80/92: John Lackland, ?1167-1216, King of England (1199-1216);
    forced by the English barons to sign the Magna Charta (1215) at
    Runnymede.
[John V]: 60/76; 61/83: 1689-1750, King of Portugal (1706-50).
John A: 62/90: see John ADAMS.
John Baptiste Lazarus: 68/143: see John Baptiste Lazarus de Theve-
    neau de FRANCY.
[John de Neufville & Sons]: 68/146: a Dutch banking house through
    which John ADAMS tried (c. 1780) to arrange an American loan.
Johnnie: 65/115; 68/144: see John Quincy ADAMS.
[John of Austria]: 80/71: 1629-79, Spanish general and statesman,
    natural son of Philip IV.
John's bro.: 64/101: see Elihu ADAMS.
Johnson: 32/8: William, 1771-1834, appointed associate justice of the
    U.S. Supreme Court (1804) by Thomas JEFFERSON.
Johnson: 34/17: Colonel Richard Mentor, 1780-1850, member of the
    House of Representatives (1807-19; 1829-37) and the U.S. Senate
    (1819-29); Vice-President (1837-41).
Johnson: 66/126: Joshua, American merchant who settled in England
    before the Revolution; first U.S. consul at London (1785-97); father
    of Louisa Catherine, who married John Quincy ADAMS (1797).
Johnson, Sam: 69/153: William Samuel, 1727-1819, American jurist
    and educator; member of the CONTINENTAL CONGRESS (1784-
    87) and the U.S. Senate (1789-91); president of Columbia College
    (1787-1800).
Johnson, Sam: 80/79: Samuel, 1709-84, the English lexicographer,
    critic, and poet; edited Shakespeare (8 vols., 1765).
joli quart d'heure, (nella Malatestiana): 74/24: (Fr) pleasant quarter-
    hour (It) (in the TEMPIO of the MALATESTA).

Jones: 66/131: see Sir Thomas JONES.

Jones: 80/77; 83/111: lieutenant and Provost Officer, DTC, Pisa.

Jones, James: 37/36: brother-in-law of DeWitt CLINTON.

Jones, Paul: 65/119; 68/143: John Paul Jones, 1747-92, naval officer serving America during the Revolution.

[Jones, Sir Thomas]: 66/131: d. 1692, English jurist, chief justice of the Common Pleas; he was dismissed in 1686 by JAMES II for refusing to rule in favour of the dispensing power of the Crown in the HALES case.

jongleur: 23/109; 55/39: (Fr) one who sings the songs composed by a troubadour.

Jordaens: 80/89: Jacob, 1593-1678, Flemish painter.

Jordan: 6/21; 24/111: river in Palestine.

Joritomo: 58/62: or Yoritomo, 1146-99, the first true Shogun in Japanese history; he assumed sovereign power in 1185. A great and constructive statesman, he inaugurated a system of military government which ran the affairs of Japan in disregard of the emperor.

José, Padre: 77/44: see Padre José ELIZONDO.

[Joseph II]: 32/9: 1741-90, King of Germany (1764-90) and Holy Roman Emperor (1765-90).

Joseph of Austria: 32/9: see JOSEPH II.

Journal de l'Empire: 34/16: French newspaper (c. 1815).

Journal des Débats: 38/42: French newspaper, controlled by the COMITE DES FORGES.

joven: 6/21: (Pr) young.

Joyce: 38/37; 74/[11], 25; 76/34; 77/51: James, 1882-1941, the Irish novelist.

Jozefff: 80/84: poss. a waiter in the WIENER CAFE.

J. Q.: 80/85: see John QUINN.

J. Q. A.: 34/17; 62/94; 64/104: see John Quincy ADAMS.

Juan of Austria: 80/71: see JOHN OF AUSTRIA.

Juana, Doña, la loca: 78/61: 1479-1555, daughter of Ferdinand of Aragon and Isabella of Castile; mother of Emperor Charles V; driven mad by the death of her husband, Philip (1506).

Judas's tree: 24/111: according to tradition, the tree on which Judas hanged himself.

Judith: 80/82: see Judith GAUTIER.

Juffusun, Tommy: 60/76: see Thomas JEFFERSON.

Jugoslavian: 80/84: Yugoslavian, the language.

Julia the Countess: 24/114: prob. a member of the Tassoni family of Ferrara, which owned the SCHIFANOJA at one time. Text reference is to the fact that the Schifanoia once was used as a tobacco factory; the Italian verb, conciare, means to tan hides, or to cure tobacco, hence the confusion of tannery in the text. For recent history of the Schifanoia, see R. Longhi, "Il Palazzo Estense di Schifanoia dal sec. XIV al sec. XX," Rivista di Ferrara, July 1935.

Juliet: 38/39: the character in Shakespeare's play, Romeo and Juliet.

Julius Caesar: 80/80: the play by Shakespeare.

Jupiter: 74/16: the Roman equivalent of ZEUS.

jura ordo...aequitas leges: 67/140: (L) rights order...equity laws. (See: Livy, Annals, III, 63).

jure regalia: 67/136: (L) jura...: royal rights. (See: John Adams, Works, IV, 107).

Justinian: 65/119; 70/157; 77/44; 78/57: Justinian I, 483-565, Byzantine Emperor (527-65); his greatest accomplishment was the codification of Roman law, done under his direction by Tribonian, called the Corpus Juris Civilis.

Justinian, Bernard: 26/122: see Bernardo GIUSTINIAN.

Juventus: 29/142: (L) the age of youth, personified.

Juxta fluvium Huai acies ordinatur nec mora: 53/16: (L) By the river HOAI the battle line is drawn up without delay. (See: A. Lacharme, Confucii Chi-King, III, 3, 9, stanza 4; Classic Anthology, 263).

K

K, Mr.: 74/6: DTC, Pisa.

Kabir: 77/52: ?1450-1518, Hindu mystic poet in the time of the Lodi
kings.

Kagekiyo: 74/20: character in the Noh play, Kagekiyo, by Motokiyo.
(See: Translations, 315-322).

Kahn: 18/80; 20/94: see KUBLAI KHAN.

Kai fong: 58/68: Kai-fong-fu (Kaifeng), capital of HONAN province.

Kai Moirai' Adonin: 47/30, 33: (Gr) And the FATES (cry over)
ADONIS. (See: Appendix A).

Kaiser: 48/34: see WILLIAM II, of Germany.

Kait: 80/80:

Kaiyuen: 58/63: (Kai-yüan), a city in S Manchuria.

kaka pharmak edōken: 39/43: (Gr) she (CIRCE) had given them dreadful drugs. (See: Appendix A).

Kakemono: 83/111: (Jap) a painted scroll.

[Kalb, Johann]: 68/142: 1721-80, known as Baron de Kalb; a German
army officer commissioned major general in the Continental Army
(1777-80), killed at the battle of Camden.

Kalda: 60/75: see KALDAN.

[Kaldan]: 60/74, 75: (Galdan) d. AD 1697. Chief of the ELEUTES,
a nomadic tribe to the north-west of China. In 1680 Kaldan became khan of his people and invaded the territory of the KALKAS;
however, Emperor KANG-HI declared himself on the side of the
Kalkas. Daring the emperor's power, Kaldan invaded the Chinese frontier in 1691; he was beaten but not crushed. When he invaded China again (1695) his forces were destroyed by the imperial troops, who used cannon. Kaldan poisoned himself.

Kaldans: 60/75: the people ruled by KALDAN; the ELEUTES.

Kaldan war: 60/74: see KALDAN.

Kalkas: 59/72; 60/74: (Khalkans) a nomadic tribe to the north and
north-west of China; the Kalkas were Mongols and traced themselves back to GENGHIS KHAN.

Kalon Aoidiaei: 39/43: (Gr) she sings beautifully. (See: Appendix
A).

kalos k'àgathos: 33/11: (Gr) a perfect gentleman. (See: Appendix
A).

Kalüpso: 20/94: see CALYPSO.

kalypygous: 43/11: callipygous: having shapely buttocks.

Kang: 53/14; 55/37: see KANG-OUANG.

Kang: 59/72: see KANG HI.

Kang Hi: [49/39]; 59/71, [72], 73; 60/74, 75, 76, [78], 79; 61/82:
(K'ang Hsi) (reign: 1662-1722), second emperor of the Manchu
dynasty to rule over China. In 1675 the Manchu dynasty was
threatened by the revolt of the Three Feudatories (one of them
OU-SAN-KOUEÏ); but by 1681 Kang-hi had re-established a firm
rule over all China and, two years later, over Formosa. He extended the Empire to the borders of Kokand and Badakhshan and
into Tibet. He was a patron of the Jesuits, whom he employed
(especially VERBIEST) to survey the Empire, study astronomy,

and cast cannon; but later, fearing their propaganda and the possible influence of the Pope on the government of China, he re-
stricted their activities. A great patron of literature and scholar-
ship, the emperor directed the writing of the Imperial Dictionary
and the great Concordance of all literature. Kang-hi was an emperor in the tradition of YAO, CHUN and YU.

Kang Ouang: 53/14, [15; 55/37]: (K'ang Wang) (reign: 1078-52), a
    weak emperor, but one who was supported by strong ministers.

Kang-wang: 53/14, 15: see KANG OUANG.

Kanouen: 56/51: Kanouensing (Kan Wên-hsing) d. AD 1297, the com-
    mander of the city of TCHANG-TCHÉOU; he was attacked and
    killed by TCHIN TIAOUEN. His wife, OUANG-CHI, preferred to
    die on his funeral pyre than to marry his murderer.

Kansas: 28/135.

Kant: 16/71: Immanuel, 1724-1804, the German philosopher.

Kao: 54/22: see KAO-HOANG-TI.

Kao: 54/29: see KAO-TI.

[Kao-hoang-ti]: 54/22, 23: (Kao Huang Ti) (reign: 202-195), found-
    er and first emperor of the HAN dynasty; known formerly as
    LIEOU-PANG. On the whole he was an able emperor and one
    provided with many wise ministers -- to whom he listened most
    of the time; he established a firm foundation for the Han dynasty.

Kao Ti: 54/23: see KAO-HOANG-TI.

[Kao-ti]: 54/29: (Kao Ti) (reign: 480-83), first emperor of the Ch'i
    dynasty (480-503); he is said to have seemed deficient in some of
    the more heroic.qualities; an unimportant ruler.

Kao Tseu: 54/28: see KAO-TSOU-OU-TI.

Kao Tseu: 54/31, 32; 56/54: see KAO-TSOU.

Kao-tsou: 54/28: see KAO-TSOU-OU-TI.

[Kao-tsou]: 54/31, 32; 56/54: (Kao Tsu) (reign: 618-26), first em-
    peror of the TANG dynasty; he established schools and stabilized
    the monetary units. Although the Tartars invaded the Empire,
    Kao-tsou's son, Shih Min, drove them out of the Empire; Shih
    Min did much to establish the Tang dynasty and became its sec-
    ond emperor, ruling under the name TAÏ-TSONG.

[Kao-tsou]: 55/39: (Kao Tsu), imperial title of CHÉKING-TANG.

[Kao-tsou]: 55/39, 40(?): (Kao Tsu), imperial title of LIEOU-TCHI-
    YUEN.

[Kao-tsou-ou-ti]: 54/28: (Kao Tsu Wu Ti) (reign: 420-23), former-
    ly LIEOU-YU, known generally as Wu Ti, the founder of the Liu
    SUNG dynasty; he proved to be a good emperor, but did not live
    long enough to be effective.

Kao-Yao: 53/10, [19(?)]; 78/59: (Kao Yao) d. BC 2204, a famous
    minister under Emperor CHUN; said to have been the first to in-
    troduce laws for the repression of crime.

Kardomah: 80/80: tea rooms in Piccadilly, London.

Karikon: 40/49: Caricus Murus, a town on the coast of North Africa
    founded by HANNO, just south of the promontory of SOLOIS.

Karxèdoniōn Basileos: 40/51: (Gr) The King of the CARTHAGINIANS.
    (See: Appendix A).

Kasgar: 61/85: Kashgar, city in W Sinkiang province W China, became a part of China in 1759; the chief city of Chinese Turkistan.

Kashmir: 19/87: Indian state in N India on the Sinkiang and Tibet frontier.

Kashmiri: 78/58: of KASHMIR.

Katholou: 74/19: (Gr) generalities. (See: Appendix A).

Katin: 77/42: Katyn, village west of Smolensk, occupied by the Germans during W. W. II. In 1943 the Germans said that the mass grave of some 10,000 Polish officers had been discovered near Katyn and claimed the Russians had massacred them; the Russians denied the charge but refused to allow an investigation. Later the Russians accused the Germans of the massacre.

KEI MEN RAN KEI/KIU MAN MAN KEI/ JITSU GETSU KO KWA/ TAN FUKU TAN KAI: 49/39: (Ch in Jap transliteration) How bright and colorful the auspicious clouds,/ Hanging gracefully;/ Let sun and moon be thus resplendent/ Morn after morn. (See: Fu Sheng, Shang-shu ta chuan).

Keith: 79/65: poss. William Keith, 1838-1911, American painter.

Keith, Sir William: 71/162: 1680-1749, British colonial governor of Pennsylvania and Delaware (1714-26).

Kensington: 80/81: the Royal Borough of Kensington, London.

Kent: 37/31: James, 1763-1847, American jurist, chief justice of the New York State Supreme Court (1804-14), judge of the New York State Court of Chancery (1814-23). His decisions as judge of the Chancery Court were instrumental in reviving equity, which had largely lapsed in America after the Revolution.

Kernes: 74/14: DTC, Pisa.

Kettlewell: 74/22: prob. John Kettlewell, a student at St. John's College, Oxford, c. 1910.

c   [Keynes, John Maynard]: 22/101, 102: 1883-1946, the English econo-
c   mist.

K. H.: 76/39: see Katherine HEYMAN.

Khan: 20/94: see KUBLAI KHAN.

Khardas: 79/66:

Khieu: 13/58: see JAN CH'IU.

Khieu Tchi: 13/58: see JAN CH'IU.

Khitan (Khitans): 55/38, 39, 41, 42, 45; 56/47: (Kitan), a Mongol tribe to the north of China, near Korea. By AD 907 the Khitans had become very strong under the chieftain YÉ-LIU-APAOKI, who proclaimed himself emperor of an independent kingdom with the dynastic title of Liao ("iron"). The Khitans encroached on the Empire until China was divided at the Yellow River; KAÏ FONG became the capital of the Empire, and PEIPING became for the first time a metropolis and the Khitan capital.

Kiang: 53/18; 54/27; 55/40; 56/50, 53; 74/3: the YANGTZE river. Present day maps make no distinction between the Kiang (or Blue River) and the Yangtze; formerly, the upper reaches of the river, as far as the lake of Tungting Hu (in Hunan province) were known as the Kiang, and the river from the lake to its mouth on the East China Sea was called the Yangtze.

Ki, Uncle: 53/11: (Ki Tzŭ) fl. BC 1153, the uncle of Emperor CHEOU-SIN and his first minister; a man of true merit.

Kiang-nan: 56/54; 58/68: (Chiang-nan), an old province of China,
    roughly the area of the present provinces of Anhwei and Kiangsu.
Kiang-ping: 57/60: (Chiang Ping) d. AD 1521, a military adventurer
    who became the favorite of Emperor OU-TSONG. He corrupted
    the emperor by providing him with pleasures and, in 1520, at-
    tempted to murder him. After Ou-tsong's death Kiang-ping was
    ambushed and killed by order of Emperor CHI-TSONG; his entire
    family was also killed and his property confiscated.
Kian King: 56/53: prob. error for NANKING (See: Mailla, Histoire
    Générale, X, 4).
Kiao-Chan: 53/8: (Chiao-shan), a mountain in the district of Chung-
    pu, in the province of SHENSI.
Kiao-hoang: 60/76, 78: (Ch) Kiao-hoa-hoang (Chiao-hwa-huang):
    the sovereign pontiff of the prosperous religion; (the Pope of the
    Roman Catholic Church).
Kiassé: 56/50: Kia-ssé-tao (Kai Ssŭ-tao) fl. AD 1273, a minister
    and military officer under Emperor LI-TSONG. He made a se-
    cret treaty with KUBLAI KHAN in 1259, representing the emperor
    as willing to pay a tribute to the Mongols to insure peace. Kublai
    accepted the treaty and turned his troops north, but Kia-ssé-tao
    attacked the rear of the Mongol troops. For this treachery,
    Kublai vowed to ruin the SUNG dynasty. Kia-ssé-tao was minister
    to two other emperors: Tu Tsung (reign: 1265-67) and K'ung Ti
    (reign: 1275-76). His attempts to deal with the Mongols, either
    by diplomacy or armed force, never seemed to do the Sung much
    good. He died disgraced.
Kia-Y: 54/23: (Kia I) fl. BC 178, member of the court of HIAO-OUEN-
    TI and head of the office of tax collection.
Ki-chan: 53/17: (Ki-shan), a mountain in China which was destroyed
    by the earthquakes that appeared as evil omens during the reign
    of YEOU-OUANG; the mountain was said to be the cradle of Yeou's
    family.
Kieï-kou: 54/32: (Chieh-ku), a barbarian tribe, obviously European,
    to the west of China; these people had red hair and blue eyes, they
    were tall and had a martial air. "The such like had never been
    seen in China before."
Kien: 56/49: see KIEN-TCHÉOU.
Kien: 61/84: see KIEN LONG.
Kien Long: 61/[84], 85: (Ch'ien Lung) (reign: 1736-1795), fourth son
    of Emperor YONG-TCHING. He was an excellent administrator
    and is often compared to his grandfather, KANG-HI. After ten
    years of reorganizing the government, Kien-long put down a re-
    volt of the aborigines in W China, forced Burma and Nepal to pay
    tribute, established Chinese supremacy over Tibet, and main-
    tained friendly relations with western nations. The emperor was
    an indefatigable poet and published a total of 33,950 pieces; his
    work is very correct, but rather mediocre. Under his patronage,
    historical works, encyclopedias, and library catalogues were
    printed.
Kien-ouen: 57/57: see KIEN-OUEN-TI.
[Kien-ouen-ti]: 54/30: (Ch'ien Wĕn Ti) (reign: 550-52), a puppet

emperor set on the throne by ambitious nobles who needed a
prince of the royal blood to head the Empire; but Kien-ouen-ti's
usefulness was soon over and he was murdered.

[Kien-ouen-ti]: 57/57: (Ch'ien Wên Ti) (reign: 1399-1403), second
emperor of the MING dynasty and grandson of HONG-VOU. He
was a weak emperor and unable to deal with the rebellions of his
uncle the Prince of Yen, fourth son of Hong-vou. In 1403 the
Prince of Yen took Nanking, the capital. Kien-ouen-ti was about
to kill himself, when he was told of a chest which Hong-vou left
to be opened in such an emergency; in the chest were the dress
of a Buddhist priest, a diploma, a razor, and money. Kien-ouen-
ti, dressed as a Buddhist monk, escaped to a monastery in
SZECHWAN, where he lived for 35 years until he was discovered
during the reign of YNG-TSONG. The Prince of Yen took the
throne, ruling under the name YONG-LO.

[Kien-tchéou]: 56/49: (Ch'ien-ch'ou), a large town in SZECHWAN
province.

Kien Ti: 57/57: see KIEN-OUEN-TI.

Kientsong: 58/68: see TCHANG-HIEN-TCHONG.

Kieou: 53/12: Kieou-heou (Chiu Hou) c. BC 1147, a noble serving
Emperor CHEOU-SIN. His daughter disapproved of the evil emperor and his concubine, TAN-KI, so they had her killed,
quartered, and served up to her father for dinner.

Ki-kié: 54/21: (Chi Chieh) fl. BC 279, commander of the forces of
the Prince of Yen.

Kimball, Dexter: 38/37: 1865-1955?, economist and writer; author
of Industrial Economics (1929).

Kimmerian lands: 1/3: land of the mythical Cimmerians; it lies at
the entrance of hell and is always shrouded in darkness of mist
and cloud. (See: Odyssey, XI, 14-19).

Kin: 55/45, 46, 47; 56/48; 58/67: (Chin), a Tartar tribe formerly
known as the NUTCHÉ. In 1114 AKOUTA, chieftain of the Nutché,
proclaimed himself an emperor and gave the name of Kin ("gold")
to his dynasty. The Kin dynasty lasted 1115-1234.

[King]: 24/113: see CHARLES VII of France.

King: 30/148: see PEDRO I of Portugal.

King: 34/16: see LOUIS XVIII of France.

King: 41/55: see LOUIS XVI of France.

King: 41/55; 65/117, 119; 69/151: see LOUIS XVI of France.

King: 65/124: see GUSTAVUS III of Sweden.

King: 66/131: see JAMES I of England.

King: 66/131: see JAMES II of England.

King: 67/136: see CHARLES I of England.

King: 69/150: see GEORGE III of England.

King: 77/51: prob. VICTOR EMANUEL.

king, the: 54/22: see SHIH CHING and SHU CHING.

King of England: 68/148: see GEORGE III.

King of Etruria: 44/20: see LOUIS, Duke of Parma.

King of Khitan: 55/42: see YÉ-LIU-LONG-SIU.

King of Korea: 58/67: see YINDSOO HIENWUN.

King of Naples: 32/9: see FERDINAND I.

King of Ragona: 8/28; 9/35: see ALFONSO V, King of Aragon.
King of Rome: 34/16: see François Charles Joseph NAPOLEON.
King of Sardinia: 32/9: see VICTOR AMADEUS III.
King of Spain: 32/9: see CHARLES IV.
King of Spain: 68/147: see CHARLES III.
King of the Franks: 68/141: see LOUIS XVI of France.
"King Otreus, of Phrygia,/ That king is my father.": 23/109; [25/119]:
    from Homeric Hymn V, To Aphrodite, 111-112.
King: 62/94; 69/153: Rufus, 1755-1827, American statesman, mem-
    ber of the CONTINENTAL CONGRESS (1784-87) and of the U. S.
    Senate (1789-96), minister to Great Britain (1796-1804), again
    U. S. Senator (1813-25). He was a strong supporter of HAMILTON.
King-Ho: 53/15: (King or Ching), river of China, rises in NE Kansu
    province, N central China, and flows to the Wei river in central
    SHENSI.
King Kong: 53/18: (Ching Kung) d. BC 578, the Prince of Tçin (Ch'in)
    and a powerful warrior.
King Kong: 53/19: (Ching Kung) 547-489, the Duke of Tsi.
King Ouang: 53/19: see KING WANG.
King St.: 62/88: a street in Boston, Massachusetts.
Kingtcheou: 56/47: (Ching-ch'ou), the capital city and seventh de-
    partment of SHENSI province.
King Ti: 57/58: (Ching Ti) (reign: 1450-57), came to the throne after
    his brother, YNG-TSONG was captured by the Mongol invaders;
    King-ti regarded his position as a permanent one and did not
    wish to give it up when his brother was released by general YU-
    KIEN. But before he could establish the succession upon his son,
    King-ti died and Yng-tsong returned to the throne.
King Wang: 53/19: (Ching Wang) (reign: 519-475), emperor during
    the major portion of the life of CONFUCIUS; he was known as the
    "Reverential.
Kin Lusiang: 56/48: (Chin Li-hsiang) 1232-1303, a scholar at the
    court of the SUNG; after the fall of the Southern Sung dynasty in
    1280, he retired to Mt. Jen where he collected many disciples.
    He wrote a history of early China and many commentaries on the
    Classics.
Kio-feou-hien: 53/8: (Chüo-fou-hsien), near the city of Yen-chou-fu
    in SHANTUNG province.
[Kiong-tchéou]: 56/49: (Chiung-ch'ou), a large town in SZECHWAN
    province.
Kipling: 82/104: Rudyard, 1865-1939, the English writer.
Kirké: 39/44; 74/15: (Gr) CIRCE. (See: Appendix A).
Kirkh: 39/44: see KIRKÉ.
Kitson: 77/51: Arthur, 1860-1937, British writer, interested in
    Social Credit.
Klab, de: 68/142: see Johann KALB.
Klages: 75/28: Charles, 19th century French composer and guitarist.
Knecht gegen Knecht: 76/41: (Ger) Vassal against vassal.
Knower: 37/36: Benjamin, fl. 1827, friend of Martin VAN BUREN,
    active in New York State politics.
Knox: 78/59: Philander Chase, 1853-1921, American political leader,

member of the U. S. Senate (1904-09; 1917-21); one of the opposition to the entry of the U. S. into the League of Nations.

Koba, Kumrad: 74/23; 84/118: see Joseph STALIN. (Koba is what
Stalin was called as a boy in Georgia; it means "the Bear"; Kumrad is borrowed from E. E. Cummings' poem No Thanks).

Koen: 55/42: (Kun) fl. BC 2297, Earl of Ch'ung and father of the
Great YU. He was minister of works under Emperor YAO and
was appointed to drain the Empire after the great overflow of the
HOANG-HO in 2295. He worked for nine years and accomplished
little, so in 2286 his son was appointed to the task; after another
nine years, Yu succeeded.

Kohinoor: 77/52: Koh-i-noor, the famous Indian diamond, now among
the British crown jewels.

Kokka: 74/11: Urquell, "ex-diplomat, ex-imperial staff officer."
(See: Guide to Kulchur, 83).

Kolschitzky: 48/34: Georges François Koltschitzky de Szombor, fl.
1683, an interpreter for a commercial company of the East who
was employed to spy on the Turkish forces during the siege of
Vienna (1683). As payment he was granted a patent to open the
first coffee house in Vienna and was given a quantity of coffee
found in the Turkish camp.

Kong: 53/16: see KONG-OUANG.

Kong: 54/31: see KONG-TI.

Kong: 56/49: see KIONG-TCHÉOU.

Kong: 58/65: see KONG-YEOU.

[Kong-ouang]: 53/16: (Kung Wang) (reign: 946-34), sixth emperor
of the CHOU dynasty.

Kongpei: 56/52: Kongpésouï (Kungpêsui) fl. AD 1354, an officer in
the imperial troops under Emperor CHUNTI.

Kong-Tchang: 13/59: see KUNG YEH CHANG.

[Kong-ti]: 54/31: (Kung Ti) (reign: 618-19), last emperor of the
Soui dynasty. Depressed by rebellion and the coming end of his
dynasty, Kong-ti took to drink; he killed his ministers, for he
feared rebellion, and was himself murdered.

Kong Yeou: 58/65: Kong-yeou-té (Kung Yeou-tê) fl. AD 1633, a rebel
against the MING dynasty who joined forces with the Manchu leader TAÏ-TSONG.

Königsberg: 51/45: town, NW Prussia; residence of Immanuel KANT.

Koré: 3/11; 17/78; [74/20; 76/35; 79/68]; 83/111: (Gr) Daughter; a
reference to PERSEPHONE. (See Appendix A).

Korea: [54/32; 55/45; 56/53]; 58/62, 63, [67, 68].

Kosouth: 38/39: Ferencz Lajos Akos Kossuth, 1841-1914, Hungarian
statesman, leader of the Independence Party.

[Ko-tsé-hing]: 56/54: (Kuo Tzŭ-hsing) d. AD 1355, one of the more
successful rebels who arose during the reign of Emperor CHUNTI;
he captured Anhwei province and proclaimed himself generalis-
simo. His nephew, TCHU-YUEN-TCHANG, joined him for a
time, but later left to form an independent rebellion of his own.

Kouang Ou: 54/26: Kouang-ou-ti (Kuang Wu Ti) (reign: 25-58), first
emperor of the After HAN dynasty. His reign was a series of
wars, for there were rebellions within the Empire and Tartars

attacking from without. Kouang-ou-ti was a successful warrior and also had sympathy for scholars and literary men.

Koublai: 55/45: see KUBLAI KHAN.

Kou-choui: 54/31: (Ku-shui), a river in SHANTUNG province.

Koué: 55/41: (Ch) (kue): the constellation ANDROMEDA.

Koué-fei: 54/34: see YANG-KOUÉ-FEI.

Kouei: 59/71: (Kuei or Kuei Wang) d. AD 1662. About 1646 he was proclaimed "last" emperor of the MING dynasty and set up a government in the southern provinces. However, the Manchus were determined to destroy all Ming power, and Kouei was soon in flight, pursued by the armies of OU-SAN-KOUEI. In 1662 Kouei retreated to Yunnan province and, sure of no mercy from the Manchus, strangled himself with a silk cord.

Kouémen: 57/57: (Kue-men), a gate of the city of Nanking, or perhaps the underground passage through which Emperor KIEN-OUEN-TI escaped from Nanking in AD 1403.

Kouetchin: 56/53: see FANG-KOUÉ-TCHIN.

Koulihan: 54/32: Kou-li-kan (Ku-li-kan), a nation to the north-west of China and north of the Caspian Sea.

Kouo-tsé-y: 54/35: (Kuo Tzŭ-i) 697-781, one of the most famous Chinese generals; he served four emperors: HIUEN-TSONG, SOU-TSONG, TAÏ-TSONG, and TÉ-TSONG. His campaigns against the Tartars were successful, and he proved an able governor of various cities and provinces; unlike most officials, his loyalty to the Empire was never questioned. His name is mentioned in the famous NESTORIAN tablet.

Koupelin: 60/74: see Philippe COUPLET.

Kourbang tourha: 58/66: (Kur-bang-turha), a town in Inner Mongolia.

K.P.: 80/91: Kitchen Police, U.S. army term.

Kreffle, Mrs.: 28/134: a pseudonym for a Mrs. Kraft whom Pound knew in Madrid (1906).

Krupp: 38/41: Alfred, 1812-87, German industrialist, head of the Krupp Works at Essen and began the manufacture of ordinance there; his type of breech-loading rifle was adopted by the Prussian army in 1861.

Krupp: 38/41: the Krupp Works at Essen, Germany.

[Krupp von Bohlen und Halback, Gustav]: 38/41: 1870-1950, husband of Bertha Krupp, elder daughter of Friedrich Alfred Krupp. During World War I he was president of the Council of Trustees of Krupp's.

Kuai, Mt.: 56/47:

Kuan Chung: 80/77: Kuan Tzŭ, 7th century BC, a statesman of the principality of CHI; although he increased the political prestige of his kingdom, CONFUCIUS considered that he did so without raising its moral status. (See: Analects III, xxii; XIV, xviii).

Kuanon: 74/6, 13, 21; 77/50; 81/97: prob. (Ch) Kuan-yin, (Jap) Kwannon: Chinese goddess of mercy.

Kublai Khan: 18/80; [20/94; 55/45]; 56/50, 51, 52, 53, 54: 1214-94. In 1260 he became emperor of the Mongols and in 1280 emperor of all China, giving the dynasty he founded the name YUEN. Kublai led few military expeditions after he became emperor of

China, and his reign was generally one of peace. In 1285 paper
money in the form of bank-notes was made current. Kublai was
often under the influence of his ministers, particularly AHAMA
and SANG-KO.

Ku ching: 58/63: see TCHANG-KU-TCHING.

Kujak: 56/49: (Kuyak Khan) (reign: 1242-48), a Mongol king, son of
OGOTAI KHAN, who held a magnificent court in Tartary and led
his forces as far as eastern Europe.

Kukano: 56/49: Koukanor (Kuku-nor) prob. the area in W China known
today as Ch'ing-hai province, or Kuku-nor province.

Kumasaka: 74/20; 79/63: the ghost in Ujinobu's Noh play, Kumasaka.
(See: Translations, 249-255).

Kung: 13/58, 59, 60; 52/4; 53/18, 19, 20; 54/31, 34; 55/40, 44; 56/49,
52; 61/80; 67/137; 77/46: (K'ung) see CONFUCIUS.

Kung-fu-tseu: 53/18, 19, 20; 54/22, 30; 55/39; 56/51; 57/58, 59; 58/66;
60/76; 76/32; 77/42: (K'ung Fu Tzŭ), see CONFUCIUS.

Kung-Sun Chow: 83/110: (Kung-sun Ch'ow), Book II of the works of
MENCIUS.

[Kung Yeh Ch'ang]: 13/59: a son-in-law of CONFUCIUS. (See: Analects V, i).

Ku'shoot: 38/39: see Ferencz Lajos Akos KOSOUTH.

Ku Tchang: 58/63: see TCHANG-KU-TCHING.

Kuthera: 79/69: see CYTHERA.

kylin: 77/43: prob. variant of kaolin(e) [Ch: kao-ling] an extremely
pure white clay, used in the formation of porcelain paste.

Kyrie eleison: 79/67: (Gr) Lord have mercy.

L

L, Tom: 74/22: see Thomas Edward LAWRENCE.

la bella Torre: 74/14: (It) the beautiful tower.

la bonne soupe fait le bon soldat: 80/82: (Fr) good soup makes a good
soldier.

La Cara: amo: 76/37: (It) the dear one: (L) I love.

Lacedaemon: [11/50]; 26/123: Sparta, the ancient city of the Peloponnesus, Greece.

lacking that treasure of honesty/ which is the treasure of states: 77/48:
from The Great Digest, X, xxiii.

La Clara a Milano: 74/3: (It) Clara (PETACCI) at Milan.

La Cour de Londres éludera autant et aussi long qu'elle peut/ l'aveu
direct/ ou indirect de l'indépendence des Etats Unis: 69/150:
(Fr) the Court of London will avoid as long as it can/ the ad-
mission direct/ or indirect of the independence of the United
States.

ladies from West Virginia: 28/134: Miss Ada and Miss Ida Mapel,
American sisters from West Virginia; they were residents at
the boarding house in Spain at which Pound stayed on his trip
in 1906.

Ladro: 74/16: (It) thief, rogue; prob. reference to a cat in the DTC,
Pisa.

Lady de X: 80/79: prob. Lady Augusta Gregory, 1852-1932, the Irish
poet and playwright.

Lady Lucan: 65/124: poss. Margaret Bingham, Countess of Lucan,
d. 1814; most famous for her paintings, celebrated by Horace
Walpole.

l'aer tremare: 74/22: (It) the air trembles. (See: Sonnets and Ballate of Guido Cavalcanti, 28).

Lafayette: 31/5; 68/142, 144; 69/151, 153: Marie Joseph Paul Yves
Roch Gilbert du Motier, Marquis de Lafayette, 1757-1834,
French statesman and officer; served as major general in the
Continental army (1777); supported American interests in France.
In his service in Virginia, Lafayette was associated with Daniel
MORGAN of the Virginia riflemen.

Lafitte: 65/117: Château Laffitte, a wine of Bordeaux.

la France dixneuvième: 74/13: (Fr) nineteenth century France.

Lakedaemon: 11/50: see LACEDAEMON.

Lalage: 50/43: common name of courtesans, used as term of endear-
ment. (See Horace; Odes, I, 22, 23).

lama: 56/52: 58/64, 66; 60/74, 75: Tibetan priests; introduced into
the palace of CHUNTI in 1353.

L'ami de tout le monde: 34/20: (Fr) everybody's friend.

[Lamont, Thomas William]: 19/86, 87; 40/48(?): 1870-1948, American banker; member of the firm of J. P. Morgan and Co.

Lampascus: 26/124: Lampsacus, ancient Greek colony in Mysia on
the Hellespont.

Lancaster: 80/94: the House of Lancaster; the English Royal House
derived from John of Gaunt, who was created Duke of Lancaster
in 1362; Lancastrian kings were Henry IV, HENRY V and HENRY VI.

Landon: 77/51: Alfred Mossman, 1887-   , American business man
    and politician; governor of Kansas (1933-37); Republican nomi-
    nee for President of the United States (1936).
Landor: 82/101: Walter Savage, 1775-1864, the English poet and
    prose writer.
Lane: 74/6: DTC, Pisa.
Lang: 56/49: see LANG-TCHÉOU.
Lang-tchéou: 54/34: (Lang-ch'ou), a city in Honan province, China.
[Lang-tchéou]: 56/49: (Lang-ch'ou), the modern city of Paoning,
    Szechwan province, China.
Languor has cried unto languor: 29/143: poss. variation of Psalms
    42, 7: Deep calleth unto deep.
Lanier: 77/49: Sidney, 1842-1881, the American poet and musician;
    among his better poems is The Symphony, in which he discusses
    the relationship between trade and human values.
Lanvin: 74/13: the Parisian dress designer.
Lao: 58/64: see LAOIST.
Laoist: 57/59; 58/64: a follower of LAO-TSE, founder of Taoism.
Laomedon: 80/84, 85: the legendary king of Troy for whom
    POSEIDON built the walls of Troy; the god was cheated of his
    pay and in revenge sent a sea monster to ravage the land.
"Laomedon, Ahi, Laomedon": 80/84: from T. Sturge Moore, The
    Rout of the Amazons.
Lao Tse: 54/28: (Lao-tzŭ), c. 604-531, one of China's most famous
    teachers, popularly regarded as the founder of the Taoist sect.
    His teachings centered on returning good for evil and looking
    forward to a higher form of life; in his interpretation of Tao, the
    "Way", he professed to have found the clue to all things human
    and divine. Central to his teaching is the Doctrine of Inaction,
    which states, "Do nothing, and all things will be done." Later,
    pure Taoism became mixed with magic, astrology, alchemy
    and the search for an elixir of life.
la pastorella dei suini: 76/38: (It) the little shepherdess of the hogs.
la persecution contre M. Van Berckel/ et ses complices/ ...de ne
    pas presser votre depart/ les affaires...crise...temps pour-
    rait/ but des Anglais outre celui d'amuser la république d'Hol-
    land: 68/148: (Fr) the persecution against M. VAN BERCKEL/
    and his associates/ ...not to rush your departure/ business...
    crisis...time could/ object of the English beyond that of amus-
    ing the Republic of Holland. (See: John Adams, Works, VII,
    334-336).
la qual manda fuoco: 63/99: (It) which sends fire. (See: Cavalcanti,
    Donna mi prega).
l'ara sul rostro: 76/34: (It) the altar on the rostrum.
Larmann, Maxy: 16/71: an invented name of no particular reference.
La Rochefoucauld, Duke de: 31/5; 65/124; [78/59]; 81/96: La Roche-
    foucauld-Liancourt, Duc François Alexandre Frédéric de, 1747-
    1827, French politician and philanthropist; member of the States-
    General (1789).
La Rupe: 76/31: La Rupe Tarpeia, a wineshop in Rome, originally
    near the supposed Tarpeian Rock, but now moved.

la scalza: Io son' la luna: 76/31: (It) the barefooted one: I am the
    moon.
La Serra: 11/49: prob. a castle, taken from Sigismondo MALATESTA
    by the peace terms imposed by PIUS II (c. 1460).
Latin: 59/73; 71/166; 76/33; 77/51, the language.
Latio: 78/57: (L) LATIUM.
Latium: 9/41; 78/56, [57]: ancient country on the Tyrrhenian Sea,
    Italy.
Latour: 65/117: Château Latour, a wine of Bordeaux.
lattittzo: 22/106: (It) lattizzo: the skin of a suckling animal, similar
    to ermine.
laudate pueri: 43/11: (L) praise (God), boys.
laudatores temporis acti: 15/64: (L) admirers of bygone days. (See:
    Horace, Ars Poetica, V, 173).
[Laurance, John]: 69/153: 1750-1810, Revolutionary soldier and
    statesman; member of the House of Representatives (1789-93);
    U. S. Senator (1796-1800); active supporter of HAMILTON's
    monetary policies.
Laurencin, Marie: 80/90: 1885-   , the French painter.
Laurens: 68/142, 147: Henry, 1724-92, American Revolutionary
    statesman; member of the Second CONTINENTAL CONGRESS
    and its president (1777-78); sent (1780) as U. S. commissioner
    to the Netherlands; was captured by the British and imprisoned
    in the Tower of London until exchanged for Cornwallis (1781).
    With Laurens was captured a copy of the U. S.-Dutch treaty,
    which England used as a pretext for war against the Netherlands.
Laurentius: 30/149: reference to Lorenzo de' MEDICI, founder of
    the Laurentian Library in Florence.
Lauro: 21/96: see Lorenzo de' MEDICI.
[Laval, Pierre]: 84/117: 1883-1945, premier of Vichy France (from
    April 1942).
la vecchia sotto S. Pantaleone: 76/30: (It) the old lady under ST.
    PANTALEONE.
la vieille de Candide: 74/16: (Fr) Candide's old woman. (See:
    Voltaire, Candide, XI-XII).
Lawes: 81/97, 98: Henry, 1596-1662, the English musician and com-
    poser; noted for his masques and airs for voice.
Lawrence, J.: 69/153: see John LAURANCE.
[Lawrence, Thomas Edward]: 74/22: Lawrence of Arabia, 1888-
    1935, the British archaeologist, soldier and writer.
Lawrence, W.: 74/22: William George Lawrence, 1889-1915, young-
    er brother of T. E. LAWRENCE; Will Lawrence invited Pound
    to St. John's College, Oxford, to speak on Provençal poetry.
    (See: Sir Ernest Baker, The Home Letters of T. E. Lawrence
    and His Brothers, 393, 395-397).
Lazarus, John Baptiste: 68/143: see John Baptiste Lazarus de The-
    veneau de FRANCY.
League of Cambrai: 51/46: 1508-1510, a league of the forces of Maxi-
    milian I, Louis XII of France, Pope Julius II, Ferdinand V of
    Aragon and several Italian towns against Venice; the League
    was temporarily successful.

Léang: 54/30; 57/59: (Liang), the tenth dynasty (502-557).

Léang-ki: 54/27: (Liang Ki) d. AD 159, uncle of Emperor Han Chung
    Ti (reign: 145-146); Léang-ki and the queen dowager, Léang,
    became great powers in the Empire. Léang-ki served as prime
    minister under HAN-HOUON-TI; he sent poisoned cakes to
    those who insulted him, and was not very well liked. Finally
    Han-houon-ti sent three thousand men to put Léang-ki to death;
    Léang-ki saw what was up, and ate one of his own cakes. All
    the members of his house were slain and his treasure became
    the emperor's.

Leao: 55/45: (Liao), the name of the dynasty of the KHITAN Tartars;
    the dynasty lasted from 907-1125, during which time the Khitans
    controlled much of northern China from their capital at Peiping.
    After the capture of Peiping by the KIN Tartars, the house of
    Leao was diminished to a minor dynasty known as the Western
    Liao (1125-1168).

le beau monde gouverne: 77/42: (Fr) society governs.

Leber: 80/81, 82: prob. Albert Leber, a confectioner in Notting Hill,
    London, c. 1915.

Leboeuf: 38/41: Edmond, 1809-88, French soldier and statesman,
    minister of war (1869-70); marshal of France (1870); disgraced
    in the Franco-Prussian War and retired.

le bonhomme Staline: 74/23: (Fr) simple STALIN.

Le corps des négociants de cette ville/ souhaitant joindre leurs accla-
    mations a ceux de toute la nation/ J. Nollet, Schiedam/ 'On m'a
    dit que ces Messieurs de Schiedam/ donnent ce repas de cent
    couverts/ et qu'il y aura beaucoup de personnes de Rotterdam':
    69/150 -151: (Fr) the businessmen of this city/ wishing to add
    their acclamations to those of the whole nation/ J. NOLLET,
    SCHIEDAM,/ 'I have been told that these gentlemen of Schiedam/
    are giving this repast for á hundred people/ and that there will
    be many people from Rotterdam.' (See: John Adams, Works,
    VII, 576).

le donne ei cavalieri: 20/95: (It) the women and the gentlemen.

Lee: 37/33: William, American consul at Bordeaux during the Pres-
    idency of MONROE (1817-25).

Lee, A.: 65/118; 68/143; 70/158: Arthur, 1740-92, American diplo-
    mat; appointed in 1776 by the CONTINENTAL CONGRESS as one
    of the three commissioners to negotiate a treaty with France;
    he became suspicious of his associates, Benjamin FRANKLIN
    and Silas DEANE, and circulated charges against them. After
    the treaty was signed (1778), Deane was recalled; he chaíged in
    return that Lee did not have the confidence of the French for-
    eign minister. Lee was then recalled in 1779. Lee served in
    the Continental Congress (1781-85), was a member of the
    Treasury Board (1784-89), and was among those who opposed
    the adoption of the Constitution.

Lee, Frank: 31/6: Francis Lightfoot, 1734-97, American statesman;
    member of the CONTINENTAL CONGRESS (1775-79), signer of
    the DECLARATION of Independence.

[Leopold II]: 33/11; 44/17, 21; 50/40, 41; 52/3: 1747-92, Holy Roman
    Emperor (1790-92). As Grand Duke of Tuscany (1765-90), he
    was Leopold I.
[Leopold II]: 50/43: 1797-1870, Grand Duke of Tuscany (1824-59);
    was son of FERDINAND III of Tuscany; grandson of LEOPOLD
    II, Holy Roman Emperor.
Leopold, Duke: 52/3: see LEOPOLD II, Holy Roman Emperor.
Leopold, Peter: 50/40: see LEOPOLD II, Holy Roman Emperor.
Leopoldine: 50/41: reference to the Leopoldine reforms, carried out
    by LEOPOLD II, Holy Roman Emperor, who as Leopold I of
    Tuscany reorganized the Tuscan government, bringing about
    extensive changes in taxation, criminal punishment, and church
    affairs.
Leopoldo: 50/43: (It) LEOPOLD II of Tuscany.
Leopoldo, Pietro: 44/17, 21; 50/41: see LEOPOLD II, Holy Roman
    Emperor.
Leou Lean: 56/53: see TCHIN-YEOU-LEANG.
Le Paradis n'est pas artificiel: 74/16; 76/38; 77/46; 83/106: (Fr)
    Paradise is not artificial. (Poss. variation of Baudelaire, Les
    Paradis Artificiels).
le/ personnel manque: 62/90: (Fr) the personnel is lacking.
le plus grand t... de ce pays-ci/ entêté comme une: 65/123: (Fr)
    the biggest t... of this country/ stubborn as a.
Le Portel: 80/93; 82/101: French fishing port on the Strait of Dover.
Lesbia: 74/6: Clodia, wife of the consul Metellus Celer; a notorious
    profligate celebrated by Catullus, who referred to her as Lesbia.
lèse majesty: 44/21: (Fr) lèse-majesté: high treason.
les gradins/ quarante-trois rangées en calcaire: [4/16]; 12/53;
    [29/145; 78/59]: (Fr) the steps/ forty-three tiers made of lime-
    stone.
Les hommes ont je ne sais quelle peur étrange/ ...de la beauté: 80/89:
    (Fr) men have I don't know what strange fear/ ...of beauty.
Les membres de la Société Bourgeoise/ de Leeuwarde: 69/152: (Fr)
    the members of the SOCIÉTÉ BOURGEOISE of LEEUWARDE.
les moeurs passent et la douleur reste./ "En casque de crystal rose
    les baladines": [78/58]; 80/82: (Fr) customs go and pain re-
    mains./ "In pink crystal helmets, the mountebanks."
les six potences/ Absouldre, que tous nous vueil absoudre: 74/5: (Fr)
    the six gallows/ Absolve, may you absolve us all. (See: Villon,
    Epitaphe de Villon: Mais Priez Dieu que tous nous veuille ab-
    souedre).
Lesterplatz: 80/79: (Ger) LEICESTER SQUARE.
Let backe and side go bare: 80/93: from the 16th century lyric Jolly
    Good Ale and Old, attributed to William Stevenson.
Le Temps: 38/42: the newspaper in Paris.
Lethe: 74/27; 77/50: the river of forgetfulness in Hades.
"Let her go back to the ships...": 2/6: from Iliad, III, 158-160.
Letizia: 44/22: Maria Letizia Ramolino, 1750-1836, mother of
    NAPOLEON.
Levant: 26/122: the name given to that region, from Egypt to Turkey,
    along the E shores of the Mediterranean.

Le vieux commode en acajou: 7/25: (Fr) la vieille...: the old ma-
     hogany chest.
Levine: 28/139: Charles A., American pilot who, as a novice flyer,
     crossed the Atlantic in 1927; his plane, the Columbia, was al-
     most wrecked during the crossing, but his luck held and he and
     his co-pilot reached Europe.
Leviticus: 74/12, 18; 76/32: the Book of Leviticus in the Bible.
Lévy: 20/89: Emil, 1855-1918, German philologist; author of Pro-
     vençal supplement dictionaire (8 vol., 1892-1925).
[Lévy-Bruhl]: 38/39: Lucien, 1857-1939, French philosopher, his-
     torian and anthropologist.
Lewinesholme: 35/23:
Lewis, P. Wyndham: 78/57; 80/84, 85: Percy Wyndham, 1884-1957,
     the British writer and painter.
Lewis, Sinc.: 84/116: Sinclair, 1885-1953, the American novelist.
Lexington: 33/11; 50/40; 62/90; 64/105; 65/122; 66/127; 67/136: see
     LEXINGTON AND CONCORD, battles of.
[Lexington and Concord, battles of]: 33/11; 50/40; 62/90; 64/105;
     65/122; 66/127; 67/136: the opening engagements of the Ameri-
     can Revolution, 19 April 1775.
Lexington Avenue: 74/25; 80/86: the street in New York.
lex Rhodi: 46/28; 78/57: (L) the law of RHODES.
Lex salica! lex Germanica: 42/3: (L) the SALIC LAW! the German-
     ic law.
Leyden: 62/92: the industrial town of S Holland province, SW Nether-
     lands.
Leyden Gazette: 62/92: a Dutch newspaper, published in LEYDEN,
     in 1782.
Li: 54/24: see LI-KOUANG.
Li: 56/54: see LI-SIANG-KOUE.
li: 57/58; [58/65; 59/72]: (Ch) a measure of length, amounting to
     approximately 1890 feet.
Liang: 53/18: see SIANG-TCHONG.
libeccio: 74/16: (It) the south wind.
Liberans et vinculo ab omni liberatos: 29/141: (L) And freeing from
     every chain those who have been liberated.
Libertatem Amicitiam Fidem: 62/93: (L) Liberty, Friendship,
     Loyalty. (See: John Adams, Works, I, 432-33; Adams' motto
     was Libertatem, amicitiam, fidem retinebis).
Liberty Tree: 64/105: an elm which stood on Washington Street in
     Boston, on which unpopular persons were hung in effigy during
     the STAMP ACT agitation.
libraio: 24/114: (It) bookseller.
Library: 16/71: see LONDON LIBRARY.
libris septem...summam, scutorum: 43/12: (L) in seven books,
     the sum of crowns.
Li-Chan: 54/29: Liü-chan (Lu-shan), a mountain in Kiangsi province
     near Lake Po-yang; the residence of the scholar Lei-tsé-tsong
     (Lei Tzǔ-tsung), who refused to leave his mountain once he had
     seen to the courses of study at the academies founded by OUEN
     TI in AD 438. (See: Mailla, Histoire Générale, V, 44, 45).

Li-Chi: 54/31: (Li Shih) d. AD 623, daughter of Emperor KAO-TSOU;
    in 617 she raised an army and came to the aid of her father in
    his struggles to gain the Empire; her husband was Chai Shao, a
    general in the army of Kao-tsou.
Li-ching: 54/35: (Li Shêng) fl. AD 787, a captain in the imperial
    troops who had great success against the Tartars. In 787 it was
    discovered that he was having an affair with a daughter of Emperor
    SOU-TSONG. Li-ching became a remittance man in Kwangtung.
Li-Chun: 55/36: (Li Shun) 778-821, Chinese emperor, son of Emper-
    or TCHUN-TSONG, whom he succeeded in 806; ruled under the
    name HIEN-TSONG.
Lido: 48/37; 76/39: town on the N end of the island outside the La-
    goon of Venice.
Lido Excelsior: 80/87: hotel on the LIDO, Venice.
Lidya: 79/66: see Lydia YAVORSKA.
Lieou Ju: 55/44: (Liu Ju) fl. AD 1084, historian at the court of Em-
    peror CHIN-TSONG; one of those who helped SSÉ-MA-KOUANG
    compile the TSÉ-TCHI TONG-KIEN.
Lieou-kin: 57/[59], 60: (Liu Chin) d. AD 1510. He and seven other
    palace eunuchs conspired to gain control over the young Em-
    peror OU-TSONG by pandering to his tastes and enjoyments.
    So successful was the scheme that in 1508 the emperor decreed
    that all petitions had to pass through the hands of Lieou-kin.
    However, the emperor's uncle raised a rebellion and asked
    Lieou-kin's death as the price of peace. The emperor consent-
    ed to imprison the eunuch, but when great amounts of treasure
    were found in his house, the emperor ordered Lieou-kin's exe-
    cution.
[Lieou-ngan]: 54/24: (Liu An) fl. BC 130, Prince of HOAI-NAN; a
    leader of the literary revival during the reign of HAN-OU, al-
    though the Prince had little inclination toward the classics.
    (See: Mailla, Histoire Générale, III, 26).
Lieou-pang: 54/21, 22: (Liu Pang) 247-195, one of the two leaders of
    a revolt against the TSIN dynasty. It had been agreed that the
    first of the two generals to reach the capital should gain the
    principality of Tsin; Lieou-pang arrived first and Emperor TSE-
    YNG surrendered. However, the second general, HIANG-YU,
    was not satisfied with his bargain, and there were wars from
    206 to 202 between the two. In 202 Lieou-pang defeated Hiang-
    yu and became emperor, founding the HAN dynasty and taking
    the title of KAO-HOANG-TI.
Lieou Pi: 55/36: (Liu Pi) d. AD 806, a governor in SZECHWAN
    province who raised a rebellion because the territory under his
    control was not increased. Defeated in his first major battle
    against imperial troops, Lieou-pi, with all of his family, was
    sent to the capital and executed.
[Lieou-siuen]: 56/50: (Liu Hsüan) fl. AD 1286, the minister of
    KUBLAI KHAN who persuaded the emperor to give up his plans
    to conquer Japan.
Lieou-Tchin: 54/27: (Liu Chin) fl. AD 263, son of the Minor HAN
    emperor, Han Hou-chu (reign: 223-64).

Lieou-Tchi-Yuen: 55/39, 40(?): (Liu Chih-yüan) d. AD 948, a distinguished general and governor of SHANSI province under Emperor Chi Wang (reign: 934-37). When the emperor ordered
his troops to attack the KHITAN Tartars, Lieou-tchi-yuen refused, knowing the imperial troops could not withstand the
Khitans. After the Khitans withdrew from Kaifeng, the imperial capital, Lieou-tchi-yuen was proclaimed emperor by his
army. He ruled under the name Kao Tsu (reign: 947-48), and
founded the After HAN dynasty.

[Lieou-té]: 54/24; 84/116(?) (Liu Tê) fl. BC 130, Prince of HO-KIEN;
a leader of the literary revival during the reign of HAN-OU,
the Prince spent much money and effort to recover and restore the Chinese classics. (See: Mailla, Histoire Générale,
III, 26)

Lieou-Tsong: 54/28: (Liu Tsung) fl. AD 317, king of HAN.

Lieou-Y: 54/28: (Liu I) fl. AD 282, a highly respected advisor of
Emperor TÇIN-OU-TI.

Lieou-yu: 54/28: (Liu Yü) 356-422, the founder of the SUNG dynasty.
In 399 he enlisted in the imperial army and was given a command of seventy men; so able was he that by 416 he was made
commander-in-chief and Duke of SUNG. In 419 he caused Emperor TÇIN-NGAN to be strangled and set up the latter's brother, Chin Kung Ti, as emperor. After sixteen months, Chin
Kung Ti abdicated, and Lieou-yu took the throne with the title
KAO-TSOU.

Lieou-yu-y: 61/81: (Liu Yü-i) fl. AD 1725, an imperial examiner in
letters for the province of SHANSI; he dealt successfully with a
famine in his province and gained the approval of Emperor
YONG-TCHING.

Lieu: 57/59: see LIEOU-KIN.

Lieutenant Governor: 64/101: see Thomas HUTCHINSON.

[Lightfoot, Robert]: 1716-94, a loyalist of Rhode Island; judge of the
British Court of Vice-Admiralty for the Southern District of
North America.

Ligur' aoide: 20/89, 94: (Gr) a clear sweet song. (See: Appendix
A).

[Liguria]: 74/22: region along the NW coast of Italy from Tuscany
to France.

"like an arrow,...the precise definition": 77/46: from The Unwobbling Pivot, XIV, 5; and poss. from Analects, XIII, iii, 1-7.

Li-ké-Yong: 55/38: (Li K'o-yung) d. AD 908, a distinguished commander of the imperial troops. His campaigns against the Turfan invaders (a barbarian tribe in the province of Sinkiang, W
China) were so successful that Emperor Chao Tsung (reign:
889-905) made him Prince of TÇIN in 895.

Li Ki: 54/24; 61/82: (Li Chi) the Book of Rites compiled by the Elder
and Younger Tai (fl. 1st-2nd century BC) from documents said
to have come from CONFUCIUS and his disciples; the text was
often revised and not completed until the 2nd century BC.

Liki: 55/36: (Li Ki) fl. AD 807, a governor of a department in the
province of KIANG-NAN who accumulated and hoarded the

treasure of six departments; the emperor ordered that the money
be put back in circulation to stimulate commerce.

Li Kiang: 55/37: (Li Chiang) fl. AD 812, a minister of Emperor
HIEN-TSONG.

Li koen: 58/65: prob. Li-kieou-tching (Li-chiu-chêng), a large town
in N China.

Li-kouang: 54/24: (Li Kuang) fl. BC 144, a commander of the NW
frontier of China whose task it was to guard against the Tartar
tribes, or HIONG-NOU.

Likoue: 58/68: Li-koué-tching (Li Kue-cheng) fl. AD 1644, commander of Peiping. After the death of Emperor HOAI-TSONG, he
was forced to surrender the city to LI-TSE-TCHING, but he first
demanded permission to give the emperor and empress a full
imperial funeral.

Lilas, Les: 74/11: Closerie des Lilas, restaurant in Paris, at the
corner of Boulevard Saint-Michel and Boulevard des Montparnasse.

Lilibullero: 74/12: Lillibullero, a song mocking the Irish Catholics,
popular in England during the revolution of 1688; the whole song
itself.

Lili Marlene: 79/62: the most popular German war song of World
War II.

Limoges: 74/3: manufacturing and commercial city of Haute-Vienne
department, W central France.

Lindaraja: 74/25: prob. Lindaraxa, the Zegri princess in Gines
Perez de Hita's Guerras Civiles de Granada.

Lindhauer: 74/20: Gustave Landhauer, 1870-1919, German statesman;
his government lasted seven, not "less than five," days.

Ling Kong: 53/18: (Ling Kung) d. BC 608, Prince of TÇIN; "without
virtue, without sense, his heart turned naturally to evil." (See:
Mailla, Histoire Generale, II, 155).

Ling Ti: 54/28: see HAN-LING.

Lin hing: 53/15: Lü-hing, Chapter XXV of the SHU CHING. (See:
section 21 of Chapter XXV).

Linus: 74/6: Saint Linus; Pope (?67-76).

Lin-Yun: 55/36: (Lin Yün) fl. AD 806, a military officer serving
under the rebel LIEOU-PI. He objected to the rebellion of his
superior, and Lieou-pi ordered him to be beheaded; but Lin-yun
was so brave that he was given his freedom.

[Li-ouang]: 53/16: (Li Wang) (reign: 878-841), known as the "Stern
One." He was remorseless in his treatment of those who opposed him and was avaricious, always seeking money to carry
out his cruel plans. Finally his people rose in rebellion, and
Li-ouang fled to SHENSI.

Li-ouen: 56/56: Li-ouen-tchong (Li Wen-chung) d. AD 1384, one of
the best military officers serving Emperor HONG-VOU.

[Liou-ouang]: 55/39: (Liu Wang), imperial title of LI TSONGKOU.

Lipan: 58/62: (Li Pan) d. AD 1618, king of the Koreans.

Lipus, Don: 6/22: a son of Farinato de FARINATI.

Lir: 2/6: Mamannan mac Lir, a Celtic sea god.

Li Sao: 56/47; 58/68; [80/75]: prob. the long Chinese poem by Ch'ü
Yüan (343-290).

Li Saou: 80/75: see <u>LI SAO.</u>
Lisboa: 30/148: a district of Portugal; also Portuguese for LISBON.
Lisbon: 44/20: the capital of Portugal.
Lisbon: 69/153: a sweet, light-colored wine, produced in Estrema-
    dura and shipped from Lisbon, Portugal.
lisciate con lagrime/ politis lachrymis: 76/40: (It) smoothed with
    tears/ (L) with polished tears.
[Li-siang-kouế]: 56/54: (Li Hsiang-kuei) fl. AD 1355, a fighting
    companion of TCHU-YUEN-TCHANG.
Li-ssế: 54/21: (Li Ssŭ) d. BC 208, prime minister of Emperor TSIN-
    CHI. Li-ssế convinced the emperor that all the unrest in the
    kingdom was the result of scholarly research and writing;
    he also suggested that it might be nice if all history could
    be destroyed so that Tsin-chi could appear as the "first
    emperor" of China. All existing literature was ordered
    destroyed -- excepting only works on agriculture, medicine,
    and divination.
Lisses: 34/18: prob. text should read: ...from Europe, two Misses
    <u>(Wright)</u>. (See: John Quincy Adams, <u>Diary</u>, 330); poss. text
    should read: ... from Europe to U. S. (or <u>Uni</u>. Ss).
Li-ssế Yuen: 55/39: (Li Ssŭ-yüan) 866-934, the adopted son of LI-
    KÉ-YONG. Like his father, he was a brilliant general and did
    much to preserve the After TANG dynasty. At the death of his
    half-brother, LI-TSUN-HIU, he was proclaimed emperor by the
    army; he ruled under the name MING-TSONG.
Liszt: 28/135: Franz von, 1811-1886, the Hungarian composer.
Litse: 58/68, 69: see LI-TSÉ-TCHING.
[Li-tsé-tching]: 58/68, 69: (Li Tzŭ-ch'êng) 1606-45, a rebel against
    the MING dynasty. At the head of an army of brigands, he over-
    ran parts of Hupeh and Honan provinces (1640) and captured
    SHENSI province (1642). In 1644 he proclaimed himself first
    emperor of the Great Shun dynasty and marched on Peiping;
    the city fell and Emperor HOAÏ-TSONG killed himself. But
    OUSAN enlisted the aid of the MANCHUs and drove Li-tsé-tching
    out of Peiping. When Li-tsé-tching was slain in battle, the
    Manchus were left in control of China and established the
    Ch'ing dynasty (1644-1912).
Li Tsong: 56/50: (Li Tsung) (reign: 1225-1265), fifth emperor of the
    Southern SUNG dynasty. He broke his treaty with the MONGOLs
    and attacked them in 1234; thereafter his reign was one of al-
    most continual war with the Mongols.
Li Tsongkou: 55/39: (Li Ts'ung-k'o) 892-936, commanding general
    of the imperial guards who later (934) came to the throne as
    the fourth emperor of the After TANG dynasty, ruling under the
    name Liu Wang). (reign: .934-36). His dynasty fell to the
    KHITAN Tartars.
[Li-tsun-hiu]: 55/38, 39: (Li Ts'un-hsü) d. AD 926, the son of LI-
    KÉ-YONG. He overthrew the After LIANG dynasty, and in 923
    set himself up as the first emperor of the After TANG dynasty,
    ruling under the name Chuang Tsung (reign: 923-26). He
    waged successful wars against the KHITAN Tartars, regaining

the province of SZECHWAN for the Empire. Finally he gave
himself up to sensuality and was assassinated by an actor.

Litterae nihil sanantes: 33/11: (L) Literature curing nothing.

Little, A.: 80/71: DTC, Pisa.

Littleton: 63/98: Sir Thomas, ?1407-81, English jurist and writer
on the law. His work Tenures (1481 or 82) is the earliest printed treatise on English law; the text is the basis of COKE's commentary known as Coke upon Littleton.

Little Turtle: 71/162: Meche Cunnaqua, d. 1812, Chief of the Mohegan
Indians.

Litvinof: 52/3: Maxim Maximovich Litvinov, 1876-1951, the Russian
revolutionist and statesman.

Liu Ch'e: 7/25: Liu Chi, d. AD 1375, Chinese poet and painter.

Liu-Heou: 54/23: (Lu Hou) (reign: 187-179), the wife of KAO-HOANG-
TI. She dominated her son, HIAO-HOEI-TI, during his reign,
and after his death she continued to rule the Empire by placing
puppet kings on the throne. She was an adept murderess, but
an able ruler.

Liu-hoei: 55/43: (Lu Hui) fl. AD 1069, a minister of Emperor CHIN-
TSONG; opposed the reforms of OUANG-NGAN-CHE.

[Liu-hoei-king]: 55/43: (Lu Hui-ching) fl. AD 1069, a minister of
Emperor CHIN-TSONG; supported the reforms of OUANG-NGAN-
CHE.

Liveright, H.: 80/83: Horace Brisbin, 1886-1933, American publisher and theatrical producer; with Albert Boni founded the firm of
Boni and Liveright (1918).

Liverpool: 65/113: port city of Lancashire, NW England.

Livingston: 33/10; 65/111, 125: Robert R., 1746-1813, American lawyer and statesman; member of the CONTINENTAL CONGRESS
(1775-77; 1779-81); one of the committee which drafted the
DECLARATION of Independence; first U. S. Secretary of Foreign Affairs (1781-83); U. S. minister to France (1801-04).

Livorno: 44/22; 50/40: (Leghorn) port and capital city of Livorno
province in W Tuscany, Italy.

Li Wang: 53/16: see LI-OUANG.

lixitae: 40/49: see LIXTAE.

Lixos: 40/49: the river in NW Africa by which HANNO stopped in
his periplus; also name of the town established there -- the
modern Larache.

Lixtae: 40/49, 50: the nomadic people of the LIXOS river area, NW
Africa.

Lixtus mountain: 40/49: the mountain area to the north of the LIX-
TAE, source of the LIXOS river.

Li-yen: 54/34: (Li Yen) fl. AD 779, a mandarin serving in the government of Emperor TÉ-TSONG.

Li-yo: 54/24: the Li Yo, a Chinese treatise on ceremonies and music.

LL.G.: 74/22: see David LLOYD GEORGE.

[Lloyd George, David]: 74/22: 1863-1945, the British statesman;
prime minister (1916-22).

Lloyd, L.: 71/164: James Lloyd, 1769-1831, U.S. Senator from
Massachusetts (1808-13).

Loca Montis: 42/8; 43/12: [(L) the regions of the mountain]; name
    given to shares in the MONTE NUOVO.
locanda: 81/96: (It) inn.
Locke: 50/40; 67/137: John, 1632-1704, the English philosopher.
Loco Signi: 42/4: (L) in lieu of a sign (signature, seal).
Lodge: 78/59: Henry Cabot, 1850-1924, American legislator; mem-
    ber of the House of Representatives (1887-93) and of the Senate
    (1893-1924); when chairman of the foreign affairs committee of
    the Senate, he was opposed to the Peace Treaty and the League
    of Nations (1919).
Loica: 28/136:
Lois: 6/21: see LOUIS VII of France.
Lolli, Gorro: 10/43; [26/122]: a nephew of Enea Silvio de PICCOLO-
    MINI; Lolli served as the Sienese emissary to Sigismondo
    MALATESTA.
Lolme: 67/140: John Louis de, 1740-1806, Swiss lawyer; author of
    The Constitution of England (1771).
Lombardo, Pietro: 45/23; [74/8]: 1435-1515, Italian architect and
    sculptor; among his most famous works is the tomb of Dante
    at Ravenna.
[Lombardo, Tullio]: 76/38: ?1455-1532, Italian architect and sculp-
    tor, son of Pietro LOMBARDO; among his works are the VEN-
    DRAMINI tomb in Venice and four marble angels in Venice.
Lon Coto: 61/82: see LONG-COTO.
London: 16/71; 35/23; 40/48; 41/55; 46/27; 48/34; 52/7; 62/88; 64/105;
    65/124, 125; 66/129; 68/147; 69/152; 70/158; 71/163, 165; 74/11;
    76/31; 78/59; 80/79; 81/95; 82/101.
London Chronicle: 66/129: not the London paper established in 1757;
    prob. a reference to the parliamentary debates and court de-
    cisions during the reign of JAMES I.
London Library: 16/71: in St. James's Square, London; founded 1841.
[London Times]: 41/55: England's most important newspaper.
Long Champ: 65/118: Longchamp, the racecourse of Paris, in the
    Bois de Boulogne.
[Long-coto]: 61/82: (Lung Coto) fl. AD 1725, a near relation of Em-
    peror YONG-TCHING and a prince of the Empire. In 1725 he
    was accused of extortion and embezzlement and sentenced to the
    rock pile in Tartary. In 1727 he was recalled by the Tribunal
    of Criminal Affairs and sentenced to death; sentence later com-
    muted to life imprisonment.
Lope de Vega: 78/60: Felix, 1562-1635, the Spanish dramatic poet.
Lordly men are to earth o'ergiven: 74/10: from The Seafarer. (See:
    Translations, 209).
Lord of Arimnium: 9/36: see Sigismondo MALATESTA.
Lord of Manchu: 58/65: see TAÏ-TSONG.
Lord of the Fire: 52/4, 5: a spirit in ancient Chinese religion.
Lords: 62/91: see HOUSE OF LORDS.
Lords of the Mountains: 52/5: spirits in ancient Chinese religion.
Lorenzaccio: 5/19; 7/27: see Lorenzino de'MEDICI.
Lorenzino: 5/19; 26/126: see Lorenzino de'MEDICI.
Lorenzo: 26/127: prob. Lorenzo LOTTO.

Lorenzo: 78/56: see Lorenzo de'MEDICI.

[Lorimer, George Horace]: 81/97: 1868-1937, American journalist; editor in chief of the Saturday Evening Post (1899-1936).

Loring: 80/73: Frederic Wadsworth, 1848-71, American writer, poet and journalist.

Lorraine: 50/42: region and former province in E France.

Lo Sordels si fo di Mantovana: 2/6; [6/22; 16/68]; 36/30: (It) The SORDELLOs are from MANTUA.

lotophagoi: 20/93: (Gr) lotus-eaters. (See: Appendix A).

Lottieri, Zan: 10/42: Zanobi Lottieri. (See: Archivio Storico Italiano, Ser. IV, iii, Pt. 2, 184-197).

[Lotto, Lorenzo]: 26/127: 1480-1556, the Venetian painter.

Lou: 53/14, 18, 19; 55/40: (Lü), the State of Lou was established by Tan, the Duke of Chou, in BC 1122; his son made his capital at Kieh-fu (in Shantung province, NE China) about 1115 and was called Duke Lou. Lou was the birthplace of CONFUCIUS.

Lou: 54/22: see LOU-KIA.

Lou: 55/39: (Lü), a principality in Shansi.

Lou-chi: 56/50: Lou-chi-jong (Lü Shih-jong) d. AD 1285, a dishonest minister who served KUBLAI KHAN; he was known as the "second AHAMA." His intrigues gained him so many enemies that he was finally condemned to death; he was butchered and thrown into the street.

Loudon, Lord: 71/160: see John CAMPBELL.

Louis: 6/21: see LOUIS VII of France.

Louis: 44/20: see LOUIS, Duke of Parma.

Louis: 64/101: see LOUIS XV of France.

[Louis VII]: 6/21: ?1121-1180, King of France (1137-80); married ELEANOR of Aquitaine (1137), marriage annulled (1152).

Louis XI: 10/46; 18/81: 1423-83, King of France (1461-83).

Louis XV: [64/101]; 65/117: 1710-74, King of France (1715-74).

Louis XVI: 32/9; [41/55; 65/117, 119; 68/141; 69/151]: 1754-93, King of France (1774-92).

[Louis XVIII]: 34/16: 1755-1824, King of France (1814-15; 1815-24).

[Louis, Duke of Parma]: 44/20: d. 1803, son-in-law of Charles IV of Spain; made king of Etruria in 1801.

Louisburg: 64/103: Louisbourg, port city of E Nova Scotia, Canada.

louis d'or: 55/38: a French gold coin.

Louisiana: 71/161.

Louis Quatorze: 77/46: Le Siècle de Louis XIV by Voltaire (1751).

Lou-kia: 54/22: (Lü Chia) fl. 2nd-3rd century BC, a diplomat in the service of Emperor KAO-HOANG-TI. He was sent to give the seal of office to Chao T'o (who had proclaimed himself Prince of Yuei) and to receive his declaration of allegiance. Lou-kia was so successful that the emperor appointed him minister of state. He left an account of his travels throughout the kingdom.

Lourpee: 28/133, 134: prob. a pseudonym for an unsuccessful French painter.

Louses of Parleymoot: 62/88: Houses of PARLIAMENT.

Lou Tai: 53/11: (Lü-t'ai), the "Stag Tower" built by Emperor CHEOU-SIN for his mistress, TAN-KI.

Lou-tchéou: 54/34: (Lü-ch'ou), a city, prob. in northern China.

[Lou-teng-yun]: 58/67: (Lü Têng-yün) fl. AD 1635, an officer of the imperial army serving Emperor HOAÏ-TSONG; he fought engagements against the Manchu forces then invading China.

Lovelace: 80/91: Richard, 1618-67, the English poet.

Lovell: 82/101: DTC, Pisa.

Lowell: 77/47: Amy, 1874-1925, the American poet and critic.

Lo Yang: 53/12; [54/30]: city in N Honan province, E central China; founded in BC 1108; served as capital of several dynasties; also known as Honan.

L.P.: 76/38: prob. Le Paradis..., quoted in text three lines above.

L. Sieuen: 56/50: see LIEOU-SIUEN.

Lucca: 44/21; 50/42; 76/37; 78/61: capital of Lucca province, Tuscany, central Italy.

Lucifer: 74/3: name of the planet Venus when it is the morning star; also Satan, the fallen angel.

Lucina: 74/9: a minor Roman deity of childbirth; an aspect of Juno, who is the goddess of childbirth.

Lucrezia: 9/38: see Lucrezia MALATESTA.

Lucrezia: 38/37; 74/24: prob. Lucrezia BORGIA.

Luff, Tommy: 74/23:

lukoi oresteroi ede leontes: 39/43: (Gr) mountain wolves and lions. (See: Appendix A).

luna, la: 74/8: (It) the moon.

Luoghi: 42/5; 43/13, 15: (It) places.

luogo di contratto: 35/25: (It) place where deals are made.

Lussurioso incestuoso, perfide, sozzure ac crapulone, / assassino, ingordo, avaro, superbo, infidele/ fattore di monete false, sodomitico, uxoricido: 10/45: (It) Lustful, incestuous, perfidious, filthiness and great guzzling, / murderer, greedy, stingy, proud, unfaithful/ maker of false money, sodomist, uxoricide.

Lutèce: 80/83: Lutetia Parisiorum, ancient name for Paris.

Luther: 46/28: Martin, 1483-1546, the German religious reformer.

lux enim/ ignis est accidens: 83/106: (L) for light/ is an attribute of fire. (See: Grosseteste, De luce seu de inchoatione formarum, ed. Baur, 51, 56).

Lux enim per se omnem in partem: 55/44: (L) For light of herself into every region. (See: Grosseteste, De luce seu de inchoatione formarum, ed. Baur, 51).

luxuria: 26/122; [37/33]: (L) luxury.

luxuria sed aureis furculis: 37/33: (L) luxury but with golden forks.

luz: 80/75, 90: (Sp) light.

Luzerne, Chevalier de: 65/125; 68/145: Anne César Chevalier de la Luzerne, 1741-91, French diplomat; ambassador to America (1779-83); played a major role in the Paris peace conference; ambassador to England (1788-91).

ly: 58/65; 59/72: see LI.

Lyaeus: 2/8: a name for DIONYSUS, especially connected with his role as the god of wine and ecstasy.

Lycabs: 2/9: Lycabas, a member of the crew that attempted to ab-

duct DIONYSUS. (See: Ovid, Metamorphoses, III).
Lycurgus: 68/141: 9th century BC, a Spartan lawgiver.
Lydia: 5/17: ancient country in the center of W Asia Minor.
Lyman, Colonel: 71/164: prob. William Lyman, d. 1811, brigadier-
    general of the Massachusetts militia during the Revolution;
    member of the Massachusetts legislature (1787) and senate
    (1789); member of the House of Representatives (1793-97).
Lynx (Lynxes): 79/68, 69: the lynx is an animal sacred to DIONYSUS.
Lytton: 82/101: see Edward Robert BULWER-LYTTON.

M

M.: 74/14: poss. Robert McAlmon, 1895-1955, American novelist
   and poet; poss. Benito MUSSOLINI.
Mabel: 80/85: see Mabel BEARDSLEY.
McAllister: 80/91: DTC, Pisa.
Macao: 59/71; 60/76: island west of the mouth of the Pearl river,
   Kwangtung province, SE China.
Maccoboy: 37/32: the Americanization of Macouba, a town of
   Martinique which was one of the principal foreign sources of
   snuff in the 18th and 19th centuries.
Mac D.: 14/62: see Thomas MACDONAGH.
[Macdonagh, Thomas]: 14/62: 1878-1916: Irish patriot engaged in
   the 1917 rebellion of Ireland; executed; member of the Celtic
   Renaissance movement in literature.
[MacDonald, James Ramsay]: 79/64: 1866-1937, the British states-
   man.
Macer: 39/44: prob. Macareus, a companion of EURYLOCHUS.
   (See: Ovid, Metamorphoses, XIV, 223 ff).
MacGorvish's bank: 18/83: poss. either Barclay's or Westminster
   Bank, London.
McHenry: [62/96]; 70/155: James, 1753-1816, American politician;
   during the Revolution served as aid to General WASHINGTON
   and to LAFAYETTE; member of the Continental Congress
   (1783-86); delegate to the Constitutional Convention (1787); Sec-
   retary of War (1796-1800). While a member of John ADAMS'
   cabinet, McHenry remained loyal to the interests of Alexander
   HAMILTON.
ma che si sente dicho: 67/137: (It) but that is felt, I say. (See:
   Cavalcanti, Donna mi prega).
Ma Chi: 54/26: (Ma Shih) fl. AD 77, mother of Emperor Han Chang
   Ti (reign: 76-89); her wisdom and virtue aided the young emperor when he took the throne at the age of eighteen.
McIntosh, Captain: 65/116: captain of the English ship MARTHA,
   which was captured by the BOSTON in 1778.
[Mackay, Elsie]: 28/140: 1894-1928, English aviatrix and screen
   actress; daughter of James Lyle Mackay, Viscount Inchcape
   (head of Peninsular and Oriental Steamship Co.); married to
   Dennis WYNDHAM (1917-22). In 1928 she accompanied Capt.
   Walter HINCHLIFFE on his disastrous flight across the Atlantic.
McKean, Thos.: 71/163: Thomas, 1734-1814, American statesman;
   member of the CONTINENTAL CONGRESS (1774-83) and its
   president (1781); signer of the DECLARATION of Independence;
   governor of Pennsylvania (1799-1808).
Mackintosh, Sir James: 34/16: 1765-1832, English scholar who defended the French Revolution in his Vindiciae Gallicae (1791);
   as a member of Parliament (1812-32), he supported penal and
   parliamentary reforms.
Maclay: 69/154: William, 1734-1804, American statesman; as a
   member of the Senate (1789-91), he was a strong opponent of
   HAMILTON's financial measures.

McLocherty: 48/35:

Macmillan Commission: 46/27: MacMillan Committee, a British
    committee on finance and industry (1929) under the chairman-
    ship of Lord MacMillan. The Committee placed major blame
    for the depression not on the maintenance of the gold standard
    itself, but upon the short-sighted handling of it by major nations
    and upon the gold hoarding policies of the U. S. and France.

Macmorral: 67/135: Dermod Mac Murrough, ?1110-1171, King of
    LEINSTER.

MacNarpen and Company: 22/102: pseudonym for Macmillan and
    Company, the publishers.

madama la marxesana: 24/110: (It) madam the marchioness. (See:
    Parisina MALATESTA).

Madame la Porte Parure: 35/25: [(Fr) the Wearer of Adornment]:

Madeira: 64/104: largest island of the group W of Morocco.

Madeira: 69/153: wine made on the island of MADEIRA; malmsey,
    sercial, and bual are the best known.

Madison: 31/4; 34/17; 69/154: James, 1751-1836, fourth President of
    the U. S.; member of the CONTINENTAL CONGRESS (1780-83),
    the Constitutional Convention (1787); as a member of the House
    of Representatives (1789-97), Madison led the Democratic-Re-
    publican party opposition to HAMILTON's financial measures;
    Secretary of State (1801-09); President (1809-17).

Madonna, the: 4/16; 24/111; 44/17; 83/113.

Madonna in hortulo: 4/16; [74/26]: (L) Madonna in the Garden,
    painting by STEFANO da Verona.

Madri': 80/71: see MADRID.

Madrid: 65/121; [80/71]: the capital of Spain.

maelid: 3/11; 79/67, 69: a fruit-tree nymph.

[Maensac, Austors de]: 23/108: brother of Pieire de MAENSAC.

Maensac, Pieire de: 5/18; 23/108, [109]: Pieire de, a poor knight of
    Auvergne; he and his brother, Austors, divided their posses-
    sions: Austors received the castle and Pieire became a trouba-
    dour. Pieire ran away with the wife of Bernart de TIERCI, tak-
    ing her to the castle of ROBERT, Dauphin of Auvergne. When
    de Tierci tried to regain his wife, the Dauphin protected Pieire
    and defeated de Tierci's attack. (See: Make It New, 26-27).

Maestro di pentore: 8/28: (It) Master of painting. (See: Piero dei
    FRANCHESHI).

Magazine Politique Hollandais: 62/92: a Dutch newspaper, published
    c. 1782.

Magdalen: 74/23: Magdalen College of Oxford University.

mag duce dono/ felicitatem dominante et Ferd. I: 43/10: (L) to the
    great duke/ gracious lord and sovereign and FERDINAND I.

magis decora poeticis fabulis: 71/166: (L) more suitable to poetic
    myths. (See: Livy, Praefatio 6).

Magnabucis, D. Michaeli de: 24/111: Notary Public of Ferrara (1427).

Magna Charta: 66/130: the charter which the English barons forced
    King JOHN to sign on 15 June 1215 at Runnymede.

magna Nux animae: 74/14, [15, 16]: (L) the great (Gr) night (L) of
    the soul. (See: St. John of the Cross, Dark Night of the Soul).

Magnifice ac poten: 9/39: (L) to the magnificent and potent.

Magnifice ac potens domine, domini mi singularissime, / humili rec-
    omendatione permissa: 9/40: (L) To the magnificent and potent
    lord, my most excellent lord,/ a humble advice permitted.

Magnifico, compater et carissime: 8/30: (L) Magnificent, my father
    and most dear.

Magnifico exso. Signor Mio: 9/37: (L) Magnificent most excellent.
    (It) My Lord.

Mahammedans: 46/27: see MOHAMMEDANS.

Mahamou: 57/57: (Mahamu) d. AD 1418, chief of the YUEN Mongols;
    he paid homage to Emperor YONG-LO.

Mahomet: 67/137: see MOHAMMED.

Mahomet VI Yahid Eddin Han: 48/34: see MOHAMMED VI.

[Maia]: 76/37; 79/70: mother of HERMES.

Maintenon, de: 81/96: Françoise d'Aubigné, Marquise, 1635-1719,
    mistress and second wife of Louis XIV of France.

maison Alma-Tadema: 80/86: (Fr) ALMA-TADEMA house.

Maison Quarée: 31/4: Maison Carrée. (See: NISMES).

Mais, qu'est-ce qu'on pense, / De la metallurgie, en Angleterre,
    qu'est-ce qu'on/ Pense de Metevsky?: 18/82: (Fr) But, what
    is thought/ of metallurgy in England, what do they/ think of
    METEVSKY?

maistre: 54/34: (O Fr) master.

Major, the: 46/25: see Clifford Hugh DOUGLAS.

Make it new...Day by day make it new: 53/11: from The Great Di-
    gest, II, 1. (See: Appendix B).

Malacca: 57/57: roughly, the area of the Malay Peninsula.

Malaspina, Marquis Antony Mary: 42/7: fl. 1622, member of the
    Malaspina, an ancient family of Tuscany.

Malatesta: 9/35: see Sigismondo MALATESTA.

Malatesta: 9/38: see Sallustio MALATESTA.

Malatesta: 26/121; 30/149: the Malatesta family of Rimini, promi-
    nent from the 13th to the 16th century.

Malatesta, Carlo: 24/111; 26/124: ?1364-1429, man of letters and
    patron of the arts; uncle of Sigismondo MALATESTA.

[Malatesta da Verrucchio]: 8/32: 1212-1312, called "Old Mastiff";
    great-great grandfather of Sigismondo MALATESTA. (See:
    Inferno, 27, 46).

[Malatesta, Domenico]: 10/47; 11/49; 16/69; 23/107: 1418-65, young-
    er brother of Sigismondo, known popularly as Malatesta Novello:
    "Novvy."

[Malatesta, Galeazzo]: 8/32; 9/35: Lord of Pesaro and cousin of
    Sigismondo; known as l'Inetto (the Unfit); in 1444 he allowed
    Alessandro SFORZA to overrun and capture Pesaro; it has been
    claimed that Galeazzo sold the city to Sforza.

[Malatesta, Galeazzo Roberto]: 8/33: 1411-32, brother of Sigis-
    mondo and heir to the lordship of Rimini; he retired to a
    cell and lived the life of an ascetic, leaving Sigismondo,
    then twelve years old, to deal with the enemies of the
    Malatesta family.

[Malatesta, Giovanni]: 11/50: a son of Sigismondo MALATESTA.

[Malatesta, Lucrezia]: 9/38: a daughter of Sigismondo MALATESTA
      by Isotta degli ATTI.
Malatesta, Novello: 16/69: see Domenico MALATESTA.
[Malatesta, Pandolfo]: 9/39; 10/44: d. 1427, Lord of FANO, father
      of Sigismondo.
[Malatesta, Paolo]: 8/32: ?1247-83?, son of MALATESTA DA
      VERRUCCHIO; brother of Giovanni Malatesta; the lover of
      Francesca da Polenta (See: Inferno, 5).
[Malatesta, Parisina]: 8/32; 20/90; 24/110: d. 1425, wife of Niccolò
      d'ESTE, daughter of Carlo MALATESTA. When Niccolò dis-
      covered that Parisina was having an affair with his natural son,
      Ugo ALDOBRANDINO, he had them both beheaded.
Malatesta, Roberto: [11/48, 50]; 24/111: d. 1482, known as The Mag-
      nificient, son of Sigismondo. In 1463 he was forced to surrender
      Fano, which he had held four months, to Federico d'URBINO, who
      commanded the forces of PIUS II. During the War of Ferrara
      (1480-84) Roberto fought for the Papacy, and was acclaimed as
      the deliverer of the Church when he saved Rome for Sixtus IV.
[Malatesta, Sallustio]: 9/38, 39; 20/94; 74/26: 1448-1470, son of
      Sigismondo MALATESTA and Isotta degli ATTI; Sallustio was
      murdered by his half-brother, Roberto MALATESTA.
[Malatesta, Sigismondo]: 8/28, 29, 31, 32, 33; 9/34, 35, 36, 37, 39,
      41; 10/42, 43, 44, 45, 46; 11/48, 49, 50, 51, 52; 17/79; 26/123,
      124, 125; 74/3; 76/30, 37; 80/90: Sigismondo Pandolfo Mala-
      testa, 1417-68, patron of the arts, built the TEMPIO MALATES-
      TIANO in Rimini; made war against Pope PIUS II and was ex-
      communicated (1460); lost all possessions except Rimini (1463).
Malatesta, Sigismund: 8/28; 9/36: see Sigismondo MALATESTA.
Malatesta, Sigismundus: 10/44: see Sigismondo MALATESTA.
Malatesta de Malatestis ad Magnificum Dominum Patremque/ suum:
      9/39: (L) Malatesta of the Malatestas to his Magnificent Lord
      and Father.
Malatestiana: 74/24: the TEMPIO MALATESTIANO.
Malatestis: 11/50; 76/40; 80/79; 83/107: see the MALATESTA family.
Malatestis, Malatesta de: 9/39: see Sallustio MALATESTA.
Malatestis, Sigismundus Pandolphus de: 8/29: see Sigismondo
      MALATESTA.
Malemorte: 6/22: Malemorte-sur-Corrèze, village in Corrèze de-
      partment, S central France; site of a once important castle.
Malesherbes: 65/117, 125: Chrétien Guillaume de Lamoignon de,
      1721-94, French statesman and writer on politics and law;
      banished by LOUIS XV but recalled (1774) by LOUIS XVI, minis-
      ter of the interior (1775-76).
Malespina, Simone: 11/48: Simone Malaspina, a captain in the forces
      of Sigismondo MALATESTA.
mal hecho: 10/46: (Sp) poorly done.
Mallarmé: 80/82: Stéphane, 1842-98, the French symbolist poet.
Mallevadoria: 42/5: (It) guarantee.
Malmaison: 74/14: a château near Paris; residence (1809-14) of the
      Empress Josephine, and later of Maria Christina of Spain and
      of the Empress Eugénie.

Malta: 80/76: the British island in the Mediterranean.

Mana aboda: 78/57: title of a poem by T. E. HULME (see: Personae, 252); aboda (Heb): work, achievement.

Manchester: 46/28: manufacturing city, Lancashire, NW England.

Manchester Cardiff: 18/82: railroad line in England, running from
Manchester to Cardiff, Wales.

Manchu: 57/60; 58/65, 67, 68, 69; 59/70, 71; 60/78; 61/81: a Tartar
tribe originally descended from the NUTCHÉ Tartars. The
Manchu power was established in 1587 by Nurhachu; in 1644 the
Manchu brought about the fall of the Ming dynasty and established the Ch'ing dynasty (1644-1912).

Mandarin(s): 54/25, 27, 34; 55/37, 41, 44; 56/52; 57/57; 58/66, 67;
59/72; 60/76; 61/80, 82, 83, 84: members of the mandarinate,
the scholar ruling class, or civil service, of China which rose
about BC 600. The mandarins were disliked, but respected,
by the people of China.

manes: 52/5; 60/76: (L) spirits of the dead.

Manes: 74/3: ?216-276?, the Persian sage, founder of the sect of
MANICHEANS; for his teaching he was condemned and cruci-
fied.

Manet: 74/13; 80/82: Édouard, 1832-83, the French painter.

Manfredi, Astorre: 9/34: member of the ruling Manfredi family of
Faenza.

[Mangu Khan]: 56/49: (reign: 1249-59), emperor of the Mongols;
he put down all feudal opposition to his rule, reduced the tax
burden, and curbed the power of the nobles. In 1259 he invaded
SZECHWAN province and besieged Ho-chou (60 miles N of
Chungking); the city resisted, and when plague broke out
in the Mongol ranks, the soldiers killed Mangu Khan and
retired.

Manhattan: 12/53; 19/84; 28/134; 74/25; 80/73: the borough of New
York city.

Manicheans: 23/109; 36/29; 74/7: followers of the religious system
founded by MANES; it is a system based on a dualism of good
and evil, of a Good and an Evil One, both of equal power, exist-
ing in the universe.

Manilla: 60/77: Manila, former province of the Philippine Islands;
the city of Manila on SW Luzon.

Manitou: 79/66, 67: the Algonquian Indian name for the natural
power which permeates all things.

man seht: 80/89: (Ger) one sees.

Mansfield, Lord: 67/136: see William MURRAY.

Mansour: 57/60: (Mansur) fl. AD 1522, a prince of the Tartar tribes
which occupied the area of Turfan, in Sinkiang province, W
China.

Mantegna: 3/12: Andrea, 1431-1506, Italian painter who worked for
the Gonzaga family of Mantua doing frescoes (1460-1506).

Mantova: 26/127: (It) MANTUA.

Mantovana: 2/6; 6/22; 36/30: (It) MANTUA.

Mantua: [2/6; 6/22]; 9/34; 10/43; 26/123, 126 [127]; 35/25; [36/30]:
capital of Mantova province, Lombardy, N Italy.

Manuel: 26/124: Manuel I Comnenus, 1120-80, emperor of the East-
    ern Roman Empire; his reign was marked by military victories
    against Italians, Venetians, Serbs, and Turks, but he was de-
    feated by the Seljuks in Phrygia (1176).
[Manutius, Aldus]: 30/148: 1450-1515, Italian printer and classical
    scholar; founder of the Aldine Press and of the New Academy,
    a group of Hellenic scholars.
Manxman: 80/81: an inhabitant of the Isle of Man.
Mao, T. C.: 53/19: see CHAO-TCHING-MAO.
Mao-chi: 54/24: (Mao-shih), the SHIH CHING.
Ma questo...è divertente: 41/52: (It) but this...is amusing.
Marblehead: 71/164: town in NE Massachusetts, on the Atlantic coast.
marble narrow for seats: 7/24: from Ovid, Artis Amatoriae, I, 139-
    142.
Marcebrus: 28/137: Marcabru, a 12th century Gascon troubadour.
March: 35/25: see MARCHES.
Marches: 9/35; [35/25]: the region in central Italy extending from
    the eastern slopes of the Apennines to the Adriatic coast.
Marchese, the: 20/90; 24/112; see Niccolò d'ESTE.
marchesini: 24/110: prob. (It) marks.
Marchesini, John: 25/116: fl. 1328, Ducal notary of Venice.
Marconi: 38/37: Marchese Guglielmo, 1874-1937, the Italian physicist.
Marecchia: 8/30, 32: the river in Italy.
Marengo: 50/41: village in Alessandria province, NW Italy; scene of
    the battle in which NAPOLEON defeated the Austrians (14 June
    1800).
Marescotti, Caloanes: 42/8: prob. a member of the Sienese BALÍA.
    c. 1622.
Mare Tirreno: 74/13: (It) the Tyrrhenian Sea.
Margaret: 77/49:
Margarita: 24/111: see Margarita d'ESTE.
Margherita: 77/49:
Margot: 80/71: see Margot ASQUITH.
Maria: 43/11: the Virgin Mary.
Maria: 83/107:
[Maria Francisca]: 32/9: 1734-1816; Maria I, Queen of Portugal
    (1777-1816); she was both sickly and weak-minded.
Maria Maddalena: 42/6; 43/16: see MARIA MAGDALENA.
[Maria Magdalena]: 42/3, 5, 6, 7, 8; 43/9, 13, 14, 15, 16: fl. 1622,
    mother of FERDINAND II of Tuscany, sister of Ferdinand II,
    Holy Roman Emperor. Since her son became Grand Duke of
    Tuscany at the age of ten, she served not only as his guardian
    (tutrice), but also as royal regent; hence the references in let-
    ters quoted to Their Highnesses, meaning mother and son.
Marie de Parma: 50/43: see MARIE LOUISE.
[Marie Louise]: 50/42, 43: 1791-1847, the daughter of Emperor
    Francis I of Austria; second wife of NAPOLEON. She was also
    known as Marie da Parma.
Marietta: 37/35:
Maritain: 77/50; 80/83: Jacques, 1882-   , the French neo-Thomist
    theologian and philosopher.

Marius: 42/7: father of Livio PASQUINI.
Marius: 71/165: Gaius, 159-86, the Roman general.
Marmaduke, John: 46/26: poss. Marmaduke William PICKTHALL.
Marotti, Virginia: 28/133: see Virginia SENNI.
Marozia: 20/92: d. 945, wife of Alberic I, Prince of Rome; mistress of Pope Sergius III.
Marquis of Ferrara: 26/123: see Niccolò d'ESTE.
Marquis of Mantova: 26/127: see Gian Francesca GONZAGA.
Mars: 30/147; 36/27; 48/37; 50/41: the Roman god of war; also the planet Mars.
Marshall: 32/9; 37/33, 35; 70/155, 156: John, 1755-1835, the American jurist; one of the American commissioners to France (1797-98); member of the House of Representatives (1799-1800); Secretary of State (1800-01); Chief Justice of the Supreme Court (1801-35). Marshall established the basic principles of Constitutional interpretation by his decisions.
martes zibbeline: 55/41; 58/63: (Fr) martre zibeline: sable.
Martha: 65/116: an English merchant ship, commanded by Captain McINTOSH, which was captured (1778) by the BOSTON, an American ship commanded by Captain Samuel TUCKER.
Martial: 5/20: 1st century AD, the Roman epigrammatist.
Martin: 77/50: Joseph William, 1884-   , American politician; member of the House of Representatives (from 1925); Republican party leader in the House since 1939.
Martineau: 34/20: Harriet, 1802-76, English novelist and economist; author of many books, including Illustrations of Political Economy (1832-34).
Martinique: 28/137; 65/112: island in the Windward Islands, West Indies.
Martin's: 64/103: an inn between Salem and Boston, Massachusetts.
Maryland: 31/3, 4: a middle Atlantic state of the U.S.A.; the MASON-DIXON line which forms the border between Maryland and Pennsylvania, is often used to indicate the division between the North and the South of the U.S.
Maryland, the: 31/3: an American ship which was directed to bring Thomas PAINE from France to America (c. 1787).
Marx: 19/84; 46/28; 48/34; [71/166(?)]: Karl, 1818-83, German political philosopher.
Masefield: 82/102: John, 1878-   , the English poet laureate (since 1930), playwright and novelist.
Ma se morisse! / Credesse caduto da sè, ma se morisse: [5/20]; 7/27: (It) But if he should die! / Believed fallen by himself, but if he should die. (See: Varchi, Storia Fiorentino, III, 262).
Masnatas et servos: 6/22: (L) domestics and slaves.
ma soeur et/ cousine: 44/20: (Fr) my sister/and cousin.
Mason and Dixon: 77/49: Mason and Dixon Line: the boundary between Pennsylvania and Maryland; surveyed by the English astronomers Charles Mason and Jeremiah Dixon (1763-67).
Mass: 77/45: the performance of the sacrament of the Eucharist in the Catholic Church.
Massachusetts: 65/109, 110, 113; 67/134, 138; 74/25: the New England state.

[Massachusetts Colonial Charter]: 64/108: the charter granted first
    (1628) to the New England Company and then (1629) to the Mass-
    achusetts Bay Company. Although once annulled (1684), the
    charter formed the basis of Massachusetts government until the
    state constitution was adopted (1780).
[Massachusetts Colonial Legislature]: 64/108: a legislative body
    consisting of a lower house, the House of Representatives, and
    an upper house, the Council.
[Massachusetts State Constitution]: 66/131; 67/138: written in large
    part by John ADAMS (1779), adopted (1780).
Mastai: [28/139]; 50/43: Giovanni Maria Mastai-Ferreti, 1792-1878,
    Pope Pius IX (1846-78); fled Rome in the insurrection of 1848,
    restored by the French (1850); became an extreme reactionary
    and supported the House of Savoy.
Masters Deputies: 43/9: members of the Sienese BALÍA.
"Master thyself, then others shall thee beare": 81/99: variation of
    Chaucer, Ballade of Good Counsel: "Reule wel thyself, that
    other folk canst rede." (Robinson, 631) (See: M. E. SPEARE,
    The Pocket Book of Verse, 1, where the line is rendered:
    "Subdue thyself, and others thee shall hear.").
Mastin: 8/32: (It) mastiff. (See: MALATESTA DA VERRUCCHIO).
Ma-tchéou: 54/32: (Ma Ch'ou) fl. AD 637, a minister serving Em-
    peror TAI-TSONG.
Mathews, Elkin: 82/101, 102: London publisher; published several
    of Pound's early works, 1908-1916.
Mathieu: 58/64: see Mathieu RICCI.
Matlock: 71/161: Timothy Matlack, d. 1829, American Revolutionary
    statesman; assistant secretary to the Continental Congress
    (1775); member of the Pennsylvania constitutional convention
    (1776) and of the committee to draft the constitution of Pennsyl-
    vania.
Matteo: 74/15: see Matteo de' PASTI.
Mattias Passion: 35/22: the Passion according to St. Matthew by
    Johann Sebastian BACH (1729).
Maukch: 77/42:
Mauleon, Savaric de: 5/18; [48/37]: d. 1236, French warrior and
    troubador whose loyalties vacillated between Henry III of
    England and Louis VIII of France. (See: "Troubadors, their
    sorts and conditions" in Literary Essays, 94-108).
Mauregato: 65/120: a town in Astorga, Spain.
Maurie: 74/11: see Maurice HEWLETT.
Mava: 39/44: prob. inv.: a sea deity.
Max: 46/26: Max Beerbohm, 1872-1956, the English writer and
    caricaturist.
[Maxim, Hiram Stevens]: 18/81: 1840-1916, inventor of the Maxim
    automatic gun.
[Maxwell, Mary Elizabeth Braddon]: 80/86: 1837-1915, British
    novelist.
Maya: 76/37: see MAIA.
Mazzei: 68/145: Philip, 1730-1816, Italian physician who came to

Virginia in 1773; he was a strong supporter of the American
Revolution and was an American agent in Italy (1779-83).
Mead: 74/24: G. R. S., 1863-1933, English writer; editor of The
Quest, a quarterly review.
Meath: 67/135: former kingdom in Leinster province, Ireland.
Medicea: 78/56: (L) of the MEDICI.
Medici: 8/32; 26/125; 43/16; 50/40; [78/56]: Italian family powerful
in Florence and Tuscany from the 14th to the 16th centuries.
[Medici, Alessandro de']: 5/19; 7/27; 84/117: 1511-1537, Duke of
Florence (1531-37); murdered by his kinsman Lorenzino de'
MEDICI because of his tyrannical rule.
Medici, Cosimo: [10/43; 21/96, 97]; 26/123, [124]: Cosimo de'
Medici, 1389-1464, Florentine banker, patron of the arts, and
ruler of the Florentine Republic; called Pater Patriae; founder
of the elder branch of the Medici family.
[Medici, Cosimo I de']: 41/55: 1519-1574, Grand Duke of Tuscany
(1569-74).
[Medici, Francesco de']: 74/5: 1541-1587, Grand Duke of Tuscany
(1574-87); son of Cosimo I de' Medici.
Medici, Giohanni: 8/28: Giovanni de' Medici, 1360-1428, Florentine
merchant and founder of the Medici family; from his two sons
COSIMO (1389-1464) and Lorenzo (1395-1440) derive the two
great branches of the family.
[Medici, Giovanni de']: 8/30: 1421-1463, favorite son of Cosimo de'
MEDICI.
[Medici, Giuliano de']: 21/97: d. 1478, brother of Lorenzo de'
Medici; stabbed to death by Bernardo Bandini and Francesco de
Pazzi.
Medici, Lauro: 21/98: see Lorenzo de' MEDICI.
[Medici, Lorenzino de']: 5/19; 7/27; 26/126: 1515-1547, grandson of
Lorenzo the Younger (1463-1507); murdered his distant kinsman,
Alessandro de' MEDICI, in 1537.
[Medici, Lorenzo de']: 21/96, 98; 26/126; 78/56: 1449-92, known as
Lorenzo il Magnifico; Florentine statesman, ruler and patron
of arts and letters; one of the great figures of the Italian
Renaissance.
[Medici, Piero de']: 21/96: 1416-69, Italian merchant prince, son
of Cosimo de' MEDICI.
Medici, Pietro de: 43/14: poss. Pietro de' Medici, 1554-1604, son
of Cosimo I de' MEDICI, Grand Duke of Tuscany.
Medici bank: 8/32; 26/125: the Medici Bank in Florence, established
by Cosimo de' MEDICI.
Medicis, Lorenzo de: 26/126: see Lorenzo de' MEDICI.
Medon: 2/9: a member of the crew which tried to abduct DIONYSUS
as he was on his way to NAXOS. (See: Ovid, Metamorphoses,
III, 671).
Medusa: 15/66: one of the three Gorgons; her face turned to stone
anything that met its gaze.
Meerkemaer: 68/147: fl. 1780, a Dutch broker employed by the bank-
ing house of VAN STAPHORST.
Me Hercule!: 80/87: (L) By Hercules!

Melagrana: 79/68, 69: (It) pomegranate.

Melchizedek: 18/82: a pre-Aaronic and pre-Levitical priest-king to whom Abraham paid tithes; a prototype of the high priest.

Meli: 40/49: Melitta, town on the Atlantic coast of North Africa, founded by HANNO; just south of AKRA.

Mellon: 38/38: Andrew William, 1855-1937, American financier; largely interested in coal, coke and iron industries as well as international banking; U. S. ambassador to Great Britain (1932-33).

meminisse juvebit: 70/158: (L) meminisse juvabit: it will be pleasant to recall. (See: Aeneid, I, 203).

Memling: 45/24; 51/44; 76/33: Hans, ?1430-95, painter of the early Flemish school.

Memnons: 17/77: Memnon, son of Tithonus and EOS; a large statue near Thebes, Egypt (supposed to be of Memnon), was reputed to produce a musical sound when struck by the light of dawn.

mémoires des académies/ des sciences de Paris: 60/78: (Fr) memoirs of the Academies/ of Sciences of Paris. (See: Mailla, Histoire Générale, XI, 364).

Memphis: 7/26: the ancient city of Egypt.

Mencius: 54/24; 78/58: (Mêng-tzǔ or Mêng K'o) 372-289, Chinese philosopher who was a follower of CONFUCIUS; author of the second of the Four Books of the Chinese classics, the Book of Mencius.

Mencken, Henry: 81/96: Henry Louis, 1880-1956, the American editor, author and critic.

Mendoça, de: 26/126: poss. Diego di Mendozza, ambassador to Rome from Charles V, Holy Roman Emperor.

Menelaus: 5/18: husband of HELEN of Troy.

Menelik: 18/82, 83; 80/88: Menelik II, 1844-1913, Emperor of Ethiopia (1889-1913); in a war with Italy (1896) Menelik freed Ethiopia from Italian control.

Mengko: 56/49: see MANGU KHAN.

Meng Kong: 56/49: (Meng Kung) d. AD 1246, an officer of the imperial troops serving Emperor Li Tsung (reign: 1225-65). Mengkong was the leader of several imperial campaigns against the Mongol.

menie: 3/12: (ME) meynee: household, retinue, army.

Meniñas, Las: 80/71: painting by VELÁSQUEZ, in the Prado.

[Mensdorff-Pouilly-Dietrichstein, Count Albert von]: 19/87: 1861-1945, Austro-Hungarian ambassador to London (1904-14).

mens sine affectu: 62/89: (L) a mind without feeling (passion). (See: John Adams, Works, I, 114, where the phrase is quoted from a work by Algernon Sidney).

Mercury: 77/49: the Roman equivalent of the god HERMES; the caduces of Mercury, the insignia of the medical branch of the U. S. Army, is a wing-topped staff with two snakes winding about it.

Merino: 33/10; 44/21: a breed of sheep which originated in Spain; known for its very fine and heavy wool.

merrda: 78/57: (It) merda: excrement.

Merry Mount: 62/87: by 1627, the new name of Mt. WOLLASTON.
mes compliments: 80/82: (Fr) my compliments.
Messiah: 34/18: a poem by Alexander POPE, first published in The
      Spectator, no. 378 (14 May 1712).
Messiah: 38/38: a savior.
Messina: 27/129: capital of Messina province in NE Sicily; the great
      earthquake at Messina occurred on 28 December 1908, when
      90 percent of the buildings were destroyed.
Metastasio: 78/56: Pietro, 1698-1782, Italian poet and dramatist;
      court poet at Vienna from 1729.
Metathemenon Te Ton/ Krumenon: 74/18; [76/41; 77/46; 78/59]: (Gr)
      if those who use a currency give it up in favour of another. (See:
      Appendix A).
Metello: 61/83: Alexandre Metello-Souza-y-Menezes, fl. 1726, Por-
      tuguese ambassador to Emperor KANG HI of China. Metello
      and the Jesuit Antoine Magalhaens reached Peiping in 1727 and
      tried to make a treaty that would give the Portuguese special
      privileges in the China trade. The emperor assumed, however,
      that the two had merely come to pay tribute to him, and the
      talks on trade had no result.
Metevsky, Sir Zenos: 18/80, 81, 82; 38/37: see Sir Basil ZAHAROFF.
Metternich: 50/41, 42: Clemens Wenzel Nepomuk Lothar, Fürst von,
      1773-1859, the Austrian statesman, intimately involved in the
      Congress of Vienna (1815).
Meudon: 66/126: SW suburb of Paris on the Seine; the château, built
      by Louis XIV, surrounded by the Forêt de Meudon.
meum est propositum: 80/85: (L) it is my intention.
Miaco: 58/62: the present city of Kyoto, Japan; established as the
      capital of Japan (AD 784) and remained officially the capital
      until 1869 when the government was removed to Tokyo.
Miao Haokien: 56/51: (Miao Hao-chien) fl. AD 1318, author of a work
      on the cultivation of mulberry trees and the production of silk;
      Emperor GIN-TSONG had copies of the work circulated among
      the provinces.
mia pargoletta: 80/84: (It) my little girl.
Micah: 84/118: fl. BC 710, Hebrew prophet; author of the book of
      Micah. (See: Micah, 4, 5).
Midas: 21/99; 78/59: the legendary king of Phrygia whose touch
      turned things to gold.
Middle Kingdom: 53/12; 77/45: one of the many names for the Chi-
      nese Empire; others are: Flowery Kingdom and Celestial
      Empire.
Middletown: 64/107: city in S Connecticut, S of HARTFORD.
Midland: 33/13: the Midland Bank, in England.
Mie: 56/49: Meï-tchéou (Mei-ch'ou), a large town in SZECHWAN
      province, China.
Mifflin: 65/113: Thomas, 1744-1800, American Revolutionary officer
      and statesman; member of the CONTINENTAL CONGRESS
      (1774-76; 1782-84) and its president (1783); aide-de-camp to
      General WASHINGTON (1775), rose to the rank of major general
      later; member of the Constitutional Convention (1787).

"mi-hine eyes hev": 80/76: from Julia Ward Howe, Battle Hymn of
    the Republic.
Mihites: 71/164: poss. (L) milites: soldiers.
Milan: 8/29, 32; 9/35, 37; 21/98; 24/110; 44/20; [74/3; 75/29]: capi-
    tal of Milano province, Lombardy, N Italy.
Milano: 74/3; 75/29: (It) MILAN.
Milé Buddha: 56/52: Mille (or Maitrêya) Buddha or the Goddess of
    Mercy, a reincarnation of BUDDHA. During the reign of Em-
    peror CHUNTI there was much unrest, many famines, earth-
    quakes, and heavenly disturbances; when the emperor started
    work on the diversion of the Hwang-Ho, there was a surge of
    popular resentment and it was rumoured that Buddha was soon
    to descend to save China from the Mongol dynasty. This ru-
    mour was used for political purposes by the WHITE LILY SO-
    CIETY.
mille cinquecento cavalli/ E li homini di Messire Sigismundo/ non
    furono che mille trecento: 11/48: (It) and fifteen hundred
    horses/ and Messer Sigismondo's (MALATESTA) men/ were
    only thirteen hundred.
millessimo: 25/116: (It) year.
mille tre cento cavalli: 11/48: (It) thirteen hundred horses.
Mills bomb: 46/25: the Mills hand grenade used by British and Al-
    lies in World War I; invented by Sir William Mills.
Milton: 34/15; 67/137; 68/141: John, 1608-74, the English poet.
Mi mise, il mio sposo novello: 20/93: (It) My recently betrothed
        sent me. (See: St. Francis of Assisi, Cantico Secondo, stan-
        za 1: Lo mio sposo novello).
[Min]: 53/10: fl. BC 2119, Empress of Siang (2146-2118), mother of
    Emperor CHAO KANG.
minestra: 78/56: (It) soup.
Ming: 56/51, 53; 57/60; 58/63, 65, 67, 68; 60/76; 61/86: the twenty-
    first dynasty (1368-1649).
ming: [74/7]; 84/117: (Ch) clear, bright. (See: Appendix B).
Ming histories: 61/86: the Ming Chi Kang Mu, a history of the MING
    dynasty; this work, finished in 1742, did not receive imperial
    approval, and the T'ung Chien Kang Mu San Pien was substi-
    tuted for it in 1775. Emperor KIEN-LONG's redaction of the
    Ming histories was published under the title Yu Chih Kang
    Chien.
Ming Kong: 53/20: see MIN-KONG.
Ming Ouan: 56/53: Ming-ouang (Ming Wang), the dynastic title
    assumed by HAN-LIN-EUL.
Ming rebellion: 60/76: the Ming forces which resisted the Manchu
    Emperor Shun Chih throughout his reign (1644-62).
Ming T'ang: 52/5: the "Temple of Light" (or "Wisdom"); the temple
    where the imperial family of China worshipped its ancestors.
Ming Tsong: 55/39: (Ming Tsung) (reign: 926-34), proclaimed em-
    peror by the army but refused for a time to function as any-
    thing but regent. In 932 the art of printing was discovered; the
    nine classics were printed by imperial orders from wooden
    blocks and sold to the public.

Ministro degli Esteri: 44/20: (It) Minister of Foreign Affairs.
[Min-kong]: 53/20: (Min Kung) d. BC 478, Prince of TCHIN.
Min Ti: 54/28: see TÇIN-MIN-TI.
Minto, Lord: 50/43: see Sir Henry George ELLIOT.
Mi pare che avea decto hogni chossia: 9/38: (It) It seems to me
    that he had said everything. (The original of this, reproduced
    in Yriarte, Un Condottiere au XVe Siècle, 159, reads: a detto
    al mio parere ogni cossa).
mi porta fortuna: 74/24: (It) brings me good luck.
Mirabel: 65/122, [125]: Comte Montagnini, fl. 1782, minister pleni-
    potentiary of Victor Amadeus III, King of Sardinia.
Miranda: 62/95: Francisco de, 1750-1816, Venezuelan revolutionist
    and leader of the Venezuelan struggle for liberty; in 1806 he
    sought foreign aid and led an expedition to the Venezuelan coast,
    but the military venture was a failure; he was a commander of
    the forces during the revolution of 1810 and was dictator for a
    short time.
Miranda: 77/49: prob. the character in Shakespeare's The Tempest.
Mir sagen/ Die Damen/ Du bist Greis: 83/113: (Ger) The ladies say
    to me,/you are an old man.
Miscio: 77/47: see Miscio ITO.
Miseria servitus, ubi jus vagum: 68/142: (L) Misera...Slavery is a
    misery, where rights are undefined. (See: John Adams, Works,
    VI, 230 note).
Mississippi: 34/16; 37/33; 65/112; 71/161, 165: principal river of the
    U. S.
Missouri: 37/34: central state of the U. S.; capital is Jefferson City.
Mitchell: 34/15: Samuel Latham Mitchill, 1763-1831, American
    physician, historian, student of natural history, and statesman;
    served for a time as Professor of Chemistry and Natural
    History at Columbia College, edited several volumes of the
    Medical Repository, wrote a Life of Tammany, the Indian
    Chief; member of the House of Representatives (1801-04; 1810-
    13) and of the Senate (1804-09).
Mitchell, Weir: 80/85: Silas Weir Mitchell, 1829-1914, American
    physician; author of several volumes of poetry and fiction;
    founder of the FRANKLIN INN CLUB.
Mithras: 76/30: Mithra, ancient cultic god of Iran and India; by the
    2nd century AD, the worship of Mithra had spread throughout
    the Roman Empire, largely because the cult was popular with
    the Roman legions. Mithraism consisted of an ethic based on
    loyalty, on a mystery cult, and on rituals of blood baptism
    and a sacred banquet.
mitrailleuse: 16/71: (Fr) machine gun.
mit Schlag: 80/84: (Viennese idiom) with whipped cream.
Mitsui: 38/38, 42: the central bank of Japan.
Mitteleuropa: 35/22, 23: Central Europe, especially that portion of
    Europe which the advocates of Pan-Germanism proposed to
    form into an empire.
Mitylene: 26/123; 82/103: see MYTILENE.

m'l'a calata: 9/37: (It) he put that on me; he fooled me.
M. Magdalene: 42/8: see MARIA MAGDALENA.
Mme la Duchess d'Agen a 5 ou 6 enfants/ contre la coutume du pays:
       65/118: (Fr) Madame the Duchess d'AYEN has five or six
       children/ contrary to the custom of the country.
Mocenigo: 35/26: Tommaso Mocenigo, 1343-1423, doge of Venice
       (1414-1423).
Mockel: 78/58; 80/82: Albert Henri Louis, 1866-1945, Belgian-French
       poet and critic; founder and editor (1886-92) of the journal LA
       WALLONIE, magazine of the Belgian symbolists.
mode, la: 65/123: (Fr) fashion.
Modena: 24/110, 113, 114: capital of Modena province, N central
       Italy.
Modon Brandos: 26/123: prob. Modon, a Greek town in Morea, S of
       Mavarino.
modus vivendi: 51/45: (L) way of life.
Moffat: 64/108: Thomas Moffatt, d. after 1779, loyalist of Rhode
       Island; comptroller of the customs at New London (c. 1770);
       left America in 1775.
Mogol (Mogols): 56/50, 51: see MONGOL.
Mogul (Moguls): 56/48, 52, 55; 58/66, 67, 68: see MONGOL.
Mohamed: 22/103, 104: see MOHAMED BEN ABT EL HJAMEED.
Mohamed Ben Abt el Hjameed: 22/103, [104]: prob. a merchant in
       Gibraltar, c. 1908.
[Mohammed]: 67/137: 570-632, Arabian prophet; founder of the
       Mohammedan religion.
[Mohammed II]: 26/121: c. 1430-1481, Ottoman sultan (reign: 1451-
       1481).
[Mohammed VI]: 48/34: 1861-1926, last Ottoman sultan (1918-22);
       deposed in 1922 when Turkey became a republic.
[Mohammedans]: 46/27; [55/46]; 60/74, [75]: followers of the
       prophet MOHAMMED.
Mohammeds: 55/46; 60/75: see MOHAMMEDANS.
Molü: 47/31; [53/9]: (Gr) moly. (See: Appendix A).
mondo, il: 48/35: (It) the world.
Mongol (Mongols): 35/24; 55/[41, 45], 46; 56/48, 50, 51, [52], 53,
       54, 55; 58/63, [66], 67, [68]; 60/75: the wandering barbarian
       tribes which occupied a vast territory to the north of China;
       they were unified and brought to political prominence under the
       leadership of GHENGHIS KHAN.
Mongrels: 55/45, 46; 58/63, 66: see MONGOL.
Mong-tsé: 54/24: (Mêng-tzŭ), Chinese form of MENCIUS.
Mongul: 58/66: see MONGOL.
Monroe: 74/14: DTC, Pisa.
Monroe: 34/[17], 18; 37/33; 41/56: James, 1758-1831, fifth presi-
       dent of the U. S.; member of the Continental Congress (1783-
       86), and of the U. S. Senate (1790-94); minister to France
       (1794-96) and to England (1803-07); Secretary of State (1811-17)
       and of War (1814-15); President (1817-25).
Monsieur Adams...il y a cent ans que je/ ne vous ai vu: 34/15: (Fr)
       Mister ADAMS (John Quincy), I haven't seen you for a hundred

years. (See: J. Q. Adams, Diary, 83).
[Montagu, George]: 65/125: 1737-88, fourth Duke of Manchester;
    English ambassador to France to treat for peace (1783).
Montagu, Sir: 77/52: see Montagu Collet NORMAN.
Monte: 42/3, 5, 7; 43/10, 15: (It) mountain, collection, heap, (bank).
    (See: MONTE DEI PASCHI).
Montecello: 21/98: see MONTICELLO.
Monte Cogruzzo: 11/49: prob. a castle, taken from Sigismondo
    MALATESTA by the peace terms imposed by PIUS II (c. 1460).
Monte de Firenze, vacabile: 43/13: (It) Bank of Florence, vacant
    (idle).
Monte dei Paschi: 41/55; [42/3, 5, 6, 7, 8; 43/10, 12, 13, 14, 15;
    44/17, 20]: the Sienese bank, founded in 1624 and still in
    existence; the "Mountain of the Pastures" bank, with credit
    backed by the Sienese public lands, the pastures of the Marem-
    ma,as security, was established under a grant from FERDI-
    NAND II of Tuscany. (Also called in text: BANK, MONTE,
    MONTE NUOVO, MONTE PASCHALE, MOUNT, MOUNTAIN,
    NEW MONTE, NEW MOUNT, and NEW MOUNTAIN).
Montefiore: 11/51: a town in Garfagnana, N Tuscany.
Monte Gioiosa: 80/79: prob. Giojosa, a town of Sicily on the N coast;
    built at the foot of the mountain on which stood Giojosa Vecchio
    (Old Giojosa).
Monteluro: 9/34: village NE of Florence.
Monte non vacabilis publico: 42/7: poss. (Medieval L) the public
    (funds) of the Monte (dei Paschi) will not remain idle.
Monte Nuovo: 43/14: (It) the New Mountain or MONTE DEI PASCHI.
[Monte Odoriso]: 36/30: one of the five castles in the Abruzzi;
    given to SORDELLO for his services by CHARLES I of Naples
    and Sicily (1269).
Monte Paschale: 43/14: see MONTE DEI PASCHI.
Montepulciano: 52/4: erroneous reference to Montemassi, town in
    central Italy, SW of Siena. (See: RICCIO).
[Monte San Silvestro]: 36/30: one of the five castles in the Abruzzi;
    given to SORDELLO for his services by CHARLES I of Naples
    and Sicily (1269).
Montfort, Simone de: [23/109]; 83/106: Simon IV de Montfort
    l'Amaury, ?1160-1218, count of Montfort and earl of Leicester;
    leader of the crusade against the ALBIGENSES (1209-29),
    killed at the siege of Toulouse.
Monthieu: 68/143: John Joseph de, fl. 1780, a business partner of
    BEAUMARCHAIS and connected with RODERIQUE HORTALEZ
    & CO.; Monthieu arranged the sale and rental of armed vessels
    to America during the Revolution.
Monticello: [21/98]: 31/5: the residence of Thomas JEFFERSON;
    near Charlottesville, Virginia.
Montino: 83/107:
monumento di civile sapienza: 44/21: (It) monument of civil wisdom.
Moore: 64/108: Sir Francis, 1558-1621, English law reporter; his
    most important work, often called "Moore's Reports," is
    Cases Collect and Report (1663).

Moore, Tom: 82/102: Thomas, 1779-1852, the Irish poet.

Moore, T. Sturge: 80/85: Thomas Sturge, 1870-1944, the English poet.

Mordecai, Charlie: 71/166: poss. Karl MARX.

More, Sir Thos: 68/141: Sir Thomas, 1478-1535, the English states- man, humanist and author.

Morea: 11/50; 26/123; 32/7: the Peloponnesus, south part of the mainland of Greece. In 1464 Sigismondo MALATESTA led an unsuccessful crusade against the Turks in Morea.

mores: 55/46; 76/31: (L) customs.

Morgan: 68/142: Daniel, 1736-1802, American Revolutionary soldier; captain of a company of Virginia riflemen.

Morgan: 40/47, 48: John Pierpont, 1837-1913, the American banker and financier.

Morgan: 71/165: William, 1750-1833, author of The Memoirs of the Life of the Rev. Richard Price (1815).

[Morgenthau, Henry]: 74/17: 1856-1946, American diplomat; am- bassador to Turkey (1913-16) and to Mexico (1920).

[Morgenthau, Henry Jr.]: 74/17: 1891-   , U. S. Secretary of the Treasury (1934-45).

Morocco: 66/126: region in NW Africa.

Morosini: 3/11: the Palazzo Morosini, Venice.

Morris, Gouverneur: 34/17: 1752-1816, American statesman; mem- ber of the Continental Congress (1778-79) and of the Constitu- tional Convention (1787); member of the Senate (1800-03); a very influential figure in New York state politics.

Morris, Robt: 69/153: Robert, 1734-1806, American financier and statesman; member of the Continental Congress (1776-78); signer of the DECLARATION of Independence; member of the Senate (1789-95).

Morse: 34/21: Samuel Finley Breese, 1791-1872, the American artist and inventor.

mortaretti: 44/18: (It) mortaletto: a small mortar used for firing a bonfire.

Mortier: 68/147: fl. 1780, a Dutch broker employed by the banking house of VAN STAPHORST.

Moscou: 34/16: .see MOSCOW.

Moscow: 16/75; 33/13; [34/16; 38/38; 80/75]: the Russian city.

Moses: 71/163: the Hebrew prophet and lawgiver.

Mosqu: 80/75: see MOSCOW.

Most Serene M. Dux: 43/9: reference to FERDINAND II of Tuscany.

motu proprio: 44/17: (L) of his own desire.

Mou: 53/15: see MOU-OUANG.

Mou: 55/37: see MOU-TSONG.

Mougden: 55/66; 61/86: (Mukden), city in S Manchuria which con- trols the north-to-south trade in S Manchuria; became the Manchu capital in 1625, served as the base for the Manchu invasion of China (1644), was capital during the Manchu rule over China (1644-1912).

Mount: 42/5, 7; 43/12, 15; 44/17, 20: see MONTE DEI PASCHI.

Mount: 43/9: see MOUNT OF PITY.

Mountain: 42/8; 43/12: see MONTE DEI PASCHI.

Mt Alban, Lord: 42/8: Montalbano, member of the Sienese BALÍA (c. 1622).

Mount of Pity: 42/4, [5]; 43/9, [12]: Monte di Pietà, a Sienese bank with credit based upon personal collateral; a kind of pawnshop; in existence before and finally merged with MONTE DEI PASCHI. (Also called in text: HOCK SHOP, PAWN SHOP, MOUNT, and PITY).

Mt Tai Haku is 300 miles from heaven...pine needle carpet: 56/47: from the Chinese of Li Po.

Mou-Ouang: 53/15: (Mu Wang) (reign: 1001-946), fifth emperor of the CHOU dynasty; famous for his military campaigns. He decreed that punishments might be redeemed by a money payment, and some three thousand offenses were made expiable by this method.

Mouquin: 74/11, 25; 76/31: a famous restaurant in New York, c. 1900.

Mou-Tsong: 55/37: (Mu Tsung) (reign: 821-25), an inept emperor who was too fond of amusement and who let eunuchs run the government; he died of drinking various concoctions, among which he hoped to find the elixir of life.

Mou Ye: 53/12: (Muh) the battle field in the north of HONAN, in the country of K'i, where the forces of WU WANG and CHEOU-SIN met; in this battle (BC 1122) Emperor Cheou-sin was defeated and the CHANG dynasty brought to an end. (See: Classic Anthology, ode 236).

Mozarello: 5/20: a poetaster of the time of Pope Leo X (1513-21).

Mozart: [26/128]; 41/54; 76/34; 78/58: Wolfgang Amadeus, 1756-91, German composer.

Mukden: see MOUGDEN.

multa: 79/65: (It) fine, penalty.

Münch: [75/28]; 80/88: Gerhardt, 20th century pianist; often played concerts in Rapallo.

munditiis: 80/72: (L) neatness.

murazzi: 25/117: (It) walls.

Murphy: 35/23:

Murray: 62/95; 70/155, 156: William Vans, 1760-1803, appointed minister to the Hague (1798), replacing John Quincy ADAMS; was instrumental in preparing the way for recognition of an American minister to France.

Murray's barracks: 62/88: the barracks in Brattle Street, Boston, where the 29th Regiment of His Majesty's Regulars were quartered (1770).

[Murray, William]: 67/136: 1705-93, first earl of Mansfield; English jurist and parliamentary debater.

Muscou: 38/38: see MOSCOW.

muscovites: 59/73: Russians.

Musée de Cluny, le: 80/83: the Cluny Museum, a 14th-15th century Gothic and Renaissance structure in Paris, built by Pierre de Chaslus, abbot of Cluny; it houses a collection of French art of the Middle Ages and the Renaissance.

Museo del Prado: [80/71]; 81/95: the Prado, Spanish national museum of painting and sculpture, in Madrid.

Muses: 74/23: the nine Greek goddesses who were patrons of the
        arts and sciences.
mus ingens, ingens, noli meum granum comedere: 56/48: (L) huge,
        huge mouse, don't eat my grain. (See: A. Lacharme, Con-
        fucii Chi-King, I, 9, 7, p. 47; Classic Anthology, 113).
Muss: 81/97: see Benito MUSSOLINI.
Mussolini: 41/52, [53], 54; [52/3]; 78/55; [80/73, 75; 81/97; 84/117]:
        Benito, 1883-1945, the Italian dictator (1922-45).
Mustafa: 22/103, 105: prob. a merchant in Gibraltar, c. 1908.
Mutholini: 80/75: see Benito MUSSOLINI.
Mycenian: 7/26: reference to Mycenae, ancient city on the plain of
        Argos.
"My Lady of Ventadour...": 6/22: for the sources of this lyric, see
        Carl Appel, Bernart von Ventadorn (1915), numbers 7:4-5; 8:1-2;
        12:8; 22:63; 44:50.
Myo Cid: 3/11: see Ruy DIAZ.
[Mytilene]: 26/123; 82/103: the island of Lesbos, in the Aegean.

N

Nadasky: 80/91; 82/101: DTC, Pisa.

Naishapur: 15/66: Nishapur, town in NE Iran; birthplace of Omar
 Khayyam. (See: Rubaiyat, stanza 8).

Nana: 54/29: in the legends which gathered about the historical
 BUDDHA, she is said to have been a virgin who miraculously
 gave birth to Buddha after the figure of the Supreme Being appeared to her in the form of a white elephant.

Nancy: 80/73, 88: poss. Nancy CUNARD.

Nan-hai: 54/22: see NAN-YUEI and CHAO-T'O.

Nanking: 59/71: city in W Kiangsu province, E China, on the south
 bank of the Yangtze; founded by the MING dynasty in 1368 and
 served as the Ming capital (1368-1403); known as the Southern
 Capital.

Nan-koan: 58/63: (Nan-k'ou), the "South Pass" a few miles north of
 Nankow, Hopeh province in NE China; also the tribe of NUTCHÉ
 Tartars which takes its name from the region of the pass.

Nankoen: 58/63: see NAN-KOAN.

Nantasket: 64/106: Nantasket Beach, village in E Massachusetts.

Nantes: 65/119: manufacturing and commercial city of Loire-Inféri-
 eure department, NW France.

Nan-Young: 13/59: (Nan Jung), a disciple of CONFUCIUS. (See:
 Analects, V, i).

Nan-yuei: 54/[22], 23: (Nan-yüeh), the State of Yuei (Yüeh) in
 Honan province, E central China, along the Hwang Ho.

Napishtim: 25/119: Uta-napishtim, a character in the Babylonian
 epic, Gilgamish; he reveals to Gilgamish "knowledge deep-
 hidden." (See: Gilgamish, Tablet XI).

Naples: 5/20; 8/32; 10/42, 43, 46; 21/96, 98; 32/9; 54/26; [74/26];
 78/56: the seaport of S Italy.

Nap'oiiiii: 74/26: see NAPLES.

Napoleon: 18/80; 24/114; 33/10; 34/16; 41/55; 44/21; 50/43; 51/44;
 62/95; 78/55; 80/75: see NAPOLEON I.

[Napoleon I]: 18/80; 24/114; 31/6; 33/10, 11; 34/15, 16; 41/55; 44/21;
 50/41, 43; 51/44; 62/95; 71/163, 164; 78/55; 80/75: Napoleon
 Bonaparte, 1769-1821, Emperor of the French (1805-14).

[Napoleon II]: 34/16: François Charles Joseph Napoleon, 1811-32,
 son of NAPOLEON I and MARIE LOUISE; titular king of Rome.

Napoleon III: [16/71; 38/41]; 74/25: Charles Louis Napoleon Bonaparte, 1808-73, known as Louis Napoleon; Emperor of the
 French (1852-71); called Barbiche because of his goatee.

Napoleon Barbiche: 16/71; 38/41: see NAPOLEON III.

Napoli: 21/96: see NAPLES.

Napper: 80/80: DTC, Pisa.

Narf, Lard: 62/88: see Fredrick NORTH.

Nascita, La: 74/24: (It) the birth; reference to the Birth of Venus
 by Sandro BOTTICELLI.

Nassau St.: 12/53: street in New York City.

Nataanovitch: 35/22:

natae praelibati margaritae/Ill. D. Nicolai Marchionis Esten. et

[151]

Sponsae: 24/111: (L) Margaret, daughter of the afore-named
   illustrious Lord Niccolò, Marquis of ESTE, and his wife.
Natalie: 80/83; 84/117: prob. Natalie Clifford BARNEY.
natural burella: 69/153: (It) natural dungeon. (See: Inferno, 34,
   98).
naturans: 47/31: (L) in accord with nature; natural action.
Nauphal: 6/21: Néaufles-Saint-Martin, district of Normandy; location of an important fortress in the Middle Ages.
Nausikaa: 78/60: Nausicaa, daughter of the Phaeacian king, Alci-
   nous, in Odyssey (VI); Odysseus approaches her as she is playing ball on the beach, just after she had finished washing the
   household linen.
nautilis biancastra: 74/21: prob. (It), nautilo biancastro: a white-
   colored shell; poss. that in BOTTICELLI's painting of Venus.
Navighero: 5/20: prob. Andrea Navagero, 1483-1529, Venetian poet
   and epigrammatist; poss. a reference to the work Navgervis,
   Sive de Poetica Dialogus by Girolamo FRACASTOR.
Navy Board: 65/114: Navy Board of the Eastern Department, the
   American Continental Navy board of direction; established in
   Boston (1777) upon the recommendation of John ADAMS.
Naxos: 2/7; 24/111; 78/56: largest island of the Cyclades, in the
   Aegean Sea; the island was once a center for the worship of
   DIONYSUS.
N. Carolina: 62/90; 69/153; 74/3: see NORTH CAROLINA.
nec accidens est: 74/27: (L) and is not an attribute.
nec benecomata: 74/15; [76/38]: (L) nor fair-tressed. (See: An-
   dreas Divus, trans., Odyssey, XI).
nec ivi in harum/ Nec in harum ingressus sum: 39/44; [74/14, 17]:
   (L) nor went I to the pigsty/ Nor into the pigsty did I enter.
   (See: AC EGO IN HARUM).
Necker: 68/147: Jacques, 1732-1804, French statesman; minister of
   finance (1776-81), director-general of finance (1788-90).
nec lupo committere agnum: 70/159: (L) nor entrust a lamb to a
   wolf. (See: John Adams, Works, IX, 571).
nec personae: 76/36: (L) nor people (individuals).
Nec Spe Nec Metu: 3/12: (L) With neither hope nor fear. (The motto
   was in the rooms of Isabella d'Este in the Ducal Palace, Mantua).
Nedham: 67/137: Marchamont, 1620-78, English political writer;
   author of The Case of the Commonwealth of England Stated (1650).
Neestho: 20/91: (Gr) let her go. (See: Appendix A).
Negus, the: 80/88: title of the sovereign of Ethiopia; see HAILE
   SELASSIE.
Nekuia: 74/9: (Gr) The Evocation of the Dead; name of the Eleventh
   book of the Odyssey. (See: Appendix A).
nel clivo ed al triedro: 76/30: (It) in the slope and at the corner.
Nel fuoco/ D'amore mi mise, nel fuoco d'amore mi mise: 20/92-93:
   (It) In the fire/ of love he put me, in the fire of love he put me.
   (See: St. Francis of Assisi, Cantico Secondo, where text reads:
   In foco amor mi mise).
nell' anima: 42/3: (It) in the soul.
Nel paradiso terrestre: 22/102: (It) In the terrestrial paradise.

Nelson: 80/71: DTC, Pisa.

Nelson, Colonel: 67/138: Thomas, 1738-89, American Revolutionary patriot; colonel in the 2nd Regiment of Virginia; member of the Continental Congress (1775-77), signer of the DECLARATION of Independence, governor of Virginia (1781).

nel tramonto: 21/98: (It) in the sunset.

Nel ventre tuo, o nella mente mia: 29/144: (It) In your belly, or in my mind.

Nemi: 74/16; 77/45; [80/73(?)]: Lake Nemi, a small crater lake in the Alban Hills of Latium, Italy; here was the sacred grove and the temple of Diana, guarded by a priest who held the post until he was killed by another who sought the office. (See: Frazer, The Golden Bough).

nemo obstabat: 12/54: (L) nobody prevented it.

Nenni: 80/73: prob. NEMI.

nenuphar: 55/44; 77/50: (Fr) water-lily.

Nenuphar: 55/44: prob. a reference to TCHEOU-TUN-Y; one of his best known writings is a satire, veiled under the symbolism of flowers, in which the writer identifies himself with the water-lily (nenuphar), "the Lady Virtue sans pareille."

N.E.P.: 74/19: New Economic Policy of the U.S.S.R., instituted by LENIN in 1921.

nephew: 26/121: see Gorro LOLLI.

nepotes Remi magnanimi: 74/17: (L) grandsons (descendents) of the great-souled REMUS.

ne povans desraciner: 80/81: (O Fr) not being able to uproot.

Neptune: 1/5; [47/30]; 80/84; 82/102; 83/106: the Roman god of the sea.

Neptunus: 47/30: (L) NEPTUNE.

Nerea: 17/76: poss. reference to the Nereïds, sea-maidens who were the daughters of Nereus, Homer's "Old Man" of the sea.

[Neroni, Dietisalvi]: 21/96: d. 1482, a wealthy citizen of Florence who conspired to overthrow the Medici rule of Florence after the death of Cosimo de' MEDICI (1464). Neroni, acting as financial advisor to Piero de' MEDICI, advised Piero to call in all his debts; this caused Piero to lose much of his popularity and gained for him a reputation of avarice. In 1466 Neroni's plot was uncovered and he was exiled from Florence.

neschek: 52/3, 4: (Heb) neshek: usury.

neson amumona: 20/94: (Gr) a noble island. (See: Appendix A).

Nestorians: 54/35: members of the Nestorian Church, originally the ancient church of Persia, which is related to Catholicism but not of the Catholic communion. The greatest period of Nestorian expansion was from the 7th to 10th centuries, when missions were sent to India and China; in 631 they brought Christianity into China. The famous Nestorian tablet (in Sian, SHENSI province) is a record, in Chinese and Syriac, of the progress of Christianity in China from 631 to 781, when the tablet was erected.

Nestorno, Giovan: 11/48: Giovanni di Toma, an officer in the forces of Sigismondo MALATESTA.

Neuchâtel: 67/140: a Swiss Canton, in the Jura Mountains.

Neufchastel: 6/21: Neufchâtel, town NE of Rouen, France; chief
    town of the Bray region.

Neufville: 68/146: see JOHN DE NEUFVILLE & SONS.

Neville: 67/137: Henry, 1620-94, English political writer; author of
    Discourses Concerning Government (1698).

Nevsky: 16/75; 19/86; 74/11; 76/31; 78/58: the Nevsky Prospekt in
    St. Petersburg; at the end of the Nevsky Prospekt is the
    Znamenskays Place, the site of the Moscow station.

Newbolt, Sir Henry: [12/53?]; 74/11; 80/85: Sir Henry John Newbolt,
    1862-1938, the English poet.

new bridge: 76/38: the Accademia Bridge, Venice.

New Discourse, the: 54/22: prob. LOU KIA's record of his travels
    about the Chinese Empire when he was minister of state for
    Emperor KAO-HOANG-TI.

New England: 62/87; 65/109; 76/39.

New England Coffee House: 70/158: a restaurant in London.

Newfoundland: 34/16.

New Hampshire: 64/102.

New Jersey: 65/111.

New Monte: 42/6; 43/13: see MONTE DEI PASCHI.

New Mount: 43/13, 14: see MONTE DEI PASCHI.

New Mountain: 42/5: see MONTE DEI PASCHI.

New York: 28/138; 34/17, 20; 37/[31], 35; 46/25; [62/90, 94; 64/108];
    65/109; [77/42]: New York State.

New York: [79/67]; 80/86: New York city.

[New York State Convention]: 37/31: a convention called to amend
    the constitution of New York State (August-November 1821).

Ney: 34/16; 50/42: Michel, 1769-1815, French soldier in the Revolu-
    tionary and Napoleonic armies; created marshal of France
    (1804); commanded the Old Guard at Waterloo (1815); tried, con-
    demned for treason and shot.

[Ngaïycou-chilitala]: 56/56: (Ai'yco Shihlitala) d. AD 1378, King of
    the Mongols; he was the successor of Emperor CHUNTI, who,
    after the Yüan dynasty fell, retreated to Korea and ruled the
    Mongol tribes there.

Ngan: 54/26: see TCHANG-NGAN.

Ngan: 55/42, 43, 44, 45: see OUANG-NGAN-CHÉ.

Ngan-yong: 54/34: Ngan-yong-tching (Ang-yung-chêng), a city in
    northern China.

Niccolo: 24/113, 114: see Niccolò d'ESTE.

Nice: 18/82: city of SE France, on the Mediterranean.

Nicea: 7/26: poss. reference to the "Nicean barks" of Poe's poem,
    To Helen, therefore reference to Helen (ELEANOR of Aqui-
    taine and HELEN of Troy).

Nicolao: 27/130: fl. 1133, a sculptor who worked on the Duomo of
    Ferrara.

Nicoletti: 74/5; 76/36: prob. the Prefect at GARDONE.

Nicolo: 82/104: see Niccolò d'ESTE.

nient' altro: 74/12: (It) nothing else.

Niger: 74/15: the river in W Africa.

nihil humanum alienum: 64/106: (L) nothing human is foreign. (See:
    Terence, Heauton Timorumenos, 77: Homo sum: humani
    nihil a me alientum puto).
Nik-ia-su: 56/48: see NINKIASSOU.
Nile: 5/17; 21/99: the river in Egypt.
nimium amorata in eum: 29/142: (L) too much enamoured of him.
Nine Urns of Yu: 53/18: see NINE VASES OF YU.
Nine vases of Yu: 53/12, [18]: the nine vases which Emperor YU
    had cast in bronze and engraved with a geographical descrip-
    tion of the nine provinces of the Empire; the vases were to be
    found in the capital of CHOU, the principality.
"nineties, the": 28/135: the 1890's.
Ninghia: 56/55: (Ningsia), a province in W Inner Mongolia.
[Ninkiassou]: 56/48: (Ninchiassu) (reign: 1225-34), Emperor of
    the KIN dynasty; his reign was one of almost continual war with
    the Mongols of OGOTAI KHAN.
Nipchou: 59/72, 73: (Nerchinsk), town in the S central Chita Region
    of the U.S.S.R., on the Shilka river. In 1689 the Treaty of
    Nerchinsk between China and Russia was signed here; the
    treaty required Russia to withdraw from the AMUR valley
    region, and served to check Russian colonization in that area
    to some extent.
Nippon: 58/62, 63: (Jap) JAPAN.
nisi forsitan epicureae: 10/44: (L) except, perhaps, the Epicurean.
Nismes: 31/4: Nîmes, a manufacturing and commercial city of Gard
    department, S France; noted for its ancient Roman buildings,
    among which is a Corinthian temple (the Maison Carrée) which
    was restored in 1789 and converted into a museum (1832).
Noah, Mordecai: 34/18, 21: 1785-1851, American journalist and
    diplomat; as U. S. consul to Tunis and special agent to Algiers
    (1813-15), he gained the release of Americans held prisoner by
    Algerian pirates; founder and editor of several New York news-
    papers; surveyor of the Port of New York (1829-33).
Noailles: 65/118: a distinguished French family; head of the family
    during the time John ADAMS was in France was Philippe de
    Noailles, Duc de Mouchy (1715-94), marshal of France, guil-
    lotined in 1794.
Noel, Noel, the green holly: 80/93: poss. variation of Shakespeare,
    As You Like It: "Heigh ho! sing, heigh ho! unto the green
    holly."
No hay amor sin celos/ Sin segreto no hay amor: 78/61: (Sp)...Sin
    secreto...: There is no love without jealousy/ Without secrecy
    there is no love. (Sin Secreto No Hay Amor is a play by Lope
    de Vega, 1624).
Noi ci facciam sgannar per Mussolini: 41/52: (It) We'd have our throats
    cut for MUSSOLINI. (See: Jefferson and/or Mussolini, 26).
Noigandres: 20/89, 90: (Pr) a term of uncertain meaning: from a
    song of Arnaut DANIEL, Er vei vermeills, vertz, blaus,
    blancs, gruocs; the last line of the first strophe ends with the
    following: "E jois le grans, e l'olors d'enoi gandres." (See:
    Lavaud, Les Poesies d'Arnaut Daniel, (1910) 81, for a note on

the meaning of gandres).

Nollet, J.: 69/150: Jacobus, fl. 1780, an official of the city of
    SCHIEDAM, Holland.

noman: 74/4, [8; 80/77]: the name Odysseus assumes when with
    the Cyclops. (See: Odyssey, IX, 336).

nominatim: 62/94: (L) namely, expressly.

Non combaattere: 76/39; 83/109: (It) Non combattere: don't fight.

nondum orto jubare: 29/145: (L) before sunrise.

non è una hontrada è un homplesso: 80/75: (It: Tuscan dialect) non
    è una contrada è un complesso: it is not a country, it's a com-
    plex.

non intendeva di quella materia: 43/15: (It) he did not understand
    such matter.

non vi sed saepe legendo: 64/106: (L) not by violence but by frequent
    reading. (See: John Adams, Works, II, 248).

[Norman, Montagu Collet]: 77/52: 1st Baron Norman of St. Clere,
    1871-1950, English financier; governor of the Bank of England
    (1920-44).

Normandia, Duchess of: 6/21: see ANOR.

Nor seeks the carmine petal to infer/ Nor is the white bud Time's
    inquisitor: 80/94: variation of Tennyson, a song from The
    Princess: Now sleeps the crimson petal, now the white.

[North, Frederick]: 62/88; 71/165: 2nd Earl of Guilford, 1732-92,
    English statesman; prime minister under George III (1770-82).
    As prime minister, North made himself the agent of the king's
    plans to control the American colonies; supported the STAMP
    ACT and the tax on tea.

North, Lord: 62/88; 71/165: see Frederick NORTH.

North, the: 34/20; 79/67: in general, that part of the U. S. north
    of the MASON-DIXON line and the Ohio River.

North American Union: 34/20: the United States of America.

North Carolina: [62/90]; 65/113; [69/153; 74/3].

North River: 71/161: the HUDSON RIVER.

Northwestern railway: 22/101: pseudonym for the Northern Pacific
    Railroad, an American railway system from Duluth and St.
    Paul, Minnesota, to Seattle, Washington, and Portland, Oregon;
    chartered by special act of Congress (1864); construction began
    (1870) and the railway was opened in 1883. Of the land granted
    by the U. S. government for the construction of the Northern
    Pacific, over 2,500,000 undistributed acres were still held by
    the company in 1948.

Norton, Miss: 76/34:

Notes for Princesses: 54/32: a work on the lives of the princesses
    of the Chinese Empire before the time of TCHANG-SUN-CHI
    (d. AD 636), its author.

Notes on Conduct: 54/33: a treatise, consisting of twelve sections,
    on "How a king should conduct himself," written by Emperor
    TAÏ-TSONG (AD 649) for his son.

Notre Dame: 83/106: the Notre Dame de Paris.

Notre dame de Clery: 56/49: the church of Our Lady in Clery, a
    town in Loiret department, SW of Orléans.

Nous: [25/119]; 40/51: (Gr) mind, sense, wit; purpose; reason, in-
    tellect. (See: Appendix A).
Nous sommes en attendant charmés de voir/ que les états des autres
    provinces et conséquemment la/ république entière ont, à
    l'exemple des Etats de Frise/ reconnu.../ (signed) Les mem-
    bres de la Société Bourgeoise: 69/152: (Fr) Meanwhile we
    are delighted to see/ that the states of the other provinces and
    consequently the/ entire republic have, following the example
    of the States of FRIESLAND/ recognized.../ (signed) the mem-
    bers of the SOCIÉTÉ BOURGEOISE. (See: John Adams,
    Works, VIII, 56).
Novanglus: 62/90; 67/134: John ADAMS used the pen name "Novan-
    glus" [i.e. New Englander] to sign a series of articles
    (BOSTON GAZETTE, 1774-75) in which he sought to demon-
    strate that the laws of England could not be made to apply to
    the American colonies; the articles were an answer to a series
    of loyalist papers by Daniel Leonard (Massachusetts Gazette
    and Post Boy, 1774-75), who signed himself "Massachusettensis."
Nova Scotia: 63/99; 65/123: a province of Canada.
novecento: 83/113: (It) of the twentieth century.
Novvy: 10/47; 11/49; 23/107: see Domenico MALATESTA.
nox animae magna: 74/[14], 15, [16]: (L) the soul's great night.
    (See: St. John of the Cross, Dark Night of the Soul).
Nutché: 55/45; 58/63: (Nü-chên), a Tartar tribe, formerly of north
    Korea near the head waters of the Yalu River. They were long
    dominated by the KHITAN Tartars, but in AD 1114 they defeated
    the Khitan; their chieftain, AKOUTA, proclaimed the KIN dy-
    nasty of the Nutché Tartars.
Nvon so Forth, Herr: 41/54: prob. Karl VON UNRUH.
N. Y.: 64/108; 65/109; 77/42: see NEW YORK, the state.
N. Y.: 79/67: see NEW YORK, the city.
N. York: 62/90, 94; 65/109: see NEW YORK, the state.

O

Oberon: 71/162: the narrative poem by C. M. Wieland (1780).

Obit, aetatis: 50/43: (L) died, at the age of.

obligatio: 43/11: (L) obligation.

Ob pecuniae scars(c)itatem: 42/7; 43/10; 66/128: (L) on account of scarcity of money.

O'Brien: 65/120: Lewis, fl. 1780, an Irishman whom John ADAMS met in Spain.

Obsta principiis: 67/134: (L) resist the beginnings. (See: Ovid, Remed. Amor, 91).

Ocean: 2/6; [23/107]: Oceanus, in early Greek cosmology the river that encircled the plain of the earth.

Odes, the: 13/60; 53/19; 59/70: the Book of Odes, or SHIH CHING.

Odon: 78/59: see Odon POR.

Odysseus: 1/4; 6/21; 20/93; 23/107; 24/111; 39/44; 47/31; 74/3, 4, [8]; 77/45; 79/66; [80/77]: the Greek hero.

Odyssey: 80/90: the Homeric epic of the wanderings of ODYSSEUS.

Oedipus: 74/17: Greek hero who inadvertently murdered his father and married his mother; the story is told in Sophocles' Oedipus Rex.

Oedipus of the Lagunes: 76/34: prob. a Venetian publication of D'ANNUNZIO caricatures.

OEuvre de M. le Duc de Vauguyon: 65/122: text should read ouvrage ...(See: John Adams, Works, III, 285): (Fr) the work of the Duke of VAUGUYON.

Offa: 67/133: Offa II, ruler of Mercia (757-796); one of the best and most powerful of the Anglo-Saxon kings.

Offo de Paschi: 43/13: (It) Office of the PASCHI (bank).

of the two usuries, the lesser is now put down: 52/4: variation of Shakespeare, Measure for Measure, III, ii, 7: 'Twas never merry world since, of two usuries, the merriest was put dowr and the worser allowed by order of law a furred gown to keep him warm.

"...of the Wabash cannon ball": 77/52: from a popular American song, The Wabash Cannon Ball.

Ogni Santi: 76/40: a canal in Venice; Pound lived in Venice (1908) near the conjunction of the San Trovaso and Ogni Santi canals.

Ogotai: 56/47, 48, 49, 51: Ogotai Khan, 1185-1241, second Khan of the Mongols, succeeding GENGHIS KHAN in 1228. With the help of his minister, YÉLIU-TCHUTSAÏ, he gave to the Mongols and the people they conquered a regular administration, taxation, and criminal jurisprudence. In 1236 he issued paper money and started a system of regular governmental examinations. He campaigned in Korea, China, and Central Asia and managed to extinguish the KIN Tartars in 1234.

Ohio: 31/3: the river.

Ohio canal: 32/7: see CHESAPEAKE AND OHIO CANAL CO.

o-hon dit que'ke fois au vi'age/ qu'une casque ne sert pour rien/ 'hien de tout/ Cela ne sert que pour donner courage/ a ceux qui n'en ont pas de tout: [29/143]; 78/58; [80/84]: (Fr: imi-

tation of colloquial language) it is sometimes said in the vil-
lage/ that a helmet has no use/ none at all/ It is good only to
give courage/ to those who don't have any at all.
Oh to be in England now that Winston's out: 80/92: variation on
Browning, Home Thoughts from Abroad.
Oige: 18/82:
Oirishman, the: 74/7: see Johannes Scotus ERIGENA.
Oklahoma City: 28/137: capital of the state of Oklahoma.
Old Dynasty: 84/116: poss. the TCHEOU dynasty of China.
old empress: 54/33: see OU-HEOU.
old great aunt: 84/117: see AUNT F.
old Marchesa: 74/11:
old woman from Kansas: 28/135:
Old Worker's Hill: 61/82: the Shen Nung Tan ("Altar dedicated to
Shen Nung," the mythical emperor of China who invented the
plow). Commonly known as the Temple of Agriculture, situ-
ated in Peiping directly across from the Tien Tan, or "Altar
of Heaven." In 1726, Emperor YONG-TCHING revived the
ancient rites connected with the Altar of Agriculture.
Oleron: 65/116: Ile d'Oléron, an island in the Bay of Biscay; noted
for its Laws of Oleron, a medieval code of maritime laws
which forms the basis of modern maritime law.
Olibanum: 2/9: frankincense.
Olim de Malatestis: [11/50]; 76/40; 80/79; 83/107: (L) once of the
MALATESTA.
Oliver: 64/101: see Oliver CROMWELL.
Oliver: 64/108: Andrew, 1706-44, secretary and lieutenant-govern-
or of Massachusetts Colony (1756-71); stamp officer for the
STAMP ACT in Massachusetts. Oliver advocated the dispatch
of British troops to America and the prosecution of Samuel
ADAMS for his political agitation.
Oliver: 62/89; [65/109]: Peter, 1713-91, a Massachusetts loyalist.
As chief justice of Massachusetts Colony (1771-76) Oliver
agreed to accept special monetary grants from the English
Crown to the Massachusetts judiciary, and this action prompted
the legislature to impeach him; however, Governor Thomas
HUTCHINSON blocked the proceedings. In 1774 several Mass-
achusetts grand juries refused to serve under Oliver because
of his loyalist sympathies.
Olivet: 24/111: the Mount of Olives, east of Jerusalem.
olivi: 74/16: (It) olive trees.
Olivia: 78/61: see Olivia SHAKESPEAR.
olofans, l': 20/91: Olifant, Roland's horn. (See: The Song of
Roland).
Oltrepassimo: 28/139: prob. pseudonym for Prince Filippo-Massi-
miliano Massimo, 1843-1915, created first Prince Lancellotti
(1865) by PIUS IX; from his half-brother, Prince Camillo-Carlo-
Alberto Massimo, he purchased the DISCOBOLUS.
omnem...volve lapidem: 26/121: (L) turn every stone.
omnes de partibus ultramarinis: 35/25: (L) all from oversea regions.
Omnia: 74/7: (L) everything.

omnia, quae sunt, lumina sunt: 83/106: (L) everything that exists
    is light. (Poss. suggested by Grosseteste, De luce seu de
    inchoatione formarum, ed. Baur, 57, where text reads: omnia
    esse unum ab unis lucis perfectione...ea, quae sunt multa,
    esse multa ab ipsius lucis diversa multiplicatione).
once, las: 18/81: (Sp) eleven o'clock.
Ongla, oncle: 6/21: (Pr) Nail, uncle. (See: Arnaut Daniel, Lo ferm
    voler qu'el cor m'intra).
Oñis: 34/17: Don Luis de, Spanish minister at Washington in 1819;
    negotiated the treaty between the US and Spain which gave
    Florida to the US. When Spain ratified the treaty (1821) there
    was much popular sentiment against Spain in America.
"On the Alcides...hand: 82/101: (See Appendix A: ΕΜΟΣ).
operai: 38/41: (It) workmen. ·
Orage: 46/26; 80/88: Alfred Richard, 1873-1934, English journalist;
    editor of the New Age.
Oranienbaum: 34/16: town in the Leningrad Region of Soviet Russia;
    was an imperial residence 1727-1914.
orationem: 62/91: (L) oration.
Orationem/ Elegantissimam et ornatissimam/ Audivimus venerabi-
    lis in Xti fratres ac dilectissimi/ filii: 10/45: (L) ... in Xto
    fratris: We have heard a most elegant and ornate speech of
    our reverend brother in Christ and most beloved son.
Ora vela, ora a remi, sino ad ora di vespero: 24/111: (It) Now sail-
    ing, now rowing, until the (hour of) sunset. (Poss. from
    Luchino dal CAMPO).
Orbe: 41/53: town in Vaud Canton, W. Switzerland, on the Orbe
    River.
Orbem bellis, urbem gabellis, Urbanus octavus/ implevit: 43/14:
    (L) URBAN VIII filled the world with wars, the city with taxes.
Orbetello: 10/42: town of Grosseto province in Tuscany.
Orbino, Fedricho d': 9/35: see Federigo d'URBINO.
Orcum: 39/45: Orcus (L) the infernal regions; Hades.
ordine, contrordine e disordine: 41/54: (It) order, counter-order,
    disorder.
oricalchi: 1/5: (L) of copper. (See: Homeric Hymn VI To Aphro-
    dite, 9).
Orion: 52/6: the constellation.
Orleans: 74/26: town of the Loiret department, Ncentral France.
ormoulu: 40/49: ormolu, brass made to imitate gold.
Oros: 59/72: Russians.
Orosians: 59/73; 60/74: Russians.
Orsini: [9/37]; 10/42: Count Aldobrando Orsini, fl. 1440, Signore
    of Pitigliano.
Orso, Count: 50/40:
Orsola, Donna: 43/13: fl. 1622, a Sienese whore.
Ortes: 60/75: Ortos (Ordos) a Tartar tribe occupying the territory
    of Ordos, a desert region south of the Hwang Ho in Suiyuan
    province, central Inner Mongolia.
Ortolo: 74/26: see MADONNA IN HORTULO.
Oryzia mutica: 32/7: (L) short-grained rice.

O se credesse: 5/19: (It) or if he would believe. (See: Varchi, Storia Fiorentino, III, 262).

O se morisse, credesse caduto da sè: 5/19: (It) or if he would die, believed fallen by himself. (See: Varchi, Storia Fiorentino, III, 262:...o che egli non morisse...non si credesse lui esser caduto da se.

Osservanza: 80/75: (It) observance.

Ostend: 65/122: port city of W Flanders province, N Belgium.

ostendit incitatque. Vir autem...: 59/70: see DE LIBRO CHI-KING SIC CENSO....

Oswald: 65/124; 69/151: Richard, 1705-84, English statesman. In 1782 he was given authority to make peace with the American colonies at the Paris peace negotiations; however, he did not sign the definitive Treaty of Versailles (3 September 1783).

O sweet and lovely/ o Lady be good: 74/17: from the song by George Gershwin, Oh, Lady Be Good.

oth fugol ouitbaer: 27/129: the line should read SUMNE FUGOL OTHBAER.

Otis: 66/127: Samuel Allyne, 1740-1814, American statesman, member of the Constitutional Convention (1784); Secretary of the U. S. Senate (1789-1814).

Otis, James: 34/17; 63/100; 64/102, 108; 66/130; 71/165, 166; 78/60(?); 82/102(?): 1725-83, American lawyer and patriot; advocate general of Boston (1756-61) but resigned in protest against the issuing of writs of assistance; head of the Massachusetts Committee of Correspondence (1764); opposed the STAMP ACT and organized the Stamp Congress (1765); also wrote on Latin and Greek prosody.

Otreus, King: 23/109; 25/119: legendary king of Phrygia; when APHRODITE lay with ANCHISES, she told him that her father was King Otreus, for she wished to keep her identity a secret. (See: Homeric Hymn V to Aphrodite, 111ff).

"O troubled reflection/ O Throat, O throbbing heart": 82/104: from Whitman, Out of the Cradle Endlessly Rocking.

Ottavian: 9/40: see Ottaviano d'Antonio di DUCCIO.

Ou: 54/26: see KOUANG-OU-TI.

Ou: 54/28: (Wu) one of the THREE KINGDOMS; the kingdom of Wu controlled the territory south of the Yangtze.

Ou: 54/29: see HIAO-OU-TI.

Oua-chi: 57/61: (Wa Shih) fl. AD 1559, a princess of Kwangsi province; she led Chinese troops against Japanese pirates that were attacking the southeast coast of China.

Ouang Chi: 54/26: (Wang Shih) fl. AD 15; he and his five brothers were of the family of Wang Mang, the Usurper (reign: 9-23).

Ouang Chi: 56/51: (Wang Shih) d. AD 1297, wife of KANOUEN, commander of Tchang-tcheou. Rather than become the wife of TCHIN-TIAO-YEN, the murderer of her husband, Ouang Chi leapt into the funeral pyre of Kanouen. Emperor TIMOUR was much impressed by the deed and built a memorial for her.

Ouangchin: 57/57: (Wang Shên) fl. AD 1403, a Buddhist priest serving in the temple of Chin-lo-koan, outside the city of Nanking.

Ouang-mi: 54/27: (Wang Mi) fl. AD 107, a mandarin who attempted
    to bribe YANG-TCHIN.

Ouang-Ngan-ché: 55/42, [43, 44, 45]: (Wang An-shih) 1021-86, be-
    came confidential advisor and minister of state to Emperor
    CHIN-TSONG (1069). He and the emperor began reforms based
    on Ouang's new and "more correct" interpretations of the
    Classics: state administration of commerce, state support for
    farmers, compulsory military service, a state system of
    barter, a new land tax system. In the face of much opposition,
    the emperor put Ouang's reforms into practice, but Ouang
    tried to move too rapidly and lived to see all his reforms
    abolished. After his death he was disgraced and his tablet re-
    moved from the Confucian Temple.

Ouang-po: 55/40: (Wang Po) d. AD 959, a statesman, mathematician,
    and personal counselor to Emperor CHI-TSONG.

Ouang Siaopo: 55/41: (Wang Hsiao-po) fl. AD 993, a man of the
    people who roused Szechwan province to revolt against their
    governor in 993. There was little money in the province, since
    the conquering SUNG troops had carried it away a few years
    before; the mandarins were fleecing the people; the rich were
    buying up small farms and depriving the poor of land and food.
    Imperial troops soon put down the rebellion, and Emperor
    TAI-TSONG appointed a governor who improved the condition
    of the poor.

Ouang-siun: 54/27: (Wang Hsün) fl. AD 280, a general serving
    Emperor TÇIN-OU-TI; engaged in campaigns against the king-
    dom of Wu, one of the THREE KINGDOMS.

Ouang tchi: 56/50: Ouang-tchu (Wang Chu) d. AD 1282, chief officer
    of the city of Peiping. He led the conspiracy to assassinate
    AHAMA, the chief minister of KUBLAI KHAN; Ouang-tchu
    lured Ahama to the palace late at night and killed him with an
    iron mace. Kublai had Ouang executed.

[Ouang-tsai-gin]: 55/37: (Wang Tsai-jen) d. AD 847, favorite con-
    cubine of Emperor OU-TSONG.

[Ouang-tsiuen-pin]: 55/41: (Wang Chŭon-pin) fl. AD 965, a general
    serving Emperor TCHAO-KOUANG; he was in charge of the
    expedition which succeeded in overcoming the HEOU-CHOU.

Ouang Yeou: 55/39: (Wang Yeou) fl. AD 921, a rebel commander of
    the troops of LI-TSUN-HIU, Prince of Tçin; he invited the
    Khitan Tartars to attack some cities of China, which they did.

Ouan Jin: 74/4, 5: (Ch) (Wen jen): man of letters; writer.

Ouan Li: 58/62, 63: (Wan Li), title of the reign of Emperor CHIN-
    TSONG.

Ouan-soui!: 54/25; 55/39, 41; 57/57; 58/69: (Ch) (Wan-sui): Ten
    thousand years. (One of the forms of address to the Emperor
    of China).

Ouantse: 56/50: prob. Ouantçe (Wan Tzŭ) fl. AD 1291, one of
    KUBLAI KHAN's ministers of state.

Ouanyen: 56/47: (Wan-yen), family name of the rulers of the KIN
    dynasty of the NUTCHÉ Tartars.

Ouei: 54/29: (Wei), a principality in the general region of the mod-

ern Sian, a city of SHENSI province, NE central China, on the
Wei river where it joins the Hwang Ho.

Ouei-Kao: 55/36: (Wei Kao) d. AD 805, a general of the imperial
troops who won significant victories over the Tartars. As
governor of a province for 21 years he gained more fame, for
during that time the people of his province paid exactly the tax
demanded by the emperor from the province-- and no more.

Ouei-Lie: 55/44: Ouei-lié-ouang (Wei-Lieh Wang) (reign: 425-401),
during the reign of this emperor nothing much happened, except that the tripods of YU began making noises-- which meant
that the end of the TCHEOU dynasty was near.

Ouei-Tching: 54/32: (Wei Chêng) d. AD 643, an astute minister of
Emperor TAÏ-TSONG.

Ouen: 53/18: see OUEN KONG.

Ouen: 54/31: see OUEN-TI.

Ouen: 56/49: Ouen-kiang-hien (Wên-chiang-hsien), a town in
SZECHWAN province.

Ouen: 56/49: see WEN WANG.

Ouen Kong: 53/18: (Wên Kung) d. BC 609, Prince of LOU; a benevolent and capable ruler.

Ouen Ouang: 53/14: see WEN WANG.

Ouen ti: 54/29: (Wên Ti) (reign: 424-453). In spite of the opposition of the state of OUEI, he extended the power of the emper-
or over much territory. He was fond of literature and the
arts and paid attention to education by establishing national
colleges.

Ouen Ti: 54/30: see KIEN-OUEN-TI.

[Ouen-ti]: 54/31: (Wên ti) (reign: 581-605), first emperor of the
Sui dynasty (589-618). He commanded that no man should be
put to death before his case had been reported three times;
however, this led to great government corruption, for it gave
a wide margin of safety to corrupt mandarins. Because the
emperor was uneducated, he had great contempt for scholars
and classical education; he preferred simple and direct language to the rhetoric of the Classics.

Ouen Ti: 56/56: see HIAO OUEN.

Ouen Tiensiang: 56/50: (Wên T'ien-hsiang) 1236-83, one of the most
patriotic men in Chinese history; he served the last five emperors of the Southern SUNG dynasty as minister and general.
All his efforts to stem the Mongol invasions and preserve the
dynasty failed, and when the dynasty fell he was taken prisoner
(1279). Because he would not pledge his loyalty to the Mongols,
he was executed by KUBLAI KHAN.

Ouen-Tsong: 55/37: (Wên Tsung) (reign: 827-41). He began his
reign by cutting government expenditures, dismissing three
thousand women from the royal harem, and giving audiences
to his ministers every other day; but he lacked firmness of
purpose, and soon the power of the court was usurped by the
eunuchs. At this time the eunuchs became a national danger,
but all efforts to get rid of them failed.

Ouen yan Tchin hochang: 56/48: Ouanyen-tchin-ho-chang (Wan-yen

Chên Ho-shang) d. AD 1232, prince royal of the KIN dynasty
and an officer of the Kin troops during the battles between the
Kin and the Mongols.

Ou-heou: 54/33: (Wu Hou) 625-705, one of the concubines of Emperor TAÏ TSONG; after his death she became the empress of
KAO-TSONG in 656, and for the next forty years she was one
of the most important figures in Chinese political history.
Cruel and unscrupulous, she controlled two emperors and became virtual ruler of the Empire. She forced her husband to
make her co-ruler (they were known as "The Two Holy Ones")
and finally took over all his power. During the years 684-705
her son TCHONG-TSONG was nominally the emperor, but the
period is often known as the reign of Empress Ou-heou.

Ou-Kiai: 56/47: (Wu Ch'ieh) fl. AD 1135, a captain of the imperial
troops who served Emperor Kao Tsung (reign: 1127-63).

Oulo: 55/45: see CHI-TSONG.

[Ou-ouang]: 13/60; 53/12, 14: French transliteration for WU-WANG.

Ousan: 58/68, 69: Ou-san-kouei (Wu San-kuei) d. AD 1678, a commander of the imperial forces during the last years of the
MING dynasty. In 1643 Ou-san-kouei received news that Peiping had fallen to the rebel LI-TSÉ-TCHING and that the emper-
or had committed suicide; after making conditions about the
treatment of the Chinese, Ou-san gave his allegiance to the
Manchus. As a result, the Manchus captured Peiping and established their dynasty over China.

où sont les heurs: 74/11; [79/62]: (Fr) where are the (O Fr) good
times. (Variation of Villon: Où sont les neiges d'antan).

Ou-tchao: 55/40: Ou-tchao-y (Wu Chao-i) fl. AD 953, wishing to
start a college, he requested permission of the Prince of
Chou to have the SHU CHING and the SHIH CHING printed (953);
the permission was granted.

Ou Ti: 54/29: (Wu Ti) (reign: 483-94), he paid attention to the laws
of the kingdom and cut down the number of retainers at court;
however, while he worried about rebellion within the Empire,
he forgot to consider the threat of the rising power of the kingdom of OUEI.

Ou Ti: 54/30; 57/59: (Wu Ti) (reign: 503-50) founder of the LIANG
dynasty; a good emperor who helped his people during famine
and purged the court of corruption. He became a Buddhist and
imported three thousand Buddhist priests to the capital; during
his reign more than thirteen thousand Buddhist temples were
built in the Empire. In 528 Ou-ti became a Buddhist monk,
but soon his ministers asked him to attend to the business of
the Empire, and he was absolved of his vows.

Outline of the Historical View of the Progress of the Human Mind:
33/11: Esquisse d'un tableau historique des progrès de l'esprit
humain (1801-04) by CONDORCET, in which he traces the
human development through nine epochs to the French Revolution and predicts that the tenth epoch will be the ultimate per-
fection of man.

Ou-Tsong: 55/37: (Wu Tsung) (reign: 841-47). His one important

decree was that all Taoist and Buddhist priests and nuns in the
Empire should return to their homes and stop living in idleness
and immorality.

Ou Tsong: 57/60: (Wu Tsung) (reign: 1506-1521), a weak and child-
ish emperor; after he had been persuaded to execute the eunuch
LIEOU-KIN, he chose KIANG-PING, a military adventurer, as
his chief advisor. Ou-tsong came to the throne as a minor,
but as he grew older he did not grow wiser. He devoted himself to leisure and frivolity and left no heir.

Ou-yen: 54/26: prob. a confusion of Ou-han (Wu Han) and Kou-yen
(Ku Yen), both fl. AD 26, and both were Chinese generals who
were created Princes of the Empire; they were especially successful in the wars against the brigands. (See: Mailla, Histoire Générale, III, 285).

Overyssel: 62/92: Overijssel, a province in E Netherlands.

Ovid: 4/15; 7/24; [20/89]; 76/40: 43 BC- 17? AD, the Latin poet.

Ovidio: 20/89: (It) OVID.

O voi che siete in piccioletta barca: 7/26: (It) oh you who are on a
very small boat. (See: Paradiso, 2, 1).

O woman shapely as a swan: 80/74: from Padraic Colum, I Shall
Not Die for Thee in Collected Poems, 134.

Ozin (Wodin) Youriak: 56/48:

P

P: 14/62: see Patrick Henry PEARSE.

Packard: 82/102:

Paddock: 71/165: Adino, a Boston coachmaker who was John ADAMS'
captain when Adams served in the Boston civilian night watch
just after the Boston Massacre (5 March 1770).

pa della justicia: 24/113: (It) the palace of justice.

Paichen: 60/75: Sina-paicheng (Hsina-p'aishêng), prob. the modern
city of Sining (or Hsining) in Tsinghai province, W central
China.

Paine, Robert: 62/90: Robert Treat Paine, 1731-1814, American
jurist; member of the CONTINENTAL CONGRESS (1774-78) and
signer of the DECLARATION of Independence; judge of the
Massachusetts supreme court (1790-1804).

Paine, Tom: 31/3: Thomas, 1737-1809, the political philosopher.

pains au lait: 80/71: (Fr) milk rolls.

Palace of the Doges: 25/115: in the Piazza di San Marco, Venice.

[Palaeologus, John]: 26/123: 1391-1448, John VIII, ruler of the
Eastern Roman Empire (1425-1448); to obtain western aid
against the Turks he appeared at the Councils of Ferrara and
Florence (1438-39).

palatio: 43/16; 54/28, 32: (L) the palace.

palazzi: 17/76: (It) palaces, mansions.

Palgrave: 22/102: Francis Turner, 1824-97, English poet and critic;
professor of poetry at Oxford (1885-95); edited the poetry
anthology Golden Treasury of the best Songs and Lyrical Poems
in the English Language (1861, 1897).

Palgrave's Golden Treasury: 22/102: see Francis Turner PALGRAVE.

palio: 24/110: (It) race.

Palio, the: 20/90(?); 43/11; 80/74; 83/107: the horseraces held in
Siena twice a year: on the festivals of Our Lady's Visitation
(July 2) and of her Assumption (August 15), the race course is
three times around the Campo, and in the race there is one
horse representing each contrade, rival social groups which
come from different districts of Siena.

palla: 20/90: prob. PALIO.

Palla, Lunarda da: 9/39: fl. 1454, prob. tutor and secretary of
Sallustio MALATESTA, Sigismondo's son.

Palladio: 40/48; 66/127; 67/139: Andrea, 1518-80, Italian architect
who adopted the principles of Roman architecture to the re-
quirements of the Renaissance; his works include the SAN
GIORGIO MAGGIORE and the Capuchin churches in Venice.
English architects of the Georgian period developed the designs
called "Palladian."

Pallas: 21/99; 78/57: see ATHENA.

Palmer: 64/101: Joseph, 1718-88, American soldier; as a colonel of
the Colonial militia he participated in the defense of the coast
near Boston; in 1777 appointed brigadier-general and given
command of the Massachusetts militia defending Rhode Island.

Palmerston, Lord: 42/3; 52/7: Henry John Temple, 3rd Viscount

Palmerston, 1784-1865, the English statesman; prime minister
(1855-58; 1859-65).

Palux Laerna: 16/69: Palus Lernae, the swamp of Lerna where
Hercules killed the Hydra, the poisonous snake. (See: Propertius, II, xxvi, 48).

Pan: 21/99: Greek pastoral god of fertility.

Pandolfi: 9/39: see Pandolfo MALATESTA.

Pandolfo: 11/51; 26/124: see Sigismondo MALATESTA.

Pandone, Parcelio: 9/34: 1405-85, Italian poet of the court of
Naples; served Sigismondo MALATESTA at Rimini (1456) and
wrote De amore Iovis in Isottam. (See: Basinio da PARMA).

Pandulphi: 10/44: see Pandolfo MALATESTA.

panier: 7/25: (Fr) basket.

Panisks: 3/11: minor gods of the forest; half-man, half-goat; from
(Gr) Paniskos, dim. of PAN.

Paolo il Bello: 8/32: (It) Paolo the Fair. (See: Paolo MALATESTA).

Paolo Secondo: 11/51: (It) Paul II. (See: Pietro BARBO).

Pao Sse: 53/17: (Pao Ssŭ) c. 8th century BC, concubine of Emperor
YEOU OUANG; earthquakes preceded her coming to the throne,
and the great eclipse of the sun on 29 August 775 followed it.
She enslaved the emperor and incited him to the wildest acts
of folly.

papa: 60/76: (It) pope.

Papa Pio Secundo: 10/49: (It) Pope PIUS II.

Paphos: 24/111; 30/147: town on the SW coast of Cyprus; famous as
a place of the worship of APHRODITE.

Paquin: 81/99: the Parisian dress designer.

Paradiso: 38/37: the third section of Dante's Divina Commedia.

Par che e fuor di questo: 11/49: (It) it seems out of this.

Paris: 18/82; 28/134, 137; 31/4, 5; 34/16; 38/41; 41/55; 48/37; 50/41;
60/78; 62/92; 65/114, 118; 67/138; 69/151, 153; 74/17; 80/83;
83/106: the French city.

Paris: 24/111: the son of Priam, King of Troy; stole HELEN of Troy
from her husband, Menelaus.

Parisina: 8/32; 20/90; 24/110, 111: see Parisina MALATESTA.

Parliament: [62/88, 89, 91]; 64/102, 103, 104; 65/110; 66/129; 67/133,
134, 135, 136; 78/59: the legislative body of Great Britain.

parliament: 67/135: see IRISH PARLIAMENT.

[Parma, Basinio da]: 9/34; 82/102: Basinio de Basinii, ?1425-57,
poet and humanist of Rimini; born in Parma, he was a noted
student of Greek; engaged in a famous literary debate with
Parcelio PANDONE on the values of Greek studies.

Parmenesi: 35/25: people of Parma, N Italy.

Parochia S. Giovannis: 43/13: (It) the parish of SAN GIOVANNI.

Paschi: 43/13, 16: see MONTE DEI PASCHI.

Paschi di detta Città: 43/16: (It) Bank of ever mentioned city. (See:
MONTE DEI PASCHI).

Pasepa: 56/50: fl. AD 1269, a Lama who provided the Mongols with
an alphabet; in gratitude, KUBLAI KHAN raised him to the
rank of head Lama.

Pasiphaë: 39/43; 74/21: wife of Minos, King of Crete; sister of
CIRCE and mother of the Minotaur.

Pasquini, Livio: 42/4, [7]: fl. 1623, a notary of Siena.

Pasquinius, Livius: 42/7: (L) Livio PASQUINI.

Passy: 65/125: in the 18th century a village to the NW of Paris, in which the American delegation (FRANKLIN, DEANE, and Arthur LEE) stayed; now a fashionable section of Paris.

Pasti: 10/46; 26/121; [74/15]: Matteo de', d. 1468, Veronese sculptor and medalist; sent by Sigismondo MALATESTA to Candia to make a portrait of the Turkish emperor, MOHAMMED II, he was arrested by the Venetians, who suspected him of being in league with the Turks against them. He was released, however, and returned to Rimini.

"Past ruin'd Latium": 9/41: variation of W. S. Landor, Past ruined Ilion Helen lives.

Patchin: 80/86: Patchin Place, a court off Sixth Avenue, Greenwich Village, New York.

pater patriae: 62/96: (L) father of his country.

Paterson: 46/27: William, 1658-1719, British financier; chief founder of the BANK OF ENGLAND (1694).

patet terra: 16/69: (L) the earth lies open.

Patrie, la: 80/82: (Fr) the Fatherland.

patronne, la: 74/11: (Fr) the proprietress.

Paucity, Mt: 59/72: a desolate range of mountains in Manchuria; called by the Chinese the "Mountains of Poverty."

Paul, St.: 71/160: d. c. 67, the Christian apostle, missionary and martyr.

[Paul II]: 11/51: see Pietro BARBO.

Pavia: 42/7; 74/26: capital of Pavia province of Lombardy, N Italy; the Church of San Michele in Pavia is an excellent example of 12th century Lombard Romanesque architecture.

Pawn Shop: 42/5; 43/9, 12: see MOUNT OF PITY.

pax: 78/55, 56; 83/106, 107: (L) peace.

pax Medicea: 78/56: (L) the peace of the MEDICI.

pax mundi: 78/55: (L) the peace of the world.

Paxton: 64/108; 71/165: Charles, 1704-1788, British commissioner of customs at Boston and head of the Board of Commissioners; left America in 1776.

Pa Yang: 56/48: Pan-yang, poss. the city of P'ing-yang in Shansi province. (See: Mailla, Histoire Générale, IX, 485).

Pe: 58/63: Pé-koan, (P'e-k'ou) the North Pass which lies to the north of NAN-KOAN; also the tribe of NUTCHÉ Tartars which takes its name from the region of the pass.

Pea, Enrico: 80/88: 1881-1952, the Italian author.

Peabody: 40/47: George, 1795-1869, American financier and philanthropist; in 1835 he negotiated a loan from the British to save the finances of Maryland; became a London broker in 1837 and did much to promote Anglo-American relations.

Peach-blossom Fountain: 84/116:

[Pearse, Patrick Henry]: 14/62: 1879-1916, Irish author and Sinn Fein leader; commander in chief of the Irish forces in the Easter Rebellion (1916); executed after surrendering his troops.

Pecora Gallo, Margurita de: 43/14: fl. 1624, a Sienese whore.

Pedro: 30/147: see PEDRO I.

[Pedro I]: 30/147, 148: 1320-1367, King of Portugal (1357-67); son
of Alfonso IV and "husband" of Ignez da CASTRO.

Pei-kiu: 54/31: (Pei Chü) fl. AD 607; he was sent by Emperor YANG-
TI to be governor in SI-YU and turned his journey to good account by mapping the country.

[Peiping]: 56/54, 55; 57/58, 59; 58/68, 69; 60/74, 75, 76, 78:
(formerly Peking), the city in Hopeh province, NE China; capital of China during the YÜAN and subsequent dynasties.

Pé-kin: 53/14: (Pe Chin) d. BC 1063, ruler of the principality of
LOU.

Pekin: 56/54, 55; 57/58, 59; 58/68, 69; 60/74, 75, 76, 78: see
PEIPING.

Peking: 58/68: see PEIPING.

pellande: 26/123: (It) a cover.

Pellegrini: 74/20; 78/57: Giampietro Domenico, under-secretary
in the Italian Ministry of Finance (1943); appointed Minister of
Finance (20 September 1943) in the government of the SALÒ
Republic; official in the Consigliere Nazionale and the Corpor-
azione della Previdenza e del Credito.

Peloponnesus: 23/107: the south part of the mainland of Greece;
also called MOREA.

pence of Peter: 67/135: Peter's Pence, a hearth tax of one penny
to support the Papacy.

Penn, John: 67/138: ?1741-88, American Revolutionary leader;
member of the CONTINENTAL CONGRESS (1775-80) and a
signer of the DECLARATION of Independence.

Penna: 8/30: see PENNABILLI.

[Pennabilli]: 8/30: a town in the Apennines, SW of Rimini, between
Mt. CARPEGNA and the Marecchia river; home of Giovanni
MALATESTA.

Pennsylvania: 62/95; 65/111; 71/164.

Penrieth: 80/91: DTC, Pisa.

Penthesilea: 80/84: queen of the Amazons; she and her followers
came to the aid of Troy after the death of Hector.

Pentheus: 2/7, 9: grandson of CADMUS and King of Thebes; when
DIONYSUS returned to Thebes, Pentheus denied his divinity
and refused to worship him; advised by a stranger (the god in
disguise) to spy on the woman worshippers, he was torn to
pieces by them when discovered. (See: Ovid, Metamorphoses,
III, 511-733).

Peoria: 28/140: city in NW Illinois.

Pepitone: 80/92: DTC, Pisa.

Per animarla: 26/124: (It) to animate him.

per capitoli: 9/35: (It) by the chapters.

Percy: 16/70(?); 82/102: see Percy Bysshe SHELLEY.

[Percy, Lord Algernon]: 16/70: 1792-1865, the famed British naval
officer.

Perdicaris: 74/10, 25: Ion, an American who was kidnapped (1904)
by the Moroccan brigand RAIS ULI; the affair gave rise to the

slogan in America: "Perdicaris alive or Raisuli dead."
per diletto: 24/114: (It) for pleasure.
père: 58/64: (Fr) father.
Péreira: 59/72, 73; 60/75, 78: Antoine Péreyra, fl. 1689, a Jesuit
    missionary in China; he served with GERBILLON on the com-
    mission to negotiate a treaty between China and Russia (1689).
pères, les: 60/74: (Fr) the fathers (priests).
per esempio: 79/63: (It) for example.
per forza: 38/40: (It) by force.
Pergusa: 4/15: Pergus, a lake in Sicily near the city of Enna; near
    the lake PERSEPHONE was seized by Pluto and carried off.
    (See: Ovid, Metamorphoses, V, 386).
Périgueux: 80/86: capital of Dordogne department, SW France; the
    historical capital of Périgord.
Perimedes: 1/3: member of the crew of ODYSSEUS. (See: Odyssey,
    XI, 23).
periplum: 59/70; 74/3, 9, 21, 22, 25; 76/30; 77/43, 44; 82/105: (Gr)
    circumnavigation. (See: Appendix A).
Perkeo: 80/77: fl. 1720, fool in the court of Karl Philip; Perkeo's
    tub is the Great Vat of Heidelberg, which according to Scheffel's
    song was emptied by Perkeo alone; a wooden figure of Perkeo
    stands on the wall of the vat room.
per l'argine sinistra dienno volta: 69/153: (It) would turn to the left
    side. (See: Inferno, 21, 136).
per legem terrae: 66/128: (L) by the law of the land.
per naturam...vivos et pilosos: 25/116: (L) by nature...alive and
    hairy.
Pernella concubina: 29/141: (It) Pernella concubine.
per pares et legem terrae: 66/128: (L) by peers and the law of the
    land. (See: John Adams, Works, III, 471-72).
Perpetua: 80/91: St. Perpetua, d. 203, a Carthaginian martyr.
Perseis: 39/43: or Perse, mother of CIRCE and PASIPHAE.
[Persephone]: 1/4; 3/11; 17/78; 39/44; 47/30; 74/20, 21; 76/35;
    79/68, 70; 80/72; 83/111: the daughter of ZEUS and DEMETER;
    she was carried off to the lower world by Hades, but was al-
    lowed to return to the world in the spring and summer.
Persha: 82/101: DTC, Pisa.
Persia: 38/38; 40/47.
Peru: 27/130.
Perugia: 5/19; 29/145; 83/110: city in central Italy, capital of Umbria;
    site of an excellent 14th century cathedral and a fountain with
    sculptures by Nicolò and Giovanni Pisano.
pervenche: 76/37: (Fr) periwinkle.
Pèsaro: 8/32; 9/34, 35, 36: port city and capital of Pesaro e Urbi-
    no province in central Italy; it was held by the Malatesta's in
    the 13th century, then by the Sforza, and then by the dukes of
    Urbino until 1631, when it passed to the Holy See.
pesca, la: 8/31: (It) fishing.
peseta: 81/95: a Spanish monetary unit.
[Petacci, Clara]: 74/3: d. 1945, mistress of Benito MUSSOLINI.
Pétain: 79/62; 80/72: Henri Philippe, 1856-1951, marshal of France;

convicted of "intelligence with the enemy" (1945) and sentenced
to life imprisonment; during the First World War he saved
France by halting the Germans at Verdun (1916).

Petano: 77/48: poss. Coltano, near Pisa, location of the DTC, 1945.

Peter: 67/135: Saint Peter, d. 67?, the apostle.

[Peter I]: 38/41; 60/78: Peter the Great, 1672-1725; emperor (1721-
25) and tsar (1682-1725) of Russia; founder of the modern
Russian state.

Peter of Russia: 60/78: see PETER I.

Petersburg: 59/73; 68/144; 74/11: see ST. PETERSBURG.

petit: 66/128: (L) seeks.

Petrograd: 27/131: see ST. PETERSBURG.

pets-de-loup: 14/63: (Fr) university people (scholars); lit.: wolf-
farts.

[Petty, Sir William]: 69/150: 2nd Earl of Shelbourne, 1st Marquis
of Lansdowne, 1737-1805, English statesman; secretary of
state under Pitt (1766-68); attempted conciliation toward the
American colonies; first lord of the treasury and prime minister (1782-83); conceded American independence.

Pe-y: 53/16: (Pe I), the ancestral house of FEI-TSEI, who became
Prince of TSIN and founder of the house which was to become
the TSIN dynasty.

Peyan: 56/53: Poyang Hu, a lake in N Kiangsi province, SE China;
China's second largest lake, into which flows the HAN river.

Peyen: 56/53: Péyen-témour (P'eyen Temur) d. AD 1362, King of
the Koreans.

Péyen: 57/58: Péyen-tiémour (P'eyen T'iehmur) fl. AD 1450, a
Mongol general who took charge of the captured Emperor YNG-
TSONG; he also participated in the Mongol attack on Peiping
(1450).

Phaebidas: 67/139: Phoebidas, a Spartan commander, who seized
the stronghold of Thebes in Boeotia (382 BC). (See: John
Adams, Works, IV, 286).

Phaethusa: 21/100; 25/118: a daughter of HELIOS. (See: Odyssey,
XII, 132).

Pharamond: 68/142: c. 5th century BC, legendary king of the Saline
Franks; supposedly he published the code of the Salic laws,
which included penal and civil laws.

Pharisees: 33/11: one of the two great Jewish religious parties that
arose in the synagogue; they insisted on strict adherence to
the laws of the Jewish religion, both the Written and the Oral
Law. The other party, the Sadducees, accepted only the teaching of the Torah.

Philadelphia: [62/94; 65/110; 67/137]; 68/145; 69/149; [70/156]: the
city of Pennsylvania; meeting place of the First CONTINENTAL
CONGRESS (1774), Second Continental Congress (1775-76; 1777;
1778-89), Constitutional Convention (1787); served as capital of
the US (1790-1800).

Philadelphy: 62/94; 65/110; 67/137; 70/156: see PHILADELPHIA.

Philiasia: 67/139: Phliasia, the territory of Phlius, a town in the
north-east of the Peloponnesus.

Philip: 80/71: Philip IV, 1605-65, King of Spain (1621-65); his por-
      trait by VELÁSQUEZ hangs in the PRADO.
Philippines: 74/20: the Philippine Islands.
Phlegethon: 25/118; 74/28: the river of fire in Hades.
Phoenician: 79/66: the language.
Phoenician cities: 40/49: the cities on the Atlantic coast of Africa
      which were founded by HANNO: KARIKON, GUTTA, AKRA,
      MELI, ARAMBO.
Phoibos: 21/99; 29/145: see APOLLO.
Phrygia: 23/109: ancient country in W central Asia Minor.
phtheggometha/thasson: 47/30: (Gr) let us raise our voices without
      delay. (See: Appendix A).
Piacenza: 24/114: town in the region of Veneto, N Italy.
Piave: 80/87: river in NE Italy.
Piazza: 44/18: the Piazza del Duomo, Siena.
Piazza: 76/34: prob. the Piazza di San Marco, Venice.
Piazza Chapel: 44/18: (It) Chapel Square. (The Piazza del Duomo,
      Siena).
Piazza del Duomo: 44/18: (It) the Duomo (Cathedral) Square (Siena).
Picasso: 2/6: Pablo, 1881-   , the painter.
Piccadilly: 80/79: Piccadilly Circus, London.
[Piccinino, Giacomo]: 10/43, 47: d. 1465, son of Niccolò PICCINI-
      NO; an Italian condottiere, connected by marriage with Fran-
      cesco SFORZA; murdered at Naples.
Piccinino: 10/46, 47; 21/97: Niccolò, 1375-1444, Italian condottiere
      serving Fillippo Maria VISCONTI, Duke of Milan; captured
      Bologna (1438) and ruled it until 1443.
piccolo: 74/26: (It) little one.
piccolo e putino: 24/113: (It) little and small.
Piccolomini, Aeneas Silvius: 10/44, [45, 46; 11/49; 26/121]: Enea
      Silvio de, 1405-64, Pope Pius II (1458-64); an author, humanist,
      and patron of writers; in literature he is known as Aeneas
      Silvius.
Piccolomini, Nicolò: 44/22: poss. Francesco di Niccolò Piccolomi-
      ni, 1520-1604, professor of philosophy at the University of
      Siena.
Pickering, Tim: [62/96]; 63/97; 70/156: Timothy, 1745-1829, Amer-
      ican general and statesman; during the Revolution he was a
      member of the Board of War (1777) and quartermaster general
      (1780-85); Postmaster General of the US (1791-95); Secretary of
      War (1795) and then Secretary of State (1795-1800). John ADAMS
      dismissed him from his last office because Pickering's anti-
      French attitude was not in line with Adams' foreign policy and
      because of Pickering's political manipulations.
[Pickthall, Marmaduke William]: 46/26: 1875-1936, English novel-
      ist living in the Near East; he was converted to Mohammedism.
pictore: 25/120; 26/127: (L) painter.
Pien: 53/18: Pien-kuan-chi (Pien Chuan-shih), a woman of the prin-
      cipality of SONG; CONFUCIUS married her in BC 532, but
      divorced her later. (See: Mailla, Histoire Générale, II, 190).
Piero: 11/49: poss. Piero della BELLA.

Piero: 21/96: see Piero de' MEDICI.

Pierre: 23/109: see Peire de MAENSAC.

Pierre: 84/117: poss. Pierre LAVAL.

Pierre, La Marquise de: 74/11:

Pietro: 43/14: see Pietro de' MEDICI.

Pietro il Grande: 38/41: (It) Peter the Great. (See PETER I).

Pig and Piffle: 41/55: prob. the English magazine Sport and Country.

pigrizia, la: 76/32: (It) laziness.

Pi-kan: 84/117: (Pi Kan) 12th century BC, uncle of CHEOU-SIN, last
    emperor of the YIN dynasty; when Pi-kan objected to the excess-
    es of Cheou-sin, the emperor had him disembowelled on the
    spot. (See: Analects, XVIII, 1).

Pilate, Pontius: 24/111; 25/116; [74/21(?)]: fl. AD 33, procurator of
    Judea under Emperor Tiberius; tried and condemned Christ.

[Pili, Ugolini dei]: 10/46: fl. 1420, Italian soldier serving as cap-
    tain under Pandolfo MALATESTA.

Pilkington, Sir J.: 67/135: Sir John, fl. 1454; the case of Sir John
    Pilkington (32 H. VI. 25) was one which substantiated the fact
    that Ireland is a dominion separate and divided from England.
    (See: Coke, Reports, 7, 22b).

Pillars, the: 40/49; 74/3: the Pillars of Heracles. (See: STRAIT OF
    GIBRALTAR).

Pillars of (Herakles) Hercules: 40/49; 74/25: see STRAIT OF GI-
    BRALTAR.

Pills, old: 10/46: prob. Ugolino dei PILI.

Pinckney: 62/94; 63/97; 70/155; 71/161: Charles Cotesworth, 1746-
    1825, American statesman; sent to France on a special mission
    (1796-97) but because the French refused to recognize his
    status he was forced to leave France for Amsterdam; there he
    was approached by members of the French government who
    offered terms under which negotiations might start (the main
    point was the Jay Treaty); this incident became the famous XYZ
    Affair.

Ping Tching: 54/30: (P'ing-ch'êng), capital of the kingdom of OUEI
    (376-494).

pinxit: 76/40: (L) (he) painted (it).

Pinyang: 58/63: Ping-ngan (Ping-an), the modern city of Keijo (or
    Seoul) in Korea; served as capital of the Korean dynasty (1392-
    1910).

Pio: 10/45, 46; 26/121: see Aeneas Silvius PICCOLOMINI.

Pio II: 10/44: (It) Pius II. (See: Aeneas Silvius PICCOLOMINI).

Piombino: 10/46: town in Tuscany; ruled by the VISCONTI family.

Pio Nono: 50/43: (It) PIUS IX.

piquée de ce badinage: 54/28: (Fr) stung by this banter. (See: Mailla,
    Histoire Générale, IV, 500).

Pirandello: 77/47: Luigi, 1867-1936, Italian dramatist and novelist.

Pisa: 21/98; 74/5, 6, 8, 25; 76/34, 37; 77/44, 46; 84/117: capital of
    Pisa province, Italy.

Pisanello: 74/15: see Antonio PISANO.

Pisanellus: 26/126: see Antonio PISANO.

Pisani, Petrus: 76/40: (L) Peter Pisani; poss. Antonio PISANO.

[Pisano, Antonio]: 26/126; 74/15; [76/40?]: ?1397-1455, Veronese
     painter and medalist; employed by Sigismondo MALATESTA in
     the building of the Tempio; patronized by Lionello d'ESTE; also
     known as Vittore Pisano.
Pistoja: 42/7: Pistoia, town in N Tuscany, near Florence.
Pitigliano: 9/37; 10/42: see Count Aldobrando ORSINI.
Pitro, Mr.: 26/125: a blacksmith in the service of Francesco
     SFORZA.
Pitt: 64/103; 71/160: William, "the Elder Pitt," 1708-1778, the Eng-
     lish statesman; was opposed to the STAMP ACT and British
     taxation of the American Colonies.
Pitt: 66/126; 69/152: William, "the Younger Pitt," 1759-1806, the
     English statesman; prime minister (1783-1801; 1804-06).
Pity, the: 43/12: see MOUNT OF PITY.
[Pius II]: 10/44, 45, 46; 11/49; 26/121: Pope (1458-64). (See: Aeneas
     Silvius PICCOLOMINI).
Pius VI: 50/41: Giovanni Angelo Braschi, 1717-99; Pope (1775-99).
[Pius VII]: 50/42: Luigi Barnaba Chiaramonti, 1742-1823; Pope
     (1800-23).
[Pius IX]: 28/139; 50/43: Pope (1846-78). (See: Giovanni Maria
     MASTAI).
[Pius XI]: 38/37; 80/80: Achille Ambrogio Damiano Ratti, 1857-
     1939; Pope (1922-39); subprefect of the Vatican Library (1911-18),
     nuncio (1919-20); cardinal and archbishop of Milan (1921).
[Place de la Concorde]: 80/82: the square in Paris.
placet sic: 60/75: (L) it pleases thus. (placet: an affirmative vote,
     yea).
Placidia: 21/98: see GALLA Placidia.
Placuit oculis: 37/35: (L) she pleased the eyes. (See: "ET AMAVA
     PERDUTAMENTE...).
Plan of Government: 67/137: The Plan, the first of three sections
     into which Charles Francis Adams has divided John Adams'
     major works relating to the form of American government; the
     other sections are titled: The Model, The Defence. (See: John
     Adams, Works, IV, 185-VI, 217).
Plantagenet: 6/21: see HENRY II of England.
Plarr: 74/11: Victor Gustave, 1863-1929, librarian of the Royal
     College of Surgeons of England; author of In The Dorian Mood
     (1896) and other works.
Platina: 11/50: see Bartolommeo SACCHI.
Plato: 8/31; 33/12; [65/113]; 68/141; 77/47: 427-348, the philosopher.
Platonis: 65/113: (L) PLATO's.
plaustra: 9/36: (It) wagons, carts.
Pleasing to Carthegenians: Hanno...as were at end of provisions:
     40/49-51: from The Periplus of Hanno.
Pleas of the Crown: 63/99: see William HAWKINS.
Pleiades: 47/31; 56/52; 74/13: the cluster of stars in the constella-
     tion of Taurus; the seven daughters of Atlas.
Plotinus: 15/66: ?205-270, the Roman philosopher; a leader of the
     Neoplatonic school.
Plura diafana: 83/108: (L) more things diaphanous. (See: Grosse-

teste, De iride seu de iride et speculo, ed. Baur, 73).

Pluto: 1/4: a name of Hades; god of the nether world. (See: PER-
SEPHONE).

Po: 24/114; 82/104: the river in N Italy.

po'eri di' aoli: 76/40: (It) poor devils.

Poggio: 3/11: Gian Francesco Poggio Bracciolini, 1380-1459, Italian
humanist; known for his discoveries of lost Latin classics in
various monasteries.

Poicebot: 5/18; 48/37: Gaubertz, a monk of Provence who became a
troubadour. (See: Make It New, 25).

Poictiers: 4/14: see POITIERS.

Poictiers, Guillaume: 8/32: see Guillaume POITIERS.

Poitiers: [4/14]; 6/21; 76/33: formerly spelled Poictiers; city of
Vienne department W central France; site of a 12th century
Romanesque Gothic cathedral and the remains of the palace
of the former counts of Poitou.

[Poitiers, Guillaume]: 6/21; 8/32: 1071-1127, ninth Duke of Aquitaine and seventh Count of Poitiers; the earliest troubadour
whose songs are extant; the grandfather of ELEANOR of Aquitaine.

Pojalouista: 16/75: (Russ) if you please.

Pola: 24/111: or Pulj, a fortified seaport at the S tip of the Istrian
Peninsula, NW Yugoslavia; S of Trieste.

Poland: 50/42; 56/49.

Pole, Cardinal: 67/134: Reginald Pole, 1500-58; created cardinal
by Pope Paul III (1536); opposed to the divorce and religious
reforms of HENRY VIII.

Polenta: 24/113: Ostasio da Polenta; an ally of the Venetians in 1441,
he was yet deprived by them of Ravenna and exiled to Candia
with his family.

Polhonac: 4/16: Héracle III, Viscount of Polignac. His wife,
Adelaide de Claustra, was admired by Guillaume de Saint-
Didier, who addressed love-songs to her; she agreed to accept
him if so urged by her husband, whereupon Guillaume wrote
the song (Dona, ieu vos soy messatgiers) in which a husband
intercedes with his wife in the interest of a rejected lover.
The Viscount received the song, admired it, sang it to his wife,
and thus "set the feast" for Guillaume.

Poliorcetes: 9/36: (Gr) taker of cities; the epithet was applied to
Sigismondo MALATESTA by PISANELLO.

Polixena: 9/35: see Polissena SFORZA.

Polk: 74/14; 76/33; 79/67: DTC, Pisa.

Pollon d'anthropon iden: 12/54: (Gr) And of many men he saw (the
cities, and knew their mind). (See: Appendix A).

Polo: 18/80: Marco, ?1254-1324?, Venetian traveler; visited
KUBLAI KHAN in 1275 and returned to Venice in 1295. In 1296
he was taken prisoner by the Genoese against whom Polo, with
the Venetians, was fighting; he dictated his memoirs while in
prison in Genoa.

Polumetis: 9/36: (Gr) of many counsels. (See: Appendix A).

poluphloisboios: 74/5: (Gr) loud-roarings. (See: Appendix A).

Pomona: 79/68: the old Italian goddess of fruit trees.

Ponce: 76/34: Juan Ponce de León, ?1460-1521, Spanish governor
of Puerto Rico and discoverer of Florida, which he found while
looking for the Fountain of Youth (Easter Sunday 1513).

Pondo: 11/49: locality in central Italy; taken from Sigismondo MALA-
TESTA by the peace terms imposed by PIUS II (c. 1460).

Pone metum,/ Metum, nec deus laedit: 25/[117], 118, [119]: (L)
Lay aside fear,/ fear, nor does God harm. (See: Tibullus,
III, x, 15).

Pong: 56/49: Pong-choui-hien (Pêng-shui-hsien), a town in Szechwan province.

Pongchan: 55/41: (Peng-shan), a district city in the province of
Szechwan.

Pontius: 74/21: prob. Pontius PILATE.

Pope: 5/20: see LEO X.

Pope: 28/139: see PIUS IX.

Pope: 38/37: see PIUS XI.

Pope: 50/42: see PIUS VII.

Pope: 61/81: see BENEDICT XIII.

Pope: 34/18; 66/127; 68/141: Alexander, 1688-1744, the English poet.

Popolo...ignorante: 41/52: (It) ignorant people.

populariser, dépopulariser: 70/158: (Fr) to popularize, depopularize.

[Por, Odon]: 78/59: 1883-   , Italian writer on social and economic
problems and on Italian Fascism.

Port: 69/153: the wine.

Portagoose boss: 61/83: see JOHN V of Portugal.

Portagoose king: 60/76: see JOHN V of Portugal.

Portagoose prelates: 58/62: Portuguese Jesuit missionaries in
Japan.

Porta Romana: 44/19: a gate in Siena.

Portoferraio: 50/41: seaport of Elba Island; where Napoleon lived
during his exile (1814-15).

porto franco: 44/22: (It) free port.

Portugal: 12/55; 35/25; 44/20; 65/121, 124; 69/153.

Portuguese Queen: 32/9: see MARIA FRANCISCA.

Poseidon: 2/9; 8/31; [40/49]: Greek god of the sea.

Poseidōnos: 40/49: (Gr) POSEIDON.

Possum: 74/3, 14; 81/96: see T. S. ELIOT.

Possum ego naturae/ non meminisse tuae!: 20/89: (L) Can I forget
thy nature! (See: Propertius, II, xx, 28).

Potemkin: 35/23: Grigori Aleksandrovich, 1739-91, Russian statesman; the chief favorite of Catherine II, he was created field
marshal in 1784; constructed a fleet in the Black Sea; created
prince of Tauris (1787).

Potomac: 31/4; 71/161: the river in Virginia.

[Pound, Ezra Loomis]: 24/112; 42/3; 62/96; 64/106; 76/36; 79/66:
1885-   , scriptor cantilenae.

[Pound, Thaddeus Coleman]: 21/97; 22/101: 1833-1914, grandfather
of Ezra POUND.

pourvou que ça doure: 55/40: (Fr) provided that it lasts.

pouvrette et ancienne oncques lettre ne lus: 74/14: (Fr) povrette et

ancienne oncques lettre ne leuz: poor and old never did I read
a letter. (See: Villon, Testament, "Ballade Pour Prier
Nostre Dame").
Pownall: 67/134: Thomas, 1722-1805, colonial governor of Massa-
chusetts (1757-60).
Poyning: 67/135: see Sir Edward POYNINGS.
[Poynings, Sir Edward]: 67/135: 1459-1521, English soldier and
diplomat; as governor of Ireland, he summoned the Drogheda
Parliament (1494) that enacted Poynings's law providing that
every act of that parliament must be approved by the English
privy council to become valid.
Poyning's law: 67/135: see Sir Edward POYNINGS.
Prado: 80/71: see MUSEO DEL PRADO.
Praedis, Ambrogio: 45/24; 51/44: see Ambrogio de PREDIS.
praemunires: 70/156: (Law) offenses made punishable by forfeiture
of property and imprisonment; also the form of writ for prose-
cuting such offenses.
Prataline: 11/49: locality in central Italy, taken from Sigismondo
MALATESTA by the peace terms imposed by PIUS II (c. 1460).
pratis nemoribus pascuis: 36/30: (L) meadows, woodlands, pastures.
Prayer: hands uplifted...and pities those who wear a crown: 64/101:
from The Fourth Satire of Dr. John Donne, versifyed by Alex-
ander Pope; variation of Henry IV, part 2, III, i, 31.
Pré Catalan: 76/31: a restaurant in the Bois de Boulogne, Paris.
Predappio: 74/15: town in NE Italy, where MUSSOLINI was born.
[Predis, Ambrogio de]: 45/24; 51/44: ?1455-1506?, Milanese por-
trait and miniature painter.
Prefect, the: 76/36: see NICOLETTI.
Prefetto: 76/36: (It) prefect.
Premier Brumaire: 44/20: 22 October 1800.
"Prepare to go on a journey": 79/66: from Odyssey, X, 490.
preraphaelite: 80/86: a society of artists formed in England in 1848
and known as the Pre-Raphaelite Brotherhood; the original
members were Holman Hunt, John E. Millais, D. G. Rossetti,
James Collinson, Thomas Woolner, Frederick George Stephens,
and W. M. Rossetti.
Presente: 78/57: (It) present.
President: 34/17: see James MONROE.
President: 34/20: see Martin VAN BUREN.
President: 37/33, 34: see Andrew JACKSON.
President: 62/94: see George WASHINGTON.
President of Magdalen: 74/23: prob. Sir Herbert Warren, 1853-1930,
president of Magdalen College, Oxford (1885-1928).
Presqu'isle: 66/126: Presque Isle, once a military fort in N Maine,
first controlled by the British in Canada and then relinquished
to the Americans; now a village.
Preston: 62/88; 64/105, 106; 71/166: Thomas, captain of the British
troops involved in the Boston Massacre (1770); he was defended
by John ADAMS, who obtained an acquittal.
prete: 80/75; 83/106: (It) priest.
Priapus: 79/67, 69: god of fertility; son of DIONYSUS and APHRO-
DITE.

Price: 70/158; 71/165: Richard, 1723-91, Welsh moral and political philosopher; attacked the British policy toward the American Revolution in his Observations on Civil Liberty and War with America (1776); was a friend of Benjamin FRANKLIN and John ADAMS.

Primavera: 76/30: a reference to Giovanna, the lady of Guido CAVALCANTI, to whom he addressed some of his ballate. (See: La Vita Nuova, XXIV, 20-23).

[Primo de Rivera, Miguel]: 38/39: 1870-1930, Spanish general and dictator.

Primrose: 41/55: one of the three principal characters in René CREVEL's Les Pieds dans le plat (1933), where she is Lady Primerose, marquise of Sussex.

Primus: 44/20: (L) the first in rank.

Prince de Penseurs: 27/129; 80/84: (Fr) prince of thinkers. (See: Jean-Pierre BRISSET).

Prince Imperial: 54/28: see TÇIN-HOEI-TI.

Prince of Hiong-nou: 54/25: see HOU-HAN-YÉ.

Prince of Hoai-nan: 54/24: see LIEOU-NGAN.

Prince of Ho-kien: 54/24: see LIEOU-TÉ.

Prince of Lou: 53/14: see PÉ-KIN.

Prince of Lou: 55/39: see LI-TSONGKOU.

Prince of Orange: 66/128: see WILLIAM III of England.

Prince of Ouei: 54/29: see TO-PA-TAO.

Prince of Tai: 54/23: see HIAO-OUEN.

Prince of Tçin: 55/38: see LI-KÉ-YONG.

Prince of Tsin: 53/16: see FEI-TSEI.

Princes Mogul: 58/67: the princes of the Mongolian tribes which, in AD 1635, formed a confederation under the hegemony of TAÏ-TSONG, the Manchu leader.

Princess: 61/85: see HIAO-CHING, HIEN-HOANG-HÉOU.

Prince Tartar: 54/25: see HOU-HAN-YÉ.

Prince Tçin: 55/39: see LI-TSUN-HIU.

Princeton: 65/109: the city in New Jersey.

Principe, the: 28/139: (It) the prince. (See: Prince OLTREPASSI-MO).

prise: 76/34: (It) prize.

Prishnip: 19/85: prob. Gavrilo Princip, who assassinated Francis Ferdinand at Sarajevo (28 June 1914).

Procuratio nomine patris: 24/110: (L) procuration in the name of the father.

Programma di Verona, il: 78/56: (It) the Program of Verona, the manifesto detailing the principles of action of the Fascist Republican Party, SALÒ Republic, October 1943.

pro hac vice: 70/156: (L) in return.

[Propertius, Sextus]: 5/17; [20/89]: ?50-15?, the Latin poet.

Properzio: 20/89: (It) PROPERTIUS.

proposito: 78/60: (It) purpose; à propos.

prore: 29/146: (It) prows (of ships).

Proserpine: 1/4; 47/30: see PERSEPHONE.

Proteus: 2/10: a sea-deity; the guardian of the herds of POSEIDON; he had knowledge of future events and would disclose this knowledge if one could catch and hold him while he changed shape.

Protot, Robert: 38/42: prob. Robert Pinot, Secrétaire Général du COMITÉ DES FORGES in the first World War, serving under the presidency of François de WENDEL; author of Le Comité des Forges de France au service de la nation (Août 1914-Novembre 1918) published in 1919.

Provençal: 20/89: the language.

Province, the: 65/109: the royal province of New York, established 1685-1776; the area of the present state of New York.

Province House: 69/150: the official building of the Province of Friesland, the Netherlands.

Provveditore: 44/22: (It) manager.

Prussia: 32/9; 38/41; 56/49.

Prussian minister: 65/122: see Baron de THULEMEYER.

Psellos: 23/107: Michael Constantine Psellus, 1018-1105?, Byzantine philosopher, politician, writer, and early Neoplatonist.

Ptierstoff: 19/87: see Aleksandr Konstantinovich BENCKENDORFF.

[Puccini, Giacomo]: 80/88: 1858-1924, the Italian composer.

puiné: 29/141: (Fr) younger.

Pujo: 40/48: Arsène Paulin, 1861-1939, American lawyer and legislator; member of the House of Representatives (1903-13), chairman of the House Committee on Banking and Currency (1911-13) and head of the so-called "money trust" investigation.

Pujol, Mme: 74/6: poss. a landlady in Provence.

Purtheo, Aloysius: 9/36: fl. 1450, prob. Benedictine abbot of the basilica SANT APOLLINAIRE, Ravenna; he agreed, for 200 gold florins, to allow Sigismondo MALATESTA to take marble from the church and use it in the TEMPIO.

Puvis: 80/84: Pierre Puvis de Chavannes, 1824-98, French muralist; some of his best work is in the Sorbonne and the Panthéon.

Pym, Bill: 66/128: William, a pseudonym used by a writer on the side of the English in the London Evening Post (1765); John ADAMS answered Pym under the pseudonym of Earl CLARENDON.

Pyrenees: 28/137: the mountain range on the French-Spanish border.

Q

qua al triedro, / e la scalza: 76/30: (It) here at the corner, / and
the barefooted one.

Quackenbos (or Quackenbush): 74/25: prob. a resident in a New
York boarding house, c. 1890. (See: Indiscretions, in Quarterly Review of Literature, V, 2 (1949) 125).

quadam nocte: 9/36: (L) on a certain night.

Quade, Mons: 12/54: an associate of Baldy BACON; for further
description of Quade, see: Pavannes and Divisions, 45-46.

Quali lochi sono questi: 11/49: (It) what places are these.

Quan ben m'albir e mon ric pensamen: 36/30: (Pr) When I consider
well in my courtly thought. (See: Sordello, III, 17).

quand vos venetz al som de l'escalina: 84/117: (Pr) when you come
to the top of the stair. (See: Purgatorio, 26, 146: que vos
guida al som de l'escalina).

Quand vous serez bien vieille: 80/84: (Fr) When you are very old.
(See: Ronsard, Sonnets pour Hélène, II, 42).

Quarterly Review: 34/19: published (London) since 1809; the reference is to the issue for November 1829.

quasi tinnula, / Ligur' aoide: Si no'us vei, Domna don plus mi cal, /
Negus vezer mon bel pensar no val: 20/89: (L) as if ringing
(Gr) clear, sweet song: (Pr) If I see you not, Lady with whom
I am most concerned, / Not seeing you is not the reward for my
fair thought. (See: Catullus, LXI, 12-13; Odyssey, XII, 183).

quatorze Juillet: 74/12: (Fr) 14 July (Bastille Day, 1945).

quattrocento: 78/58; 79/63; 83/113: (It) of the fifteenth century.

Queen: 66/126: see CHARLOTTE SOPHIA.

Queen: 67/136: see ELIZABETH I.

Queen: 83/106: see ERMENTRUDE.

Que la lauzeta mover': 6/22: (Pr) When I see the lark on the move.
(See: Bernart de Ventadorn, no. 43).

Qu'est-ce qu'on pense...?...On don't pense: 18/82: (Fr) What do
they think?...They don't think.

Que tous les mois avons nouvelle lune: 80/88: (Fr) That every
month we have a new moon.

que vos vers expriment vos intentions, / et que la musique conforme:
53/9: (Fr) that your verses express your intentions, / and that
the music conform. (See: Mailla, Histoire Générale, I, 93).

quia impossible est: 74/20: (L) is it impossible?

Qu'il fit la sottise de Moscou: 34/16: (Fr) That he did the folly of
Moscow. (See: J. Q. Adams, Diary, 104).

qu'ils veillèrent à la pureté du langage / et qu'on n'employât que des
termes propres: 60/78-79: (Fr) that they looked to the purity
of the language/ and that one should use only suitable terms.
(See: Mailla, Histoire Générale, XI, 365).

Quincey: 33/10, 12: see QUINCY.

Quincy: [33/10, 12]; 71/162: city in E Massachusetts, 8 miles S of
Boston; birthplace and home of John ADAMS and John Quincy
ADAMS; earlier called MERRYMOUNT and Mt. WOLLASTON.

Quincy: 63/99: prob. Edmund Quincy, 1703-88, friend of John

ADAMS; father-in-law of John HANCOCK and Jonathan Sewall.
(See: Adams, Works, II, 81).

Quincy: 64/105; 70/157: Josiah, Jr., 1744-75, American lawyer;
with John ADAMS he served as counsel for Captain PRESTON
in the Boston Massacre affair of 1770; known for his political
pamphlets written in support of the Revolution; younger brother
of Samuel QUINCY, the loyalist.

Quincy, Saml: 63/98: Samuel, 1735-89, American lawyer and friend
of John ADAMS; became solicitor-general of Massachusetts
under the Crown; a loyalist, he left the country in 1776.

Quindecennio: 54/28: (It) fifteen-year period.

quindi Cocito, Cassio membruto: 69/153: (It) then COCYTUS,
CASSIO with powerful limbs. (See: Inferno, 34, 52 and 67).

Quinn, John: [12/55, 56]; 80/85: 1870-1924, American lawyer;
authority on modern Irish literature and drama; collector and
patron of modern art.

Qui se faisait si beau: 19/84: (Fr) Who made himself so handsome.

Qui son Properzio ed Ovidio: 20/89: (It) Here are PROPERTIUS
and OVID.

quocunque aliunde: 43/11: (L) wherever else.

R

Rabateau, Jehan: 24/113: member of the Council of CHARLES VII of France.

Rabindranath: 77/52: see Sir Rabindranath TAGORE.

Ragona: 8/28; 9/35: see ARAGON.

Ragusa: 16/70; 35/26; 74/26: a port of Dalmatia; from 1205 to 1358 under the control of Venice.

raison: 77/50: (Fr) reason, right.

Rais Uli: 74/10, 25: Ahmed ibn-Muhammed Raisuli, 1875-1925, Moroccan brigand who kidnaped Walter Harris, Ion PERDICAR-IS (1904), and Sir Harry Maclean (1907); to avoid war with America and England, the sultan of Morocco met the ransom demanded by Raisuli.

Ram and Bull: 77/53: reference to the ram (March) and bull (April) in the astrological frescoes in the SCHIFANOJA, Ferrara.

Rambottom, Georgio: 9/38: Georgio Ranbutino, fl. 1454, a stone mason working on the TEMPIO of Sigismondo MALATESTA.

Ramona, Romano: 77/49: DTC, Pisa.

Ramsey: 79/64: see James Ramsay MACDONALD.

Ranger, the: 68/143: the ship commanded by John Paul JONES in 1777.

Ran-ti: 4/15: (Jap) Ran-tai for (Ch) Lan-t'ai: "Orchid Tower Palace." (See: SO-GIOKU).

Rapallo: 62/88, 96; 80/78: town of Liguria, NW Italy, on the Gulf of Rapallo; residence of Pound (1924-1945).

Rapin: 67/133: Paul de Rapin de Thoyras, 1661-1725, French historian; author of Histoire d'Angleterre (8 vols., 1723) covering English history up to the accession of William and Mary.

Raquel: 3/12: a Jewish merchant whom Ruy DIAZ, noted for his cunning, cheated.

Ravenna: 9/36: town of Ravenna province, N Italy.

R. C.: 74/4: Roman Catholic.

Read: 67/133: George, 1733-98, American constitutional lawyer from Delaware; Daniel Leonard, John ADAMS' opponent in the NOVANGLUS correspondence, studied law with him.

rectus in curia: 32/7: (L) right in point of law.

Red Caps, the: 56/53: see WHITE LILY SOCIETY.

Redentore: 83/110: (It) Redeemer.

Redimiculum Metellorum: 74/9: (L) ...Matellarum: a Chaplet of Chamber-pots; title of a book of poems published (1930) by Basil BUNTING.

Red Lion: 65/111: an inn between Philadelphia and Bristol, Pennsylvania.

Red Square: 80/75: the square in Moscow.

Reeve: 63/98: Sir Thomas, d. 1737, English jurist; author of Lord Chief Justice Reeve's Instructions to his Nephew concerning the study of law.

Regalia principis: 67/133: (L) the rights royal of a prince. (See: John Adams, Works, III, 545).

Regent's canal: 77/44: a canal along the north edge of Regent's Park, London.

Regents Park: 80/86: Regent's Park in London.

reges sacrificioli: 58/62: (L) priests with kingly functions.

reges, seniores et populus: 68/141: (L) kings, elders, and people.

Reggio, Bernardo: 11/48: Bernardo da Reggio, an officer in the
    forces of Sigismondo MALATESTA.

Regis optimatium populique: 68/141: (L) of the king, of the aristo-
    crats, of the people too. (See: Polybius, Fragm., VI; quoted
    by Jonathan Swift, A Discourse of the Contests and Dissensions
    between the Nobles and Commons of Athens and Rome; quoted
    by John Adams, Works, IV, 383).

regnicoles: 57/60: (Fr from L) inhabitants of a kingdom.

Reile: 44/20: Honoré Charles Michel Joseph, 1775-1860, aide-de-
    camp to NAPOLEON (1808).

Reithmuller: 82/103: Richard Henri Riethmueller, 1881-1942?, in-
    structor in German at the University of Pennsylvania (1905-07);
    author of Walt Whitman and the Germans (1906).

Relaxetur: 26/121: (L) Let him be released.

Rembrandt: 80/89: Rembrandt Harmensz van Rijn, 1606-69, the
    Dutch painter.

remedium: 69/151: (L) remedy, redress.

rem eorum saluavit: 9/35: (L) saved their state.

Remi: 74/17: (L) REMUS.

Re Militari: 26/121: see DE RE MILITARI.

remir: 20/90: (Pr) (I) look.

[Remus]: 74/17: with his brother, ROMULUS, a founder of the city
    of Rome.

Rena, Orazzio della: 42/6, 8; 43/14, 16: Horatio or Horace, fl. 1622;
    prob. associated with the guardians of FERDINAND II of Tus-
    cany.

Rennert: 20/89; 28/135: Hugo Albert, 1858-1927, scholar of Ro-
    mance languages, University of Pennsylvania; Pound was his
    student (1905-06).

Replevin: 46/28: (Law) the return to, or recovery by, a person of
    goods or chattels wrongfully taken or detained, upon giving
    security to try the matter in court and return the goods if de-
    feated in the action.

repos donnez à cils/ senza termine furge Immaculata Regina/ Les
    larmes que j'ai creées m'indondent/ Tard, très tard je t'ai
    connue la Tristesse: 80/91: (Fr) give rest to (O Fr) those/
    (It) without end acts (L) Immaculate Queen/ (Fr) The tears
    that I created flood me/ Late, very late have I known you,
    Sadness. (See: Villon, Grand Testament, rondeau after stanza
    165).

representatives: 83/114: see HOUSE OF REPRESENTATIVES.

Republic, the: 78/56: the SALÒ Republic, as distinguished from the
    monarchy of occupied Italy, 1943-45.

Republic, The: 84/116: by Charles BEARD (1943).

Republican Party: 40/48: formerly the Whig Party; the present day
    Republican Party was founded in 1854. It is often called the
    party which represents the interests of big business.

Resanesi: 35/25: people of Resina, a city on the bay of Naples; the
    site of ancient Herculaneum.
res non verba: 82/103: (L) objects not words.
Respectons les prêtres: 44/19: (Fr) Let us respect the priests.
res publica: 21/96: (L) republic.
Revmo Monsignore: 11/49: see Aeneas Silvius PICCOLOMINI.
rex: 74/7: (L) king.
Rheingrave: 65/122: see Rhinegrave de SALM.
Rhine: 80/77: river of Germany.
Rhode Island: 65/121; 66/127: the north Atlantic state.
Rhodes: [24/111; 26/123; 46/28]; 67/140; [74/22; 78/57]: the island
    in the Aegean Sea; in antiquity a center of trade.
Rhodez: 4/13: Rodez, an ancient town in Provence.
Rhodi: 46/28; 78/57: (L) of RHODES.
Rhodon: 74/22: (L) RHODES.
Rhodos: 24/111; 26/123: see RHODES.
Rhumby, Mr.: 48/35:
Rhys: 74/23: Ernest, 1859-1946, English editor and writer.
Rialto: 25/115; 26/124: the bridge in Venice.
Ricarda: 24/113: Ricciarda. (See: Marchese SALUZZO).
Ricci: 58/63, [64]: Mathieu or Matteo, 1552-1610, founder of the
    modern Catholic missions of China; he arrived at Macao in 1582.
    One of his most important acts was to determine the correct
    Chinese name for God; he decided that TIEN and CHANG TI
    were accurate. Without pronouncing on the meaning of these
    terms, CLEMENT XI decided on T'ein-chu (actually the name
    of one of the eight demi-gods of ancient Chinese mythology);
    modern sinologists have confirmed Ricci's opinion. This con-
    fusion of terms greatly hindered the Christianization of China.
    Ricci died in Peiping, and is the only foreigner mentioned by
    name in the dynastic histories of China.
Riccio: 52/4: Guido, Sienese hero at the siege of Montemassi; Simone
    Martini's fresco of him (1328) is in the Palazzo Publico, Siena.
Richard: 6/22: see RICHARD I of England.
Richard: 53/18: see RICHARD III of England.
[Richard I]: 6/22: Richard Coeur de Lion, 1157-99; King of England
    (1189-99).
[Richard III]: 53/18: 1452-85; King of England (1483-85).
Richardson, Roy: 84/115: captain in charge of Prisoner Training,
    DTC, Pisa.
Richelieu, Rue: 65/118: Rue de Richelieu, street of Paris; runs
    past the Bibliothèque Nationale and the Palais Royal to the
    Louvre.
Richmond: 80/86: suburb of London.
Riley, Whitcomb: 80/88: James Whitcomb Riley, 1849-1916, the
    American poet.
Rimini: 8/31; 9/[36, 37], 39; 11/51; 24/110, 111; 26/123; 80/75, 80;
    83/106: (Ariminum), seaport of Forli province, N Italy; seat of
    the MALATESTA family.
Rimini bas reliefs: 83/106: prob. a reference to the bas reliefs in
    the TEMPIO of Sigismondo MALATESTA.

Rio Grande: 28/136: river in the southwest US.
ripa del Palazzo: 25/116: (It) side of the Palace.
risotto: 80/79: (It) boiled rice.
Rites, the: 58/64: see TRIBUNAL OF RITES.
Ritz-Carlton: 74/25: the hotel in New York.
Rivera: 38/39: see Miguel PRIMO DE RIVERA.
Rives, Amber: 74/12: Amélie Rives (Princess Troubetzkoy), 1864-
     1945; author of The Quick and the Dead.
Roane: 37/35: Spencer, 1762-1822, American jurist and political
     writer; served as judge of the General Court.(1789) and in 1794
     was elected to the Virginia Court of Appeals. A Jeffersonian
     Republican, he asserted the supremacy of the states.
Robbia, de la: 80/75: Della Robbia, the Florentine family of sculp-
     tors and ceramicists; their terra cotta enamels bear the name
     Della Robbia ware.
[Robert]: 5/18; 23/109: 1169-1234, Dauphin of Auvergne; he pro-
     tected the troubadour Piere de MAENSAC against the attack of
     Bernart de TIERCI.
Robert: 11/50: see Roberto MALATESTA.
Roberto: 11/48: see Roberto MALATESTA.
Robert's: 74/11; 76/31: a restaurant, prob. in Paris.
Robinson Crusoe: 32/8: by Daniel Defoe (1719).
Rocca: 9/34: the fortress which Sigismondo MALATESTA built at
     Rimini; started in 1437, finished 1446.
Rocca Sorano: 11/50: (It) Castle of Sorano.
Rochefoucauld: 78/59: see LA ROCHEFOUCAULD.
Rodenbach: 80/90: Georges, 1855-1898, Belgian poet of the symbol-
     ist group; associated with the 19th century Belgian literary re-
     vival.
Rodendo con denti una bachetta che havea in mani: 24/112: (It) Chew-
     ing with his teeth a stick he had in his hands.
Roderique Hortalez: 68/143: Roderique Hortalez & Co., a mock
     company set up by BEAUMARCHAIS to sell military supplies
     to the American colonies during the Revolution.
Rogers: 82/102: Samuel, 1763-1855, the English poet.
Rogier: 33/12: Charles Latour, 1800-85, Belgian statesman; opposed
     union with the Low Countries; premier of Belgium (1847-52).
Rohan, La Comtesse: 77/50: prob. the Duchesse de Rohan, fl. 1924,
     French writer and painter.
Roi, le: 34/16: see LOUIS XVIII.
Roi je ne suis, prince je ne daigne: 77/51: (Fr) I am not the king,
     I do not condescend to be the prince. (From the motto of the
     House of Rohan: Roi ne puis, prince ne daigne, Rohan suis.)
Rokku: 4/16: see TAI HAKU.
Roma: 60/78; 77/51; 78/56: (It) ROME.
Roma, Agniolo da: 11/48: Agnolo, an officer in the forces of Sigis-
     mondo MALATESTA.
Romagna: 8/32; 24/110; [28/133; 35/25]; 81/97: region of Italy which
     now forms the provinces of Bologna, Ferrara, Ravenna, and
     Forli.
Romagnolo: 28/133: pertaining to ROMAGNA.

Romains: 80/84: Jules; pseudonym of Louis Farigoule, 1885-   ;
   the French writer.
Romancero: 35/25:
[Romano, Alberic da]: 29/141, 142: Podesta of Treviso; brother of
   Cunizza da ROMANO.
Romano, Cunizza: 6/22; [29/141, 142; 74/16, 21; 76/30; 78/61]:
   Cunizza da Romano, fl. 1228, married to Ricciardo di SAN
   BONIFAZZIO (c. 1222). Between 1227-29 she had an intrigue
   with SORDELLO, who was staying at Treviso with her brother,
   Ezzelino III of Romano; at the request of her brother, Sordello
   abducted her -- primarily for political reasons. In 1265, when
   about 67 years old, she executed a deed of manumission, giv-
   ing freedom to a number of slaves, at the house of the CAVAL-
   CANTI.
Romano, Eccelin da: 29/142: Ezzelino II of Romano, father of
   Cunizza da ROMANO.
Romano, Pietro: 74/8: see Pietro LOMBARDO.
Romano, Tullio: 76/38: see Tullio LOMBARDO.
Roman Road: 43/16: prob. the Cassian Way, a northern inland
   route from Rome to Lucca.
Romans: 10/47; 48/36; 65/113.
Romanzoff: 34/15, 16: Count Nicolas-Petrovitch, 1754-1826, Russian
   statesman; minister of foreign affairs for ALEXANDER I of
   Russia (1807-14).
Roma profugens Sabinorum in terras: 77/51; 78/56: (L) fleeing from
   Rome to the land of the SABINES.
Rome: 7/24; 9/38; 20/90; 24/111; 34/16; [60/78]; 67/135; [77/51;
   78/56].
Rome: 64/108: George, d. after 1788, loyalist and merchant of New-
   port, Rhode Island during the Revolution he served as a con-
   tractor for the royal forces.
Romei, Laodamia delli: 24/113: c. 1430, a judge's wife who, ap-
   parently, had committed adultery; under the edict (1425) of
   Niccolò d'ESTE, she was beheaded.
Romeo: 38/39: the character in Shakespeare's play Romeo and
   Juliet.
romerya: 5/18: (Pr) pilgrimage to Rome.
Romuli: 65/113: (L) ROMULUS.
[Romulus]: 65/113: with his brother, REMUS, a founder of the city
   of Rome.
Ronald, Sir: 80/88: Sir Ronald Storrs, 1881-   , British administra-
   tor and historian.
Ronaldson: 32/8: James, 1768-1842, American printer and typo-
   grapher who established a type foundry in Philadelphia in 1796.
Ronsard: 80/83: Pierre de, 1524-85, the French poet.
ronzino baiectino: 9/39: (It) the little bay nag.
Roosevelt, F. Delano: 46/29: Franklin Delano Roosevelt, 1882-1945,
   President of the United States (1933-1945).
Rops: 64/107: Mrs. Ropes, fl. 1772, wife of Judge Ropes, a friend
   of John ADAMS.
Rospigliosi: 50/42: Count Rospigliosi, fl. 1814, Austrian regent in
   Tuscany.

Rossetti: 80/88: Dante Gabriel, 1828-82, the English painter and
    poet; founder and leader of the Pre-Raphaelite school of paint-
    ing (1848).
Rostovseff: 78/58: Michael Ivanovich Rostovtzeff, 1870-1952, Amer-
    ican historian; professor of classical philology and ancient his-
    tory at St. Petersburg (1901-18), professor of ancient history
    at U. of Wisconsin (1920-25) and at Yale (1925-39); author of
    History of the Ancient World (1924-26), Social and Economic
    History of the Hellenistic World (1941).
[Rothschild, Mayer Amschel]: 74/17: 1743-1812, usually considered
    to be the founder of the house of Rothschild.
Rothschilds: 40/48; 46/27; 48/35; 80/79: the house of Rothschild, a
    family of international bankers, founded by Mayer Amschel
    ROTHSCHILD.
Rotterdam: 19/86; 69/151: the city in the Netherlands.
Rourke: 67/135: Tiernan O'Rourke, d. 1172, king of Breifne and
    ruler of part of Meath (1144); in 1152 his wife was carried off
    by Dermod MacMurrough (See: MACMORRAL).
Rouse: 74/4: William Henry Denham, 1863-1950, British educator
    and classical scholar; translated Homer (1939) and much East
    Indian literature.
Rousselot: 77/50: Abbé Jean Pierre, 1846-1924, French pioneer in
    experimental phonetics and in the study of dialect as related
    to geography and genealogy; author of Précis de Prononciation
    Française (1902).
Routledge: 62/91: see Edward RUTLEDGE.
Rowe: 71/160: John, fl. 1774, an important merchant of Boston.
Roy, le: 24/113: see CHARLES VII.
Rubens: 80/89: Peter Paul, 1577-1640, the Flemish painter.
Rubicon: 80/80: the river of N central Italy, just north of RIMINI.
ruffiane: 26/124: (It) procuresses.
Rufiano: 11/49: poss. Rufina, a village of Firenze province, Tus-
    cany, central Italy; or Ruffano, a town in southern Italy.
Ruggles: 63/99: Timothy, 1711-95, a prominent Massachusetts
    loyalist.
Rummel, W.: 80/71: Walter Morse Rummel, 1887-1953, German
    pianist and composer; especially interested in 12th-13th century
    French songs.
Runing Mede: 66/127: Runnymede, a meadow on the south bank of
    the Thames in Surrey, S England; the MAGNA CHARTA was
    signed here by King JOHN in 1215.
Rupe Tarpeia: 74/21: the Tarpeian Rock, the cliff in Rome where
    criminals and traitors were hurled to their death; the exact
    location of the rock is disputed.
Rush: 65/113; 68/145; 70/157: Benjamin, ?1745-1813, American
    physician and political leader; member of the CONTINENTAL
    CONGRESS (1776-77) and signer of the DECLARATION of In-
    dependence; surgeon in the Continental Army (1777-78), mem-
    ber of the Pennsylvania constitutional ratification convention
    (1787), treasurer of the US Mint (1797-1813).

Rushworth: 67/133: John, ?1612-90, English historian; author of
   Historical Collections (8 vols. 1659-1701), a work covering the
   period 1618-48.
Russell: 42/3: Lord John, 1792-1878, English statesman; prime
   minister (1846-52).
Russell: 71/163: Jonathan, 1771-1832, American diplomat; charge
   d'affaires in England when the War of 1812 broke out; one of
   the five American commissioners who negotiated the treaty
   of Ghent with Great Britain in 1814.
Russia: 18/81; 27/129; 34/15; 59/72, 73; 60/74, 78; 70/157; 74/19.
Russian, the: 34/15: the Russian army of Emperor ALEXANDER I.
Rutledge: [62/91]; 65/111: Edward, 1749-1800, American lawyer;
   member of the CONTINENTAL CONGRESS (1774-77) and signer
   of the DECLARATION of Independence; member of the South
   Carolina legislature (1782-96) and governor of South Carolina
   (1798-1800); brother of John RUTLEDGE.
Rutledge: 65/110: John, 1739-1800, American statesman; member of
   the CONTINENTAL CONGRESS (1774-76; 1782-83); governor
   of South Carolina (1779-82); associate justice of the US Supreme
   Court (1789-91), appointed Chief Justice (1795) but the appoint-
   ment was not confirmed.
Ruyter, De: 62/92: Michel Adriaanszoon de Ruyter, 1607-76, Dutch
   admiral and naval hero; active in the cause for Dutch freedom.

S

S : 10/42: see Sigismondo MALATESTA.
S. A.: 12/55: see SOUTH AMERICA.
S. A.: 42/3: Su Altezza (It) Your Highness.
S. A.: 67/138: see Samuel ADAMS.
Saave: 4/16: (L) salve: hail!
[Sabines]: 77/51; 78/56: the ancient people of Italy.
Sabinorum: 77/51; 78/56: (L) of the SABINES.
[Sacchi, Bartolommeo]: 11/50: Latin name: Platina, 1421-81,
    Italian humanist and historian.
saccone: 28/139: (It) a straw mattress.
sacerdos: 29/141; 80/80: (L) priest.
Sachs: 75/28: Hans, 1495-1576, the German Meistersinger of Nurem-
    berg.
[Sackville, John Frederick]: 62/93: Duke of Dorset, 1745-99;
    English ambassador-extraordinary and plenipotentiary to
    France (1783-89).
Sacrum, sacrum, inluminatio coitu: 36/30; [74/13]: (L) a sacred
    thing, a sacred thing, the cognition of coition.
Sadakichi: 80/73: see Sadakichi HARTMANN.
Sadducees: 80/75: a sect of Jews at the time of Christ; urban and
    aristocratic, the Sadducees were firm upholders of the pre-
    scriptions of the Law and were religiously conservative, deny-
    ing immortality and resurrection.
[Sade, Hippolyte de]: 71/162: d. 1780, appointed Chef d'Escadre of
    France in 1776; a distinguished naval commander.
s'adora: 20/89: (It) it is adored.
Sadowa: 38/41: the village in Czechoslovakia where the Austrians
    suffered a major defeat in the Franco-Prussian War.
saeculorum: 80/91: (L) of the ages.
saeculorum Athenae: 74/16: (L) immemorial of ATHENA.
saeva: 76/40: (L) cruel.   .
Sage of Concord: 28/134: see Ralph Waldo EMERSON.
Sagittarius: 52/6: the southern constellation represented as a cen-
    taur shooting an arrow.
Sagramoro: 9/38: Sacramoro Sacramori, fl. 1454, counsellor and
    secretary to Sigismondo MALATESTA.
[Sagundino, Nicoló]: 26/121, 122: spokesman at Rome for the
    Venetian Senate; charged by the Venetians to try to make peace
    between Pope PIUS II and the MALATESTA family.
sainfoin: 65/121: a kind of hay.
Saint Archangelo, Petracco: 11/48: Petraccio da Sant'Arcangelo,
    a captain in the forces of Sigismondo MALATESTA.
S. Bartolomeo: 80/78: prob. SAN BARTOLOMEO IN GALDO.
Saint Boniface, Richard: 6/22; 29/142: see Count Ricciardo di SAN
    BONIFAZZIO.
St Catherine's chapel: 44/17: in the church of San Domenico, Siena.
St. Clement of Alexandria: 14/62: Titus Flavius Clemens, ?150-
    220?, Greek theologian of the early Christian church.
S. Domenico: 44/17: San Domenico, a church in Siena.

St Etienne: 83/106: the Basilica of St. Étienne, a 12th century
     church in Périgueux.
St. George: 26/126; 43/11: d.c. 303, Christian martyr; adopted in
     the time of Edward III as the patron saint of England.
St George: 43/11: prob. a reference to a figure of St. George as
     patron saint on a Sienese cart.
S. Gionni: 43/16: see SAN GIOVANNI.
S. Giorgio: 28/133: see SAN GIORGIO MAGGIORE.
[S. Girolamo degli Schiavoni]: 5/19, 20: a church on the Tiber near
     which the body of Giovanni BORGIA floated; a witness near the
     church saw the cloak of Borgia floating and the assassins throw-
     ing stones on it to make it sink.
Saint Hilaire: 45/24; 51/44: church in Poitiers, France; built in the
     11th century.
St Jago de Cuba: 70/155: see SANTIAGO DE CUBA.
St James: 69/[150], 152: the Court of St. James's, London.
St James Campostella: 65/120: a church in Galicia where there is
     a shrine to St. James; a famous object of pilgrims during the
     Middle Ages.
[St. John, Henry]: 68/144: Viscount Bolingbroke, 1678-1754, Eng-
     lish statesman, orator and author; his best known work is the
     Idea of a Patriot King (1749)
[St. John of the Cross]: 64/16: Juan de Yepis y Alvarez, 1542-91,
     the Spanish mystic.
St John's eve: 35/25: 23 June, midsummer.
St Joseph: 66/126: a military fort on the Great Lakes; John ADAMS
     requested the English to relinquish it to the Americans.
Saint-Libin: 32/7:
St. Louis Till: [74/18]; 77/51: American soldier, DTC, Pisa,
     where he was executed.
St. Mark: 26/122: patron saint of Venice; the flag of St. Mark is
     the Venetian standard.
St. Mary's: 66/126: a military fort on the Great Lakes; John
     ADAMS requested the English to relinquish it to the Americans.
St. Nicholas: 25/116: Church of St. Nicolo dei Mendicoli, originally
     built in the 7th century, but restored many times since; it is
     on the Campo S. Nicolo in Venice.
S. Pantaleone: 76/30: prob. the Church of S. Pantalon, on the
     Campo S. Pantalon, Venice.
St Peter's: [10/43]; 31/6; 46/28; [74/26(?)]: St. Peter's Church
     in Rome.
St. Petersburg: 19/87; [27/131]; 38/41; [59/73; 68/144; 74/11]: the
     Russian city.
S. Pietri: 10/43: (It) ST. PETER'S.
S. Pietro: 74/26: poss. ST. PETER'S or SAN PIETRO IN VINCOLI.
St Trophime: 45/24; 51/44: church in Arles, Provence; constructed
     11th-15th century.
St. Valentine's day: 66/129: 14 February.
St What's his name: 83/107:
Sala: 68/142: river in the Netherlands, the north mouth of the
     Rhine; Sala, its ancient name, is applied to the inhabitants

along its banks: the Salian Franks; the modern name of the
    river is Ijssel.
Saladin: 6/21: ?1137-93, the Moslem warrior and great opponent of
    the Christian crusaders.
Salamis: 74/7, 9, 18; 77/46; 79/64: island E of Greece, in the Gulf
    of Aegina; off Salamis the allied Greek fleet defeated the
    Persians (480 BC).
Salazar: 79/67: DTC, Pisa.
Salem: 48/35; 63/100; 64/103: the city in Massachusetts; once an
    important center of fishing, shipping, and ship-building.
[Salic Law, the]: 42/3: the laws of the Salian Franks, first com-
    piled (c. 508-11) by Clovis I; the code was the fundamental law
    of the Merovingian and Carolingian rulers and the early Holy
    Roman emperors. (See: SALA).
Salisbury plain: 80/93: a tract of land in Wiltshire, S England, near
    the city of Salisbury.
salita: 80/78: (It) ascent, rising path.
salite: 43/11: (It) rising ground.
[Salm, Rhinegrave de]: 65/122: one of the negotiators of the Treaty
    of Paris (1783).
Salmacis: 4/15: the water nymph who loved Hermaphroditus. (See:
    Ovid, Metamorphoses, IV, 285-388).
Salò: 78/56: the Salò Republic, founded in northern Italy in October
    1943, a remnant of the Fascist regime.
salotto: 27/130: (It) parlor.
Salustio: 20/94; 74/26: see Sallustio MALATESTA.
Saluzzo, Marchese: 24/113, Sallusto, whose daughter, Ricciarda di
    Sallusto, married (1431) Niccolò d'ESTE and became the mother
    of his sons, Ercole and Sigismondo.
Salviati: 76/38: prob. the Fondamenta del Banco Salviati, Venice.
Salzburg: 26/128; 78/58; 79/62: the city in Austria; famous for its
    annual Mozart festival.
Samarkand: 60/75: city in Soviet Central Asia.
Sa Mo: 58/62: Satsuma, the southern part of Kyushu Island, Japan;
    the ancient fief of the Satsuma lords.
Sanazarro: 5/20: Jacopo Sannazaro, 1456-1530, the Neapolitan poet
    who wrote about the murder of Giovanni BORGIA.
[San Bartolomeo in Galdo]: 80/78: town in Benevento province,
    Campania, S Italy.
San Bertrand: 48/37: prob. Saint-Bertrand, a village of Haute-
    Garonne department, S France.
[San Bonifazzio, Count Ricciardo di]: 6/22; 29/142: Podestà of
    Mantua and husband of Cunizza da ROMANO; when Ricciardo
    discovered the intrigue between his wife and SORDELLO, the
    poet was forced to flee to Provence. However, political troubles
    between Sordello and San Bonifazzio were equally important in
    causing his flight.
San Casciano: 41/54: San Casciano in Val di Peas, a town in Firenze
    province, central Italy; near Florence.
San-chan: 54/27: (San-shan), a mountain in the province of KIANG-
    NAN.

Sancho: 20/91: King Sancho, a character in Lope de Vega's Las Almenas de Toro. (See: Spirit of Romance, 203-204).

Sandro: 20/90; 80/89: see Sandro BOTTICELLI.

Sandro: 76/39:

Sandusky: 66/126: once a military fort on Sandusky Bay in N Ohio;
first controlled by the British in Canada and then relinquished
to the Americans.

Sandwich: 63/99: town in SE Massachusetts.

San Giorgio: 28/133: see SAN GIORGIO MAGGIORE.

[San Giorgio dei Greci]: 76/39: the Greek Orthodox Church on the
Ponte dei Greci, Venice.

San Giorgio Maggiore: [24/110]; 26/126; [28/133]; one of the islands
of Venice; also the church thereon.

San Giovanni: [42/7]; 43/12, [13]: San Giovanni di Siena, a church
of Siena.

Sangko: 56/50: (Sang Ko) d. AD 1291, served as first minister to
KUBLAI KHAN (1288-91); he was a villain, clever and apt at
flattery, who sacrificed the honor of the Empire to his own interests. He was executed in 1291.

San Gregorio: [76/39]; 83/110: church, calle del Traghetto, Venice.

San Joannij: 42/7: see SAN GIOVANNI.

San Juan: 74/16: see ST. JOHN OF THE CROSS.

San Marco: 26/122; 76/39; 79/63: the Piazza and Basilica of San
Marco, Venice.

San Marino: 67/140: the republic on the Italian peninsula

San Martino: 11/49: a locality in central Italy, taken from Sigismondo MALATESTA by the peace terms imposed by Pope PIUS
II (c. 1460).

San Petronio: 24/110: a race run at Bologna.

San Piero: 29/145: San Pietro, the church and monastery south of
Perugia.

San Pietro in Vinçoli: 10/45; [74/26(?)]: Saint Peter in Chains, a
church of Rome, on the Esquiline near the Baths of Titus; built
in 442.

San Remo: 48/34: seaport of Imperia province, NW Italy, on the
Ligurian Sea.

San Samuele: 26/124: church on the Campo San Samuele, Venice.

San Sepolchro: 78/56: Sansepolcro, town of Arezzo province, central Italy.

San Stefano dei Cavalieri: 79/64: a church in Pisa richly hung with
banners of the Turks and Arabians, trophies of the victories of
the Knights of San Stephano.

Santa Maria: 9/36: a church in Trivio; on the same site Sigismondo
MALATESTA built the TEMPIO.

Santa Maria dei Miracoli: 74/8; 76/38; [83/107]: a church in Venice;
decorated by the sculpture of Pietro and Tullio LOMBARDO.

Santa Marta: 76/33: the Romanesque-Gothic church in TARASCON.

Sant Apollinaire: 9/36: the Basilica of San Apollinare in Classe; from
the basilica, Sigismondo MALATESTA took marble for the
TEMPIO.

Santayana, George: 80/73; 81/97: 1863-1952, the American philosopher.

[Santiago de Cuba]: 70/155: seaport and capital of Oriente province in E Cuba.

Santos, José Maria dos: 12/54, 55: prob. a Portuguese merchant.

San Trovaso: 76/[39], 40: a church on the Campo San Trovaso, Venice.

San Vio: 76/38, [39]; 83/110: church of San Vio on the Campo San Vio in Venice. Also the Festival of San Vio (15 June) held in honor of the suppression of the conspiracy of Baiamonte Tiepolo; on the festival day, the doge went to the church of San Vio to give a thank offering for the deliverance of the Republic.

San Vitale: 9/41: a 6th century Byzantine church in Ravenna.

San Yin: 49/38:

San Zeno: 29/141, 142: the Bastia San Zeno, or San Zenone, in Verona.

San Zeno: 42/7; 74/26; 78/58: San Zeno Maggiore, a Romanesque church in Verona.

San Zorzo: 24/110: poss. SAN GIORGIO MAGGIORE.

Sapiens Consilij: 25/119: (L) Reverend (member) of the Council.

Sapiens Terrae Firmae: 25/119: (L) Reverend (delegate) from the Mainland.

Saracens: 24/111: term commonly used in the Middle Ages to designate the Arabs and, by extension, Moslems in general -- whether Arabs, Moors, or Turks.

Sarasate: 80/81: Pablo de, 1844-1908, Spanish violin virtuoso.

Sardegna: 50/43; 65/122, 124: (It) SARDINIA.

Sardegna: 65/124: a reference to VICTOR AMADEUS III.

Sardinia: 32/9; [50/43; 65/122, 124]: island in the Mediterranean Sea, W of Italy.

Sardinian ambassador: see Comte Montagnini MIRABEL.

Sardis: 5/17; 26/123: capital of ancient LYDIA.

Sargent: 80/90; 81/95: John Singer, 1856-1925, the American painter.

Sarlat: 6/23: a town in SW central France.

Sarnone: 84/115: DTC, Pisa.

Sarsfield, Count: 65/122: poss. a French emissary to the Hague. (See: Adams, Works, III, 283).

Sartine: 68/142, 143: Antoine Raymond Jean Gualbet Gabriel de, comte d'Alby, 1729-1801, French statesman; minister of marine (1774-80).

Sauter: 80/81: George, 1866-1937, a Bavarian portrait painter who lived in London (1895-1915).

Savairic: 48/37: see Savaric de MAULEON.

Savil, Mrs. 63/98: fl. 1758, wife of Dr. Elisha Savil, a friend of John ADAMS.

Savio: 11/49: the river in north central Italy.

Sbrigara: 11/49: a locality in central Italy, taken from Sigismondo MALATESTA by the peace terms imposed by Pope PIUS II (c. 1460).

[Scala, Can Grande della]: 78/59: 1291-1329, lord of Verona and the greatest member of the Ghibelline family that ruled Verona from 1277-1387; he was a friend and protector of DANTE.

S. Carolina: 34/19; 64/106; 65/110; 69/153: SOUTH CAROLINA.

scavenzaria: 35/24: (It) special sale.

scavoir faisans...et advenir...a haute/...à Chinon, le Roy, l'Esne
    de la Trimouill,/ Vendoise, Jehan Rabateau: 24/113: (Fr)
    making known...and to come...to high/ nobility of family and
    house...and great deeds.../ valor...affection...our aforesaid
    cousin.../ power, royal authority...he and his descendents...
    and/ as they desire to have henceforth forever in their arms
    quartering/...three golden flower-de-luce...on scalloped azure
    field.../ enjoy and use. 1431, council at CHINON, the KING,
    l'Esne de la TRIMOUILL, VENDOISE, Jehan RABATEAU.

Schacht: 52/3: Hjalmar Horace Greeley, 1877-   , German financier;
    president of the Reichsbank under Hitler.

schepens: 69/150: (Dut) sheriffs.

Schiavoni: 5/19, 20: see S. GIROLAMO DEGLI SCHIAVONI.

Schicksal, sagt der Führer: [56/54]; 62/91: Destiny, says the
    FÜHRER.

Schiedam: 69/150, 151: town in SW Netherlands.

Schifanoja: 77/51, 53: or Schifanoia, the Palazzo Schifanoia, palace
    of the ESTE, in Ferrara; famous for the frescoes of Cosimo
    TURA and Francesco del COSSA; built by Alberto d'ESTE (1391),
    extended by Borso d'ESTE.

Schlossmann: 38/39:

Schneider: 38/42: see SCHNEIDER-CREUSOT.

[Schneider, Adolphe]: 38/41: d. 1845, brother of Joseph-Eugène
    SCHNEIDER.

Schneider: 38/41: Joseph-Eugène, 1805-75, French industrialist;
    with his brother Adolphe SCHNEIDER, he organized the
    SCHNEIDER-CREUSOT iron works (1836).

Schneider Creusot: [38/42]; 41/56: Schneider-Creusot, the iron
    works organized (1836) by Joseph-Eugène and Adolphe
    SCHNEIDER; once the world's largest steel plant.

Schoeney's daughters: 2/6: Schoeneus' daughter, Atalanta. (See:
    Ovid, Metamorphoses, X, 560-707). (Schoenyes is the spelling
    in Arthur Golding's translation of the Atalanta episode, Meta-
    morphoses).

Schöners: 74/11; 76/31: a restaurant, poss. in Bolsano, Italy.

Schorn, Henry: 69/149: the widow of Henry Schorn provided John
    ADAMS with a secret mailing address in Amsterdam (1781).

Schuyler, Filippo: 69/153: Philip John Schuyler, 1733-1804, Ameri-
    can statesman; member of the US Senate (1789-91); a supporter
    of Alexander HAMILTON's financial program.

Schuylkill: 77/44: the river in Pennsylvania.

Schweighauser: 65/118; 68/143: fl. 1778, a French commercial agent
    at Brest with whom John ADAMS, representing the American
    government, had dealings.

Scilla: 47/30: see SCYLLA.

Scios: 2/7: Chios, a large Ionian island off the coast of Asia Minor;
    claimed to be the birthplace of HOMER.

Scirocco: 74/3; 76/31; 77/43: a hot southeast wind in the Mediterra-
    nean areas.

Scorpio: 52/5, 6; 58/18: the southern constellation.
Scotland: 67/136.
Scott, G.: 79/62, 67: DTC, Pisa.
Scott: 63/97: Sir Walter, 1771-1832, the English novelist.
Scott: 34/21: Winfield, 1786-1866, American soldier; Whig candidate
    for the Presidency in 1852.
Scottch Kirrrk: 76/39: the Scotch Presbyterian Church in Venice.
Scotus: 83/106: see Johannes Scotus ERIGENA.
Scotus Erigena: 74/7: see Johannes Scotus ERIGENA.
Scudder's Falls: 77/44: on the SCHUYLKILL, N of Philadelphia.
scudo: 42/3: (It) crown. (a monetary unit, varying in value with
    locality and date).
Scylla: 47/[30], 32: the sea-monster, living in a cave opposite
    Charybdis; she had six heads, each with a triple row of teeth,
    and barked like a dog. (See: Odyssey, XII, 80-100).
Seance Royale: 34/16: (Fr) royal interview (one held by LOUIS XVIII
    in 1815).
se casco, non casco in ginocchion': 77/51: (It) if I fall, I do not fall
    on my knees.
Se-choui: 53/9: (Se-shui), river in KIANG-NAN; joins the HOANG-HO.
Second Baronet: 28/139:
[Second National Bank of the United States]: 37/32, 33, 34, 35, 36:
    the central bank of the US which acted as a fiscal agent for the
    government and also conducted a general commercial business.
    The bank, capitalized at $35,000,000 and operating twenty-five
    branches, grew especially prosperous under the management of
    Nicholas BIDDLE; its prosperity drew to it much criticism from
    the frontier, and many claimed that it was too powerful and that
    it operated in the interests of the East alone. The bank's at-
    tempt to renew its national charter was defeated during the ad-
    ministration of JACKSON. The First National Bank, established
    by Hamilton, lasted 1791-1811; the second bank from 1816 to 1836.
secretissime: 26/122; 34/18: (It) very secretly.
Sed aureis furculis: 26/122: (L) but with golden forks.
Sed et universus quoque ecclesie populus: 27/130: (L) And the whole
    population of the church, too.
Sedgwick: 69/153: Theodore, 1746-1813, American jurist and states-
    man; member of the CONTINENTAL CONGRESS (1785-88), the
    House of Representatives (1789-96; 1799-1801), and of the Senate
    (1796-99).
Segundino, Nicolo: 26/121, 122: see Nicolò SAGUNDINO.
Segur, Mount: 23/109; 48/37; 76/30; 80/88, 90: site of a castle in
    Provence which was besieged during the Albigensian crusade.
Seignory: 26/127: the ruling body of Venice.
Seignory: 43/13: the ruling body of Siena.
Seine: [38/37]; 77/50: the river in France.
seipsum seipsum diffundit, risplende: 55/44: (L) itself, it diffuses
    itself, (It) it shines. (See: Grosseteste, De luce seu de inchoa-
    tione formarum, ed. Baur, 51).
Seitz: 80/91: a captain in the Provost section, DTC, Pisa.
Selinga: 59/72: town on the border between Russia and Manchuria.

[Sellaio, Jacopo]: 20/90; 80/89: 1422-93, the Florentine painter.
Selsey: 80/86: prob. Selsey Bill, headland on the S coast of England.
Selvo: 26/122: Domenigo Selva, Doge of Venice (1071-81).
selv' oscura: 23/108: (It) dark forest. (See: Inferno, 1, 2).
semina motuum: 80/78: (L) seeds of motion.
Semiramis: 44/21: the ship that took Maria Anna Elisa BONAPARTE,
    Grand Duchess of Tuscany, from Lucca (1814).
Senate: 34/18, 20; 37/34; 62/93, 94, 95; 70/155; 78/59; 83/113, 114:
    see UNITED STATES SENATE.
Senate: 80/75: see IRISH SENATE.
Senén: 43/9: (L) of the Sienese.
Senensis: 42/7; 43/10: (L) Sienese.
senesco/ sed amo: 80/71: (L) I am getting old, but I love.
Senesi: 10/42: (It) the Sienese.
Senis: 42/7; 43/13: (L) at SIENA.
Senna: 38/37: (It) SEINE.
Sennin: 4/16: Chinese spirits of the air.
Senni, Virginia: 28/133: née Marotti, prob. Venetian woman whose
    life and that of her son was saved by the operation of Dr.
    WALLUSCHNIG (1925).
Sensaria: 25/120; 83/110: (It) brokerage.
Se pia,.../ O empia, ma risoluto/ E terrible deliberazione: 5/[19],
    20: (It) If pious.../ or impious, but decided/ and terrible de-
    liberation. (See: Varchi, Storia Fiorentina, III, 262).
Sequit bonorum descriptio: 24/111: (L) There follows a description of
    property.
Serenely in the crystal jet: 74/27: poss. variation of Verlaine,
    Clair de Lune.
serenissimo D^{no}: 43/9: (L) to the most serene Lord.
Sergeant XL: 76/35: Sergeant Lauterback, Disciplinary Sergeant,
    DTC, Pisa.
Sergeant, Jonathan: 67/138: Jonathan Dickinson Sergeant, 1746-98,
    American lawyer; New Jersey delegate to the first CONTINENT-
    AL CONGRESS (1774).
Sero, sero: 25/118; 62/91: (L) too late, too late.
Serpentine: 80/94: the lake in Hyde Park, London.
settant'uno R. superiore Ambrosiana: 20/89: (It) seventy-one R.
    superior Ambrosian. (a catalogue number in the AMBROSIANA).
Seu Gin: 53/8: (Sui Jen-chi), a mythical king of China who followed
    the reign of YEOU; he introduced the use of fire and wood, ac-
    counting by tying knots in string, and the beginnings of trade;
    the name means "producer of fire and wood."
Sevilla: 28/134; 80/71: (Sp) Seville, capital of Seville province and
    of Andalusia in SW Spain.
Sewall: 63/100: Stephen, 1704-60, American jurist; judge of the
    supreme court of Massachusetts in 1739 and chief justice in
    1752; he was opposed to the British WRITS OF ASSISTANCE.
sexaginta quatuor nec tentatur habere plures: 11/51: (L) sixty-four,
    nor tries to get any.
Sextus: 5/17; 20/89: see Sextus PROPERTIUS.
Sforza: 9/35: see Francesco SFORZA.

Sforza: 26/125: see Alessandro SFORZA.

Sforza, Alessandro: 9/34, [35, 37; 26/125]: 1409-73, Lord of Pesaro
    and Cotignola, brother of Francesco SFORZA; it is assumed
    that he obtained PESARO (1444) through some rather underhand-
    ed agreement with Galeazzo MALATESTA, whose granddaughter,
    Constanza Varna, he married.

[Sforza, Drusiana]: 10/43: daughter of Francesco SFORZA; married
    to Giacomo PICCININO.

Sforza, Francesco: 8/[29, 31], 32; [9/35, 36, 37]; 10/43, [46]: 1401-
    66, Italian condottiere; overthrew the Ambrosian republic (1447)
    and obtained the dukedom by force and strategy; ruled Lombardy
    and other parts of north Italy until his death. Married Bianca
    Maria VISCONTI (1441).

Sforza, Franco: 10/43: see Francesco SFORZA.

[Sforza, Galeazzo Maria]: 21/98: 1444-1476, Fifth Duke of Milan
    (1466-76); son of Francesco SFORZA and Bianca Maria VIS-
    CONTI, hence the portmanteau name given him in the text:
    "Galeaz Sforza Visconti."

[Sforza, Polissena]: 8/32; 9/35: d. 1449, natural daughter of Fran-
    cesco SFORZA; in 1441 Sigismondo MALATESTA married her
    to cement his alliance with Sforza; eight years later she died,
    believed to have been poisoned by Sigismondo.

shagreen: 55/45: the rough skin of the shark; shagreen leather.

Shah Nameh: 77/52: Shah Namah, the great Persian epic (the book
    of kings) written by FIRDAUSI (c. 1010).

[Shakespear, Olivia]: 78/61: mother-in-law of Ezra Pound.

Shakespeare: 34/15, 19; [80/79]: William, 1564-1616, the English
    poet.

shamen: 54/29: shamans, those who practice shamanism; in this
    case BUDDHISTS.

Shanghai: 28/136; 79/67: Shanghai: the Chinese city.

[Shansi]: 61/81: province in NE China; one of the Five Northern
    Provinces.

Shantung: 53/8; [56/54]; 57/58; 58/68: province in NE China; one of
    the Five Northern Provinces.

sha-o: 74/[17], 18: (Shao) the Succession Dance, which mimed the
    peaceful accession of Emperor CHUN (Shun). (See: Analects:
    III, xxv; VII, xiii; XV, x).

[Shaw, George Bernard]: 46/26: 1856-1950, the Irish playwright.

Shelbourne: 69/150: see Sir William PETTY.

[Shelley, Percy Bysshe]: 16/70(?); 82/102(?), 1792-1822, the English
    poet.

[Shensi]: 56/47; 58/66: province in NE central China; one of the Five
    Northern Provinces.

Shenstone: 66/127: William, 1714-63, the English poet.

Shepard, Bill: 80/90: William Pierce Shepard, 1870-1948, professor
    of Romance Languages at Hamilton College, New York; teacher
    of Pound (1903-05).

Sherman: 65/113: Roger, 1721-93, American jurist and statesman;
    judge of the Connecticut superior court (1766-67; 1773-88); mem-
    ber of the CONTINENTAL CONGRESS (1774-81; 1783-84) where

he supported John ADAMS' proposals to negotiate a treaty with
France; signer of the DECLARATION of Independence; member,
House of Representatives (1789-91) and the Senate (1791-93).

[Shih Ching]: 13/60; 54/22, 24; 59/70: the Book of Odes, supposedly
collected and edited by CONFUCIUS.

Shirley: 67/133; 71/160: William, 1693-1771, English lawyer and governor of Massachusetts Colony (1741-49; 1753-56); in 1754 he
started the issuing of WRITS OF ASSISTANCE in the colony.

Shogun: 58/62: the Japanese title of commander-in-chief; the title
arose in the 8th century during the wars against the Ainu. The
shoguns became a quasi-dynasty which held the real civil and
military power in Japan, while the imperial dynasty was theor-
etically and ceremoniously supreme.

[Shu Ching]: 53/15; 54/22, 24: the Book of History, supposedly collected and edited by CONFUCIUS.

Shun: 56/49, 55; 57/59; 58/66; 74/7, 17, 18, 20; 77/45: see CHUN.

Shun's music: 74/17: see SHA-O.

sia: 74/8: (It) either.

Siam: 60/76: the country in SE Asia.

Siang: 53/18: (Hsiang), the territory in central Hunan province, SE
central China, that is watered by the Siang river.

[Siang-tchong]: 53/18: (Hsiang Chung) d.c. BC 609, son of OUEN
KONG and successor to LOU; however, after his father's death,
Siang was killed by a relative, who usurped the dukedom.

siano soddisfatti: 43/10: (It) get satisfaction.

Siao: 54/29: see SIAO-TSÉ.

Siao-ho: 54/21, 22: (Hsiao Ho) d. BC 193, the advisor of LIEOU-PANG,
Prince of Han; much of Lieou-pang's success in founding the
HAN dynasty is due to the efforts of Siao-ho, who kept the army
supplied, provided accurate maps, and helped to create a new
penal code.

[Siao-tsé]: 54/29: (Hsiao Tzŭ), the son of KAO-TI; in AD 483 he became emperor under the name Wu Ti (reign: 483-494). However,
the reference may be to Siao-tsé-leang (Hsiao Tzŭ-liang), who
was the son of Emperor Wu Ti and who did collect antique vases;
this Siao became emperor in 494, ruling less than a year, under
the name Chao Nieh.

Siberia: 65/125.

Sicheus: 7/26, 27: Sichaeus, Dido was married to Sichaeus, who was
her uncle and a priest of Heracles; he was murdered for his
treasure by Dido's brother, Pygmalion.

Sicily: 25/115; [80/81]; 82/102.

sic: beneplacitu nostro/ Ad regis nutum duratura: 66/131: (L)...
beneplacito...: thus: in accordance with our (royal) good
pleasure/ to endure at the King's command. (See: Coke, Institutes, IV, 74; John Adams, Works, III, 521, 524).

sic in lege: 61/80: (L) thus in the law.

Sic loquitur eques: 28/139: (L) thus speaks the knight.

Sic loquitur nupta/ Cantat sic nupta: 39/46: (L) so the bride speaks,
so she sings.

si com' ad Arli: 80/86: (It) so as at ARLES. (See: Inferno, 9, 112).

si come avesse l'inferno in gran dispitto: 79/65: (It) as he greatly
    despised hell. (See: Inferno, 10, 36).

Siculus, D.: 67/139: see DIODORUS SICULUS.

Sidg: 9/35, 37; 11/49: see Sigismondo MALATESTA.

Sié: 53/17: (Sie) town in the principality of Chin, in SHANSI province,
    NE China.

Sieff: 74/17: Israel Moses, British merchant; reputed anonymous
    owner of the London tabloid, the Daily Mirror, during the late
    1930's.

Siena: 9/37; 10/42, 44; 21/98; 29/141; 42/3, 4, 5, 6, 7, [10]; 43/9,
    10, 11, 13, 14, 16; 44/19, 22; 52/3; 77/46: city, Tuscany, cen-
    tral Italy.

Siesina, Island of: 26/126:

Sigismondo: 10/43: see Sigismondo MALATESTA.

[Sigismund V]: 9/34: 1368-1437, Holy Roman Emperor (1433-37).

Sigismund: 9/41; 10/43, 46: see Sigismondo MALATESTA.

Sigismundi: 10/43: see Sigismondo MALATESTA.

Sigismundo: 8/31, 32, 33; 9/34, 35, 36; 10/42, 45; 11/48, 49, 52;
    16/69; 17/79; 26/123, 125; 74/3; 76/30, 37; 80/90: see Sigis-
    mondo MALATESTA.

Sigismundo da Rimini: 26/123: (It) Sigismondo of RIMINI. (See:
    Sigismondo MALATESTA).

Sigismundo's Temple: 76/37: see the TEMPIO.

Sigismundus: 10/44: see Sigismondo MALATESTA.

signorinas: 83/110: (It) young ladies.

Signor...si: 24/112: (It) Sir...yes.

Siki: 74/23: Battling Siki, a light heavyweight boxing champion of
    the 1920's, a Senegalese of brutish strength.

Silenus: 79/66: a satyr, sometimes described as the son of Hermes
    or Pan; companion of DIONYSUS; sometimes known as a musi-
    cian.

Silk War: 16/70: war between Venice and Ragusa at the beginning of
    the 15th century; Pandolfo MALATESTA led the Venetians
    against Ragusa in 1420, but did not capture it.

Silla: 77/43: locality in the African Sudan, west of Timbuctoo and
    on the Niger; final stop of the FASA in the reincarnation of
    WAGADU.

S'il règne un faux savoir: 65/125: (Fr) if a false knowledge reigns.
    (See: John Adams, Works, III, 362, where he quotes from the
    Mercure de France (February 1783): s'il y regne un faux savoir,
    pire que l'ignorance...).

Simone: 23/109: see Simon de MONTFORT.

simplex munditiis: 80/72: (L) plain in her neatness. (See: Horace,
    Odes, I, 5).

simul commorantes: 25/115: (L) lingering together.

Sinbu: 58/62: see JIMMU TENNO.

since affectu: 62/89: (L) sine affectu: without feeling (passion).

Singki: 56/52: (Hsing Chi) d. AD 1352, a commander of the imperial
    troops serving Emperor CHUNTI; his sudden death from a
    wound gave the rebels against the throne an unexpected victory
    in Kiangsi province.

Sin/jih/jih/sin: 54/24: (Ch) daily renovation (reformation). (See: Appendix B).

Si no'us vei, Domna don plus mi cal,/ Negus vezer mon bel pensar no val: 20/89: (Pr) If I see you not, Lady with whom I am most concerned,/ Not seeing you is not the true reward for my fair thought. (See:Appel's Bernart von Ventadour, 235).

Sin star: 53/19: prob. Antares, a star in the Chinese constellation of Sin. (See: Mailla, Histoire Générale, II, 222).

Sintien: 54/35: (Hsin-tien) prob. a town close to Ch'ang-an, the capital of the TANG dynasty, in Shensi province. (See: Mailla, Histoire Générale, VI, 350).

Sin-yu: 54/22: (Ch) NEW DISCOURSE.

Si pulvis nullus.../Erit, nullum tamen excute: 7/24: (L) even if there is no dust.../ brush it off. (See: Ovid, Ars Amatoria, I, 151).

Siracusa: 77/45; 80/90: (It) SYRACUSE.

Sirdar: 74/11, 14; 78/58: a restaurant, prob. in Paris.

sirenes: 76/38: prob. a reference to the four marble angels in Venice carved by Tullio LOMBARDO.

Sirens: 1/5; 70/156; [74/21; 79/66]: the mythical creatures who had the power of drawing men to destruction by their song. ODYSSEUS escaped them by plugging the ears of his men with wax and having himself lashed to the mast of his ship. (See: Odyssey, XII). According to one legend, the Sirens drowned themselves in a fit of pique after Odysseus escaped them.

Si requieres monumentum: 46/28: (L) if you require(?) a memorial.

Siria: 74/10: village in Arad province, western Rumania.

Sirmio: 76/36; 78/56: Sermione, a peninsula and village in Brescia province of Lombardy, N Italy.

sistrum: 17/78: an Egyptian metal rattle.

Sitalkas: 74/15; 78/57: a Thracian king of the tribe of Odrysae, d. 424 BC.

Si tuit li dolh ehl planh el marrimen: 80/94: (Pr) Si tuit li dolh elh plor elh marrimen: If all the griefs, tears and anguish and the pain. (See: Bertran de Born, Planh on the death of Henry the young King).

Si tuit li dolh el plor/ tuit lo pro, tuit lo bes: 84/115: (Pr) If all the grief and the tears/ all the worth, all the good. (See entry above for source).

Siuen: 53/16, 17: see SIUEN-OUANG.

Siuen: 55/37, 38: see SIUEN-TSONG.

Siuen-ouang: 53/16, [17]: (Hsüan Wang) (reign: 827-781), a good emperor who put himself under the guidance of trustworthy counselors; although the kingdom was bothered by attacks from barbarians, Siuen managed for some time to repel them with the royal troops. (See: Mailla, Histoire Générale, II, 35).

[Siuen-tsong]: 55/37, 38: (Hsüan Tsung) (reign: 847-60). An emperor of intelligence and decision, he became known as the second TAÏ-TSONG.

Siun: 54/25: see HAN-SIUEN-TI.

Siu-tcheou: 53/9: (Siu-ch'ou), a department of the province of KIANG-NAN.

6th Anne chap. xxxvii section 9: 66/129: an Act of Parliament (1707)
    which provided for the encouragement of trade with America.
Si-yu: 54/25, 31: (Hsi-yu), a large region of western China, outside
    the limits of SHENSI province; the territory of the Tartars.
Slaughter: 78/57; 84/115: DTC, Pisa.
Sligo: 52/7; 77/51; 80/85: seaport of county Sligo in N Eire on Sligo
    Bay.
Slonimsky: 77/47: Henry Slominsky, 1884-   , author of Heraklit
    und Parmenides (1912).
Smaragdos, chrysolithos: 7/25: (L) emeralds, topazes. (See: Pro-
    pertius, II, xvi, 43).
Smith: 28/136: William Brooke, a young painter Pound knew in Phil-
    adelphia (c. 1905); Pound dedicated A Lume Spento (1908) to him.
Smith, Adam: 40/47: 1723-90, Scottish economist; author of Inquiry
    into the Nature and Causes of the Wealth of Nations (1776).
Smith, Robert: 31/4: 1757-1842, US Secretary of the Navy (1801-09)
    and Secretary of State (1809-11). President MADISON requested
    Smith to resign his last post because his foreign policy was not
    in accord with Madison's and because Madison could not stand
    his prose style.
Smith, W.: 69/153: William Loughton Smith, ?1758-1812, American
    statesman; member House of Representatives (1789-97); US
    minister to Portugal (1797-1801). He was a supporter of HAM-
    ILTON's financial policies and a heavy speculator in government
    paper.
Snag: 74/8; 76/32; 77/51: nickname of a prisoner in a "security cage"
    near Pound; DTC, Pisa.
Snot: 62/96: see James McHENRY.
Snow: 74/22: Herbert Kynaston, 1835-1910, editor of Theocritus and
    teacher of Greek at Eton. He changed his name from Snow.
S.O.: 43/12: Standard Oil.
Soane et Loire: 38/41: Saône-et-Loire, a department in E central
    France.
Sobr' un zecchin: 78/55: (It) on a golden coin.
Sochy-lism: 77/42; [78/60]: socialism.
Société Bourgeoise: 69/152: an early form of the chamber of com-
    merce, but having a more direct control over the actions of the
    government.
Socrates: 67/137: ?470-399, the Greek philosopher.
Soffici: 42/8: prob. a member of the Sienese BALÍA (c. 1622).
So-Gioku: 4/15: Sung Yü, 3rd and 4th century, Chinese poet. (See:
    The Man-Wind and the Woman-Wind in Waley, 170 Chinese
    Poems, 41).
Sogliano: 11/49: a locality in central Italy, taken from Sigismondo
    MALATESTA by the peace terms imposed by Pope PIUS II
    (c. 1460).
Soho: 80/80: a district in London.
soi disant: 74/7: (Fr) supposedly.
Soldan of Egypt: 21/98: Kait Bey (Qā'it Bāy), sultan, 1468-96.
soldi: 24/111: soldo: small Italian coin.

soll deine Liebe sein: 83/107: (Ger) is to be your love.

Solois: 40/49: a promontory on the Atlantic coast of North Africa; HANNO stopped there on his periplus.

solons: 84/115: members of the US SENATE.

Somnus: 20/94: the Roman god of sleep. (See: Ovid, Metamorphoses, XI, 592).

Soncino: 82/102: see Hieronymus SONCINUS.

Soncinus, Hieronymus: 30/149; [82/102]: Gerolamo Soncino, Italian printer of the 16th century.

Song: 53/16: (Sung) poss. the principality founded in BC 1113 by Emperor TCHING-OUANG.

Son of Heaven: 52/4, [7]: a title of the emperor of China; poss. reference to CHANG-TI.

son père: 74/20: (Fr) his father.

Sons of Liberty: 64/104, 106: groups which organized throughout the American Colonies to resist enforcement of the STAMP ACT (1765).

sont/ l'in...fan...terie koh/lon-/i-ale: 28/137: (Fr) they are the colonial infantry.

[Soong, Charles Jones]: 74/4: d. 1924, member of the prominent Soong family of China; he was a Methodist missionary in Shanghai and made his fortune as a Bible manufacturer and salesman.

Sorano: 10/42; 11/50: a town of Tuscany in the province of Grosseto.

Soranzo, John: 25/115: Giovanni Soranzo, Doge of Venice (1312-28).

Soranzo, Sorantia: 25/116: daughter of Giovanni SORANZO, Doge of Venice; she was exiled from Venice in 1320 and permitted to return only to attend her father when he was ill (1328).

Sordello: 2/6; [6/23]; 29/142; 36/30: ?1180-1255?, Italian troubadour who lived much of his life in Provence; son of a poor cavalier, Sier ESCORT. He came to the court of Count Ricciardo di SAN BONIFAZZIO, fell in love with the Count's wife, Cunizza da ROMANO, and helped her brothers to abduct her; he was then forced to flee to Provence. Later he took military service with CHARLES I of Naples and Sicily. Sordello's most important poem is the planh on the death of Blacatz. (See: Purgatorio, 6 and 7; Browning's Sordello; and Make It New, 27).

Sordello: 2/6: the poem by Robert Browning (1840).

Sordellum: 6/23: (L) SORDELLO.

Sordellus de Godio: 36/30: Sordello da GOITO, Podestà of Mantua; generally thought to be the same person as SORDELLO.

Sordels: 2/6; 6/22; 16/68; 36/30: the family of SORDELLO.

sorella la luna: 74/3: (It) sister moon.

Sorella, mia sorella, / che ballava sobr' un zecchin': 77/53; [78/55]: (It) sister, my sister, / who danced over a golden coin.

Sorrento: 37/33, 35: seaport, Bay of Naples.

So-shu: 2/6, 9: poss. a reference to the Chinese poet Li Po (d. AD 762); or to Chuang Tzŭ (So-shu is the Japanese version), who was a Taoist philosopher of China (fl. 4th century BC).

sotto le nostre scoglie: 76/30: (It) under our old rags.

Souan yen: 53/8: (Suan Yen) fl. BC 2722, one of the favorite governors of Emperor CHIN-NONG.

Soui: 54/30: (Sui), a feudal principality of China.

Soui: 54/30, 31, 32: (Sui), the twelfth dynasty (589-605).

Sounou: 61/83: (Su Nu or Surniama) d. AD 1724, a prince of royal
   blood and descended from an older branch of the Manchu princes
   than was Emperor YONG-TCHING. Sounou was regarded as a
   threat to the throne and spent most of his life in exile, serving
   as general of the eastern Tartars.

Sou-ouei: 54/30: (Su Wei) fl. AD 580, advisor to YANG-KIEN, the
   Duke of Soui.

Sousa, De: 77/50: Robert de Souza, 1865-1946, a minor French symbolist poet.

sous les lauriers: 8/28: (Fr) under the laurels.

souterrain: 80/91: (Fr) underground, subway.

South, the old: 46/25; 74/25: used in reference to the aristocracy of
   the Southern states of the US before the Civil War (1861-65).

[South America]: 12/55; 38/37; 71/164.

Southampton: 80/93: the English city.

[South Carolina]: 34/19; 64/106; 65/110; 69/153.

South Chariot: 53/12: more commonly called the "south-pointing
   chariot"; the ancestor of the mariner's compass, said to have
   been invented by TCHEOU KONG.

South Country: 56/53: prob. a reference to the area comprising the
   modern province of Anhwei; this region was the birth place of
   TCHU-YUEN-TCHANG, founder of the MING dynasty.

Southern Barbarians: 54/23: the tribes of the region of YUEI, a state
   in Honan province along the Yellow River. All barbarian tribes
   to the south went under the generic name of the Nan.

South Han: 55/41: or Nan-han, roughly the area of the provinces of
   Kwangsi and Kwangtung in SE China; this principality lasted
   from 905-971.

South Horn: 40/50: the estuary of four small rivers on the SW coast
   of Sierra Leone, W Africa.

South Ming: 58/65: see MING dynasty.

South Seas: 65/112.

Sou Tsi: 53/20: (Su Chi) fl. BC 288, a member of the court of
   TCHAO-SIANG-OUANG who thought it badinage when the prince
   divided China into two parts and called himself "l'empereur
   d'occident."

Sou-tsin: 53/20: (Su Ch'in) d. BC 317, a Taoist philosopher who was
   for a time a minister of the State of TSIN. He tried to organize
   a confederation of the Six States against the growing power of
   Tsin; he succeeded and gained great wealth and power. He then
   became minister of the State of Yen, but was involved in an intrigue with the queen-dowager and was assassinated.

Sou Tsong: 54/34: (Su Tsung) (reign: 756-63). At the start of his
   reign the barbarians held both the eastern and western capitals
   of the Empire; his reign was one of continual wars with barbarians and rebels, but he was served by able generals.

Spagna: 84/116: (It) SPAIN.

Spahlinger: 27/129: Henry, 1882-   , Swiss bacteriologist; inventor
   of an anti-tuberculosis serum.

Spain: 5/18; 8/32; 32/9; 34/15, 17; 44/20; 50/42; 65/111, 119, 120, 121; 68/147; 71/165; 74/11; 80/84; [84/116].

Spanish dictator: 38/39: see PRIMO DE RIVERA.

Sparta: 11/50, 51; [20/94; 26/123; 68/141]: or Lacedaemon, the ancient city of Greece.

Spartans: 68/141: people of SPARTA.

Spartha: 20/94; 68/141: see SPARTA.

Speare: 80/91: Morris Edmund, 1884-   , American educator and literary scholar; edited The Pocket Book of Verse (1940).

Spencer, Ambrose: 37/31: 1765-1848, American lawyer and politician who was associated with DeWitt CLINTON's Republican party machine in the politics of New York State; chief justice of the New York supreme court (1819-23); member of House of Representatives (1829-31).

Spencer, H.: 80/90: Ezra Pound's instructor at the Cheltenham Military Academy, Ogontz, Pennsylvania (1898).

Spensers: 62/89: see Hugh le DESPENSER, the elder and the younger.

Speranzo, Nic.: 25/117: prob. member of the Consiglio de' DIECI.

Spewcini: 80/88: see Giacomo PUCCINI.

spezzato: 74/16: (It) broken.

Spielhaus: 79/62: (Ger) theatre (the Spielhaus in SALZBURG).

spilla: 20/93: (It) pin, brooch.

Spinder: 19/84:

Spinello: 11/49: a locality in central Italy, taken from Sigismondo MALATESTA by the peace terms imposed by Pope PIUS II (c. 1460).

spingard: 11/48: (It) spingarda: swivel-gun, or a military catapult.

Spire, André: [77/50]; 81/96: 1868-   , French writer and strong advocate of Zionism.

spiriti questi? personae?: 76/37: (It) ghosts these? (L) people?

Spirit of Heaven: 58/65: see CHANG-TI.

Spirit of Mountains: 52/7: spirit of the ancient Chinese religion.

Spiritus veni/ adveni: 74/21-22: (L) come spirit, / come.

Sponsa Cristi: 74/3: (L) the Bride of Christ: (the Church); reference is to Sponsa Christi mosaics in the church of S. Maria in Trastevere, Rome.

Sposa, La: 74/3: (It) The Bride (the Church).

S.P.Q. Amst. faustissimo foedere juncta: 69/152: (L) Senate and People of Amsterdam -- in very fortunate union joined.

"Spring and Autumn, the": [54/24]; 78/61: Spring and Autumn Annals, the Ch'un Ch'iu. This, the last of the Five Classics, is a chronological record of the chief events in the State of LOU (Lu) between 722-484; it is generally regarded as the work of Confucius, whose native state was Lou.

S.P. Senensis ac pro eo amplissim/ Balia Collegium civices vigilantiae/ totius civitatis: 43/10: (L) ...Collegium civicae: The Senate and People of SIENA and on their behalf the most honorable BALÍA, the College of civic vigilance of the entire city.

Squero: 76/40: (It) shipyard.

Ssé-kouang: 55/44: see SSÉ-MA KOUANG.

Ssé-ma: 55/43: see SSÉ-MA KOUANG.

Ssé-ma Kouang: 55/[43], 44: (Ssŭ-ma Kuang) 1019-1086, a distin-
      guished statesman, historian and scholar. He was minister of
      state under Emperor Gin Tsung (reign: 1023-64) and an impor-
      tant minister under his successor, Emperor CHIN-TSONG.
      Ssé-ma-kouang was a zealous opponent of the reforms of OUANG-
      NGAN-CHÉ, and when Chin-tsong refused to part with the lat-
      ter, Ssé-ma retired to private life. In 1085 he returned to the
      government, but died a few months later. His greatest work
      was the TSÉ-TCHI TONG-KIEN, A Comprehensive Mirror for
      the Aid of Government, which was finished in 1084 after more
      than twenty years of work; he wrote another history of thirty-
      five centuries of Chinese culture, a dictionary, and a number
      of miscellaneous papers.
Ssetcheou: 56/54: (Ssŭ-ch'ou), a town near the modern city of Feng-
      yang in the province of Anhwei.
Ssétchuen: 55/41: see SZECHWAN.
Stadtholder, the: 65/123, 125: see WILLIAM V, Prince of Orange.
stadtholder: 67/140: (Dut) chief of state.
Stadtvolk, Pa.: 28/138:
stagirite: 74/22: a native of Stagira, here ARISTOTLE.
Stael, Madame de: 34/16: Anne Louise Germaine Necker, baronne
      de Staël-Holstein, 1766-1817, French-Swiss woman of letters;
      she lived in Switzerland, France, Russia and England, always
      collecting about her a group of brilliant people.
Stalin: 52/3; 74/4, 23; 84/118: Joseph Vissarionovich Dzhugashvili,
      1879-1953, Russian statesman and Communist leader.
Staline: 74/23: (Fr) STALIN.
Stambouli: 12/67: Stambul, the oldest part and main Turkish resi-
      dential section of Istanbul.
Stammbuch of Sachs: 75/28: (Ger) genealogical record of SACHS
      (perhaps of the Hans Sachs family, or of the meistersingers of
      all ages).
Stamp Act: 64/102; 66/128, 129: a revenue law passed by the English
      Parliament (1765) which extended the British stamp tax to
      America and required all publications and legal documents
      issued in the colonies to bear a stamp. The result was violent
      opposition throughout the Colonies, culminating in the Stamp
      Act Congress, which met on 7 October 1765 in New York City
      and petitioned the King and Parliament to remove the tax.
      Fearing the loss of trade with the Colonies, the British repealed
      the act in 1766.
Staphorst: 68/147; 69/151: see VAN STAPHORST.
star chamber: 57/59: a court of secret session.
Starcher: 84/115: DTC, Pisa.
staria senza più scosse: 74/13: (It) it would rest without further
      tossing. (See: Inferno, 27, 63).
State Convention: 37/31: see NEW YORK STATE CONVENTION.
State House: 71/165: the State House, Boston.
States, the: 78/57; 83/114: the US.
State Trials: [64/105]; 71/165: prob. State Trials and Statutes at
      Large by John Seldon.

stati fatti Signoria: 43/13: (It) was made into Seignory.

statuum quorum: 69/151: (L) of the condition of which.

Stealing of the Mare, the: 78/60: title of one of a cycle of romances
      by Abu Obeyd, translated from the Arabic by Lady Anne Blunt
      and put into English verse by Wilfred Scawen BLUNT; published
      in London (1892).

Steele: 78/57: Lt. Colonel John Steele, commanding officer of the
      DTC, Pisa.

Stef: 84/118: see Lincoln STEFFENS.

Stefano: 4/16: Stefano da Verona, 14th-15th century Veronese painter.

Steff: 19/86: see Lincoln STEFFENS. (See his Autobiography, 730-
      32).

Steffens, Lincoln: [19/86]; 84/118: Joseph Lincoln, 1866-1939, the
      American journalist.

[Steno, Michele]: 25/117: Doge of Venice (1400-13).

Stephen, order of: 43/11: The Order of St. Stephen, a chivalric order
      founded by Cosimo I de' MEDICI after the battle of Marciano,
      in 1554, on the feast of St. Stephen, Pope and Martyr; the Dukes
      of Tuscany were the hereditary Grand Masters of the Order.

stg: 66/126: sterling.

Stickney: 80/73: Trumbull, 1874-1904, the American poet.

Stile senese: 43/16: (It) in the Sienese style.

Stone Cottage: 83/112: Stone Cottage, Coleman's Hatch, Sussex,
      where Yeats and Pound spent several winters (1913-1916).

Stonolifex: 26/123:

Stony Hill: 66/127: Stony-field Hill, a part of Stony Acres, John
      Adams' property in BRAINTREE, Massachusetts.

Stourbridge: 66/126: municipal borough of Worcestershire, W cen-
      tral England, on the Stour.

Stowe: 66/126: a town in Oxfordshire, outside Buckingham, England.

[Strait of Gibraltar]: 40/49; 74/3, 25.

Strasbourg: 16/70: the French city.

Stratford: 66/126: Stratford on Avon, Warwickshire, England.

Stretti: 3/11; 27/130: (It) embraced one another (a popular Italian
      song).

Strozzi, Filippo: 10/42: 1426-91, banished by the Medici, he returned
      to Florence in later years and began to build the famous Strozzi
      Palace.

Stuarda, la: 74/24; 80/93: (It) the Stuart. (See: Mary STUART).

[Stuart, Mary]: 74/24; 80/93: Mary Queen of Scots, 1542-87; ruled
      in Scotland (1561-68). The reference is probably to the murder
      of David Rizzio (1566), an Italian who was Mary's chief advisor.

Stufa, Agnolo della: 8/29: Florentine ambassador sent to Sigismondo
      MALATESTA.

Stupro, caede, adulter,/ homocidia, parricidia ac periurus,/ pres-
      bitericidia, audax, libidinosus: 10/44: (L) in debauchery,
      slaughter, an adulterer/ a homicide, a parricide, and a per-
      jurer,/ killer of old men, bold, licentious.

stuprum, raptum/ I.N.R.I. Sigismund Imperator, Rex Proditorum:
      10/46: (L) debauchery, rape/ Jesus of Nazareth, King of the
      Jews, Sigismondo Emperor, King of Traitors.

Sturge M.: 80/85: see T. Sturge MOORE.

styrax: 20/92: (L) storax: a balsam used in perfumery.

Su: 56/54: see SU-SIANG-KOUÉ.

Sub annulo piscatoris, palatium seu curiam Olim de Malatestis: 11/50:
(L) By the ring of the fisherman, the palace or court once of the
MALATESTAs.

sub conditione fidelitates: 64/101: (L) under condition of faith; on
trust. (See: John Adams, Works, II, 149, where the phrase
is quoted from a work of Strykius).

Subillam/ Cumis ego occulis meis/ ...tu theleis respondebat illa/
apothanein: 64/106: (L) Sibyl/at CUMAE I with my own eyes/...
(Gr) What do you want? (L) She replied: (Gr) To die. (See:
Petronius, Satiricon, XLVIII, 8; and Appendix A).

Suen fou: 58/65: see SUEN-HOA-FOU.

Suen-hoa-fou: 58/[65], 66: (Suan-hwa-fu), city near Peiping, in the
province of Hopeh.

Suen Te: 58/63: see SUEN-TI.

[Suen-ti]: 58/63: (Suan Ti) (reign: 569-83), fourth emperor of the
Ch'ên dynasty.

suffestes: 68/141: (L) sufes (-fetis): the name of the highest magistrate in Carthage.

suis fils d'un pauvre laboureur: 56/54: (Fr) I am the son of a poor
workingman. (See: Mailla, Histoire Générale, X, 1).

sul Piave: 80/87: (It) on the PIAVE.

Sulpicia: 25/117, 118: fl. BC 40, the niece of Messalla Corvinus; she
was a Roman poet whose six short pieces on her passion for
Cerinthus are included in volume III of the works of Tibullus.

Sultan: 21/98: MOHAMMED II.

Suma: 74/21: village on Oska Bay, near Kobe, Japan; here GENJI
spent his years of exile from the court. (See: Lady Murasaki,
The Sacred Tree; and the Noh play Suma Genji in Translations,
232).

summa: 57/57: (L) the whole, totality; a treatise covering the whole
of a field.

summus justiciarius: 67/133: (L) chief justice. (See: John Adams,
Works, IV, 544).

sumne fugol othbaer: [27/129]; 77/45: (OE) sumne fugel oþbaer: the
ship (or bird) carried one of them away. (See: The Wanderer,
line 82).

Sumus in fide/ Puellaeque canamus/ sub nocte: 39/45: (L) We have
the protection.../ ...and girls let us sing (the praise of).../
beneath the night. (See: Catullus, XXXIV, 1-4 and Virgil,
Aeneid, VI, 268).

Sung, Charlie: 74/4: see Charles Jones SOONG.

Sung: 53/18: an important Chinese state that occupied the lower part
of the valley of the HOAI river; lasted 1113-285.

Sung: 54/28, 29: the eighth dynasty (420-23); known as the Liu Sung
dynasty.

Sung: 55/40, 45, 46; 56/47, 48, 51; 57/59: the nineteenth dynasty
(960-1280); the dynasty is divided into two parts: the Sung (960-
1127) and the Southern Sung (1127-1280).

Sung: 56/50, 51: the Southern SUNG, second part of the nineteenth
    dynasty (1127-1280).
Sung, pseudo: 56/52: see WHITE LILY SOCIETY.
Sun-hao: 54/27, 28: (Sun Hao) d. AD 283, ruler of the kingdom of
    OU, which controlled the territory south of the Yangtze. Em-
    peror TÇIN-OU-TI spent many years trying to bring the king-
    dom under his rule, and succeeded in 280; Sun-hao was a cruel
    king, and his people finally revolted to join the emperor.
Sun land: 58/62: see JAPAN.
Sun Te: 55/38: Sun-té-tchao (Sun Tê-chao) fl. AD 901, first general
    of the Empire during the reign of Emperor Chao Tsung (reign:
    889-905). He freed the emperor from the control of the eun-
    uchs and had several of them executed. In gratitude, the em-
    peror made his family an affiliate of the royal house.
Sunt lumina: 74/7, 8: (L) are lights. (from Johannes Scotus Erigena).
Sun-tong: 54/23: (Sun Tung) fl. 202-195, a member of the court of
    Emperor KAO-HOANG-TI whose task it was to write on the
    ceremonies and usages of the rites.
Sun up; work...Imperial power is? and to us what is it?: 49/39: an
    ancient Chinese lyric, the Sun up song. (See: Shen Tê-ch'ien,
    Origins of Ancient Poetry, 1).
superbo Ilion: 23/109: (It) superb TROY.
Surrender of Breda: 80/[71], 87: painting by VELÁSQUEZ, hanging
    in the Prado, Madrid.
[Su-siang-kouê]: 56/54: (Su Hsiang-kuei) fl. AD 1355, a fighting
    companion of TCHU-YUEN-TCHANG.
Sussex: 83/112: the county in S England.
Su Ta: 56/54, 56: (Su Ta) d. AD 1385, served as the lieutenant of
    TCHU-YUEN-TCHANG during his struggles to found the MING
    dynasty; when Tchu became emperor (under the name HONG-
    VOU), Su-ta became his advisor.
Sweden: 32/7; 41/56.
Swedenborg, Emanuel: 77/50: 1688-1772, the Swedish scientist,
    philosopher and religious writer.
Sweetland: 79/67: DTC, Pisa.
Swift-amoursinclair: 33/14: Swift and Armour are American meat
    packers. Upton Sinclair, 1878-   , American novelist and
    politician exposed the Chicago meat packing industry in The
    Jungle (1906).
Swift men as if flyers, like Yangtse...: 53/16: from Shih Ching, ode
    263, stanza 5.
Swinburne: 80/86; 82/101: Algernon Charles, 1837-1909, the English
    poet.
Sylla: 71/165: or Sulla, 138-78, the Roman general,noted for his
    cruelty.
Sylva: 34/19: a book on practical arboriculture by John EVELYN
    (1664).
sylva nympharum: 17/77: (L) the wood of the nymphs.
Symons: 80/72, [89]: Arthur, 1865-1945, the British poet and liter-
    ary critic.
Syntagma: 31/6: the Syntagma Philosophicum by Pierre Gassendi.
    (See: GOSINDI).

Syracuse: 8/31; 43/12; [77/45; 80/90]: seaport, SE Sicily.

Syrinx: 53/8: a nymph pursued by PAN; when she changed into a tuft of reeds, Pan fashioned the reeds into his pipes -- thus, the pipes of Pan.

Syrus: 77/43: Publilius Syrus, a writer of Latin mimes and maxims in the first century BC.

[Szechwan]: 55/41: a province in S central China.

T

T.: 66/127: prob. Thomas Trask, one of John ADAMS' farm hands at
    BRAINTREE.
Tabarin: 80/72: the Bal Tabarin, a night club in Montmarte, Paris.
Tacitus: 67/139; 68/141: Publius Cornelius, 55-120?, the Roman his-
    torian.
tael: 54/26, 27, 35; 57/60; 61/84, 85: a Chinese coin.
[Tagore, Sir Rabindranath]: 77/52: 1861-1941, the Bengali poet;
    awarded the Nobel Prize for Literature (1931).
Tagus: 12/54: the river in Spain and Portugal.
Tai: 54/23: (T'ai), a feudal state in the province of SHANSI, lasted
    c. BC 350-100.
Taï: 54/32, 33: see TAÏ-TSONG.
Taï: 55/40: see TAÏ-TSOU.
Taï: 58/65, 66: see TAÏ-TSONG.
Taï Chan, Mt.: 54/30: see TAISHAN.
Taï chen: 58/66: (T'ai Shên) fl. AD 1643, a Mongol prince who allied
    himself with the Manchu leader TAÏ-TSONG during one of the
    latter's many raids on SHANSI province.
Tai Haku, Mt.: [4/16]; 56/47: prob. Taihoku, mountain peak in South
    Kankyo province of N Korea.
Tai-hia: 53/20: (Ch) Tai-hoa: mountains. (See: Mailla, Histoire
    Générale, II, 259).
Tailhade: 78/58: Laurent, 1854-1919, the French poet.
Tai Ming: 56/53: (Ch) (Ta Ming): the Great MING (dynasty).
Taiping: 56/53: a city and district in the old province of KIANG-NAN;
    now a city in the modern province of Anhwei.
Taipou: 56/52: Taï-pouhoa (T'ai Pu-hoa) d. AD 1352, a scholar and
    military officer serving Emperor CHUNTI; he successfully en-
    countered the rebels against the throne on several occasions but
    finally died in battle.
Taishan, Mt.: [54/30]; 74/5, 6, 7, 8, 9, 10, 12, 15, 21, 27; 77/43,
    53; 80/73; 81/95; 83/108: (Tai or T'ai Shan), a sacred mountain
    of China in W Shantung province, 32 miles S of Tsinan; there
    are many shrines on the road to the top, on which stand the
    temples.
Taishan-Chocorura: 83/108: see TAISHAN. Mount Chocorua, a peak
    in E New Hampshire, in the Sandwich Range of the White Mount-
    ains.
Taitong: 58/66: (Tai-tung), city in SHANSI province, just inside the
    northern border between China and Inner Mongolia.
Taï Tsong: 54/31, 32, 33; 55/38, [44]; 56/54: (T'ai Tsung) (reign:
    626-649), one of China's most remarkable emperors. A disci-
    ple of Confucius, he noted that when emperors were attached to
    Taoism or Buddhism they brought about the downfall of their
    dynasties and said, "Just as wings are necessary for the birds
    and water for the fishes, so I put my trust in the teachings of
    the sages of our country." He cut government costs, reduced
    taxes, built libraries, aided scholars, and saw that his people
    had more than enough for their daily needs. In 645 he invaded

Korea, but could not bring it completely into the Empire. In
649 he composed <u>NOTES ON CONDUCT</u>.

Tai Tsong: 55/41: (T'ai Tsung) (reign: 977-998), a mild but decisive
emperor who governed with economy. His first important act
was to suppress the state of Northern HAN (979), a task his
brother, TAI-TSOU, had not completed. But Tai-tsong was unable to check the KHITAN Tartars or to stop a dangerous alliance between the Khitan and NUTCHÉ Tartars. He was a student of history, honored Confucius and studied the Classics.

[Taï-tsong]: 56/47, 48, 49, 51: (T'ai Tsung), imperial title of
OGOTAI Khan.

Tai Tsong: 58/65, 66, 67, 68: (T'ai Tsung or T'ein Ts'ung) 1591-
1643 (reign: 1625-43), son of TAI TSOU (1559-1626), who was
the founder of the Manchu power. In 1635 Tai-tsong proclaimed
himself Emperor of China, although the MING dynasty still held
Peiping. In 1636 he established the Manchu rule as the Ch'ing
dynasty, conquered Mongolia and gained much of the Empire.
He modeled his government after the Chinese, especially in the
matter of holding public examinations, but denationalized the
Chinese by abolishing some of their customs.

Taï-Tsou: [50/40, 41]; 56/54: (T'ai Tsu) (reign: 960-76), founder
of the SUNG dynasty. He was serving as a general under Emperor CHI-TSONG when his troops invested him with the yellow
robe of emperor. His greatest accomplishment was the restor-
ation of the Empire; he reclaimed Southern Han, Heou-chou,
Szechwan and other provinces for the throne, and only Northern
Han resisted his attacks. He encouraged the study of literature,
revised the law courts, changed the criminal code, and stabi-
lized the economy.

[Taï-tsou]: 55/38: (T'ai Tsu or Chu Wên) (reign: 907-13), first emperor of the After Liang dynasty (907-60). When the last emper-
or of the TANG dynasty made him Prince of Liang, Taï-tsou
assumed much of the emperor's power and assassinated him in
907. Taï-tsou's reign was troubled by rebellions and invasions
of the KHITAN Tartars.

Taï-Tsou: 55/40: (T'ai Tsu) (reign: 951-54), founder and first emperor of the After CHOU dynasty. Although his reign was dis-
turbed by the rebellious Prince of Han, Taï-tsou proved to be
an able administrator and leader. He was a patron of literature
and honored the memory of Confucius by saying, "Confucius is
the master of a hundred generations of emperors."

Tai-Tsou: 55/45: (T'ai Tsu), the imperial title of GENGHIS KHAN.

Tai Tsou: 58/66: (T'ai Tsu or Nurhachu) 1559-1625 (reign: 1616-25),
the real founder of the Manchu power; he consolidated the tribes
of Inner Mongolia and brought most of the territory north of the
Great Wall under his control. In 1625 he established the Manchu capital at Mukden.

Takasago: 4/15: seaport of S Honshu, Japan; there two pines grow
that are inhabited by the spirits of an old man and his wife,
symbolic of long life and conjugal loyalty.

Talbot: 80/93: an extinct breed of dog; perhaps the name comes from

the Talbot family of England, on whose crest appears the figure
of a dog.

Talleyrand: 44/19; 50/42; 62/95; 70/155: Charles Maurice de Talley-
rand-Périgord, 1754-1838, French statesman; created grand
chamberlain by Napoleon (1804); helped to restore the Bourbons
after Napoleon's fall; instrumental in organizing the Quadruple
Alliance (1834). The agents in the XYZ Affair were reputed to
be those of Talleyrand (who was minister of foreign affairs, 1797-
1807) but he denied any connection with them.

Tamerlan: 34/16: an opera with music by P. Winter and text by E.
Morel de Chêfdeville (based on Voltaire's Orphelin de la Chine)
first performed: Paris, c. 1802.

Tami: 76/40: poss. Tami Koumé, Japanese painter, of whom see
Letters, passim; poss. reference to Tomi, a Roman outpost on
the Black Sea, S of the Danube, where OVID spent his ten years
of exile and where he died.

Tammany Hall: 34/17: the New York City headquarters of the Tammany Society of New York (founded 1786), the major force in
New York politics until the elections of 1932.

Tamuz: 47/30: see ADONIS.

Tan Aoidan: 29/144: (Gr) song. (See: Appendix A).

Tancred: 82/102, 103: Frederic W., a member of the Hulme-Flint
poetry group (c. 1909).

Tancreds, Jerusalem and Sicily: 82/102: reference to Tancred (d.
1194), King of Sicily; and Tancred (?1078-1112), Norman hero
of the First Crusade who distinguished himself in the capture
of Jerusalem.

Taney: 37/35, 36: Roger Brooke, 1777-1864, American jurist; US
Attorney General (1831-33), Secretary of the Treasury (1833-34),
Chief Justice of the Supreme Court (1836-64). He is most
famous for his decision in the Dred Scott case (1857) when the
Supreme Court held that Scott (an American Negro who held
that he had obtained his freedom by residing in free territory)
was not a citizen and not entitled to any standing in court.

Tang: 53/11: see TCHING-TANG.

Tang: 54/31; 55/44; 56/51, 52; 57/59; 74/4: (T'ang) the thirteenth
dynasty (618-907)

Tang: 55/39: (T'ang), the After T'ang, the fifteenth dynasty (923-36).

Tang: 55/40: (T'ang), the Southern T'ang, a principality in the province of Kiangsu, E China; formerly this region was the principality of OU (Wu), but in AD 937 the princes of Wu changed their
name to T'ang.

Tang: 55/46: (T'ang), village in the province of Honan, near the modern city of Nanyang.

Tang dance: 56/52: a dance called the "Tang" in the text because the
dancers wore headdresses like those of the TANG dynasty. (See:
Mailla, Histoire Générale, IX, 608).

Tangier: 74/10, 25; [84/117]: the seaport of NW Morocco.

Tangiers: 84/117: see TANGIER.

T'ang Wan Kung: 78/58: title of Book III of the works of Mencius,
(See: Mencius, III, I, iii, 6-7).

tanka: 74/17: prob. the Japanese verse form of five lines; the first
    and third have five syllables, the others seven.
Tan Ki: 53/12: (T'a Chi) d. BC 1122, an evil woman who was the con-
    cubine of Emperor CHEOU-SIN; after WU WANG's victory at
    MOU YE, she was executed -- "to the delight of nearly every-
    one who knew her."
Tan mare fustes: 20/91: (O Fr) tant mar fustes: So unfortunately
    you were. (See: Chanson de Roland, 2034).
tanta novità: 10/45: (It) so much innovation.
Tan Tchin: 54/29: see FAN-TCHIN.
Tant las fotei com auzirets/ Cen e quatre vingt at veit vetz: 6/21:
    (Pr) And I had them as often as you shall hear/ 120 and eight
    times. (See: William of Poitiers, Farai un vers, pos mi
    sonelh, 79).
Tao: 55/44: see TAOIST.
Taoist (Taoists, Taotse, Taozers): 54/27, 28, 29, 31, 34; 55/37,
    38, 42, 44, 45; 56/47, 48, 56, 57, 58; 57/59; [58/64]; 60/74;
    61/80: believer in Taoism, supposedly founded by LAO-TSE
    (c. BC 604). Taoism is essentially a religion of inaction, of
    mystical contemplation of the Tao -- the way the universe
    functions or the path which natural events take. Later Taoism
    became a seeking for long life and for the elixir vitale. The
    Taoist idea of a laissez faire government was in direct contra-
    diction to the Confucian ethic.
Taotse (Taotses, Taotssé): 54/29; 55/37; 60/74: see TAOIST.
Taouen: 60/75: Ta-ouan (Ta-wan), a principality in SHENSI province;
    according to legend, the horses of Ta-ouan were celestial
    (TIEN-MA) and their sweat was the color of blood.
Taozer (Taozers): 54/31, 34; 55/37, 38, 42, 44, 45; 56/47, 48, 56;
    57/58, 59: see TAOIST.
Tarascon: 76/33: a town of Bouches-du-Rhône department in SE
    France.
Tarentum: 11/48, 49: (L) Taranto; a seaport, SE Italy.
Tariff League: 50/43: the Italian customs league.
tartar: 59/73: the language.
Tartar king: 54/25: see HOU-HAN-YÉ.
Tartar lord: 55/45: see AKOUTA.
Tartars: 53/16, 17; 54/24, 25, 26, 28, 29, 30, 31, 33, 34, 35; 55/37,
    39, 40, 41, 42, 45; 56/47; 57/57, 58, 60; 58/63, 65, 66, 67;
    59/70, 71: the northern barbarians or Huns; the nomadic tribes
    on the borders of Chih-li, Shansi, and Kansu provinces. By
    the end of the third century BC the Tartars, or HIONG-NOU,
    had formed a nation composed of many nomadic tribes. In BC
    142 they crossed the Great Wall and gained control of much of
    Shansi province. By BC 33 the Empire had divided the Tartars
    into small tribes, most of which offered at least token homage
    to the emperor.
Tartars, West: 53/16: a western tribe of barbarians, the K'iang,
    which lived to the west of Kansu; they defeated the forces of
    SIUEN-OUANG in the battle of "The Thousand Acres" (BC 788).
Tartar war: 54/26: the wars between the Chinese Empire and the
    Tartars, during the first century AD.

Tartary: 56/47; 58/66; 60/75, 78; 65/123: or Tatary, an indefinite
region in Asia and Europe, from the Sea of Japan to the Dnieper
river, controlled at various times by the Tartar tribes. The
Tartars which invaded China occupied the area beyond the
northern boundaries of Shensi, Shansi and Hopeh provinces.

Tarviso: 29/142: Treviso, (L) Tarvisium, city of Treviso province,
N Italy; seat of the Lombard duchy in the early Middle Ages;
home of Ezzelino III of ROMANO.

Tatile: 78/56:

Tatler, The: 19/85: a British magazine devoted to gossip about the
upper classes.

Taverna: 76/31: a restaurant in Venice.

Taylor: 70/157: John, 1703-66, English jurist and scholar; author
of Elements of Civil Law (1755).

Taylor, John: 67/138: 1753-1824, a printer and political writer of
Caroline County, Virginia; in 1814 he printed a letter of John
ADAMS' written to John Penn (1776); author of An Inquiry into
Principles and Policy of the Government of the United States
(1814).

Tçé-tchéou: 55/40: (Tz'ŭ-ch'ou), city near Liuchow in Kwangsi
province, SE China; in AD 954 the Northern Han attacked Liuchow and Emperor CHI-TSONG engaged the Han troops near
Tçé-tchéou.

tcha: 62/87: (Ch) (ch'a): tea. (See: Appendix B).

tchang: 53/13: (chang), a unit of measurement; 141 inches.

Tchang: 53/16: (Chang), river which rises in Shensi province and
flows NE parallel to the Hwang Ho, joining it on the Great Plains.

Tchang: 54/28: Ouang-tchang (Wang Chang) fl. AD 290, a Chinese
officer. (See: Mailla, Histoire Générale, IV, 192-193).

Tchang: 54/34: see TCHANG-SIUN.

Tchang Chi: 57/60: (Chang Shih) fl. AD 1521, Empress dowager,
mother of Emperor OU-TSONG. At the death of her son, who
left no heir, she called a council to name the next emperor.
CHI-TSONG, grandson of Emperor HIEN-TSONG, was chosen.

[Tchang-hien-tchong]: 58/69: (Chang Hsien-chung) fl. AD 1643, a
rebel chieftain with a reputation for extreme cruelty. (See:
Mailla, Histoire Générale, X, 479).

[Tchang-ku-tching]: 58/63: (Chang Chü-chêng) d. AD 1582, a scholar
and statesman who was tutor to Emperor Mu Tsung (reign:
1567-73) and regent over Emperor CHIN-TSONG. He central-
ized the government, promoted peace and order in the Empire,
and tried to balance the budget. Often accused of taking bribes,
he was deprived of his titles and property in 1584.

Tchang-ngan: 54/25, 26: (Changan), the modern city of Sian in
Shensi province, NE China; it was the capital of the Empire
under the HAN dynasty.

Tchang-siun: 54/34: (Chang Hsŭn) fl. AD 756, a commander of imperial troops serving Emperor SOU-TSONG; he is best known
for his defence of YONG-KIEU during a siege.

Tchang star: 56/53: (Chang), the Chinese constellation of Tchang
(Hydra).

Tchang-sun Chi: 54/32: (Chang Sun-shih) d. AD 636, the empress
    of TAÏ-TSONG. She was one of the great queens of China; like
    her husband she was a foe of Taoism and Buddhism; at her
    death she asked the emperor not to build her a great tomb be-
    cause it would cost the people too much. She wrote a work on
    the lives of the princesses who had been on the throne before
    her time.
Tchang tcheou: 56/51: (Changchow), the modern city of Lungki in
    Fukien province, SE China, on the left bank of the Saikoe river.
Tchang-tsong: 54/23: (Chang Tsung) fl. 202-195; a member of the
    court of Emperor KAO-HOANG-TI who studied the theory of
    music.
Tchan-y: 53/20: Tchang-y (Chang I) fl. BC 313, a Chinese condotti-
    ere who served the States of OUEI, TSIN and Chou during the
    feudal wars near the end of the TCHEOU dynasty.
Tchao-hou: 61/85: Tchao-hoeï (Chao Hui) fl. AD 1759, a general of
    the imperial troops serving Emperor KIEN-LONG; he was re-
    sponsible for the success of the campaigns to put down the
    ELUTES who, under the leadership of Amursana, revolted
    against the Empire and attempted to take the district of Ili in
    Sinkiang province.
Tchao Kouang: 55/40: Tchao-kouang-yin (Chao K'uang-yin) see TAÏ-
    TSOU (960-76).
Tchaomed: 60/75: Tchao-modo (Chaomoto), a town to the north
    of the Gobi desert; here FEYANKOU defeated KALDAN, leader
    of the ELUTES.
Tchao-ouang: 53/15: (Chao Wang) (reign: 1052-01), an emperor who
    allowed the government to become weak and the prosperity of
    the country to decline; he was drowned while crossing the River
    Han, probably the victim of a plot.
Tchao Siang: 53/20: Tchao-siang-ouang (Chao Siang-wang) fl. BC
    288, Prince of TSIN; in his many wars with the other feudal
    states of China he did much to weaken the TCHEOU dynasty and
    prepare the way for the TSIN dynasty.
Tchao-tso: 54/23: (Chao Tso) fl. BC 170, minister of war in the
    court of Emperor HIAO-OUEN-TI.
Tchen-yu: 54/25: (Chên-yu), the title which the Tartars gave to their
    kings.
Tcheou: 53/14, 17, 18, 19, [20]; 54/21, 24; 55/42, 44; 56/51, [54, 55;
    84/116(?)]: (Chou), the third dynasty (1122-255).
Tcheou Kong: 53/12, 14; 54/32; 57/57, 59: (Chou Kung) d. BC 1105,
    Duke of Chou, advisor to his brother WU WANG and regent for
    his nephew TCHING-OUANG. His activities, devoted wholly to
    the welfare of the state, aided greatly in establishing the
    TCHEOU dynasty; he is credited with the invention of the
    SOUTH CHARIOT. Tcheou-kong is one of the measuring sticks
    for the greatness of any ruler.
Tcheou-li: 54/24: (Ch) (Chou-li): Rites of the Chou Dynasty.
Tcheou Tun-y: 55/44: (Chou Tun-i) 1017-73, a scholar and philosoph-
    er who held small posts in the government; his chief works are

elucidations of the mysteries of the <u>Book of Changes,</u> or <u>I</u>
<u>Ching,</u> which is ascribed to WÊN WANG.

Tcheu: 56/55: see TCHEOU.

Tchi: 13/38: <u>Tsêng Hsi</u>, a disciple of Confucius and father of Tsêng
Tzu, the most important of the disciples. (See: <u>Analects,</u> XI,
25).

Tchin: 53/19: (Chin), a powerful feudal state in the southern half of
Shansi, NW of Honan, on the Yellow river.

Tchin: 55/42: see TCHIN-TSONG.

Tching: 53/10, 11: see TCHING-TANG.

Tching: 53/19: (Ching), a principality of feudal China near the present city of Kaifeng in Honan province, E central China.

Tching: 61/84: see YONG-TCHING.

Tching brothers: 56/53: see TCHIN-YEOU-LEANG.

Tching-gintai: 54/33: (Chêng Jen-t'ai) fl. AD 662, a general of the
imperial troops serving Emperor Kao Tsung (reign: 650-84);
he was sent to deal with the Tartar tribes which had been attacking the borders of the Empire -- his campaign was a success.

Tching mao: 60/76: see TCHIN-MAO.

Tching ouang: 53/13; 55/37; 57/57: (Chêng Wang) (reign: 1115-1078),
son of WU WANG; second emperor of the TCHEOU dynasty; he
fostered cultivation and reclamation, brought good men into the
government, and regulated the measure of money and cloth.

Tching Tang: 53/10, 11; 56/49: (Ch'êng T'ang) (reign: 1766-53), the
founder of the Shang dynasty (1766-1122); he was a model king
who subordinated every passion and feeling to the good of his
people; in time of drought he coined money so the people could
buy grain, but there was no grain to buy until his sacrifices
were accepted by Heaven and rain fell. On his wash basin he
inscribed the admonition: <u>Make it new.</u>

Tching-tcheou: 55/38: poss. the city of <u>Ting-tcheou</u> (Ting-ch'ou) in
Hopeh province, N China.

[Tching-tsong]: 56/51, 53: (Chêng Tsung), imperial title of TIMOUR
Khan.

Tchinkiang: 59/71: <u>Tching-kiang</u> (Chinkiang), city and port of Kiangsu province, E China.

Tchin-kin: 56/50: (Chên Chin) d. AD 1285, son of KUBLAI KHAN and
prince royal of the Empire. He was a model of all virtues and
manners, learned in the humanities and the arts of war and ruling; his early death was a great loss to the Empire.

Tchinkis: 55/46; 56/47: <u>Tchinkis-han</u> (Ghingiz Khan) see GENGHIS
KHAN. It is said that 'Tchinkis' is an imitation of the cry of a
celestial bird, which no one has ever seen but which will herald
great happiness when it does appear.

Tchin-li: 56/53: (Ch'ên Li) fl. AD 1363, second son of TCHIN-YEOU-
LEANG; after his father was defeated at the battle of Lake Poyang, Tchin-li was allowed by TCHU-YUEN-TCHANG to retain
the family estates.

[Tchin-mao]: 60/76, 77: (Chên Mao) fl. AD 1717, a second-class
mandarin holding a military command in Kwangtung and serv-

ing as viceroy of Canton. In 1717 he memorialized Emperor
KANG-HI to drive the Christian missionaries from the Empire
and to expel the European merchants from MACAO. The emperor, insulted by the actions of CLEMENT XI, proclaimed that
no missionary could stay in China without special imperial permission and persecuted those who did not comply.

Tchin Ouang: 56/49: see TCHING-TANG.

Tchin-Song: 55/41: see TCHIN-TSONG.

Tchin Tiaouen: 56/51: Tchin-tiao-yen (Chên Tiao-yen) fl. AD 1297,
a brigand in the south of China who gathered a large band of
vagabonds; he attacked the city of Tchang-tchéou (in Fukien
province) and killed KANOUEN, the commander of the city.

Tchin-tsong: 55/41, [42]: (Chên Tsung) (reign: 998-1023), a capable emperor but a devout Taoist, whose superstition led him
to disgrace. K'ou Chun, a brilliant general and statesman,
forced the emperor to fight the Khitan Tartars and to make peace
with them by promising an annual tribute of one hundred ounces
of silver and two hundred pieces of silk. When court intrigues
ousted K'ou Chun, the emperor fell into the hands of ministers
who used his superstition to their advantage. Three books, reputed to be from heaven, were presented to the emperor, who
was so impressed by this supposed honor that he ordered a
great temple built; the temple took seven years to build and cost
so much that some date the decline of the SUNG dynasty from
this event. By 1020 the emperor was insane and his power in
the hands of eunuchs.

[Tchin-yeou-gin]: 56/53: (Ch'ên Yu-jen) fl. AD 1363, brother of
TCHIN-YEOU-LEANG; he took part in the battle of Lake Poyang
(1363) in which his brother was defeated by TCHU-YUEN-
TCHANG, founder of the MING dynasty.

[Tchin-yeou-leang]: 56/53: (Ch'ên Yu-liang) d. AD 1363, commander
of an independent revolutionary force during the general revolu-
tions of the reign of Emperor CHUNTI. In 1358 he proclaimed
himself Prince of Han and styled himself emperor of a "Han"
dynasty; by 1363 his power in China was second only to that of
TCHU-YUEN-TCHANG, the great revolutionary leader who
founded the MING dynasty. In 1363 the two forces met in a
battle on Lake Poyang, and Tchin-yeou-leang was killed by a
stray arrow and his army routed; his two brothers, TCHIN-
YEOU-GIN and Ch'en yu-kuei were associated with him in his
career.

[Tchoang-tsong]: 55/38, 39: (Chuang Tsung), imperial title of LI-
TSUN-HIU.

Tchong: 54/26: prob. Fan-tchong (Fan Chung) fl. AD 22, a bandit
leader. (See: Mailla, Histoire Générale, III, 248 ff).

Tchong: 54/33: see TCHONG-TSONG.

Tchong: 56/49: see TCHONG-KING-FOU.

Tchongking: 55/42: see TCHONG-KING-FOU.

[Tchong-king-fou]: 55/42; 56/49: (Chung-ching-fu), the modern city
of Chungking in SZECHWAN province, China.

[Tchong-tsong]: 54/33: (Chung Tsung) (reign: 684-710), a weak emperor who was controlled by women. His mother, OU-HEOU, ruled the Empire until 705; and from 705-710 the emperor was ruled by his wife, Wei, who wanted to be a second Ou-heou; Wei was murdered in 710.

tchu: 53/13: (Ch) (chu): 1/24 of a TAEL.

Tchu: 55/38: see TAÏ-TSOU.

Tchuen: 53/10: Tchuen-hio (Chuan Hsü) (reign: 2514-2436), the fifth of the legendary emperors of China; grandson of HOANG TI.

Tchun: 55/36: see TCHUN-TSONG.

Tchun-tsiou: 54/24: the Ch'un Ch'iu, or SPRING AND AUTUMN Annals.

Tchun-tsong: 55/36: (Chun Tsung or Li Sung) (reign: AD 805), a mild and good man, but ill with an incurable disease when he came to the throne. After eight months he abdicated in favour of his son, who ruled under the name HIEN-TSONG.

Tchu-ouen: 56/56: (Chu Wên) 1383-1403, grandson of Emperor HONG-VOU and prince royal; he succeeded his grandfather, taking the title of KIEN-OUEN-TI.

Tchu-yé: 58/64, 65: Tchu-yé-yuen (Chu Yeh-yuan) fl. AD 1622, commander of imperial forces in Shantung serving Emperor Hsi Tsung (reign: 1621-27); he inflicted heavy losses on the rebel forces during the rebellions of 1622.

[Tchu-yuen-tchang]: 56/53, 54: (Chu Yüan-chang) 1328-99, founder of the MING dynasty. He was a Buddhist novice, but when the Buddhists were forced to disband some monasteries, Tchu-yuen-tchang offered his services to Kuo Tzŭ-hsing (d. 1355), one of the leaders of the revolutionary WHITE LILY SOCIETY; he later parted from Kuo Tzŭ-hsing and proclaimed himself Prince of Wu (1364). From this time he led the major force seeking the overthrow of Emperor CHUNTI and the Mongol dynasty. In 1367 he proclaimed himself Emperor of China, founded the Ming dynasty, and called himself HONG-VOU.

Tçin: 53/17: see TSIN.

Tçin: 54/27, 28: (Chin), the seventh dynasty (265-420); it is divided into the Western Chin (265-317) and the Eastern Chin (317-420).

Tçin: 55/38, 39: (Chin), a principality in the province of Shansi.

Tçin: 56/51: (Chin), the Western Chin dynasty (265-317); the first part of the TÇIN.

Tçin Hiao: 54/28: Tçin-hiao-ou-ti (Hsiao Wu Ti) (reign: 373-97). His reign was plagued with civil wars, for TÇIN was declining in power and the SUNG dynasty was about to appear. This emperor is noted for his poor knowledge of female psychology.

[Tçin-hoai-ti]: 54/28: (Hwai Ti) (reign: 307-13), a very intelligent emperor who was versed in the arts of government, but he had no success in war with the Prince of the Eastern Sea (who was to bring the Eastern TÇIN into prominence). The emperor had such poor results in battle that he was deposed.

[Tçin-hoei-ti]: 54/28: (Hui Ti) (reign: 290-307), son of TÇIN OU TI; he was rather feeble-minded and his reign was one of unrest, mostly caused by his advisors.

[Tçin-min-ti]: 54/28: (Min Ti) (reign: 313-17). His reign was dis-

turbed by Tartar attacks; in 317　the Tartars captured the capital and made the emperor a prisoner.

Tçin Ngan: 54/28: Tçin-ngan-ti (An Ti) (reign: 397-419), an emper-
or who was little better than an idiot. However, the reference
may be to Tçin-ngai-ti (Ai Ti) (reign: 362-66), who is known
as the "Sad and Sorrowful Emperor" and wasn't much better
than Tçin-ngan-ti.

Tçin Ou: 54/28: see TÇIN OU TI.

Tçin Ou Ti: 54/27, [28]: (Wu Ti) (reign: 265-90), founder of the
Western TÇIN dynasty; his most important act was the overthrow of the kingdom of OU, one of the THREE KINGDOMS.

Tçin Tching: 54/28: Tçin-tching-ti (Ch'eng Ti) (reign: 326-43), not
a bad man himself, but he came to the throne at the age of five
and had incompetent and cruel advisors.

Te, admirabile: 50/40: (L) Thee, admirable.

teatro romano: 80/83: (It) Roman theatre.

Te cavero la budella del corpo! / El conte levatosi: / Io te cavero la
corato a te!: 10/43: (It) I will carve the guts right out of you!
And the Count rising: / I'll tear the liver out of you!

Te cavere le budelle/ La corata a te: 81/96: (It) I'll cut your guts
out/ (and I) yours!

Te Deum: 44/17: (L) Thee, God (a Christian hymn sung on all oc-
casions of thanksgiving).

Te fili Dux, tuosque successores/ Aureo anulo: 26/124: (L) Thee,
my son the Duke, and thy successors/ with a golden ring.

T.E.H.: 16/71: see Thomas Ernest HULME.

Te Kouang: 55/39: see YÉ-LIU-TÉ-KOUANG.

Télémaque: 34/16: a ballet, prob. based on the opera Télémaque by
Adrien Boieldieu; first performed in St. Petersburg, 1808.

Tellus: 47/32; 77/46, 51; 79/65; 83/111: the Roman divinity of the
Earth.

Tellus-Helena: 77/51: a combination of TELLUS and HELEN of Troy;
the divinity of fertility, and a semi-goddess of destruction.

telo rigido: 20/91: (L) with rigid javelin; with hardening of the arch-
ery.

Témougin: 55/45: (Temuchin), the personal name of GENGHIS KHAN.

Tempio: [8/32]; 9/35, 36; [74/24; 76/37]; 80/75: the Tempio Malatestiano in Rimini; the early Renaissance style building was begun 1446 (or 1447), consecrated 1450, and work was suspended
in 1455. To build his Tempio, Sigismondo MALATESTA se-
cured some of the best artists and craftsmen of Italy: Leon
Battista ALBERTI, Agostino di DUCCIO, Pier della FRANCES-
CA, and PISANELLO. (For a complete description see: Cor-
rado Ricci, Il Tempio Malatestiano, Rome: 1925).

Temple: 64/108; 71/165: Sir John, an English agent in Boston (1776).

Temple, the: 79/66: the Inner Temple or the Middle Temple, among
the Inns of Court.

templum aedificavit: 8/32: (L) built a temple. (See: the TEMPIO).

tempora, tempora...mores: 76/31: (L) time (ages), time...customs.
(See: Cicero, O tempora! O mores!).

temporis acti: 80/77: (L) bygone days. (See: Horace, Ars Poetica,
173).

Tempus loquendi, / Tempus tacendi: 31/3; [74/7]: (L) There is a time
    to speak, / there is a time to be silent; (inscribed on the tomb
    of Isotta degli ATTI in the TEMPIO).
Ten Bou: 56/49: prob. Outoubou (Wutubu) (reign: 1214-25), emperor
    of the KIN dynasty; his reign was one of almost continual war
    with the Mongols of GENGHIS KHAN.
Teng: 55/46: (Têng), village in the province of Honan, near the
    modern city of Nanyang.
Tengtcheou: 55/43: (Têng-ch'ou), the modern city of Penglai on the
    N coast of Shantung Peninsula in Shantung province, NE China.
Teng-tchi: 54/26: (Têng Chê) fl. AD 107, refused to be made a prince,
    but later returned to the court to aid the government of Emper-
    or HAN-NGAN-TI.
Tengyun: 58/67: see LOU-TENG-YUN.
Tenkate: 68/147: the Messrs. Tenkate, Amsterdam brokers (1780).
Tennyson: 80/86: Alfred, 1st Baron Tennyson, 1809-92, the English
    poet.
Ten of the Baily: 8/29, 30: see DIECI DELLA BALÍA.
Ten Seo Daisin: 58/62: (Tensio Dai Sin or in Japanese Amaterasu-
    o-mi-kami), the Japanese Goddess of the Sun, chief goddess of
    the Shinto religion; her descendents became the emperors of
    Japan.
TenShi: 49/39: (Jap) Son of God; poss. a place name.
10th District: 76/39: the Tenth Congressional district of Massachu-
    setts; a reference to George Holden TINKHAM, who represented
    the district in the House of Representatives.
Teofile: 76/31: see Théophile GAUTIER.
Téou-Chi: 54/27: (T'ou Shih) fl. AD 168, queen dowager; appointed
    regent over the Emperor HAN-LING-TI; she was the daughter
    of the prime minister, Tau Bu.
Teoui-tchéou: 55/40: Tsouï-tchéou-tou (Ts'ui Ch'ou-tu) fl. AD 952,
    an officer of the imperial troops serving Emperor TAÏ-TSOU.
ter flebiliter: [4/13]; 78/55: (L) thrice mournfully. (See: Horace,
    Odes, IV, xii, 5).
Terminus: 48/37: the "great god Terminus," the sacred boundary
    stone which stood in the great temple of the Capitoline Jupiter
    in Rome.
Ter pacis Italiae: 24/112: (L) Three times of the Italian peace.
ter pacis Italiae auctor: 24/112: (L) three times author of the Italian
    peace.
Terpsichore: 74/23: the Muse of the dance.
Terra: 82/104: (L) Earth.
terra...carta: 25/120: (It) (of the) world...document.
Terracina: 39/45; 74/13: seaport of Latium in central Italy, just SE
    of the Pontine Marshes; was an ancient town on the Appian
    Way, and the ruins of an ancient temple to Jupiter are found
    there.
terrene: 8/30; 10/46: (L) land, realm.
Terreus: 4/16; 82/103: Tereus, legendary King of Thrace. (See:
    ITYS).
testibus idoneis: 10/45: (L) according to suitable witnesses.

Té Tsong: 54/34, 35: (Te Tsung) (reign: 780-805), a weak but ami-
    able emperor. His ministers urged him to obtain revenue by
    finding new taxes and to abolish the three existing taxes: land
    tax, compulsory labor, and payment in kind; the new tax was an
    annual collection in money. Once the emperor became aware
    of the condition of the peasants, he gave much attention to mak-
    ing their lot easier, but his ministers prevented him from ac-
    complishing many of his aims. He was a poet and wrote his im-
    perial decrees in verse.
Tethnéké: 23/109: (Gr) he is dead. (See: Appendix A).
teuke: 61/85: a piece of money used by the Russians in W Asia; about
    the value of one TAEL of silver in China.
Tevere: 74/24: (It) TIBER.
[Thacher, Oxenbridge]: 63/98, 100; 64/103, 106: 1720-65, American
    lawyer and member of the Massachusetts general court; associ-
    ated with James OTIS and Stephen SEWALL in the controversy
    over the Boston WRITS OF ASSISTANCE (1763).
Thales: 77/46: c. 636-546, the Greek Milesian philosopher.
Thames: 70/159; 74/15: the English river.
Thatcher, Oxenbridge: 63/98; 64/103, 106: see Oxenbridge THACHER.
that man: 21/97; 22/101; 28/138: see Thaddeus Coleman POUND.
that 1908 medico: 28/136: prob. William Carlos WILLIAMS.
Thayer, Oxenbridge: 63/100: see Oxenbridge THACHER.
Thebae: 83/111: see THEBES.
Theban(s): 1/4; 68/141: see THEBES.
[Thebes]: 1/4; 68/141; 83/111: the ancient Greek city; TIRESIAS was
    from Thebes.
The empty armour shakes as the cygnet moves: 4/15: variation of
    Ovid, Metamorphoses, XII, 143-45.
The evil that men do lives after them: 80/79: from Julius Caesar,
    III, ii, 79.
theign: 48/38: (OE) servant.
the imprint of the intaglio....what is poured into it: 79/64: variation
    of Paradiso, 13, 67-69.
their Highnesses: 42/5, 8; 43/14, 15, 16: see FERDINAND II of Tus
    cany and MARIA MAGDALENA.
Themis Conditor: 71/163: (Gr) law, justice, right (L) the founder.
Theodora: 77/44:
Theognis: 33/10: Theognis of Megara, an aristocratic elegiac poet
    of the 6th century BC whose best known work is the Elegies to
    Kyrnos, in which he considers the values of the aristocratic
    man in human affairs.
Théophile: 80/82: see Théophile GAUTIER.
Theresa: 68/143: a French ship carrying cargo to South Carolina
    during the Revolution (1778) and belonging, so he claimed, to
    BEAUMARCHAIS' firm RODERIQUE HORTALEZ & CO; but the
    ownership of the vessel was disputed by M. MONTHIEU. "There
    is no...but ignorance": 80/79: from Twelfth Night, IV, ii, 45.
the sage/ delighteth in water...with the hills: 83/107: from Analects,
    VI, xxi.
The scarlet curtain throws a less scarlet shadow: 7/25: from Gold-

ing's translation of Ovid's Metamorphoses, X, 586-96. (See: Literary Essays, 235-37).

These fragments you have shelved (shored): 8/28: variation of T. S. Eliot, The Waste Land: These fragments I have shored against my ruins.

Theseus: 6/21, 23: the Greek hero, son of Aegeus; his most famous exploit was the slaying of the Minotaur.

The ship landed in Scios...: 2/7-10: from Ovid, Metamorphoses, III, 597-691.

The slavelet is mourned in vain: 5/20: from Martial, V, 37.

Thessalonians, First: 74/12: the book in the Bible.

thethear: 81/97: (Sp) cecear: lisping; to pronounce Spanish c in the Castilian manner, th.

Thetis: 76/37: a Nereid; mother of Achilles.

the yellow bird: 79/65: from Ta Hsio, III, 2; Shih Ching, ode 230. (See: Appendix B).

"This wind, sire, is the king's wind,...No wind is the king's...": 4/15 -16: from Sung Yü, The Man-Wind and the Woman-Wind. (See: Waley, 170 Chinese Poems, 41).

Thiy: 78/59:

"Thkk, thgk"/ of the loom...under olives: 39/43: variation of Odyssey, X, 254.

Tholomeno, Don Joas: 65/122: see Don Joas Theolomico de ALMEIDA.

Thomas bank: 74/15: the THAMES.

Thomas, Tony: 60/75: Antoine, fl. 1691, Jesuit misionary in China.

Thompson: 66/127: James Thomson, 1700-1748, the Scottish poet; author of the Seasons (1726-1730).

"those girls": 3/11: from Browning, Sordello, III, 698.

"Thou shalt purchase the field with money": 74/18; [76/32]: from Jeremiah, 32,25.

[Thrace]: 4/16: ancient country on the E Balkan Peninsula, SE Europe.

Three Kingdoms: 54/27: the Epoch of the Three Kingdoms, 221-265. During this period there were three minor dynasties: the Minor Han (221-263), the Wei (220-260) and the Wu (222-64). The kingdom of Wei embraced the central and northern provinces; Wu controlled the provinces south of the Yangtze, and Han ruled the province of Szechwan. This was a period of great battles, of heroes, and of chivalry, a period much like that of King Arthur.

Three Towers: 54/30: built by Emperor HEOU-TCHU.

Thseng-sie: 13/58: Têng Hsi, a disciple of Confucius. (See: Analects, XI, xxv).

Thucydides: 67/139: ?471-400?, the Greek historian.

[Thulemeyer, Baron de]: 65/122: minister from Prussia at the Paris Treaty conference (1783).

Thumiatehyon: 40/49: Thymiaterium, city founded by HANNO, just south of the Strait of Gibraltar and north of SOLOIS.

Thumon: 62/91: (Gr) soul, life, strength, courage, mind. (See: Appendix A).

Tian: 13/58: Tien or Tsêng Hsi, a disciple of Confucius. (See: Ana-
lects, XI, xxv).
Tiber: 5/18, 20; [74/24]: (It) Tevere, the Italian river.
Tiberius: 38/39: Tiberius Julius Caesar Augustus, 42 BC-37AD,
second Roman Emperor (14-37 AD).
Tibet: 60/78.
Tician: 25/119, 120: see TITIAN.
Tician de Cadore: 25/120: (It) TITIAN of CADORE.
Tiémour: 57/58: see PÉYEN.
Tiemoutier: 56/52: (Tiehmutiehr or Temudar) d. AD 1322, minister
of state under Emperor GIN-TSONG and prime minister under
Emperor Ying Tsung (reign: 1321-23). Tiemoutier was an un-
scrupulous minister who grew rich by his official robberies.
After his death Ying Tsung deprived him of all his honors and
started to put his followers to death. Alarmed, some of them
plotted to assassinate the emperor; they did in 1323.
Tien: 54/29: (Ch) (T'ien): Heaven. (See: CHANG TI).
Tien-cheou, Mt.: 57/60: (T'ien-shou), a range of hills NW of Peiping where were situated the tombs of the MING emperors.
Tien Hing: 55/37: (T'ien Hsing) fl. AD 812, a minister of Emperor
HIEN-TSONG.
Tien ma: 60/75: (Ch) (T'ien-ma): Heaven horse.
Tienouan; 56/52: Tien-ouan (T'ien-wan), the name of the dynasty
which Siu-cheou-hoei (Hsü Shou-hui) attempted to found (1351-
57); his revolt against CHUNTI was successful for a time, but
he was captured and killed c. 1357. (See: Mailla, Histoire
Générale, IX, 594). The name of the general who "beat the
rebels" in the text was Tong-pu-siao (Tung Pu-hsiao) fl. 1352.
(See: Mailla, Histoire Générale, IX, 600).
Tien-tan: 54/21: (T'ien Tan) fl. BC 279, a soldier, and later a commander of the forces of TSI.
Tientsin: 58/64; [61/80]: city of E Hopeh province in NE China, at
the junction of the Pie and the Grand Canal.
Tientsing: 61/80: see TIENTSIN.
Tiepolo, Lorenzo: 26/122: Doge of Venice (1268-75).
Tierci, de: 5/18; 23/109: Bernart, nobleman of Provence; his wife
was stolen away by Piere de MAENSAC. (See: Make It New,
27).
tiers Calixte: 10/46: (Fr) the third CALIXTUS.
tiers état: 65/125: (Fr) third estate; the people, commons.
Tigullio: 74/17; 77/51: the Gulf of Tigullio, Italy.
Ti Ko: 53/8: (Ti Ku) (reign: 2436-2366), a ruler noted for his justice
and interest in his people; he attained fame by being the first
emperor to have more than one wife.
Ti Koen: 58/64: poss. Tien-ki (T'ien-ki) the name given to the reign
of Emperor HI-TSONG.
Till: 74/8: see ST LOUIS TILL.
Tilsit: 34/15: city, formerly of East Prussia, a port on the Niemen;
under Russian administration since 1945. The treaties which
constitute the Peace of Tilsit were concluded there on 7 and 9
July 1807. After having won the battle of Friedland, Napoleon I

met Alexander I of Russia for a conference at Tilsit (25 June
1807); France made peace with Russia and gave Russia a free
hand in its design on Finland, but the pact was broken in 1812.

Time: 74/12: the American news magazine.

Times: 41/55: the London Times.

Timon of Athens: 63/99: the play by Shakespeare.

Timour: 56/51, 53: Timour Khan (reign: 1295-1308), grandson of
KUBLAI KHAN, whom he succeeded to the throne. Timour was
an honest ruler who tried to promote the welfare of his people;
he improved the administration, reformed the system of select-
ing officials, curbed the power of the nobility, expelled dishonest officials and cut down bribery. In 1303 he was confined
to his bed and the government was run by palace ladies and corrupt officials.

[Ting-tsong]: 56/49: (Ting Tsung), imperial title of KUJAK Khan.

Tinkey, Mrs.: 77/47: evidently the landlady of Miscio ITO.

Tinkham: [74/11; 76/39]; 78/59; [80/87]: George Holden, 1870-1956,
member of the House of Representatives from Massachusetts
(1915-43); a conservative and isolationist.

Tip: 37/33: see William Henry HARRISON.

Tipa: 60/75: or Deva, the title of the viceroy who governs Tibet for
the Grand Lama.

Tippecanoe clubs: 34/20: political organizations working for the election of William Henry HARRISON and John TYLER in the presidential campaign of 1840; they were running against Martin VAN
BUREN. The slogan of the Whig party was "Tippecanoe and
Tyler too." Harrison was called "Tippecanoe" because of the
battle with the Indians which he fought on the Tippecanoe river
(7 November 1811).

tira libeccio: 74/21: (It) the south-west wind blows.

Tiresias: 1/3, 4; 2/9; [39/44]; 47/30; [80/72]; 83/111: the legendary
Greek seer associated with the royal house of Cadmus. In
Hades, Tiresias informs ODYSSEUS the way he must go to return
to Ithaca. (See: Odyssey, X, XI; Ovid, Metamorphoses, III).

Tiro: 74/21: see TYRO.

Tirol: [35/22; 38/39; 74/19], 26; 83/113: or Tyrol, former province
of Austria; now Italian; includes the Bavarian Alps on the N border and the Ötztaler Alps in the center.

Tirreno: 74/13: (It) TYRRHENIAN SEA.

tisane: 39/43: (Fr) a decoction of herbs.

Titania: 20/94; 21/100: epithet of CIRCE. (See: Ovid, Metamorphoses, XIV, 382 and 438).

[Tithonus]: 74/13: son of Laomedon and brother of Priam; he was
loved by Eos, who asked that Zeus grant him immortality; Tithonus was granted immortal life but without immortal youth,
so he became old and shrivelled and is said to have turned into
a grasshopper.

Titian: 25/119, [120]: Tiziano Vecellio, 1477-1576, the Venetian
painter.

Titus: 78/57: Titus Flavius Sabinus Vespasianus, 40-81, Roman emperor (79-81).

T. J.: 31/3, 5; 33/10, 11; 69/152: see Thomas JEFFERSON.

T. L.: 74/22: see Thomas Edward LAWRENCE.

Toc: 7/26: (Fr) imitation.

Todero: 76/38: the column of St. Theodore in the Piazza di San
    Marco, Venice, where the statue of Theodore stands on a croco-
    dile.

to forge Achaia: 74/[22], 25: from Hugh Selwyn Mauberley.

toh pan: 80/89: (Gr) the all. (See: Appendix A).

To Kalon: 58/64: (Gr) the beautiful. (See: Appendix A).

Tola, octroi...decime: 35/26: Tola(?); octroi (Fr) town dues, toll-
    house; decime (Fr) 1/10 of a franc.

Tolfa: 10/46: town in central Italy, famous for its alum mining in-
    dustry.

Tolomei: 43/15: an ancient Sienese family.

Tolosa: 76/30; 80/81: poss. (L) Toulouse, the city on the Garonne,
    France; prob. Tolosa, a town of Guipuzcoa, Spain.

Tom: 69/154: see Thomas JEFFERSON.

Tom: 77/52: DTC, Pisa.

Tomczyk, Miss: 82/102:

Tompkins: 37/31: Daniel D., 1774-1825, American politician; gover-
    nor of New York (1807-16); Vice President of the US (1817-25).
    He was closely allied with the DeWitt CLINTON political fac-
    tion of New York.

Ton: 58/66: Tou-ché-kéou (Tu-shih-k'ou), a gorge north of Shansi
    province, leading from Inner Mongolia into China.

Tong: 56/54: see TONG-PING-TCHANG.

[Tong-ping-tchang]: 56/54: (Tung Ping-chang) fl. AD 1355, a fight-
    ing companion of TCHU-YUEN-TCHANG.

Tonkin: 60/76: region in N French Indo China; once a part of China.

Topa: 54/30: see TOPA-HONG.

Topa-hong: 54/[29], 30: (Toba Hung) d. AD 499, the Tartar emper-
    or of OUEI; rebelled against the Empire in 489 but later made
    peace. He was known for the reverence he gave to the ancient
    emperors and to Confucius.

Topas: 54/29: the people of TOPA-HONG.

To-pa-tao: 54/29: (Toba Tao) d. AD 452, prince of the kingdom of
    OUEI; a very important and powerful ruler of the time, who
    paid much attention to the state of education in his domain. One
    day he entered a Buddhist monastery and found the priests all
    drinking whiskey and the monastery full of weapons -- so he
    abolished the Buddhists of his kingdom.

Topeka: 28/134, 135: the city in Kansas.

tornsel: 18/80: prob. (It) tornese: of Tours; a minor coin of base
    silver or copper, struck in many of the Italian states prior to
    the unification.

Toro: 20/91: town in ZAMORA province, NW Spain.

Toro, las almenas: 20/91: (Sp) the battlements of TORO; Las Al-
    menas de Toro is a play by Lope de Vega (1618).

Torquato: 74/24: Torquato Tasso, 1544-95, the Italian poet.

Torrano: 11/49: a locality in central Italy, taken from Sigismondo
    MALATESTA by the peace terms imposed by Pope PIUS II
    (c. 1460).

Torre! Torre! Civetta!: 80/74: (It) Tower! Tower! Screech owl! (See: TOWER OF PISA).

Torwaldsen: 74/25: Bertel Thorwaldsen, 1770-1844, the Danish sculptor; one of his best known works is the statue of a lion at Lucerne, Switzerland.

Tory (Tories): 63/99; 70/156: the loyalist party in America during the Revolution.

[to sacrifice to a spirit not one's own is flattery]: 77/45: from Analects, II, xxiv, 1.

Tosch: 80/81: name of a dog.

To study with the white wings of time passing...not when they are at harvest: 74/15-16: from Analects, I: i, 1-2; ii, 2; iii, v.

Toth: 80/91: DTC, Pisa.

totis viribus: 71/161: (L) with all my strength.

Toto: 56/52: (T'o-t'o) 1313-55, minister of state under Emperor CHUNTI and one of that emperor's few honest ministers. Toto attempted to quell the rebellions of the rising MING, but court intrigue hindered his efforts. His campaign against the rebels was stopped by a decree stripping him of all honors and sending him into exile; in 1355 he was poisoned, but by 1363 his reputation was again honored. He is also known for his historical studies, particularly for his history of the KIN Tartars.

toujours: 77/42: (Fr) always, forever.

toujours Pari': 83/106: (Fr) forever PARIS.

Tou-kou-hoen: 54/31: (Tu-ku Hun), a Tartar tribe which occupied the territory around Lake Koko Nor in Tsinghai province, W central China.

Touli-Kahn: 54/30: Touli-kohan (Tuli Kohan) fl. AD 593, leader, or Kohan, of the Tu-chüei, a Tartar tribe in northern China; he was given the daughter of Emperor OUEN-TI.

Tour, la: 68/147: see TOWER OF LONDON.

Tournon, Maillard de: 60/76: Charles-Thomas Maillard de Tournon, 1668-1710, titular Patriarch of Antioch who, in 1704, was sent to China by Pope CLEMENT XI with the title of Patriarch of the Indies and Legate. He arrived in Canton in 1705 and published the decretal of Clement XI condemning Chinese ancestor worship.

Tou-san: 54/34; 55/37: (Tu-san), a Tartar tribe; or Tartars in general.

tout crédit soit d'un peuple soit d'un particulier/ ...de deux choses/ l'opinion de la bonne foi/ et de la possibilité/ ou il se trouve de faire face: 68/148: (Fr) all credit whether of a people or an individual/ ...of two things/ the opinion as to the good faith/ and as to the chances/ of his meeting. (See: John Adams, Works, VII, 344).

Tout dit que pas ne dure la fortune: 76/34: (Fr) Everything says that fortune doesn't last.

Tou-yu: 54/27: (Tu Yu) fl. AD 247, an officer of Emperor TÇIN-OU-TI who proposed to build a bridge over the Hwang Ho; he also led an attack against the kingdom of OU.

tovarisch: 27/131, 132; 74/8: (Russ in Fr transliteration) comrade;
      in a comradely fashion.
Tower, the: 74/6, 8, 21; 76/33: see TOWER OF PISA.
Tower of Hananel: 74/18: in the north corner of Jerusalem, on the
      wall.
Tower of London: 68/147; [80/92]: the ancient fortress, prison and
      royal residence in London.
[Tower of Pisa]: 74/6, 8, 21, 25; 76/33; 80/74: the Campanile of
      Pisa; the leaning tower.
Tower of Ugolino: 74/[9], 14, [16, 25; 79/64]: the Torre Della Fame
      (Tower of Famine) in Pisa, in which UGOLINO della Gherades-
      ca, his sons and grandsons were imprisoned and starved to
      death; it stood at the north side of the Piazza degl'Anziani.
      (See: Inferno, 33).
Towers of Pisa: 74/[14, 21], 25: there are several, but the two
      most famous are the Torre Della Fame (the TOWER OF UGO-
      LINO) and the Campanile (The Leaning TOWER OF PISA).
trabesilis: 25/115: (L) with wooden beams, timbered.
Trachulo: 10/42: Servulo, court poet of Sigismondo MALATESTA.
Tracy: 71/166: see Comte Antoine Louis Claude DESTUTT DE TRACY.
"Trade, trade, trade": 77/49: prob. from Sidney Lanier, The
      Symphony.
Train, Francis: 74/25: George Francis Train, 1829-1904, American
      merchant and writer.
Trapier: 64/106: an acquaintance of John ADAMS. (See: Adams,
      Works, II, 249).
Trastevere: 74/3, 24: · district in Rome, across the Tiber from the
      main city.
Trattoria degli Apostoli (dodici): 74/26: (It) Inn of the Apostles
      (twelve).
Trebizond: 26/123: an offshoot of the Byzantine Empire which in-
      cluded Georgia, the Crimea, and the S shore of the Black Sea.
Tre cento bastardi ... bombardi: 24/112: (It) Three hundred gun
      salute...bombards.
Tre donne intorno alla mia mente: 78/61: (It) Three women on my
      mind.
Tree of Visages: 4/15: prob. an invention; poss. a reference to the
      tsuboki or Camellia Japonica, the flowers of which are often
      likened to human heads in Japanese poetry.
treize rue Gay de Lussac: 80/88: (Fr) 13, rue GAY-LUSSAC (Paris).
[Tribunal of Rites]: 58/64: a commission set up in 1601 by Emperor
      CHIN-TSONG to consider the merits of Christianity when the
      Jesuit missionary Mathieu RICCI came to the court. The Tri-
      bunal rejected Christianity and recommended that the mission-
      ary be sent back to his own country. However, the emperor
      allowed him to remain at court.
Tribune: 28/136: prob. the New York Herald Tribune, Paris edition.
Trieste: 28/135: the seaport at the head of the Adriatic Sea.
Trimouill: 24/113: Georges de la Tremouille, d. 1433, favourite and
      prime minister of CHARLES VII of France (1425-33); he was
      an enemy of Joan of Arc and aided in handing her over to the
      English.

Trinacrian: 80/81: (L) <u>Trinacria</u>: three-pointed; a poetical name
        for Sicily.
trine as praeludio: 79/70: poss. (It) <u>trino as preludio</u>: threefold
        (in trinity) as prelude.
Trinity, the: 34/20: the Father, the Son, and the Holy Ghost.
Trist: 41/56: Eliza House, fl. 1785, a friend of Thomas JEFFERSON;
        she cared for Jefferson's daughter while he was in Europe.
Tristano: 24/110: (It) Tristram; poss. the version of the story of
        Tristram and Isolde by Thomas of Britain (c. 1185) in Norman
        French verse; the earliest extant version. (See: <u>Spirit of Ro-
        mance</u>, 79).
Tritons: 29/141: legendary Greek mermen.
Trivio: 9/36: in Rimini; site of the TEMPIO.
Troas: 79/63; 80/81: the Troad, territory surrounding the ancient
        city of TROY.
Troezene: 6/23: <u>Troezen</u>, a plain on the NE extremity of Argolis;
        home of Aethra, mother of THESEUS.
Trompette: 65/117: a château near Bordeaux.
Tropismes: 23/107: (Fr) tropisms.
[Trotsky, Leon]: 16/74: 1877-1940, the Russian Bolshevik leader,
        negotiated the treaty of Brest-Litovsk.
Trotzsk: 16/74: see Leon TROTSKY.
Trovaso: 76/39: see SAN TROVASO.
[Trowbridge, Edmund]: 64/103: 1709-93, Massachusetts jurist; pre-
        sided at the Boston Massacre trial (1770); remained neutral in
        the Revolution. (He changed his name from Goffe).
Troy: 4/13; 5/18; 20/90; 23/109; [79/66]; 82/103: the ancient city.
[Truman, Harry S.]: 84/118: 1884-   , President of the United States
        (1945-52).
Tsai: 53/19: (Ts'ai), a small feudal state situated on the river HOAI
        in Honan province, E central China.
Tsai: 55/45: see TSAÏ-KING.
Tsaï-gin: 55/37: see OUANG-TSAÏ-GIN.
Tsai King: 55/45: (Ts'ai Ching) 1046-1126, a partisan of OUANG-
        NGAN-CHÉ; in 1107 he became lord high chamberlain under
        Emperor HOEÏ-TSONG and gained control of the administration.
        He filled all posts with his own men, made oppressive changes
        in the salt tax and coinage, and led the Empire into expensive
        wars; he was several times degraded but always managed to
        work his way back to power. Tsaï-king is known in Chinese
        history as "the Chief of the Six Traitors."
Tsao: 53/19: a principality of feudal China in Shantung province
        (1122-501).
Tsehing: 56/54: see KO-TSÉ-HING.
Tsé-ho: 54/31: (Tzŭ-ho), city on the northern border of Shansi prov-
        ince.
Tseng: 80/73: <u>Tzu Kung</u>, disciple of Confucius; important in Chinese
        interstate diplomacy (495-68). (See: <u>Mencius</u>, III, I, iv, 13).
Tseou-kou: 54/26: prob. <u>Tcheou-kien</u> (Ch'ou Chien) fl. AD 27, a
        Chinese bandit leader. (See: Mailla, <u>Histoire Générale</u>, III,
        290-291).

Tsé Tchin: 53/19: prob. name of a Chinese emperor. (See: Mailla, Histoire Générale, II, 211).

[Tsé-tchi tong-kien]: 55/44: (Tzŭ-chih t'ung-chien commonly called T'ung-chien or Mirror of History), a history of China from the fifth century BC down to the beginning of the Sung dynasty, AD 960; SSÉ-MA-KOUANG was editor and chief author; the work, begun before 1064, was completed in 1084 and presented to Emperor CHIN-TSONG. The history was later abridged and cast in a new form and given the title Tsé-tchi-tong-kien kang-mou (Tzŭ-chih t'ung-chien kang-mu or Kang-mu).

Tsé-tchi tong kien hang mou: 55/44: see TSÉ-TCHI TONG-KIEN.

Tseu-lou: 13/58: Tzu-lu, a disciple of Confucius. (See: Analects, XI, xxv).

Tse-Yng: 54/21: (Tzŭ Ying) (reign: BC 206), son of EULH-chi-hoang-ti and last emperor of the TSIN dynasty; he held the throne forty-six days and then surrendered it to LIEOU-PANG, Prince of Han, who allowed Tse-yng safe conduct from the palace.

Tsi: 53/19: (Chi), a feudal state comprising a large part of northern Shantung and southern Chihli (1122-265); the Duke of Tsi mentioned is prob. Ching Kung (fl. 547-489).

Tsié-mé: 54/21: (Chieh-me), town in the province of Shantung.

Tsievitz: 35/22:

Tsin: 53/16: (Ch'in), a city, once the capital, of Kansu province, N China.

Tsin: [53/17]; 54/21: (Ch'in), the fourth dynasty (255-206)

Tsin Chi: 54/21: Tsin-chi-hoang-ti (Ch'in Shih Huang Ti) (reign: 246-209), fourth emperor of the TSIN dynasty to rule all of China and the real founder of its power.

Tsing: 49/39: (Ch'ing), the twenty-second dynasty (1616-1912); the reference is prob. to KANG HI, fourth emperor of the Ch'ing dynasty.

Tsing-chin: 55/41: (Ch'ing-shên), city in Szechwan province; known later as Koan-hsien.

Tsing-mo: 53/9: Tsing-mao, a Chinese herb. (See: Mailla, His· toire Générale, I, 74).

Tsiuenpiu: 55/41: see OUANG-TSIUEN-PIN.

Tsiun-Y: 54/34: (Chün-i), prob. a village in Honan province.

Tso-kieou-min: 54/24; [55/44]: (Tso Chiu-min or Tso) fl. 5th century BC, a disciple of Confucius; he wrote a commentary on the SPRING AND AUTUMN Annals (or CH'UN CH'IU) of Confucius. Tso has been canonized as the "Father of Prose," for he expanded the brief entries of Confucius into dramatic episodes. His commentary is known as the Tso Chuan.

Tso kieou ming: 55/44: see TSO-KIEOU-MIN.

Tsong: 55/44: see TAÏ-TSONG.

tsong-ping: 60/76: (Ch)(tsung-ping): brigadier-general.

Tsunhoa: 58/65: (Tsun-hwa) a fortified city in the province of Hopeh; in AD 1629 the city fell to the Manchu forces during their march on Peiping.

Tsu Tsze: 80/73: Tzu Hsi, 1835-1908, Empress dowager of China and actual ruler (1898-1908). (See: Guide to Kulchur, 8ln).

Tucker, Sam: 65/114, 115, 116, 117: Samuel, 1747-1833, American
  naval officer; as captain of the Franklin and the Hancock he
  preyed on British shipping during the Revolution; he was commander of the frigate Boston which carried John ADAMS to his
  post as commissioner to France (1778).

Tu Diona: 47/30: (Gr) You DIONE. (See: Appendix A).

Tudor: 80/94: royal family that ruled England from 1485-1603.

Tudor, William: 71/167: 1779-1830, author of Biographical Memoir
  of the Life of James OTIS (Boston: 1823).

Tudor indeed is gone and every rose: 80/94: variation of the Rubaiyat V: Iram indeed is gone with all his Rose.

Tuft: 64/104: Cotton Tufts, 1732-1815, American physician; a friend
  of John ADAMS, whose affairs he administered while Adams
  was in London.

Tuilleries: 34/16: Tuileries, former palace in Paris; while seldom
  used as a royal residence before the Revolution, Napoleon made
  it his chief residence, as did Louis XVIII.

Tully: 63/99: see CICERO.

Tung Kieou: 53/8: (Tun-chiu), a place near the department of Ta-
  ming-fu in the province of Chihli, NE China.

Tura, Cosimo: 24/114; 79/63: or Cosmé, c. 1430-95, Italian painter
  of murals; a leader of the Ferrarese school and court painter
  to Borso and Ercole d'ESTE; one of the SCHIFANOJA mural-
  ists.

Turchum: 26/121: see MOHAMMED II.

Turgenev: 80/72: Ivan Sergeyevich, 1818-83, the Russian novelist.

Turgot: 31/5; 65/119; 67/140; 68/141: Anne Robert Jacques, 1727-81,
  the French economist.

Turin: 44/30: city, Torino province, NW Italy.

Turk: 55/40: prob. a reference to LIEOU-TCHI-YUEN, who was
  originally a Chato Tartar before he became emperor.

Turkey: 24/112; 41/56.

Turkish war: 48/34: the siege of Vienna (1683).

Turner: 80/91: DTC, Pisa.

turris eburnea: 21/99: (L) tower of ivory. (See: Litany of the
  Blessed Virgin).

Tuscany: 2/7; [3/11]; 8/30; [33/11; 43/12; 44/17]; 50/41, 42: region
  of central Italy. During the 12th and 13th centuries the region
  was divided into small republics and then united under the
  MEDICI dukes of Florence; later it passed to the HOUSE OF
  LORRAINE, and subsequently to Sardinia and the kingdom of
  Italy.

tu theleis respondebat...: 64/106: see SUBILLAM CUMIS EGO OC-
  CULIS MEIS....

tutrice: 42/6, 8; 43/9, 16: (It) guardian.

24 E 47th: 12/53; 80/86: poss. the residence of Pound's AUNT F(rank).

29th Styschire: 62/88: (poss. Styx + shire) the 29th Regiment of His
  Majesty's Foot was quartered in Boston in 1770. (See: John
  Adams, Works, I, 97).

Tyciano da Cadore: 25/119: see TITIAN.

Tyler: 34/21; 37/33: John, 1790-1862, tenth President of the United
    States (1841-45); Vice-President (1841), succeeding to the presi-
    dency on the death of President William Henry HARRISON (4
    April 1841).
Tyler: 74/14; 76/33; 79/67: DTC, Pisa.
Tyler, Wat: 33/11: or Walter, d. 1381, English leader of the Peas-
    ants' Revolt (1381) in protest against the Statute of Laborers and
    the poll tax.
Tyndarida: 5/18: a reference to HELEN of Troy, whose mother was
    Leda, wife of Tyndareus; also a reference to the wife of Bernart
    de TIERCI.
Tyro: 2/6, 10; 7/25; 74/9, [21]: daughter of Salmoneus; loved by
    Poseidon, who visited her disguised as the Thessalian river,
    Enipeus.
Tyrol: 35/22; 38/39; 74/19: see TIROL.
[Tyrrhenian Sea]: 74/13.
Tyson, Jo: 29/143:

Ubaldo: 78/58: see Ubaldo degli UBERTI.

[Uberti, Farinata degli]: 6/22; 78/58: d. 1264, Florentine Ghibelline leader who was banished to Siena (1258) and recaptured Florence from the Guelphs in 1260; he is called the "Savior of Florence;" his daughter married Guido CAVALCANTI (1266 or 67). (See: Inferno, 10).

[Uberti, Ubaldo degli]: 78/58: friend of Ezra Pound; a descendent of Farinata degli UBERTI; a resident of Genoa.

Uberton (Gubberton): 46/26: prob. reference to Surbiton, a town on the Thames, Surrey, England.

Uccello, Paolo: 74/25: Paolo di Dono, c. 1396-1475, Florentine painter; one of the "realists" of the 15th century.

Udine: 41/54: city of Friuli province in NE Italy; in World War I it was an Italian military base of operation against Austria (1915-18); occupied by Austrian troops in October 1917.

'udor: 83/109: (Gr) water. (See: Appendix A).

Ugo: 24/110, 112: see Ugo ALDOBRANDINO.

Ugolino: 74/14, 16; 79/64: Ugolino della Gheradesca, ?1220-89, Ugolino da Pisa; conspired to seize power in Pisa but was imprisoned and his wealth confiscated (1274); escaped and allied himself with the Guelphs of Florence and Lucca, then at war with Pisa, and regained his property (1276). After committing other treasons against Pisa, he, his two sons and two grandsons were imprisoned in the tower of Gualandi (since called Torre Della Fame) and starved to death. (See: Inferno, 33).

Uhlan, the young: 41/53, 54: see Fritz von UNRUH.

Ukraine: 67/140.

Ulster: 80/74, 82: the northernmost of the four historic provinces of Ireland.

ultimo febbraio: 26/126: (It) last of February.

Un' abbondanza che affamava: 50/40: (It) a plenty that kept you hungry. (See: Zobi, Storia Civile, I, 403: l'affamatrice abbondanza).

una compagna d'Adamo. Come si fesse?: 22/102: (It) a mate for ADAM. How to make her?

una grida: 35/25: (It) a proclamation.

Una niña de nueve años: 3/11: (Sp) a nine year old girl.

una nuova messa/ (dodicesimo anno E.F.)/ bella festa: 48/36: (It) a new mass/ (12th year of the Fascist Era)/ beautiful ceremony.

una pace qualunque: 41/54: (It) just any peace.

Un centavo, dos centavos: 12/53: (Sp) one cent, two cents.

"Un curé déguisé.../ Me parait un curé déguisé." A la porte/"Sais pas, Monsieur, il me parait un curé déguisé": 77/50: (Fr) "A disguised priest.../ Seems to me like a disguised priest." At the door/"(I) don't know, Sir, he seems like a disguised priest to me."

Undertree: 58/62, 63: see HIDEYASHI TOYOTOMI.

undsoweiter: 12/55; 40/47: (Ger) and so forth.

Un fontego: 61/81: (It) a chamber.

Union: 71/161: see UNITED STATES.
United States (U. S.; U. S. A.): 34/16, 19, [20]; 37/35; [46/29;
    62/92]; 65/121; 67/139; 68/145, 146; 69/149, 150, 151,
    152; 70/156; [71/161; 83/114].
U. S. Constitution: 37/35; 67/139: see CONSTITUTION OF THE
    UNITED STATES
U. S. N. A.: 62/92; 69/105: the United States of North America.
[United States Senate]: 34/18, 20; 37/34; 62/93, 94, 95; 70/155;
    78/59; 83/113, 114: the upper house of the CONGRESS OF THE
    UNITED STATES.
Unkle G.: 76/39: see George Holden TINKHAM.
un libro franxese che si chiama Tristano: 24/110: (It) a French book
    called TRISTANO.
un peu interessantes: 34/15: (Fr) somewhat interesting.
Un peu moisi, plancher plus bas que le jardin: 7/24: (Fr) A bit mil-
    dewed, floor(ing) lower than the garden. (See: Flaubert, Un
    Coeur Simple).
Unruh, von: [41/53, 54]; 48/34: Fritz von Unruh, 1885- , German
    playwright, poet and novelist; officer in World War I.
[Unruh, Karl von]: 41/54: German military officer; father of Fritz
    von UNRUH.
un sorriso malizioso: 10/43: (It) a malicious smile.
Untel, Monsieur: 38/38: (Fr) Mr. so-and-so.
un terzo cielo: 76/36: (It) a third atmosphere. (See: Paradiso, 8,
    37: il terzo cielo).
until I end my song: 74/15: from Spenser, Prothalamion.
Upward, Allen: 74/15; 77/47; 78/57: 1863-1926, British novelist and
    journalist.
Urban VIII: 43/10, [14]: 1568-1644; Pope (1623-44).
Urbanus: 43/14: see URBAN VIII.
Urbino, Federico d': [9/35, 36, 37]; 10/43, 45; 11/49: Federigo da
    Montefeltro, 1422-82, First Duke of Urbino; a great Italian con-
    dottiere and politician, but more famous as a patron of arts and
    letters.
Urochs: 74/6, 9: aurochs, the European bison.
Ussel: 74/6, 14; 76/30: town in Corrèze department, S central
    France; near VENTADOUR.
Usura: [15/64]; 45/23, 24; 46/28, 29; 50/42; 51/44, 45; 78/59, 60:
    (L, It) usury.
Usuria: 15/64: (L) usury.
usury (usurers): 12/55; 14/63; [19/84]; 44/22; 46/27; [48/34]; 51/44;
    52/4; 55/45; 50/75; 74/7, 18, 19; 76/41; 78/59, 60.
Ut animum nostrum purget...: 59/70: see DE LIBRO CHI-KING SIC
    CENSO....
utilité publique, motif trop élevé: 59/71: (Fr) public usefulness, too
    elevated a motive.
Utrecht: 62/92; 68/147: province in central Netherlands; the capital
    city thereof.
Uzano, Nic: 21/97; 41/53: Niccolò da Uzzano, d. 1432, Florentine
    statesman; as the leader of the aristocratic party of Florence,
    he was opposed to the growing power of the MEDICI; he was one

of the few truly honest and disinterested men in Florentine politics of the day.

V

vacabile: 43/13: (It) that which is to be vacant.

Vada: 9/37; 41/52: village of Livorno province, Tuscany, central Italy.

vadit pars: 25/117: (L) a part goes.

Vai soli: 74/9: prob. (It) Mai soli: never alone.

Val Cabrere: 48/37: Valcabrère, village in the department of Haute-Garonne, S France.

Valcaire: 65/120: Valcarce, river in León province, Spain.

Val di Chiana: 44/22: Valle di Chiana, the valley of the Chiana river in central Italy.

Valencia: 3/12: region and ancient kingdom in eastern Spain; became an independent Moorish kingdom (11th century); held by Ruy DIAZ (1094-99); finally reconquered from the Moors in 1238 by James I of Aragon.

Valenciennes: 65/123: city of Nord department, N France.

Valent: 30/148: Valenzia, city of Alessandria province, Piedmont, NW Italy.

Valturibus, Roberto de: 11/52: see Roberto VALTURIO.

Valturio: 9/35; [11/52]; 26/121; 54/29; 57/58: Roberto, d. 1489, Italian engineer and author; engineer on the Great ROCCA of Sigismondo MALATESTA; as Sigismondo's first secretary he urged Malatesta to support Florence rather than ALFONSO V of Aragon; author of De Re Militari (1472).

Van: 37/33: see Martin VAN BUREN.

Van Berckel: 65/122; 68/148: Engelbert François, 1726-96, pensionary of Amsterdam and a friend of the American cause against England; a party to the first negotiations for a trade treaty between America and the Netherlands (1779).

Van Buren, Martin: 34/19, 20, 21; 37/31, 32,[33], 34, 35, 36; 46/28; 48/34: 1782-1862, eighth President of the United States. Member of the US Senate from New York (1821-28), governor of New York (1829); US Secretary of State (1829-31); Vice-President of the US (1833-37); President (1837-41). In 1840 Van Buren was the unsuccessful Democratic candidate for the presidency, and in 1848 he was defeated on the Free-Soil ticket.

Van Capellen: 62/92: see Joan Derk van der CAPELLEN TOT DEN POL.

Vandenberg: 84/118: Arthur Hendrick, 1884-1952, member of the US Senate from Michigan (1928-52); he was leader of the Senate "isolationist bloc" before World War II, but later served as a US delegate to the United Nations conference in San Francisco (1945).

Van den Santheuvel, Baron]: 65/122: deputy from Holland at the Paris Peace Conference (1782).

Vanderberg, Barham: 16/72: an invented name.

Van der Capellen: 65/122; 68/147: see Joan Derk van der CAPELLEN TOT DEN POL.

Vanderpyl: [7/25]; 74/13; [80/88]: Fritz-René, 1876-   , Dutch writer living in Paris at 13, rue Gay-Lussac; author of books on art.

[235]

vani: 41/52: (It) rooms (of houses).

Van Myden: 63/98: Van Muyden's Short Treatise on the Institutions of Justinian.

Vanni: 11/50: see Giovanni MALATESTA.

Vanoka: 20/95: prob. an invented name.

Van Renselaer: 37/31: Stephen Van Rensselaer, 1764-1839, American army officer and politician; Lieutenant Governor of New York (1795-1901); member of the House of Representatives (1822-29); associated with DeWitt CLINTON's Republican party machine in New York State.

Vans M: 70/155: see William Vans MURRAY.

Van Staphorst: 62/92; [68/147]; 69/150, [151]: Nicholas and Jacob, fl. 1780, directors of the Dutch banking house having their name.

Van Tzin Vei: 33/13: (Wang Ching-wei) 1885-1944, a Chinese statesman; a disciple of Sun Yat Sen, he broke with the Kuomingtang and became puppet ruler of Manchuria (1939-44).

Van Vloten: 68/147; 69/151: Van Vlooten, fl. 1780, a Dutch broker.

Varchi: 5/19, 20: Benedetto, 1503-65, Italian historian; author of Storia Fiorentino (published 1721), a history of Florence, 1527-38, commissioned by Cosimo de' MEDICI.

Vashinnt(t)onn: 50/40, 41: see George WASHINGTON.

Vatican: 28/139; 38/37; 80/80: the Papal residence, Rome.

Vauban: 65/117: Sebastien le Prestre, Marquis de Vauban, 1633-1707, French military engineer; commissary general of fortifications (1678), marshal of France (1703).

Vaughn: 65/124: Benjamin Vaughan, 1751-1835, British diplomat; a friend of Benjamin FRANKLIN, he sided with the Colonists during the Revolution and unofficially promoted concilliation in the Anglo-American negotiations of 1782; settled in America in 1796.

Vauguyon: 65/122: Paul François, duc de la, 1746-1828, French diplomat; ambassador to Holland (1770) and to Spain (1784-90).

Vechii, Orazio: 79/63: Orazio Vecchi, ?1550-1605, Italian composer; known especially for his L'Amfiparnasso: Commedia Armonica.

Velásquez: 80/87, 89; 81/95: Diego Rodriguez de Silva y Velásquez, 1599-1660, the Spanish painter.

veleno: 74/15: (It) poison.

Ven der Kemp: 68/147: François Adriaan Van der Kemp, 1752-1829, Dutch scholar and soldier who migrated to New York; friend of John ADAMS.

Vendoise: 24/113: a councillor of CHARLES VII of France.

Vendome: 56/49: Vendôme, town in Loir-et-Cher department, N central France.

Vendramin: 76/38: Cardinal Francesco (elected 1605), Venetian cleric. The Palazzo Vendramin is on the Campiello della Chiesa in Venice; it once contained a magnificent art collection.

Venerandam: 1/5: (L) compelling adoration. (See: Georgius Dartona Cretensis' Latin translation of Homeric Hymn VI, To Aphrodite).

Venere, Cytherea "aut Rhodon"/ vento ligure, veni: 74/22: (It) VENUS, (L) CYTHERA "or Rhodes"/ (It) Ligurian wind, come.

Venetijs: 26/127: (L) at VENICE.

Venezia: 21/96; 48/37: (It) VENICE.

Veneziana: 76/39: (It) woman of Venice.

Venezuela: 34/17.

Venice: 5/19; 8/30; 10/42, 46; 11/50; 21/96; 24/110, 112, 113; 25/115, 116; 26/123, 126, [127]; 35/25, 26; 40/47; 44/21; [48/37]; 50/42; 67/140; 74/25; 76/39: (Venezia).

Ventadour: 6/22; 27/132; 74/6, 14; 80/87, former duchy in the department of Corrèze, S central France; near Limousin.

Ventadour, Lady of: 6/22: Alice of Montpellier, wife of EBLIS III vicomte of Ventadour; the Provençal troubadour Bernart de Ventadour (1148-95) belonged to the court of Ventadour, but when Eblis discovered Bernart making songs to his wife he banished the troubadour and locked Alice in a tower; Bernart later joined the court of ELEANOR of Aquitaine.

Venter venustus, cunni cultrix: 39/43: (L) belly beautiful, cunning in country matters.

vent'uno Maggio: 24/112: (It) May 21st.

Venus: 27/131; [74/22]; 79/67: see APHRODITE.

Verbiest: 60/74, 77, 78: Ferdinand, 1623-88, Jesuit missionary in China. He arrived in Peiping in 1660 and introduced the Chinese, whose astronomy was largely Ptolemaic, to the systems of Copernicus and Galileo; he was also employed by Emperor KANG-HI as a mathematician and a cannon founder. Verbiest's plea that Chinese priests be ordained, that they be allowed to say a vernacular Mass, and that ancestor worship be tolerated, was not granted by Rome.

verde colore predeletto...ziparello: 24/110: (It) green beloved color ...(?).

Verdun: 16/72; 48/34; 80/72: fortified town in NE France, in Lorraine on the Meuse; site of the longest and bloodiest battle of World War I in which Marshal PÉTAIN repulsed the Germans (1916).

Vergennes: 41/55; 65/121; 68/143, 144, 145, 146; 69/149, 151; [70/155]; 71/161: Comte Charles Gravier de, 1717-87, French statesman; minister of foreign affairs under Louis XVI (1774-87).

Verjaring/ van den veldslag by Lexington/ Eerste Memoire dan den Heer Adams/ Indruk of de Hollandsche Natie: 65/122: (Dut) Concerning/ the battle of LEXINGTON/ First memoir by Mr. ADAMS/ Impression of the Dutch Navy. (See: John Adams, Works, III, 279).

Verlaine: 74/27; 80/72: Paul, 1844-96, the French poet.

Vermont: 70/157.

Vernon, W.: 65/114: William, 1719-1806, American merchant; in 1777 appointed chairman of the Navy Board of the Eastern Department.

ver novum, canorum, ver novum: 39/43, [45]: (L) fresh spring, melodious, fresh spring.

Verona: 29/142; 35/25; 78/56, 59: city of Verona province, NE Italy; among its buildings is an ancient Roman amphitheater.

Verres: 14/62: Gaius, c. 120-43, Roman administrator whose corruption astonished even the Romans.

Versailles: 33/10; 65/125; 69/152: city S of Paris where Louis XIV
    built the palace known as Versailles.
Versailles: 69/152: the Court of Versailles, at VERSAILLES.
versalzen: 74/18: (Ger) to oversalt; to spoil.
vers le Noël: 80/83: (Fr) around Christmas.
Verucchio: 8/32: Verrucchio, town and castle 10 miles S of Rimini,
    Italy.
Vervennes: 70/155: see Comte Charles Gravier de VERGENNES.
vespa, la: 83/110, 111: (It) the wasp.
Vesuvius: 37/33, 35; 80/73: the volcano on the east side of the Bay
    of Naples.
Vetta: 77/51: (It) summit.
Vexis: 6/21: Vexin, ancient district of France, N of the Seine and
    the Oise.
via Balbo: 78/55; 80/75: via Caesar Balbo, a street in Rome.
Via del Po: 24/114: (It) road of the PO.
viae stradae: 5/17: (L) streets.
Via Sacra: 29/141: (It) prob. a street in Verona.
Vicenza: 42/7: capital of Venezia Euganea, NE Italy.
[Vickers]: 18/81(?); 38/37(?): the international armament makers;
    Vickers has controlling interests with firms in many countries
    besides England and has (or had) connections with MITSUI,
    SCHNEIDER, etc.
[Victor Amadeus III]: 32/9; 65/124: 1726-96; King of Sardinia (1773-
    96).
Victor Emanuel: 61/82; [77/51(?)]: Victor Emmanuel II, 1820-78;
    King of Italy (1861-78).
Victoria: 34/20; 35/26(?); 37/33; 41/53: Alexandrina Victoria, 1819-
    1901; Queen (1837-1901).
Vidal: 4/14, 16: Peire, fl. 1175-1215, Provençal troubadour; followed
    Richard Coeur de Lion on the Third Crusade (1189-92); it is
    said that when he loved Loba de Perrautier he dressed in wolf-
    skins and was almost killed by hounds during a hunt.
Vidas: 3/12: a Jewish merchant whom Ruy DIAZ, noted for his cun-
    ning, cheated.
videt et urbs: 78/60: (L) he saw and cities. (See: Raphael of Vol-
    terra, trans. Odyssey, I, 2: qui mores hominum multorum
    vidit et urbes, quoted in Literary Essays, 265).
videlicet alligati: 43/9: (L) namely bound servants.
Vidkun: 84/117: Vidkun Quisling, 1887-1945, Norwegian politician who
    collaborated in the German conquest of Norway (1940) and be-
    came head of the government under the German occupation.
viels: 8/32: viell, an early form of the medieval viol.
Vienna: 19/87; 28/35; 34/18; 35/22; 38/39; 48/34; 50/41; 68/144;
    69/150; 74/26.
vigneron: 21/79: (Fr) wine-grower.
Vildrac: 80/84: Charles, 1882-   , the French poet and playwright.
Villa Catullo: 74/5: the villa on Lake Garda, Italy, where Catullus
    lived for a time; it was here that he wrote his salutation to the
    promontory of SIRMIO.
Villa Falangola: 37/33, 35: the villa in Sorrento where Martin VAN

BUREN lived (c. 1854) after his retirement from public life.
vingt à v.ngtcinq navires dans le bassin/.../ magazins de la ville
    sont remplis,/ journée d'un homme 15s/ et nourri: 65/122:
    (Fr) twenty to twenty-five ships in the basin/.../ warehouses
    (or armories) of the city are filled/ a man's day (is worth) 15
    sous,/ including food. (For this extract from the journal of
    Count SARSFIELD for 5 June 1782, see John Adams, Works,
    III, 283).
vino rosso: 76/40: (It) red wine.
Vio: 76/39: see SAN VIO.
Virgil: 34/15: Publius Vergilius Maro, 70-19, the Roman poet.
Virgin: 43/9, 11, 12; 58/64; 76/39: the Virgin Mary.
Virgin, the: 80/71: Coronation of the Virgin, a painting by VELÁS-
    QUEZ in the Prado, Madrid.
Virginia: 64/106; 67/137, 138; 68/145; 70/156.
Virgo: 52/4: a constellation due south of the handle of the Dipper;
    the Virgin, represented as a woman holding in her left hand a
    spike of grain.
virtù: 74/7: (It) virtue, power.
Vischer: 65/123: Visscher, fl. 1780, a pensionary of The Hague.
Visconti, Bianca: 8/31: Bianca Maria Visconti, 1423-68, daughter
    of Filippo Maria VISCONTI; married Francesco SFORZA (1441).
[Visconti, Filippo Maria]: 9/36: 1392-1447, Duke of Milan; warred
    with Venice and Florence; his daughter, Bianca Maria VISCON-
    TI, married Francesco SFORZA, who took over the dukedom of
    Milan.
Visconti, Galeaz Sforza: 21/98: prob. Galeazzo Maria SFORZA.
Visigoths: 65/119: one of the tribes of West Goths; founded the Visi-
    gothic kingdom in Spain, southern France and Africa.
Viterbo, Paulo: 11/48: Paulo da Viterbo, an officer in the forces of
    Sigismondo MALATESTA.
Vitruvius: 67/139: Marcus Vitruvius Pollio, fl. 1st century BC,
    Roman architect whose work served as one of the models for
    Renaissance architecture.
Viva: 44/17, 18: (It) Hurrah!
Vivante: 52/3: Leone, 1887-   , Italian author and critic; author of
    English Poetry (1950). Vivante lives in a villa on a hill outside
    Siena.
Vlaminck: 74/13: Maurice, 1876-1905, the French painter, writer
    and printmaker.
Vlettmann: 19/85:
Voce-profondo: 20/91: (It) deep-voiced.
voce tinnula: 3/11; 28/137: (L) with ringing voice. (See: Catullus,
    LXI, 13).
Vogliamo: 11/50: (It) we want.
voi che passate per questa via: 76/39: (It) you who pass through this
    street (you who go in this way).
Voi, popoli transatlantici admirabili: 50/41: (It) You, admirable
    transatlantic people.
Voisin: 74/11; 76/31; 77/47: a restaurant in Paris.
Volpe: 76/39; 80/87: Giuseppe Volpi, Count di Misurata, 1877-1947,

Italian statesman and financier; member of the Italian delegation
to the Paris Conference (1919); minister of finance (1925-29).

volpe, la: 22/102: (It) the fox.

Voltaire: 65/118; 77/46: François Marie Arouet de, 1694-1778, the
French philosopher.

Von Moltke: 80/81: Helmuth Karl Bernard, Graf von Moltke, 1800-
91, Prussian field marshal; was responsible for the successes
of the Prussian army in the Danish War (1864), the Austro-
Prussian War (1866) and the Franco-Prussian War (1870-71).

Von Tirpitz: 74/21; 77/42: poss. Alfred von Tirpitz, 1849-1930, German admiral.

vous êtes très mal élevé/...Tiens, elle te le dit...: 80/83: (Fr) you
are very badly brought up (ill-mannered)/...Look, she's telling
you....

Vous voudrez citoyen: 44/20: (Fr) You will be willing, citizen.

W

Wadsworth, Jeremiah: 69/153: 1743-1804, American soldier and politician; Commisary General of the Continental Army (1778-79); member of the House of Representatives (1789-95).

[Wagadu]: 74/8; 77/43: the name of the spiritual strength among the FASA. "For in itself., Wagadu is not of stone, not of wood, not of earth. Wagadu is the strength which lives in the heart of man." (See: Leo Frobenius, Erlebte Erdteile, VI, 42).

Walcott: 71/164: see Oliver WOLCOTT.

Walden, Lord H. de: 33/12: Charles Augustus Ellis, 6th Baron Howard de Walden, 1799-1868, English diplomat; minister to Stockholm (1832-33), Lisbon (1833-46) and Brussels (1846-68).

Wales: 66/132; 67/135: part of the United Kingdom of Great Britain and Northern Ireland; made an English principality (1284), incorporated with England during the reign of Henry VIII.

Walker, Jimmy: 38/37: James John, 1881-1946, the American political leader; mayor of New York city (1925-32).

Wall, the: 54/21, 31: see GREAT WALL OF CHINA.

Waller: 81/98: Edmund, 1606-87, the English poet.

Wallonie, La: 78/58: a Belgian literary magazine. (See MOCKEL).

Walls: 82/101; 83/110: DTC, Pisa.

Wall St.: 12/54: street in New York city; center of the financial district.

Walluschnig, Dottor Aldo: 28/133: prob. an Austrian doctor in Venice, c. 1925.

Walter: 80/71: see Walter Morse RUMMEL.

Walterplatz: 83/113: the Waltherplatz, principal square in BOLSANO; there is a statue of Walther von der Vogelweide there.

wan: 80/79: (Ch) (wên): culture. (See: Analects, IX, v, 2; Pound translates the word as "the precise knowledge;" Legge as "the Cause of truth; the arts of peace--music, dancing, literature-- as opposed to the arts of war").

Wan, King: 77/45: prob. WEN WANG.

Wang: 13/60: see WU WANG.

Wonjina: 74/4; 77/52: Wondjina, in Australian native legend, the son of a god who created the world by speaking the names of objects; but Wondjina created too many things, so his father took his mouth away. In Australia the wondjina figures, ground drawings, have no mouths; the aborigines believe that there would be a deluge if their wondjina figures had mouths; thus Wondjina is a type of rain god.

Warenhauser: 22/101: pseudonym for Frederick Weyerhaeuser, 1834-1914, American capitalist, known as the "Lumber King"; about 1900 he purchased approximately a million acres of lumber land in Washington and Oregon from the NORTHERN PACIFIC Railroad.

War Office: 62/94: the department of the US Secretary of War.

Warren: 70/156: Mercy, 1728-1814, wife of James WARREN and sister of James OTIS; noted as a woman of letters; author of political satires, verse and dramas. John ADAMS was particularly amused by her satire on the Boston Tea Party.

Warren, J.: 65/114: James, 1726-1808, Massachusetts political leader; paymaster general of the Continental Army (1775-76); member of the Navy Board (1776-81); member of the Massachusetts
governor's council (1792-94). Husband of Mercy WARREN.

Washington: 37/32; 63/97; 84/115: Washington, D.C.

Washington, G.: 31/3, 5; 33/12; 34/16, 18; 50/40, 41; 62/91, 92, 93,
94, 95, 96; 65/109, 110, 111, 121; 70/157, 158; 71/166; 79/64:
George, 1732-99, first President of the United States. Served
with the British forces during the French and Indian Wars (1752-
58), receiving the rank of colonel; retired (1759) to Mount Vernon, Virginia. Member of the CONTINENTAL CONGRESS
(1774-75); elected to command all Continental armies (1775), resigned commission (1783). President (1789-97).

Washington, J.& M.: 74/14; 76/33; 80/71; 84/115: DTC, Pisa.

Washington's army: 70/157: see CONTINENTAL ARMY.

Waterloo: 80/75: town of Brabant province, Belgium, just south of
Brussels; the battle of Waterloo was fought just south of here
on 18 June 1815.

Watson: 77/42: a shopkeeper in Clinton, New York, c. 1904.

Wattle (Wattle-wattle): 9/35, 37; 10/43: see Francesco SFORZA.

Watts Dunton: 82/101: Theodore Watts-Dunton, 1832-1914, the English
poet, novelist, and critic; friend of Rossetti and Swinburne,
whose life Watts-Dunton regulated; Swinburne lived with him
from 1879-1909.

Wazir: 35/26: Vizier, a high executive officer, usually a minister
of state, of various Mohammedan countries, especially of the
former Turkish empire.

Webb: 71/160: Daniel, English soldier; commander of the British
forces in America (1756); succeeded shortly by James ABER-
CROMBIE; Webb served in the French and Indian Wars.

Webster, Dan.: 34/19, 20, 21; 37/32, [33], 36: Daniel, 1782-1852,
the American lawyer and statesman; member of the House of
Representatives (1813-17; 1823-27) and of the Senate (1827-41;
1845-50); Secretary of State (1841-43) under TYLER and again
(1850-52) under Fillmore. Webster opposed President JACK-
SON on the Second National Bank issue (1833).

[Wechel, Christian]: 1/5: fl. 1538, the printer of the Latin version
of the Odyssey translated by Andreas DIVUS.

Wei: 84/117: Wei Tzŭ, 12th century BC, viscount of the principality
of Wei. He was the step-brother of CHEOU-SIN, last sovereign of the YIN dynasty; Wei became so disgusted with the cruelty of his kinsman that he retired from the court and left the
kingdom. (See: Analects, XVIII, 1).

Wein, Weib, Tan Aoidan: 29/144: (Ger) Wine, Woman, (Gr) Song.
(See: Appendix A).

Wellington: 33/11; 50/42; 78/60; [79/64(?); 80/75(?)]: Arthur
Wellesley, 1st Duke of Wellington, 1769-1852, British general
and statesman; defeated Napoleon at Waterloo (1815).

Wells: [42/3]; 46/26: Herbert George, 1866-1946, the English writer.

Wendel, François de: 38/42: 1874-1949, president of the COMITÉ DES FORGES.

Wen Wang: 53/11, 14; [56/49; 77/45(?)]: (Wên Wang) 1231-1135, the title of canonization of Ch'ang, Duke of Chou, known as the Chief of the West; ruler of the principality of CHI, in Shensi. Thrown into prison by CHEOU-SIN as dangerous to the throne, he spent the time writing the Book of Changes (I Ching). Wen Wang, the father of WU WANG, is considered one of the great men of China, standing against the corruption of his age.

Wester, Dan: 37/33: see Daniel WEBSTER.

West Horn: 40/50: the modern bay of Bissau, the chief port of Portuguese Guinea, W. Africa.

West Indies: 64/107; 71/167.

Westminster: 14/62; 83/114: Westminster Palace or House of Parliament, London.

west mountain: 16/68: the mountain of Purgatory. (See: Purgatorio, 3).

Weston: 62/87: Thomas, ?1575-1644?, English merchant and adventurer; organized the expedition of colonists which settled an area near Mt. WOLLASTON in Massachusetts (1625).

West Virginia: 28/134.

"What shall add to this whiteness?": 80/73: from Mencius, III, I, iv, 13.

"Whether in Naishapur or Babylon": 15/66: from Rubaiyat, stanza 8.

Whigs: 33/12: the Whig party, one of the dominant political parties of the United States during the second quarter of the 19th century.

Whistler: 80/81, 82, 90: James Abbott McNeill, 1834-1903, the American painter.

White: 80/91; 84/115: lieutenant in the Provost Section, DTC, Pisa.

White House: 64/104: the first house of John and Abigail ADAMS in Boston (1768).

[White Lily Society]: 56/52, 53: a secret society which arose in China (1351) in opposition to the Mongol dynasty. Ostensibly the society was organized to worship the MILE BUDDHA, or Goddess of Mercy, who was to free China from the Mongols, but actually the society was used to raise a rebellion against Emperor CHUNTI. Hai Shan, the leader of the "White Lily," pretended to be a descendent of the SUNG dynasty, and at a great meeting he sacrificed a white horse and black cow and had all those who would follow his standard wear a red cap.

Whiteside: 74/14; 79/63: the negro turnkey at the DTC, Pisa; used by the Provost Section to handle the solitary cells and "security cages."

Whitman: 80/73, 86, 91; 82/104: Walt, 1819-92, the American poet.

Whitney: 38/37: Richard, 1888-   , New York banker and stock broker.

Who even dead, yet hath his mind entire!: 47/30: from Odyssey, X, 493.

Wiener Cafê: [18/81(?)]; 80/84, 85: a restaurant near the British Museum, London.

Wigmore: 79/62: the Wigmore Gallery, Marylebone, London.
Wi'let, Miss: 38/38: prob. Violet HUNT.
Wilkes: 79/64: poss. John Wilkes, 1727-97, English reformer.
William: 66/128: see WILLIAM III of England.
William: 74/11; 80/85; 82/103: William Butler YEATS.
William B.Y.: 79/65: William Butler YEATS.
William, Uncle: 77/51; 80/83; 83/106, 107, 111: William Butler YEATS.
[William II]: 48/34: 1859-1941, German emperor and king of Prussia
       (1888-1918).
William III: [66/128], 131; 71/167: 1650-1702; king of England (1689-
       1702).
[William V]: 65/123, 125: 1748-1806, Prince of Orange; Stadtholder
       of the Netherlands (1751-95).
Williams, Bill Carlos: [28/136(?)]; 78/61: William Carlos, 1883-
       the American poet.
Williams, J.: 65/118: Jonathan, 1750-1815, American diplomat and
       army officer; lived abroad from 1776-85 and acted at times as
       a purchasing agent for the Colonies; superintendent of West
       Point (1805-12). He was the grandnephew of Benjamin FRANK-
       LIN.
William's old "da": 80/85: see John Butler YEATS.
Willin(c)k(s): 62/92; 66/126; 69/151: Wilhem and Jan Willinks, direc-
       tors of the Dutch banking house having their name (c. 1780).
Willing, Thomas: 69/153: 1731-1821, American banker and statesman;
       member of the Continental Congress (1775-76); president of the
       First Bank of the United States (1791-1807); a supporter of
       HAMILTON's financial policies.
Willkie, Wendell: 77/51: Wendell Lewis, 1892-1944, American law-
       yer and business executive; Republican nominee for President
       of the US in 1940.
Willy: 76/31: see William Butler YEATS.
Willy: 78/58; 80/81, 82: see Henri GAUTHIER-VILLARS.
Wilson, Thomas: 74/6, 14; 77/47(?); 78/60(?): DTC, Pisa.
Wilson, Woodrow: 38/38; 78/60: 1856-1924, the twenty-eighth Presi-
       dent of the United States (1913-21).
Wimbledon: 16/71: the suburb of London.
Winston: 41/54; 80/92; 84/118: see Winston CHURCHILL.
Winston's mama: 41/54: see Jennie JEROME.
Winter and summer...to remember her: 6/23: from Sordello (ed.
       Marco Boni, Bologna, 1954, p. 15): Atretan dei ben chantar
       finamen....
Wiseman: 80/91: DTC, Pisa.
Wiseman, William: 80/91: poss. Sir William George Wiseman, 1885-
       , British diplomat.
with a bang not with a whimper: 74/3: variation of Eliot's line from
       The Hollow Men: Not with a bang but a whimper.
With Dirce in one bark convey'd: 82/103: from W. S. Landor, Dirce:
       ...With Dirce in one boat convey'd.
with the golden crown, Aphrodite...thou with dark eyelids: 1/5: from
       Homeric Hymn VI, To Aphrodite. (Prob. a translation from
       the Latin version of Georgius Dartona Cretensis).

"With us there is no deceit": 80/78: see the Noh play, Hagoromo, in
     Translations, 312.
W. L.: 74/22: see William George LAWRENCE.
Woburn Buildings: 82/102: at 18, Woburn Place, London; home of
     W. B. Yeats.
Woburn Farm: 66/126: prob. Woburn, the estate of the Duke of Bed-
     ford in Bedfordshire, SE central England.
[Wolcott, Oliver]: 62/96; 71/164: 1760-1833, American lawyer and
     politician; succeeded Alexander Hamilton to serve as US Secre-
     tary of the Treasury in the cabinet of John Adams (1795-1800).
Wolf: 71/160: James Wolfe, 1727-59, a major general in the British
     forces; commanded expedition against Montcalm at Quebec.
Wolfgang Amadeus: 26/128; [78/58]: see Wolfgang Amadeus MOZART.
Wollanston, Capn: 62/87: see Captain WOLLASTON.
Wollanston, Mt.: 64/105: see Captain WOLLASTON.
[Wollaston, Captain]: 62/87; 64/105: (neither his dates nor Christian
     name survive); an English adventurer and colonist who settled
     an area within the limits of what is now QUINCY, Massachusetts,
     and gave it the name of Mount Wollaston (1625).
Woodstock: 66/126: municipal borough of Oxfordshire, central Eng-
     land.
Wopkins, W.: 69/152: fl. 1783, an official of the State of Friesland,
     the Netherlands; member of the SOCIÉTÉ BOURGEOISE estab-
     lished at LEEUWARDE.
Wordsworth: 83/112: William, 1770-1850, the English poet.
Wörgl (Woergl): 41/55; 74/19; 78/60: a small town in the Austrian
     Tyrol which in the early 1930's issued its own money, a form
     of the stamp script first proposed by Silvio GESELL. (See:
     A Visiting Card, 15).
Writ(s) of Assistance: 63/100; 71/160: a writ, authorized by the stat-
     ute of 12 Charles II (1672),issued to an official to aid in the search
     for smuggled or uncustomed goods -- in practice, a general
     search warrant. Writs of Assistance were issued in Boston
     (1761) to allow English port agents to discover smuggled goods;
     they were not very effective, and served to stir up much dis-
     content against the British.
Wurmsdorf: 19/87: see Count Albert von MENSDORFF-POUILLY-
     DIETRICHSTEIN.
Wu Wang: [13/60]; 53/12, 14: 1169-1115, the title under which Fa, son
     of WEN WANG, was canonized. Continuing his father's battles
     against Emperor CHEOU-SIN, Wu Wang assembled a great army
     and defeated the emperor at Mêng-chin, in Honan, ending the
     Shang (or Yin) dynasty; he ruled (1122-1115) as the first emperor
     of the TCHEOU dynasty.
Wymans, Dr.: 28/138:
Wymmes: 74/20: text should read Wemyss; poss. Sir Henry Colville
     Barclay Wemyss, 1891-   , British army officer.
Wyndham: 78/57: see Percy Wyndham LEWIS.
[Wyndham, Dennis]: 28/140: fl. 1922, English actor; married to
     Elsie MACKAY (1917-1922); the marriage was ended by an annul-
     ment.

Wythe: 65/112, 113; 67/137; 68/145: George, 1726-1806, American jurist and statesman; member of the CONTINENTAL CONGRESS (1775-77) and signer of the DECLARATION of Independence.

X

Xaire: 84/117: (Gr) Hail! (See: Appendix A).

X. and B. Central: 19/87: the New York, New Haven and Hartford Railroad; controlled by J. P. MORGAN. (See: Lincoln Steffens, Autobiography, 590).

Xarites: 27/131; [74/21; 80/79]: the Charites, the GRACES. (See: Appendix A).

Xbre Monte Paschale, fatto Signoria: 43/14: (It) in December the MONTE DEI PASCHI, by act of the Seignory (governing body).

Xembre: 43/16: December.

Xrestes: 40/50: Chretes River, the modern St. Jean river on the NW coast of French West Africa.

Xtertn, Mr.: 46/26: see G. K. CHESTERTON.

Xthonos: 83/111: (Gr) of the earth. (See: Appendix A).

Xtians (Xtns, Xtianity): 58/62; 59/71, 73; 60/76; 61/80, 83; 76/32: CHRISTIANS, CHRISTIANITY.

X------y: 80/72: prob. DTC, Pisa.

X,Y,Z: 70/155: the XYZ Affair; an incident in the diplomatic relations between America and France (1797-98). The American commission to France, Charles Cotesworth PINCKNEY, John MARSHALL and Elbridge GERRY, accused the agents X, Y, and Z of suggesting that a bribe of £50,000 in the form of a loan to France would be welcomed by the Directory and particularly by TALLEYRAND. The uproar created by the incident in the United States aided those who wished to destroy Franco-American relations and to be more friendly toward England, the reverse of John ADAMS' foreign policy. Although Talleyrand never admitted that the agents were his, it is generally thought that they were.

Y

Yai: 56/50, 51: (Yai-shan), a small island in a bay 30 miles S of Hsin-hui, Kwangtung province. This island served as the last stronghold of the Southern SUNG dynasty. In 1279 the Mongol fleet attacked the island, defeating the Sung fleet, killing Emperor Ti Ping (reign: 1271-79) and ending the Southern Sung; KU-BLAI KHAN then became ruler of all China.

Yang: 54/31: see YANG-TI.

Yang-Hou: 54/27: (Yang Hu) d. AD 278, an important general serving Emperor TÇIN-OU-TI; since the emperor needed to take the kingdom of OU, one of the THREE KINGDOMS, in order to control all China, Yang-hou was directed to plan the campaign, but he died before accomplishing his task.

Yang-Kien: 54/30: (Yang Chien) the personal name of Emperor OUEN-TI.

Yang-kien: 54/30: (Yang Chien) fl. AD 580, created prime minister and Duke of SOUI by Emperor Suan Ti (reign: 569-83). Yang-kien was an able soldier and statesman and prepared the way for the SOUI dynasty, which takes its name from his title. OUEN-TI, first emperor of the Soui, was his son.

[Yang-koué-feï]: 54/34: (Yang Kuei-fei) d. AD 756, the favorite concubine of Emperor HIUEN-TSONG and second in importance to the empress. During the revolt of the imperial troops, the soldiers demanded the death of Yang-koué-feï, whom they accused of political intrigue. Although unwilling, the emperor finally consented to her death; she was strangled and her body shown to the soldiers, who promptly returned to their duty. But the event so saddened the emperor that he resigned the throne that same year.

Yang Lo: 57/57: see YONG-LO.

Yang-long: 57/57: Yang-yng-long (Yang Ying-lung) fl. AD 1403, a member of the court of Emperor KIEN-OUEN-TI; helped the emperor to escape from Nanking.

Yang Siun: 54/28: (Yang Hsün) fl. AD 289, the father-in-law of Emperor TÇIN-OU-TI. When the emperor became occupied with the entertainments of the court, which had originally belonged to SUN-HAO, Yang-siun was told by the emperor to govern the kingdom.

Yang-tchin: 54/26, 27: (Yang Chên) d. AD 124, a philosopher of Shensi province who came to be known as the "Confucius of the West." At the age of 50 he yielded to repeated requests to come out of retirement and became a governor in Shantung. His old friend OUANG-MI came, bringing the usual present of money to a superior, but Yang-tchin refused.

Yang Tchong: 54/26: (Yang Chung) fl. AD 76, a member of the privy council of Emperor Han Chang Ti (reign: 76-89).

Yang Ti: 54/31: (Yang Ti or Yang Kuang) (reign: 605-18), moved the imperial capital to Loyang and began building palaces, gardens and canals, employing, it is said, two million men. Although his canals in the provinces of Hupeh, Shantung, and Honan were

[248]

designed primarily to facilitate state progresses, they greatly
improved commerce in the north. But the emperor paid more
attention to gracious living than to ruling the empire.

Yangtse: 53/16; [54/27; 55/40; 56/50, 53; 74/3]: the principal river
of China (See also KIANG).

Yao: 53/9, 14, 19; 54/24; 55/42, 44; 56/48, 49, 55; 57/59; 58/66;
74/7, [18, 20]: (reign: 2357-2259), the son of TI-KO; a ruler
so benevolent that the weather was favorable toward him; he
commanded the royal astronomers to create an agricultural
calendar. Yao, like CHUN, is one of the ideal emperors of
Chinese history, one of the standards against which all emperors are measured, and at his death there were three years of
mourning before Chun took the throne.

Yaou: 74/20: see YAO.

Yaou chose Shun...nor dazzled thereby: 74/20: from Analects, VIII,
xviii.

Yash (Jassey): 19/87: a commercial town in NE Romania.

[Yavorska, Lydia]: 79/66: 1874-1921, Russian-born actress, once
married to Prince Vladimir Bariatinsky; acted in London (1910-
21).

y cavals armatz: 7/24; 80/87: (Pr) and horses all armed. (See:
Bertran de Born, Bien me plait le doux temps de printemps).

Yeats, J. B.: 80/[85], 86: John Butler Yeats, 1839-1922, the Irish
artist; father of W. B. YEATS.

Yeats, Judge: 37/35: Joseph C. Yates, governor of New York State
(1822-24).

Yeats, W.B.: 41/55; [74/11; 76/31; 77/51; 79/65]; 80/[74], 82, [83,
85], 89; 82/102, [103]; 83/106, [107, 111]: William Butler Yeats,
1865-1939, the Irish poet.

Yé Hihien: 57/57: (Yeh Hsi-hsien) fl. AD 1403, a member of the
court of Emperor KIEN-OUEN-TI; helped the emperor to escape
from Nanking.

Yeiner Kafé: 18/81: poss. the WIENER CAFE.

Yeliou Apaoki: 55/38: see YÉ-LIU-APAOKI.

Yeliu: 56/47, 49: see YÉLIU TCHUTSAÏ.

Yeliu: 56/50: see YÉ-LIU-YEOUCHANG.

[Yé-liu-apaoki]: 55/38, 39: (Yeh-lü O-pao-chi or Yeh-lü Cho-li-
chih) d. AD 926, Chieftain of the KHITAN Tartars. Until 907
the Khitans had recognized the emperor of China as their suzer-
ain, but in this year Yé-liu-apaoki proclaimed himself emperor
of an independent kingdom with the dynastic title of Liao and began encroaching on the territory of the Empire.

[Yé-liu-hiéou-co]: 55/41: (Yeh-lü Hsiu-co) d. AD 998, governor of
the region of Yen, which is around the city of Peiping (once
called Yen as well); he was a general of the Khitan Tartars and
is known for his humanity and his just and liberal administration.

[Yé-liu-long-siu]: 55/42: (Yeh-lü Lung-hsü) d. AD 1031, king of the
KHITAN Tartars. In 1004 he led his troops into the Empire,
taking over a large area; he was met by the imperial troops and
after several battles was persuaded to make a peace which was
honorable both for himself and Emperor TCHIN-TSONG (1006).

Yéliu Tchutsaï: 55/46, 47, 49: (Yeh-lü Ch'u-ts'ai) 1190-1244, a
KHITAN Tartar who served as advisor to GENGHIS KHAN and
to OGOTAI Khan. Yéliu was largely responsible for the organization of regular administration among the Mongols, for a
system of taxation and of criminal law. When paper money was
issued in 1236 it was due to Yéliu's advice that the issue was
limited to 100,000 ounces of silver. A patron of literature and
a student of Confucius, he did much to civilize the Mongols.
After his death some suspected that he had grown rich in the
government; but when his house was searched all that could be
found were some musical instruments, pictures and several
thousand books.

[Yé-liu-te-kouang]: 55/39: (Yeh-lü Tê-kuang) d. AD 947, second
son of YÉ-LIU-APAOKI; in 926 he succeeded to the throne of
the KHITAN Tartars (the Liao dynasty) and in 936 he agreed to
help CHÉ-KING-TANG gain the Empire in return for territory
in Chihli and Shansi provinces. The revolt was successful, and
Yé-liu-te-kouang, the "Father-Emperor," received a yearly
tribute from Ché-king-tang, the "Child-Emperor."

[Yé-liu-yeouchang]: 56/50: (Yeh-lü Yeu-shang) fl. AD 1287, a
scholar who received permission from KUBLAI KHAN to re-
open the Imperial College, which had not been in operation
since the time of OGOTAI Khan.

Yenkeli: 60/76: (Ch) Yankee; name given to English in the Orient.

Yen Yen: 54/29: Yen-yen-tchi (Yen Yen-chih) d. AD 456, although
of peasant stock, he rose to be prime minister of the Empire
under Emperor OU-TI; he was a model of modesty, frugality
and disinterestedness.

Yeou: 53/8: (Yu Tsao-chi) a mythical king of China; he followed the
reign of the great trinity of powers who ruled 18,000 years
each. Yeou taught men to build houses, and his name means
"nest having."

Yé-ouang: 56/56: (Yeh Wang) fl. AD 1375, an admiral serving Emperor HONG-VOU; he won several victories over the Mongols.

Yeougin: 56/53: see TCHIN-YEOU-GIN.

Yeou Ouang: 53/17: (Yu Wang) (reign: 781-770), a thoroughly bad
and unprincipled emperor who was under the influence of the
Lady PAO SSÉ; before Yeou's death many of his feudal chiefs,
outraged by his wickedness, refused to obey his orders and began to act as independent lords. After Yeou, the TCHEOU dynasty began to decline rapidly.

yerqui: 61/85: Yerquen, a petty court in the Bukhara region, W.
Asia.

Yésien: 57/58: (Yeh Hsien) d. AD 1454, commander of the Mongol
forces which invaded the Empire (1449), captured Emperor
YNG-TSONG and attacked Peiping (1450). In 1453 he seized
supreme power over the Mongols but was killed in a battle with
a rival.

"Ye spirits who of olde were in this land...": 8/30: from a poem
written by Sigismondo Malatesta to praise Isotta degli Atti.

yidd (yitt, yit): 41/52; 52/3; 74/17: (from Ger: Jude) a Jew.

Yin: [53/13]; 84/117: the SHANG dynasty (1766-1121); the name of the
     dynasty was changed to Yin about BC 1401.
[Yindsoo Hienwun]: 58/67: king of Korea (1623-49).
Y-king: 53/12: (I Ching), better known as the classic Book of Changes,
     written by WEN WANG while in prison at Yu-li.
y Las Hiladeras: 80/71: (Sp) Las Hilanderas: and The Spinners; a
     painting by VELÁSQUEZ, in the Prado, Madrid.
Yn: 53/11: see I YIN.
Yng-che: 57/60: (Ch) (Ying-shih): the Five Sisters.
Yng P: 53/19: Yng-pi (Ying Pi) fl. BC 492, natural son of Ling Kung,
     Prince of OUEI. When his father offered to make Yng-pi his
     successor to the title of Ouei, Yng-pi refused it, saying that
     his birth made him too low to accept the honor.
Yng star: 53/19: a Chinese star. (See: Mailla, Histoire Générale,
     II, 222).
Yng-Tsong: 57/57, 58: (Ying Tsung) (reign: 1437-50; 1457-65). He
     came to the throne at the age of eight years and, although his
     mother tried to provide a responsible guardian, the young em-
     peror was much influenced by the eunuch Wang Chin. In 1449
     Wang Chin precipitated a war with the Mongols, who invaded
     Shansi, defeated the troops commanded by Wang Chin, and cap-
     tured the emperor. KING-TI was made emperor in his brother's
     place, but in 1457 Yng-tsong returned to the throne and execut-
     ed many who had served his brother.
Yntsa: 60/76: (Ch) Indians; Eastern Indians, though text reference
     is to the French.
Yo Lang: 54/30: see LO YANG.
Yong: 61/82, 83: see YONG-TCHING.
Yong-kieu: 54/34: poss. Yong-kieou (Yung-chiu), a city in Honan
     province, China.
Yong Lo: 57/57: (Yung Lo) (reign: 1403-1425). As the Prince of
     Yen, he dethroned his nephew, Emperor KIEN-OUEN-TI, in 1403
     and took the throne himself. He repopulated areas devastated
     by war, drew up a penal code, and sent missions to Java, Su-
     matra, Siam and Ceylon. A patron of literature, he had com-
     piled a gigantic encyclopedia, known as the Yung Lo Ta Tien,
     which included many commentaries on the Classics.
Yong Tching: 61/78, 80, 81, 82, 83, 84, 85: (Yung Chêng) (reign:
     1723-35), fourth son of Emperor KANG-HI. His first act was
     to degrade and confine his brothers so to reduce contention for
     the succession. He then turned against the Christian mission-
     aries, some of whom had supported other candidates for the
     throne, and confined them to either Peiping or Macao. In 1732
     he thought to expel all Christians, but finding that they taught
     filial obedience (a central doctrine of Confucius) he left them
     alone, stipulating, however, that no more missionaries should
     enter the country. He was careful for the people's welfare and
     avoided wars, although he did expand the Empire to the Laos
     border.
York: 80/94: the English royal house of York, one branch of the
     Plantagenets which came into prominence with Richard Planta-

genet, 3rd Duke of York (1411-60); Yorkist kings of England were
  Edward IV (1461-70; 71-83), Edward V (1483), Richard III (1483-85).
Yorke, Sir Jo.: 68/147: Joseph Yorke, Baron Dover, 1724-92, Eng-
  lish diplomat; ambassador to The Hague (1751-80).
[Y-ouang]: 53/16: (I Wang or I) (reign: 934-09), son of KONG-
  OUANG and seventh emperor of the TCHEOU dynasty; during
  his reign barbarian tribes made frequent incursions into China.
Youi-leang-fou: 53/16: (Youi Liang-fu) fl. BC 860, one of the first
  officers of the Empire under Emperor LI-WANG.
Young: 71/161: Thomas, ?1731-1777, American Revolutionary patriot
  and physician; member of the Constitutional Convention of
  Pennsylvania (1776) and member of the committee that drafted
  the constitution of Pennsylvania.
Your eyen two wol sleye...: 81/98: from Merciles Beaute, attributed
  to Chaucer (Robinson, 638).
Y(Y)our H(H)ighness: 42/3, 5, 6:   see FERDINAND II of Tuscany and
  MARIA MAGDALENA.
Your Highness: 48/35: prob. Queen VICTORIA.
Your Majesty: 44/20, 21: see Maria Anna Elisa BONAPARTE.
Yo-Y: 53/20: (Yo I) fl. BC 285, minister of the feudal state of Yen
  (lasted 1122-265) near Peiping.
'Yperionides: 23/108: (Gr) son of HYPERION. (See: HELIOS) (See:
  Appendix A).
Yriarte: 10/44: Charles Émile, 1832-98, French historian; author of
  Un condottiere au XVe siècle (1882), a study of Sigismondo
  MALATESTA.
Ysaÿe: 80/81: Eugène, 1858-1931, Belgian violin virtuoso.
Yseut: 8/30: see ISOLDE.
Ytis: 4/14: see ITYS.
Y Tsong: 55/38: (I Tsung) (reign: 860-74), an emperor who had
  little common sense, preferring his own pleasures to govern-
  ing his people; during his reign there were rebellions and bar-
  barian invasions.
Yu: 53/8, 9, 10, 11, 12, 18, 19; 54/24; 55/42; 56/48, 49; 58/66; 74/7:
  (Ta Yü or Great Yü) (reign: 2205-2197), founder and first emperor of the HIA dynasty. It was CHUN who first brought Yu
  to the attention of Emperor YAO, and Yu was assigned the task
  of controlling the flood waters of the Yellow River (2286); he
  was so successful that Chun had him serve as his viceregent
  and he was offered the throne in place of Chun's son. Like Yao
  and Chun, Yu is one of the standards by which all Chinese emperors are measured.
Yu: 74/18: see YAO.
Yuan Jang: 13/58, 59: (Yüan Jang), it is not determined just what
  relation existed between Confucius and Yuan Jang, whether Yuan
  was an old rogue or a young disciple of Confucius. (See: Analects, XIV, xlvi, Legge's interpretation and Waley's differ).
Yu-chan: 53/9: (Yü-shan), a mountain in the province of KIANG-NAN,
  E China.
Yuei: 53/17: (Yüeh or Yü-yüeh), a kingdom or principality in S China;
  lasted c. BC 722-220 AD.

Yuen: 54/30: (Yüan), in AD 496 TOPA-HONG, ruler of OUEI,
 changed the name of his family from To-pa to Yuen.
Yuen: 55/39: see LI-SSÉ-YUEN.
Yuen: 56/47, 50, 51, 53, 54, 56; 58/67: (Yüan), the twentieth dynas-
 ty (1206-1368). This dynasty of Mongol emperors was established
 in 1206 by GENGHIS KHAN; in 1280, under KUBLAI KHAN, the
 Yuen began its control over the entire Chinese Empire.
Yu-en-mi: 79/65: poss. you-and-me.
Yuentchang: 56/53, 54: see TCHU-YUEN-TCHANG.
Yuen-yen: 53/13: a precious stone, perhaps jade. (See: Mailla,
 Histoire Générale, I, 335).
Yukien: 57/58: (Yü Ch'ien) 1398-1457, a minister of Emperor KING-
 TI. The only person who kept his head when Emperor YNG-
 TSONG was captured by the Mongols (1450), he defended Peip-
 ing, the capital, against the invaders and succeeded in driving
 them beyond the Great Wall. On the death of King-ti (1457),
 Yng-tsong returned to the throne and had Yukien executed for
 supporting King-ti; this was an injustice for Yukien had done
 great service to the Empire and had made Yng-tsong's return
 from captivity possible.
Yukiou: 56/53: Yu-kiué (Yü Chiüe) d. AD 1358, commander of the
 city of Ngan-king (Anking) in Anhwei province; killed while defending the city from the rebels against Emperor CHUNTI.
Yu-lin: 54/31: (Yü-lin), city in N China near the Great Wall; on
 the N border of Shensi province.
Yun-nan: 61/83: (Yunnan), a province in S China.
Yupingtchi: 54/29: (Yü Ping-chih) fl. AD 448, president of the judi-
 cial tribunal under Emperor OUEN-TI. He sought after justice
 so ardently and with such severity that he ruined multitudes of
 poor people; finally the emperor had to remove Yu-ping-tchi
 from his office.
Yusuf: 22/103, 104, 105: a tourist guide whom Pound met in Gibraltar, 1908.
Yu-Tchong: 56/47: (Yü Chung) fl. AD 1135, governor of King Ch'ou,
 a department of the province of Shensi.
Y-wang: 53/16: see Y-OUANG.
Y-yang: 54/23: Y-yang-hien (I-yang-hsien), a town and region near
 the modern city of Loyang in Honan province, E central China.

Z

Zagreus: 17/76, 77; 77/53: see DIONYSUS.

[Zaharoff, Sir Basil]: 18/80, 81, 82; 38/37: 1850-1938, European munitions magnate; started selling arms (c. 1876) for Nordenfeldt & Co., later joined with Maxim, an early competitor, and both joined with Vickers (by 1913); Zaharoff also had interests in oil, international banks, and newspapers.

zaino, il: 78/56: (It) the knapsack.

Zamberti, Zuane: 26/127: prob. Guiliano Giamberti Sangallo (1445-1516) Italian architect.

Zamora: 20/91: city of Zamora province, NW Spain.

Zanzibar: 80/80: the British protectorate off Tanganyika, E Africa.

Zarathustra: 74/16: see ZOROASTER.

Zattere, le: 83/110: a street in Venice, off the Giudecca.

Zeeland: [62/92]; 65/122: a province in SW Netherlands, composed of several small islands.

Zefalonia: 24/111: see CEPHALONIA.

Zeitgeist: 50/43: (Ger) spirit of the time.

Zeland: 62/92: see ZEELAND.

Zeno: 29/141: see SAN ZENO.

Zenos, Sir: 18/81: see Sir Basil ZAHAROFF.

Zephyr: 74/13: see ZEPHYRUS.

Zephyrus: 25/118; 47/32; 74/[13], 22, 27: in Greek mythology the personification of the West Wind.

Zeus: 11/50; [23/108; 71/167]; 74/8, [16]; 81/95: the Greek god.

Zezena: 11/50: see CESENA.

Ziani: 26/124: Sebastiano, Doge of Venice (1172-78); when Venice defeated the naval forces of Barbarossa, Pope Alexander III gave to Ziani a ring with which he and his successors should wed the Adriatic Sea each year on the day of the Ascension.

ZinKwa: 56/49:

Zion: 74/7; 76/32: part of Jerusalem; defined in the Bible as the City of David. The name is symbolic of Jerusalem, or the Promised Land, and of the Messianic hope of Israel.

Ziovan: 83/110: prob. a Venetian named Giovanni whom Pound knew; perhaps a gondolier.

Zoagli: 46/25; 76/37; 80/92; 83/107: a town on the Ligurian coast, NW Italy, a few miles south of RAPALLO.

Zobi: 50/40, 41, 43: Antonio, 1808-79, Italian historian; author of Storia Civile della Tosca, 1737-1848 (1850-52), a history of Tuscany.

Zoe: 20/92: d. 1050, a Byzantine empress who poisoned her husband, Romanus III, took the throne and married Michael the Paphlagonian.

Zohanne: 24/110: Johanne, prob. a servant of Parisina MALATESTA.

Zojas y Hurbara, la Marquesa de las: 18/81: poss. Madame Maria del Pilar Antonia-Angela-Patrocinio-Simona de Muquiro y Bernete, widow of Villafranca de los Caballeros, whom Sir Basil ZAHAROFF, then seventy-five years old, married in 1924.

[Zondadari, Anton-Felice]: 44/19: Cardinal-Archbishop of Siena (1795-1823).

Zoroaster: 67/137; [74/16]: fl. 5th century BC, a religious teacher
    of ancient Persia; he was the founder of Zoroastrianism, origi-
    nally a kind of fertility religion; it later developed a more com-
    plex cosmogony and eschatology, deriving from the struggle of
    the Zoroastrian supernatural spirits.
Zothar: 17/78; 20/92: prob. an invented name.
Zubly: 65/111, 112: John Joachim, 1725-81, American clergyman,
    prominent in colonial affairs; delegate to the CONTINENTAL
    CONGRESS (1775), although he was more a loyalist in sentiment
    than a revolutionary; author of several political pamphlets:
    The Stamp Act Repealed (1766), The Law of Liberty (1775).
Zuliano: 11/50: poss. reference to Aeneas Silvius PICCOLIMINI.
Zupp: 80/92: DTC, Pisa.
Zwischen die Volkern erzielt wird: 51/45: (Ger) between the (two)
    peoples (a modus vivendi) is achieved.
Zwol: 62/92: Zwolle, city of Overijssel province in E Netherlands,
    on the Ijssel river.

APPENDIXES

APPENDIX A: GREEK

Appendix A contains all Greek expressions in the Cantos, whether in Greek or Roman script, arranged in the order of the Greek alphabet.

The following is a key to abbreviations used in Appendix A:

Barker: The Politics of Aristotle, trans. by Ernest Barker (Oxford 1946)

L&S: H. G. Liddell and Robert Scott, A Greek-English Lexicon, 9th ed., (Oxford 1940)

Lyra Graeca: Lyra Graeca, ed. and trans. by J. M. Edmonds, rev. ed., 3 vols. (Loeb Classical Library 1928-1940)

OBGV: The Oxford Book of Greek Verse (Oxford 1931)

Appendix A was prepared by Professor Frederic Peachy, Reed College.

Agathos: 33/11: (ἀγαθός): "good: well-born, gentle; brave, valiant; capable; good (in moral sense)" (L&S).
Agalma: 40/49: (ἄγαλμα): "glory, delight, honour; pleasing gift; statue in honour of a god, sculpture; statue, portrait, picture; image" (L&S).
ἀγλαὸς ἀλάου πόρνη Περσεφόνεια: 80/72. The words are a jumble, not a quotation. ἀγλαός is an adj. (nom. masc. sing., fem. ἀγλαή) meaning "splendid, shining, bright; beautiful, famous, noble" (L&S). ἀλαοῦ would be the gen. masc. sing. of ἀλαός, blind. πόρνη means whore (nom. sing.). The words do not construe, and it is hard to define what associations they have for Pound. He seems to be calling PERSEPHONE the blind man's whore; and obviously he has the same idea in mind when he writes ΚΟΡΗ, 'ΑΓΛΑΟΣ 'ΑΛΑΟΥ in 74/20. The following line, "Still hath his mind entire", points to the Homeric passage, Odyssey X, 493-495 (cf. 39/44), which lies at the source: μάντιος ἀλαοῦ, τοῦ τε φρένες ἔμπεδοί εἰσι· / τῷ καὶ τεθνηῶτι νόον πόρε Περσεφόνεια/ οἴῳ πεπνῦσθαι· (the Poet is speaking of Tiresias, "the blind prophet of steadfast mind; though he is dead, Persephone has granted him alone possession of his faculties"). πόρνη looks like a wilful corruption of Homeric πόρε (has granted). (Faber ed.: πόρη).
'ΑΘΑΝΑΤΑ: 76/40: (ἀθάνατα): immortal. Epithet of APHRODITE in Sappho's poem to the goddess, and anaphora of the words

ΠΟΙΚΙΛΟΘΡΟΝ', 'ΑΘΑΝΑΤΑ two lines above. Pound knew this poem by heart (See: Literary Essays, 205).

alixantos, aliotrephes, eiskatebaine: 23/107: (ἀλίξαντος) "worn by the sea" (L&S); (ἀλιοτρεφής) "feeding in the sea, sea-reared" (L&S); (εἰσκατέβαινε) he went down into. The passage from which these words come show Pound to be construing, with the aid of Liddell & Scott's Abridged Greek-English Lexicon, Stesichorus' fragment on the setting sun. εἰσκατέβαινε is from the fragment itself (see next entry). In the Abridged Lexicon, the definitions of ἅλιος are immediately preceded by that of ἀλίξαντος, and immediately followed by that of ἀλιοτρεφής.

"Ἅλιος δ' 'γπεριονίδας δέπας ἐσκατέβαινε χρύσεον/ "Οφρα δὶ ὠκεανοῖο περάσας/ ποτὶ βένθεα/ νυκτὸς ἐρεμνᾶς/ . . . ποτὶ ματέρα, κουριδίαν τ' ἄλοχον/ παῖδάς τε φίλοις. . . . ἔβα δάφναισι κατάσκιον : 23/107-8. The above quotation may be translated: "The Sun, Hyperion's child, stepped down into his golden bowl, and then, after crossing the stream of Ocean, [he reached] the depth of black [and holy] night, and joined his mother, his faithful wife and his dear children. [Meanwhile the son of Zeus] entered [on foot] the laurel-shaded [grove]." The words omitted by Pound are set in brackets. The son of Zeus is HERACLES, and the fragment refers to the hero's tenth labor, in which he journeyed to the West in the Sun's boat in search of the cattle of GERYON. The complete (and more correct) text may be cited from Lyra Graeca II, fr. 8, p. 34 (See: OBGV, no. 161): 'Λέλιος δ' 'Υπεριονίδας δέπας ἐσκατέβαινεν/ χρύσεον, ὄφρα δι' 'Ωκεάνοιο περάσας/ ἀφίκοιθ' ἱερᾶς ποτὶ βένθεα νυκτὸς ἐρεμνᾶς/ ποτὶ ματέρα κουριδίαν τ' ἄλοχον παῖδάς· τε φίλους·/ ὁ δ' ἐς ἄλσος ἔβα δάφναισι κατάσκιον ποσίν/ παῖς Διός.

'Ἀλλ' ἄλλην χρὴ πρῶτον ὁδὸν τελέσαι, καὶ ἱκέσθαι/ Εἰς 'Λΐδαο δόμομς (Faber ed.: δόμους) καὶ ἐπαινῆς Περσεφονείης'/ Ψυχῇ χρησομένους (Faber ed.: χρησομένος) Θηβαίου Τειρεσίαο/ Μάντιος (Faber ed.: Μάντηος) 'αλαοῦ του τε φρένες ἔμπεδοι εἰσι·/ Τῷ καὶ τεθνειῶτι νόον πόρε Περσεφόνεια/ [οἴῳ πεπνῦσθαι· τοὶ δὲ σκιαὶ ἀΐσσουσιν.] : 39/44. The quotation, marred by typographical errors, is from Odyssey X, 490-495, as Pound himself indicates in the right-hand margin; only he left out the last line, 495, which is added above in brackets. The lines may be translated: "But first you must accomplish another journey, and come to the house of Hades and awesome PERSEPHONE, to consult with the soul of Theban TIRESIAS, the blind prophet of steadfast mind; though he is dead, Persephone has granted him alone possession of his faculties, while the other shades are witless." These are the words of CIRCE to ODYSSEUS.

Anaxiforminges: 4/13: (ἀναξιφόρμιγγες): lords of the lyre. The unique epithet is from Pindar Olympian II, 1. The poem starts with the words: 'Λναξιφόρμιγγες ὕμνοι, τίνα θεόν, τίν' ἥρωα, τίνα δ' ἄνδρα κελαδήσομεν; -- "Hymns that are lords of the lyre, what god, what hero, what man shall we sing of?" For the associations of the word and the passage, see: Personae, 189 and Letters, 91 and passim.

ἄρχειν καὶ ἄρχεσθαι: 67/140: (Faber ed.: ἄρχειν)καὶ: to rule and to be ruled. The words constitute a theme in Greek political thought, going back as far as Solon (see L&S s.v. ἄρχω, 4), and reappearing in Aristotle Politics 1254a 21: "Ruling and being ruled . . .

not only belongs to the category of things necessary, but also to
that of things expedient'' (Barker's translation). Barker sum-
marizes the chapter (I. v) thus: ''There is a principle of rule
and subordination in nature at large: it appears especially in the
realm of animate creation. By virtue of that principle, the soul
rules the body; and by virtue of it the master, who possesses the
rational faculty of the soul, rules the slave, who possesses only
bodily powers and the faculty of understanding the directions
given by another's reason. . .'' See: Politics 1277b 15 (III. iv).

Ἀφροδίτη ; Ἀφροδίτην : 76/37; 79/69: APHRODITE (nom. and accus.
case forms).

ἄχρονος : 80/77: without time, independent of time.

βροδοδάκτυλος: 74/22: the adj. ροδοδάκτυλος, rosy-fingered, is the
Homeric epithet of Ἠώς, Dawn. βροδοδάκτυλος is the Aeolic form,
found in Sappho as the epithet of σελάννα (σελήνη), the moon: Lyra
Graeca I, fr. 86, 246 (See: OBGV, no. 145).

βροδοδάκτυλος Ἠώς: 80/89: (in Homer, ροδοδάκτυλος Ἠώς): rosy-fingered
Dawn. Pound uses the Aeolic form βροδοδάκτυλος, apparently in
reminiscence of Sappho (see preceding entry).

γέα ; Gea: 77/46, 79/65, 82/104: earth. γέα is the Ionic form of Attic
γῆ, Homeric γαῖα.

Gignetei kalon: 21/99: (γίγνεται καλόν): a beautiful thing is born (or, it
becomes beautiful).

γλαυκῶπις: 79/68: ''(in Homer, epithet of ATHENA, probably) with
gleaming eyes'' (L&S).

γλαύξ: 79/64: ''the little owl, Athene noctua, (so called from its)
glaring eyes ... (freq. as emblem of ATHENA)'' (L&S).

γλαύξ, γλαυκῶπις: 74/16: little owl, with gleaming eyes. See two preceding entries, and note in context that the olive is sacred to
ATHENA who created it, and that γλαυκῶπις, like γλαυκός, is used
to describe the sheen of the olive.

δακρύων ; ΔΑΚΡΥΩΝ; Dakruōn: 76/38, 76/40, 82/105, 83/110: weeping
(present participle, nom. masc. sing., of δακρύω; or possibly,
gen. pl. of δάκρυον, tear).

δεινὰ εἶ, Κύθηρα: 79/70: you are fearful, CYTHERA (Faber ed.: δεινα, εἰ
Κύθηρα).

Δημήτηρ : 77/48: DEMETER.

Δίγενες/ Digenes; Digenes, διγενές: 48/35; 74/3: text should read
digonos, δίγονος (See note by Alan Neame, The European, 4 (June
1953) 42, authorization for which is noted op. cit., 41). The
meaning is: twice-born; digonos is attested as an epithet of
DIONYSUS with just that meaning.

Δρυάς : 83/108: Dryad (tree-nymph).

Εἰδὼς : 81/98: knowing. εἰδώς is the participle of οἶδα, I know; Pound
seems in context to be using it as a gerund.

ΕΙΚΟΝΕΣ : 74/24: (εἰκόνες): pictures, images.

ΕΙΚΩΝ ΓΗΣ: 14/62: (εἰκὼν γῆς): picture, or image, of the earth.

εἰς χθονίους: 83/111: (accent χθονίους): to those (or the gods) of the
nether world.

hekasta: 74/19: (ἕκαστα) : particulars. From Aristotle, Nicomachean
Ethics 1143b 4: ἐκ τῶν καθ' ἕκαστα γὰρ τὰ καθόλου (for generalities

arise from particulars). The context shows Pound to have two
passages of the Ethics in mind: VI. xi. 4-7, and I. iii. 5-8 when
he says that philosophy is not for young men. For the former,
see: Guide to Kulchur, 329.

Ἕλανδρος and Ἑλέπτολις: 7/24: Destroyer of men and Destroyer of
cities. Pound's ELEANOR puts him in mind of Aeschylus'
HELEN (Ἑλένα), whom the chorus, playing upon her name, call
ἑλέναυς ἕλανδρος ἑλέπτολις (Agamemnon 689-690).

helandros kai heleptolis kai helarxe: 46/29: (ἕλανδρος καὶ ἑλέπτολις καὶ
ἑλάρχη): (usury) destroys men, and destroys cities, and destroys
government. The first two epithets are from Aeschylus' description of HELEN (see preceding entry), the third is coined
by Pound on the same pattern, from ἑλ- plus ἀρχή (note that Pound
likes to transcribe χ by x).

ἐλέησον Kyrie eleison: 79/67: (Κύριε ἐλέησον): have mercy, Lord have
mercy (from the Orthodox liturgy, and the Roman mass).

ἑλέναυς and ἑλέπτολις: 2/6: destroyer of ships and destroyer of cities
(see above, Ἕλανδρος etc.).

Ἑλέναυς, ἕλανδρος, ἑλέπτολις: 7/25: destroyer of ships, destroyer of men,
destroyer of cities (see above, Ἕλανδρος etc.).

ἐμὸν τὸν ἄνδρα : 82/104: ἐμόν my, τὸν ἄνδρα man. Three words from the
refrain to the first part of Theocritus II (lines 17, 22, 27, 32, 37,
42, 47, 52, 57, 63): ἴυγξ ἕλκε τὺ τῆνον ἐμὸν ποτὶ δῶμα   τὸν ἄνδρα ("little
wheel, bring that man back to my house"). Cf. 81/96.

ΕΜΟΣ ΠΟΣΙΣ . . . ΧΕΡΟΣ : 82/101: my husband. . .hand. The words are
from Aeschylus Agamemnon 1404-1406, Clytemnestra speaking:
οὗτός ἐστιν Ἀγαμέμνων, ἐμὸς/ πόσις, νεκρὸς δὲ τῆσδε δεξιᾶς χερός,/ ἔργον δικαίας
τέκτονος ("This is Agamemnon, my husband, dead by my right
hand, and a good job"). See: Literary Essays, 267-275. "On
the ALCIDES' roof/ like a dog" comes from the Watchman's
words in line 3 of the same play: στέγαις Ἀτρειδῶν ἄγκαθεν, κυνὸς δίκην--
although "Alcides'" (instead of Atreidae's) is obscure.

Entha hieron Poseidonos: 40/49: (ἔνθα ἱερὸν Ποσειδῶνος): There (stands)
a temple of Poseidon. From Hanno's Periplus (text in Geo-
graphici Graeci Minores, ed. C. Müller).

ἐνὶ Τροίη: 79/66: in Troy. From the song of the SIRENS to
ODYSSEUS, Odyssey XII, 189-190: ἴδμεν γάρ τοι πάνθ᾽ ὅσ᾽ ἐνὶ Τροίη
εὐρείη/ Ἀργεῖοι Τρῶές τε θεῶν ἰότητι μόγησαν ("for we know all the labors
which Greeks and Trojans performed on the plains of Troy, at
the gods' will"). (See: Personae, 187).

ἐντεῦθεν: 82/105: thence, thereupon.

Epi purgo: 20/91: (ἐπὶ πύργῳ): upon the wall. Iliad III, 153: τοῖοι ἄρα
Τρώων ἡγήτορες ἧντ᾽ ἐπὶ πύργῳ   (So sat the Trojan leaders upon the
wall). From the passage in which the old men of Troy speak of
Helen; cf. below, Neestho.

es thalamon Ἐς θάλαμόν: 39/44: into the bedroom. From Odyssey X,
340. CIRCE invites ODYSSEUS to bed with her, and he asks:
"How can you expect me to do as you say, when you have turned
my companions into swine in this house, when you have me here,
and with treachery in your heart suggest that I go in the bedroom
and climb your bed, only to make me in my nakedness a coward

and no man at all?'' (Faber ed.: θάλαμον).

εσσομένοισι : 74/24: (aspirate ἐσσομένοισι): for generations to come (the form is Homeric, dat. masc. pl. of future participle of verb to be). Probable source, Odyssey XI, 76, from the speech of ELPENOR in the underworld, when he begs ODYSSEUS to pay him funeral honors on his return to CIRCE'S realm, to plant in his memory the oar he used pull.

Euné kai philoteti ephata Kirkh Εὐνῆ καὶ φιλότητι, ἔφατα Κίρκη : 39/44: making love in bed, said CIRCE. From Odyssey X, 335-336. When Circe fails to bewitch ODYSSEUS, she invites him to sheathe his sword; then they may climb into bed, and there make love and know each other. εὐνῇ καὶ φιλότητι is an Homeric phrase frequently recurring to describe the act of love. ἔφατα should read ἔφατο; the word is necessarily elided in Homer, ἔφατ', and Pound's morphology is not letter-perfect. "Kirkh" is a Poundian transliteration in which the -h represents the letter eta (Η, η).

ἔφατα πόσις ἐμὸς : 82/104: she said my husband. ἔφατα (for ἔφατο, see preceding entry) is Homeric. πόσις ἐμός looks like an anaphora of Clytemnestra's words in Agamemnon 1404-1405: see above, ΕΜΟΣ ΠΟΣΙΣ.

Ἡ θεὸς, ἠὲ γυνή. . . . φθεγγώμεθα θᾶσσον   e theos e guné....ptheggometha thasson: 39/43: either a goddess or a woman...let us raise our voices without delay. The line is Odyssey X, 228: ἢ θεὸς ἠὲ γυνή· ἀλλὰ φθεγγώμεθα θᾶσσον. Polites is speaking to Odysseus' companions on CIRCE'S threshold.

Ἡέλιον τ' Ἡέλιον : 15/67: and the Sun, the Sun. ἠέλιος is the Homeric form of ἥλιος.

ἦθος : 79/64, 84/117: "custom, usage; disposition, character; bearing; nature" (L&S).

ΗΛΙΟΝ ΠΕΡΙ ΗΛΙΟΝ : 74/9: (ἥλιον περὶ ἥλιον): the sun around the sun. (Faber ed.: ΗΛΙΟΝ ΠΕΡΙΗΛΙΟΝ)

Ἥλιος : 79/70: the Sun.

ἥλιος, ἅλιος, ἄλιος = μάταιος : 23/107: ἥλιος, sun; ἅλιος (A), of the sea (adj.); ἄλιος (B), fruitless, idle; μάταιος, vain, empty, idle. Pound has just quoted two lines of Stesichorus, in which the Doric form ἅλιος for ἥλιος is used. He looks up ἅλιος in his Abridged Greek-English Lexicon, and finds that there are three definitions: (1) Dor. for ἥλιος; (2) Lat. marinus; (3) = μάταιος, deriv. uncertain. Cf. above, alixantos etc.

Eri men ai de kudoniai: 39/45: (Ἦρι μὲν αἴ τε Κυδώνιαι) : In the spring the quinces. A fragment of Ibycus begins with these words, Lyra Graeca II, fr. 1. p. 84 (see: OBGV, no. 164). See: Personae, 87.

ΘΕΛΓΕΙΝ : 74/15: (θέλγειν, infinitive of θέλγω): to enchant, bewitch, which is what CIRCE, to whom Pound again returns, did; also, in Homer, to cheat, cozen (see L&S).

θέμις: 80/71: "law (not as fixed by statute, but) as established by custom; justice, right" (L&S)

Thumon: 62/91: (θυμόν, accus. sing. of Homeric θυμός, with many meanings): "soul, spirit; breath, life, strength; desire; temper; courage; anger; heart; mind" (L&S).

Ἴακχε, Ἴακχε, χαῖρε: Iacchos, Iacchos, hail. Iacchos is a mystic name
of DIONYSUS.

Ἴακχος, Io! Κύθηρα, Io!: 79/67: Iacchos, Io! CYTHERA, Io! See
preceding entry, and below, Io! and Κύθηρα.

Ἴυγξ. . . . ἐμὸν ποτὶ δῶμα τὸν ἄνδρα: 81/96: Little wheel .... man to my
house. Cf. above, ἐμὸν τὸν ἄνδρα. In this idyll, which is a dramatic
monologue, a girl is trying to cast a spell upon her faithless
lover, and using a magic wheel.

ἰχώρ: 79/69; 82/104: "ichor, the juice, (not blood, that flows in the
veins of gods; later simply,) blood" (L&S).

Io!: 79/67: (ἰώ): "exclamation, chiefly in dramatic poetry (lyric);
freq. repeated, esp. in invoking aid, often with names of gods"
(L&S).

Katholou: 74/19: (καθόλου): generalities. See above, hekasta.

καὶ Ἴδα, θεά: 77/49: and Ida, goddess. Ida is the hill in the Troad
where the marriage of Anchises and Aphrodite was consummated,
also the scene of the judgment of Paris.

Καὶ Μοῖραι᾽ Ἄδονιν/ Kai Moirai᾽ Adonin: 47/30, 33: And the Fates -
(cry over) ADONIS. From Bion's Lament for Adonis, of which
lines 93-94 read: αἰαῖ δ᾽ ὀξὺ λέγοντι πολὺ πλέον ἢ τύ, Διώνα᾽/καὶ Μοῖραι
τὸν Ἄδονιν ἀνακλαίοισιν ἐν Ἀιδα ... (The Graces utter their shrill cry
even louder than you, Dione; and the Fates weep for Adonis in
the world below). This, at any rate is Pound's reading of the
lines, though the text is doubtful, and mss. and edd. are at con-
siderable variance. What Pound means by the apostrophe after
Μοῖραι is obscure. (Faber ed.: καὶ Μοῖρα τ᾽ Ἄδονιν).

κακὰ φάρμακ᾽ ἔδοκεν/ kaka pharmak edoken: 39/43, 74/15: she (Circe)
had given them dreadful drugs. From Odyssey X, 213: τοὺς αὐτὴ
κατέθελξεν, ἐπεὶ κακὰ φάρμακ᾽ ἔδωκεν ([wolves and lions] that she had
bewitched, for she had given them dreadful drugs).

καλλιπλόκαμα: 77/45: with beautiful locks. καλλιπλόκαμος is an adj.
with the same ending for masc. and fem. (Pound here gives a
solecistic fem. form), and used of persons only: so in the Iliad
of DEMETER and THETIS, and Pindar of HELEN in Olympian
III, 1.

καλὸν ἀοιδιάει/ Kalon aoidiaei: 39/43: she sings beautifully. Sc. the
woman in CIRCE'S house. From the words of Polites, Odyssey
X, 227.

kalos k'àgathos: 33/11: (καλὸς κἀγαθός): "originally denotes a perfect
gentleman; but later in a moral sense, a perfect character"
(L&S).

Karxèdoniōn Basileos: 40/51: (Καρχηδονίων βασιλέως): of the king of the
Carthaginians. From Hanno's Periplus.

Kirkê: 74/15: (Κίρκη): CIRCE.

Κόρη; Kore: 79/68; 83/111: Daughter, i.e., PERSEPHONE, Daughter
of DEMETER.

ΚΟΡΗ, ἈΓΛΑΟΣ ἈΛΑΟΥ: 74/20: Daughter, the blind man's
shining...(?). Cf. above, ἀγλαὸς ἀλάου κτλ. Κόρη is PERSEPHONE,
while ἀλαοῦ seems to refer to TIRESIAS. ἀγλαός is masc., and
does not properly construe with Κόρη, fem.

Κόρη, Δελιὰ δεινά: 76/35: Daughter (PERSEPHONE), dread DELIA

Κόρη , maiden, daughter, is used of other maiden deities, but esp. of the Daughter of DEMETER, Persephone. Δελιά seems to be written for Δηλία, i.e., ARTEMIS, virgin goddess of Delos.

Κόρη καὶ Δήλια καὶ Μαῖα : 79/70: Daughter (PERSEPHONE) and Delia (Artemis, cf. preceding entry) and Maia (mother of Hermes).

Κύδιστ' ἀθανάτων, πολυώνυμε,/ παγκρατὲς/ αἰεὶ/ Ζεῦ, φύσεως ἀρχηγέ,/ νόμου μέτα πάντα/ κυβερνῶν : 71/167: (for παγκρατὲς read παγκρατὲς): Most honored of the immortals, worshipped under many names, all-powerful always, Zeus, first cause of nature, who govern all things with law. These are the first two lines (dactylic hexameters, which Pound has divided in his own way) of Cleanthes' Hymn to Zeus, OBGV no. 483.

Κύθηρα: 77/46: CYTHERA; Aphrodite is usually Κυθέρεια, Cytherea, so named from the city Cythera in Crete, or from the island of Cythera. But Pound calls the goddess herself Cythera.

Κύθηρα δεινά : 76/34, 80/89, 84/116: dread (or fearful) CYTHERA.

Κύπρις : 76/36: Cypris (the Cyprian goddess), i.e., APHRODITE.

Κύπρις 'Αφροδίτη : 79/70: Cypris Aphrodite (cf. preceding entry).

λιγύρ' : 74/17: (nom. fem. sing. of the adj. λιγυρός, elided): clear, shrill. Cf. "the sharp song;; in the live above, and next entry.

Ligur' aoide: 20/89, 94: (λιγυρ' ἀοιδή) : clear, sweet song. As of the Sirens in Odyssey XII, 183. Cf. preceding entry.

λύκοι ὀρέστεροι, ἠδὲ λέοντες/ lukoi oresteroi ede leontes: 39/43: mountain wolves and lions. From Odyssey X, 212: in CIRCE'S realm were mountain wolves and lions, which she held in thrall, after giving them dreadful drugs.

lotophagoi: 20/93: (λωτοφάγοι) : lotus-eaters. Odyssey IX, 82-104.

Maya: 76/37: (Μαῖα) : Maia, mother of Hermes (presumably in this context).

μεταθεμένων τε τῶν χρωμενων ; Metathemenon te ton krumenon;

ΜΕΤΑΘΕΜΕΝΩΝ ; Metathemenon: 53/19; 74/18; 76/41; 77/46; 78/59: The words are taken from a context in Aristotle, Politics 1257b 16: ὀτὲ δὲ πάλιν λῆρος εἶναι δοκεῖ τὸ νόμισμα καὶ νόμος παντάπασι, φύσει δ' οὐδέν, ὅτι μεταθεμένων τε τῶν χρωμένων οὐδενὸς ἄξιον οὐδὲ χρήσιμον πρὸς οὐδὲν τῶν ἀναγκαίων ἐστί , . . . "In opposition to this view there is another which is sometimes held. On this view currency is regarded as a sham, and entirely a convention. Naturally and inherently (the supporters of the view argue) a currency is a nonentity; for if those who use a currency give it up in favour of another, that currency is worthless, and useless for any of the necessary purposes of life" (Barker's translation; the words underlined translate the Greek μεταθεμένων τῶν χρωμένων). The recurrence of the phrase out of context always points to the context itself: Aristotle on property and the art of acquisition, Politics I. viii-xi. Because Pound's economics are often thought to be medieval (in both the chronological and the derogatory sense), it might be well to quote a passage from Barker's Introduction (pp. lv-lvi), showing clearly the historical filiation of economic thought: "...The theory of the polis included studies to which we should now give a separate existence -- in particular the theory of economics... There is much writing on"economics"

in the fourth century. It dealt partly with household management
(the literal meaning of oikonomia), and partly with public economy or state finance. There is the Oeconomicus of Xenophon,
which gave inspiration to Ruskin; there is an Oeconomica falsely
ascribed to Aristotle; there is a treatise by Xenophon On the
Revenues of Athens; there is economic theory in the Republic
and the Laws of Plato; there is the famous and profoundly influential theory of exchange and of interest in the first book of the
Politics, which affected so deeply the canonists of the Middle
Ages. Such economic theory, which in turn is subordinated to
(or, perhaps one should rather say, is the crown of) ethics,
admits of no isolation of the economic motive, and of no abstrac-
tion of economic facts as a separate branch of enquiry. It is a
theory of the ways in which households and cities can properly
use the means at their disposal for the better living of a good
life. Wealth, on this basis, is a means to a moral end; as such a
means, it is necessarily limited by the end, and it must not be
greater -- as equally it must not be less -- than what the end
requires. This is not socialism; but it is a line of thought in-
imical to capitalism..." The frequent allusions in the Cantos to
the text of the Politics is an indication of the latter's importance
in the formulation of Pound's thought; Pound has gone back from
medieval economic scripture to the source, which he has com-
pulsed in the original.

Molü; μῶλυ : 47/31; 53/9: moly, the magic herb which Hermes gave
    to ODYSSEUS (Odyssey X, 305) to counteract the drugs of
    CIRCE.

Neestho: 20/91: (νεέσθω) : let her go back (imperative 3rd sing. of
    νέομαι, return). From Iliad III, 159 (cf. above, Epi purgo): ἀλλὰ
    καὶ ὣς τοίη περ ἐοῦσ' ἐν νηυσὶ νεέσθω ("But even so, and such though she
    be, let her take ship and go back"). The old men of Troy,
    seated upon the wall, are speaking of HELEN.

Nekuia: 74/9: (Νέκυια) : The Evocation of the Dead, the name of the
    eleventh book of the Odyssey. TYRO and ALCMENA are among
    the dead whom Odysseus sees in the underworld: Tyro at XI,
    235, and Alcmena at XI, 266.

neson amumona; ΝΗΣΟΝ ᾿ΑΜΥΜΟΝΑ : 20/94; 76/41: (νῆσον ἀμύμονα) : a
    noble island. From Odyssey XII, 261-262: αὐτίκ' ἔπειτα θεοῦ ἐς
    ἀμύμονα νῆσον/ ἱκόμεθ' . . . ("We came next to a noble island belong-
    ing to a god", i.e., Thrinakia, where Odysseus' companions
    killed the cattle of the Sun).

νους; Nous: 25/119; 40/51: (νοῦς): "mind, sense, wit; heart; resolve,
    purpose; reason, intellect; mind as the active principle of the
    universe" (L&S). (Faber ed.: νόος)

Νύξ : 74/16: Night.

Ho Bios: 20/92: (ὁ βίος): Life.

οἱ βάρβαροι; hoi barbaroi: 76/37: the barbarians.

ΟΙ ΧΘΟΝΙΟΙ: 83/111: (οἱ χθόνιοι) : the gods of the nether world; or
    simply, those of the world below.

ΟΎ ΤΙΣ ; οὔ τις : 74/3, 4, 8; 80/77: (Οὖτις): Noman. This is the name
    for himself that ODYSSEUS gives the Cyclops in Odyssey IX, 366.

Pallas Δίκη : 78/57: (Παλλάς): Pallas (who art) Justice. Pallas is
Athena, and Dikê Justice. Pound seems to be invoking the goddess, using Dikê as her epithet.

πάντα ῥεῖ: 80/90; 83/107: all things flow (as Heraclitus is said to
have said: See: Guide to Kulchur, Index, passim).

periplum: 59/70; 74/9, 21, 22, 25; 76/30, 77/43, 44; 82/105:
(περίπλους) : circumnavigation. Periplus also designates an account of a coasting voyage, such as that of Hanno. Note, however,
that Pound always writes "periplum".

Περσεφόνεια: 74/21; 83/111: PERSEPHONE (Homeric form of
Περσεφόνη).

ΠΟΙΚΙΛΟΘΡΟΝ', 'ΑΘΑΝΑΤΑ: 76/40: richly enthroned, immortal. The
opening words of Sappho's hymn to APHRODITE, Lyra Graeca
I, fr. 1, p. 182 (OBGV, no. 140): Ποικιλόθρον' ἀθάνατ' 'Αφρόδιτα
("Immortal Aphrodite on your many-splendored throne"). Cf.
above, 'ΑΘΑΝΑΤΑ.

πολλά παθεῖν : 76/35: to experience, or suffer, much. See: Odyssey
I, 4: πολλὰ δ' ὅ γ' ἐν πόντῳ πάθεν ἄλγεα ὃν κατὰ θυμόν (and his heart ex-
perienced many sufferings upon the sea).

Pollon d'anthropon iden: 12/54: (πολλῶν δ' ἀνθρώπων ἴδεν) : and of many
men he saw (the cities, and knew their mind). From Odyssey I,
3: πολλῶν δ' ἀνθρώπων ἴδεν ἄστεα καὶ νόον ἔγνω.

Polumetis; πολύμητις: 9/36; 78/60: of many counsels (stock Homeric
epithet of Odysseus).

poluphloisboios: 74/5: (πολυφλοίσβοιο): loud-roarings. πολυφλοίσβοιο is
the genitive of the adj. πολύφλοισβος, an Homeric epithet of the sea,
e.g. in Iliad I, 34: βῆ δ' ἀκέων παρὰ θῖνα πολυφλοίσβοιο θαλάσσης (silently
he made his way to the shore of the loud-roaring sea). Pound
has made a noun out of the genitive form of the adj., and made it
plural by adding an -s (in diminutive loud-roarings). See:
Personae, p. 181.

ποτὶ βένθεα/...: 23/108. See above, "Ἅλιος δ' 'γπεριονίδας κτλ.

'ΡΕΙ ΠΑΝΤΑ: 74/11: (ῥεῖ πάντα): all things flow. Cf. above, πάντα ῥεῖ.

ΣΕΙΡΗΝΕΣ: 74/21: (Σειρῆνες): SIRENS (Odyssey XII, 142-200).

Σίγα μαλ' αὖθις δευτέραν : 5/19: Silence once more a second time. The
words are taken out of two lines in Aeschylus Agamemnon, 1344-
1345: ΧΟ. σῖγα· τίς πληγὴν ἀυτεῖ καιρίως οὐτασμένος ;/ ΑΓ. ὤμοι μάλ' αὖθις,
δευτέραν πεπληγμένος (Chorus: "Silence! Who cries that he is struck
a mortal blow?'' Agamemnon (within): "Ah! once more, I am
struck a second time!'').

Σίγα, σίγα: 5/19: Silence, silence! Cf. preceding entry.

τάδ' ὧδ' ἔχει: 58/69: That's how it is. The last words of Clytemnestra's
speech, Aeschylus Agamemnon 1401-1406 ("This is Agamemnon,
my husband, dead by my right hand, and a good job. That's how
it is''). Cf. above, ΕΜΟΣ ΠΟΣΙΣ.

Tan aoidan: 29/144: (τὰν ἀοιδάν): Song (accus. with definite article of
ἀοιδή, in the Doric form with α, perhaps in reminiscence of
Theocritus, e.g. I, 62).

Tethneke: 23/109: (τέθνηκε): he is dead.

ΤΙΘΩΝΩΙ: 74/13: (Τιθωνῷ, dative of Τιθωνός): to Tithonus (husband of
Eos, the Dawn, granted immortal life by Zeus, but not immortal
youth).

τίς ἀδικεῖ: 76/39: Who wrongs (you)? Apparently a reminiscence of
    APHRODITE'S question to Sappho, Lyra Graeca I, fr. 1, p. 184
    (OBGV, no. 140): τίς τ', ὦ Ψαπφ', ἀδικήει;
To kalon: 58/64: (τὸ καλόν): the beautiful.
τὸ πᾶν: 80/89: the all, the whole.
Τυ Διώνα/ Tu Diona; Τυ Διώνα, Και Μοῖραι/ Tu Diona, Kai Moirai: 47/30,
    33: you, Dione; you, Dione, and the Fates. From Bion's Lament
    for Adonis, 93-94: cf. above, Και Μοῖραι' Ἄδονιν. Dione was the
    mythical mother of APHRODITE, but the name in this context
    would designate Aphrodite herself. (Faber ed.:Τυ Διώνα, Και Μοῖρα)
tu theleis...apothanein: 64/106: (read τί θέλεις; ἀποθανεῖν): ''What do
    you want?'' ''To die.'' From Petronius Satiricon XLVIII, 8:
    ''Nam Sibyllam quidem Cumis ego ipse oculis meis uidi in
    ampulla pendere, et cum illi pueri dicerent: Σίβυλλα, τί θέλεις;
    respondebat illa: 'Αποθανεῖν θέλω.'' Cited by Eliot in his epigraph
    to The Waste Land.
ὕδωρ, "ΥΔΩΡ, Hudor, 'udor: 83/106, 107, 109: water.
"ΥΛΗ, ὕλη: 30/148, 35/25, 77/49: ''wood, woodland, wood cut down,
    stuff, material, matter'' (L&S).
ὑπὲρ μόρον: 80/90: beyond what is destined μόρος, fate or destiny, is
    Homeric: the phrase is used, e.g., in Odyssey I, 34, 35).
'Yperionides: 23/108: ('Υπεριονίδης): son of Hyperion, i.e., Helius,
    the Sun.
ὑπὸ χθονὸς: 77/46: under the earth.
φαίνεταί μοι: 74/23: He seems to me. Sappho's poem ''To Anactoria'',
    Lyra Graeca I, fr. 2, p. 186 (OBGV, no. 141) begins with the words:
    Φαίνεταί μοι κῆνος ἴσος θεοῖσιν (''A very god he seems to me ...'').
φαίνε-τ-τ-τ-τττ-αί μοι: 74/22: the quotation of the preceding entry,
    stuttered.
phtheggometha thasson/ φθεγγώμεθα θᾶσσον: 47/30: (Faber ed.: θᾶσσον):
    let us raise our voices without delay. From Odyssey X, 228: cf.
    above, Ἡ θεὸς ἠὲ κτλ.
Phoibos: 21/99: (Φοῖβος): Phoebus, i.e. Apollo (the name is supposed
    to signify Bright or Pure).
Xaire: 84/117: (χαῖρε): hail.
ΧΑΡΙΤΕΣ: 74/21; 80/79: (Χάριτες): the GRACES.
χθόνια γέα, Μάτηρ: 74/13: nether earth, Mother. The poets often speak
    of Mother Earth. γέα is Ionic for γῆ, μάτηρ Doric for μήτηρ.
ΧΘΟΝΙΟΣ: 82/104: (χθόνιος): beneath the earth, nether; or sprung from
    the earth, earth-born (the adj. is in its nom. masc. sing. form).
χθόνος; ΧΘΟΝΟΣ; Xthonos: 77/43; 82/104; 83/111: (accent χθονός, gen.
    of χθών): of the earth.
Ψυχάριον ἀι βάσταξον νεκρὸν: 77/44: (read ψ. εἶ βάσταζον ν.): You are a
    tiny soul supporting a corpse. Saying attributed to Epictetus in
    the Meditations of Marcus Aurelius IV, 41.

APPENDIX B: CHINESE

Appendix B contains all Chinese expressions in logographic form, arranged in sequence by canto numbers. Italicized phrases without specific source are from the Cantos; where other sources are drawn upon, explicit reference is given. ALL CAPS indicate cross reference to the appropriate entry in the General Index. Underlined location references indicate sources of material quoted from the Cantos.

正 (chêng⁴   51/46; 60/79; 66/128; 68/146: to regulate + the name: to define the correct terms; to rectify the names or terms: a true definition.

名 ming²)

止 (chih³)   52/7: to stop, to desist.

堯 (Yao²)   53/9; 56/48,55: the name of the emperor, YAO.

舜 (Shun⁴)   53/9; 56/48,55: the name of the emperor, SHUN.

禹 (Yü³)   53/9; 56/48: the name of the emperor, YU.

皋 (Kao¹   53/10: the name of the emperor, KAO-YAO.

陶 yao²)

新 (hsin¹   53/11: new + daily + new: to renovate, to make new daily: Day by day make it new; Confucius, 36: as the sun makes it new/ day by day make it new/ Yet make it new again.

[269]

日 jih⁴

日 jih⁴

新 hsin¹)

夏 (Hsia⁴)   53/11: name of the Hsia (HIA) dynasty.

周 (Chou¹)   53/14, 20; 56/55: name of the Chou (TCHEOU) dynasty.

仲 (Chung⁴   53/18; 56/54: an alternative name of CONFUCIUS.

尼 ni⁴)

新 (Hsin¹)   54/24: new. (See 53/11).

仁 jên²   仁 (jên²   55/36: virtuous + men + use + wealth +(to) develop + themselves + un + virtuous + men + use + themselves + (to) become + prosperous: Confucius, 83: The humane man uses his wealth as a means to distinction, the inhumane becomes a mere harness, an accessory to his takings.

者 chê³   者 chê³

以 i³   以 i³

              財 ts'ai²

              發 fa¹

身 shên[1]　　身 shên[1]

發 fa[1]　　不 pu[4]

財 ts'ai[2])

漢 (Han[4])　　56/55: name of the HAN dynasty.

變 (pien[4])　　57/59: to transform, to change: <u>a word to make change</u>.

福 (fu[2])　　61/84: prosperity: <u>the Happiness ideogram</u>.

茶 (ch'a[2])　　62/87: tea.

正 (chêng[4])　　63/98; <u>67/133</u>: upright, true, exact, straight: <u>clear as to definitions</u>.

中 (chung[1])　　<u>70/159</u>; 76/32; 77/42; 84/118: the middle; the axis, center, pivot: <u>I am for balance</u>; <u>Confucius</u>, 103: <u>an axis round which something turns</u>.

明 (ming[2])　　74/7; <u>84/117</u>: bright, clear, intelligent; to understand, to cleanse, to illustrate: <u>these are distinctions</u>; Confucius, 20: <u>the sun and moon, the total light process, the radiation, reception and reflection of light; hence, the intelligence</u>. Bright, brightness, shining.

莫 (mo[4])　　74/8: not, do not, there is not.

誠 (ch'êng)　　76/32: honesty, sincerity: <u>the word is made perfect</u>; Confucius, 20: <u>the precise definition of the word, pictorially the sun's lance coming to rest on the precise spot verbally</u>.

先 (hsien¹   <u>77/43</u>: before + after: first and last, succes-
              sive: <u>what precedes and what follows</u>.

後 hou⁴)

何 (ho²   <u>77/43</u>; 80/76: how far: <u>how is it far, if you</u>
              <u>think of it?</u>; (See <u>Analects</u>, IX, xxx, 2).

遠 yüan³)

旦 (tan⁴)   77/44: the dawn.

口 (k'ou³)   <u>77/44</u>: the mouth: <u>is the sun that is the god's</u>
              <u>mouth</u>.

非 (fei¹   77/45: (it is) wrong + that + spirit + (thus) +
              sacrifice + (it is) flattery + besides: it is
              flattery for a person to sacrifice to a spirit
              which does not belong to him: <u>not one's own</u>

其 ch'i²   <u>spirit and sacrifice is flattery bi gosh</u>; to
              sacrifice to a spirit not one's own is flattery
              <u>(sycophancy)</u>; (See <u>Analects</u>, II, xxiv, 1).

鬼 kuei³

而 erh²

祭 chi⁴

之 chih¹

諂 ch'an³

也 yeh³)

志 (chih⁴) 77/45: will, purpose: directio voluntatis, as lord over the heart; Confucius, 22: the will, the direction of the will.

符 (fu² 77/46: agree with + token, credential; a warrant, commission; note: on 77/54 the phrase is translated: halves of a tally stick, which is translation of only the fu²; see Mathews, A

節 chieh²) Chinese-English Dictionary (Revised, American Edition, 1943) index 1922, example 7, p. 283.

成 (ch'êng²) 77/53: to complete: bringest to focus.

道 (tao⁴) 78/60: a path, the truth; the doctrine, the way; Confucius, 22: the process....an orderly movement under lead of the intelligence.

辭 (tz'u² 79/64: speech, words; an expression or phrase, message + intelligent, successful; to succeed: to succeed in saying exactly what you wish to say; what matters is / to get it across; see

達 ta²) Mathews, op. cit., index 5956, example 17, p. 852: In language it is simply required that it conveys the meaning.

Note: 达 is error for 達

黃 (huang² 79/65: yellow + bird + stops (alights, perches, comes to rest); see Confucius, 39: yellow bird...comes to rest; Classic Anthology, ode 230, p. 143.

鳥 niao³

止 chih³)

犬 (ch'uan³) 80/77: dog.

仁 (jên[2])   82/103: perfect virtue, humanheartedness:
              humanitas; Confucius, 22: humanity, in the
              full sense of the word, "manhood." The man
              and his full contents.

勿 (wu[4]   83/110: do not + assist + to grow: don't work
              so hard, which see in General Index; see
              Mathews, op. cit., index 7208, example 5, p.
              1076: let it grow naturally.

助 chu[4]

長 chang[3])

APPENDIX C: CHRONOLOGY

Appendix C contains all dates mentioned in the Cantos, set in the framework of a more complete chronological survey. Underlined annotations are from the Cantos; those in brackets are interpolated.

B.C.

2837: 53/8:	Fou Hi taught men to grow barley.
2611: 53/8	
2500-2400: 53/9	
1766: 53/10:	Tching Tang opened the copper mine ... / made discs with square holes in their middles
1231: 53/11:	After five hundred years came then Wen Wang
1106: 53/12	
1079: 53/13	
1078: 53/13	
1053: 53/15	
860: 53/16	
479: 53/19:	Died Kung aged 73
279: 54/21	
213: 54/21	
202: 54/22; 56/51:	Then were HAN
179: 54/23	
157: 54/24	
146: 54/24	
49: 54/26:	The text of books reëstablished

A.D.

33: 25/116:	Also a note from Pontius Pilate dated the ''year 33''
77: 54/26	
107: 54/26	
159: 54/27	
175: 54/27:	and the books were incised in stone
265: 56/51	
274: 54/27	
317: 54/28:	HOAI TI was deposed, MIN TI taken by tartars
396: 54/28	
444: 54/29	
448: 54/29	
460: 54/29	
503-550: 54/30	
581: 54/30:	Came the XIIth dynasty: SOUI

A.D.
 618: 54/31; 56/51
 635: 54/32
 643: 54/32
 662: 54/33
 713-756: 54/33: Honour to HIEUN 'to hell with embroideries,/
                      to hell with the pearl merchants'
 726: 54/34

 756: 54/34
 805: 54/35; 55/36
 820: 55/37
 846: 55/38
 860: 55/38
 923: 55/39: Thus came TçIN into Empire/ calling themselves
                  later TANG
 934: 55/39
 947: 55/39
 950: 56/51
 953: 55/40

 978: 55/41: TAI TSONG brought out the true BOOKS
 993: 55/41
 [996: death of Hugh Capet]
1004: 55/41
1022: 55/42
1042: 55/42
1069: 55/42
1084: 55/44: offered the/ HISTORY, called/ Tsé-tchi tong kien
                  hang mou
 [1152: Eleanor of Aquitaine marries Henry of Anjou, later
       Henry II of England]
1157: 55/45

1172: 55/45
1175: 26/124: first bridge in Rialto
1176: 26/124
1219: 55/46
1225-1265: 56/50
1251: 43/10
1255: 25/115
1265: 29/142: Free go they all as by full manumission/ All
                  serfs of Eccelin my father da Romano
1266: 25/115
1266 (?): 25/116
 [1270: Siena conquered by Charles I of Anjou]

1278: 56/50
1295: 56/50: KUBLAI died heavy with years
 [1310: Council of Ten of Venice established]
1312-1320: 56/52

A.D.
 1323: 25/116
 1335: 25/117
 1340: 25/117: Council of the lords noble, Marc Erizio/ Nic.
                 Speranzo, Tomasso Gradonico
 1344: 25/117
 1361: 40/47

 1362: 40/47
 1368: 56/51,53,54: Came MING thus to KianKing
 1384: 56/56
 1385: 56/56
 1386: 56/56
  [1395: Gian Galeazzo Visconti made duke of Milan]
 1401: 35/25
 1403: 57/57
 1409: 25/117; 57/57
 1413: 24/111

 1415: 25/117; 57/57
 1422: February: 24/110: Thus the book of the mandates
 1423: 35/26 [Francesco Foscari becomes Doge of Venice]
 1425: 21 May: 24/112 [death of Parisina Malatesta, wife of
                 Niccolò d'Este]
 1427: 27 November: 24/110
 1429: 21/96: [death of Giovanni di Ricci de' Medici]
 1430: 57/57; 58/63
 1431: 24/113
 1432: 24/113
 1434: 21/97   [Medici family establishes control of Florence]

 1438: 2 January: 26/123: they came here/ ...mainly to see the
                 greek Emperor: [Council of Ferrara-Florence.]
      25 January: 26/123
      February: 26/123
      8 March: 26/125
  [1440: death of Ginevra d'Este, wife of Sigismondo Malatesta]
 1441: 23/113 [Francesco Sforza marries Bianca Maria Visconti]
 1442: 41/53
      September: 8/32: married him (Sigismundo) his
                 (Francesco's)/ daughter
 1445: 16 March: 9/34
      October: 8/32

 1446: 11/50: And he gone out into Morea,/ Where they sent
             him to do in the Mo'ammeds
  [1447: end of Visconti rule in Milan upon death of Bianca
             Maria Visconti; the Tempio Malatestiana begun]
 1448: November: 8/32
 1449: 7 April: 8/29
      December: 8/32

A.D.

1450: 8/32:   and never quite lost till '50,/ and never quite lost
                 till the end in Romagna; [Francesco Sforza be-
                 comes duke of Milan]
     December: 8/32
1452: 57/58:   In '52 was Emperor's grain ration
     5 August: 8/30
1453: 14 August: 26/126

1454: 20 December: 9/37, 39:   [letters written to Sigismondo
                 Malatesta]
     21 December: 9/38
     22 December: 9/39
1459: 57/58:   Died Yukien the restorer, that had so vile a
                 reward
  [1460: Sigismondo Malatesta excommunicated by Pope Pius II]
1461: 2 December: 26/121
1462: August: 11/48: [Urbino and Papal troops defeat Malatesta
                 at Mondolfo]
     12 October: 26/121
     28 October: 26/122
     12 December: 26/126
  [1468: death of Sigismondo Malatesta]

1469: December: 21/96 [death of Piero de' Medici]
  [1470: death of Isotta degli Atti, third wife of Sigismondo
                 Malatesta]
  [1471: death of Borso d'Este]
  [1473: Sistine Chapel built by Pope Sixtus IV]
  [1494: Medici expelled from Florence]
1497: 57/59:   and in '97 they made a law code
1503: August: 30/149: And in August that year died Pope
                 Alessandro Borgia
1505: 57/59
1511: 15 August: 26/127
1512: 57/60:   [Medici control of Florence restored]

1513: 31 May: 25/119,120:
1516: 5 December: 25/120 [Concordat between Pope Leo X
                 and Francis I of France]
1522: 11 August: 25/119
1527: 46/28:   Thereafter art thickened. Thereafter design went
                 to hell.
  [1534: death of Pandolfo Malatesta]
1536: 56/60   CHI-TSONG did rites at the MING tombs
1537: 25/120
1538: 1/5:   In officina Wecheli, 1538, out of Homer
1548: 26 February: 26/126: was killed in this city/ Lorenzo de
                 Medicis
     29 February: 26/126
  [1569: Cosimo I de'Medici becomes Grand Duke of Tuscany]

A.D.
    1578: 58/62
    1591: 43/13
    1600-1813: 71/163: can remember no British friendship/ during
                        the years that you indicate
    1621: 43/14:   to provide WORK for the populace
    1622: 42/5,8; 43/9,11,12: as long as the MOUNT endure/ there
                        first was the fruit of nature/ there was the
                        whole will of the people
        January: 43/13,14
        2 January: 42/6; 43/16: which date goes in the Sienese
                        calendar
        3 January: 43/13
        6 January: 43/13
        March: 43/13: Donna Orsola of wherever removed from
                        the book/ of the Sienese public women
        4 March: 43/11
        24 March: 43/13: again appeared black money from
                        Florence
        22 December: 43/15
        29 December: 42/6
        30 December: 42/6; 43/16: TTheir HHighnesses gratified/
                        the city of this demand to/ erect a New Monte

    1623: 43/13
        July: 42/4,8
        18 July: 42/4
    1624: 42/8
        21 June: 43/14
        16 July: 43/14: Monte Nuovo, committee to arrange it
        November: 42/3: a mount, a bank, a fund a bottom an/
                        institution of credit
    1625-1635: 58/66: TAI TSONG, son of TAI TSOU, ruling from
                        Mougden
    1626: May: 43/14: more stew about the black money (lead money)
    1628: 19 March: 62/87: [New England Company formed]

    1635: 58/68
    [1644: Ch'ing or Manchu dynasty begins]
    1645: 59/71:   and the Nankings set up a new emperor
    1655: 59/70
    1662: 60/79
    1664: 59/71:   And in the '64 they putt out the Xtians
    1669: 60/77:   PERMIT only Verbiest and his colleagues
    1676: 43/15
    1679: 43/15
    1680: 43/15

    1693: 60/74:   [French Jesuits established in Peiping]
    1694: 46/27   [Bank of England founded]
    1699: 60/75

A.D.
    1700: 49/39:   came Tsing to these hill lakes
    1707: 14 February: 66/129
    1720: 60/78
    1722: 60/78
    1725: 61/80:   Public works for the unemployed
    1735: 61/84:   Died 1735 at 58 [Yong Tching]/ in the 13th year
                        of his reign
          19 October: 62/87: Born 1735; 19th Oct. old style
          30 October: 62/87: 30th new style John Adams

    1736: 61/85
    1739: 71/162
    1745: 71/160
    1749: 43/16
    1750: 50/40:   the arts gone to hell by 1750
    1752: 64/101
    1754: 67/133; 71/163: Mr Shirley in 1754 confided to Dr Franklin
                        a secret/ that is a scheme for taxing the colo-
                        nies by act of Parliament
    1755: 71/165
    1758: 63/98
    1759: 71/160

    1760-1775: 33/11: (the Revolution) …was in the minds of the
                        people
    1760: 63/100:   [accession of George II of England]
    1761: 70/157; 71/160: In '61 came writs of assistance
    1764: 71/163
    1765: 66/128   [Stamp Act becomes law in the colonies: 22 March]
          1 November: 64/102
    1766: 44/17; 77/46
          December: 32/7
    1767: 64/108   [Townshend Acts; Monticello built]
          11 July: 64/104: J.Q.A. Born July eleventh
          1 October: 64/104

    1768: 64/104, 108   [British troops sent to Boston to meet colo-
                        nial unrest]
          17 January: 66/128
          17 June: 66/129
    1769: 64/104, 108
          December: 64/105
    1770: 62/89:   [Boston Massacre: 5 March; John Adams defends
                        Captain Preston: October]
    1771: 64/107
    1772: 21 December: 66/130
    1773: 31/6; 64/108; 67/133; 70/156: [Boston Tea Party: 16
                        December] the sea nymphs/ Hyson, Congo,
                        Bohea

A.D.

1774: 62/90; 69/149; 70/158; 71/160,163,166: [First Continental
              Congress assembles: 5 September]
      9 February: 62/90: 9 Feb to end of that year probably
      very laborious/ Birth of a Nation
      7 June: 62/90
      17 September: 65/110: America will support Massachusetts
      1 December: 65/110
1775: 67/137 [Second Continental Congress convenes: May]
      17 April: 67/136
      19 April: 67/136: [battles of Lexington and Concord]
      September: 65/111
      20 October: 65/112

1776: 67/137,138
      6 April: 65/113 [Congress opens ports to all countries not
              subjects of Great Britain]
      12 May: 62/91
      7 June: 62/91
      2 July: 62/91 [Richard Henry Lee's resolution declaring
              independence adopted by Congress]
1777: 33/11; 68/142 [John Adams appointed commissioner to
              France: 28 November]
      12 June: 65/114
      August: 26/128
      September: 65/114
      11 November: 65/114

1778: 65/114   [France recognizes American independence: 6
              February; John Adams begins ten-year residence
              in Europe as American diplomat; Articles of
              Confederation adopted]
      19 February: 65/114
      1 March: 65/116
      June: 21/98
1779: March: 33/10 [John Adams appointed minister plenipoten-
              tairy]
1780: 65/120, 121; 68/145 [John Adams appointed minister to
              the United Provinces]
      6 January: 69/150
      February: 68/146
      11 May: 69/151
      17 July: 68/146
      12 November: 68/147
      24 December: 65/121
      25 December: 68/148
      31 December: 69/149

1781: 1 January: 69/149 [Surrender of Cornwallis at Yorktown:
              19 October]
      February: 33/12

A.D.
>   4 December: 69/150
> 1782: 50/40; 62/92; 65/123: Birth of a Nation; [Martin Van
>   Buren born]
>   January: 65/125
>   25 January: 69/150
>   19 April: 62/92: John got his answer and recognition
>   26 April: 69/150
>   5 August: 69/150
>   14 September: 65/122: Independence of America is assured
>   29 September: 69/151
>   October: 62/92
>   7 October: 69/151: Treaty ready by monday (J.A. to
>   Jefferson)
>   8 October: 65/122 [John Adams completes treaty with
>   United Provinces]: a treaty of commerce, by no
>   arts or disguises
>   7 November: 69/151 [John Adams and other American
>   negotiators in Paris, working on treaty with
>   England]
>
> 1783: 44/17; 71/163 [Great Britain recognizes American inde-
>   pendence: 3 September]
>   3 May: 65/125
>   17 May: 65/125
>   27 October: 66/126
> 1784: 22 June: 66/126 [Congress ratifies peace treaty with Great
>   Britain: 14 January]
> 1785: 31/6; 44/17; 70/158 [John Adams appointed Minister to
>   Court of St. James's]
>   27 May: 69/152
>   August: 41/55
>   19 August: 69/152
> 1786: 19 April: 66/127: anniversary of the battle of Lexington
>
> 1787: 31/4,17; 67/139; 69/153 [Constitutional Convention: 25
>   May-17 September]
>   2 August: 31/4
> 1788: 62/92; 63/99 [John Adams relieved of appointment to
>   Court of St James's; returns to America]
>   2 May: 31/5
> 1789: 71/161 [French revolution; storming of the Bastille: 14
>   July]
> 1790: 19 April: 70/158
> 1791: 50/41; 70/155: J.A. vice president and president of the
>   senate
>   10 November: 50/41: end of representative government/
>   18th Brumale, 10th of November
> 1792: 44/19   [death of Leopold II, Holy Roman Emperor]
> 1795: 62/94
>   18 June: 62/94

A.D.
___

1796-1854: 62/95: <u>no president chosen against Pennsylvania</u>
1796: 44/19 [John Adams elected President]
    18 July: 66/127
1798: 70/155 [Alien and Sedition Acts]
    1 July: 70/155
1799: 44/19 [Tuscany invaded by Napoleon; Ferdinand III flees]
    18 February: 62/95
    26 April: 44/19
    · 28 June: 44/19: <u>came men of Arezzo/ past the Porta</u>
                    <u>Romana and went into the ghetto/ there to sack</u>
                    <u>and burn hebrews</u>
    3 July: 44/19
1799: (?): 18 December: 44/20

1800: 44/19; 50/41; 71/164,166: <u>JOHN ADAMS/ FOR PEACE/</u>
                      <u>1800</u>
    14 June: 50/41: [Napoleon defeats the Austrians at
                Marengo]
    22 October: 44/20
    28 December: 70/156: <u>I leave the state with its coffers full</u>
                [John Adams prepares to leave the Presidency]
1801: 50/41 [Tuscany becomes Kingdom of Etruria under
            Louis, Duke of Parma]
    4 March: 63/97 [Thomas Jefferson inaugurated as
            President]
1804: 65/114 [Napoleon crowned emperor at Paris: 2 December]
1806: 74/25
1807: 5 December: 44/21 [Maria Louise of Tuscany deposed]
1808: 71/160 [Tuscany annexed to France with Maria Anna
            Elisa, sister of Napoleon, made Grand Duchess
            the next year]

1809: 34/15; 71/161 [John Quincy Adams appointed minister to
            Russia]
1811: 4 January: 34/15
    16 April: 31/5
1812: 14 August: 34/16 [declaration of war between U.S. and
            Great Britain: 18 June]
    1812 (?): 15 November: 33/12
1813: 31/5; 71/162: <u>Taxes laid, war supported. This must be</u>
    15 November: 31/6
1814: 31/6; 67/138 [U.S. peace commission meets British at
            Ghent: 8 August; Treaty of Ghent signed 24
            December]
    July: 71/163
1815: 33/11; 71/164,165: <u>"Our correspondence is considered a</u>
            <u>curiosity by both parties"/ Adams to Jefferson;</u>
            [Congress of Vienna]
    18 March: 34/16

A.D.

        20 March: 34/16: <u>The King, Bourbon, left the Tuilleries</u>
        13 November: 33/10

1818: 71/167
1819: 67/137
1820: 34/17; 83/107 [John Quincy Adams serving as Secretary
            of State under Monroe: 1817-1825]
        18 January: 34/17: I (J.Q.A.) called at the President's
        25 December: 34/18: <u>read aloud after breakfast</u>/ <u>from</u>
            Pope's "Messiah"
1821: 37/31   [Napoleon dies: 5 May]
1823: 12 June: 32/8
1824: 2 October: 34/18 [Ferdinand III of Tuscany dies; John
            Quincy Adams elected President]
1825: 63/97
1826: 34/19   [deaths of John Adams and Thomas Jefferson:
            4 July]

1828: 26 May: 34/19
1829: March: 34/19 [John Quincy Adams leaves Presidency;
            Andrew Jackson inaugurated]
      November: 34/19; 37/33
      December: 37/33 [President Jackson raises question of
            the continuance of the Bank of the United States:
            8 December]
      13 December: 34/19
1830: 37/34   [Jackson again attacks Bank of the United States:
            6 December]
      October: 37/33
1831: 9 November: 34/19: "I took seat Number 203": [John
            Quincy Adams goes to House of Representatives,
            serving from 5 December 1831-23 February
            1848]
1832: 2 March: 34/20 [Bank of the United States presents to
            Congress an application for renewal of its
            charter: 9 January]
      3 March: 34/20

1834: 37/35
1837: 13 April: 34/20 [Martin Van Buren inaugurated President]
      May: 37/33 [panic begins as New York banks suspend
            specie payments: 10 May]
  [1838: Henry Adams born]
1842: 33/12; 38/41: <u>Said Herr Krupp (1842): guns are a merchan-</u>
            <u>dise</u>/ <u>I approach them from the industrial end.</u>
1843: 21 December: 34/21
1847: 38/41
1848: 33/13   [John Quincy Adams dies while speaking on the
            House floor: 23 February]

A.D.

1849: 33/13
1850: 50/43; 67/139 [Clay's Compromise of 1850]

1854: 21 June: 37/35
1858: 40/47:   THE MOST GLORIOUS MR./D'ARCY/ is per-
               mitted for 50 years to dig up the subsoil of/
               Persia.
1859: 30 October: 50/43 [Leopold II, Grand Duke of Tuscany,
               deposed]
1860: 76/31
1861: 46/27   [Fort Sumter fired upon, beginning Civil War: 12
               April]
1862: 33/12, 13
1864: 33/12; 46/27
1868: 38/41:   Austria had some Krupp cannon;/ Prussia had
               some Krupp cannon
1870: 19/84; 28/139 [outbreak of Franco-Prussian war]
1871: 33/12

1874: 38/41
1876: 40/48
1880: 74/13; 76/31
1885-1900: 38/41: produced ten thousand cannon/ to 1914, 34
               thousand
   [1885: Ezra Pound born: 30 October]
   [1886: death of Charles Francis Adams: 21 November]
1900: 38/41
   [1901: death of Queen Victoria]
1904: 77/43:   I'll tell you wot izza comin'/ Sochy-lism is
               a-comin'
1906: 81/95

1907: 40/48
1908: 27/130; 28/136; 41/54 [Pound begins European residence]
1909: 27/130
1910: 27/130; 74/22; 77/50
1912: 74/26
1914: 38/40,41; 41/54; 77/47; 80/84: [Archduke Franz Ferdinand
               of Austria assassinated: 28 June]
       May: 38/38: "Will there be war?" "No, Miss Wi'let,/ On
               account of bizschniz relations."
1915: 80/80:   a street demonstration/ in Soho for Italy's entry
               into combat
1917: 81/95   [U.S. declares war on Germany: 6 April]
1918: 42/3   [end of World War I: 11 November]

1919: 46/25   [D'Annunzio occupies Fiume: 12 September]
1920: 27/130; 78/59
   [1922: Mussolini marches on Rome: 28 October]
1923: 33/13; 38/39

A.D.
    1924: 74/11   [Pound establishes residence at Rapallo, Italy]
    1925: 74/4   [Publication of A Draft of XVI Cantos]
        23 May: 28/133
    1926: 48/34
    1927: 27/130; 38/39
    1929: 38/37   [New York Stock Market crashes: October]
    1932: 37/31   [Franklin D. Roosevelt elected President]

    1933: 41/52,56
    1935: 46/29   [Italy invades Ethopia: 2 October]
    1937: 54/26
    1938: 74/5; 84/117: vide the expedition of Frobenius' pupils about
                1938
    1939: 84/115: [Germany invades Poland: 1 September]
      [1940: Pound begins broadcasts over Radio Rome]
      [1941: Japanese attack U.S. fleet at Pearl Harbor: 7 December]
      [1943: Allied troops occupy Rome; Italy surrenders; Mussolini
                deposed: 25 July]
    1945: 74/8; 84/118: [Pound confined at Disciplinary Training
                Center near Pisa; Mussolini executed by Italian
                Partisans: 20 April; end of World War II]
        25 June: 74/12:
        14 July: 74/12: Haec sunt fastae/ Under Taishan
        8 September: 82/103: the cricket hops/ but does not chirrp
                in the drill field
        October: 84/115
        8 October: 84/115: Si tuit li dolh el plor/ ... tuit lo pro,
                tuit lo bes
      [November: Pound returned to U.S.]

APPENDIX D: GENEALOGY

Appendix D contains the following genealogical and related materials:
 a. Genealogical tables of Italian Renaissance families important
    in the Cantos
    1. The House of Este
    2. The House of Sforza
    3. The House of Visconti
    4. The House of Malatesta
    5. The House of Montefeltro
    6. The House of Medici: Elder Branch
    7. The House of Medici: Younger Branch
 b. The Emperors of China
 c. The Rulers of England [Edgar to Elizabeth II]
 d. The Rulers of France [Pepin the Short to Napoleon III]
 e. The Rulers of Tuscany [Cosimo de' Medici to Ferdinand IV]
 f. The Renaissance Papal Succession [Calixtus III to Benedict
    XIII]
 g. The Presidents of the United States
Names in ALL CAPS are mentioned in the Cantos and are annotated
in the General Index.

THE HOUSE OF ESTE:

ALBERTO
1347-1393
m. (a) Giovanna de'Roberti
   (b) Isotta Albaresani

(b) NICCOLÒ III
1383-1441
Twelfth Marquis of Ferrara
m. (a) Gigliola da Garrara, 1397
   (b) Parisina MALATESTA, 1418
   (c) Ricciarda da SALUZZO, 1431

Ugo ALDOBRANDINO
(natural)
1405-1425

LEONELLO
(natural,
legitimated)
1407-1450
Thirteenth
Marquis of
Ferrara
m. (a) Margherita
       Gonzaga
   (b) Maria
       d'Aragona

BORSO
(natural)
First Duke
of Modena
(1452) and
Ferrara
(1471)

(b)GINEVRA
1419-1440
m. Sigismondo
   MALATESTA

MARGARITA
(natural)
d. 1452

(c)ERCOLE I
1431-1505
Second Duke
of Ferrara
and Modena
m. Leonora
   d'Aragona,
   1473

Isabella
1474-1539
m. Gian Francesco
   GONZAGA

Beatrice
1475-1497
m. Lodovico
   Sforza

ALFONSO I
1476-1534
Third Duke of
Ferrara and Modena
m. (a) Anna Sforza, 1491
   (b) Lucrezia BORGIA, 1502

Ippolito I
1479-1520
Cardinal

(b)Ercole II
1508-1559
Fourth Duke of
Ferrara and Modena
m. Renée o? France

Alfonso
(by Laura Dianti)
1527-1587
m. Giulia della Rovere

Alfonso II
1533-1597
Fifth Duke of
Ferrara and Modena

Lucrezia
1535-1598
m. Francesco Maria II
   della Rovere, Duke
   of Urbino

Luigi
1538-1586
Cardinal

Cesare
1562-1628
Duke of Ferrara, 1597
Duke of Modena, 1597-1628
m. Virginia de' Medici

THE HOUSE OF SFORZA:

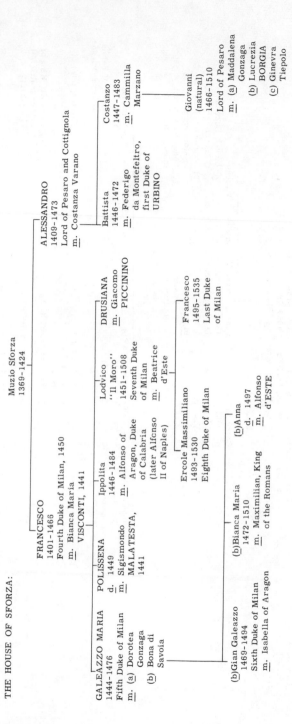

Muzio Sforza
1369-1424

FRANCESCO
1401-1466
Fourth Duke of Milan, 1450
m. Bianca Maria
VISCONTI, 1441

ALESSANDRO
1409-1473
Lord of Pesaro and Cottignola
m. Costanza Varano

GALEAZZO MARIA
1444-1476
Fifth Duke of Milan
m. (a) Dorotea
Gonzaga
(b) Bona di
Savoia

POLISSENA
d. 1449
m. Sigismondo
MALATESTA,
1441

Ippolita
1446-1484
m. Alfonso of
Aragon, Duke
of Calabria
(later Alfonso
II of Naples)

Lodvico
"Il Moro"
1451-1508
Seventh Duke
of Milan
m. Beatrice
d'Este

DRUSIANA
m. Giacomo
PICCININO

Battista
1446-1472
m. Federigo
da Montefeltro,
first Duke of
URBINO

Costanzo
1447-1483
m. Cammilla
Marzano

(b)Gian Galeazzo
1469-1494
Sixth Duke of Milan
m. Isabella of Aragon

(b)Bianca Maria
1472-1510
m. Maximilian, King
of the Romans

Ercole Massimiliano
1493-1530
Eighth Duke of Milan

(b)Anna
d. 1497
m. Alfonso
d'ESTE

Francesco
1495-1535
Last Duke
of Milan

Giovanni
(natural)
1466-1510
Lord of Pesaro
m. (a) Maddalena
Gonzaga
(b) Lucrezia
BORGIA
(c) Ginevra
Tiepolo

THE HOUSE OF VISCONTI:

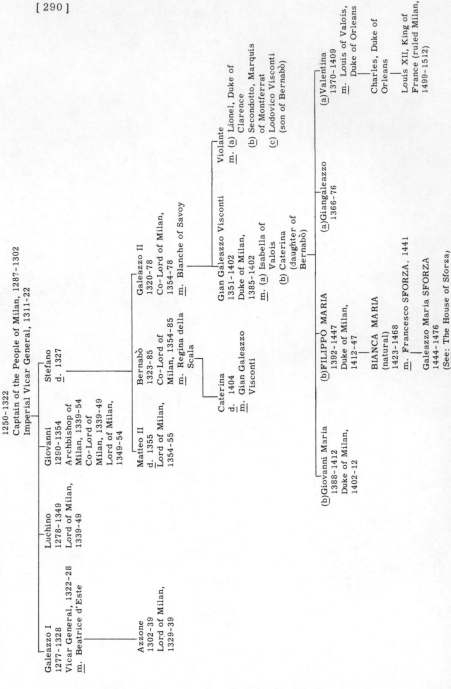

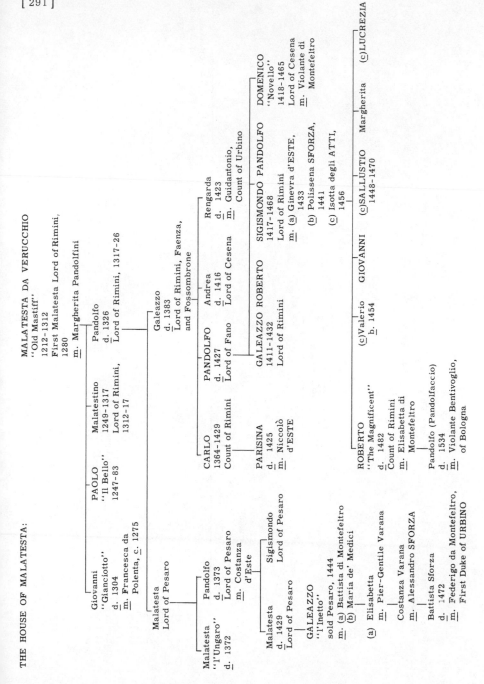

THE HOUSE OF MONTEFELTRO:
Counts and Dukes of Urbino

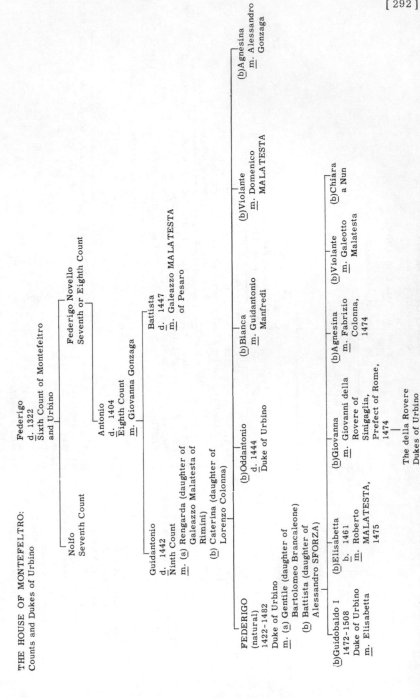

Federigo
d. 1322
Sixth Count of Montefeltro
and Urbino

Nolfo
Seventh Count

Federigo Novello
Seventh or Eighth Count

Antonio
d. 1404
Eighth Count
m. Giovanna Gonzaga

Guidantonio
d. 1442
Ninth Count
m. (a) Rengarda (daughter of
    Galeazzo Malatesta of
    Rimini)
    (b) Caterina (daughter of
    Lorenzo Colonna)

FEDERIGO
(natural)
1422–1482
Duke of Urbino
m. (a) Gentile (daughter of
    Bartolomeo Brancaleone)
    (b) Battista (daughter of
    Alessandro SFORZA)

(b)Oddantonio
d. 1444
Duke of Urbino

Battista
d. 1447
m. Galeazzo MALATESTA
    of Pesaro

(b)Guidobaldo I
1472–1508
Duke of Urbino
m. Elisabetta

(b)Elisabetta
b. 1461
m. Roberto
MALATESTA,
1475

(b)Giovanna
m. Giovanni della
    Rovere of
    Sinigaglia,
    Prefect of Rome,
    1474

The della Rovere
Dukes of Urbino

(b)Agnesina
m. Fabrizio
    Colonna,
    1474

(b)Violante
m. Galeotto
    Malatesta

(b)Chiara
a Nun

(b)Bianca
m. Guidantonio
    Manfredi

(b)Violante
m. Domenico
    MALATESTA

(b)Agnesina
m. Alessandro
    Gonzaga

THE HOUSE OF MEDICI: Elder Branch

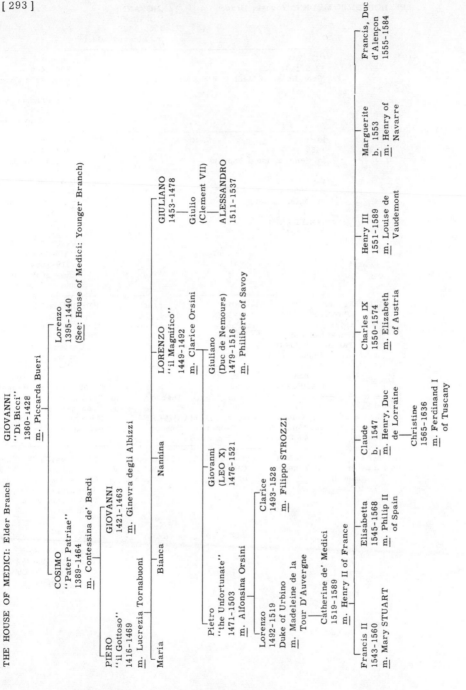

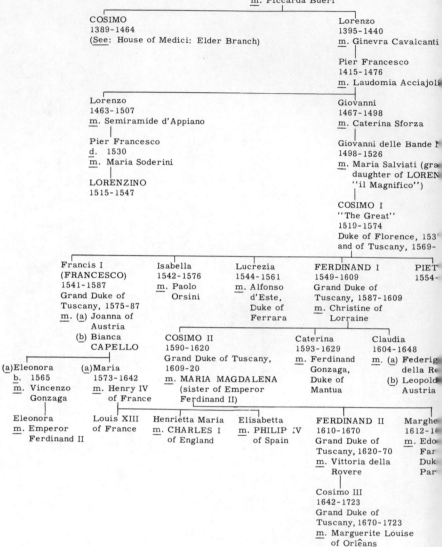

GIOVANNI
"Di Bicci"
1360-1428
m. Piccarda Bueri

COSIMO
1389-1464
(See: House of Medici: Elder Branch)

Lorenzo
1395-1440
m. Ginevra Cavalcanti

Pier Francesco
1415-1476
m. Laudomia Acciajoli

Lorenzo
1463-1507
m. Semiramide d'Appiano

Pier Francesco
d. 1530
m. Maria Soderini

LORENZINO
1515-1547

Giovanni
1467-1498
m. Caterina Sforza

Giovanni delle Bande N
1498-1526
m. Maria Salviati (gra
daughter of LOREN
"il Magnifico")

COSIMO I
"The Great"
1519-1574
Duke of Florence, 153
and of Tuscany, 1569-

Francis I
(FRANCESCO)
1541-1587
Grand Duke of
Tuscany, 1575-87
m. (a) Joanna of
Austria
(b) Bianca
CAPELLO

Isabella
1542-1576
m. Paolo
Orsini

Lucrezia
1544-1561
m. Alfonso
d'Este,
Duke of
Ferrara

FERDINAND I
1549-1609
Grand Duke of
Tuscany, 1587-1609
m. Christine of
Lorraine

PIET
1554-

(a)Eleonora
b. 1565
m. Vincenzo
Gonzaga

(a)Maria
1573-1642
m. Henry IV
of France

COSIMO II
1590-1620
Grand Duke of Tuscany,
1609-20
m. MARIA MAGDALENA
(sister of Emperor
Ferdinand II)

Caterina
1593-1629
m. Ferdinand
Gonzaga,
Duke of
Mantua

Claudia
1604-1648
m. (a) Federig
della Re
(b) Leopold
Austria

Eleonora
m. Emperor
Ferdinand II

Louis XIII
of France

Henrietta Maria
m. CHARLES I
of England

Elisabetta
m. PHILIP IV
of Spain

FERDINAND II
1610-1670
Grand Duke of
Tuscany, 1620-70
m. Vittoria della
Rovere

Marghe
1612-1
m. Edo
Far
Duk
Par

Cosimo III
1642-1723
Grand Duke of
Tuscany, 1670-1723
m. Marguerite Louise
of Orléans

THE EMPERORS OF CHINA

The chronological table of the emperors of China is divided into four columns:

1. The date of an emperor's accession to the throne.
2. The imperial title of the emperor, as it is spelled in the French orthography of Mailla, Histoire Générale de la Chine.
3. The imperial title of the emperor, as it is spelled in standard Wade orthography.
4. The name under which the emperor is listed, if at all, in Herbert A. Giles, A Chinese Biographical Dictionary.

Imperial titles printed in ALL CAPS in column two are to be found in the General Index and are listed under the first element of the name, whether in parentheses or not; elements in parentheses indicate a dynastic name appended by Pound to the imperial title.

The transliteration of French orthography into the Wade System has been done in accordance with the tables in Bernard Karlgren, "A Mandarin Phonetic Reader in the Pekinese Dialect," Archives d'Etudes Orientales, XII.

THE LEGENDARY PERIOD

Age of the Five Rulers

	1.	2.	3.	4.
BC	2953	FOU-HI	Fu Hsi	Fu Hsi
	2838	CHIN-NONG	Shên Nung	Shên Nung
	2698	HOANG-TI	Huang Ti	Huang Ti
	2598	CHAO-HAO	Shao Hao	
	2514	TCHUEN-hio	Chuan Hsü	
	2436	TI-KO	Ti Ku	
	2366	Ti-tchi		
	2357	YΛO	Yao	Yao
	interregnum of mourning			
	2255	CHUN	Shun	Shun

First Dynasty: The Hsia
(BC 2205-1766)

BC	2205	YU	Yü	Ta Yü
	2197	Ti-Ki		
	2188	Tai-khang		
	2159	Tchong-khang		
	2146	Ti-siang		
	2119	Han-tsou		
	2079	CHAO-KANG	Shao Kang	
	2057	Ti-chou		
	2040	Ti-hoai		
	2014	Ti-mang		
	1996	Ti-sié		
	1980	Ti-pou-kiang		
	1921	Ti-kiong		
	1900	Ti-kin		
	1879	Kong-kia		
	1848	Ti-kao		
	1837	Ti-fa		
	1818	Li-koué		

Second Dynasty: The Shang
(BC 1766-1121)

BC	1766	TCHING-TANG	Ch'êng T'ang	Ch'êng T'ang
	1753	Tai-kia		
	1720	Ou-teng		
	1691	Tai-keng		
	1666	Siao-kia		
	1649	Yong-ki		
	1637	Tai-tching		
	1562	Tchong-ting		
	1549	Ouai-gin		
	1534	Ho-tan-kia		
	1525	Tsou-y		
	1506	Tsou-sin		

BC 1490   Ou-kia
   1465   Tsou-ting
   1433   Nan-keng
   1408   Yang-kia
   1401   Poan-keng   (changed name of the Shang dynasty to Yin)
   1373   Siao-sin
   1352   Siao-y
   1324   Ou-ting
   1265   Tsou-keng
   1258   Tsou-kia
   1225   Lin-sin
   1219   Keng-ting
   1198   Ou-y
   1194   Tai-ting
   1191   Ti-y
   1154   CHEOU-SIN   Chou Hsin   Chou Hsin

SEMI-HISTORICAL AND HISTORICAL PERIOD

Third Dynasty: The Chou
(BC 1122-255)

BC 1122   OU-OUANG   Wu Wang   Wu Wang
   1115   TCHING-OUANG   Chêng Wang
   1078   KANG-OUANG   K'ang Wang
   1052   TCHAO-OUANG   Chao Wang
   1001   MOU-OUANG   Mu Wang   Mu Wang
    946   KONG-OUANG   Kung Wang
    934   Y-OUANG   I Wang
    909   HIAO-OUANG   Hsiao Wang
    894   Y-ouang
    878   LI-OUANG   Li Wang
    841   interregnum of CONG-HO
    827   SIUEN-OUANG   Hsüan Wang
    781   YEOU-OUANG   Yu Wang
    770   Pping-ouang
    719   Houan-ouang
(Historical period begins about BC 781-719)
    696   Tchouang-ouang
    681   Hi-ouang
    676   Hoei-ouang
    651   Siang-ouang
    618   Khing-ouang
    612   Khouang-ouang
    606   Ting-ouang
    585   Kien-ouang
    571   Ling-ouang
    544   King-ouang
    . . .   Tao-ouang
    519   KING-OUANG   Ching Wang
    475   Yuen-ouang
    468   Tching-ting
    440   Gae-ouang
    440   Ssé-ouang

BC 440 Cao-ouang
    425 OUEÏ-LIÉ-ouang   Wei-lieh Wang
    401 Gan-ouang
    375 Lie-ouang
    368 Hien-ouang
    320 Chin-tsing-ouang
    314 Nan-ouang
    255 Tcheou-kun

Fourth Dynasty: The Ch'in
(BC 255-206)

BC 255 Tchao-siang-ouang
    250 Hiao-ouen-ouang
    249 Tchoang-siang-ouang
    246 TSIN-CHI-hoang-ti   Ch'in Shih Huang Ti   Shih Huang Ti
    209 EULH-chi-hoang-ti   Êrh Shih Huang Ti   Hu Hai
    206 TSE-YNG   Tzǔ Ying   Tzǔ Ying

Fifth Dynasty: The Former Han
(BC 206-AD 25)

BC 202 KAO-HOANG-TI   Kao Huang Ti   Liu Pang
    194 (HIAO) HOEI-TI   (Hsiao) Hui Ti   Liu Ying
    187 LIU-HEOU   Lü Hou   Lü Hou
    179 (HIAO) OUEN-ti   (Hsiao) Wên Ti   Liu Hêng
    156 (HIAO) KING-ti   (Hsiao) Ching Ti   Liu Ch'i
    140 (HAN) OU-ti   (Han) Wu Ti   Liu Ch'ê
     86 (HAN) TCHAO-TI   (Han) Chao Ti   Liu Fu-ling
     74 Lieou-ho
     73 (HAN) SIUEN-TI   (Han) Hsüan Ti   Liu Hsün
     48 (HAN) YUEN-ti   (Han) Yüan Ti   Liu Shih
     32 Tching-ti
      6 Ngai-ti
AD   1 (HAN) PING-ti   (Han) Ping Ti   Liu K'an
      6 Ju-tsě-yng-kui-nie
      9 Ouang-mang
     23 Lieou-hiuen

Fifth Dynasty: The After Han
(AD 25-221)

AD   25 KOUANG-OU-ti   Kuang Wu Ti   Liu Hsiu
     58 (HAN) MING-ti   (Han) Ming Ti   Liu Chuang
     76 Tchang-ti
     89 (HAN) HO-TI   (Han) Ho Ti   Liu Chao
    106 Chang-ti
    107 (HAN) NGAN-ti   (Han) An Ti   Liu Yu
    125 Pé-king-heou
    126 Chun-ti
    145 Tchong-ti
    146 Tché-ti
    147 (HAN) HOUON-TI   (Han) Huan Ti   Liu Chih

AD   168   LING-TI   (Han) Ling Ti   Liu Hung
      190   Hien-ti

THE EPOCH OF THE THREE KINGDOMS
(AD 221-265)

Sixth Dynasty: The Minor Han

AD   221   Tchao-lié-ti
      223   Han-heou-tchu

The Wei Dynasty

AD   220   Ouen-ti
      227   Ming-ti
      240   Ti-fang
      254   Ti-maou
      260   Yuen-ti

The Wu Dynasty

AD   222   Ta-ti
      252   Hoei-ki-ouang
      258   King-ti
      264   Ou-tching-heou

Seventh Dynasty: The Western Chin
(AD 265-317)

AD   265   (TÇIN) OU-TI   (Chin) Wu Ti   Ssŭ-ma Yen
      290   (TÇIN) HOEI-TI   (Chin) Hui Ti   Ssŭ-ma Chung
      307   (TÇIN) HOAI-TI   (Chin) Hwai Ti   Ssŭ-ma Chih
      313   (TÇIN) MIN-TI   (Chin) Min Ti   Ssŭ-ma Yeh

Seventh Dynasty: The Eastern Chin
(AD 317-420)

AD   317   Yuen-ti
      323   Ming-ti
      326   (TÇIN) TCHING-ti   (Chin) Ch'êng Ti   Ssŭ-ma Yen
      343   Kang-ti
      345   Mou-ti
      362   Ngai-ti
      366   Fi-ti or Y-ti
      371   Kien-ouen-ti
      373   (TÇIN) HIAO-ou-ti   (Chin) Hsiao Wu Ti   Ssŭ-ma Yao
      397   (TÇIN) NGAN-ti   (Chin) An Ti   Ssŭ-ma Tê
      419   Koung-ti

EPOCH OF DIVISION BETWEEN NORTH AND SOUTH

Eighth Dynasty: The Liu Sung
(AD 420-479)

AD	420	(KAO-TSOU) OU-TI	(Kao-tsu) Wu Ti	Liu Yü
	423	Chao-ti		
	424	OUEN-TI	Wên Ti	Liu I-lung
	453	HIAO-OU-TI	Hsiao Wu Ti	Liu Chün
	465	Fi-ti		
	466	Ming-ti		
	473	Fi-ti		
	477	Chun-ti		

Ninth Dynasty: The Ch'i
(AD 480-503)

AD	480	KAO-TI	Kao Ti	Hsiao Tao-ch'êng
	483	OU-TI	Wu Ti	Hsiao Tsê
	494	Ti-tchao-nié		
	494	Ti-tchao-ouen		
	494	Ming-ti		
	499	Ti-paou-kuen		
	501	Ho-ti		

Tenth Dynasty: The Liang
(AD 503-557)

AD	503	OU-TI	Wu Ti	Hsiao Yen
	550	KIEN-OUEN-TI	Chien Wên Ti	Hsiao Kang
	552	Yu-tchang-ouang		
	552	Yuen-ti		
	555	King-ti		

Eleventh Dynasty: The Ch'ên
(AD 557-589)

AD	557	Ou-ti		
	560	Ouen-ti		
	567	Fi-ti		
	569	SUEN-TI	Suan Ti	Ch'ên Hsü
	583	HEOU-TCHU	Hou Chu	Ch'ên Shu-pao

Twelfth Dynasty: The Sui
(AD 589-618)

AD	581	OUEN-TI	Wên Ti	Yang Chien
	605	YANG-TI	Yang Ti	Yang Kuang
	618	KONG-TI	Kung Ti	
	619	Kong-ti		

Thirteenth Dynasty: The T'ang
(AD 618-907)

AD				
AD	618	KAO-TSOU	Kao Tsu	Li Yüan
	626	TAÏ-TSONG	T'ai Tsung	Li Shih-min
	650	Kao-tsong		
	684	TCHONG-TSONG	Chung Tsung	Li Hsien
	684	OU-HEOU	Wu Hou	Wu Hou
	705	TCHONG-TSONG	Chung Tsung	Li Hsien
	710	Joui-tsong		
	713	HIUEN-TSONG	Hsüan Tsung	Li Lung-chi
	756	SOU-TSONG	Su Tsung	Li T'ing
	763	Tai-tsong		
	780	TÉ-TSONG	Tê Tsung	Li Kua
	805	TCHUN-TSONG	Chun Tsung	Li Sung
	806	HIEN-TSONG	Hsien Tsung	Li Shun
	821	MOU-TSONG	Mu Tsung	Li Hêng
	825	King-tsong		
	827	OUEN-TSONG	Wên Tsung	Li Han
	841	OU-TSONG	Wu Tsung	Li Yen
	847	SIUEN-TSONG	Hsüan Tsung	Li Shên
	860	Y-TSONG	I Tsung	Li Ts'ui
	874	HI-TSONG	Hsi Tsung	Li Yen
	889	Tchao-tsong		
	905	Tchao-siuen-ti		

Fourteenth Dynasty: The After Liang
(AD 907-923)

AD				
AD	907	TAÏ-TSOU	T'ai Tsu	Chu Wên
	913	Yn-ouang		
	913	Mo-ti		

Fifteenth Dynasty: The After T'ang
(AD 923-936)

AD				
AD	923	TCHOANG-TSONG	Chuang Tsung	Li Ts'un-hsü
	926	MING-TSONG	Ming Tsung	Li Ssŭ-yüan
	934	Min-ti		
	934	LIOU-OUANG	Liu Wang	Li Ts'ung-k'o

Sixteenth Dynasty: The After Chin
(AD 936-947)

AD				
AD	936	KAO-TSOU	Kao Tsu	Shih Ching-t'ang
	944	Tsi-ouang		

Seventeenth Dynasty: The After Han
(AD 947-951)

AD				
AD	947	KAO-TSOU	Kao Tsu	Liu Chih-yüan
	948	Yn-ti		
	951	Kiang-yn-kong		

Eighteenth Dynasty: The After Chou
(AD 951-959)

AD	951	TAÏ-TSOU	T'ai Tsu	Kuo Wei
	954	CHI-TSONG	Shih Tsung	Kuo Jung
	959	Kong-ti		

Nineteenth Dynasty: The Sung
(AD 960-1127)

AD	960	TAÏ-TSOU	T'ai Tsu	Chao K'uang-yin
	977	TAÏ-TSONG	T'ai Tsung	Chao Huang
	998	TCHIN-TSONG	Chên Tsung	Chao Hêng
	1023	GIN-TSONG	Jen Tsung	Chao Chên
	1064	Yng-tsong		
	1068	CHIN-TSONG	Shên Tsung	Chao Hsü
	1086	Tché-tsong		
	1101	HOEÏ-TSONG	Hui Tsung	Chao Chi
	1126	Kin-tsong		

Nineteenth Dynasty: The Southern Sung
(AD 1127-1280)

AD	1127	Kao-tsong		
	1163	Hiao-tsong		
	1190	Koang-tsong		
	1195	Ning-tsong		
	1225	LI-TSONG	Li Tsung	Chao Yün
	1265	Tou-tsong		
	1275	Ti-hien		
	1276	Toan-tsong		
	1278	Ti-ping		

Twentieth Dynasty: The Yüan or Mongol
(AD 1206-1368)

AD	1206	TAÏ-TSOU	T'ai Tsu	Genghis Khan
	1228	TAÏ-TSONG	T'ai Tsung	Ogotai Khan
	1242	TING-TSONG	Ting Tsung	Kuyak Khan
	1249	HIEN-TSONG	Hsien Tsung	Mangu Khan
	1260	CHI-TSOU	Shih Tsu	Kublai Khan

(in 1280 Kublai Khan became emperor of all China)

	1295	TCHING-TSONG	Chêng Tsung	Timour Khan
	1308	Ou-tsong		
	1312	GIN-TSONG	Jen Tsung	Ayuli Palpata
	1321	Yng-tsong		
	1324	Tai-ting		
	1329	Ming-tsong		
	1329	Ouen-tsong		
	1333	Ning-tsong		
	1333	CHUN-TI	Shun Ti	Tohan Timur

Twenty-first Dynasty: The Ming
(AD 1368-1644)

AD			
1368	HONG-VOU	Hung Wu	Chu Yüan-chang
1399	KIEN-OUEN-TI	Chien Wên Ti	Chu Yün-wên
1403	YONG-LO	Yung Lo	Chu Ti
1425	GIN-TSONG	Jen Tsung	Chu Kao-chih
1426	Suen-tsong		
1437	YNG-TSONG	Ying Tsung	Chu Ch'i-chên
1450	KING-TI	King Ti	Chu Ch'i-yü
1457	Yng-tsong		
1465	HIEN-TSONG	Hsien Tsung	Chu Chien-shên
1488	HIAO-TSONG	Hsiao Tsung	Chu Yu-t'ang
1506	OU-TSONG	Wu Tsung	Chu Hou-chao
1522	CHI-TSONG	Shih Tsung	Chu Hou-tsung
1567	Mou-tsong		
1573	CHIN-TSONG	Shên Tsung	Chu I-chün
1620	Kouang-tsong		
1621	Hi-tsong		
1628	HOAÏ-TSONG	Huai Tsung	Chu Yu-chien
1644	Chi-tsou-tchang-ti		

Twenty-second Dynasty: The Ch'ing
(AD 1616-1912)

AD			
1616	TAÏ-TSOU	T'ai Tsu	Nurhachu
1625	TAÏ-TSONG	T'ai Tsung	T'ein Ts'ung
1644	CHUN-TCHI	Shun Chih	Shun Chih
1662	KANG-HI	Kang Hsi	K'ang Hsi
1723	YONG-TCHING	Yung Chêng	Yung Chêng
1736	KIEN-LONG	Ch'ien Lung	Ch'ien Lung

(The China Cantos and the Histoire Générale de la Chine stop at the
year 1780; the names of the remaining emperors of the Ch'ing dynasty
are given in only the Wade transliteration.)

1796	Chia Ch'ing
1820	Tao Kuang
1851	Hsien Fêng
1861	T'ung Chih
1875	Kuang Hsü
1908	Hsüan T'ung

On January 1, 1912, Sun Yat-sen entered the republican capital, Nanking;
he assumed the presidency of the provisional government and brought
the dynastic history of China to an end.

RULERS OF ENGLAND

EDGAR	959-75	Harold I Harefoot	1035-40
Edward the Martyr	975-78	Hardecanute	1040-42
Ethelred II the Unready	978-1016	EDWARD THE	
Edmund Ironside	1016	CONFESSOR	1042-66
Canute	1016-35	Harold II	1066

William I the Conqueror	1066-87	Edward VI	1547-53
William II Rufus	1087-1100	Mary	1553-58
Henry I Beauclerc	1100-35	ELIZABETH I	1558-1603
Stephen	1135-54	JAMES I	1603-25
HENRY II	1154-89	CHARLES I	1625-49
RICHARD I Coeur de		(Commonwealth, 1649-60)	
Lion	1189-99	CHARLES II	1660-85
JOHN Lackland	1199-1216	JAMES II	1685-88
Henry III	1216-72	WILLIAM III and Mary	1689-1702
EDWARD I Longshanks	1272-1307	ANNE	1702-14
Edward II	1307-27	George I	1714-27
Edward III	1327-77	George II	1727-60
Richard II	1377-99	GEORGE III	1760-1820
Henry IV Bolingbroke	1399-1413	George IV	1820-30
HENRY V	1413-22	William IV	1830-37
HENRY VI	1422-61	VICTORIA	1837-1901
EDWARD IV	1461-83	EDWARD VII	1901-10
Edward V	1483	George V	1910-36
RICHARD III	1483-85	EDWARD VIII	1936
Henry VII	1485-1509	George VI	1936-52
HENRY VIII	1509-47	Elizabeth II	1952-

RULERS OF FRANCE

Merovingian and Carolingian Kings

Pepin the Short	751-768	Henry I	1031-1060
Charlemagne (Holy	768-814	Philip	1060-1108
Roman Emperor, 800-14)		Louis VI	1108-1137
Louis I	814-40	Louis VII	1137-1180
Charles I the Bald (Holy	840-77	Philip II	1180-1223
Roman Emperor as		Louis VIII	1223-26
CHARLES II		LOUIS IX	1226-70
Louis II	877-79	Philip III	1270-85
Louis III	879-82	Philip IV	1285-1314
Carloman	879-84	Louis X	1314-16
Charles II the Fat (Holy	884-887	John I	1316
Roman Emperor as		Philip V	1316-22
Charles III)		Charles IV	1322-28
Odo, Count of Paris	888-98		
Charles III the Simple	893-923	House of Valois	1328-1589
Robert I	922-23		
Rudolf, Duke of Burgundy	923-36	House of Bourbon	
Louis IV	936-54		
Lothair	954-86	Henry IV	1589-1610
Louis V	986-87	Louis XII	1610-43
		Louis XIV	1643-1715
		LOUIS XV	1715-74
### Capetian Line		LOUIS XVI	1774-92
		Louis XVII (nominal	1793-95
Hugh CAPET	987-96	king only)	
Robert II	996-1031		

The Republic		The Restoration	
National	20 Sept. 1792-26	LOUIS XVIII	1814-24
Convention	Oct. 1795	Charles X	1824-30
The DIRECTORY,	27 Oct. 1795-9	Louis Philippe	1830-48
	Nov. 1799		
		The Second Republic	
The Consulate	1799-1804	Louis Napoleon, President	1848-52
First Empire		The Second Empire	
NAPOLEON I,	1804-15	NAPOLEON III	1852-70
Bonaparte		(Louis Napoleon)	

THE GRAND DUKES OF TUSCANY

Medici		Leopold I (Holy	1765-90
		Roman Emperor as	
COSIMO I	1569-74	LEOPOLD II)	
Francis I	1575-87	FERDINAND III	1790-99;
FERDINAND I	1587-1609		1814-24
COSIMO II	1609-20	(Tuscany included in the kingdom of	
FERDINAND II	1620-70	Etruria and ruled under the duchy	
Cosimo III	1670-1723	of Parma, 1801-7)	
Giovan Gastone	1723-37	(Tuscany annexed to France by	
		Napoleon, 1807-14)	
Lorraine		LEOPOLD II	1824-59
		Ferdinand IV	1859-60
Francis I (Holy	1737-65	(Tuscany incorporated into Sardinia,	
Roman Emperor)		1860)	

SUCCESSION OF RENAISSANCE POPES

211.	CALIXTUS III	1455-58		230.	Urban VII	1590	
212.	PIUS II	1458-64		231.	Gregory XIV	1590-91	
213.	PAUL II	1464-71		232.	Innocent IX	1591	
214.	Sixtus IV	1471-84		233.	Clement VIII	1592-1605	
215.	Innocent VIII	1484-92		234.	Leo XI	1605	
216.	ALEXANDER VI	1492-1503		235.	Paul V	1605-21	
217.	Pius III	1503		236.	Gregory XV	1621-23	
218.	Julius II	1503-13		237.	URBAN VIII	1623-44	
219.	LEO X	1513-21		238.	Innocent X	1644-55	
220.	Adrian VI	1522-23		239.	Alexander VII	1655-67	
221.	Clement VII	1523-34		240.	Clement IX	1667-69	
222.	Paul III	1534-49		241.	Clement X	1670-76	
223.	Julius III	1550-55		242.	Innocent XI	1676-89	
224.	Marcellus II	1555		243.	Alexander VIII	1689-91	
225.	Paul IV	1555-59		244.	Innocent XII	1691-1700	
226.	Pius IV	1559-65		245.	CLEMENT XI	1700-21	
227.	St. Pius V	1566-72		246.	Innocent XIII	1721-24	
228.	Gregory XIII	1572-85		247.	BENEDICT XIII	1724-30	
229.	Sixtus V	1585-90					

PRESIDENTS OF THE UNITED STATES

President		Term of office
1. George WASHINGTON	1732-1799	1789-97
2. John ADAMS	1735-1826	1797-1801
3. Thomas JEFFERSON	1743-1826	1801-09
4. James MADISON	1751-1836	1809-17
5. James MONROE	1758-1831	1817-25
6. John Quincy ADAMS	1767-1848	1825-29
7. Andrew JACKSON	1767-1845	1829-37
8. Martin VAN BUREN	1782-1862	1837-41
9. William Henry HARRISON	1773-1841	1841
10. John TYLER	1790-1862	1841-45
11. James Knox Polk	1795-1849	1845-49
12. Zachary Taylor	1784-1850	1849-50
13. Millard Fillmore	1800-1874	1850-53
14. Franklin Pierce	1804-1869	1853-57
15. James BUCHANAN	1791-1868	1857-61
16. Abraham Lincoln	1809-1865	1861-65
17. Andrew Johnson	1808-1875	1865-69
18. Ulysses Simpson Grant	1822-1885	1869-77
19. Rutherford Birchard HAYES	1822-1893	1877-81
20. James Abram Garfield	1831-1881	1881
21. Chester Alan Arthur	1830-1886	1881-85
22. Grover Cleveland	1837-1908	1885-89
23. Benjamin Harrison	1833-1901	1889-93
24. Grover Cleveland	1837-1908	1893-97
25. William McKinley	1843-1901	1897-1901
26. Theodore Roosevelt	1858-1919	1901-09
27. William Howard Taft	1857-1930	1909-13
28. Woodrow WILSON	1856-1924	1913-21
29. Warren Gamaliel Harding	1865-1923	1921-23
30. Calvin Coolidge	1872-1933	1923-29
31. Herbert Clark Hoover	1874-	1929-33
32. Franklin Delano ROOSEVELT	1882-1945	1933-45
33. Harry S. TRUMAN	1884-	1945-53
34. Dwight David Eisenhower	1890-	1953-

APPENDIX E: QUOTATION INDEX

Appendix E contains an index to literary quotations in the Cantos, arranged by authors and works quoted. Quotations are indexed by initial identifying words only. Full quotations and source annotations will be found in the General Index. Quotations in Greek or Chinese script are indicated by location only; the full quotations will be found in Appendixes A and B. Where more than one quotation from the same Greek source appears on a page in the Cantos, the number of quoted items follows in parenthesis.

Aeschylus: hac dextera: 82/101. helandros: 46/29. On the Alcides':
    82/101. [Greek]: 2/6. 5/19. 7/24. 7/25. 58/69. 82/101.
    82/104.
Alcamo, Ciullo d': aulentissima: 79/64.
Alysoun: Betueen April: 39/45.
Aristotle: hekasta: 74/19. Katholou: 74/19. Metathemenon: 74/18;
    78/59. [Greek]: 53/19; 76/41. 67/140.
Baudelaire, Charles: Le Paradis: 74/16; 76/38; 77/46; 83/106.
Bible:
    I Corinthians: and the greatest: 74/12.
    Jeremiah: buy the field: 76/32. from the tower: 74/18. Thou
        shalt: 74/18.
    John: in principio: 74/5.
    Leviticus: in meteyard: 74/12, 18; 76/32.
    Micah: each one: 74/13, 21; 76/32; 78/57; 79/65; 84/118.
    Psalms: Languor: 29/143.
Bion: Kai Moirai: 47/30, 33. Tu Diona: 47/30, 33. [Greek]: 47/30,
    33.
Born, Bertran de: Si tuit: 80/94; 84/115. y cavals: 7/24; 80/87.
Browning, Robert: Hard night: 5/18. Oh to be: 80/92. those girls:
    3/11.
Campo, Luchino dal: Ora vela: 24/111.
Catullus: brings the girl: 5/17. Da nuces: 5/17. Hymenaeus Io:
    4/15. quasi: 20/89. Sumus in: 39/45. voce: 3/11; 28/137.
Cavalcanti, Guido: A Lady: 36/27-29. dove sta: 63/99; 76/30, 35.
    e fa di: 74/26; 78/59. Formando di: 27/129. formato: 70/156;
    74/24. in quella: 63/99. l'aer: 74/22. la qual: 63/99. ma
    che: 67/137.
Chanson de Roland: Aoi: 79/68; 81/97. Tan mare: 20/91.
Chaucer: Be glad poor: 82/103. Compleynt: 30/147. Master thy-
    self: 81/99. Your eyen: 81/98.
Cicero: Faece: 65/113. optime modice: 67/139-140. tempora:
    76/31.
Cleanthes: [Greek]: 71/167.
Colum, Padraic: O woman: 80/74.
Confucius:
    Analects: A good: 53/12. as under the: 78/59. Chose Kao-yao:
        78/59. How is it far: 77/43, 51; 79/66. in discourse:

79/64. Sha-o: 74/18. Shun's music: 74/17. the sage:
83/107. To study: 74/15-16. wan: 80/79. Yaou chose:
74/20. [Chinese]: 77/43; 80/76. 77/45.

Classic Anthology: agit: 53/17. Campestribus: 53/17. He
heard: 53/17. Juxta: 53/16. mus ingens: 56/48. Swift
men: 53/16. the yellow: 79/65. [Chinese]: 79/65.

Great Digest: lacking that treasure: 77/48. Make it: 53/11.
Sin jih: 54/24. the yellow: 79/65. [Chinese]: 53/11.
55/36. 74/7; 84/117. 76/32. 77/45. 78/60. 79/65.
82/103.

Unwobbling Pivot: like an arrow: 77/46. [Chinese]: 70/159;
76/32; 77/42; 84/118.

Daniel, Arnaut: e l'olors: 20/90. e lo soleis: 4/15. e quel: 7/26.
Noigandres: 20/89, 90. Ongla: 18/81.

Dante:
Canzoniere: Al poco: 5/20.
De Vulgari Eloquentia: directio: 77/45.
Divina Commedia:
Inferno: Caina: 5/19. così discesi: 80/77. cosi Elena:
20/92. E biondo: 7/27. Io venni: 14/61. Mastin: 8/32.
natural burella: 69/153. per l'argine: 69/153. quindi:
69/153. selv': 23/108. si com': 80/86. si come:
79/65. staria: 74/13.
Purgatorio: a guisa: 32/9. con gli: 7/24. consiros:
83/107. quand vos: 84/117. west mountain: 16/68.
Paradiso: ch'intenerisce: 74/9. che mai da: 39/44. il
duol: 38/37. O voi: 7/26. the imprint: 79/64. un
terzo: 76/36.
La Vita Nuova: e che fu: 76/30.

Eliot, T. S.: and the pleasure: 83/112. Grishkin: 77/44. These
fragments: 8/28. with a bang: 74/3.

Epictetus: [Greek]: 77/44.

Erigena, Johannes Scotus: authority comes: 36/29. sunt lumina:
74/7, 8.

Flaubert, Gustave: Contre le lambris: 7/24. Un peu: 7/24.

Ford, Ford Madox: and all: 74/11.

Fu Sheng: Kei men: 49/39.

Grosseteste, Robert: lux enim ignis: 83/106. Lux enim per: 55/44.
omnia, quae: 83/106. Plura: 83/108. Seipsum: 55/44.

Hagoromo: With us: 80/78.

Hanno: Entha: 40/49. Karxèdoniōn: 40/51. Pleasing to: 40/49-51.

Heraclitus: [Greek]: 80/90; 83/107.

Hesiod: Begin thy plowing: 47/31.

Homer:
Hymns: V, To Aphrodite: Bearing the golden: 1/5. King
Otreus: 23/109; 25/119. VI, To Aphrodite: Cypri: 1/5.
oricalchi: 1/5. Venerandam: 1/5. with the golden: 1/5.
Iliad: Epi: 20/91. Let her go: 2/6. Neestho: 20/91. peur de:
20/91. poluphloisboios: 74/5.
Odyssey: Ad Orcum: 39/45. And by: 2/6. And then went:
1/3-5. benecomata: 76/38. es thalamon: 39/44. Eunè:

APPENDIX F: SOURCE CHECKLIST

Appendix F contains a selective checklist of the major literary and historical sources of the Cantos. In one sense, a lifetime of reading provided sources for the Cantos; the various source notes attached to entries in the General Index offer evidence of the range of Pound's reading. But certain works proved of special importance to his poem, and it is these, selected from the larger whole, that this checklist presents.

A. Literary Sources.

    The Agamemnon of Aeschylus; Camoens: Lusiad; the poems of Catullus; the works of Cavalcanti; the Divina Commedia, La Vita Nuova, Il Canzoniere, and De Vulgari Eloquentia of Dante; Homer's Odyssey, especially in the Andreas Divus (1538) edition; the Odes of Horace; Ovid's Metamorphoses; the Provençal poets, especially Bernart de Born, Arnaut Daniel, Sordello, and Bernart de Ventadour; the Elegies of Propertius; Poems and Fragments of Sappho; Villon; and Virgil's Aeneid, in the translation of Gavin Douglas.

B. Miscellaneous Sources

    Aristotle: Politics, I; Confucius: Analects, Great Digest, and Unwobbling Pivot in editions by James Legge and Jean Pierre Guillaume Pauthier; the Classic Anthology: Seraphim Couvreur's edition; Johannes Scotus Erigena: De Divisione Naturae; Robert Grosseteste's De luce seu inchoatione formarum and De iride seu de iride et speculo; The Periplus of Hanno; The Life and Works of Mencius, edited by James Legge; the De Modo Usurarum, vol. II, of Claudius Salmasius; Roberto Valturio's De Re Militari; and Benedetto Varchi: Storio fiorentino.

C. Historical Sources

    The following historical sources are known to have been the specific editions used by Pound.

Adams, John, The Works of John Adams, second president of the United States: with a life of the author, notes and illustrations, by his grandson Charles Francis Adams. 10 vols. Boston, 1852-65.
Adams, John Quincy, The Diary of John Quincy Adams, 1794-1845, ed. by Allan Nevins, New York & London, 1928.
Battaglini, Francesco Gaetano, "Della Vita e de' Fatti di Sigismondo Malatesta, Commentario del conte Francesco Gaetano Battaglini," Basini Parmensis Poetae Opera Praestantiora, II, 259-698. Rimini, 1784.

Broglio, Gaspare, "Cronaca" (a manuscript life of Sigismondo
    Malatesta) in the Gambalunga Library, Rimini.
Clementini, Cesare, "Vita di Sigismundo Pandolpho," Raccolto
    Istorico della Fondazione e dell'Origine e Vita de' Malatesti,
    II, 296-481. Rimini, 1617.
Confucius: Confucius, Confucii Chi-King: sive liver carminum
    (Alexandre de Lacharme, ed. & tr.), Stuttgart & Tübingen, 1830.
Frobenius, Leo, Erlebte Erdteile, 7 vols. Frankfort a. M.,
    1925-29. and Douglas C. Fox, African Genesis, New York,
    1937.
Jefferson, Thomas, The Writings of Thomas Jefferson.   20 vols.
    Washington, D.C., 1903.
Mailla, Joseph-Anne Marie Moyriac de, Histoire Générale de
    la Chine, ou annales de cet Empire: translation of the Tong-
    kien-kan-mou. 12 vols. (vol. 13 by l'Abbé Grosier) Paris,
    1777-85.
Monte dei Paschi documents:
    Il Monte dei paschi di Siena e le aziende in esso riunite.
         Note storiche raccolte e pub. per ordine della Deputazi-
         one ed cura del presidente, conte Niccolò Piccolomini...
         Siena, 1891-1919.
Soranzo, Giovanni, Pio II e la politica italiana nella lotta contro
    i Malatesti (1457-1463), Padua, 1911.
Tonini, Luigi, Rimini nella Signoria de' Malatesti, vol. II,
    Rimini, 1880.
Van Buren, Martin, The Autobiography of Martin Van Buren,
    Annual Report of the American Historical Association, 1918,
    vol. II, Washington, D.C. 1920.
Yriarte, Charles Émile, Un condottiere au XVe Siècle. Rimini;
    études sur les lettres et les arts à la cour des Malatesta
    d'après les papiers d'état des archives d'Italie, Paris, 1882.
Zobi, Antonio, Storio civile della Toscano del   MDCCXXXVII
    al MDCCCXLVIII, Firenze, 1850-52.

APPENDIX G: TEXT COLLATION

The Annotated Index is based on the New Directions edition of the Cantos, second printing, second state, dated 1948, released 1952. The text of the Faber edition (1954) offers evidence of corrections, clarifications and deletions important to the study of the poem. Appendix G contains the results of a collation of the two texts. Certain minor variations have been omitted: (1) Faber's full spelling of obscenities; (2) variations caused by differences in the conventions of British and American spelling and punctuation; and (3) variations that derive from typographical, not textual, decisions. It is, of course, impossible to know with certainty which variations are deliberate decisions of Pound, which are the result of a Faber editor, and which are uncorrected errors of a Faber compositor; until a definitive text is established, students of the poem must work with an uncertain and shifting text and make it do. These notes, then, are presented with a necessary caveat.

Location data gives the canto, page and line number on page in the New Directions edition; this is followed by the full line from the Faber text or descriptive information. Entries marked by an asterisk are authorized by the errata note following page 576 in the Faber edition.

The provisional collation prepared by Mr. Guy Davenport for the Pound Newsletter served as a point of departure for this textual study.

1/3/5:	Heavy with weeping, so winds from sternward
3/13:	Covered with close-webbed mist, unpiercèd ever
3/29:	Souls out of Erebus, cadaverous dead, of brides,
5/2:	'Lose all companions.' Then Anticlea came.
2/6/23:	That by the beach-run, Tyro,
9/31:	So-shu churned in the sea, So-shu also, [line is not set off by spacing]
3/11/19:	Or: the gray steps lead up under the cedars.
4/13/17:	Et ter flebiliter, Itys, Ityn!
15/23:	Saffron sandal so petals the narrow foot: Ὑμην,
15/24:	Ὑμεναι ὦ, Aurunculeia! Ὑμην, Ὑμεναι ὦ,
15/25:	The scarlet flower is cast on the blanch-white stone.
15/26:	So-Gioku saying:
15/27:	'This wind is the king's wind,
15/30:	That Ran-ti opened his collar:
16/12:	The barge scrapes at the ford,
5/17/2:	Ecbatan, the clock ticks and fades out,
17/5:	Down in the viæ stradæ, toga'd the crowd,

5/17/6:	[deleted]
17/7:	and from parapet looked down.
17/8:	To North was Egypt,
17/9:	the blue deep Nile
17/13:	[deleted]
17/14:	Iamblichus' light, and
18/5:	North wind nips on the bough.
18/6:	[deleted]
18/8:	So many things are set abroad and brought to mind
18/20:	'Came lust of woman upon him,
19/14:	'O empia? For Lorenzaccio had thought to stab in the open,
19/31:	Σίγα, σίγα.
20/8-10:	Fracastor had Zeus for midwife,/ Lightning served as his tweezers,/ Al poco giorno ed al gran cerchio d'ombra,/ Cotta, D'Alviano talk out with Navighero,
6/21/15:	'Ongla, oncle' turned Arnaut,
23/10:	Theseus from Troezene,
23/11:	Whom they wd. have given poison
7/24/7:	And then the phantom of Rome,
24/15:	To Dante's 'ciocco', brand struck in the game.
25/14:	My lintel, and Liu Ch'e's.
27/8:	But Eros drowned, drowned, heavy, half dead with tears
27/13:	[opposite this line, in margin] Desmond Fitzgerald
8/31/19:	Talking of the war about the temple of Delphi,
9/37/5:	Mr Feddy has done it (m'l'a calata) has sunk it.'
10/46/12:	And the tiers Calixte was dead, and Alfonso, Alfonse le roi, etc.
*11/49/6:	Said: 'Par che è fuor di questo...Sigis...mundo.'
12/53/13:	Nicholas Castaño in Habana,
55/11:	John Quinn
56/1:	Said John Quinn:
13/60/1:	And Kung said "Wan ruled with moderation,
60/7-8:	[deleted]
15/64/20:	the beast with a hundred legs, USURA
65/5:	..........e, broken
66/11:	Keep your eyes on the mirror!
67/5:	"Ἠέλιον τ' "Ἠέλιον
16/70/9:	[opposite this line, in margin] Plarris narrations
75/24:	Thus we used to hear of it at the opera,
17/76/10:	Moving there, with the oak-wood behind her,
78/28:	the cohort of her dancers.
18/80/15:	And all this costs the Khan nothing,
81/5:	[followed by line spacing]
82/16:	On the Manchester-Cardiff have been fitted with
83/5:	Take the French regimental badges off their artillery
83/13:	And so old Fowler went out there,
19/85/4:	The stubby fellow: 'Perfectly true,
85/6:	'Can't move 'em with a cold thing like economics.'
86/3:	"Das thust du nicht, Albert!"
87/3:	I said: 'You buy your damn coal from our mine.'

```
  19/87/14:    And next to him his nephew Mr. Mensdorf,
*    87/15:    And old Benckendorff, for purely family reasons,
     87/19:    And Mensdorf had his from Vienna,
     87/22:    And Mensdorf was just reaching into his pocket,
  20/89/3:     Negus vezer mon bel pensar no val.
     89/5:     The viel held close to his side;
     89/6:     And another: s'adora.
     89/13:    And Rennert had said: 'Nobody, no, nobody
     89/27:    And I said: 'I dunno, sir,' or
     91/3:     And he said: 'Some bitch has sold us
     91/10:    [opposite this line, in margin] Roland
     91/20:    'God, what a woman!
     91/28:    'Este, go' damn you,' between the walls, arras,
  22/101/4:    [opposite this line, in margin] T.C.P.
    101/29:    And C.H.D. said to the renowned Mr. Bukos:
    101/30:    'What is the cause of the H.C.L.?'
    101/30:    [line is followed by inserted line] (The high cost of
                  living) and Mr. Bukos,
    102/12:    And Mr. Hobson wrote in to the office:
    102/18:    Upon Cohen's Thesaurus. Nel paradiso terrestre
    105/26:    An' I said to him: Yusuf! Yusuf's a damn good feller.
  23/107/26:   ('Derivation uncertain.' The idiot!
    108/5:     Precisely
    108/5:     [line followed by half line] the selv' oscura
    108/8:     'Yperionides!
    109/29:    And she said: 'Otreus, of Phrygia,
    109/30:    'That king is my father. . .'
    109/31:    and I saw then, as of waves taking form,
  24/113/10:   [opposite this line, in margin] Este armes from the K.
                  of France
    114/24:    [opposite this line, in margin] scifanoja
  25/117/3:    [opposite this line, in margin] 'Who fleed the lion's
                  rump?'
    117/13:    [no space follows this line]
    117/16:    [followed by line spacing]
    119/3:     And thought then: the deathless,
    119/7:     Casting his gods back into the νόος.
    119/10:    'King Otreus, my father...'
  26/121/16:   'The book will be retained by the council'
    123/5:     The goldsmiths and jewelers company
    124/5:     Aureo annulo, to wed the sea as a wife,
    127/25:    Zamberti has often spoken of it to yr Sublimity, I
  27/129/6:    Pas, sumne fugol othbaer:
  28/134/17:   From the Señora at 300 pesetas cost to the latter
    134/28:    While the ladies from West Virginia
    136/17:    Never cherr terbakker!
    139/22:    '...ah read-it?'
    140/6:     Nor for the code of Peoria.
    140/7-11:  [deleted]
  29/142/26:   You begin by making the replica.'
    143/12:    'With heads down now, and now up.'
```

144/27:   Quar noi vezon so qu'ieu vuelh.
30/149/4: Il Papa morì.
           [Title page to Cantos 31-41]   A DRAFT OF
                                                   CANTOS XXXI-XLI

                                                      JEFFERSON
                                                    NUEVO MUNDO
  32/7/15: ...pour l'exciter, et à tailler des croupières to the
            Anglois...
     7/18: mainly munitions.
     7/18: [line followed by space and line of dots] ....
     8/14: keep accounts, and here they begin to labour,
     8/17: along with Robinson Crusoe, Creeks, Cherokees, the
            latter
 33/10/1:   Quincy, Nov. 13, 1815
    10/23: [followed by line spacing]
    11/7:   [opposite this line, in margin] Pietro Leopoldo
    12/6:   to keep in countenance the funding and banking system...
 34/15/6:   'En fait de commerce ce (Bonaparte) est un étourdi,'
            said Romanzoff. . .
    16/29: [line spacing following this line deleted]
    19/6:   in tumbler number 2, and in tumbler number 1,
            planted ....
    21/16: [in pyramid following this line]

                                                   /\
                                                  /CITY\
                                                 / OF \
                                                /ARRARAT \
                                               /FOUNDED BY\
                                              /MORDECAI NOAH\
                                             /_____\

 21/25-26: CONSTANS PROPOSITO....
            JUSTUM ET TENOCEM
 35/24/1:   'get an i - d e - a , I-mean-a biz-nis i - d e - a.'
    24/2:   dixit sic felix Elias.
    25/35: [following this line, an inserted line] from all lands
            beyond the sea.
    26/1:   Needing salt, made their peace with Venice
    26/4:   'Where 'ave I 'eard that nyme?'
 36/29/12: [opposite this line, in margin] hagoromo
    29/24: Erigena was not understood in his time
    29/28: So they dug for, and damned Scotus Erigena
    29/33: [following this line, an inserted line] not quite in a
            vacuum.
 37/31/14: Ambrose (Mr.) Spencer, Mr Van Rensselaer
    31/12: [opposite this line, in margin : a vertical line]
    32/18: not to be lashed save by court. . . . Land
    33/5:   'Tip an' Tyler
    33/6:   We'll bust Van's biler......'
    33/7:   brought in the vice of luxuria, sed aureis furculis,
    33/31: '30 million' said Mr Dan Webster 'in states on the
            Mississippi
    36/2:   'Able speech by Van Buren.'
 38/38/17: Because of that bitch Minny Humbolt

42/18:   'faire passer ses affaires
42/19:   avant celles de la nation.'
39/43/30: é theos ée guné .... phtheggōmetha thasson
44/8:   Εἰς Ἀΐδαο δόμους καὶ ἐπαινῆς Περσεφονείης
44/9:   Ψυχῇ χρησομένος Θηβαίου Τειρεσίαο
44/10:   Μάντηος ἀλαοῦ τού τε φρένες ἔμπεδοί εἰσι·
44/10:   [opposite this line, in margin] XLVII
44/23:   Euné kai philoteti ephata Kirke
44/26:   Ἐς θάλαμον
44/30:   Under the portico Kirke: . . . .
45/20:   From star-up to the half-dark
40/48/10: Belmont representing the Rothschild
48/24:   'we cdnt. have stopped it (the panic).'
49/1:   (AGALMA, haberdashery, clocks, ormoulu, brocatelli,
49/11:   30 thousand aboard them with water and wheat, in
           provision.
49/12:   Two days beyond Gibel Tara, layed in the wide plain
51/4:   Killed flayed, brought back their pelts into Carthage.
51/10:   the νόος, the ineffable crystal:
41/52/10: Story told by the mezzo-yitt
52/13:   will come in for 12 million.
52/17:   DO with that money?
52/23:   because you are all for the confino.'
52/24:   'Noi ci facciam scannar per Mussolini'
53/17:   to keep up with your letters.'
53/30:   In den Deutschen Befreiungskriegen, by Wilhelm Baur
55/14:   Pays to control the Press, for its effect on the market
55/34:   to the consumer   72 (idem)
          Title page to Cantos 42-51   THE FIFTH DECAD OF
                                              CANTOS

                              SIENA
                    THE LEOPOLDINE REFORMS
42/3/3:   Palmerston, to Russell re/ Chas. F. Adams)
3/4:   'And how this people CAN in this the fifth et cetera
3/5:   year of the war, leave that old etcetera up
3/6:   there on that monument!' 'H.G.' to E.P. 1918
3/6:   [opposite this line, in margin] Wells
6/22:   approbations as follows.
7/22:   ob pecuniae scarcitatem
43/10/17: ob pecuniae scarsitatem
11/8:   alias: serve God with candles
11/34:   ducatorum? no. ducentorum
12/15:   but the S.O. man (Standard Oil)
13/6:   [opposite this line, in margin] Celso Cittadini
13/24:   on the gabelle and/or on the dogana
14/12:   implevit. The Pope filled . . . .
15/18:   to creditors be paid 2/3rds under that, frozen assets
44/18/30: torch flares grenades and they went to the Piazza del
           Duomo
20/25:   aide de camp, general Reile who will deliver this letter.

21/7:   'You,' 'She,' 'she' all to Majesty)
21/23-22/1: [Faber reads who for ND that throughout these
             lines]
45/24/17:   CONTRA NATURA
46/26/21:   "Camel driver said: 'I must milk my camel.'
26/23:   And the camel driver said: 'It is time to drink milk.
47/30/4:   [opposite this line, in margin] XXXIX
30/14:   φθεγγώμεθα θᾶσσον
30/28:   καὶ Μοῖρα τ' Ἄδονιν
30/29:   KAI MOIRA T' ADONIN
32/7:   Scilla's white teeth less sharp.
33/1:   καὶ Μοῖρα τ' Ἄδονιν
33/2:   KAI MOIRA T' ADONIN
33/5:   τυ Διῶνα, καὶ Μοῖρα
33/6:   TU DIONA, KAI MOIRA
33/7:   καὶ Μοῖρα τ' Ἄδονιν
33/8:   KAI MOIRA T' ADONIN
48/34/14:   sixteen, I think, and whenever; Von Unruh
35/5:   Διγενες
35/29:   err' u' nimbecile; ed ha imbecillito
37/23:   Hauled off the butt of that carcass, 20 feet up a tree
             trunk.
37/26:   Employed, past tense; at the Lido, Venezia,
37/30:   and if wind was, the old man placed a stone.
49/38/19:   [space following this line deleted]
38/24:   [followed by line spacing]
50/42/20:   .... on the throne of England, ...on the Austrian sofa
42/28:   Two sores ran together, Gentz, Metternich,
42/29:   Hell pissed up Metternich
43/9:   [followed by line spacing]
43/15:   Mastai, Pio Nono. D'Azeglio went into exile
43/22:   [followed by line spacing]
51/44/23:   It destroys the craftsman; destroying craft
45/5:   or duck widgeon; if you take feather from under the wing
45/30:   sang Geryone: I am the help of the aged;
52/4/3:   [following this line, an inserted line] ('Pericles,' near
             the beginning.)
5/27:   The fish-ward now goes against crocodiles
7/19:   [Chinese character, chih[3], following this line is deleted]
53/13/12:   saying this is my will and my last will:
13/33:   Ten seven eight ante Christum)
15/15:   Tchao ouang that hunted across the tilled fields
15/17:   as a tiger against me,
16/7:   And in this time was the horse dealer Fei-tsei
20/25:   [below Chinese character following this line] chou[1]
55/36/18:   [Chinese characters following this line have sound des-
             ignations; read down right column, then left: jên[2]/
             che[3]/ 1[3]/ tsui[2]/ fa[2-5]/ shên[1],/ pu[4-5]// jên[2]/che[3],/
             1[3]/shên[1]/fa[2-5]/tsui[2]]
40/17:   Chou coin was of iron, like Sparta's,
43/10-15:   [vertical line in margin]

45/13:   and redeemed these notes at one third/
46/4:   and saw a green unicorn speaking,
46/16:   [line followed by Chinese character]

徹
ch'e 4.5

56/56/22:   [line followed by Chinese character]

孝
hsiao⁴

57/58/11:   Yésien, Péyen Tiémour came up under
                the walls at Pekin
61/4:   [line followed by Chinese character]

金
chin¹

58/63/18:   and fur of martes zibbelines
63/27:   And on tother side, was Undertree making war in Korea
65/7:   red belt for the princes of blood
65/11:   Li koen, vicery, has spent all his money, not paying the
                troops
66/16:   and he made a Berlitz, Manchu, chinese and mogul
67/8:   Whereupon TAI TSONG wrote him: I will send a
                thousand
68/18:   and human meat sold in market.
69/16:   [line followed by Chinese character]

平
p'ing²

59/71/21:   and took in Gallileo's astronomy,
73/29:   [line followed by Chinese character]

敬
ching⁴

60/79/8:   [line followed by Chinese character]

樂
yueh⁴·⁵

61/82/15:   your briefs shd/ be secret and sealed
                and your Emperor
84/13:   but to profit on other men's loss (Antoninus)
84/14:   is no better than banditry
62/87/22:   'Passion of orthodoxy is fear, Calvinism has no other
                agent
88/20:   Gent standing in his own doorway got 2 balls in the arm
88/25:   BE IT ENACTED/ guv'nor council an' house of
                assembly
89/14:   sine affectu in 1770, Bastun.
92/18:   for the U.S.N.A. (of North America) letters of credence/
92/18:   [line followed by half-line] we say that he is to be now
94/4-5:   [opposite these lines, in margin: a vertical line]
63/97/1:   towards sending of Ellsworth
98/6:   Vol. Two (as the protagonist saw it:)
64/101/26: to be burnt on an hill, and his house broken open. . .
105/1-4:   [opposite these lines, in margin: a vertical line]

65/109/28: but an American, Patrick Henry
110/16: now avows bribery to be part of her system
122/12: Don Joas Tholomeno: 'Independence of America is
           assured
122/13: Sept. 14th '82,'
122/14: Mirabel (Sardegna) 'only why dont they acknowledge it?'
124/11: I will write home at once on this subject.'
125/6: which inflexibility has been called vanity. Policy
125/13: such is Doc Franklin (May 3rd 1783).
125/14: A composed man
66/128/31: [opposite Chinese characters]   正 chêng^4

                                                             名 ming^2

129/33: Small field pieces <u>happened</u>, said
           Governor Hutchinson
130/19: freeholders and other inhabitants (Cambridge 21 Dec.
           '72)
67/133/21: CHÊNG
137/2: (note to the 1819 edition 'NOVANGLUS')
137/3: A PLAN OF GOVERNMENT
140/28: ἄρχειν καὶ ἄρχεσθαι
68/143/16: I beg leave you permit this to remain. . . .'

146/7: Chêng^4 正

           Ming^2 名

147/34: integral branch of the sovreignty
69/154/11: smelt it or before he told long Tom about it.
70/155/13: in aim to have quintuple directory . . . . Vergennes'
           friends
158/17: 'seeks information from all quarters, and judges more
71/161/4: no history of those decades '89 to '09
167/4: Don't it remind you of alderman Beckford
167/16: κυβερνῶν.
74/4/22: [space following this line is deleted]
5/30: Absouldre, que tous nous veuil absoudre
7/15: sd/ Isaiah. Not out on interest said David rex [rest of
           line deleted]
9/21: are never alone ΉΛΙΟΝ ΠΕΡΙΗΛΙΟΝ
15/14: with a printing press by the Thames bank'
18/32: ask . . . [rest of line deleted]
*   20/22: Glass-eye Wemyss treading water
21/5: under such canvas
22/15-22: [deleted]
27/13: est agens and functions dust to the fountain pan
           otherwise
*75/28/6: Ständebuch of Sachs in yr/ luggage
76/31/3-4: la scalza: ''Io son' la luna/ and they have broken my
           house''

34/11:   has, if equalled at moments (? synthetic'ly)

40/20:   [note that here and elsewhere Faber text has large
          lower case omega for upper case.]

77/46/15:   the b........ bank has; pure iniquity

77/49/3:   [space following this line is deleted]

50/17:   who wrapped up De Sousa's poem (fine oreille)

50/18:   "Un curé déguisé; sd/ Cocteau's of M.......

50/19:   'Me paraît un curé déguisé' A la porte

50/20:   Sais pas, Monsieur, il me paraît un curé déguisé.

51/12:   as in the insets at the Scifanoja

52/8:   'And with the return of the gold standard' wrote Sir
          Montague

52/14:   and the snot press and periodical tosh do not notice this

78/53/3:   to Rostovtzeff (is it Rostovtzeff?)

58/15:   a ceux qui n'en ont point de tout

*   59/10:   Griffith said, years before that,: 'Can't move 'em with

60/3:   [Chinese character moved to center of page]

61/8:   be visible to the sergeants

79/63/30:   (Janequin per esempio, and Orazio Vecchii or Bronzino)

64/7:   [Chinese character on this line reads]   達

64/25:   and if Attlee attempts a Ramsay

65/26:   of fat fussy old women

70/9:   δεινὰ, εἰ Κύθηρα

70/15:   κύφηρῦ

70/18:   [space after this line is deleted]

*80/71/28:   Breda, the Virgin, Los Boracchos

*   71/30:   y Las Hilanderas?

72/8:   ἀγλαος ἀλάου πόρη Περσεφόνεια

72/23:   Petain defended Verdun while Blum . . .

72/24:   [deleted]

72/32:   simplex munditiis, as the hair of Circe;

74/26:   But if a man don't occasionally sit in a senate

75/24:   and is buried in the Red Square in Moscow

77/19:   [Chinese character (ch'üan^3) set opposite this and
          following three lines]

*   78/11:   disse: Io son' la luna.'

79/33:   'The evil that men do lives after them'

82/14:   syndical organization

83/9:   can it have been the old Ecole Militaire?

83/12:   (that was M.......)

83/18:   at an angle, say about 160 degrees

84/5:   (o-hon dit quelquefois au vi'age)

87/1:   in wake of the saracen

88/18:   Fritz still roaring at treize rue Gay Lussac

91/14:   Les larmes que j'ai créés m'inondent

81/95/6:   [line followed by inserted line] (Kings will, I think,
          disappear)

96/11:   Possum observed that the local folk dance

98/11:   If Waller sang or Dowland played,

99/8:   [line followed by inserted line] What thou lov'st well
          shall not be reft from thee

81/100/7:   all in the diffidence that faltered.
82/103/19:   [space following this line deleted]
   104/26:   μυστήριον, mysterium
   104/28:   lay in the fluid.
83/112/27:   (Summons withdrawn, sir.)
84/118/14:   the last appearance of [deleted] in that connection
   118/20:   Poco, poco.   δῖα ὑφορβά

APPENDIX H: CORRELATION TABLE

The Annotated Index is keyed to the New Directions edition of the Cantos, second printing, second state. For readers of the Faber and Faber edition, Appendix H offers a correlation table, comparing the pagination of the New Directions and Faber editions.

ND	Faber	ND	Faber	ND	Faber	ND	Faber
1/3	7	43	47-48	83	87	123	128-129
4	8-9	44	48-49	19/84	88	124	129-130
5	9	45	49-50	85	89-90	125	130-131
2/6	10	46	50-51	86	90-91	126	131-132
7	10-11	47	51	87	91-92	127	132-133
8	11-12	11/48	52-53	88	92	128	133
9	12-13	49	53	20/89	93	27/129	134
10	13-14	50	54-55	90	94-95	130	135-136
3/11	15-16	51	55	91	95-96	131	136-137
12	16	52	56	92	96-97	132	137
4/13	17-18	12/53	57	93	97-98	28/133	138
14	18	54	58	94	98-99	134	138-139
15	19	55	59	95	99	135	140-141
16	20	56	60-61	21/96	100	136	141-142
5/17	21	57	61	97	101-102	137	142-143
18	21-22	13/58	62-63	98	102-103	138	143-144
19	22-23	59	63-64	99	103-104	139	144-145
20	24	60	64	100	104	140	145
6/21	25-26	14/61	65-66	22/101	105	29/141	146
22	26-27	62	66-67	102	106-107	142	147-148
23	27	63	67	103	107-108	143	148-149
7/24	28	15/64	68-69	104	108-109	144	149-150
25	29	65	69-70	105	109-110	145	150-151
26	30-31	66	70-71	106	110	146	151
27	31	67	71	23/107	111-112	30/147	152
8/28	32	16/68	72-73	108	112-113	148	152-153
29	33-34	69	73-74	109	113-114	149	154
30	34-35	70	74-75	24/110	115	---------------	
31	35-36	71	75-76	111	116-117	31/3	157
32	36-37	72	76-77	112	117-118	4	157-158
33	37	73	77-78	113	118-119	5	159-160
9/34	38	74	78-79	114	119	6	160
35	39-40	75	79	25/115	120	32/7	161-162
36	40	17/76	80	116	121-122	8	162-163
37	41-42	77	81	117	122-123	9	163
38	42-43	78	81-82	118	123-124	33/10	164-165
39	43	79	83	119	124-125	11	165-166
40	44	18/80	84-85	120	125	12	166-167
41	45	81	85-86	26/121	126	13	167-168
10/42	46	82	86-87	122	126-127	14	168

ND	Faber	ND	Faber	ND	Faber	ND	Faber
34/15	169	43/9	224-225	13	277-278	58/62	330-331
16	169-170	10	225-226	14	278-279	63	331-332
17	171-172	11	226-227	15	279-280	64	332-333
18	172-173	12	227-228	16	280-281	65	333-334
19	173-174	13	228-229	17	281-282	66	334-335
20	174-175	14	229-230	18	282-283	67	335-336
21	175-176	15	230-231	19	283-284	68	336-337
35/22	177	16	231-232	20	284-285	69	337-338
23	177-179	44/17	233-234	54/21	286-287	59/70	339-340
24	179-180	18	234-235	22	287-288	71	340-341
25	180-181	19	235-236	23	288-289	72	341-342
26	181	20	236-237	24	289-290	73	342-343
36/27	182-183	21	237-238	25	290-291	60/74	344-345
28	183-184	22	238	26	291-292	75	345-346
29	184-185	45/23	239	27	292-293	76	346-347
30	185-186	24	240	28	293-294	77	347-348
37/31	187	46/25	241-242	29	294-295	78	348-349
32	188-189	26	242-243	30	295-296	79	349
33	189-190	27	243-244	31	296-297	61/80	350-351
34	190-191	28	244-245	32	297-298	81	351-352
35	191-192	29	245	33	298-299	82	352-353
36	192-193	47/30	246-247	34	300-301	83	353-354
38/37	194-195	31	247-248	35	301	84	354-355
38	195-196	32	248-249	55/36	302	85	355-356
39	196-197	33	249	37	303-304	86	356-357
40	197-198	48/34	250-251	38	304-305	62/87	357-358
41	198-199	35	251-252	39	305-306	88	358-359
42	199-200	36	252-253	40	306-307	89	359-360
39/43	201	37	253-254	41	307-308	90	360-361
44	202-203	49/38	255-256	42	308-309	91	361-362
45	203-204	39	256	43	309-310	92	362-363
46	204	50/40	257	44	310-311	93	363-364
40/47	205-206	41	258-259	45	311-312	94	364-365
48	206-207	42	259-260	46	312-313	95	365-366
49	207-208	43	260	56/47	314-315	96	366-367
50	208-209	51/44	261-262	48	315-316	63/97	368-369
51	209	45	262-263	49	316-317	98	369-370
41/52	210	46	263	50	317-318	99	370-371
53	210-212	--------------		51	318-319	100	371
54	212-213	52/3	267-268	52	319-320	64/101	372-373
55	213-214	4	268-269	53	320-321	102	373-374
56	214	5	269-270	54	321-322	103	374-375
--------------		6	270-271	55	322-323	104	375-376
42/3	217	7	271	56	323-324	105	376-377
4	218-219	53/8	272-273	57/57	325-326	106	377-378
5	219-220	9	273	58	326-327	107	378-379
6	220-221	10	274	59	327-328	108	379-380
7	221-222	11	275-276	60	328-329	65/109	381-382
8	222-223	12	276-277	61	329	110	382-383

ND	Faber	ND	Faber	ND	Faber	ND	Faber
111	383-384	70/155	431-432	33	483-484	77	532-533
112	384-385	156	432-433	34	484-485	78	533-534
113	385-386	157	433-434	35	485-486	79	534-535
114	386-387	158	434-435	36	486-487	80	535-536
115	387-388	159	435	37	487-488	81	536-537
116	388-389	71/160	436-437	38	488-489	82	537-539
117	389-390	161	437-438	39	489-490	83	539-540
118	390-391	162	438-439	40	490-492	84	540-541
119	391-392	163	439-440	41	492	85	541-542
120	392-394	164	440-441	77/42	493-494	86	542-543
121	394-395	165	441-442	43	494-495	87	543-544
122	395-396	166	442-443	44	495-496	88	544-545
123	396-397	167	443	45	496-497	89	545-546
124	397-398	---------------		46	497-498	90	546-547
125	398-399	74/3	451-452	47	498-499	91	547-548
66/126	400-401	4	452-453	48	499-500	92	548-549
127	401-402	5	453-454	49	500-501	93	549-550
128	402-403	6	454-455	50	501-502	94	550-551
129	403-404	7	455-456	51	502-503	81/95	552-553
130	404-405	8	456-457	52	504-505	96	553-554
131	405-406	9	457-458	53	505	97	554-555
132	406	10	458-459	54	506-507	98	555-556
67/133	407-408	11	459-460	78/55	508-509	99	556-557
134	408-409	12	460-461	56	509-510	100	557
135	409-410	13	461-463	57	510-511	82/101	558
136	410-411	14	463-464	58	511-512	102	559-560
137	411-412	15	464-465	59	512-513	103	560-561
138	412-413	16	465-466	60	513-514	104	561-562
139	413-414	17	466-467	61	514-515	105	562
140	414-415	18	467-468	79/62	516-517	83/106	563-564
68/141	416-417	19	468-469	63	517-518	107	564-565
142	417-418	20	469-470	64	518-519	108	565-566
143	418-419	21	470-471	65	519-520	109	566-567
144	419-420	22	471-472	66	520-521	110	567-568
145	420-421	23	472-473	67	521-522	111	568-569
146	421-422	24	473-474	68	522-523	112	569-570
147	422-423	25	474-475	69	523-524	113	570-571
148	423-424	26	475-477	70	524-525	114	571
69/149	425-426	27	477	80/71	526-527	84/115	572-573
150	426-427	75/28	478	72	527-528	116	573-574
151	427-428	29	479	73	528-529	117	574-575
152	428-429	76/30	480	74	529-530	118	575-576
153	429-430	31	481-482	75	530-531		
154	430	32	482-483	76	531-532		

ADDITIONS AND CORRECTIONS

The second printing of the Annotated Index permits the following
additions and corrections.
    New entries are marked by the sign ++
    Entries previously unannotated are marked by the sign +
    Unmarked entries either add material to previous notes, or
correct errors of fact or typography.

+ Adelphi: 74/12: prob. to be combined with Adelphi 62/93, in the
    sense of the Adelphi buildings, London, built by the Brothers
    ADAM.
Ainley: 77/47: prob. Henry Ainley, who created the role of Cuchu-
    lain in Yeats' At The Hawk's Well, in which he wore a mask.
    (See: W. B. Yeats, Letters, 607, 609-611.) Miscio ITO played
    the role of the Guardian of the Well.
Aïulipata: 56/52: Aiyulipalipata, . . .
Amaril-li: 79/62: prob. the solo madrigal of Giulio Caccini, heard
    by Pound at Salzburg.
Aristotle: 36/29; 74/19, 22. . . .
Atthis: 5/18: prob. one of the girls of whom Sappho sang. (See:
    Mary Barnard, Sappho, 40.)
avènement révolution . . . : 33/13: avènement révolution. . . .

barbarisci: 24/110: (It) Barbary horses.
Bard, Jo: 81/96: Joseph Bard. . . .
Barzun: 77/50: prob. Henri-Martin Barzun, 1881-   , French
    writer. (See: Letters, 134.)
British Statutes: 64/105: The Statutes at Large from Magna Carta
    to the thirtieth year of King George II (vols. 1-6) ed. by H. B.
    Cay. From the 31st year of King George 2nd to the 13th year
    of King George 3rd (vols. 7-9) ed. by O. Ruffhead. London: 1758-
    73.

Carson: 84/116: prob. the G. C. Carson, a miner, whom the Pound
    family knew c. 1910.
Cayohoga: 31/3: the Cuyahoga River, eastern Ohio. Jefferson spells
    it Cayahoga and Cayohoga in his correspondence about a pos-
    sible canal between Lake Erie and the Ohio River.
[Ché-pou-kiu-atchen]: 54/32: . . . first officer or Che-li-sa. . . .
Chrysophrase: 17/76: chrysoprase, . . .
ciocco: 5/17; 7/24: (It) log, brand, firewood.
Contre le lambris . . . / . . . baromètre: 7/24: . . .
Corles, Mr.: 35/22:
così discesi . . . : 80/77: (It) thus I descended through the spiteful
    air /. . . .

Cul de Sac: 31/5: the cul-de-sac Tête-bout. ...

D. de M.: 9/38: poss. Domenico MALATESTA, but see Yriarte, Un
    Condottiere au XVe Siècle, 396, 397.
 + DeLara: 80/79: prob. Isidore de Lara, 1858-1935, English composer.
Demattia: 84/115: ...
++ Detroit: 66/126: the military fort at Detroit, controlled by the British,
    1784.
Deux Avares, Les: 65/117: ...
diaspre: 20/95: (O Fr) a kind of silk figured in flowers or arabesques.
Dulac: 80/81: Edmund, 1882-1953, ...
++ Dulac, papa: 80/82: father of Edmund Dulac.

E difficile, / ... : 21/97: . . . to live in wealth/without having status. . . .
[Elliot, Gilbert]: 50/43: 1782-1859, second earl of Minto. He was
    special envoy to Sardinia and Tuscany (1847-48). (See: Zobi,
    Storia civile della Toscana, 236, for an account of his evviva of
    30 October 1847.)
[Ermentrude]: 83/106: . . . ERIGENA compared her to ARACHNE.
"et amava ... : 9/41: ... (and the ornament of Italy) ... pulchra
    aspectu, plurimis. . . .
Et/ En l'an trentunième ... : 56/56: . . . And just as for Prince
    OUEN TI of HAN in former times, / make the obsequies for me.
Excideuil: 80/88: . . . near Périgueux.

Falange, La: 80/83: prob. La Phalange, the Parisian literary maga-
    zine.
Fei-tsei: 53/16: . . . a descendant of Yih, an official of the great
    CHUN. Fei-tsei was given charge of Emperor HIAO-OUANG's
    studs. . . .
fiolo del Signore: 24/110: (It) son of the Lord.

gabelle: 43/13; 44/21: (It) duties, taxes, customs fees.
Gardone: 74/5; 76/36; 78/56: Gardone Riviera, on Lake Garda.
Gin Cheou: 54/30: Gin-cheou-kong (Jen Shou Kung), the celebrated
    palace of "Long-lived Benevolence" completed by OUEN-TI in
    AD 596. (See: Mailla, Histoire Générale, V, 489.)
Goedel: 78/56; 79/62: Carl Goedel, member of the English section
    of the Ente Italiana Audizione Radiofoniche during 1942-43 and
    later with the propaganda agencies of the SALÒ Republic; Pound
    was associated with him, especially during the period of the
    Salò regime.
gonfaron/ ... : 26/122: (Pr) banner (battle pennon)/ . . .

Hanover: 37/36: . . . a royal family of England (1714-1901).

++ in gran dispitto: 77/51: (It) with great scorn. (See: <u>Inferno</u>, 10, 36.)
[Isolde]: 8/30: . . . of Tristram and Isolde.

Jackson, Colonel: 80/82: a Joseph Jackson, whom Pound knew in
    London, 1908.
Jepson: 74/11; 78/60: . . .
Jew (Jews): . . . (delete 65/112). . . .

++ Know then. . . . Evil king is known by his imposts: 52/4-7: from the
    <u>LI KI</u>.
Kouémen: 57/57: . . . a gate of Nanking.
[Krupp von Bohlen und Holbach, Gustav]: 38/41: . . .
++ Kung walked: 13/58: see addition to Appendix E: Confucius, below.

Lady Lucan: 65/124: Margaret Bingham. . . .
Lawrence, W.: 74/22: . . . (See: Sir Ernest Barker's foreword in
    <u>The Home Letters</u>.)
Lilas, Les: 74/11: . . . Boulevard du Montparnasse.
Li Sao: 56/47 . . . : the Li Sao or "Falling into Trouble," a collec-
    tion of poems by Ch'ü Yüan (343-290). (See: H. A. Giles, A <u>His-</u>
    <u>tory of Chinese Literature</u>, 50-53.)
+ Loica: 28/136: the reference is to Florence Farr, who created the
    role of Louka in Shaw's <u>Arms and the Man</u>; she died in Ceylon in
    1917. (See: Virginia Moore, <u>The Unicorn</u>, 239, 252.)
Long Champ: 65/118: <u>Longchamp</u>, in the late 18th century the fashion-
    able concourse in the Bois de Boulogne.
Lucina: 74/9: Diana Lucina, the moon.
luxuria sed aureis furculis: [26/122]; 37/33: . . .

[Mackay, Elsie]: 28/140: . . . In 1928 she accompanied Capt. Walter
    Hinchliffe. . . .
marchesini: 24/110: prob. (It) of the marquess; from the marquess's
    account.
Mead: 74/24: . . . <u>The Quest</u>, a quarterly review concerned with theo-
    sophy and hermeticism.
++ Michilimakinac: 66/126: the military fort at the Strait of Mackinac,
    controlled by the British, 1784.
Mihites: 71/164: . . . ; or poss. play on the (L) <u>mihi</u>, thus <u>egoists</u>.
    (See: Adams, <u>Works</u>, X, 119).
Minto, Lord: 50/43: see Gilbert ELLIOT.
Mi pare che avea . . . : 9/38: (It) seems to me that she has said every-
    thing. . . .
Monte non vacabilis publico: 42/7: . . . will not expire.
++ monumentum: 46/28: (L) memorial.

Nenni: 80/73: Pietro Nenni, 1891-   , leader of the Italian Socialist
    Party.

Neuchâtel: 67/140: a monarchical republic, later (1815) a part of
   Switzerland. (See: Adams, Works, IV, 374-377.)
New Discourse: 54/22: the Sin-Yu (Hsin Yü) by LOU-KIA, a work on
   the Classics; part of the general literary reconstruction that took
   place after the book burning of LI-SSÉ. (See: Mailla, Histoire
   Générale, II, 514.)
++ Nicolo (ainé) Pitigliano: 29/141: see Niccolò ORSINI (below).

++ [Orsini, Niccolò]: 29/141: 1442-1510, Lord of Pitigliano, son of
   Aldobrando ORSINI.

   palla: 20/90: (It) ball; reference is to court tennis.
   Par che e fuor di questo: 11/49: (It) he seems lost   (out of it).
 + Peach-blossom Fountain: 84/116: an allegory by T'ao Ch'ien (365-
      427). (See: H. A. Giles, A History of Chinese Literature, 50-53).
   pellande: 26/123: (It) outer garments with long sleeves, richly deco-
      rated.
++ Pernella: 29/141: Penelope Orsini, d. c. 1465, mistress of Aldobrando
   ORSINI; she was killed by his son, Niccolò ORSINI.
   Phlegethon: 25/118; 75/28: . . .
   Piccolomini, Nicolò: 44/22: Count Niccolò Piccolomini, editor of the
      Monte dei Paschi documents. (See: Appendix F.)
++ Pitigliano: 9/37; 10/42; 29/141: the seat of the ORSINI family.
   placet sic: 60/75: (L) petition thus.
   plaustra: 9/36: (L) wagons, carts.
   Psellos: 23/107: . . . politician, writer, and Neoplatonist.

   Regis optimatium . . . : 68/141: . . . A Discourse on the Contests
      and Dissensions. . . .
 + Rhumby, Mr.: 48/35: pseudonym for Bainbridge Colby, Secretary of
      State under Wilson, 1920.
   Robert's: 74/11; 76/31: the New York restaurant.

   saccone: 28/139: (It) penitential robe of sackcloth. (See: John Drum-
      mond in Russell, An Examination of Ezra Pound, 115-116.)
   [St. John of the Cross]: 74/16: . . .
   St. Louis Till: [74/8] . . .
   Salò: 78/56: the city on Lake Garda, seat of the Salò Republic, founded
      in Northern Italy in October 1943, a remnant of the Fascist regime.
   sed aureis furculis: 26/122; [37/33]: . . .
   Selsey: 80/86: the town, near the tip of Selsey Bill, S coast of England.
   sexaginta quatuor . . . : 11/51: . . . nor tries to get any more.
   simul commorantes: 25/115: (L) living together.
   sobr' un zecchin: 78/55: (It) on a golden coin   (sequin).
   sotto le nostre scoglie: 76/30: (It) under our crags.
   souterrain: 80/91: (Fr) underworld.
   State Trials: 71/165: A Complete Collection of State-Trials and Pro-
      ceedings for High Treason, and other crimes and misdemeanours,

from the reign of King Richard II. to the reign of King George I. (8 vols.).

+ Stonolifex: 26/123: poss. transcription error for (Gr) skeuophylax; in classical Greek it means storekeeper, but later sense might have taken it to mean keeper of the religious materials (vestments, icons, etc.). (See: Mansi, Amplissima Collectio Conciliorum, vol. 31A, column 495 for an account of the Patriarch's entourage and the mention of this term.) Also possible confusion with (Gr) stolos, equipment.

Suma: 74/21: village on Osaka Bay. . . .

superbo Ilion: 23/109: (It) proud Troy.

Tami: 76/40: prob. reference to Tomi. . . .

Tant las fotei . . . : 6/21: (Pr) . . . / 180 and eight times. . . .

Taoist . . . : 54/27 . . . for the elixir vitae. . . .

Tçin Ngan: 54/28: the reference is to Tçin-ngai-ti (Ai Ti) (reign: 362-66). . . .

Télémaque: 34/16: prob. the set ballet of the opera Télémaque . . . first performed in St. Petersburg, 1806.

Tempus loquendi,/ Tempus tacendi: 31/3; [74/7]: . . .; this was also Sigismondo MALATESTA's personal motto. (See: Yriarte, Un Condottiere au XVᵉ Siècle, 213). The phrase comes from Ecclesiastes, iii, 7.

++ "The fifth element: mud": 34/16: from Napoleon's remark: "God—besides water, air, earth and fire—has created a fifth element—mud."

++ Thetis: 36/30: a locality in the Abruzzi, Italy.

Tolosa: 76/30; 80/81: (L) Toulouse, the city on the Garonne; residence of the elder Dulac.

Tosch: 80/81: Papa Dulac's dog.

++ two halves of the tally: 83/104: see Appendix B, 77/46.

++ "Tyke 'im up ter the bawth": 80/86: see Ford Madox Ford, Portraits from Life, 186-187.

Vai soli: 74/9: . . . ; or poss. Pound also has in mind the Latin phrase, vae soli, woe to the solitary man. (See: Translations, 407.)

verde colore predeletto . . . ziparello: 24/110: (It) green beloved color . . . embroidered short jacket (from giubberello, which in Venetian dialect becomes ziparello).

ver novum, canorum . . . : 39/43, [45]: (L) fresh spring, melodious, fresh spring. (See: Pervigilium Veneris, I, 2: ver novum, ver iam canorum, ver renatus orbis est.)

viel(s): 8/32; 20/89: vielle. . . .

Warenhauser: 22/101: . . . in Washington and Oregon from the Northern Pacific Railroad.

Wiener Café: [18/81?]; 80/84, 85: the Vienna Cafe, formerly at Hart Street and Holborn, London.

Yash (Jassy): 19/87: also Iasi, a commercial. . . .

Yu-en-mi: 79/65: reference is to the Youanmi Gold Mines, Ltd., promoted by Herbert Hoover in 1912.

Zobi: 50/40, 41, 43: . . . author of Storia civile della Toscana. . . .
Zohanne: 24/110: Giovanni da Rimini, favorite jockey of Parisina
    MALATESTA. (See: E. G. Gardner, Dukes and Poets in Ferrara,
    35.)

Appendixes

A. ῞ΥΛΗ, ὔλη : 30/148; 35/25; 77/49: . . . also in gnostic cosmology,
   matter (as opposed to spirit, light).

D. Rulers of France: House of Valois: 1328-1589:

Philip VI	1328-50	Louis XII	1498-1515
John II	1350-64	Francis I	1515-47
Charles V	1364-80	Henry II	1547-59
Charles VI	1380-1422	Francis II	1559-60
CHARLES VII	1422-61	Charles IX	1560-74
LOUIS XI	1461-83	Henry III	1574-89
Charles VIII	1483-98		

E. Alysoun: Betuene Aprile: 39/45.
++ Bible: Ecclesiastes: Tempus loquendi: 31/3; 74/7.
++ Confucius: Analects: Canto XIII is a pastiche from the Analects,
   with translation and paraphrase mixed together. The sources are
   as follows: lines 3-30: Analects IX, ii; XI, xxv; lines 31-37: XIV,
   xlvi; lines 38-42: IX, xxii; lines 45-51: XIII, vi, xiii; lines 56-
   62: XIII, xviii; lines 63-66: V, i; lines 67-77: XVI, xiii.
++ Dante: Inferno: in gran dispitto: 77/51.
++ Li Ki (Li Chi, Book of Rites): Know then . . . Evil king is known
   by his imposts: 52/4-7.
   Mencius: . . . [Chinese]: 83/110.
++ Pervigilium Veneris: ver novum: 39/43, 45.

F. Miscellaneous Sources:

++ Li Ki (Li Chi, Book of Rites).

Historical Sources:

Yriarte, Charles Émile, Un condottiere au XVe Siècle. . . .
Zobi, Antonio, Storia civile della Toscana. . . .